BASEBALLHQ.COM'S **2013**

MINOR LEAGUE
BASEBALL
ANALYST

ROB GORDON AND JEREMY DELONEY | BRENT HERSHEY, EDITOR | EIGHTH EDITION

TRIUMPH
BOOKS

This book is available in quantity at special discounts for your group or organization. For further information, contact:

Triumph Books LLC
814 North Franklin Street
Chicago, Illinois 60610
(312) 337-0747
www.triumphbooks.com

Printed in U.S.A.
ISBN: 978-1-60078-741-6

Cover design by Brent Hershey
Front cover photograph by Tim Heltman/USA TODAY Sports Images

Acknowledgments

Jeremy Deloney:

I feel fortunate and blessed to be asked to come back for my fourth edition of the *Minor League Baseball Analyst*. Co-writing a book has its privileges, but it also can be challenging. Granted, I think about baseball virtually all year, but putting pen to paper—as antiquated as that sounds—is an entirely different animal. As an avid and passionate college hoops fan, I have to put my television viewing on hold for the purposes of writing, but I'm glad I do it. I'm not one to boast or talk about myself, but I am very proud to see my name on the cover of a book. Of course, there are several people to whom I owe plenty of gratitude and thanks.

My wife, Amy, who continues to amaze me with her love and support. She sacrifices a great deal while I pursue my passion. We've been happily married for 13 years and I sometimes wonder how she puts up with my fervent and enthusiastic love of sports. I'm not sure that's what she signed up for, but she seems to understand. She is an incredible wife, mother, and human being and I feel blessed to have her by my side through all of life's adventures. I cannot be more amazed at her selfless nature, love of life, and calming ways. I am very appreciative of all she does for me and our family and I look forward to growing old with her, assuming she sticks around as I slowly lose my precious hair.

My oldest son, Owen, who has plenty of success ahead of him. He's more a fan of basketball than baseball at this point, though I believe deep down he may be starting to come around. The kid can crush my 45 mph fastball into the next yard and has legitimate three-point range. Regardless of what his passion ultimately becomes, I will continue to support him and be his biggest fan. I'm proud to be his old man.

My middle son, Ethan, who is a happy and enthusiastic kid. He makes me laugh with his funny anecdotes and he impresses me with his compassion and zest for life. He isn't very much into sports, but that's OK with me. I want him to do what he likes to do and I will always support him. He loves his Legos and video games which seem to be common staples among kids his age. I'm proud to call him my son.

My daughter, Madeline, who is my little sweetie. I'm certain my wife would share that Madeline has me wrapped around her finger and it is probably true. I simply can't say no to her. She is a smart and beautiful little girl. I cannot help but smile whenever she is around. I could have a bad day at work and I'll be able to forget everything when I see her when I walk in the door. I'm proud to be her dad.

My parents, Bill and Nancy, for all they have ever done for me and my family. I'm honored when people have commented that my dad and I are similar. I'm sure some of the crude and sophomoric humor may not be appreciated by all, but I can always count on my dad for a few chuckles. I have gotten my work ethic from my parents and I hope to pass that along to my kids. My parents are incredible human beings and I'm very blessed to be their son.

My brothers, BJ and Andy, who are more than family to me. We take an annual baseball trip which is always one of the highlights of the year. One cannot scoff at sitting in ballparks and indulging in beers and hot dogs all the while talking sports. Both of my brothers are successful in their careers and have wonderful wives and kids who adore them. Sure, we were quite competitive and quarrelsome as kids, but I think we've grown to like each other now (though I still remember the needless injuries playing knee football in the family room or being the unfortunate victim of the "What is the capital of Thailand?" gag). They are some really cool dudes.

The folks at BaseballHQ.com who have been extremely instrumental in my writing career. I can still recall the day I received an email from Deric McKamey who was interested in talking to me about potentially joining the team at BHQ. Ron Shandler has a very well-respected name in this industry and for good reason—he's simply the best in the business. Brent Hershey and Ray Murphy provide extraordinary leadership and organization to the team and I feel very fortunate that they welcome me back every year.

Rob Gordon, who has co-written this book for the past four years. I respect him a great deal and I always look forward to his insights and opinions on baseball. Though we don't always agree with each other's assessments, I learn from him, which enhances my work.

I also want to thank the readers of this book. It goes without saying, but this book wouldn't exist without your support. Thank you!

Rob Gordon:

Producing this book continues to be a labor of love, but would not have been possible without the support of family, friends, and the wonderful folks at BaseballHQ.com.

In 2003 Ron Shandler gave me the opportunity to do something I'd wanted to do all of my life—write about baseball. Ron is one of the smartest baseball people I've ever had the pleasure of meeting. But beyond that, Ron has been very supportive, friendly, and loyal—and I owe him a huge thank you for giving Jeremy and I the chance to write and publish this book.

Deric McKamey took me under his wing, showed me the ropes, and spent countless hours explaining what scouts look for and how to break down a player's strengths and weaknesses. Deric's total recall of the most obscure minor league players still amazes me. Deric has moved on to bigger and better things in professional baseball, but his imprint on the structure and content of this book lives. It was nice to see Deric in Toledo and at the 2012 First Pitch Forum in Arizona.

Jeremy Deloney and I are now in our fourth edition of the MLBA and each year I'm more and more impressed with his comprehensive and astute knowledge of the minor leagues. Jeremy sees tons of games in the MWL and elsewhere and is able to quickly and concisely analyze a player's potential. Jeremy continues to be one of the best and most insightful baseball writers working today. Now that he lives in Michigan, I will work on convincing him to root for the Wolverines instead of the Buckeyes—but I'm not optimistic. This book would not be possible without the countless hours and sleepless nights he puts into it.

I would also think to thank Brent Hershey. Brent served as our editor at BaseballHQ.com throughout the year and throughout the production of this book. Without his sage advice and careful attention to detail, the writing and analysis here would not be as clear, accurate, or as concise as it is. Brent also knows a great deal about minor leaguers and probably sees as many games as I do. Brent's work is largely behind the scenes, but it has been an invaluable addition.

Many other baseball people provided invaluable support and encouragement over the years. They include Jeff Barton, Jim Callis, John Sickels, Ray Murphy, Rick Wilton, Patrick Davitt (who does a great job with BaseballHQ Radio), Todd Zola, Greg Ambrosius, Jason Grey of the Tampa Bay Rays, Joe Sheehan, Jesse Goldberg-Strassler with the Lansing Lugnuts, Jeff Erickson, Lawr Michaels, Jason Griffin of the Toledo Mudhens, Mark Murray of the St. Louis Cardinals, Brian Walton, Jason Collette, Kimball Crossley with the Toronto Blue Jays, Tim Heaney, Eric Karabell with ESPN, Steve Moyer, Phil Hertz (Go Blue!), Jock Thompson, and Doug Dennis, who continues to be one of the funniest baseball writers working today.

Some day someone will write a story about Baseball Unlimited. Until then I'll just have to thank the league—Michael Hartman, Steve Hartman, Michael Cooney, Bob Hathaway, Doug Hathaway, Raj Patel, Derald Cook, Todd Hooper, Dave Dannemiller, Ted Maizes, Nick Gleckman, Greg Murrey, Randy Jones, and John Mundelius. You guys rock and may BU live forever!

The kids from Dearborn Baseball have been a blast to coach. Watching them go from T-ball to kids pitch to travel ball over the past eight years has been incredible. There is no bigger reward than teaching kids about baseball and good sportsmanship. 15-0 and league champs this year—way to go, boys! Thanks to coaches Aaron Richardson and Bob Werth.

I would also like to thank Craig Cotter and the guys at Michigan Strategy Baseball. Their commitment to teaching the kids baseball and softball is a welcome addition to baseball in Southeast Michigan and has been fun to watch.

My oldest son Bobby starting playing travel baseball this year with the Dearborn Heights Knights. His head coach Brad Ebben took the boys on this first-year travel team to another level. They all improved and learned good sportsmanship along the way. Thanks Brad—the kids had a great experience. I'd also like to thank assistant coaches Rob Stockman and Rob Curtis. Can't wait for 2013.

My colleagues at the University of Michigan, Wayne State University, and Siena Heights University are too numerous to mention by name but you have all been very supportive, particularly David Smith, John Stratman, Michael Hartman, Joe Turrini, and Mark Guevara who have been my companions at numerous opening day games in Detroit and listened to me drone on endlessly about the next "can't miss prospect" and the importance of a quality change-up. Also a big thank you to Andy Wible, Susan Gass, Tim Webb, Ching-Yune Sylvester, David Brawn, Scott McClure, Chris Bass, Craig Regester, Liz Faue, Tim Dodd, Allison Friendly, and Bill Blackerby.

I would especially like to thank my family. My two boys—Bobby and Jimmy—make the sky bluer, the sun brighter, and the crack of the bat all the more sweet. My mother Sandra Bovenkerk Gordon took me on an annual birthday trip to Chicago to see the Cubs play and drove me to countless baseball practices and little league games and my father Robert W. Gordon III took me to Chicago to see the great Roberto Clemente play in his last season and has shared my passion for the game of baseball. My sister Susan Arntson helped raised me and tried to keep me out of trouble. Thank you! She has an amazing family. Her husband Jeff and her kids Rachael, Josh, Marrisa, and Jake seem like more than just regular family.

Finally – a huge thank you to my amazing and beautiful wife Paula Jean Walker-Gordon. Not only has she has been incredibly supportive and tolerant throughout this process, but she is a complete wiz at MS Excel and helped me compile all of the data that appears in this book. This may sound like a cliché, but I really would not have been able to do this without her in my life.

TABLE OF CONTENTS

by Jeremy Deloney

Welcome to the 2013 *Minor League Baseball Analyst*, the eighth edition of BaseballHQ.com's annual prospect book. Our old friend Deric McKamey—now a scout with the St. Louis Cardinals—was the originator of the book and did an unbelievable job for the first four editions. Rob Gordon and I have co-written the last four with the help of the terrific crew at BaseballHQ.com. We know that you demand excellence and we strive to put a quality product in your hands. We hope you enjoy the contents as much as we do.

I remember the days when following minor league baseball was quite difficult. Prior to the onset of the Internet, I waited by the mailbox for the latest edition of Baseball America. I recall *USA Today Baseball Weekly* had a section devoted to minor league baseball as well. Now with major media outlets covering this sport, along with hundreds of blogs and websites, the competition has grown exponentially.

We truly appreciate the thirst for prospect information and we enjoy bringing our assessments to you. While we also understand there are several other qualified prospect sites and outlets, we encourage you to make the MLBA a staple of your annual routine, whether it be consulting the book or enjoying the daily and weekly analysis via BaseballHQ.com. Rob and I have done this for a long time, and our connections within the game and own scouting experience allow us to bring you the best prospect coverage available. You can be assured that the opinions herein are our own; we don't simply regurgitate information from other outlets and re-package it.

The general format of the book has generally been constant over the years with a few wrinkles here and there. Some of the essay topics are similar to themes from years past and that is by design. We will continue to provide prospect assessments on nearly 1,000 players along with a voluminous amount of statistical analysis. Everyone loves prospect lists and we've got more lists for your enjoyment. As always, we aren't looking for you to agree with everything Rob and I bring to you, but our goal is to provide different perspectives and opinions that may challenge you to look a little closer.

It is customary for me to state that selecting the nearly 1,000 players is the most difficult thing about writing this book. Given the number of prospects currently in the minor leagues as well as international signees, there are lots to choose from. There are likely to be some players that would rank in a Top 1,000 list that you won't see in this book. This is by design. We want to include players who are close to reaching the majors, but may not have the ceiling of a 17-year-old international player. There are several call-ups during the season that may cause readers to scurry for their 2013 MLBA to look for instant analysis. (Of course, you could always check out BaseballHQ.com for the daily call-ups report.) There is plenty of time for a 17 or 18-year-old prospect to appear in future editions of the book. It is safe to assume, however, that the best prospects are in this book.

When splitting up the duties of the book, we've looked at different ways of doing it, but we've always come back to Rob taking the National League and me focusing on the American League. As the Astros are now in the AL, I had to brush up on my knowledge of the Houston organization from top to bottom. These roles don't imply that Rob doesn't have a say in the inclusion or exclusion of players from the AL or me not sharing my opinion on the NL. This book is a testament to team effort, not only from Rob and I, but from the entire minor-league crew at BaseballHQ.com. Brent Hershey, Chris Mallonee, Colby Garrapy and Chris Lee all have contributed in significant ways, whether it be scouting games during the season, assessing prospects for this book, or in some cases, contributing an essay. We all bring a different perspective to this edition and we hope it shows in the end result.

BaseballHQ.com's rating system has garnered several questions and comments since it was introduced in 2007. The Potential Ratings is a two-part system in which a player is assigned a number rating based on his upside potential (1-10) and a letter rating based on the probability of reaching that potential (A-E). A 10 implies a Hall of Fame potential whereas a 1 is a minor league roster filler. Certainly you will not find a player less than 6 in the 2013 MLBA. The MLBA is filled with prospects of varying probability ratings, however.

The rating system is not an "end all, be all" system; there are times in which the argument could be made that an 8A player may actually be a 9D player. We rate players first by the upside potential. If a position player offers five tools or the potential for five tools, that player will get a high number assigned. If that same player has a history of poor performance or is in the lower depths of the minors, he may be assigned a low letter rating. Our goal isn't to squelch debate; rather it is to shed light on a player's ultimate potential. What is the difference between an 8A and a 9D? Good question, and one that is difficult to answer. This depends on such factors including, but not limited to, his athleticism, tools, ability to improve, and historical performance. Ratings can and will change, depending on the aforementioned factors. Our goal is to give you a snapshot of a player's ultimate upside and likelihood of success.

Don't think of this book as just about stats. While there are a ton of stats to enjoy, the defining aspects are the essays and prospect profiles. This is what we hope sets us apart from other baseball annuals. The essays and profiles attempt to add a little color to the black-and-white statistics and answer "why" or "how" those stats came to be. Additionally, analyzing minor league prospects is all about projection several years down the road.

The meat and potatoes of the book continue to be the hitter and pitcher profiles. We bring you expanded stats, tool assessments, expected arrival dates, draft info, potential roles, and their ultimate rating. While a player's skills may improve or regress from year to year, our goal is to quantify and measure a player at one certain point in time. Equally important as the statistical tables is the tool analysis. Over-analysis of statistics in the minor leagues can be a dangerous proposition. Not only are there severe hitters/pitchers environments, but these are mostly still young players who are developing their bodies and their games. Don't get too caught up in a hitter's BA or a pitcher's ERA—look deeper at their skills and how their tools project. That's where Rob and I come into play. It's one thing to look at an OBP and draw conclusions. It's another thing to provide reasons why the OBP is at a certain level and why it may get better or get worse.

Evaluating a hitter is based on several factors, including but not limited to, bat speed, pitch recognition, plate discipline, power, and the ability to use the entire field. These factors can be evident in a player's stats, but some cannot. How does a player make adjustments? Does he have a loose swing with projection? Is he solely a fastball hitter who struggles with breaking stuff? There can be a lot of noise in statistical evaluation of a hitter. Park factors, age vs. level, hidden injuries, and a player's makeup can be such distractions. The job of a scout is to filter out the noise and gauge a player's future worth. Of course, we expect some disagreement from time to time. But isn't that part of the fun?

Pitching assessment also has its challenges. Certain statistics paint a colorful picture. ERA, Dom, Ctl, HR per game, and Cmd are very valuable. But how does an ERA in the hitter-friendly California League compare to an ERA in the spacious ballparks of the Florida State League? The pitcher profiles in the MLBA attempt to paint a picture beyond what the stats may say. Take a look at the types of pitches and their velocities that are provided in the book. Evaluating pitching can be much more difficult than

hitters. Often times, a pitcher's command simply clicks and the prospect sees his status rise considerably. Sometimes, a pitcher loses his pitchability and can't throw strikes. We attempt to determine if those skills can return.

One significant change to this year's edition is the HQ100. The 2012 edition's Top 100 list was solely a combination of mine and Rob's individual Top 100 lists. This year's HQ100 is the by-product of five individuals. It was a fascinating exercise to see how similar—and how different—each list was to one another. None of us looked at any other list prior to formulating our own. We'll share both my list and Rob's list in this year's book. Take the time to compare our lists to the HQ100. We hope to do the same in future editions.

The Top Prospects By Position will also be formulated directly from the HQ100 as opposed to previous editions of the MLBA which were predicated on an individual writer's opinions. The Top Prospects By Organization continue to be the lists of Rob (NL) and I (AL).

We hope you enjoy the eighth edition of the MLBA. We work very hard for several months to bring you the best product we can provide. Whether you are a fantasy baseball fanatic or simply a baseball fan, we welcome any opinions, ideas, constructive criticisms, or feedback. Enjoy!

2012 Arizona Fall League Wrap-up

by Rob Gordon and Brent Hershey

There are lots of reasons for one to be careful with Arizona Fall League statistics. For one, it's a very small sample; the season is just 32 games long. Second, it's set in Phoenix, a high-altitude area that often inflates offensive performances. And third, it's always been a hitters-heavy league, and 2012 was no exception.

What follows is a subjective list of the 10 Best and 10 Worst statistical performances from the 2012 Arizona Fall League, and why they should or shouldn't matter to a prospect's overall ranking or future outlook.

10 Best Performances

George Springer (OF, HOU)
2012 stats: .302/.383/.526 with 21 doubles, 24 HR, 62 BB/156 K, and 32 SB in 506 AB between High-A and Double-A
AFL stats: .286/.412/.500 with 4 HR, 13 BB/20 K in 70 AB
Why it matters/Why it doesn't: Springer had a monster season in the CAL, but scuffled in a late-season promotion to Double-A. There were no concerns about his raw power, but needed to prove it would translate outside of the CAL, and with a .500 Slg in the AFL, he did just that. He also struck out 20 times; his contact rate going forward remains something to watch.

Matt Skole (1B/3B, WAS)
2012 stats: .291/.426/.559 with 28 doubles, 27 HR, 99 BB/133 K, and 11 SB in 413 AB between Low-A and High-A
AFL stats: .305/.419/.525 with 3 HR, and 13 BB/18 K in 59 AB
Why it matters/Why it doesn't: Skole fell to the 5th round in the 2011 draft amid concerns about a power drop. His answer in his first full season? Twenty-seven home runs in just over 400 AB. Skole is blocked at 3B by Ryan Zimmerman and Anthony Rendon, so he mostly played 1B in the AFL and looked shaky. But his bat is legit, with plus power and good plate discipline.

Nick Franklin (2B/SS, SEA)
2012 stats: .278/.347/.453 with 32 doubles, 11 HR, 48 BB/106 K in 472 AB between Double-A and Triple-A
AFL stats: .338/.422/.519 with 2 HR, 12 BB/15 K in 77 AB
Why it matters/Why it doesn't: Franklin's position on the field is the big takeaway from his AFL season: he played the entire time at second base after splitting time at both MIF positions during the year. He looked more comfortable than in his 2011 AFL season, and still profiles as a gap-power bat that should have value even at 2B. His improved Eye at the plate is also a positive development.

Anthony Rendon (3B, WAS)
2012 stats: .233/.363/.489 with 8 doubles, 6 HR, and 23 BB/29 K in 133 AB between rookie ball, High-A, and Double-A
AFL stats: .338/.436/.494 with 15 BB/14 K and 6 SB in 77 AB
Why it matters/Why it doesn't: Rendon needed to prove he could stay healthy and hit for an extended period of time. He missed most of 2012 with his second serious ankle injury. He looked 100%, had his longest active stint as a professional, and raked over his last 10 games (15-for-33 with 8 BB/5 K). He was one of the most impressive players and has regained his elite prospect status.

Mike O'Neill (OF, STL)
2012 stats: .359/.458/.440 with 24 doubles, 5 triples, 0 HR, 78 BB/26 K, and 10 SB in 418 AB between High-A and Double-A
AFL stats: .368/.463/.397 with 11 BB/11 K, and 2 SB in 68 AB
Why it matters/Why it doesn't: Despite being one of the better hitters in the minors, O'Neill won't appear on anyone's top 100 list. Listed at 5'9" 170, he might be even smaller, but is a hitting machine. He had an amazing 3.00 Eye during 2012, striking out just 26 times. He plays hard, runs well, and hits to all fields. He has very little power and will still have to prove himself at every level.

Rymer Liriano (OF, SD)
2012 stats: .280/.350/.417 with 32 doubles, 8 HR, 32 SB, 41 BB/119 K in 465 AB between High-A and Double-A
AFL stats: .319/.376/.505 with 4 HR, 6 SB, 6 BB/21 K in 91 AB
Why it matters/Why it doesn't: Liriano's prospect buzz is growing, but this might be a slight case of AFL inflation. He struggled somewhat in Double-A (.712 OPS, 183 AB) after a mid-season promotion, but many feel his doubles will grow into HR soon. The addition of his speed should put him on your fantasy radar—though his poor Eye (0.34 in 2012) indicates that he's not quite ready yet. The power is real, though.

Zach Collier (OF, PHI)
2012 stats: .269/.333/.399 with 13 doubles, 6 HR, 11 SB, 26 BB/60 K in 283 AB at High-A
AFL stats: .371/.461/.532 with 3 SB, 12 BB/10 K in 62 AB
Why it matters/Why it doesn't: Former first-round pick (2008) was playing for his 40-man roster spot, which he achieved shortly after the AFL season. Was fifth in the league in BA, but has yet to meet expectations at any full-season level (2012's .733 OPS was a career best). He'll move up to Double-A in 2013, where improvement on his career ct% of 75% will be the true test. Still has tools and the body (6-2, 185) to dream on, but it's time to produce.

Robbie Erlin (LHP, SD)
2012 stats: 3-3 with a 2.82 ERA, 16 BB/80 K, and a .248 BAA in 60.2 IP between rookie ball and High-A
AFL stats: 2-1 with a 2.28 ERA, 6 BB/31 K in 23.2 IP
Why it matters/Why it doesn't: After a June elbow strain caused him to miss the season, he came to the AFL to show his readiness to contend for a 2013 rotation spot. He did that, even in the hitter-friendly AFL. Not overpowering, he has good command of three solid offerings, locates well, and keeps hitters off balance. He should get his shot come March.

Chase Anderson (RHP, ARI)
2012 stats: 5-4, 2.86 ERA, 25 BB/75 K, and a .238 BAA in 104 IP at Double-A
AFL stats: 3-1, 3.47 ERA, 9 BB/26 K and a .218 BAA in 23.1 IP
Why it matters/Why it doesn't: Impressive numbers, but Anderson will be 25 by mid-February. His best pitch is a change-up that he can throw for strikes in any count. With the lack of a plus fastball (low 90s), Anderson is more likely to profile as a middle reliever than impact starter. He's definitely not in the Skaggs/Bradley class of ARI SP prospects.

Seth Blair (RHP, STL)

2012 stats: 1-3, 4.58 ERA, 16 BB/13 K and a .264 BAA in 19.2 IP at Rookie ball and High-A

AFL stats: 2-1, 2.25 ERA, 14 BB/22 K and a .236 BAA in 20 IP

Why it matters/Why it doesn't: Blair was making up for lost time, as a tumor on his pitching hand cut his 2012 short. A former supplemental first-round pick, he has a four-pitch mix highlighted by a lively mid-90s FB, a good change-up and some deception in his delivery. Needs to work on throwing strikes consistently, but could be an up-and-comer in 2013 if health cooperates.

10 Worst Performances

Dellin Betances (RHP, NYY)

2012 stats: 6-9, 6.44 ERA, 99 BB/124 K and a .281 BAA in 131.1 IP at Double-A and Triple-A

AFL stats: 1-3, 5.25 ERA, 4 BB/15 K and .271 BAA in 12 IP

Why it matters/Why it doesn't: Betances pitched exclusively out of the bullpen in the AFL. Given the much better BB/K numbers, he may be a better fit there, as some scouts have said for the past couple of years. Opposing hitters teeing off on him is still the main concern (BAA), but with a hulking frame like his (6-8, 260), he'll continue to get chances to succeed.

Grant Green (2B/OF, OAK)

2012 stats: .296/.338/.458 with 26 doubles, 15 HR, 33 BB/75 K, and 13 SB in 524 AB at Triple-A

AFL stats: .273/.364/.424 with 2 HR, and 10 BB/19 K in 66 AB

Why it matters/Why it doesn't: Green was the 13th overall pick in the 2009 draft, but still doesn't have a clear position. He was drafted as a SS, moved to CF, and came to the AFL to play 2B. Green struggled at the keystone and is looking more like a super utility player, though one with above-average power and a bit of speed.

Matt Curry (1B, PIT)

2012 stats: .287/.354/.479 with 34 doubles, 11 HR, 45 BB/108 K, and 4 SB in 401 AB between Double-A and Triple-A

AFL stats: .253/.366/.342 with 1 HR, 13 BB/23 K in 79 AB

Why it matters/Why it doesn't: While Curry continues to put up respectable numbers, it looks like his power isn't going to be enough for a full-time role. His bat looked very pedestrian in the AFL, and at 24, his window of opportunity is small. He's unlikely to convince the Pirates he's ready to contribute anytime soon.

Tim Beckham (SS, TAM)

2012 stats: .256/.325/.361, 10 doubles, 6 HR, 29 BB/71 K in 285 AB at Triple-A

AFL stats: .244/.282/.359, 2 doubles, 1 HR, 5 BB/29 K in 78 AB

Why it matters/Why it doesn't: Making up time due to a drug suspension, Beckham did little to change the "bust" perception attached to his #1 draft pick status (2008). Horrible plate discipline and middling power continued. Many feel that his future is either as a second baseman or just a utility player. He's still just 22, but will likely head back to Triple-A in 2013 for more seasoning.

Hak-Ju Lee (SS, TAM)

2012 stats .261/.336/.360, 15 doubles, 10 triples, 4 HR, 37 SB, 51 BB/102 K in 475 AB at Double-A

AFL stats: .247/.344/.272, with 3 SB, 11 BB/21 K in 81 AB

Why it matters/Why it doesn't: Whispers about the impotence of Lee's bat get a little louder. His game is superb defense and impressive SB numbers, but with just one extra-base hit in 81 AB in the AFL, even his 12 bb% might not be enough for fanalytic relevance. Still has to hit a little bit to get on base. Can handle the game with the glove, but the bat may hold him back.

Austin Romine (C, NYY)

2012 stats .243/.333/.408 with 5 doubles, 4 HR, 14 BB/16 K in 103 AB across three levels

AFL stats: .222/.342/.286 with 12 BB/13 K in 63 AB

Why it matters/Why it doesn't: A spring training back injury took away his outside shot to break camp with the Yankees. For the most part, Romine showed little of the double-digit HR pop of his earlier career—which continued in Arizona. His plate patience in both the regular season and AFL is a new wrinkle, but for him to stick and make a fantasy impact, his power has to return.

Edward Salcedo (3B, ATL)

2012 stats: .240/.295/.412 with 26 doubles, 17 HR, 33 BB/130 K, and 23 SB in 471 AB at High-A

AFL stats: .140/.197/.267 with 5 BB/22 K, and 5 SB in 86 AB

Why it matters/Why it doesn't: Salcedo has more than enough power, but his overly aggressive approach at the plate and sub-par defense limit his potential. He continued to show some secondary skills in the AFL (5 SB) but was over-matched at the plate and his actions at 3B were abysmal. A move to another position is likely.

Joe Panik (SS, SF)

2012 stats: .297/.368/.402 with 27 doubles, 7 HR, 10 SB, 58 BB/54 K in 535 AB at High-A

AFL stats: .205/.295/.269 with 4 SB, 10 BB/7 K in 78 AB

Why it matters/Why it doesn't: Panik is a gap-to-gap hitter with solid fundamentals and great batting eye. Some question whether he'll be able to stick at SS, but for now he makes all the plays in the field. His success in 2012 came in the high-octane CAL, so he'll need to prove himself at Double-A. Chalk up his horrible AFL to fatigue after 600+ plate appearances during the regular season.

Aaron Westlake (1B, DET)

2012 stats: .249/.320/.391 with 35 doubles, 9 HR, 47 BB/105 K, and 4 SB in 465 AB at Low-A

AFL stats: .194/.216/.347 with 3 HR, 2 BB/17 K in 72 AB

Why it matters/Why it doesn't: Westlake was a 3rd round pick in 2011 and was considered an advanced hitter with good pop and the ability to hit for average. Two years later, Westlake has failed to move past the MWL and needed something to jump-start his career. Unfortunately Westlake looked overmatched against less than stellar pitching and at 24 years old, his future looks bleak.

Jarred Cosart (RHP, HOU)

2012 stats: 6-7 with a 3.30 ERA, 51 BB/92 K, and a .250 BAA in 114.2 IP between Double and Triple-A

AFL stats: 0-3, 6.50 ERA, 9 BB/15 K, and a .313 BAA in 13 IP

Why it matters/Why it doesn't: Despite mid- to high-90s power stuff, Cosart has yet to have a true breakout. He failed to take advantage of the AFL and struggled with control. He still has time to figure things out, but the pitching-thin Astros might be forced to bring him to the majors and the results might not be pretty.

Poor Performers from the 2011 Draft

by Brent Hershey

It's a testament to the uniqueness of the 2011 MLB draft that finding out-and-out disappointments following a draftee's first full season is a bit of a challenge. Led by the initial quartet—Cole, Hultzen, Bauer, Bundy—it's more difficult to find picks from the draft's first round (typically this column's scope) that haven't been pleasant surprises. Even players that haven't quite lived up to early expectations (Bubba Starling, Corey Spangenberg come to mind) can't really be classified as "poor performers."

So for this year's exercise, we'll stretch our player pool to include the first-round supplemental picks. For one reason or another, the players below have gotten off to a slow start in their pro careers. But as several members of last year's list remind us (Delino DeShields, Aaron Sanchez, Luke Jackson), they're only a year and a half away from being one of the top 60 players in the draft. Some of these will regain their top-prospect status, while others might not.

Jed Bradley (LHP, MIL) finished his first full season at High-A Brevard County with a 5-10 record and a 5.53 ERA. More troubling, he gave up 136 hits in 107 IP and registered just a 5.0 k/9. A college lefty with good size (6-4, 225) and a history of high strikeout numbers, Bradley started quickly (2.79 ERA in five April starts), but then battled some mechanical issues and was shut down in early August with arm fatigue. He'll likely head back to High-A, where he'll attempt to re-establish his prospect status.

Levi Michael (2B/SS, MIN) also struggled in the Florida State League, finishing at .246/.339/.311 after an impressive career at the University of North Carolina. Michael came into the draft touted for his disciplined hitting approach and modest power, but both were inconsistent in his debut. His ultimate position is still to be determined; it was thought he could handle shortstop though he split time between both middle infield positions in 2012. Michael did have a better second half hitting for average and getting on base, though he failed to generate much power out of his 5-10, 180-lb frame.

Kevin Matthews (LHP, TEX) got 15 starts at Low-A Hickory, and though his ERA was passable (4.38), he continued to have problems with control. Matthews walked 64 in 74 IP in 2012, and over his professional career has a 7.2 bb/9. Though he was signed out of a UVA commitment and is still just 20 years old, Matthews has a lot of work to do in commanding his arsenal. Many scouts think that his ultimate home will be in the bullpen.

Brandon Martin (SS, TAM) has struggled with the stick in his two rookie-league assignments so far, hitting .255 in the GCL in 2011, and .209 in in the Appalachian League in 2012. He did hit 10 HR in 2012, and while his bat speed is sufficient for fastballs, pitchers soon caught on and fed him a steady diet of breaking stuff. With the leather, Martin has been a stellar defender, leading APPY shortstops in assists, putouts and double plays. For fantasy purposes, Martin has to hit to warrant a farm spot.

Larry Greene's (OF, PHI) batting average and on-base numbers don't look horrible (.272/.373) in 257 New York Penn League at-bats, but it's the lack of over-the-fence power (just 2 HR) that is surprising. The Georgia high-schooler was known for his mammoth shots, but showed up to spring training in questionable condition and it took his bat a while to get going. He did, though, hit 22 doubles and put on displays in batting practice, giving scouts and Philadelphia hope that with better focus and more reps, he'll mature into a power stud. His defense will never be a strong suit, as he's slow in left field, but improvement in his bat could alleviate concerns. He'll advance to low-A Lakewood (SAL) in 2013.

Michael Kelly (RHP, SD) never got on track in 2012, posting 18 walks but 14 strikeouts and a 7.53 ERA in 14 IP at Low-A Fort Wayne to begin the season. The Padres obviously rushed Kelly as a 19-year-old, but when they re-assigned him to their rookie-level team in Arizona, he barely fared better—44 IP, 54 H, 25 BB, 37 K and a 7.11 ERA. Kelly has a great pitcher's frame at 6-4, 185, but only has a low-90s fastball at the moment. Until his curve and change-up improve, Kelly will continue to struggle.

Dwight Smith (OF, TOR) turned down a Georgia Tech commitment to sign with the Jays, but his first full season in the system—41 games in the APPY league followed by 18 games at Vancouver—did not go well (.212/.279/.315). Known best for his pure hitting ability rather than his questionable speed or power, Smith still earned solid grades for continually making solid contact. In a system with several more advanced OF prospects, the whispers that Smith worked out some at second base in the fall instructional league make some sense. His status could take a step forward in 2013.

Kes Carter (OF, TAM) totaled less than 150 AB in the Gulf Coast and Midwest leagues in 2012, but his dismal line at Bowling Green (.228/.363/.346) isn't as bad as it looks. He got on base with a discerning eye (0.68 bb/k), stole nine bases and legged out two triples. He still grades out as a good centerfielder, but at 22 years old, needs to stay healthy and start accumulating AB. He'll go back to Low-A Bowling Green in 2013,

Grayson Garvin (LHP, TAM) suffered through an injury-plagued season, didn't pitch after June 11, and eventually succumbed to Tommy John surgery. The results weren't pretty—5.05 ERA in 11 appearances (10 starts)—but the underlying peripherals were a bit more encouraging before the injury. Though listed at 6-6, 225, there were some concerns about Garvin's lack of strikeout ability, though he fanned Florida State League batters at a 7.2 k/9 clip. For now, all bets are off until he returns (probably late in 2013, if at all), but his big-college pedigree (Vanderbilt) and Tampa's excellent track record developing starting pitchers at least give him a shred of chance long-term. But he'll need to prove his health first.

James Harris (OF, TAM) has viewed as a project when taken with the 60th overall pick in 2011, and his combined numbers in two seasons of rookie-level ball bear that out. Combined, he has a .174 batting average, though his 10% walk rate will give him ample on-base opportunities should his batting average improve. A chiseled athlete with above-average speed, he's still learning the proper technique on the basepaths (just 6 SB in 14 attempts in 2012). Harris will play most of 2013 at 20 years old, and will likely stay in extended spring training and then be assigned to rookie-level or short-season team. He's raw, but too young to give up on.

2012 First-Year Player Draft Recap

by Jeremy Deloney (AL) and Rob Gordon (NL)

AMERICAN LEAGUE

BALTIMORE ORIOLES

As is customary for this organization, the Orioles selected a nice mix of pitchers and position players as well as college and prep players. They signed 10 of their top 11 selections, though the overall success will be determined by the very top. RHP Kevin Gausman (1st) was the fourth overall pick and could reach the big leagues as soon as 2014. He has proven success with his power repertoire and only needs to polish his secondary offerings. RHP Branden Kline (2nd) gives Baltimore another high upside arm to dream on. The best position players are led by prep SS Adrian Marin (3rd) and college 1B Christian Walker (4th). Both are capable of producing solid offensive results while Marin has legitimate secondary skills with his speed and defense. Walker could also advance quickly due to his polished approach and feel for contact.

Sleeper: RHP Josh Hader (19th) was not considered a top prospect entering the draft, but he found a great deal of success upon signing, going 2-0 with a 1.88 ERA, 2.8 Ctl, and 15.1 Dom between rookie ball and short-season ball. He has a long, lean frame with lots of projection.

Grade: C+

BOSTON RED SOX

The Red Sox focused on pitching in this draft and were able to select a solid mix of prep arms and more polished collegiate pitchers. However, their first selection was SS Deven Marrero (1st) who was coming off of a disappointing season at Arizona State. Few draftees can match his defensive attributes and he could make an impact with the bat with a few adjustments. Their next eight selections were pitchers, including two intriguing college arms in LHP Brian Johnson (1st) and RHP Pat Light (supplemental 1st). Both are strike-throwing machines and Light is capable of reaching the mid-to-high 90s on occasion. RHP Jamie Callahan (2nd) is the type of prep pitcher who could stay in short-season ball for a few years to iron out his mechanics and realize the power potential expected of him. The highest upside of anybody in this class is RHP Ty Buttrey (4th) who has a tall and projectable frame with solid present velocity. He could develop into a #2-type starter with a plus fastball and curveball combination. Outside of Marrero, there isn't much promise with any position player selected.

Sleeper: RHP Justin Haley (6th) has a big body with nice velocity. He uses his height to pitch on a downhill plane and induce a high amount of groundballs. He lacks a true out pitch, though he commands his fastball well. He posted a 1.89 ERA, 4.3 Ctl, and 8.9 Dom with Lowell of the short-season NY-Penn League.

Grade: B

CHICAGO WHITE SOX

The White Sox didn't spend a ton of money in signing their draft picks, but they got good value with their selections. This could be one of the more underrated draft classes and they will need their top two selections to pan out. OF Courtney Hawkins (1st) and 1B Keon Barnum (supplemental 1st) give them two power hitting sluggers that project to middle-of-the-order run producers. Hawkins made it all the way to High-A as an 18-year-old and he brings several promising tools to the table. Barnum is more of a bat-only prospect, but the power is exciting. He'll need to make more contact and improve his pitch recognition to realize the pop. 2B Joey DeMichele (3rd) is an advanced infielder who can put bat to ball and run well. He could be a fast-mover in this organization. Another quality infielder is 2B Micah Johnson (9th), but he doesn't offer as much contact as DeMichele, though he has plus speed. RHPs Chris Beck (2nd) and Brandon Brennan (4th) highlight the pitchers of the White Sox selections and both have upside of mid-rotation starters.

Sleeper: C Sammy Ayala (17th) was expected to be selected much higher. He offers excellent size, strength, and power potential, though he has plenty of work to do behind the dish.

Grade: C+

CLEVELAND INDIANS

After selecting a college hitter in OF Tyler Naquin in the first round, the Indians opted for three high school performers who have healthy upsides. Naquin is a virtual shoo-in to reach the majors based upon his polished all-around game, though he lacks ideal power to be a corner outfielder. RHP Mitch Brown (2nd) headlines the trio of promising prep stars and he could end up being a steal in the second round. RHP Kieran Lovegrove (3rd) provides lots of projection and potential and will likely be a long-term project. The Indians are excited about OF D'Vone McClure (4th) who has great athleticism and could develop into an offensive behemoth with added strength and consistency. There isn't much depth outside of the first four picks, though a few such as RHP Dylan Baker (5th), OF Josh Schubert (7th), and 1B Nelson Rodriguez (15th) could pay dividends down the road.

Sleeper: RHP Jacob Lee (9th) had a stellar pro debut in short-season ball by throwing strikes and getting hitters to chase his curveball out of the strike zone. He may not have much upside, but could eventually make it to the majors as a reliever.

Grade: C

DETROIT TIGERS

The Tigers have been known to select players who have dropped in the draft due to signability concerns and the expectation was they would do the same this year with their first pick not coming until pick #91. While prep RHP Jake Thompson (2nd) was selected where he was projected, he gives the Tigers a high-ceiling pitcher that could eventually front a rotation one day. OF Austin Schotts (3rd) had the best pro debut in the system even after moving from SS to CF upon signing. After selecting Schotts, Detroit didn't pick a high school player again until the 18th round. Their meager draft pool forced them to pick signable college players, though a few have excellent potential. RHP Drew VerHagen (4th) is a hard-throwing sinkerballer who keeps the ball on the ground, while LHP Joe Rogers (5th) could reach the majors as a situational reliever unless the Tigers wish to develop him as a starter. By no means was this a great draft, but they added a few quality arms to an organization in desperate need of pitching prospects.

Sleeper: OF Jake Stewart (9th) has good tools and athleticism, but didn't produce much at Stanford. He has sufficient power potential and he runs very well.

Grade: C-

HOUSTON ASTROS

No other organization can boast the quality the Astros obtained in this particular draft. From high upside prep stars to low ceiling college players, they selected a healthy mix. With the second highest bonus pool, Houston was able to draft and sign their top 11 picks. SS Carlos Correa (1st) was the first overall pick and he has scary upside with both the bat and glove. Complementing him was a nifty pick in RHP Lance McCullers Jr (supplemental 1st) who is only a refined change-up away from being a legitimate top-of-the-rotation arm. After those two, the Astros opted for a few near-sure things with INF Nolan Fontana (2nd) from the University of Florida and RHP Brady Rodgers (3rd) from Arizona State. Fontana walked 65 times while fanning only 44 times in 49 games with Low-A Lexington. Rodgers doesn't own a true out pitch, but throws strikes and locates with precision. In the fourth round, the Astros went well over slot to select 3B Rio Ruiz, a high school infielder who could be the steal of the draft. Much of the money spent on McCullers and Ruiz came from the slot of Correa, who signed for well under what was expected of the #1 overall pick. While there wasn't much talent left to sign after the first six rounds, the Astros absolutely cornered the market on premium talent.

Sleeper: OF Brett Phillips (6th) has scary speed and arm strength and projects as a big league CF. The question is whether he'll be able to hit. He has a solid approach, though questionable pop.

Grade: A+

KANSAS CITY ROYALS

Picking #5, the Royals were in line to get a high-quality pitcher and they got one in RHP Kyle Zimmer (1st). He has the goods to pitch at the front of the rotation and he could get to Kansas City very quickly. He immediately becomes their top pitching prospect. The Royals were able to bolster their pitching depth with a few others shrewd selections in the next two rounds. LHP Sam Selman (2nd) and LHP Colin Rodgers (3rd) were excellent picks in their respective rounds and should be counted on to reach the majors at some point. Selman won the Pioneer League's pitcher of the year in his pro debut. Rodgers has nice pitchability and advanced command for someone his age. They didn't select a hitter until INF Kenny Diekroeger (4th) and they went over slot to sign him. He's been an enigma throughout his amateur career and the Royals hope to cultivate his talents. The best pro debut may have been from OF Alexis Rivera (10th) who eclipsed expectations with his advanced bat and solid secondary skills. Junior college OF Fred Ford (7th) has significant power upside and smashed 13 HR with short-season Burlington. Whether that power plays at an upper level remains to be seen, as he has a very long swing and difficulty making contact.

Sleeper: OF Ethan Chapman (30th) was a lightly-regarded college outfielder, but his speed and CF range should get him to the big leagues. He draws walks and understands his role as a speedster with limited power.

Grade: A-

LOS ANGELES ANGELS

Without a first or second round pick, the Angels were left with some of the scraps, but were able to snag a few useful pieces. They were able to sign 36 of their 38 selections and feed a system that ranks among the shallowest in baseball. RHP R.J. Alvarez (3rd) was their top pick and most expensive sign and he inked a contract only for $416,000. He immediately becomes one of the better pitching prospects in the system due to his quick arm that pops mid-90s velocity. Another interesting arm is RHP Mark Sappington (5th) who could convert to the bullpen and provide plenty of power. The Angels are likely to keep him as a starter for the time being. The position players lack significant tools, but there are a few who could develop into solid big league infielders. 2B Alex Yarbrough (4th) is a natural hitter who maximizes his tools with hustle and intelligence. He teamed with SS Eric Stamets (6th) to form a double-play combo at Low-A Cedar Rapids upon signing. Stamets is all about speed and defense. The highest upside among the Angels draftees could be RHP Reid Scoggins (15th) who returned from Tommy John surgery and has incredible velocity with a violent delivery.

Sleeper: RHP Yency Almonte (17th) is the type of pick that could pay off in the long-run if the Angels can cultivate his smooth delivery and projection.

Grade: D+

MINNESOTA TWINS

Blessed with the highest draft pool with which to sign draftees, the Twins took advantage by taking OF Byron Buxton (1st) with the #2 overall pick and signing him to a $6 million bonus. Minnesota has been known to choose command-oriented strikethrowers in the draft, but they went the opposite route this season. After Buxton, the Twins selected hard-throwing pitchers with five of their next six picks. RHP J.O. Berrios (supplemental 1st) has as much upside as any high school pitcher in the draft while RHP Luke Bard (supplemental 1st) and LHP Mason Melotakis (2nd) could find their way to the Twin Cities fairly quickly. RHP J.T. Chargois (2nd) profiles as a late-innings reliever while RHP Zack Jones (4th) could also earn that type of role. The Twins set out to add several pieces to their thin pitching corps and they satisfied their appetite. The position players weren't in abundance, though OF Adam Brett Walker (3rd) should supply plenty of power. They had a very productive draft and it will be interesting to see whether the change in philosophy will lead to success down the road.

Sleeper: LHP Taylor Rogers (11th) fits the Twins usual mold with his command and pinpoint fastball location. He may not have frontline velocity, but he sequences pitches and can miss bats with his curveball.

Grade: A

NEW YORK YANKEES

The Yankees were determined to add some young, exciting talent to their farm system and they did just that with some smart and shrewd selections. They added some interesting power arms while picking a few hitters who swing a good bat, but have limited secondary skills. The Yankees signed their first 20 picks, most of them from the college ranks. The first two selections, RHP Ty Hensley (1st) and OF Austin Aune (2nd), offer high upside potential. Both are terrific athletes who could make significant impacts in the near-term. Perhaps the best arm in this class belongs to RHP Corey Black (4th) who dominated hitters at short-season Staten Island and Low-A Charleston in his pro debut. He can bring serious heat—90-98 mph fastball—despite a short and thin frame. C Peter O'Brien (2nd) offers excellent power at the plate, but is limited defensively as is 1B Nathan Mikolas (3rd). A pitcher who could reach the big leagues in a hurry is RHP Nick Goody (6th) who made it to High-A in his debut and should thrive in a short-innings role.

Sleeper: LHP James Pazos (13th) is the type of arm that should make it to the big leagues on the basis of his aggressive style and demeanor. While he sits in the low-90s and lacks frontline velocity, he knows how to pitch and is effective against hitters from both sides of the plate.

Grade: B-

OAKLAND ATHLETICS

With three of the first 47 picks in the draft, the Athletics took high school infielders and all immediately become among their top prospects. Sprinkle in a few college players and this draft was among the best in baseball. SS Addison Russell (1st) along with supplemental first rounders SS/3B Daniel Robertson and 1B Matt Olson could all advance together and form an exciting infield at Low-A Beloit in 2014. All three offer quality hitting skills with solid power. Of the three, Robertson is likely the most polished prospect, but Russell's upside and Olson's power are more promising. Outside of RHP Nolan Sanburn (2nd), the Athletics didn't select many high-upside arms, but a few could become useful pieces. Sanburn and RHP Seth Streich (6th) were chosen from the college ranks and can dial up their fastballs to the mid-90s. Other solid position players selected include C Bruce Maxwell (2nd), athletic OF B.J. Boyd (4th), and 1B Max Muncy (5th).

Sleeper: RHP Kris Hall (8th) sits in the low-90s with his fastball and can complement it with two good breaking balls. He may be better as a reliever where he could advance quickly.

Grade: B+

SEATTLE MARINERS

The Mariners were able to stock up on infielders, but their first round selection will ultimately determine the success of this draft. C Mike Zunino was chosen with the third overall pick and he dazzled in his pro debut, reaching Double-A and slugging .588 with 3 HR in 51 AB. He hit .360/.447/.689 with 13 HR between short-season Everett and Double-A Jackson. There is a chance he'll reach Seattle by the end of '13. 3B Joe DeCarlo (2nd) provides another solid offensive producer along with 3B Patrick

Kivlehan (4th) who was named MVP of the Northwest League after hitting .301 with 12 HR in 282 AB. They were able to select a few excellent defensive infielders as well. SS Chris Taylor (5th) and 2B Timothy Lopes (6th) have excellent quickness and range and could provide enough offense to warrant long looks in the future. Due to the focus on offense, only two pitchers were taken in the first nine rounds. High school RHP Edwin Diaz (3rd) has above average velocity, but he has major work in front of him with his shoddy command. LHP Tyler Pike (supplemental 3rd) is virtually the opposite. He doesn't throw very hard, but has better command and polish than most high school hurlers.

Sleeper: OF Jamodrick McGruder (9th) was a 2B at Texas Tech and saw more time in the outfield upon signing. He has top-of-the-line speed and could become a significant asset defensively due to his range and arm. He will never hit for much power, but he gets on base consistently.

Grade: B

TAMPA BAY RAYS

The Rays were quite diligent in selecting players they could sign and they were able to ink 37 of their 40 selections. This is an organization that believes in toolsy players and they have no problem with letting their prospects develop at their own pace. After selecting relatively safe college 3B Richie Shaffer with their first pick, they opted for high-upside prep players with their next five selections. Though Shaffer was an easy choice, he has plus bat potential with both BA and power due to his professional approach and easy contact. There are several intriguing position players in this haul, led by OF Bralin Jackson (5th), OF Andrew Toles (3rd), and SS Spencer Edwards (2nd). Toles is a multi-talented player who has well above average speed and can be a solid defender in CF. Jackson and Edwards could take a while to develop, but both offer exciting tools. There weren't many arms selected, though RHP Damion Carroll (6th) and RHP Nolan Gannon (4th) are legitimate talents. The best pro debut belonged to the Rays last selection, RHP Nick Sawyer (40th) who posted a 0.28 ERA, 3.9 Ctl, and 16.6 Dom on three levels. He'll remain in the bullpen where his max-effort delivery provides plenty of deception.

Sleeper: C Taylor Hawkins (12th) wasn't exactly a standout in his pro debut (.182, 0 HR, 24 Ks in 55 AB), but he offers lots of power and arm strength. He needs significant polish, but the potential reward is huge.

Grade: B

TEXAS RANGERS

The Rangers love high-upside toolsy prospects and they drafted their fair share. Their first five picks were all from the high school ranks and four of them are position players. Though there is always risk in multi-tooled high school players, the Rangers have a good track record of developing them. 3B Joey Gallo (supplemental 1st) had a spectacular pro debut and won the Arizona League's MVP award after breaking the league's HR record. OF Lewis Brinson (1st) has plentiful tools and could be the system's best prospect if he develops as expected. OFs Jamie Jarmon (2nd) and Nick Williams (2nd) are also intriguing picks. Williams had a much better debut, though Jarmon has exciting potential. The pitcher with the best chance for future success is RHP Collin Wiles (supplemental 1st) who many thought would go to Vanderbilt instead of signing. He lacks velocity at present, but he has a long, lean frame that should add plenty of ticks down the road. The other pitchers selected were more for depth purposes.

Sleeper: RHP Eric Brooks (11th) is a groundball machine with good velocity and the chance to become a solid #4-type starter. He offers athleticism and a clean delivery with the ability to throw consistent strikes.

Grade: A-

TORONTO BLUE JAYS

With five of the first 60 picks in the draft, the Blue Jays focused on high upside players, particularly from the high school ranks. RHP Marcus Stroman (1st) was pegged by many draft pundits as being close to the big leagues, but a 50-game suspension for PEDs will carry over into May. He's still expected to reach Toronto towards the end of the season, if not earlier. Another impressive arm, LHP Matt Smoral (supplemental 1st), didn't pitch upon signing for $2 million because of a broken foot. Other high school pitchers selected include RHP Tyler Gonzales (supplemental 1st) who owns a big fastball and potential to become a dynamite late-innings reliever and RHP Chase DeJong (2nd) who has better secondary offerings. The key to the success of this draft may be on the shoulders of ultra-athletic OFs, D.J. Davis (1st) and Anthony Alford (3rd). Davis can fly on the basepaths and has sufficient bat speed and strength to project power down the road. Alford has a very high ceiling with plus speed and some potential to develop a feel for hitting. It is also easy to overlook 3B Mitch Nay (supplemental 1st) who has the most power in this draft class.

Sleeper: 2B Will Dupont (16th) offers nice upside, but has limited defensive skills. He slid over to 2B upon signing and could also play CF. He has excellent speed and moderate power potential to profile as an offensive-minded 2B.

Grade: A-

NATIONAL LEAGUE

ARIZONA DIAMONDBACKS

The Diamondbacks selected Stryker Trahan with the 26th overall pick in the draft and he had a nice pro debut, hitting .281 with power and good plate discipline. Trahan was drafted as a catcher and the success of this draft will hinge upon him being able to stick behind the plate. The club played it fairly safe after taking the risky Trahan, going with high school 3B Jose Munoz (2nd) and ASU right-hander reliever Jake Barrett (3rd). Barrett struggled in his pro debut, going 0-3 with a 5.84 ERA in 25 outings.

Sleeper: Evan Marzilli (OF) was a hard-nosed, grinding type player at South Carolina, but does not have the raw skills that excite scouts. He does, however, have good speed, makes consistent contact, and is a good defensive CF. Marzilli hit .332/.403/.389 with 6 SB in his debut and could develop into a solid 4th OF.

Grade: C+

ATLANTA BRAVES

The Braves signed all 10 players covered by the new slotting system and spent almost all of their $4 million draft budget. The new slotting system encouraged the Braves to move away from high upside high school prospects after the first couple of rounds, but they did get two local players in Lucas Sims (RHP), who hails from Snellville, GA and Alex Wood (LHP) from University of Georgia. Both players have questions about their ability to remain starters, but also had impressive pro debuts and can reach the upper-90s with their fastballs. The Braves also nabbed defensive-minded backstop Bryan de la Rosa (C) in the third round and the offensive-minded Josh Elander (C) in round six.

Sleeper: David Peterson (RHP) was an 8th round pick out of Charleston has a nice 92-95 mph fastball that tops out at 96 mph. He works mostly off his fastball and commands it well to both sides of the plate. His curveball and change-up are below-average and will need to improve for him to transition back into a starting role. The Braves used him in relief in his pro debut, where he was very effective, going 4-1 with a 1.93 ERA.

Grade: B

CHICAGO CUBS

The rebuilding Cubs had the 6th overall pick in the draft and two supplemental picks. They went with toolsy high school OF Albert Almora. Some scouts and analysts viewed Almora as the top player available in the draft and the Cubs were thrilled he was still available. He has 5-tool potential and was impressive in his pro debut, hitting .321 in 140 AB. The Cubs also landed Missouri State righty Pierce Johnson who has a good 92-94 mph fastball and high school right-hander Paul Blackburn who has good athleticism and some projectability. The Cubs were one of a few teams to go over their allotted budget, but not by enough to lose any future draft picks.

Sleeper: 7th round pick Stephen Bruno (SS) projects as a utility-type infielder who can play SS, 2B, and 3B if needed. He is a polished hitter and batted .361 in the NWL. Bruno has a short-compact stroke and a good understanding of the strike zone. He makes consistent contact, has moderate gap power, and could be a useful player down the road.

Grade: A

CINCINNATI REDS

Much like the Cubs, the Reds had a fairly high 1st round pick and two supplemental picks, and they opted for high school right-hander Nick Travieso and then landed outfielders Jesse Winker and UCLA standout Jeff Gelalich. At 6-2, 215 Travieso was a bit of a risky pick at #14. He has three potentially plus offerings, including a 91-94 mph fastball and a good hard slider, but doesn't have great size and struggles with control. Winker looks to have been under-rated pre-draft and was one of the more dynamic players in the Pioneer League, hitting .338/.443/.500 and Gelalich has solid all-around potential. If Travesio pans out, this could be another good draft for the Reds, but there are some risks.

Sleeper: Seth Mejias-Brean (3B) was an 8th round pick out of the University of Arizona. He has good power and solid plate discipline and fared well in his pro debut, hitting .313/.389/.536. He is a plus defender at 3B with good hands, range, and a strong arm and could be a steal this late in the draft.

Grade: C+

COLORADO ROCKIES

With the 10th overall pick the Rockies took high school CF David Dahl. Dahl was considered one of the better prep offensive players and he did not disappoint in his pro debut, hitting .379/.423/.625 with 22 2B, 10 3B, 9 HR, and 12 SB in 280 AB and was the most dynamic player in the Pioneer League. The Rockies also added Radford right-hander Eddie Butler who has a good mid-90s fastball and a plus slider. He worked as a starter in his debut, but likely profiles better as a reliever. An interesting pick-up in the 3rd round was Buffalo catcher Tom Murphy. He has a nice bat—.288/.349/.462—but isn't likely to stick behind the plate. The Rockies desperately need pitching and failed to add an impact arm in this draft.

Sleeper: Wilfredo Rodriguez (C) was a 7th round pick out of high school in Puerto Rico. You can never have too many catching prospects and Rodriguez has a nice bat and had a solid debut, hitting .319/.370/.452 in the Pioneer League. He is fairly raw defensively, but works hard and could stick at catcher.

Grade: B

LOS ANGELES DODGERS

The Dodgers new ownership has stated that they intend to restore the luster to the venerable franchise. The Dodgers were once the envy of the baseball world because of their seemingly endless supply of quality prospects, especially pitchers and international players. The new draft rules make rebuilding a farm system a longer-term project, but the Dodgers made steps in the right direction when they selected Corey Seager with the 18th overall pick. Seager is a fairly polished high school SS with a plus bat and above-average defense, though his pro future may be at 3B. They followed that up by taking switch-hitting Puerto Rican SS Jesmuel Valentin and Florida lefty Paco Rodriguez. Overall Seager is the one standout in this year's crop and the organization will look to add more depth via the international and FA market.

Sleeper: Zach Bird (RHP) signed for just $140,000 in the 9th round. He is a 6'4" high school right-hander who is long and lean and comes after hitters from a high 3/4 slot. He pitches off an 88-92 mph fastball and also has a big, looping curveball, and a change that has some potential. He struck out 10.4 per nine in his pro debut and will be worth watching.

Grade: C+

MIAMI MARLINS

The once again re-tooling Marlins had the 9th pick in the 2012 draft and opted to go with Oklahoma State lefty Andrew Heaney. Heaney isn't a flame-thrower, but rather a polished collegiate lefty who should reach the majors quickly. He has a 90-92 mph fastball, good breaking ball, and a good change-up and locates all three offerings well. The club did not have another pick until the 3rd

round where they selected high school 3B Avery Romero. Heaney is the only sure-fire impact player from this draft class.

Sleeper: Nick Wittgren (RHP) is a long, lean right-hander from Purdue and had an excellent professional debut, posting a 1.17 ERA with 5 BB/47 K in 30.2 IP. His fastball isn't plus and sits in the low-90s but he has some nice deception and a decent curveball. He notched 13 saves in 23 games and could move up quickly.

Grade: B

MILWAUKEE BREWERS

The Brewers had to wait until the 27th pick to make their first selection of the 2012 draft, but then got to pick twice and nabbed power hitters Clint Coulter (C) and Victor Roache (OF). At 6-3, 200 pounds, Coulter was one of the more physical players available and had a nice debut, hitting .302/.439/.444. He did strike out often but also drew plenty of walks (37 BB/40 K in 169 AB). Roache hit an NCAA-leaging 30 home runs at Georgia Southern in '11, but missed all of '12 with a broken wrist and remains a bit of a wild card. If healthy, he has as much power as any player in the draft. The Brewers also snagged Cal Poly star Mitch Haniger (OF) with a supplemental 1st round pick, giving the club some much needed positional depth.

Sleeper: Edgardo Rivera (OF) was an 8th round pick out of Puerto Rico. He is fairly raw, but might be one of the best runners in the system with a bit of power and the ability to hit. He had a solid pro debut, hitting .262/.356/.310 in the AZL.

Grade: A-

NEW YORK METS

The struggling Mets are in desperate need of big league position players. Not surprisingly their top three picks in the 2012 draft address that need. With the 12th overall pick the Mets selected high school shortstop Gavin Cecchini, who is the younger brother of the Red Sox Garin Cecchini. Gavin is a solid, all-around player who has the tools to stick at short, though a .246 BA in rookie ball showed holes in his swing. The Mets also took Purdue backstop Kevin Plawecki as and Arkansas SS Matt Reynolds. Unfortunately none of their top three picks looked very impressive in their debuts and lack the physicality to be impact players. The club failed to sign their second pick in round two, Teddy Stankiewicz and picked a college reliever in round three. Overall this was not a particularly impressive crop of prospects.

Sleeper: Logan Taylor (RHP) was the Mets 11th round pick out of Eastern Oklahoma State JC. At 6-5, 205 he still has some projection and already features a nice 90-94 mph fastball and a decent curve. The Mets used him exclusively in relief in his debut, where he was very effective, going 2-0 with a 0.93 ERA, 2 BB/19 K in 19.1 IP.

Grade: C-

PITTSBURGH PIRATES

The Pirates have been very aggressive in recent drafts, spending well above slot recommendations and landing high-upside players such as Josh Bell, Jameson Taillon, Stetson Allie, Clay Holmes, and Gerrit Cole. The new, firmer system established in the most recent collective bargaining agreement was meant to limit teams like the Pirates from going overboard. When Mark Appel, whom many felt was the best player available in the draft, slipped to #8, the Pirates took a chance and made him their selection. After weeks of negotiations, the two sides were not able to reach a deal and Appel returned to Stanford for his senior season. The Pirates do get a compensation pick in 2013 and were able to land Texas Tech OF Barrett Barnes (1-S) and high school catcher Wyatt Mathisen (2), but the loss of Appel makes the overall haul fairly skimpy.

Sleeper: Tyler Gaffney (OF) has nice athleticism and had a decent career as a two-sport player (football and baseball) at Stanford. He has good speed and plenty of raw strength, but was somewhat stiff in his actions due to his football-related bulk. He did, however, show a good approach at the plate with decent understanding of the strike zone and good discipline. He was surprisingly effective in his pro debut, hitting .297 with 20 BB/20 K, and 11 SB in 111 AB at State College in the NYPL.

Grade: D+

PHILIDELPHIA PHILLIES

The Phillies didn't have a first round pick and had to wait until pick #40 to make their initial selection. The organization continues to value projectable high school athletes and they did not deviate in '12. The team made RHP Shane Watson their first pick and he had a solid, if brief, debut. Watson has some nice projection left, but for now tops out at 94 mph. The club then picked Mitch Gueller at #54 and Dylan Cozens at #77. They were not able to sign their second 2nd round pick Alec Rash and then went with low-upside but inexpensive college players in rounds 6-11. The Phillies overall haul this year was relatively thin and Waston was the only top 100 player the club was able to land.

Sleeper: Hoby Milner (LHP) was the club's 7th round pick after an inconsistent career at Texas. Milner worked mostly in relief for the Longhorns and has a decent 87-90 mph fastball, a good curveball, and a decent change-up. He showed good control while in college and had a decent pro debut, going 7-3 with a 2.50 ERA, 24 BB/54 K in 68.1 IP. For now Milner will work as a starter, but could be a nice lefty reliever.

Grade: D

ST. LOUIS CARDINALS

The Cardinals rapidly improving farm system was given additional depth as they had 5 of the first 59 picks. They did an excellent job of filling organizational need and adding across the board depth. The club's first selection was Texas A&M right-hander Michael Wacha. At 6-6, 200 pounds Wacha was one of the more projectable college hurlers available. He showed a 90-93 mph fastball, but clocked in a 96 mph at times. He mixed in a good slider, a curve, and a change-up. Wacha was so effective in his debut that he progressed all the way up to Double-A and could make his MLB debut in 2013. The Cardinals also added Florida State OF James Ramsey at #23, Stanford 3B Stephen Piscotty at #36, St. Mary's 3B Patrick Wisdom at #52, and high school catcher Steve Bean at #59. The club also added Wake Forest lefty Tim Cooney

who also had a very strong debut (3.40 ERA with 8 BB/43 K). Adding a character player in CF (Ramsey), two corner guys, a finesse lefty, and an impressive catcher in Bean, the Cardinals did remarkably well.

Sleeper: Brett Wiley (2B) was the Cardinals 13th round pick out of Jefferson JC in Missouri. Wiley is a solid all-around player who has a good approach at the plate with a short, compact stroke and decent plate discipline. He has gap power and slugged .443 in his debut. He moves well with good range and a strong arm and played SS in junior college.

Grade: A

SAN FRANCISCO GIANTS

The Giants selected Mississippi State right-hander Chris Stratton with 20th pick in the draft. Stratton is a polished hurler with a 91-93 mph fastball, a plus slider, curve, and change-up. He has good command and should develop into a solid mid-rotation starter and could move up quickly. The Giants picked college players with their first five picks, highlighted by Martin Agosta (RHP) in the 2nd round and Mac Willimanson (OF) from Wake Forest in round 3. Willamson had a nice debut, hitting .342 with 7 home runs, and was one of the more impressive players in the NWL, but overall the Giants did not pick up a lot of impact talent.

Sleeper: Tyler Hollick (OF) was the Giants 14th round pick out of Chandler-Gilbert CC in Arizona. Hollick doesn't have any standout tools, but does have a solid all-around approach. He has above-average speed, plays solid defense in CF, and has a nice compact stroke at the plate. In his debut he hit .301/.441/.372 with 28 BB/27 K and 21 SB in 23 attempts.

Grade: C

SAN DIEGO PADRES

The Padres already have one of the deeper farm systems in the minors and in 2012 were able to add to that depth. The Padres used three of their first four picks to take high school hurlers: Max Fried (LHP), Zach Eflin (RHP), and Walker Weickel (RHP). Fried was a teammate of 16th overall pick Lucas Giolito at Harvard-Westlake High School in California. Fried features a 90-93 mph fastball that tops out at 95 mph, a plus curveball, and an average change-up and could quickly become one of the better LHP in the minors. Eflin had triceps tendinitis, but before the injury flashed a plus mid-90s fastball that tops out at 97 mph and Weickel is a projectable 6-6, 200 pound right-hander whose fastball is already in the 91-94 mph range. The Padres also took Stony Brook OF Travis Jankowski as a supplemental 1st round pick and he brings plus speed and excellent CF defense. The Padres had a $9.9 million draft budget and they spent all but $90,000 of it and signed their first 14 picks. If Fried and Jankowski pan out, this could be a very good draft.

Sleeper: Maxx Tissenbaum (2B) doesn't generate much scouting buzz and at 6-0, 180 he doesn't have any physical tools that stand out. He is, however, a good defender at 2B, has surprising power, good strike zone judgment, and battles in every AB. He had a nice pro debut, hitting .296/.399/.374 with 27 BB/14 K in 171 AB.

Grade: A-

WASHINGTON NATIONALS

For the past several years the Nationals have opted to take the best player available, regardless of the circumstances. So far, this approach has paid off handsomely, netting them Stephen Strasburg, Drew Storen, Bryce Harper, Anthony Rendon, Alex Meyer, and Brian Goodwin. This year was no exception as the Nationals selected high school righty Lucas Giolito, despite the fact that he sprained his UCL in March ending his senior year. The Nationals hoped that rest and rehab would take care of the problem, but Giolito logged just 2 innings before heading for Tommy John surgery in August. Giolito will miss all of 2013, but should be ready to resume his career in 2014. Prior to the injury, Giolito had a fastball that sat at 94-96 and topped out at 99 mph to go along with a plus curveball and a plus change-up. Assuming a full recover, he still has tremendous long-term potential. The Nats followed up this risky pick by going with safe college players with their next four selections—Tony Renda (2B), Brett Mooneyham (LHP), Brandon Miller (OF), and Spencer Kieboom (C).

Sleeper: Ronald Pena (RHP) was the Nationals 16th round pick out of Palm Beach State JC in Florida. Pena has a nice 90-93 mph fastball that tops out a 94 mph. He also throws a decent curve and change-up, but struggles with command and consistency. He looked good in his brief pro debut, going 1-1 with a 2.92 ERA, 1 BB/9 K in 12.1 IP.

Grade: B

2012-2013 Top 20 International Prospects

by Rob Gordon

Each year there is a bevy of talented international players who emerge on the scene. Despite the creation of the World Baseball Classic and the brief appearance of baseball as an Olympic sport, these players do not get a lot of exposure until they sign professional contracts and come to the U.S. This article will take a look at the top 20 international prospects for 2012-2013. Since the focus of the MLBA is on prospects, this list will not include international players over the age of 30, but does include international Non-Drafted Free Agents (NDFA) who have signed or remain unsigned at the time of the publication (January 2013). For each player we have provided a scouting report, an ETA to the majors, a player rating, and a brief summary of their contractual status.

Franklin Barreto (SS, TOR)

A short, athletic 16-year-old from Venezuela, he has tons of international experience from the age of 10. He is an advanced hitter with a good approach at the plate, quick hands, and the ability to make consistent contact. At 5-9, 175 he doesn't project to have much power, but he uses the whole field, with decent pop and can hit the ball into the gaps where he can use his plus speed. Defensively, he has good range but doesn't have true shortstop actions and has an average arm. Some scouts see him moving to CF due to his plus speed, but the lack of power could push him to 2B where he could develop into a Jose Altuve-type. The Blue Jays signed Barreto to a $1.45 million bonus.
MLB Debut: 2017
Potential Rating: 8C

Carlos Belen (3B, SD)

A tall, physically strong 3B from the Dominican Republic who signed with the Padres for a $1 million bonus. He has a potential impact bat with power and a good approach at the plate. He already shows good bat speed, quick hands, and a decent understanding of the strike zone. Some evaluators are not convinced that he will be able to stick at 3B as he doesn't have first-step quickness or adequate range. He does have a strong arm and decent hands, but his value takes a hit if he has to move to the OF, where he is a below-average runner. The Padres already have good depth at 3B and are attempting to stockpile as many power bats as they can, but they do need to figure out where he will play.
MLB Debut: 2018
Potential Rating: 9D

Gustavo Cabrera (OF, SF)

A physically mature Dominican who signed with the Giants for a $1.3 million bonus, many scouts considered Cabrera to be the top prospect from Latin America. He has plus, plus speed, raw power, plus bat speed, and has a decent understanding of how to hit. He is also a good defender with enough range and arm strength to play CF. He's had hamstring issues in the past, but the Giants loved his athleticism. Some scouts do have questions about his ability to hit for average and to stay balanced at the plate, but his plus raw tools make him particularly appealing.
MLB Debut: 2017
Potential Rating: 9D

Jose Castillo (LHP, TAM)

Castillo is a 17-year-old from Venezuela. At 6-4, 200 he already has an ideal pitching frame and should add strength and durability. He has a good low-90s fastball that tops out at 93-94 mph and could develop into a mid-90s heater once he fills out. He also has a decent change-up and a breaking ball that needs refinement. Nice, clean, easily repeatable mechanics with good velocity from the left-hand side. If the secondary offerings come along, he has substantial upside. The Rays inked him to a $1.55 million bonus.
MLB Debut: 2017
Potential Rating: 9E

Luis Castillo (SS, Venezuela)

Castillo is a 17-year-old shortstop from Venezuela who signed an $800,000 deal with the Blue Jays, only to have the contact voided when he failed a physical. Prior, Castillo impressed with his well-rounded game. He has good bat speed and squares the ball up well with a nice line-drive approach. Scouts feel he will develop moderate to above-average power down the road. Might not have enough speed or range to stick at SS, but does have a good arm and mobility so a move to 3B or the OF would be possible.
MLB Debut: 2018
Potential Rating: 8D

Shintaro Fujinami (RHP, Japan)

He might be the best pitching prospect without an MLB contract. The 18-year-old right-hander has a strong, durable frame and features a 90-94 mph fastball with good late life. He also has a potentially plus mid-80s slider, a splitter, and a decent change-up. He has better command than countryman Shohei Otani and has plenty of international experience from Japan's 18U world championship team. Fujinami was taken in the 1st round of the NPB draft by the Hanshin Tigers and will have to go through the traditional posting system before he is eligible to come to the U.S.
MLB Debut: ?
Potential Rating: 9D

Luiz Gohara (LHP, SEA)

Gohara is a tall, long-limbed 16-year-old left-hander from Brazil. At 6-3, 220 he already has good size and a nice 88-92 mph fastball and in instructional ball was topping out at 96 mph. He mixes in a curveball that has the potential to be a plus, a slider, and an unrefined change-up. He comes after hitters from a high ¾ arm slot, and though he hasn't faced the same level of international competition as some of the others on this list, he is a projectable lefty. He signed with Seattle for $880,000 and could be a steal at that price.
MLB Debut: 2017
Potential Rating: 9D

Tzu-Wei Lin (SS, BOS)

Considered by many the top position prospect from Asia this year, he agreed to a $2.05 million bonus. The 16-year-old is listed at 5-8, 160—small and slight. He runs very well and has good range and instincts. At the plate he good strike zone judgment and plus speed with gap power. Lin is considered a plus defender and that will be his ticket to the majors.
MLB Debut: 2018
Potential Rating: 8D

Amaurys Minier (SS, MIN)

Minier is 16-year-old switch-hitting shortstop from the Dominican Republic who signed $1.4 million deal with the Twins. At 6-2 190, he has already has good size and projects to have above-average power from both sides of the plate. Reviews of his ability to hit for average are mixed; there are concerns that he isn't as patient as he needs to be. He's played shortstop and 3B, but doesn't have the range or athleticism to stick at short and will most likely move to 3B or the OF as professional. If he can hit consistently, he has some nice long-term upside due to his above-average power.
MLB Debut: 2018
Potential Rating: 8E

Jose Mujica (RHP, TAM)

A lean, athletic 16-year-old right-hander from Venezuela, Mujica signed with the Tampa for $1 million. At 6-2, 180 he has some room for growth and already has a strong frame. Mujica has clean, easy mechanics and already features a low-90s fastball that tops out at 93 mph with late life. He also has a good sinking change-up with future potential and a slurvy, curveball that will need significant work.
MLB Debut: 2018
Potential Rating: 9E

Shohei Otani (RHP, Japan)

Otani is one of the top pitching prospects in Japan. At 6-4, 200 he is a tall, physically mature right-hander with a strong lower half who generates easy velocity. He comes after hitters with a good 92-96 mph fastball that tops out at 99 mph. He also has a good 82-85 mph slider that at times has tight spin, a splitter, and an under-developed curve. His fastball can sometimes flatten out at higher velocity. His command can be inconsistent and he is not as polished as Yu Darvish was at the same age. The 18-year-old Otani considered not entering the NPB draft and coming to the U.S. instead, but ultimately relented and was selected by the Nippon Ham Fighters and so will have to go through the traditional posting system.
MLB Debut: ?
Potential Rating: 9D

Alexander Palma (OF, NYY)

Palma is a 16-year-old OF prospect from the Dominican Republic who agreed to an $800,000 deal with the Yankees. Palma is one of the better offensive prospects in Latin America this year and he has a strong body and good athleticism. At the plate, he has plus bat speed and a balanced approach that projects to average-to-plus power. He is only an average runner and will need to work hard to stay in shape as he already has a thick lower half, but he moves well enough and has the arm strength to play RF as a professional.
MLB Debut: 2018
Potential Rating: 8D

Hiroyuki Nakajima (SS, OAK)

He agreed to a 3-year, $6.5 million deal with the Oakland A's and will take over as the club's starting shortstop. At 30, Nakajima is the oldest player on this list, but should be in contention for the

AL ROY. Nakajima has a nice line-drive approach, makes decent contact, and has above-average speed. He doesn't have much power, but is a career .300 hitter in Japan. He is a solid defender with decent range and a good arm.

MLB Debut: 2013
Potential Rating: 7B

David Rodriguez (C, TAM)
He is anoffensive-minded backstop from Venezuela with a good approach at the plate. His balanced swing and consistent contact produces moderate gap-to-gap power. Rodriguez doesn't have plus bat speed, so might not develop plus power. He has good arm strength, but is raw behind the plate, and his mobility and blocking skills need work. At 5-11, 190 he is built like a catcher and will have value if he can stick there.

MLB Debut: 2018
Potential Rating: 8D

Ahmed Rosario (SS, NYM)
Rosario is a 17-year-old shortstop from the Dominican Republic. More than any other Latin American prospect, Rosario generates mixed reactions among scouts. Some see a long, lean, athletic SS with good speed and above-average power for the position. Those that like Rosario say he has good actions, nice hands, and enough arm strength to stick as short. His detractors question both his ability to hit and to play shortstop in the majors. He does have problems with his swing, which can get long, and he needs to make more consistent contact. The Mets clearly saw a guy with 5-tool potential and love his make-up and a give him the largest bonus of any Latin player outside of Cuba when they agreed to pay him $1.75 million.

MLB Debut: 2018
Potential Rating: 9E

Hyun-Jin Ryu (LHP, LA)
The Dodgers signed the 25-year-old Ryu to a six-year, $30 million contract after paying $25.74 million to the Hanwha Eagles of the Korean Baseball Organization. Ryu has a 88-92 mph fastball that tops out at 94 mph. He mixes in a slurvy, curveball, a slow curve, a slider, and a good change-up. He isn't going to be overpowering and projects as a mid-rotation starter. Scouts are mixed on his long-term potential but the suddenly free-spending Dodgers were desperate to restock their system with talent.

MLB Debut: 2013
Potential Rating: 7C

Masahiro Tanaka (RHP, Japan)
Tanaka is one of the better pitchers active in the NPB and has recently told his team (the Rakuten Eagles) that he would like to be posted after the 2013 season. The 2011 Sawamura Award winner features a nice four-seam fastball that sits at 90-93 mph and tops out at 95 mph. He mixes in a plus 81-83 mph late-breaking slider, and a split-change. In 2012, Tanaka was 10-4 with a 1.87 ERA and 19 BB/169 K in 171 IP. He has had some injury (back) problems in the past, but is only 24 years old and could develop into a solid mid-rotation starter.

MLB Debut: ?
Potential Rating: 8C

Luis Torrens (C, NYY)
Torrens has good international experience and has played SS and 3B in the past. The 16-year-old has seen some action behind the plate, but at this point it is not known he if he can handle the position. The Yankees signed Torrens for $1.3 million and will give him a chance to develop behind the dish. Mostly they like his experience and advanced bat, as he is one of the more polished international hitters. He has a good understanding of the strike zone and the ability to drive the ball to all fields. He is a below-average runner, but moves well and has a strong throwing arm. If the move behind the plate works, Torrens has future value, but for now it is very much a work in progress.

MLB Debut: 2018
Potential Rating: 8E

Richard Urena (SS, TOR)
He was widely considered the best defensive shortstop available on the international market and the 16-year-old Dominican agreed to a $775,000 deal with the Blue Jays. At 6-1, 160 Urena is lean, quick, and athletic and has natural shortstop actions. There are definite concerns about his ability to hit; he has quick hands, but does not make much contact or have even average power. He runs the bases well, but is not a true burner. He might not hit enough to have much value.

MLB Debut: 2017
Potential Rating: 7D

Julio Urias (RHP, LA)
He is a short 16-year-old lefty from Mexico was signed by the Dodgers in August. At 6-0 Urias doesn't have the typical size you'd expect from a highly-prized international player, but he does have a fastball that sits in the upper-80 and tops and already tops out at 92 mph. He also has an advanced change-up, a cutter, and a decent curveball, all of which he locates well. His delivery and clean with easily repeatable mechanics. Urias was one of the younger players available this summer and while he doesn't have tremendous upside, he knows how to pitch and gives the Dodgers another solid pitching prospect.

MLB Debut: 2018
Potential Rating: 8D

Sleepers Outside the Top 100

by Jeremy Deloney

One of the more arduous tasks of writing about prospects is compiling a Top 100 list. While there seemingly are similar prospects on most pundits' lists, the order can be quite divergent. Most Top 100 lists feature names that have become well-known through well above average performance or sterling reputations earned from high draft selections or storied amateur pedigrees. This essay will focus on ten minor league prospects who are unlikely to be on any 2013 Top 100 list. These ten prospects have relatively high ceilings, however, and for fantasy leaguers with deep farm systems, these are names to consider after the Top 100 are gone.

He has only pitched 27 innings since coming to the United States, but 19-year-old **Miguel Almonte** (RHP, KC) has shown a mature approach to pitching and uncanny feel for his craft. With the Royals in the rookie-level Arizona League, he posted a 2.33 ERA, walked five and struck out 28. He impressed during instructional league and could be placed at Low-A Lexington to start the '13 season. With his fastball and change-up combination, he could dominate the South Atlantic League and vault his way to High-A before season's end.

Almonte's easy, loose arm action produces a clean and repeatable delivery. He throws consistent strikes and is able to spot his 89-96 mph fastball with precision. He has the confidence to use any pitch in any count and should have at least three solid-average to plus pitches when he physically and developmentally matures. With his long, wiry and projectable frame, he could add a few more ticks of velocity down the road. Like most pitchers his age, Almonte needs to throw more innings and learn to sequence his pitches better.

Though he struggled in his pro debut—.222/.282/.353 with 60 K/12 BB—20-year-old **Matt Dean** (3B, TOR), has as high a ceiling as any third baseman in the lower minors. He has legitimate talent with both the bat and glove and could make a name for himself once he gets comfortable with the professional ranks.

The tall and strong right-handed hitter exhibits above average raw power to all fields and could hit for a moderately-high BA once he learns to recognize pitches better and swing with more authority. He had a tendency to swing tentatively at hittable pitches in the '12 season. He has plenty of room to add strength to his lean frame. He possesses plus bat speed, though his swing can get long at times. Defensively, he has excellent hands and a strong arm that is playable at third base. With a few adjustments to his offensive package, Dean could break out in a major way. He's likely to begin the '13 season at Low-A Lansing where he could put up impressive numbers.

Raw pitchers can often take a long time to develop and **Victor De Leon** (RHP, STL) fits into that category. After showcasing one of the top power arms in the short-season Appalachian League, the 20-year-old could either start or relieve. With Johnson City, he started 10 games and posted a 3.25 ERA, 4.1 Ctl, and 8.5 Dom. The raw statistics may not appear dominant, but it was the development of his secondary pitches that give him significant upside.

De Leon works effectively off of his 91-95 mph fastball that often touches 97 mph. He generates his plus velocity with pure arm strength and fast arm action. He induces a lot of groundballs by using his 6'2" height and arm angle to pitch downhill. Though his heater can sometimes lack late action at higher velocities, he can blow it by hitters up in the zone. His slider has developed into a true swing-and-miss pitch that gives him a second offering to keep hitters at bay. Despite holding LHH to a .222 BA, he still has strides to make with his change-up. Without it, he could be a dynamic force at the back of the bullpen. Regardless, he needs to work on his command and fastball location. Pitching in the rotation for Low-A Peoria should give him ample opportunity to work on his overall pitch mix.

With the Orioles contending in the American League East in 2012, there was far less focus on their minor leaguers. **Nick Delmonico** (INF, BAL) was expected to begin his career in short season, but was assigned to Low-A Delmarva and had a solid pro debut. The 20-year-old left-handed hitter showed a remarkable feel for hitting and should continue to grow into his vast offensive ceiling. He batted .249/.351/.411 with 22 doubles, 11 HR and 8 SB in 338 AB. He missed some time due to a knee injury, but there are no lingering concerns.

Delmonico is a pure-hitting infielder with good power potential and keen bat control for someone his age. He puts the bat on the ball consistently with a short stroke and can leverage his strength to reach the seats. He uses the entire field in his approach and should eventually hit for a higher BA once he becomes more comfortable hanging in against left-handed pitching (.175 against lefties in '12). Delmonico will never be mistaken for a stolen base threat, but his baseball IQ and acumen gives him ability to run the bases well. His plus arm strength is his sole asset on defense and he'll need to improve his hands and range. He split time between 2B and 1B, though many in the organization see him as a 3B. Once he settles on a defensive home, his bat could get him to the majors quickly.

It would be a mistake to claim that the offensive exploits of **Tyler Goeddel** (3B, TAM) are worthy of inclusion on a Top 100 list. However, he has extremely intriguing upside predicated on his athleticism and projection. With Low-A Bowling Green, the supplemental first round pick from '11 batted .246/.335/.371 with 19 doubles, 6 HR, and 30 SB in 329 AB. Those may not be eye-popping numbers, but it was his first pro experience and he held his own as a 19-year-old in the Midwest League.

One look at his smooth actions in his 6'4" 180 pound frame and it is easy to dream on his future. He has exceptional speed for an athlete his size and he offers terrific instincts for the game. With excellent bat speed and strong hands, the right-handed hitter makes hard contact with a level swing path. Though he lacks the load and leverage in his swing to hit for present power, he has shown the ability to make adjustments and could eventually realize his plus power potential. He has some work to do with his overly aggressive approach and he could stand to pack on some muscle to his lean frame. Defensively, he exhibits a very strong arm and decent footwork to stick at 3B. However, the Rays drafted Richie Shaffer and recently traded for Patrick Leonard which might result in a position change for Goeddel, possibly to an outfield corner where he could have plus range and arm strength.

Signed out of Colombia as a non-drafted free agent in July '10, **Dilson Herrera** (2B, PIT) exceeded expectations in his first year in the United States. Between the rookie level Gulf Coast League and State College in the short-season New York-Penn League, the diminutive 18-year-old hit .286/.341/.489 with 12 doubles, 8 HR, and 12 SB in 227 AB. He drew 19 walks while fanning 47 times. Despite a 5'10" 150 pound frame, the right-handed hitter finished 2nd in the GCL in HR and SLG.

Herrera is expected to man 2B for Low-A West Virginia in '13. There are plenty of reasons to believe in his ability to rocket up prospect charts. He has well above average bat control and hand-eye coordination that allow him to make easy contact with a short, repeatable stroke. He has a tendency to expand the strike zone and get himself out by swinging at bad pitches, but his pitch recognition should improve with more professional at bats. He uses the entire field in his approach and should hit for a high BA while maintaining moderate power. Herrera also runs well with plus speed, though he needs to get on base more. He is a below average defender at present, though he ranges well to both sides. At his peak, Herrera should become an offensive-minded 2B.

A seven-figure bonus to a 9th round selection is rare, but that's what the Pirates gave **Clay Holmes** (RHP, PIT) out of an Alabama high school in '11. The 19-year-old made his pro debut with short-season State College and was among the better prospects in the circuit. The 6'5" 230 pounder held hitters to a .176 oppBA in 59.1 innings and posted a 2.28 ERA, 4.4 Ctl, and 5.2 Dom.

Though Holmes didn't dominate as much as his frame and power arm would suggest, he has greater pitchability than most his age. He pitches aggressively with his heavy 90-95 mph fastball that hitters simply couldn't elevate. With his dynamic sinker, he didn't use his curveball or change-up to get hitters to chase. He throws downhill because of his height and angle and thrives in the bottom half of the strike zone. His breaking ball and offspeed pitch were inconsistent when he used them, but both show potential to become at least average pitches in time. His curveball shows good break and he repeats the arm speed on his change-up. Whether he develops into a high strikeout pitcher remains to be seen, but a tall power-armed righty with extreme groundball tendencies has significant value.

Blessed with pure arm strength and the ability to hit triple digits on the gun, **Francellis Montas** (RHP, BOS) has excellent upside, possibly as a future closer. He'll be given every opportunity to remain as a starter, though his development could be hastened with the move to the bullpen. The 19-year-old pitched most of the season with the rookie-level Sox in the Gulf Coast League and started one game for Lowell in the NYPL. Between the two stops, he posted a 2.98 ERA, 2.6 Ctl and 9.2 Dom in 44.1 innings.

Montas throws from a ¾ slot with excellent angle and his fastball is tough to hit as it features explosive, late life. Currently, his heater is his only weapon as he lacks touch for changing speeds and struggles to get consistent spin on his breaking ball. There

is some hope in the development of his slider and he could be a dominant fastball/slider performer if he can get them to work in sync. His change-up offers very little deception. Montas throws consistent strikes despite effort in his delivery, though his fastball location and command need polish. There are certainly areas for him to focus on in '13—likely in Low-A—but if things come together for him, he could either become a #2-3 starter or a lights-out reliever.

Catchers often can take a while to develop due to the rigorous demands of the position. Because he has talent with both the bat and glove, **Michael Perez** (C, ARI) is already off to a terrific start in his pro career. With Missolua of the short-season Pioneer League, the 20-year-old batted .293/.358/.542 with 16 doubles and 10 HR in 225 AB. Though he struck out 72 times, the trade-off for his power was acceptable. Additionally, he was able to showcase his solid defensive skills.

Perez was a highly-regarded player when the Diamondbacks selected him in the fifth round of the '11 draft, but they didn't expect him to be this far along. The left-handed hitter batted .323 against lefties in '12 and has a keen ability to use the entire field. He has above average bat speed to hit for power to all fields, though he hits more HR to the pull side. Once he adds more strength, he could develop into a middle-of-the-order run producer. He may never hit for much of a BA at higher levels because he tends to swing at bad pitches, but his power can't be ignored. Defensively, he possesses a strong arm and solid-average receiving skills. He needs to clean up his footwork and work on his catch-and-throw skills, but the raw ingredients are there for Perez to evolve into one of the top all-around catchers in baseball.

Most of the players in this essay haven't yet reached Low-A, but **Matt Wisler** (RHP, SD) was a standout at that level in '12. With Fort Wayne in the Midwest League, the 20-year-old started 23 games and posted a 2.53 ERA, 2.2 Ctl, 8.9 Dom, and .227 oppBA in 114 innings. Most impressive was his ability to keep the ball in the ballpark—he yielded only 1 HR. It is expected that he'll jump to High-A Lake Elsinore of the California League where his numbers may not be as good because of the friendly hitting environments, but his overall game could lead to his placement on future Top 100 lists.

Wisler fell to the seventh round of the '11 draft due to signability concerns. He immediately found pro ball to his liking and saw his velocity increase after tweaking his delivery with the help of Padres pitching coaches. He now sits between 91-93 mph with his fastball and it touches 96 mph on occasion. Not only does it have hard sink, he throws it for strikes and is the perfect set-up for his solid complementary pitches. His curveball may be his best offering and he can either use it as a chase pitch or drop it in for strikes. Wisler's change-up has evolved into an average offering and should continue to get better as he finds consistency with his arm speed. Tall and lanky at 6'3" 175 pounds, he has room to grow and could develop more velocity down the line. Though he may not become a dominator in the big leagues, he should grow into a dependable and durable mid-rotation starter.

2013 HS Draft Class at 2012 Area Code Games

by Colby Garrapy

As a high schooler in 2008, Mike Trout suited up for the New York Yankees during the annual Area Code Games. No one could have predicted his impact on MLB just four short years later. But when he took the field in front of hundreds of MLB scouts, one thing was for sure—he was first round talent in the making.

August 5-10, 2012 marked the 26th Area Code Games (ACG) that started back in 1986 in Lodi, CA. Now held at Blair Field in Long Beach, CA each June, the ACG has become the number one showcase for high school players throughout the country. Top players compete using wood bats while scouts from every organization, along with college coaches, take notes for the upcoming draft and their recruiting class.

Not just anyone can participate in the showcase. MLB scouts nominate candidates, and an invitation-only tryout determines the players who will be representing their team, made up of players in their geographical area (i.e., the reason Trout, from New Jersey, was on the Yankees).

The result is a early look at some of the stars of the future; players that will someday be the talk of the fanalytic world. While their skills remain raw, impressions made at showcases like this affect front office decisions—and their skills are what we will eventually use to construct our fantasy rosters.

For those looking to get a jump on the high school portion of the 2013 MLB First Year Player Draft, here are some names and scouting reports from the 2012 Area Code Games:

Willie Calhoun, 2B
Benicia, CA … 5-8, 170 … L/R
Description: Calhoun plays a superb second base showing great agility, hands, and range. To accompany his above average defensive ability, his bat has above average potential with gap power and above average speed. Calhoun shows some issues with breaking stuff and should be more selective at the plate, something that will have to come with age and experience. While he can certainly handle the duties of a second baseman, sending him out in pro ball as a shortstop and letting his arm play himself off it would not be a horrible idea. His bat, though, should suffice at either position.

JP Crawford, SS
Lakewood, CA … 6-2, 180 … L/R
Description: Crawford's diversity of skills is what scouts look for in a HS shortstop. While nothing is plus, a lot of his tools have the ability to reach above average. His bat is line drive oriented with moderate pop. His strong wrists allow him to get through the zone quickly and consistently put the ball in play. His speed is average now, with room to improve. His arm can play at SS, but his instincts will be what determine his end position. Crawford does not "wow" like HS shortstops of the past, but could end up as a speedy centerfielder.

Nick Longhi, 1B/LHP
Venice, FL … 6-2, 205 … R/L
Description: Longhi came into the showcase listed as a pitcher, but after seeing his BP and first few games, it was obvious his future

is at the plate. Longhi hit the ball harder than anyone all week, driving it to all fields, inside-outing some pitches, and squaring up everything else. His quick wrists and simple short stroke allow him to get the barrel to the ball quickly, taking advantage of his plus power. While he runs like a first baseman, he has a plus arm and good instincts, which might lead to a corner outfield spot down the road. But his bat should play average to above with plus power.

Marcus Doi, OF
Mid-Pacific Institute, HI … 6-0, 185 … R/R
Description: Doi stood out throughout the showcase. He plays an average defense with an above average arm in the outfield, but with his build it would be intriguing to see what he can do at third base, taking advantage of his actions in the field. He has pull side power (hitting one HR, and almost a second in his final AB), with an aggressive hack at the plate. Like most HS hitters, he struggles at times with the breaking ball, but makes proper adjustments squaring pitches up and hitting to all fields. He runs average now with a chance to play a tick above in the future. Doi does not possess any plus tools, but is well-rounded across the board.

Garrett Luna, 3B
Magnolia, TX … 6-1, 200 … R/R
Description: Luna has the ideal build for a third baseman and his actions at the hot corner made him an exciting player to monitor. All week, Luna showed good range with a strong arm, and could grade out to above average to plus at the corner. In the box, Luna squares up pitches nicely, hitting the ball to all fields while showing pull side power and a potential to be average or better. He struggles with breaking pitches and can be overaggressive when he falls behind in the count, something advanced coaching will address. He runs a tick below average, but better underway and showed good base running instincts. Luna has the defense already, but the bat will have to play for him to stick at third.

Reese McGuire, C
Kentwood, WA … 6-1, 190 …L/R
Description: McGuire was one of the biggest names coming into the ACG, but the results at the plate did not match the buzz. He has a strong frame now, ideal for a catcher at the next level. Behind the plate he showed solid hands with average receiving skills, solidifying the likelihood that he'll stay at the position. In the batter's box, McGuire displayed a smooth stroke with quick wrists, allowing him to square up the ball and drive it to all fields. Against better breaking balls he struggled to make adjustments. While the power potential is certain, he will be a below average runner. McGuire's bat is special, but if he cannot stay behind the plate, it will diminish his future value.

Corey Simpson, C
Sweeny, TX … 6-3, 220 … R/R
Description: Power is the one tool Simpson will rely on his entire career. During the showcase he showed his ability to drive the ball with authority (huge HR, double to dead center), but off-speed pitches were an obvious weaknesses. He can hit, but will need to adjust in pro ball to reach his potential. Simpson does not show great feel for the catcher position or the ability to call games at the

next level. With his monstrous size, a move to first base will most certainly be on the horizon. In the meantime, it cannot hurt to try him behind the plate. If not, his value will lie solely on his bat and power combo.

Ian Clarkin, LHP

Madison, CA … 6-3, 190 … L/L

Description: Clarkin brings a very solid three pitch mix that projects to be average to above. His FB sits 89-91, up to 93, with an 80-81 CU, and 72-74 CB. He displays control with all three pitches and commands them effectively in the zone. His FB has some good life and should tick up some mph with further development. His CB has good depth, and with proper coaching could become a very effective out pitch. It was very surprising to see the feel he has for the CU and the fade it has, something you typically do not see from HS pitchers. With a durable frame, average to above average arsenal, and repeatable mechanics, Clarkin is a good pitching prospect.

Dustin Driver, RHP

Wenatchee, WA … 6-2, 200 … R/R

Description: Driver came in the first day and topped the charts with his FB, reaching up to 94 sitting mostly 90-92. He showed three other pitches, a cutter that sat 85-87, a 75-77 CB, and a CU around 81-83. Driver repeats his delivery well with a clean and very quick arm action. His ability to spot his pitches allow him to get ahead in counts and fool hitters with his above average FB and average CB. He shows some feel for the CU, but only a few were used (or needed) throughout the week. With his ideal size, and good mix of pitches that all show average to plus projections, Driver has the makings of middle of the rotation workhorse.

Steven Farinaro, RHP

Head-Royce, CA … 6-0, 160 … R/R

Description: For a smallish guy, Farinaro shows two quality pitches and has a third in the works. Mostly a FB/CB guy now, his FB sits 89-91 while his CB comes in at 73-75, flashing some tight break at times. At only 160 pounds, there is room to fill out, making a stronger frame and adding some to his velo. He has long arm action, but he repeats well and executes his pitches, throwing strikes with consistency. His CB has good shape and could become a serious out pitch. The development of his third pitch, a CU, and his frame's durability will be the leading indicators as to whether he stays in the rotation or is headed for a late inning reliever. Regardless, his stuff plays average to above and he profiles as a #3-4 starter or setup/closer in the bullpen.

Stephen Gonsalves, LHP

Cathedral Catholic, CA … 6-5, 185 … L/L

Description: Gonsalves has a very projectable body that should add some bulk over the next few years and add to his durability. He shows a three-pitch mix featuring an 89-91 FB, and a mid- to upper-70s CB/CU combo. While his arm action is loose and easy, his delivery has some funk to it, which creates some deception. But he also shows the ball in the back, giving hitters a good look at what is coming. He spots the FB well, but struggles finding consistency with his secondary stuff, relying heavily on his FB to get him through some trouble. His CB, though, shows good depth,

an encouraging sign going forward. Gonsalves has the pieces to be a #2-3 starter, but his ultimate outcome will depend on how he makes adjustments and develops his secondary offerings.

Brett Hanewich, RHP

Lakewood Ranch, FL … 6-3, 210 … S/R

Description: Hanewich is not a pitcher that was on many radars entering the showcase, but many left with a sound impression. He shows three pitches; a FB sitting 88-91, CB at 73-76, and a CU at 80-82. With his strong pitchers build, velocity improvements seem likely, as does his ability to be a workhorse in the rotation. Hanewich gets extremely out-front and downhill, allowing him to release the ball much closer to the plate then most. Thus, his FB plays up once it reaches the hitters. He has solid feel for his CB that shows decent depth, but he will have to develop consistency with the CU in order to reach his potential as a starter. Should Hanewich continue to repeat his delivery as he has, and show the ability to develop more consistent secondary he should be an interesting name on the draft boards in June.

AJ Puk, LHP

Cedar Rapids, IA …. 6-6, 205 … L/L

Description: For his size, Puk displayed great athleticism on the mound (and in the batter's box), while locating very efficiently with two of his three pitches. Puk sat 88-91 with his FB, 74-76 with the CB, and 79-82 with the CU. He spots the FB/CB combo well, but struggles finding his release point with his CU, something many HS pitchers struggle with. His clean and quick arm action, along with his ability to get downhill with ease should further enable his command of the zone. He can already establish first pitch strikes with two of his pitches, but if he can develop his CU into a usable third pitch, Puk's projectability as a starter will become much higher and his stock will rise.

Logan Shore, RHP

Coon Rapids, MN … 6-2, 210 … R/R

Description: Shore has an ideal pitcher's frame that he uses nicely, complementing his three pitch mix. His FB sits 90-92; his SL at 79-81. He showed a CU during warm ups, but failed to execute one during the game, likely an indication of his lack of confidence in it. He pitches from a 3/4 arm slot with a herky-jerky delivery that works. He tends to slow his arm action while throwing his SL, something he will have to learn to fix in order for it to become a useful pitch. Overall, Shore shows some signs of a legitimate pitching prospect, but his role as a starter or reliever will come down to his ability to develop his CU into a useful third pitch.

2013 College Names to Know

by Chris Lee

With many fantasy leagues allowing owners to stash amateur players, an owner is doing himself a disservice not to be at least vaguely familiar with the top college players. While a college star doesn't always translate to a big-league success story, with drastic changes to the collegiate bats in the last two seasons the guessing game has become a bit easier.

Of course, there's still difficulty for the fantasy owner, because just as is the case at the MLB level, the top players and the top fantasy players may differ. The 2013 class is tougher than usual, as there aren't a lot of can't-miss college prospects (especially in the way of hitters). But for the forward-looking owner, here are a few players to watch as the spring season starts in February.

Mark Appel, RHP
Stanford … senior … 6-5, 215

Description: Appel was a near-consensus No. 1 pick of the 2012 draft. But hiring Scott Boras always has the potential to do funny things to draft position, and so Appel fell all the way to the Pirates at No. 8. Then, Appel did something nearly unheard of for a college player picked in the first round: He declined Pittsburgh's offer of $3.8 million and returned to school.

Scouts have long loved Appel—his fastball touches the high-90s, and he has a good slider—but the numbers have never screamed "dominant ace" until last year, when his k/9 went from 7.0 to 9.5. His control has always been good, and that also improved to 2.2 bb/9 in 2012. Plus, he keeps the ball in the park—just 4 HRs the last two seasons, though the Sunken Diamond is a pitcher's park. He's got an easy, three-quarters delivery, can go nine innings without losing velocity, and has never had arm problems.

Fantasy outlook: Appel might not dominant like Tim Lincecum, David Price or Stephen Strasburg, but he should be a good pitcher worthy of ownership in mixed leagues for many years to come.

Kris Bryant, 3B
San Diego … R/R … junior … 6-5, 215

Description: Bryant hit 22 HRs as a high school senior, and though he was highly regarded then, some scouts discounted him because of a long swing. Watching him now, it's hard to find much fault; Bryant swings with a definite uppercut, but it's fluid and without a lot of wasted movement. It's certainly not a long swing for a guy his size, and he hits the ball to all fields. Bryant has played third base in college and although he's not a defensive star, he plays it reasonably well—though many see a first baseman at the professional level.

Bryant has a nice eye and excellent power, and those skills only keep improving. He hit nine homers as a freshman, 14 as a sophomore in 213 AB, and a 33/55 bb/k ratio improved to 39/38. His batting lines have been amazingly consistent, posting .365/.482/.599 as a freshman, followed by .366/.483/.671 as a sophomore. In addition, he stole nine bases in 12 attempts in 2012, but the college game is not a place to evaluate stolen bases and his speed is just average.

Fantasy outlook: A potential middle-of-the-order first baseman with some pop who won't hurt you in other categories.

Jonathan Crawford, RHP
Florida … junior … 6-1, 205

Description: Once in a blue moon in college baseball, you'll see a pitcher rise from almost total obscurity to complete domination in the flash of an eye. This happened to Crawford in the Southeastern Conference in 2012. The junior is still scratching the surface of his potential, but if you want a glimpse of what could be, check out video of the last inning of his no-hitter against Bethune-Cookman in UF's first NCAA Tournament game last season. Crawford was still hitting the high-90s with terrific movement.

The fact that Crawford only threw 3.2 innings as a freshman is less a reflection on Crawford, and more a statement about the ridiculous talent that Florida coach Kevin O'Sullivan has accumulated the past few years. In 2012, he threw 77.2 innings, with 73 strikeouts and 24 walks in 19 appearances (14 starts). That's not a lot of innings for that number of starts, but O'Sullivan has never been one to run up high pitch counts with his hurlers. Crawford's 98-pitch complete game might be a better reflection of his potential durability.

Fantasy outlook: Crawford is a high-risk, high-reward proposition. Watch him closely this spring; the Gators traditionally play a brutal schedule, so that will help get a better handle on him.

Sean Manaea, LHP
Indiana State … junior … 6-5, 215

Description: Manaea exploded in the Cape Cod League in 2012, amassing 85 strikeouts against just seven walks in 57.1 IP. The strikeout mark set the all-time league record. That followed up on his 115 K, 105 IP, 32 BB sophomore season at ISU in the Missouri Valley League, which is certainly a respectable conference.

Manaea's fastball sits in the mid-90s, and he complements it with a slider that's great at times. He's got a smooth delivery, though he needs some work on keeping the ball down.

Fantasy outlook: Manaea may have as much upside as anyone on this list, but it's also come completely out-of-the-blue, as he was a relative unknown a year ago. The good news is that some feel there's still plenty of room for improvement. If he has a good junior year, he will be rewarded with a high draft selection.

Ryne Stanek, RHP
Arkansas … junior … 6-4, 190

Description: Like Appel, Stanek is a guy who scouts like better than the stats (92.2 IP, 83 K, 36 BB as a sophomore) might suggest. The righty has a low-three-quarters delivery and a broad repertoire of pitches, none of which are necessarily dominant at this point. However, Stanek stays low in the zone and has been tough to hit, as opponents managed just a .229 average and two homers in 2012.

People seem to have differing opinions about Stanek; some describe him as "polished" and his stuff as "great" at times, but he seems to have trouble with a consistent release point and certainly hasn't dominated for any long stretches. However, the velocity seems to be creeping up in the right direction, and he's got a smooth, easy delivery.

Fantasy outlook: Stanek looks like a lesser version of Appel in that he's got a good shot to make it, but might not be a Cy Young winner. Despite a lack of dominance, some like his consistency and delivery enough that he could be considered for the No. 1 overall pick. He's certainly got room to grow and is far from a finished product, but the whole package gives him an excellent shot to become a big-league rotation guy.

Bobby Wahl, RHP

Mississippi … junior … 6-3, 210

Description: Ole Miss has recently put Lance Lynn and Drew Pomeranz in the majors, and Wahl might be next. He pitched out of the bullpen as a freshman before becoming one of the SEC's most dependable starting pitchers in 2012.

Wahl is a stocky guy with a three-quarters arm angle and a delivery that takes some effort. A slider-change-fastball guy who can touch the high-90s, Wahl fanned 104 in 99 IP and walked 32. He also gave up six home runs, but Swayze Field is also very much a hitter's park (365 to the alleys, 390 to center).

Fantasy outlook: Just about everybody expects Wahl to be a top-half-of-the-first-round guy, so he'll get a chance. However, buyer beware, as a lot of people feel that he projects as a reliever in the professional ranks.

Austin Wilson, OF

Stanford … R/R … junior …6-5, 245

Description: There aren't a lot of slam-dunk hitting prospects in this draft, and certainly not a lot of power-speed guys, but Wilson might be the best bet in this college class in that regard. Wilson is more of an old-school scout's dream (he's the classic "five-tool" player) than a modern-day sabermetric standout (his

.285/.389/.493, 24 BB, 44 K line at Stanford last year was nothing special for the college game), but there's plenty of potential here.

Wilson has the prototypical Stanford line-drive swing, and it is quite compact for a man his size. He's very strong, and should he develop a little more uppercut, there's serious home run potential here. Wilson's not a burner on the base paths, but he's at least got decent speed to go with intelligence, and picked his spots well last year (7-for-7 in steals) for a team that didn't run a lot. He's projected as a corner outfielder.

Fantasy outlook: Wilson's not going to help fantasy owners in the next couple years, and certainly not a shoe-in to become a star. But for an owner with some patience looking for a player with big upside, Wilson's not a bad bet.

Potential sleepers:

Conrad Gregor, 1B, Vanderbilt (L/L): One of college baseball's best pure hitters, the lefty hits lefties and righties equally well, and no particular pitch seems to give him fits. The questions are his defense (which improved tremendously last season) and his power (he's more of a line-drive hitter), but he's got outstanding strike-zone judgment. If the homers come, everything else suggests he's good enough to make it.

Corey Littrell, LHP, Kentucky: The 6-foot-3 lefty has been known to dominate at times, and has pitched well in a hitters' park. The junior struck out 87 in 98. 2/3 innings (with 25 walks) last year and there are some whispers that he might be the college sleeper of the entire 2013 draft.

ORGANIZATION RATINGS/RANKINGS

Each organization is graded on a standard A-F scale in four separate categories, and then after weighing the categories and adding some subjectivity, a final grade and ranking are determined. The four categories are the following:

Hitting: The quality and quantity of hitting prospects, the balance between athleticism, power, speed, and defense, and the quality of player development.

Pitching: The quality and quantity of pitching prospects and the quality of player development.

Top-End Talent: The quality of the top players within the organization. Successful teams are ones that have the most star-quality players. These are the players who are a teams' above average regulars, front-end starters, and closers.

Depth: The depth of both hitting and pitching prospects within the organization.

Overall Grade: The four categories are weighted, with top-end talent being the most important and depth being the least.

TEAM	Hitting	Pitching	Top-End Talent	Depth	Overall
Pittsburgh	A-	A	A	A-	A
St. Louis	B	A	A	A-	A
San Diego	A-	A	B	A	A-
Seattle	B+	A	A-	B+	A-
Miami	B+	A-	A-	A-	A-
Texas	A-	B	A-	A-	A-
Houston	A-	B	B+	A-	B+
Minnesota	B+	B	A	B+	B+
Boston	B	B	A-	B+	B+
Arizona	B+	B	B	A-	B+
Tampa Bay	B	B+	B+	B	B+
Chicago (N)	A	C+	A	C	B+
New York (N)	C+	B	B+	C+	B
Philadelphia	B	B-	B-	B-	B-
Toronto	C	B	B-	B-	B-
Washington	B+	C	B-	B+	B-
Cincinnati	C	B	B-	B-	B-
New York (A)	B	C	B	C	B-
San Francisco	C+	B	C	A-	B-
Atlanta	C-	B+	C	B-	C+
Kansas City	C	C+	C+	B-	C+
Colorado	B+	D	B+	C	C
Baltimore	C-	B-	B-	C-	C
Oakland	B	D	C	C-	C
Milwaukee	C+	B-	C+	C	C
Cleveland	C-	C-	C+	C-	C-
Chicago (A)	C	D	C	D	D+
Detroit	C-	D	C-	D	D+
Los Angeles (N)	C-	C	D	D	D+
Los Angeles (A)	D	D	D+	D	D

BATTERS

POSITIONS: Up to four positions are listed for each batter and represent those for which he appeared (in order) the most games at in 2011. Positions are shown with their numeric designation (2=CA, 3=1B, 7=LF, 0=DH, etc.)

BATS: Shows which side of the plate he bats from—right (R), left (L) or switch-hitter (S).

AGE: Player's age, as of April 1, 2013.

DRAFTED: The year, round, and school that the player performed at as an amateur if drafted, or where the player was signed from, if a free agent.

EXP MLB DEBUT: The year a player is expected to debut in the major leagues.

PROJ ROLE: The role that the batter is expected to have for the majority of his major league career, not necessarily his greatest upside.

SKILLS: Each skill a player possesses is graded and designated with a "+", indicating the quality of the skills, taking into context the batter's age and level played. An average skill will receive three "+" marks.

- **PWR:** Measures the player's ability to drive the ball and hit for power.
- **BAVG:** Measures the player's ability to hit for batting average and judge the strike zone.
- **SPD:** Measures the player's raw speed and base-running ability.
- **DEF:** Measures the player's overall defense, which includes arm strength, arm accuracy, range, agility, hands, and defensive instincts.

PLAYER STAT LINES: Player statistics for the last five teams that he played for (if applicable), including college and the major leagues.

TEAM DESIGNATIONS: Each team that the player performed for during a given year is included.

LEVEL DESIGNATIONS: The level for each team a player performed is included. "AAA" means Triple-A, "AA" means Double-A, "A+" means high Class-A, "A-" means low Class-A, and "Rk" means rookie level.

SABERMETRIC CATEGORIES: Descriptions of all the sabermetric categories appear in the glossary.

CAPSULE COMMENTARIES: For each player, a brief analysis of their skills/statistics, and their future potential is provided.

ELIGIBILITY: Eligibility for inclusion is the standard for which Major League Baseball adheres to; 130 at-bats or 45 days on the 25-man roster, not including the month of September.

POTENTIAL RATINGS: The Potential Ratings are a two-part system in which a player is assigned a number rating based on his upside potential (1-10) and a letter rating based on the probability of reaching that potential (A-E).

Potential

10:	Hall of Famer	5:	MLB reserve
9:	Elite player	4:	Top minor leaguer
8:	Solid regular	3:	Average minor leaguer
7:	Average regular	2:	Minor league reserve
6:	Platoon player	1:	Minor league roster filler

Probability Rating

- A: 90% probability of reaching potential
- B: 70% probability of reaching potential
- C: 50% probability of reaching potential
- D: 30% probability of reaching potential
- E: 10% probability of reaching potential

SKILLS: Scouts usually grade a player's skills on the 20-80 scale, and while most of the grades are subjective, there are grades that can be given to represent a certain hitting statistic or running speed. These are indicated on this chart:

Scout Grade	HR	BA	Speed (L)	Speed (R)
80	39+	.320+	3.9	4.0
70	32-38	.300-.319	4.0	4.1
60	25-31	.286-.299	4.1	4.2
50 (avg)	17-24	.270-.285	4.2	4.3
40	11-16	.250-.269	4.3	4.4
30	6-10	.220-.249	4.4	4.5
20	0-5	.219-	4.5	4.6

CATCHER POP TIMES: Catchers are timed (in seconds) from the moment the pitch reaches the catcher's mitt until the time that the middle infielder receives the baseball at second base. This number assists both teams in assessing whether a base-runner should steal second base or not.

1.85	+
1.95	MLB average
2.05	−

Adams, David — 45 — New York (A)

EXP MLB DEBUT: 2013 | POTENTIAL: Reserve INF | 7C

Bats R Age 26
2008 (3) Virginia
Pwr ++
BAvg +++
Spd ++
Def ++

Year	Lev	Team	AB	R	H	HR	RBI	Avg	OB	Slg	OPS	bb%	ct%	Eye	SB	CS	x/h%	Iso	RC/G
2009	A+	Tampa	231	37	65	7	41	281	354	498	852	10	83	0.67	3	4	46	216	6.20
2010	AA	Trenton	152	31	47	3	32	309	382	507	889	11	80	0.58	5	2	45	197	6.80
2011	Rk	GCL Yankees	56	13	24	1	11	429	475	643	1118	8	82	0.50	2	1	42	214	9.41
2011	A+	Tampa	52	6	16	0	4	308	357	365	723	7	85	0.50	0	2	19	58	4.48
2012	AA	Trenton	327	44	100	8	48	306	378	450	828	10	84	0.72	3	1	31	144	5.86

Fundamentally-sound infielder who has seen limited action last three years due to foot injury. Exhibits level, compact stroke with solid gap power. Has strength to reach seats, but doubles will be name of game. Below average speed limits SB and has limited range. Owns strong arm and turns double play.

Adams, Matt — 3 — St. Louis

EXP MLB DEBUT: 2012 | POTENTIAL: Starting 1B | 8B

Bats L Age 24
2009 (23) Slippery Rock
Pwr ++++
BAvg +++
Spd +
Def ++

Year	Lev	Team	AB	R	H	HR	RBI	Avg	OB	Slg	OPS	bb%	ct%	Eye	SB	CS	x/h%	Iso	RC/G
2009	A-	Batavia	130	16	45	4	27	346	397	523	920	8	84	0.52	0	0	33	177	6.78
2010	A	Quad Cities	464	71	144	22	88	310	356	541	897	7	83	0.42	5	1	44	231	6.38
2011	AA	Springfield	463	80	139	32	101	300	356	566	922	8	81	0.44	0	1	41	266	6.68
2012	AAA	Memphis	258	41	85	18	50	329	366	624	990	5	78	0.26	3	1	47	295	7.51
2012	MLB	St. Louis	86	8	21	2	13	244	286	384	669	5	72	0.21	0	0	38	140	3.64

Adams has big-time power and had a chance to win the starting 1B job when Berkman went down, but an elbow injury closed that window. Has solid bat speed and good plate discilpine that gives him the tools to hit for average and power. Had another solid year in the minors, but has yet to carve out a role in the majors.

Adrianza, Ehire — 6 — San Francisco

EXP MLB DEBUT: 2013 | POTENTIAL: Backup SS | 6C

Bats B Age 23
2006 NDFA, D.R.
Pwr +
BAvg ++
Spd +++
Def ++++

Year	Lev	Team	AB	R	H	HR	RBI	Avg	OB	Slg	OPS	bb%	ct%	Eye	SB	CS	x/h%	Iso	RC/G
2009	A	Augusta	388	54	100	2	46	258	330	327	658	10	83	0.64	7	1	20	70	3.82
2010	A+	San Jose	445	70	114	3	35	256	327	348	676	10	80	0.54	33	15	26	92	4.01
2011	A	Augusta	143	18	33	3	17	231	317	378	694	11	78	0.56	3	2	42	147	4.26
2011	A+	San Jose	230	34	69	3	27	300	364	470	833	9	80	0.50	5	1	43	170	6.02
2012	AA	Richmond	451	52	99	3	32	220	285	310	595	8	80	0.46	16	4	30	91	2.94

One of the more athletic SS in the minors. Has plus speed that leads to good range. Also has a plus arm and can make all the plays. The only concern is if he will hit enough to play full-time. He had a good stint in the CAL in '11, but is not consistent at the plate and struggled at Double-A.

Aguilar, Jesus — 3 — Cleveland

EXP MLB DEBUT: 2014 | POTENTIAL: Starting 1B | 7D

Bats R Age 23
2007 FA (Venezuela)
Pwr ++++
BAvg ++
Spd +
Def ++

Year	Lev	Team	AB	R	H	HR	RBI	Avg	OB	Slg	OPS	bb%	ct%	Eye	SB	CS	x/h%	Iso	RC/G
2010	A-	Mahoning Val	123	8	30	2	17	244	306	366	672	8	77	0.39	2	0	37	122	3.82
2011	A	Lake County	349	58	102	19	69	292	357	544	901	9	72	0.36	1	0	47	252	6.91
2011	A+	Kinston	113	12	29	4	13	257	323	389	712	9	75	0.39	1	0	24	133	4.21
2012	A+	Carolina	368	63	102	12	58	277	356	454	810	11	75	0.49	0	1	38	177	5.72
2012	AA	Akron	72	12	21	3	13	292	400	500	900	15	67	0.54	0	0	43	208	7.53

Big and physical hitter with plenty of power and loft. Continued to hit LHP while showing improved contact. Advancing quickly with bat, but plate discipline is poor and stiff swing can be exploited by good pitching. Secondary skills further behind. Very slow and below average hands at 1B. Has decent arm strength.

Ahmed, Nick — 6 — Atlanta

EXP MLB DEBUT: 2014 | POTENTIAL: Backup SS | 7C

Bats R Age 23
2011 (2) Connecticut
Pwr +
BAvg ++
Spd ++++
Def ++++

Year	Lev	Team	AB	R	H	HR	RBI	Avg	OB	Slg	OPS	bb%	ct%	Eye	SB	CS	x/h%	Iso	RC/G
2009	NCAA	Connecticut	191	34	55	2	20	288	346	366	713	8	86	0.65	11	3	18	79	4.41
2010	NCAA	Connecticut	267	57	80	4	43	300	368	375	743	10	88	0.94	34	8	15	75	4.86
2011	NCAA	Connecticut	183	51	61	2	35	333	416	448	864	12	90	1.44	23	6	25	115	6.54
2011	Rk	Danville	248	46	65	4	24	262	342	379	721	11	81	0.65	18	6	29	117	4.60
2012	A+	Lynchburg	506	84	136	6	49	269	333	391	725	9	80	0.48	40	10	34	123	4.58

Tall, skinny SS who had an impressive full-season debut. Has a solid approach at the plate with gap power, but did strike out in 20% of AB and needs to put the ball into play more. Has above-average speed that results in good range with soft hands and a quick, strong throwing motion.

Alberto, Hanser — 6 — Texas

EXP MLB DEBUT: 2015 | POTENTIAL: Starting SS | 8C

Bats R Age 20
2009 FA (DR)
Pwr ++
BAvg ++++
Spd ++++
Def ++++

Year	Lev	Team	AB	R	H	HR	RBI	Avg	OB	Slg	OPS	bb%	ct%	Eye	SB	CS	x/h%	Iso	RC/G
2011	A-	Spokane	187	21	50	0	16	267	301	321	622	5	92	0.60	7	1	18	53	3.37
2012	A	Hickory	246	37	83	4	38	337	383	463	846	7	91	0.82	15	4	27	126	5.89
2012	A+	Myrtle Beach	279	36	74	4	34	265	270	362	632	1	90	0.07	9	3	23	97	3.11

Quick and athletic infielder with skills requisite of big league SS. Makes routine plays with quick hands and plus range. Owns strong, accurate arm to form plus defender. May not profile for pop, but makes easy contact with short swing and has strength to mash doubles. Above average speed that should bring loads of SB.

Alcantara, Arismendy — 6 — Chicago (N)

EXP MLB DEBUT: 2015 | POTENTIAL: Starting SS | 7D

Bats B Age 21
2008 NDFA, D.R.
Pwr +
BAvg ++
Spd +++
Def +++

Year	Lev	Team	AB	R	H	HR	RBI	Avg	OB	Slg	OPS	bb%	ct%	Eye	SB	CS	x/h%	Iso	RC/G
2010	A-	Boise	219	29	62	3	24	283	314	402	716	4	76	0.19	7	3	23	119	4.21
2011	A	Peoria	369	45	100	2	37	271	301	352	654	4	79	0.21	8	8	21	81	3.41
2012	A+	Daytona	331	47	100	7	51	302	340	447	787	5	82	0.31	25	4	27	145	5.09

Short, switch-hitting SS from the D.R. had a nice state-side debut. Features good speed but has only moderate power. Makes consistent contact, but doesn't walk much and his swing mechanics are not smooth. A bit of a late bloomer, but one worth watching.

Alfaro, Jorge — 23 — Texas

EXP MLB DEBUT: 2016 | POTENTIAL: Starting C | 9D

Bats R Age 20
2010 FA (Colombia)
Pwr ++++
BAvg ++
Spd ++
Def +++

Year	Lev	Team	AB	R	H	HR	RBI	Avg	OB	Slg	OPS	bb%	ct%	Eye	SB	CS	x/h%	Iso	RC/G
2011	A-	Spokane	160	18	48	6	23	300	317	481	798	2	66	0.07	1	0	33	181	5.48
2012	A	Hickory	272	40	71	5	34	261	302	430	732	6	69	0.19	7	3	44	169	4.71

Muscular backstop who missed time early with hamstring issue. Tendency to lengthen swing and get jumpy in box, but has plus raw power based on bat speed and plate coverage. Uses entire field, though Ks a lot. Shows athleticism and has potential to be solid defender. Maintains ideal catch and throw skills.

Alford, Anthony — 8 — Toronto

EXP MLB DEBUT: 2017 | POTENTIAL: Starting OF | 8E

Bats R Age 18
2012 (3) HS (MS)
Pwr ++
BAvg +++
Spd ++++
Def ++

Year	Lev	Team	AB	R	H	HR	RBI	Avg	OB	Slg	OPS	bb%	ct%	Eye	SB	CS	x/h%	Iso	RC/G
2012	Rk	GCL Blue Jays	18	1	3	1	1	167	250	333	583	10	78	0.50	4	0	33	167	2.48

Muscular and athletic prospect who needs lots of development, but payoff could be huge. Owns tools, highlighted by plus speed. Should grow into average power with added loft. Owns OK approach and plus speed could be enhanced by drawing more walks. Plays rangy CF with average arm, but crude on jumps.

Almonte, Zoilo — 79 — New York (A)

EXP MLB DEBUT: 2013 | POTENTIAL: Starting OF | 7B

Bats B Age 24
2005 FA (DR)
Pwr +++
BAvg ++
Spd +++
Def +++

Year	Lev	Team	AB	R	H	HR	RBI	Avg	OB	Slg	OPS	bb%	ct%	Eye	SB	CS	x/h%	Iso	RC/G
2010	A	Charleston (Sc)	227	33	63	10	35	278	339	485	823	8	71	0.32	7	6	40	207	5.84
2010	A+	Tampa	238	26	62	3	26	261	326	366	691	9	73	0.35	8	1	26	105	4.13
2011	A+	Tampa	259	38	76	12	54	293	369	514	882	11	77	0.52	14	4	39	220	6.57
2011	AA	Trenton	175	23	44	3	23	251	307	377	684	7	74	0.31	4	1	34	126	3.94
2012	AA	Trenton	419	64	116	21	70	277	318	487	804	6	75	0.24	15	4	39	210	5.26

Overall solid outfielder who has shown steady progress and finished 3rd in EL in HR. Hits much better from left where compact swing makes clean contact with more pop. Leverage in stroke allows for average power. Plate discipline is concern and can be jammed inside. Ability to play OF with average range.

Almora, Albert — 8 — Chicago (N)

EXP MLB DEBUT: 2016 | POTENTIAL: Starting CF | 9D

Bats R Age 19
2012 (1) HS, FL
Pwr +++
BAvg ++++
Spd +++
Def +++

Year	Lev	Team	AB	R	H	HR	RBI	Avg	OB	Slg	OPS	bb%	ct%	Eye	SB	CS	x/h%	Iso	RC/G
2012	Rk	Arizona Cubs	75	18	26	1	13	347	364	480	844	3	89	0.25	5	1	27	133	5.57
2012	A-	Boise	65	9	19	1	6	292	292	446	738	0	92	0.00	0	1	42	154	4.32

Was one of the more polished players in the '12 draft and had an excellent debut. Has above-average bat speed with a nice line-drive approach. He squares the ball up consistently and should develop above-average power. Defensively has good range and has a plus throwing arm for CF. Has tremendous potential.

Altherr, Aaron
8 | **Philadelphia** | EXP MLB DEBUT: 2014 | POTENTIAL: Starting CF | **7D**

Bats R Age 22
2009 (9) HS, AZ
Pwr ++
BAvg ++
Spd ++++
Def +++

Year	Lev	Team	AB	R	H	HR	RBI	Avg	OB	Slg	OPS	bb%	ct%	Eye	SB	CS	x/h%	Iso	RC/G
2010	Rk	GCL Phillies	115	12	35	1	15	304	322	400	722	3	81	0.14	10	3	23	96	4.14
2010	A-	Williamsport	94	11	27	0	10	287	343	426	769	8	86	0.62	2	3	37	138	5.22
2011	A	Lakewood	147	20	31	1	15	211	266	272	538	7	68	0.23	12	0	23	61	1.89
2011	A-	Williamsport	269	41	70	5	31	260	294	375	670	5	81	0.25	25	4	27	115	3.59
2012	A	Lakewood	420	65	106	8	50	252	314	402	717	8	76	0.37	25	8	39	150	4.44

Yet another toolsy Phillies prospect with size and speed. Has good raw power, but it doesn't translate to game action. Continues to move up despite the lack of a breakout. Struggles with off-speed and breaking balls, but shows a willingness to drive the ball to all parts of the field. Still a work in progress.

Amaral, Beau
8 | **Cincinnati** | EXP MLB DEBUT: 2015 | POTENTIAL: Backup CF | **6C**

Bats L Age 22
2012 (6) UCLA
Pwr +
BAvg ++
Spd +++
Def +++

Year	Lev	Team	AB	R	H	HR	RBI	Avg	OB	Slg	OPS	bb%	ct%	Eye	SB	CS	x/h%	Iso	RC/G
2012	Rk	Billings	234	55	69	1	24	295	343	376	719	7	88	0.63	20	2	20	81	4.48

Scrappy, heady CF whose tools might be a bit short at the pro level. Works hard and puts the bat on the ball consistently. He has a short, compact stroke, but doesn't have much power. Does have above-average speed and is a smart runner. He is a good defender in CF who reads the ball well off the bat, but only an average arm.

Amaya, Gioskar
4 | **Chicago (N)** | EXP MLB DEBUT: 2015 | POTENTIAL: Starting 3B/2B | **7C**

Bats R Age 20
2009 NDFA, Venezuela
Pwr ++
BAvg ++++
Spd ++
Def ++

Year	Lev	Team	AB	R	H	HR	RBI	Avg	OB	Slg	OPS	bb%	ct%	Eye	SB	CS	x/h%	Iso	RC/G
2011	Rk	Cubs	204	37	77	0	36	377	415	510	925	6	81	0.33	13	8	25	132	6.96
2012	AAA	Iowa	1	1	1	0	0	1000	1000	2000	3000	0	100	1.00	0	0	100	1000	27.71
2012	A-	Boise	272	61	81	8	33	298	374	496	870	11	76	0.51	15	5	32	199	6.57

Short, athletic 2B has one of the more polished bats in the system. Has a quick bat, good strike zone judgment, and makes consistent contact. Doesn't have much power, but did hit 8 home runs in '12. Move from SS to 2B was a good one as speed and range were not enough for SS but work fine at 2B where has good instincts.

Anderson, Jake
9 | **Toronto** | EXP MLB DEBUT: 2016 | POTENTIAL: Starting OF | **8D**

Bats R Age 20
2011 (1-S) HS (CA)
Pwr +++
BAvg ++
Spd +++
Def ++

Year	Lev	Team	AB	R	H	HR	RBI	Avg	OB	Slg	OPS	bb%	ct%	Eye	SB	CS	x/h%	Iso	RC/G
2011	Rk	GCL Blue Jays	37	9	15	2	7	405	463	622	1085	10	78	0.50	2	0	27	216	8.98
2012	Rk	Bluefield	191	25	37	3	13	194	238	304	541	5	62	0.15	3	3	38	110	1.95

Lean and projectable OF who offers tools and loads of potential despite less than stellar season. Needs to become more patient and read breaking balls. Repeats balanced swing and likes to use whole field. Should realize power potential due to plus bat speed. Projects well in RF despite average arm because of instincts.

Anderson, Lars
37 | **Arizona** | EXP MLB DEBUT: 2010 | POTENTIAL: Platoon 1B | **6B**

Bats L Age 25
2006 (18) HS (CA)
Pwr ++
BAvg +++
Spd ++
Def +++

Year	Lev	Team	AB	R	H	HR	RBI	Avg	OB	Slg	OPS	bb%	ct%	Eye	SB	CS	x/h%	Iso	RC/G
2011	AAA	Pawtucket	491	65	130	14	78	265	368	422	789	14	76	0.67	5	0	36	157	5.61
2011	MLB	Boston	5	2	0	0	0	0	0	0	0	0	40	0.00	0	0	0	0	
2012	AAA	Pawtucket	340	49	88	9	52	259	364	415	778	14	74	0.63	1	0	38	156	5.50
2012	MLB	Boston	8	1	1	0	0	125	125	125	250	0	63	0.00	0	0	0	0	
2012	AAA	Columbus	56	4	11	0	7	196	308	286	593	14	68	0.50	0	0	45	89	3.05

Tall and lean prospect who has spent most of last 3 years in Triple-A. Offers size, bat speed, strength, and hand-eye coordination, but hasn't developed power as expected. Swing lacks loft and continued struggles against LHP could lead to platoon role at best. Possesses excellent glovework at 1B and has seen action in LF.

Anderson, Leslie
37 | **Tampa Bay** | EXP MLB DEBUT: 2013 | POTENTIAL: Reserve 1B/LF | **7E**

Bats L Age 31
2010 FA (Cuba)
Pwr +++
BAvg ++
Spd +
Def ++

Year	Lev	Team	AB	R	H	HR	RBI	Avg	OB	Slg	OPS	bb%	ct%	Eye	SB	CS	x/h%	Iso	RC/G
2010	A+	Charlotte	84	13	22	3	11	262	295	405	700	5	93	0.67	0	1	27	143	4.09
2010	AA	Montgomery	181	24	55	6	25	304	367	475	842	9	85	0.64	3	1	33	171	5.91
2010	AAA	Durham	122	14	40	2	13	328	354	418	772	4	84	0.25	0	0	18	90	4.74
2011	AAA	Durham	462	46	128	13	65	277	308	413	722	4	87	0.35	2	3	29	136	4.22
2012	AAA	Durham	444	63	137	14	56	309	347	450	797	6	87	0.46	0	3	26	142	5.13

Smooth-swinging natural hitter who finished 3rd in IL in BA. Set career high in HR, though has contact-oriented approach designed to use whole field. Can catch up to good FB and recognizes pitches. Doesn't draw many BB and offers no speed. Plays 1B and LF and is fringy at both.

Aplin, Andrew
8 | **Houston** | EXP MLB DEBUT: 2015 | POTENTIAL: Fourth OF | **6B**

Bats L Age 22
2012 (5) Arizona State
Pwr ++
BAvg +++
Spd +++
Def ++++

Year	Lev	Team	AB	R	H	HR	RBI	Avg	OB	Slg	OPS	bb%	ct%	Eye	SB	CS	x/h%	Iso	RC/G
2010	NCAA	Arizona State	89	25	30	0	14	337	459	416	874	18	89	2.00	7	2	17	79	7.11
2011	NCAA	Arizona State	137	22	39	1	19	285	368	416	784	12	89	1.20	3	5	33	131	5.61
2012	NCAA	Arizona State	219	48	66	5	27	301	376	470	846	11	95	2.17	6	2	35	169	6.25
2012	A+	Lancaster	104	19	27	3	13	260	287	423	710	4	85	0.25	4	3	33	163	4.06
2012	A-	Tri City	164	38	57	4	25	348	431	537	967	13	87	1.09	20	7	32	189	7.73

Polished and athletic OF who is known more for defense than offense. Had scintillating debut by making consistent, hard contact and controlling strike zone. Only projects to gap power as lacks load and trigger in swing for consistent long balls. Plays outstanding CF defense with plus instincts and a strong, accurate arm.

Arcia, Oswaldo
9 | **Minnesota** | EXP MLB DEBUT: 2013 | POTENTIAL: Starting OF | **9D**

Bats L Age 22
2007 FA (Venezuela)
Pwr ++++
BAvg ++++
Spd ++
Def +++

Year	Lev	Team	AB	R	H	HR	RBI	Avg	OB	Slg	OPS	bb%	ct%	Eye	SB	CS	x/h%	Iso	RC/G
2011	Rk	GCL Twins	8	1	4	0	1	500	500	875	1375	0	88	0.00	0	0	50	375	11.77
2011	A	Beloit	71	18	25	5	18	352	425	704	1129	11	77	0.56	2	2	56	352	9.78
2011	A+	Fort Myers	213	27	56	8	32	263	293	460	753	4	75	0.17	1	1	43	197	4.61
2012	A+	Fort Myers	207	22	64	7	31	309	378	517	895	10	78	0.51	1	3	41	208	6.76
2012	AA	New Britain	262	54	86	10	67	328	393	557	950	10	76	0.45	3	2	41	229	7.51

Thick-bodied OF who flew under radar and established career high in 2B and HR. Owns natural hitting approach that allows him to wait for good pitches to drive. Has strength and bat control to realize BA and power. Has some swing and miss to game and is below average runner. Good RF with avg range and strong arm.

Arenado, Nolan
5 | **Colorado** | EXP MLB DEBUT: 2013 | POTENTIAL: Starting 3B | **9D**

Bats R Age 22
2009 (2) HS, CA
Pwr +++
BAvg +++
Spd ++
Def +++

Year	Lev	Team	AB	R	H	HR	RBI	Avg	OB	Slg	OPS	bb%	ct%	Eye	SB	CS	x/h%	Iso	RC/G
2009	Rk	Casper	203	28	61	2	22	300	352	404	756	7	91	0.89	5	2	28	103	4.97
2010	A	Asheville	373	45	115	12	65	308	342	520	862	5	86	0.37	1	3	47	212	5.93
2011	A+	Modesto	517	82	154	20	122	298	356	487	844	8	90	0.89	2	1	36	190	5.89
2012	AA	Tulsa	516	55	147	12	56	285	335	428	763	7	89	0.67	0	2	33	143	4.95

Struggled with consistency and failed to duplicate his breakout. Power spike didn't carry over to AA and raises concerns. Nice inside-out swing with a quick stroke and makes consistent contact. Hasn't struck out more than 58 times since turning pro. Continues to improve defensively and is now above average with a strong throwing arm.

Arias, Junior
5 | **Cincinnati** | EXP MLB DEBUT: 2015 | POTENTIAL: Backup 3B | **6D**

Bats R Age 21
2009 NDFA, D.R.
Pwr ++
BAvg +
Spd +++
Def ++

Year	Lev	Team	AB	R	H	HR	RBI	Avg	OB	Slg	OPS	bb%	ct%	Eye	SB	CS	x/h%	Iso	RC/G
2010	Rk	Reds	195	44	56	6	25	287	329	482	811	6	70	0.21	4	3	38	195	5.70
2011	Rk	Billings	219	47	55	8	30	251	311	452	763	8	66	0.26	7	5	45	201	5.25
2012	A	Dayton	361	52	75	7	35	208	249	313	562	5	73	0.21	28	7	28	105	2.16

Tall, athletic player has not developed as anticipated. Has good raw tools, but has made little progress. Struggles with breaking balls and doesn't make enough contact. Does have good speed and stole a career high 28 bases, but hit just .208 in the MWL. Has a strong arm and size for 3B, but there is plenty of work to be done.

Arteaga, Humberto
6 | **Kansas City** | EXP MLB DEBUT: 2016 | POTENTIAL: Starting SS | **7C**

Bats R Age 19
2010 FA (Venezuela)
Pwr +
BAvg +++
Spd ++
Def ++++

Year	Lev	Team	AB	R	H	HR	RBI	Avg	OB	Slg	OPS	bb%	ct%	Eye	SB	CS	x/h%	Iso	RC/G
2011	Rk	Royals	213	30	54	0	28	254	284	324	608	4	82	0.23	8	2	24	70	2.91
2012	Rk	Burlington	234	40	64	2	29	274	300	380	681	4	87	0.29	7	3	28	107	3.82

Lean and smooth INF with potential Gold Glove defensive ability. Hands and instincts advanced for age and range is well above average. Makes throws from deep in hole with arm strength. Offers little power and doesn't run well. Makes contact with controlled stroke, but rarely draws walks. Bat must improve to play at next level.

Asche, Cody — 5 — Philadelphia
EXP MLB DEBUT: 2014 | POTENTIAL: Starting 3B | 8D

Bats L Age 23
2011 (4) Nebraska
Pwr ++
BAvg +++
Spd +++
Def ++

Year	Lev	Team	AB	R	H	HR	RBI	Avg	OB	Slg	OPS	bb%	ct%	Eye	SB	CS	x/h%	Iso	RC/G
2010	NCAA	Nebraska	209	32	65	10	58	311	363	522	884	8	77	0.35	1	2	35	211	6.37
2011	NCAA	Nebraska	208	46	68	12	56	327	421	639	1061	14	80	0.83	2	1	59	313	8.99
2011	A-	Williamsport	239	14	46	2	19	192	266	264	530	9	79	0.48	0	3	28	71	2.08
2012	A+	Clearwater	255	31	89	2	25	349	378	447	825	4	85	0.32	10	2	20	98	5.48
2012	AA	Reading	263	42	79	10	47	300	354	513	868	8	79	0.39	1	1	42	213	6.23

4th round pick in '11 had a nice full-season debut, with surprising power. Has good hand-eye coordination and bat speed. Can be overly aggressive and did strike out 93 times. Is fringy at 3B where his tools are average across the board. He could be moved to a new position, but his ticket to the big leagues will be his bat.

Aune, Austin — 6 — New York (A)
EXP MLB DEBUT: 2016 | POTENTIAL: Starting 3B/RF | 9E

Bats L Age 19
2012 (2) HS (TX)
Pwr +++
BAvg ++
Spd +++
Def +++

Year	Lev	Team	AB	R	H	HR	RBI	Avg	OB	Slg	OPS	bb%	ct%	Eye	SB	CS	x/h%	Iso	RC/G
2012	Rk	GCL Yankees	139	19	38	1	20	273	361	410	771	12	68	0.42	6	4	37	137	5.65

Raw, athletic INF with semblance of five tools, but will need several years. Has upside predicated on clean stroke and plus raw power. Oozes athleticism with quick actions and avg wheels. Ample range to stick at SS, but hands may work better at 3B or OF. Can overswing and needs to clean up crude approach.

Austin, Tyler — 39 — New York (A)
EXP MLB DEBUT: 2014 | POTENTIAL: Starting 1B/OF | 8B

Bats R Age 21
2010 (13) HS (GA)
Pwr +++
BAvg ++++
Spd +++
Def +++

Year	Lev	Team	AB	R	H	HR	RBI	Avg	OB	Slg	OPS	bb%	ct%	Eye	SB	CS	x/h%	Iso	RC/G
2012	Rk	GCL Yankees	6	1	3	1	2	500	571	1000	1571	14	83	1.00	0	0	33	500	14.43
2012	A	Charleston (Sc)	266	69	85	14	54	320	403	598	1000	12	74	0.54	17	2	48	278	8.36
2012	A+	Tampa	134	20	43	2	23	321	377	478	854	8	79	0.43	6	0	37	157	6.20
2012	AA	Trenton	7	2	2	0	1	286	375	286	661	13	86	1.00	0	0	0	0	4.04

Steady, natural hitter who reached AA in first full season. Hit at least .312 every month while exhibiting solid all-around game. Uses entire field with bat control and hand-eye coordination. Hits for pop with natural strength, leverage, and patience. Avg speed plays up due to instincts and offers plus arm and avg range in OF corner.

Avery, Xavier — 78 — Baltimore
EXP MLB DEBUT: 2012 | POTENTIAL: Starting OF | 8C

Bats L Age 23
2008 (2) HS (GA)
Pwr ++
BAvg +++
Spd ++++
Def +++

Year	Lev	Team	AB	R	H	HR	RBI	Avg	OB	Slg	OPS	bb%	ct%	Eye	SB	CS	x/h%	Iso	RC/G
2010	A+	Frederick	447	73	125	4	48	280	342	389	731	9	79	0.44	28	14	28	110	4.65
2010	AA	Bowie	107	10	25	3	18	234	281	374	655	6	68	0.21	10	0	36	140	3.48
2011	AA	Bowie	557	72	144	4	26	259	318	343	661	8	72	0.31	36	14	26	84	3.71
2012	AAA	Norfolk	390	57	92	8	34	236	324	356	681	12	73	0.48	22	7	28	121	4.05
2012	MLB	Baltimore	94	14	21	1	6	223	305	340	645	10	76	0.48	6	3	38	117	3.62

Athletic and very fast outfielder reached BAL on basis of improved approach and more powerful contact. Won't become masher, but has sufficient bat speed with clean swing mechanics. Has potential to become prominent leadoff hitter, but needs to read breaking pitches better. Legitimate CF defender with ample range, but arm strength is suspect.

Baez, Javier — 6 — Chicago (N)
EXP MLB DEBUT: 2015 | POTENTIAL: Starting 3B/SS | 9C

Bats R Age 20
2011 (1) HS (FL)
Pwr ++++
BAvg +++
Spd ++
Def ++

Year	Lev	Team	AB	R	H	HR	RBI	Avg	OB	Slg	OPS	bb%	ct%	Eye	SB	CS	x/h%	Iso	RC/G
2011	Rk	Cubs	12	2	4	0	0	333	333	500	833	0	83	0.00	2	0	50	167	5.48
2011	A-	Boise	6	0	1	0	1	167	167	167	333	0	67	0.00	0	0	0	0	
2012	A	Peoria	213	41	71	12	33	333	360	596	957	4	77	0.19	20	3	38	263	7.08
2012	A+	Daytona	80	9	15	4	13	188	235	400	635	6	74	0.24	4	2	53	213	3.08

Strong, athletic SS has the tools to star. Is strong and physically mature with plus bat speed and good power. Was the best player in the MWL. Plate discipline is marginal, but has time to improve. Moves well defensively with a strong arm and improved actions and for now should be able to stick at SS. Is on the fast-track to Wrigley.

Baker, Aaron — 3 — Baltimore
EXP MLB DEBUT: 2014 | POTENTIAL: Reserve 1B | 7C

Bats L Age 25
2009 (11) Oklahoma
Pwr ++++
BAvg ++
Spd ++
Def +++

Year	Lev	Team	AB	R	H	HR	RBI	Avg	OB	Slg	OPS	bb%	ct%	Eye	SB	CS	x/h%	Iso	RC/G
2011	A+	Bradenton	386	53	109	15	73	282	356	469	825	10	76	0.48	1	2	36	187	5.82
2011	AA	Bowie	46	2	9	0	3	196	196	239	435	0	59	0.00	0	0	22	43	0.22
2012	A+	Frederick	319	44	85	22	72	266	341	549	889	10	76	0.47	7	3	51	282	6.55
2012	AA	Bowie	7	1	3	0	4	429	556	571	1127	22	71	1.00	0	0	33	143	11.33
2012	A-	Aberdeen	4	0	1	0	0	250	250	500	750	0	50	0.00	0	0	100	250	7.33

Big and strong 1B who led CAR in HR in repeat of High-A. Possesses nice approach and ability to crush RHP with pitch recognition. Power is clearly best tool, though owns nice hands and glovework at 1B. BA potential muted by inability to hit breaking balls and long swing can be exploited. Lacks foot speed to be threat on base.

Baldwin, James — 8 — Los Angeles (N)
EXP MLB DEBUT: 2015 | POTENTIAL: Starting CF | 7D

Bats L Age 21
2010 (4) HS, NC
Pwr ++
BAvg +
Spd ++++
Def +++

Year	Lev	Team	AB	R	H	HR	RBI	Avg	OB	Slg	OPS	bb%	ct%	Eye	SB	CS	x/h%	Iso	RC/G
2010	Rk	Dodgers	179	25	49	2	22	274	309	363	672	5	66	0.15	17	3	20	89	3.79
2011	Rk	Ogden	196	47	49	10	39	250	313	480	793	8	62	0.24	22	5	45	230	5.87
2012	A	Great Lakes	440	62	92	7	40	209	282	334	617	9	60	0.25	53	8	36	125	3.36

Tall, athletic OF is the son of former major league pitcher. Has tons of athleticism, but that has yet to translate to success. Has plus speed, but struggles with breaking balls and making consistent contact,striking out an alarming 177 times. Not likely to hit for much power, but covers ground well in CF, and has a strong throwing arm.

Baltz, Jeremy — 9 — San Diego
EXP MLB DEBUT: 2015 | POTENTIAL: Starting OF | 7C

Bats R Age 22
2012 (2) St. Johns
Pwr +++
BAvg +++
Spd ++
Def ++

Year	Lev	Team	AB	R	H	HR	RBI	Avg	OB	Slg	OPS	bb%	ct%	Eye	SB	CS	x/h%	Iso	RC/G
2010	NCAA	St. John's	240	64	95	24	85	396	459	771	1230	10	82	0.64	6	0	43	375	10.48
2011	NCAA	St. John's	209	42	65	6	60	311	426	483	910	17	78	0.89	7	2	32	172	7.35
2012	NCAA	St. John's	241	65	83	8	52	344	423	531	954	12	91	1.50	18	5	30	187	7.43
2012	A-	Eugene	263	44	74	5	43	281	361	414	776	11	84	0.77	12	2	31	133	5.32

Big, strong OF has a good approach with above-average bat speed and raw power. Stays balanced and makes consistent contact with good plate discipline. Should develop above-average power, hit for average, and get on base. Below average speed and defense likely limit him to LF or 1B.

Barfield, Jeremy — 9 — Oakland
EXP MLB DEBUT: 2014 | POTENTIAL: Starting OF | 7E

Bats R Age 24
2008 (8) San Jacinto JC
Pwr ++++
BAvg ++
Spd ++
Def +++

Year	Lev	Team	AB	R	H	HR	RBI	Avg	OB	Slg	OPS	bb%	ct%	Eye	SB	CS	x/h%	Iso	RC/G
2008	A-	Vancouver	251	28	68	3	41	271	339	375	714	9	83	0.62	5	3	29	104	4.48
2009	A	Kane County	404	48	106	8	52	262	341	389	729	11	76	0.49	1	5	31	126	4.67
2010	A+	Stockton	508	72	138	17	92	272	339	417	757	9	82	0.56	1	1	28	146	4.85
2011	AA	Midland	495	56	127	11	72	257	315	384	699	8	82	0.47	1	1	30	127	4.13
2012	AA	Midland	482	67	131	13	64	272	321	415	736	7	83	0.43	1	0	32	143	4.51

Tall and instinctual OF who repeated AA and was slightly better. Tweaked stroke to make more contact and still has potential to tap into plus, raw power. Has lost a step, but fits RF profile with pop, strong arm, and avg range. Still too much swing and miss and approach hasn't or won't lead to high OBP without an upgrade.

Barnes, Barrett — 8 — Pittsburgh
EXP MLB DEBUT: 2014 | POTENTIAL: Starting CF | 8C

Bats R Age 21
2012 (1-S) Texas Tech
Pwr +++
BAvg +++
Spd +++
Def +++

Year	Lev	Team	AB	R	H	HR	RBI	Avg	OB	Slg	OPS	bb%	ct%	Eye	SB	CS	x/h%	Iso	RC/G
2010	NCAA	Texas Tech	217	71	74	14	53	341	444	641	1084	16	77	0.80	12	3	47	300	9.46
2011	NCAA	Texas Tech	214	47	62	10	38	290	404	509	913	16	73	0.72	19	2	42	220	7.38
2012	NCAA	Texas Tech	206	53	67	9	49	325	416	597	1013	13	82	0.86	19	1	48	272	8.36
2012	A-	State College	125	16	36	5	24	288	373	456	829	12	83	0.81	10	6	31	168	5.87

Strong, athletic player who runs well and should be able to stick in CF though his arm is below average. Has enough bat speed and above-average power to have value. Had a solid debut in the NYPL, showing better than anticipated plate discipline, but was shut down at the beginning of August with a stress fracture in his leg.

Barnum, Keon — 3 — Chicago (A)
EXP MLB DEBUT: 2016 | POTENTIAL: Starting 1B | 8D

Bats L Age 20
2012 (1-S) HS (FL)
Pwr ++++
BAvg ++
Spd ++
Def ++

Year	Lev	Team	AB	R	H	HR	RBI	Avg	OB	Slg	OPS	bb%	ct%	Eye	SB	CS	x/h%	Iso	RC/G
2012	Rk	Bristol	43	6	12	3	8	279	354	512	866	10	70	0.38	0	0	33	233	6.37

Big and powerful prospect who swings with authority and has above avg raw power to all fields. Bat is only plus tool and will need to work on shortening swing to make better contact. Doesn't control bat well and breaking balls give him fits. Isn't a baseclogger, but lacks quickness. Plays 1B, but may move to OF due to strong arm.

Bean, Steve — 2 — St. Louis

EXP MLB DEBUT: 2016 | POTENTIAL: Starting C | 8D

Bats L Age 19 — 2012 (1-S) HS, TX
Pwr ++ · BAvg +++ · Spd ++ · Def +++

Year	Lev	Team	AB	R	H	HR	RBI	Avg	OB	Slg	OPS	bb%	ct%	Eye	SB	CS	x/h%	Iso	RC/G
2012	Rk	Johnson City	80	6	10	1	5	125	263	213	476	16	60	0.47	2	0	50	88	0.98
2012	Rk	GCL Cardinals	50	8	16	0	7	320	414	400	814	14	78	0.73	0	0	25	80	6.05

Strong, athletic backstop was one of the better defenders in the draft. Receives the ball well with good agility and a plus throwing arm. Scouts are mixed about whether he will hit and he struggled his first taste, but was better when sent down. Isn't going to hit for power, but he can shut down the running game.

Beckham, Tim — 46 — Tampa Bay

EXP MLB DEBUT: 2013 | POTENTIAL: Starting SS | 8D

Bats R Age 23 — 2008 (1) HS (GA)
Pwr +++ · BAvg +++ · Spd +++ · Def +++

Year	Lev	Team	AB	R	H	HR	RBI	Avg	OB	Slg	OPS	bb%	ct%	Eye	SB	CS	x/h%	Iso	RC/G
2009	A	Bowling Green	491	58	135	5	63	275	322	389	711	6	76	0.29	13	10	31	114	4.28
2010	A+	Charlotte	465	68	119	5	57	256	343	359	703	12	74	0.52	22	14	28	103	4.42
2011	AA	Montgomery	418	82	115	7	57	275	337	395	732	9	78	0.43	15	4	30	120	4.60
2011	AAA	Durham	106	12	27	5	13	255	275	462	737	3	73	0.10	2	1	37	208	4.32
2012	AAA	Durham	285	40	73	6	28	256	325	361	686	9	75	0.41	6	0	23	105	3.98

Athletic and quick infielder who needs to capitalize on tantalizing tools. Possesses well above average bat speed, but swing mechanics not conducive to anything more than average pop. Pitch selection is subpar, but can drive ball. Profiles as 2B with strong arm and textbook footwork.

Bell, Josh — 9 — Pittsburgh

EXP MLB DEBUT: 2015 | POTENTIAL: Starting RF | 9D

Bats B Age 20 — 2011 (2) HS, TX
Pwr ++++ · BAvg +++ · Spd ++ · Def ++

Year	Lev	Team	AB	R	H	HR	RBI	Avg	OB	Slg	OPS	bb%	ct%	Eye	SB	CS	x/h%	Iso	RC/G
2012	A	West Virginia	62	6	17	1	11	274	297	403	700	3	66	0.10	1	0	35	129	4.19

Athletic, switch-hitting OF has all the tools, but had a lackluster debut. A knee injury delayed his start and he played in just 15 games. Has plus bat speed and power to both sides. Defensively he is raw, has only average speed, and a fringy arm. Has lots of work to do, but as much raw power as any prospect in the minors.

Belnome, Vince — 4 — Tampa Bay

EXP MLB DEBUT: 2013 | POTENTIAL: Utility INF | 6D

Bats L Age 25 — 2008 (29) West Virginia
Pwr ++ · BAvg +++ · Spd ++ · Def ++

Year	Lev	Team	AB	R	H	HR	RBI	Avg	OB	Slg	OPS	bb%	ct%	Eye	SB	CS	x/h%	Iso	RC/G
2010	A+	Lake Elsinore	498	81	136	16	84	273	397	436	832	17	73	0.75	4	1	35	163	6.37
2011	AA	San Antonio	267	56	89	17	62	333	433	603	1036	15	78	0.80	0	5	42	270	8.71
2012	Rk	Padres	10	1	4	1	5	400	500	1000	1500	17	100	1.00	0	0	75	600	13.47
2012	A+	Lake Elsinore	14	2	8	1	7	571	647	1000	1647	18	86	1.50	0	0	50	429	16.19
2012	AAA	Tucson	258	28	71	5	33	275	379	384	762	14	72	0.60	5	1	24	109	5.31

An above-average hitter with good OB ability, he has moderate bat speed with a slight upper-cut swing and decent plate discipline. Handles fastballs well, but struggles with off-speed offerings. Is a career .300 hitter, with solid power, but doesn't have a clear position. Played 1B, 2B, 3B, and DH and profiles a UT player.

Beltre, Engel — 8 — Texas

EXP MLB DEBUT: 2014 | POTENTIAL: Starting OF | 8E

Bats L Age 23 — 2006 FA (DR)
Pwr +++ · BAvg ++ · Spd ++++ · Def ++++

Year	Lev	Team	AB	R	H	HR	RBI	Avg	OB	Slg	OPS	bb%	ct%	Eye	SB	CS	x/h%	Iso	RC/G
2009	AA	Frisco	14	1	1	0	1	71	71	143	214	0	86	0.00	1	0	100	71	
2010	A+	Bakersfield	263	38	87	5	35	331	358	460	818	4	87	0.32	10	7	23	129	5.33
2010	AA	Frisco	181	14	46	1	14	254	293	337	630	5	87	0.42	8	2	20	83	3.34
2011	AA	Frisco	437	64	101	1	28	231	277	300	577	6	76	0.27	16	6	22	69	2.52
2012	AA	Frisco	564	80	147	13	55	261	293	420	713	4	79	0.22	36	10	32	160	4.15

Tall and athletic, he returned to Double-A and finished second in SB. Possesses plus speed and CF defensive ability; arm strength is good. Has more tools than production, but set career high in HR and SB. Hits LHP (.308) and owns plus raw power. Needs to tone down swing-happy approach and learn to get on base more.

Benson, Joe — 8 — Minnesota

EXP MLB DEBUT: 2011 | POTENTIAL: Starting OF | 7C

Bats R Age 25 — 2006 (2) HS (IL)
Pwr +++ · BAvg ++ · Spd ++++ · Def +++

Year	Lev	Team	AB	R	H	HR	RBI	Avg	OB	Slg	OPS	bb%	ct%	Eye	SB	CS	x/h%	Iso	RC/G
2011	MLB	Minnesota	71	3	17	0	2	239	270	352	622	4	70	0.14	2	2	41	113	3.15
2012	Rk	GCL Twins	8	1	3	0	0	375	444	500	944	11	75	0.50	1	1	33	125	7.78
2012	A+	Fort Myers	33	7	10	1	8	303	395	485	880	13	73	0.56	4	0	40	182	6.90
2012	AA	New Britain	141	13	26	3	20	184	253	305	558	8	70	0.30	4	3	38	121	2.20
2012	AAA	Rochester	95	9	17	2	8	179	264	316	580	10	72	0.41	4	0	41	137	2.63

Strong, athletic OF who suffered thru nightmare season with various injuries. Plays game aggressively at plate and in field. Exhibits raw power and above avg speed, though racks up Ks with free-swinging approach. Expands strike zone and BA potential muted. Positive tools are evident, but needs to piece together.

Beras, Jairo — 9 — Texas

EXP MLB DEBUT: 2017 | POTENTIAL: Starting OF | 9E

Bats R Age 17 — 2012 FA (DR)
Pwr ++++ · BAvg ++ · Spd +++ · Def ++

Year	Lev	Team	AB	R	H	HR	RBI	Avg	OB	Slg	OPS	bb%	ct%	Eye	SB	CS	x/h%	Iso	RC/G
2012		Did not play																	

Tall, lean OF who won't begin pro career until July after suspension for providing fake date of birth. Frame and bat speed give lot to dream on. Incredible, raw power could reach 40+ HR. Runs well for size, though likely to slow down as he add strength and weight. Has raw swing that will take time, but has athleticism to get better.

Bernadina, Roderick — 789 — Baltimore

EXP MLB DEBUT: 2015 | POTENTIAL: Starting OF | 8E

Bats R Age 20 — 2009 FA (Curacao)
Pwr +++ · BAvg +++ · Spd +++ · Def +++

Year	Lev	Team	AB	R	H	HR	RBI	Avg	OB	Slg	OPS	bb%	ct%	Eye	SB	CS	x/h%	Iso	RC/G
2011	Rk	GCL Orioles	184	30	44	4	28	239	320	413	733	11	86	0.85	6	2	48	174	4.85
2012	A	Delmarva	104	8	31	2	12	298	354	394	748	8	80	0.43	3	1	19	96	4.70
2012	A+	Frederick	13	1	1	1	4	77	77	308	385	0	85	0.00	0	0	100	231	
2012	A-	Aberdeen	116	19	30	0	14	259	312	319	631	7	84	0.47	4	0	20	60	3.40

Lean, athletic OF with raw skills and potential to turn into solid performer. Can play any OF position with avg speed and arm and will likely end up in RF as he fills out. Swings and misses, though focuses on using entire field with plate coverage and strike zone judgment. Exhibits bat speed and raw power with leverage in swing.

Bethancourt, Christian — 2 — Atlanta

EXP MLB DEBUT: 2013 | POTENTIAL: Starting C | 8D

Bats R Age 21 — 2009 NDFA, Panama
Pwr ++ · BAvg ++ · Spd ++ · Def ++++

Year	Lev	Team	AB	R	H	HR	RBI	Avg	OB	Slg	OPS	bb%	ct%	Eye	SB	CS	x/h%	Iso	RC/G
2009	Rk	Danville	50	10	13	2	8	260	339	480	819	11	68	0.38	1	1	54	220	6.10
2010	A	Rome	399	31	100	3	34	251	276	331	607	3	84	0.23	11	3	24	80	2.87
2011	A	Rome	221	25	67	4	33	303	328	430	757	3	88	0.30	6	3	25	127	4.63
2011	A+	Lynchburg	166	11	45	1	20	271	284	325	609	2	79	0.09	3	2	16	54	2.66
2012	AA	Mississippi	268	30	65	2	26	243	272	291	563	4	83	0.24	8	6	12	49	2.31

Strong, defensive-minded backstop continues to impress behind the plate. Good actions with a quick release and plus throwing arm that helped nail 42% of base runners. Uses a short, compact stroke to drive the ball to all fields and should add power as he matures. Struggles to make consistent contact, but his defense remains plus.

Bichette, Dante — 5 — New York (A)

EXP MLB DEBUT: 2015 | POTENTIAL: Starting 3B | 8D

Bats R Age 20 — 2011 (2) HS (FL)
Pwr +++ · BAvg +++ · Spd +++ · Def +++

Year	Lev	Team	AB	R	H	HR	RBI	Avg	OB	Slg	OPS	bb%	ct%	Eye	SB	CS	x/h%	Iso	RC/G
2011	Rk	GCL Yankees	196	33	67	3	47	342	429	505	934	13	79	0.73	3	3	34	163	7.54
2011	A-	Staten Island	7	1	1	1	1	143	250	571	821	13	71	0.50	0	1	100	429	5.34
2012	A	Charleston (Sc)	471	67	117	3	46	248	313	331	644	9	80	0.47	3	4	26	83	3.54

Pure hitter who failed to build upon impressive '11. Bat speed slowed and was content with weak contact to opp field. Brings advanced approach with clean, textbook swing and power potential. Avg speed, but instincts give him SB potential. Can be decent 3B with agility and strong arm, though throwing accuracy needs attention.

Bird, Greg — 23 — New York (A)

EXP MLB DEBUT: 2016 | POTENTIAL: Starting 1B | 8E

Bats L Age 20 — 2011 (5) HS (CO)
Pwr +++ · BAvg +++ · Spd + · Def ++

Year	Lev	Team	AB	R	H	HR	RBI	Avg	OB	Slg	OPS	bb%	ct%	Eye	SB	CS	x/h%	Iso	RC/G
2011	Rk	GCL Yankees	12	0	1	0	0	83	154	83	237	8	67	0.25	0	0	0	0	
2012	Rk	GCL Yankees	49	9	14	0	5	286	417	367	784	18	73	0.85	0	0	21	82	5.95
2012	A-	Staten Island	40	4	16	2	8	400	478	650	1128	13	75	0.60	0	0	38	250	10.09

Big and tough prospect who may end up at 1B as he lacks agility and receiving skills. Produces offensively with bat speed and strength. Draws BB with patient, professional approach and stings balls to entire field with line drive stroke. With more loft in swing, could be excellent power hitter. Long swing can be exploited.

Black, Justin — 8 — Atlanta
EXP MLB DEBUT: 2016 | POTENTIAL: Backup OF | 6C

Bats R Age 20 | 2012 (4) HS, MT
Pwr ++ | BAvg ++ | Spd +++ | Def +++

Year	Lev	Team	AB	R	H	HR	RBI	Avg	OB	Slg	OPS	bb%	ct%	Eye	SB	CS	x/h%	Iso	RC/G
2012	Rk	GCL Braves	132	15	24	2	7	182	285	258	542	13	59	0.35	3	4	21	76	2.06

Struggled in his pro debut but has plus speed and is a solid defender in CF. Is raw at the plate and struck out 54 times in 132 AB. He does have nice raw power and the Braves think they can turn it into game power. He played American Legion ball in Montana and he has lots of work to do.

Blash, Jabari — 9 — Seattle
EXP MLB DEBUT: 2015 | POTENTIAL: Starting OF | 8E

Bats R Age 24 | 2010 (8) Miami Dade CC
Pwr ++++ | BAvg ++ | Spd ++ | Def +++

Year	Lev	Team	AB	R	H	HR	RBI	Avg	OB	Slg	OPS	bb%	ct%	Eye	SB	CS	x/h%	Iso	RC/G
2010	Rk	Pulaski	109	21	29	5	20	266	344	477	821	11	60	0.30	1	1	41	211	6.64
2011	A	Clinton	124	13	27	3	13	218	401	347	748	23	65	0.88	5	2	33	129	5.51
2011	A-	Everett	195	26	57	11	43	292	381	574	956	13	67	0.43	10	3	53	282	8.24
2012	A	Clinton	400	71	98	15	50	245	343	433	776	13	67	0.45	13	7	41	188	5.57

Tall, muscular OF who was old for Low-A, but solid tools tough to ignore. Plays game aggressively and can hit for power due to leveraged stroke. Draws BB with patient approach, but can be passive. Owns long swing and not likely to hit for BA. Possesses below avg speed, though is OK RF with avg arm and range.

Bogaerts, Xander — 6 — Boston
EXP MLB DEBUT: 2014 | POTENTIAL: Starting 3B | 9C

Bats R Age 20 | 2009 FA (Aruba)
Pwr ++++ | BAvg +++ | Spd +++ | Def +++

Year	Lev	Team	AB	R	H	HR	RBI	Avg	OB	Slg	OPS	bb%	ct%	Eye	SB	CS	x/h%	Iso	RC/G
2011	A	Greenville	265	38	69	16	45	260	324	509	834	9	73	0.35	1	3	46	249	5.83
2012	A+	Salem	384	59	116	15	64	302	372	505	878	10	78	0.51	4	4	39	203	6.49
2012	AA	Portland	92	12	30	5	17	326	333	598	931	1	77	0.05	1	1	50	272	6.62

Tall, strong INF has huge upside predicated on plus power and athleticism. Improved selective approach gives him chance to hit for high BA with scary pop. Hit breaking balls with more authority, but Ks can be issue. May outgrow SS, but quick, loose hands and average speed playable at 3B or corner OF.

Bonifacio, Jorge — 9 — Kansas City
EXP MLB DEBUT: 2015 | POTENTIAL: Starting OF | 8C

Bats R Age 20 | 2009 FA (DR)
Pwr +++ | BAvg ++++ | Spd +++ | Def +++

Year	Lev	Team	AB	R	H	HR	RBI	Avg	OB	Slg	OPS	bb%	ct%	Eye	SB	CS	x/h%	Iso	RC/G
2010	Rk	Royals	76	9	16	0	6	211	268	342	610	7	59	0.19	1	2	31	132	3.47
2011	Rk	Burlington	236	26	67	7	30	284	329	492	821	6	75	0.28	5	6	46	208	5.71
2012	A	Kane County	412	54	116	10	61	282	330	432	762	7	80	0.36	6	3	31	150	4.86

Aggressive, pure-hitting OF who started hot, but faded down stretch. Struggles with selectivity, but continues to hit for high BA by using whole field and bat control. Power won't be realized until he exhibits more patience, but packs wallop in leveraged stroke. Secondary skills are playable, though overall game needs polish.

Borchering, Bobby — 357 — Houston
EXP MLB DEBUT: 2015 | POTENTIAL: Starting 1B/3B | 8E

Bats B Age 22 | 2009 (1) HS (FL)
Pwr ++++ | BAvg ++ | Spd ++ | Def ++

Year	Lev	Team	AB	R	H	HR	RBI	Avg	OB	Slg	OPS	bb%	ct%	Eye	SB	CS	x/h%	Iso	RC/G
2010	A	South Bend	523	74	141	15	74	270	338	423	761	9	76	0.42	1	1	34	153	4.98
2011	A+	Visalia	531	80	142	24	92	267	329	469	798	8	69	0.30	4	1	39	202	5.54
2012	A+	Visalia	307	47	85	18	60	277	337	534	872	8	69	0.29	0	2	49	257	6.59
2012	AA	Mobile	77	4	10	2	8	130	163	208	370	4	65	0.11	0	1	20	78	
2012	AA	Corpus Christi	95	11	18	4	18	189	267	389	656	10	62	0.28	1	1	56	200	3.76

Strong, powerful INF who returned to High-A and ended in AA. Long swing and aggressive approach hinder BA potential. Possesses well above avg power from both sides due to plus bat speed and wrist strength. Has decent athleticism, but lacks foot speed. Poor defender at 3B with limited range and fringy instincts.

Bostick, Chris — 46 — Oakland
EXP MLB DEBUT: 2016 | POTENTIAL: Starting 2B | 7C

Bats R Age 20 | 2011 (44) HS (NY)
Pwr ++ | BAvg +++ | Spd +++ | Def +++

Year	Lev	Team	AB	R	H	HR	RBI	Avg	OB	Slg	OPS	bb%	ct%	Eye	SB	CS	x/h%	Iso	RC/G
2011	Rk	Athletics	52	13	23	1	5	442	473	654	1127	5	77	0.25	4	0	35	212	9.61
2012	A-	Vermont	279	41	70	3	29	251	317	369	686	9	76	0.41	12	5	33	118	4.09

Athletic, advanced INF who brings a little bit of everything to the table. Despite limited size, offers strength and bat speed to project some pop. Has professional approach that allows him to see pitches and get on base. Hits hard line drives to gaps and has been menace to LHP. Not a standout defender, but has good glove.

Bowe, Theo — 8 — Cincinnati
EXP MLB DEBUT: 2014 | POTENTIAL: Backup CF | 6C

Bats L Age 22 | 2008 (21) HS, DE
Pwr + | BAvg ++ | Spd ++++ | Def ++

Year	Lev	Team	AB	R	H	HR	RBI	Avg	OB	Slg	OPS	bb%	ct%	Eye	SB	CS	x/h%	Iso	RC/G
2009	Rk	GCL Reds	101	15	29	0	9	287	374	356	730	12	79	0.67	15	4	21	69	4.86
2010	Rk	Billings	130	21	39	1	9	300	381	362	742	12	82	0.71	12	9	13	62	4.91
2011	A	Dayton	266	45	65	1	24	244	323	320	643	10	77	0.50	20	9	20	75	3.59
2012	A	Dayton	86	8	16	0	2	186	286	244	530	12	78	0.63	12	1	19	58	2.24
2012	A+	Bakersfield	373	65	117	3	39	314	388	383	771	11	81	0.63	58	28	15	70	5.22

Just 5-9, 150, but has some of the best speed in the minors. He stole 58 bases in '12 and hit .314 in the CAL. Willing to be patient at the plate and draw walks to take advantage of his speed. Has almost no power, but profiles a top-of-the-order hitter and is a plus defender in CF who gets good reads and covers ground well.

Boyd, B.J. — 8 — Oakland
EXP MLB DEBUT: 2017 | POTENTIAL: Starting OF | 8E

Bats L Age 19 | 2012 (4) HS (CA)
Pwr ++ | BAvg +++ | Spd ++++ | Def ++

Year	Lev	Team	AB	R	H	HR	RBI	Avg	OB	Slg	OPS	bb%	ct%	Eye	SB	CS	x/h%	Iso	RC/G
2012	Rk	Athletics	143	37	43	1	20	301	398	434	831	14	75	0.64	16	4	30	133	6.36

Compact, athletic OF who profiles as leadoff hitter with above avg speed and OBP ability. Had good pro debut and showed clean swing and hard contact. Power doesn't project and could benefit from being more aggressive. Has raw skills on defense where he has great range, but needs to learn nuances of OF play.

Bradley, Jackie — 8 — Boston
EXP MLB DEBUT: 2014 | POTENTIAL: Starting CF | 8A

Bats L Age 23 | 2011 (1-S) South Carolina
Pwr ++ | BAvg ++++ | Spd +++ | Def ++++

Year	Lev	Team	AB	R	H	HR	RBI	Avg	OB	Slg	OPS	bb%	ct%	Eye	SB	CS	x/h%	Iso	RC/G
2011	NCAA	South Carolina	162	32	40	6	27	247	337	432	769	12	77	0.58	2	1	43	185	5.19
2011	A	Greenville	15	2	5	1	3	333	333	600	933	0	80	0.00	0	0	40	267	6.34
2011	A-	Lowell	21	5	4	0	0	190	320	190	510	16	76	0.80	2	0	0	0	1.98
2012	A+	Salem	234	53	84	3	34	359	476	526	1001	18	83	1.30	16	6	37	167	8.65
2012	AA	Portland	229	37	62	6	29	271	367	437	804	13	79	0.71	8	3	39	166	5.77

Short, strong OF has exciting game that led to excellent production. May only have gap power, but has all-around tools for future success. No glaring weakness and has plate discipline and leadoff ability. Smashes line drives to all fields with textbook stroke and can hit LHP. Defense enhanced by plus range and instincts.

Brantly, Rob — 2 — Miami
EXP MLB DEBUT: 2012 | POTENTIAL: Starting C | 7C

Bats L Age 23 | 2010 (3) UC-Riverside
Pwr ++ | BAvg +++ | Spd ++ | Def ++

Year	Lev	Team	AB	R	H	HR	RBI	Avg	OB	Slg	OPS	bb%	ct%	Eye	SB	CS	x/h%	Iso	RC/G
2011	A+	Lakeland	146	16	32	3	18	219	245	322	567	3	88	0.29	0	0	28	103	2.48
2012	AA	Erie	180	16	56	3	24	311	354	461	815	6	91	0.71	0	3	36	150	5.55
2012	AAA	Toledo	130	11	33	0	6	254	292	285	577	5	81	0.28	0	0	12	31	2.50
2012	AAA	New Orleans	52	7	19	2	11	365	377	558	935	2	83	0.11	0	0	32	192	6.50
2012	MLB	Miami Marlins	100	14	29	3	8	290	372	460	832	12	84	0.81	1	1	38	170	5.97

Offensive minded backstop with a short, compact stroke at the plate that generates plenty of line-drives. Is a work in progress behind the plate with a decent throwing arm, but below average blocking and receiving skills. He uses the entire field with solid strike zone judgment and fared well in his MLB debut.

Brentz, Bryce — 9 — Boston
EXP MLB DEBUT: 2013 | POTENTIAL: Starting OF | 8C

Bats R Age 24 | 2010 (1-S) Middle TN State
Pwr ++++ | BAvg ++ | Spd ++ | Def ++

Year	Lev	Team	AB	R	H	HR	RBI	Avg	OB	Slg	OPS	bb%	ct%	Eye	SB	CS	x/h%	Iso	RC/G
2010	A-	Lowell	262	28	52	5	39	198	258	340	598	7	71	0.28	5	4	44	141	2.80
2011	A	Greenville	170	43	61	11	36	359	408	647	1055	8	79	0.40	2	2	39	288	8.42
2011	A+	Salem	288	48	79	19	58	274	334	531	866	8	72	0.33	1	1	44	257	6.25
2012	AA	Portland	456	62	135	17	76	296	353	478	831	8	71	0.31	7	5	36	182	5.94
2012	AAA	Pawtucket	17	0	2	0	0	118	167	118	284	6	65	0.17	0	0	0	0	

Strong outfielder who fits the RF prototype. With well above average bat speed and natural loft in swing, could produce 30+ HR down line. Improved ability to use whole field and hit for nice BA, but expands strike zone and finished 3rd in EL in Ks. Lacks foot speed and athleticism, but arm strength is asset on defense.

Brett, Ryan

Pos	Team	EXP MLB DEBUT	POTENTIAL	Rating
4	Tampa Bay	2015	Starting 2B	8C

Bats B Age 21
2010 (3) HS (WA)
Pwr + +
BAvg + + + +
Spd + + + +
Def + +

Year	Lev	Team	AB	R	H	HR	RBI	Avg	OB	Slg	OPS	bb%	ct%	Eye	SB	CS	x/h%	Iso	RC/G
2010	Rk	GCL Rays	89	8	27	0	9	303	361	404	765	8	81	0.47	12	3	26	101	5.12
2011	Rk	Princeton	240	42	72	3	24	300	368	471	839	10	90	1.08	21	3	42	171	6.13
2012	A	Bowling Green	410	77	117	6	35	285	345	393	737	8	82	0.51	48	8	25	107	4.66

Short, solid INF who finished 3rd in MWL in SB. Suspended 50 games for PED in Aug. Knows strike zone and swings at hittable pitches. Owns gap power, though unlikely to develop more despite bat speed and control. Instincts enhance plus speed, but hands and below avg arm limit upside on defense.

Brinson, Lewis

Pos	Team	EXP MLB DEBUT	POTENTIAL	Rating
8	Texas	2016	Starting OF	9D

Bats R Age 19
2012 (1) HS (FL)
Pwr + + +
BAvg + + +
Spd + + + +
Def + + +

Year	Lev	Team	AB	R	H	HR	RBI	Avg	OB	Slg	OPS	bb%	ct%	Eye	SB	CS	x/h%	Iso	RC/G
2012	Rk	Rangers	237	54	67	7	42	283	341	523	864	8	69	0.28	14	2	54	241	6.76

Long, lean OF who showed surprising polish. Still has things to iron out, but athleticism and speed are well above avg. Packs power with explosive bat speed. Owns leverage in swing and surprising pitch recognition. Needs to put bat to ball more consistently, but should improve if he shortens swing. Plays CF with plus range and strong arm.

Brito, Socrates

Pos	Team	EXP MLB DEBUT	POTENTIAL	Rating
8	Arizona	2016	Starting CF	7C

Bats L Age 20
2010 NDFA, D.R.
Pwr + + +
BAvg + + +
Spd + + +
Def + + +

Year	Lev	Team	AB	R	H	HR	RBI	Avg	OB	Slg	OPS	bb%	ct%	Eye	SB	CS	x/h%	Iso	RC/G
2011	Rk	Diamondbacks	236	29	65	1	29	275	313	360	673	5	79	0.26	18	10	17	85	3.73
2012	Rk	Missoula	279	47	87	4	39	312	360	444	804	7	74	0.29	15	9	28	133	5.57

Failed a drug test in '10, but has taken advantage of a 2nd chance. A physical player with good speed and raw power, though still raw in many phases. Plus bat speed and should add power as he matures. Plays solid defense with a strong arm and can play all three OF positions. Needs to be more selective, but his raw tools are exciting.

Brown, Gary

Pos	Team	EXP MLB DEBUT	POTENTIAL	Rating
8	San Francisco	2013	Starting CF	8C

Bats R Age 24
2010 (1) Cal State Fullerton
Pwr + + +
BAvg + + +
3.80 Spd + + + + +
Def + + +

Year	Lev	Team	AB	R	H	HR	RBI	Avg	OB	Slg	OPS	bb%	ct%	Eye	SB	CS	x/h%	Iso	RC/G
2010	NCAA	Cal St/Fullerton	210	63	92	6	41	438	461	695	1156	4	94	0.75	32	5	37	257	9.05
2010	Rk	Giants	22	6	4	0	0	182	308	227	535	15	77	0.80	2	0	25	45	2.40
2010	A-	Salem-Keizer	22	2	3	0	2	136	208	227	436	8	68	0.29	0	1	33	91	0.59
2011	A+	San Jose	559	115	188	14	80	336	387	519	906	8	86	0.60	53	19	32	182	6.63
2012	AA	Richmond	538	73	150	7	42	279	329	385	713	7	84	0.46	33	18	27	106	4.32

Struggled in 2012 after an impressive breakout season. He continues to have an exciting package of skills, highlighted by his plus speed and ability to make consistent contact. Is also a plus defender in CF who takes good routes with nice range and a strong arm. Should continue to move up quickly.

Broxton, Keon

Pos	Team	EXP MLB DEBUT	POTENTIAL	Rating
8	Arizona	2014	Starting CF	7D

Bats R Age 23
2009 (3) Santa Fe JC (FL)
Pwr + + +
BAvg +
4.25 Spd + + + +
Def + + +

Year	Lev	Team	AB	R	H	HR	RBI	Avg	OB	Slg	OPS	bb%	ct%	Eye	SB	CS	x/h%	Iso	RC/G
2009	Rk	Missoula	272	38	67	11	37	246	296	474	770	7	66	0.20	6	1	46	228	5.34
2010	A	South Bend	531	74	121	5	32	228	312	360	672	11	68	0.38	21	13	34	132	4.10
2011	A	South Bend	78	8	18	0	1	231	294	282	576	8	62	0.23	6	4	11	51	2.63
2011	A+	Visalia	406	69	102	7	44	251	350	362	712	13	65	0.44	27	8	25	111	4.74
2012	A+	Visalia	490	84	131	19	62	267	323	437	759	8	72	0.29	21	8	34	169	4.86

Toolsy OF might be the best athlete in the system. Has a quick bat and showed improved power in repeat of the CAL, but still swings and misses too often. Covers ground well in CF with a strong arm, and takes good routes. A player to keep an eye on, but below average contact is huge red flag.

Bruno, Stephen

Pos	Team	EXP MLB DEBUT	POTENTIAL	Rating
6	Chicago (N)	2015	Starting 2B	7D

Bats R Age 22
2012 (7) Virginia
Pwr + +
BAvg + + +
Spd + +
Def + +

Year	Lev	Team	AB	R	H	HR	RBI	Avg	OB	Slg	OPS	bb%	ct%	Eye	SB	CS	x/h%	Iso	RC/G
2010	NCAA	Virginia	98	30	38	3	30	388	455	592	1046	11	83	0.71	5	2	34	204	8.59
2011	NCAA	Virginia	25	4	6	0	2	240	240	320	560	0	72	0.00	0	1	33	80	2.03
2012	NCAA	Virginia	238	49	88	6	54	370	405	559	964	6	89	0.52	11	3	35	189	7.11
2012	A-	Boise	252	51	91	3	37	361	404	496	900	7	81	0.38	2	7	27	135	6.59

Though undersized, he is a hitting machine. Has a short, compact stroke and a good understanding of the strike zone and makes consistent contact with gap power. Has decent speed with a good glove and soft hands. Played SS in pro debut, but made 17 errors and could develop into a super-utility type down the road.

Buxton, Byron

Pos	Team	EXP MLB DEBUT	POTENTIAL	Rating
8	Minnesota	2016	Starting OF	9C

Bats R Age 19
2012 (1) HS (GA)
Pwr + + + +
BAvg + + +
Spd + + + +
Def + + +

Year	Lev	Team	AB	R	H	HR	RBI	Avg	OB	Slg	OPS	bb%	ct%	Eye	SB	CS	x/h%	Iso	RC/G
2012	Rk	GCL Twins	88	17	19	4	14	216	303	466	769	11	70	0.42	4	3	58	250	5.29
2012	Rk	Elizabethton	77	16	22	1	6	286	353	429	782	9	81	0.53	7	0	36	143	5.34

Toolsy, projectable OF with very high ceiling. Exhibits natural hitting skills with repeatable swing. Some length in stroke and can struggle with breaking balls. Knows strike zone and makes consistent, hard contact with plus bat speed. Plus power potential and should hit for BA. Has well above avg speed, range, and arm.

Cabrera, Yordy

Pos	Team	EXP MLB DEBUT	POTENTIAL	Rating
6	Miami	2015	Starting SS	8E

Bats R Age 22
2010 (2) HS (FL)
Pwr + + +
BAvg + +
Spd + + +
Def + + +

Year	Lev	Team	AB	R	H	HR	RBI	Avg	OB	Slg	OPS	bb%	ct%	Eye	SB	CS	x/h%	Iso	RC/G
2010	Rk	Athletics	16	3	3	0	0	188	350	250	600	20	69	0.80	0	0	33	63	3.27
2011	A	Burlington	359	59	83	6	47	231	292	368	660	8	69	0.28	23	6	39	136	3.72
2012	A+	Stockton	220	26	51	3	21	232	284	332	616	7	69	0.24	2	2	27	100	3.00

Big, strong-framed INF who missed development time with minor ailments and was acquired from OAK in Oct. Has upside with bat speed and above avg power potential. Doesn't draw many BB and inconsistent swing mechanics lead to Ks. Owns good defensive tools, but can make careless errors despite plus arm and solid range.

Calhoun, Kole

Pos	Team	EXP MLB DEBUT	POTENTIAL	Rating
789	Los Angeles (A)	2012	Reserve OF	6B

Bats L Age 25
2010 (8) Arizona State
Pwr + +
BAvg + + +
Spd + +
Def + +

Year	Lev	Team	AB	R	H	HR	RBI	Avg	OB	Slg	OPS	bb%	ct%	Eye	SB	CS	x/h%	Iso	RC/G
2010	NCAA	Arizona State	224	61	72	17	59	321	472	616	1088	22	82	1.60	7	6	42	295	9.59
2010	Rk	Orem	202	43	59	7	42	292	407	505	912	16	78	0.87	3	1	42	213	7.34
2011	A+	Inland Empire	512	94	166	22	99	324	409	547	955	12	81	0.76	20	10	39	223	7.53
2012	AAA	Salt Lake	410	79	122	14	73	298	366	507	873	10	79	0.50	12	3	42	210	6.45
2012	MLB	Los Angeles	23	2	4	0	1	174	240	217	457	8	74	0.33	1	0	25	43	0.95

Short, strong OF who bypassed AA and was on shuttle between Salt Lake and LA. Mature approach allows for selectivity and grinding out AB. Has punch to drive balls to gaps and offer some power. Lacks projection in compact frame and bat speed fringe-avg at best. Steals bases despite below avg speed and has OK range.

Calixte, Orlando

Pos	Team	EXP MLB DEBUT	POTENTIAL	Rating
6	Kansas City	2015	Reserve INF	7C

Bats R Age 21
2011 FA (DR)
Pwr + + +
BAvg + +
Spd + + +
Def + + +

Year	Lev	Team	AB	R	H	HR	RBI	Avg	OB	Slg	OPS	bb%	ct%	Eye	SB	CS	x/h%	Iso	RC/G
2011	A	Kane County	289	19	60	3	31	208	259	263	522	6	76	0.29	11	4	15	55	1.71
2012	A	Kane County	228	31	55	10	34	241	305	465	770	8	81	0.48	2	5	49	224	5.00
2012	A+	Wilmington	256	38	72	4	28	281	321	426	747	6	75	0.23	8	3	35	145	4.73

Short, wiry strong INF who increased prospect status with improved power. HR and 2B both skyrocketed as he learned to use bat speed to advantage. Crude pitch recognition and free swinging ways need to be tamed, but has good pop for middle INF. Can be careless defender at times, though has arm and range to stick at SS.

Candelario, Jeimer

Pos	Team	EXP MLB DEBUT	POTENTIAL	Rating
5	Chicago (N)	2015	Starting 3B	7C

Bats B Age 19
2011 NDFA, D.R.
Pwr + +
BAvg + + +
Spd + +
Def + +

Year	Lev	Team	AB	R	H	HR	RBI	Avg	OB	Slg	OPS	bb%	ct%	Eye	SB	CS	x/h%	Iso	RC/G
2012	A-	Boise	278	34	78	6	47	281	342	396	738	9	80	0.47	2	1	26	115	4.62

Despite being just 18, has an advanced approach at the plate and had a successful debut. Is a switch-hitter with nice bat speed and solid plate discipline. Doesn't have plus power, but makes consistent contact and should continue to hit for average as he moves up. Has moderate speed, but needs to work on his defense. He made 20 errors in 71 games.

Canha, Mark | 3 | Miami | EXP MLB DEBUT: 2014 | POTENTIAL: Backup 1B | 6C

Bats R Age 24	Year	Lev	Team	AB	R	H	HR	RBI	Avg	OB	Slg	OPS	bb%	ct%	Eye	SB	CS	x/h%	Iso	RC/G
2010 (7) UC-Berkeley	2010	NCAA	California	204	48	65	10	69	319	403	520	923	12	80	0.73	9	3	32	201	7.05
Pwr +++	2010	Rk	GCL Marlins	17	3	3	0	1	176	263	176	440	11	94	2.00	1	1	0	0	1.85
BAvg +++	2010	A-	Jamestown	53	7	14	4	9	264	339	585	924	10	75	0.46	0	0	57	321	7.02
Spd +	2011	A	Greensboro	384	72	106	25	85	276	372	529	901	13	78	0.69	7	3	44	253	6.80
Def ++	2012	A+	Jupiter	406	65	119	6	68	293	376	411	787	12	82	0.72	1	3	28	118	5.50

Had a breakout season in '11, hitting 25 HR, but failed to duplicate in '12. Has a good approach at the plate and is patient enough to wait for pitches he can drive. He has a short, compact stroke and is willing to drive pitches the other way. Doesn't have great range or hands, but isn't going to be a liability. He should fare better at Double-A.

Castellanos, Alex | 4 | Los Angeles (N) | EXP MLB DEBUT: 2012 | POTENTIAL: Starting 2B | 7B

Bats R Age 26	Year	Lev	Team	AB	R	H	HR	RBI	Avg	OB	Slg	OPS	bb%	ct%	Eye	SB	CS	x/h%	Iso	RC/G
2008 (10) Belmont-Abbey	2010	A+	Palm Beach	460	62	124	13	57	270	325	461	786	8	76	0.34	19	9	44	191	5.30
Pwr +++	2011	AA	Springfield	354	72	113	19	62	319	362	562	925	6	73	0.26	10	1	39	243	6.99
BAvg +++	2011	AA	Chattanooga	121	30	39	4	23	322	397	603	1000	11	80	0.63	4	1	56	281	8.22
Spd +++	2012	AAA	Albuquerque	344	74	113	17	52	328	408	590	998	12	75	0.54	16	8	43	262	8.26
Def ++	2012	MLB	Los Angeles (N)	23	3	4	1	3	174	174	391	565	0	65	0.00	0	0	50	217	2.08

Short, powerful 2B has surprising power. Uses a short compact stroke and good bat speed to launch balls to all fields. Can be overly aggressive at the plate and needs to make more consistent contact, but he does have good speed. Doesn't have a true position on defense and saw action at 2B, 3B, and both corner OF spots in '12.

Castellanos, Nick | 59 | Detroit | EXP MLB DEBUT: 2014 | POTENTIAL: Starting 3B/RF | 9C

Bats R Age 21	Year	Lev	Team	AB	R	H	HR	RBI	Avg	OB	Slg	OPS	bb%	ct%	Eye	SB	CS	x/h%	Iso	RC/G
2010 (1-S) HS (FL)																				
Pwr ++++	2010	Rk	GCL Tigers	24	5	8	0	3	333	429	417	845	14	79	0.80	0	1	25	83	6.48
BAvg ++++	2011	A	West Michigan	507	65	158	7	76	312	368	436	804	8	74	0.35	3	2	29	124	5.60
Spd ++	2012	A+	Lakeland	215	37	87	3	32	405	460	553	1013	9	80	0.52	3	2	26	149	8.21
Def ++	2012	AA	Erie	322	35	85	7	25	264	295	382	677	4	76	0.18	5	4	27	118	3.61

Pure-hitting prospect who crushed High-A before promotion to AA. MVP of Futures Game moved to RF to hasten ascent to big leagues. Growing into power and should continue to hit for high BA despite lack of patience. Hits to all fields and makes easy, hard contact with pitch recognition. Raw glove, but could become avg in RF or 3B.

Castillo, Phillips | 79 | Seattle | EXP MLB DEBUT: 2016 | POTENTIAL: Starting OF | 9E

Bats R Age 19	Year	Lev	Team	AB	R	H	HR	RBI	Avg	OB	Slg	OPS	bb%	ct%	Eye	SB	CS	x/h%	Iso	RC/G
2010 FA (DR)																				
Pwr +++																				
BAvg ++																				
Spd ++	2011	Rk	Mariners	170	36	51	1	27	300	357	482	839	8	64	0.25	8	5	47	182	6.87
Def ++	2012	Rk	Pulaski	201	23	42	6	23	209	257	348	605	6	70	0.22	0	1	38	139	2.73

Pure hitter with ton of projection and offensive potential. Profiles as middle of order guy with above avg power. Had poor season and struck out too often with aggressive approach. Has strike zone awareness, but expanded for more punch. Needs to add strength. Raw routes in OF need time.

Castro, Harold | 4 | Detroit | EXP MLB DEBUT: 2017 | POTENTIAL: Starting 2B | 7C

Bats L Age 19	Year	Lev	Team	AB	R	H	HR	RBI	Avg	OB	Slg	OPS	bb%	ct%	Eye	SB	CS	x/h%	Iso	RC/G
2011 FA (Venezuela)																				
Pwr +																				
BAvg +++																				
Spd ++++																				
Def ++	2012	Rk	GCL Tigers	193	24	60	1	21	311	345	420	765	5	87	0.40	15	3	28	109	4.88

Lean, athletic INF with exciting small-ball skills. Runs well and could offer loads of SB once he learns nuances. Possesses bat control and makes easy contact while using entire field. Lacks strength for power, but can lace line drives to gaps. Raw defensively with below avg arm strength, but has quickness and work ethic.

Castro, Leandro | 8 | Philadelphia | EXP MLB DEBUT: 2014 | POTENTIAL: Backup OF | 6C

Bats R Age 24	Year	Lev	Team	AB	R	H	HR	RBI	Avg	OB	Slg	OPS	bb%	ct%	Eye	SB	CS	x/h%	Iso	RC/G
2007 NDFA, D.R.	2009	A	Lakewood	66	9	10	0	6	152	211	212	423	7	77	0.33	2	1	40	61	0.64
Pwr ++	2009	A-	Williamsport	256	48	81	7	43	316	349	512	861	5	81	0.27	18	9	38	195	5.99
BAvg ++	2010	A	Lakewood	502	78	129	10	81	257	304	406	710	6	82	0.37	22	13	36	149	4.25
Spd +++	2011	A+	Clearwater	231	38	64	10	31	277	292	481	773	2	86	0.15	10	2	38	203	4.63
Def +++	2012	AA	Reading	478	66	137	10	71	287	311	427	738	3	85	0.24	13	9	34	140	4.39

Short Dominican OF put up decent numbers at Double-A. None of his tools are plus, but he does have moderate power, nice speed, and can play all three OF positions. Plate discipline is well below average and will likely limit his potential, but speed and moderate power give him a chance as a 4th OF.

Catricala, Vince | 357 | Seattle | EXP MLB DEBUT: 2013 | POTENTIAL: Starting 1B/3B | 8D

Bats R Age 24	Year	Lev	Team	AB	R	H	HR	RBI	Avg	OB	Slg	OPS	bb%	ct%	Eye	SB	CS	x/h%	Iso	RC/G
2009 (10) Hawaii	2009	Rk	Pulaski	219	33	66	8	40	301	354	493	848	8	84	0.53	6	1	36	192	5.88
Pwr +++	2010	A	Clinton	496	90	150	17	79	302	373	488	861	10	77	0.50	7	3	39	185	6.30
BAvg +++	2011	A+	High Desert	282	56	99	14	61	351	419	574	994	10	84	0.73	8	3	34	223	7.74
Spd +	2011	AA	Jackson	239	45	83	11	45	347	407	632	1039	9	80	0.51	9	1	52	285	8.45
Def +	2012	AAA	Tacoma	463	58	106	10	60	229	286	348	634	7	81	0.42	4	2	32	119	3.30

Lean, strong INF who had drastic dropoff from '11. BA, HR, and BB all regressed, but there is hope. Has decent approach with ability to make hard contact with powerful stroke. Bat speed results in good pop and has feel for hitting. Limited speed and doesn't project well with poor glove. Plays 3B, but likely to move to LF or 1B.

Cavazos-Galvez, Brian | 7 | Los Angeles (N) | EXP MLB DEBUT: 2013 | POTENTIAL: Backup OF | 7C

Bats R Age 26	Year	Lev	Team	AB	R	H	HR	RBI	Avg	OB	Slg	OPS	bb%	ct%	Eye	SB	CS	x/h%	Iso	RC/G
2009 (12) New Mexico	2011	AA	Chattanooga	411	60	114	14	61	277	298	470	767	3	85	0.19	13	11	40	192	4.67
Pwr ++	2012	Rk	Dodgers	18	4	7	1	4	389	389	778	1167	0	83	0.00	2	0	71	389	9.28
BAvg +++	2012	A+	Rancho Cuc	52	14	18	3	11	346	370	596	967	4	92	0.50	4	2	33	250	6.82
Spd +++	2012	AA	Chattanooga	78	11	13	4	11	167	226	359	585	7	78	0.35	5	0	54	192	2.48
Def ++	2012	AAA	Albuquerque	178	33	63	7	32	354	372	567	939	3	87	0.21	1	1	33	213	6.57

Good athlete, but missed time with an injury. When he wasn't hurt, he tore the cover off the ball. He can do a bit of everything, but has no standout tools. Can look great in one AB and awful in the next. Punishes mistakes, but can be beat by better pitching. Has solid power potential, runs well, can play all three OF positions.

Cecchini, Garin | 5 | Boston | EXP MLB DEBUT: 2015 | POTENTIAL: Starting 3B | 8C

Bats L Age 22	Year	Lev	Team	AB	R	H	HR	RBI	Avg	OB	Slg	OPS	bb%	ct%	Eye	SB	CS	x/h%	Iso	RC/G
2010 (4) HS (LA)																				
Pwr +++																				
BAvg ++++																				
Spd +++	2011	A-	Lowell	114	21	34	3	23	298	389	500	889	13	83	0.89	12	2	47	202	6.84
Def ++	2012	A	Greenville	455	84	139	4	62	305	388	433	821	12	80	0.68	51	6	33	127	5.99

Pure-hitting INF who obliterated Low-A pitching in first full season. Development stalled by injuries in past, but fully healthy. Possesses innate knowledge of K zone and makes easy contact with hand-eye coordination. Needs to swing with more authority to realize power and could improve against LHP. Plus arm with good hands at 3B.

Cecchini, Gavin | 6 | New York (N) | EXP MLB DEBUT: 2016 | POTENTIAL: Starting SS | 8D

Bats R Age 19	Year	Lev	Team	AB	R	H	HR	RBI	Avg	OB	Slg	OPS	bb%	ct%	Eye	SB	CS	x/h%	Iso	RC/G
2012 (1) HS, LA																				
Pwr ++																				
Bavg +++																				
Spd +++	2012	Rk	Kingsport	191	21	47	1	22	246	311	330	641	9	77	0.42	5	4	26	84	3.49
Def +++	2012	A-	Brooklyn	5	2	0	0	0	0	0	0	0	0	80	0.00	0	0			

Wiry SS was the 12th overall pick in 2012. Has the range, arm and hands to stick at SS, but is not a plus defender. Makes solid contact with good plate discipline. Has avg speed and moderate power, but should be able to hit for average. Hand injury limited his production and results should be better in '13.

Ceciliani, Darrell | 8 | New York (N) | EXP MLB DEBUT: 2013 | POTENTIAL: Backup CF | 7C

Bats L Age 23	Year	Lev	Team	AB	R	H	HR	RBI	Avg	OB	Slg	OPS	bb%	ct%	Eye	SB	CS	x/h%	Iso	RC/G
2009 (4) Columbia Basin CC																				
Pwr ++	2009	Rk	Kingsport	158	29	37	2	13	234	292	310	603	8	80	0.42	14	2	22	76	2.92
BAvg +++	2010	A-	Brooklyn	271	56	95	2	35	351	403	531	935	8	79	0.43	21	14	35	181	7.31
6.5/60 Spd +++	2011	A	Savannah	421	62	109	4	40	259	340	361	701	11	77	0.54	25	8	28	102	4.38
Def +++	2012	A+	St. Lucie	85	19	28	1	10	329	400	459	859	11	85	0.77	2	0	29	129	6.33

Solid all-around player sidelined with chronic hamstring injuries. He did see action in the AFL where he hit .258. Uses a nice line-drive approach to spray the ball, but lacks over the fence power. He does have decent plate discipline, so should be able to hit for average. Speed was a big part of his game so the injury is a concern.

Chambers, Adron — 7 — St. Louis

EXP MLB DEBUT: 2011 | POTENTIAL: Backup OF | 6B

Bats L Age 26 — 2007 (38) Pensacola JC

Pwr + | BAvg + + + | Spd + + + | Def + + +

Year	Lev	Team	AB	R	H	HR	RBI	Avg	OB	Slg	OPS	bb%	ct%	Eye	SB	CS	x/h%	Iso	RC/G
2010	AAA	Memphis	69	11	20	1	8	290	372	362	734	12	74	0.50	6	1	10	72	4.75
2011	AAA	Memphis	426	73	118	10	44	277	357	415	772	11	79	0.59	22	13	29	138	5.23
2011	MLB	St. Louis	8	2	3	0	4	375	375	625	1000	0	88	0.00	0	0	33	250	7.43
2012	AAA	Memphis	357	60	114	3	44	319	404	403	808	13	78	0.64	13	4	19	84	5.83
2012	MLB	St. Louis	54	4	12	0	4	222	288	296	584	8	67	0.28	2	1	17	74	2.73

Short, athletic OF is a solid offensive contributor, but not likely to get a chance to play full-time. Turned in another solid season at Triple-A, but struggled in limited action with the Cardinals. Moderate power likely limits him to a backup role, but speed and range in CF give him value.

Chen, Chun-Hsui — 23 — Cleveland

EXP MLB DEBUT: 2013 | POTENTIAL: Starting C | 7C

Bats R Age 24 — 2007 FA (Taiwan)

Pwr + + + | BAvg + + + | Spd + | Def + +

Year	Lev	Team	AB	R	H	HR	RBI	Avg	OB	Slg	OPS	bb%	ct%	Eye	SB	CS	x/h%	Iso	RC/G
2009	A-	Mahoning Val	195	24	42	1	19	215	323	308	631	14	78	0.74	9	2	38	92	3.64
2010	A	Lake County	218	27	68	6	39	312	362	518	880	7	83	0.45	1	1	44	206	6.37
2010	A+	Kinston	172	31	55	6	30	320	443	523	966	18	79	1.06	4	1	42	203	8.12
2011	AA	Akron	412	58	108	16	70	262	332	451	783	9	70	0.35	2	1	40	189	5.38
2012	AA	Akron	399	62	123	5	43	308	393	426	819	12	75	0.55	6	3	29	118	6.04

Short, compact C who repeated AA and hit for less power, but higher BA and more BB. Was consistent all year and exhibits natural hitting skills with moderate pop. Can become pull-conscious and has trouble with breaking balls. Thick frame limits athleticism and is subpar receiver. Will have to hit more to move to 1B full time.

Chen, Pin-Chieh — 8 — Chicago (N)

EXP MLB DEBUT: 2014 | POTENTIAL: Starting CF | 7D

Bats L Age 21 — 2009 NDFA, Taiwan

Pwr + + | BAvg + + | Spd + + + + | Def + + +

Year	Lev	Team	AB	R	H	HR	RBI	Avg	OB	Slg	OPS	bb%	ct%	Eye	SB	CS	x/h%	Iso	RC/G
2010	Rk	Cubs	168	25	49	0	17	292	367	327	694	11	89	1.05	10	7	10	36	4.44
2010	A-	Boise	22	1	7	0	2	318	400	318	718	12	91	1.50	0	1	0	0	4.82
2011	A-	Boise	229	34	69	2	30	301	370	424	794	10	81	0.57	20	6	29	122	5.52
2012	A	Peoria	464	75	120	2	51	259	346	347	693	12	83	0.79	36	14	23	88	4.41

Athletic OF from Taiwan didn't look as dynamic in the MWL. Controls the bat well with good plate discipline and is willing to take a walk. Despite struggles, he should be able to hit for average and has plus speed. Slashing stroke lets his speed play up, but limits power. Is still learning CF, but has good instincts and athleticism.

Chiang, Chih-Hsien — 79 — Texas

EXP MLB DEBUT: 2013 | POTENTIAL: Reserve OF | 6B

Bats L Age 25 — 2005 FA (Taiwan)

Pwr + + + | BAvg + + + | Spd + + | Def + + +

Year	Lev	Team	AB	R	H	HR	RBI	Avg	OB	Slg	OPS	bb%	ct%	Eye	SB	CS	x/h%	Iso	RC/G
2010	AA	Portland	438	54	114	11	65	260	309	420	729	7	85	0.48	2	0	41	160	4.50
2011	AA	Portland	321	68	109	18	76	340	387	648	1035	7	81	0.41	6	2	54	308	8.21
2011	AA	Jackson	130	11	27	0	10	208	243	262	504	4	77	0.20	1	2	26	54	1.52
2012	AA	Jackson	290	27	73	5	37	252	293	386	679	6	80	0.30	3	2	36	134	3.81
2012	AAA	Tacoma	159	14	39	2	11	245	268	321	589	3	87	0.24	0	2	21	75	2.66

Lean, athletic OF who swings aggressively and puts ball in play. Has some pull power, but goes gap to gap with hard line drives. Rarely works counts and doesn't draw many BB. Speed is a tick below avg, though he has sufficient range in OF corner. Some semblance of arm strength and decent instincts give him reserve profile.

Choice, Michael — 8 — Oakland

EXP MLB DEBUT: 2013 | POTENTIAL: Starting OF | 9C

Bats R Age 23 — 2010 (1) UT-Arlington

Pwr + + + + | BAvg + + + | Spd + + + | Def + + +

Year	Lev	Team	AB	R	H	HR	RBI	Avg	OB	Slg	OPS	bb%	ct%	Eye	SB	CS	x/h%	Iso	RC/G
2010	NCAA	Texas-Arlington	196	67	75	16	59	383	555	704	1259	28	72	1.41	12	4	39	321	12.84
2010	Rk	Athletics	7	1	0	0	0	0	222	0	222	22	71	1.00	0	0	0	0	
2010	A-	Vancouver	102	20	29	7	26	284	376	627	1004	13	58	0.35	6	1	66	343	10.05
2011	A+	Stockton	467	79	133	30	82	285	367	542	909	12	71	0.46	9	5	44	257	7.07
2012	AA	Midland	359	59	103	10	58	287	347	423	770	8	75	0.38	5	1	26	136	5.04

Big, strong OF with plus bat speed and power. Season ended in July due to broken hand. Fits profile of power-hitting OF. Improved swing mechanics and pitch recognition could lead to moderate BA. Can overswing and struggle with breaking balls. Exhibits good speed and can stick in CF.

Clarke, Chevez — 89 — Los Angeles (A)

EXP MLB DEBUT: 2015 | POTENTIAL: Starting OF | 8E

Bats B Age 21 — 2010 (1) HS (GA)

Pwr + + + | BAvg + + | Spd + + + + | Def + + +

Year	Lev	Team	AB	R	H	HR	RBI	Avg	OB	Slg	OPS	bb%	ct%	Eye	SB	CS	x/h%	Iso	RC/G
2010	Rk	Angels	162	26	35	3	16	216	278	389	667	8	66	0.25	9	2	43	173	3.97
2011	Rk	Angels	195	33	44	3	27	226	284	400	684	8	66	0.24	5	4	41	174	4.25
2012	Rk	Orem	177	34	48	3	26	271	380	384	764	15	71	0.61	11	1	29	113	5.41
2012	A	Cedar Rapids	269	38	51	6	27	190	251	305	556	8	71	0.28	11	3	33	115	2.12

Toolsy OF who is on verge of dropping off prospect lists. Hit .190 in Low-A before demotion to short-season where he was slightly better. Shows quick bat and offers raw, avg power potential. Poor pitch selectivity and needs to make better contact. Has excellent speed and will need to improve OBP to steal more bases.

Collier, Zach — 7 — Philadelphia

EXP MLB DEBUT: 2014 | POTENTIAL: Backup OF | 6C

Bats L Age 22 — 2008 (1-S) HS, CA

Pwr + + | BAvg + + | 4.10 Spd + + + | Def + + +

Year	Lev	Team	AB	R	H	HR	RBI	Avg	OB	Slg	OPS	bb%	ct%	Eye	SB	CS	x/h%	Iso	RC/G
2008	Rk	GCL Phillies	129	15	35	0	19	271	356	357	713	12	78	0.61	5	0	29	85	4.63
2009	A	Lakewood	298	40	65	0	32	218	274	319	593	7	73	0.29	13	7	35	101	2.84
2009	A-	Williamsport	137	21	31	1	13	226	274	336	610	6	69	0.21	7	0	39	109	2.98
2011	A	Lakewood	416	50	106	1	36	255	320	349	669	9	76	0.40	35	13	29	94	3.89
2012	A+	Clearwater	283	39	76	6	32	269	330	399	729	8	79	0.43	11	3	29	131	4.54

Athletic, toolsy OF continues to make progress. Was suspended for amphetamines in the middle of '11, but was latter revealed that it was Adderall ADHD. Missed the first part of the '12 season due to the suspension. Is still just 22 and has some nice tools, but needs to stay on the field and prove he can hit at Double-A.

Collins, Tyler — 79 — Detroit

EXP MLB DEBUT: 2015 | POTENTIAL: Starting OF | 7C

Bats L Age 23 — 2011 (6) Howard JC

Pwr + + | BAvg + + + + | Spd + + + | Def + +

Year	Lev	Team	AB	R	H	HR	RBI	Avg	OB	Slg	OPS	bb%	ct%	Eye	SB	CS	x/h%	Iso	RC/G
2011	Rk	GCL Tigers	3	2	1	0	1	333	600	667	1267	40	100	0.00	0	0	100	333	13.39
2011	A-	Connecticut	163	28	51	8	31	313	353	534	886	6	90	0.59	6	1	37	221	6.14
2012	A+	Lakeland	473	68	137	7	66	290	367	429	796	11	86	0.91	20	3	34	140	5.62

Compact, thick OF with all-fields approach and aggressive style. Offers moderate power that will lead to more doubles than HR. Works counts and makes hard contact with quick, compact stroke. Can be jammed inside with good FB, but recognizes and hits breaking balls. Instincts showing improvement in OF, but has below avg arm.

Colon, Christian — 46 — Kansas City

EXP MLB DEBUT: 2013 | POTENTIAL: Starting 2B | 8C

Bats R Age 24 — 2010 (1) Cal State Fullerton

Pwr + + + | BAvg + + + | Spd + + + | Def + + +

Year	Lev	Team	AB	R	H	HR	RBI	Avg	OB	Slg	OPS	bb%	ct%	Eye	SB	CS	x/h%	Iso	RC/G
2010	A+	Wilmington	245	38	68	3	30	278	314	380	694	5	87	0.39	2	4	25	102	4.01
2011	AA	NW Arkansas	491	69	126	8	61	257	320	342	662	9	90	0.90	17	7	19	86	3.91
2012	Rk	Royals	22	6	8	0	4	364	462	500	962	15	100	0.00	1	1	38	136	8.07
2012	AA	NW Arkansas	273	33	79	5	27	289	362	392	754	10	90	1.15	12	6	20	103	5.06
2012	AAA	Omaha	17	4	7	1	5	412	474	647	1121	11	94	2.00	0	0	29	235	8.96

Instinctual INF who controls strike zone and is tough out. Rarely gives in to pitchers with contact-oriented approach and plate discipline. Doesn't project to more than gap power, but has strength to hit occasional HR. Makes routine plays, but lack of range likely to lead him to 2B where avg quickness and arm are manageable.

Cone, Zach — 89 — Texas

EXP MLB DEBUT: 2015 | POTENTIAL: Starting OF | 7C

Bats R Age 23 — 2011 (1-S) Georgia

Pwr + + + | BAvg + + | Spd + + + | Def + + + +

Year	Lev	Team	AB	R	H	HR	RBI	Avg	OB	Slg	OPS	bb%	ct%	Eye	SB	CS	x/h%	Iso	RC/G
2009	NCAA	Georgia	93	20	30	4	18	323	370	548	918	7	73	0.28	3	1	37	226	7.03
2010	NCAA	Georgia	212	45	77	10	53	363	403	627	1030	6	84	0.42	13	0	38	264	7.94
2011	NCAA	Georgia	247	39	68	4	34	275	317	385	701	6	81	0.31	13	3	25	109	4.05
2011	A-	Spokane	224	37	45	4	29	201	254	339	593	7	75	0.28	11	2	47	138	2.73
2012	A	Hickory	432	66	113	17	64	262	323	461	783	8	75	0.35	10	0	42	199	5.22

Athletic OF who made slight tweaks to swing. Aggressive approach and subpar pitch recognition likely to keep BA low, but tapped into raw power with additional leverage. Has above avg speed and offers plus CF range that camouflages fringy arm. Has all tools to be prospect and needs time to put all together.

Copeland, Kolby — 8 — Miami

EXP MLB DEBUT: 2015 | POTENTIAL: Backup OF | 7D

Bats L Age 19 — 2012 (3-S) HS, LA

Pwr + + | BAvg + + + | Spd + + | Def + +

Year	Lev	Team	AB	R	H	HR	RBI	Avg	OB	Slg	OPS	bb%	ct%	Eye	SB	CS	x/h%	Iso	RC/G
2012	Rk	GCL Marlins	217	34	62	0	34	286	335	406	740	7	88	0.59	2	6	32	120	4.82
2012	A-	Jamestown	22	5	5	0	0	227	320	318	638	12	91	1.50	2	0	20	91	4.06

Strong, physical OF had a solid pro debut. Projects to have average power with a quick bat and nice approach at the plate. Understands the strike zone well. If his power develops he has the tools to develop into a good corner OF. Speed is a tick below average so sticking in CF seems unlikely.

Correa, Carlos

6 | **Houston** | EXP MLB DEBUT: 2016 | POTENTIAL: Starting SS | **9C**

Bats R Age 18
2012 (1) HS (PR)
Pwr + + +
BAvg + + + +
Spd + + + +
Def + + + +

Year	Lev	Team	AB	R	H	HR	RBI	Avg	OB	Slg	OPS	bb%	ct%	Eye	SB	CS	x/h%	Iso	RC/G
2012	Rk	GCL Astros	155	23	36	2	9	232	265	355	620	4	77	0.19	5	1	39	123	3.00
2012	Rk	Greeneville	35	5	13	1	3	371	450	600	1050	13	77	0.63	1	0	38	229	9.05

#1 overall pick in draft projects to be a star with BA and power with plus defense. Started slow but showed talent as season progressed. No weakness in game and only needs to tidy up swing and close holes. Has upside with balanced swing and plus bat speed. Should be able to stay at SS with plus range and arm.

Coulter, Clint

2 | **Milwaukee** | EXP MLB DEBUT: 2016 | POTENTIAL: Starting C | **8D**

Bats R Age 19
2012 (1) HS, WA
Pwr + + +
BAvg + + +
Spd + +
Def + +

Year	Lev	Team	AB	R	H	HR	RBI	Avg	OB	Slg	OPS	bb%	ct%	Eye	SB	CS	x/h%	Iso	RC/G
2012	Rk	Brewers	169	37	51	5	33	302	427	444	871	18	76	0.93	3	5	22	142	6.87

Athletic, large-bodied catcher with a strong bat and power potential. Put on a good offensive display in rookie ball, hitting for power and average with good strike zone judgment. Behind the plate he has a strong arm, but other aspects of being a top-rate receiver still need to be refined.

Cowart, Kaleb

5 | **Los Angeles (A)** | EXP MLB DEBUT: 2014 | POTENTIAL: Starting 3B | **9C**

Bats B Age 21
2010 (1) HS (GA)
Pwr + + + +
BAvg + + + +
Spd + +
Def + + +

Year	Lev	Team	AB	R	H	HR	RBI	Avg	OB	Slg	OPS	bb%	ct%	Eye	SB	CS	x/h%	Iso	RC/G
2010	Rk	Orem	5	1	2	1	3	400	500	1000	1500	17	60	0.50	0	0	50	600	17.17
2010	Rk	Arizona Angels	21	0	3	0	4	143	143	143	286	0	71	0.00	0	0	0	0	
2011	Rk	Orem	283	49	80	7	40	283	341	420	761	8	71	0.31	11	4	28	138	5.02
2012	A	Cedar Rapids	263	42	77	9	54	293	347	479	826	8	83	0.50	9	4	36	186	5.66
2012	A+	Inland Empire	263	48	68	7	49	259	367	426	793	15	75	0.67	5	3	38	167	5.73

Strong, athletic INF who enjoyed breakout season. Has high upside with plus bat speed and consistent swing. Can drive ball out to all fields and has improved approach to hit for high BA. Next step – improving plate coverage. Doesn't run well, but is solid defender with great footwork. Arm strength is also plus.

Cox, Zack

5 | **Miami** | EXP MLB DEBUT: 2013 | POTENTIAL: Starting 3B | **7C**

Bats L Age 24
2010 (1) Arkansas
Pwr + +
BAvg + + +
Spd + + +
Def + +

Year	Lev	Team	AB	R	H	HR	RBI	Avg	OB	Slg	OPS	bb%	ct%	Eye	SB	CS	x/h%	Iso	RC/G
2010	Rk	GCL Cardinals	15	0	6	0	1	400	438	467	904	6	80	0.33	0	0	17	67	6.63
2011	A+	Palm Beach	164	22	55	3	20	335	377	439	816	6	82	0.38	2	2	20	104	5.43
2011	AA	Springfield	352	54	103	10	48	293	346	432	778	8	80	0.42	0	1	28	139	5.04
2012	AAA	Memphis	299	27	76	9	30	254	283	421	704	4	79	0.19	1	0	42	167	3.96
2012	AA	Jacksonville	95	14	24	1	13	253	324	368	692	10	72	0.37	0	0	33	116	4.23

Short, compact 3B has not yet lived up to expectations. Had a nice pro debut, but struggled in '12. Eroding plate discipline and poor contact rate have stalled his development. A flat swing plane limits his power potential. Remains a solid defender at 3B with soft hands and good range.

Coyle, Sean

4 | **Boston** | EXP MLB DEBUT: 2014 | POTENTIAL: Starting 2B | **8D**

Bats R Age 21
2010 (3) HS (PA)
Pwr + + +
BAvg + +
Spd + + +
Def + + +

Year	Lev	Team	AB	R	H	HR	RBI	Avg	OB	Slg	OPS	bb%	ct%	Eye	SB	CS	x/h%	Iso	RC/G
2010	Rk	GCL Red Sox	10	5	2	0	0	200	273	300	573	9	90	1.00	0	0	50	100	3.13
2011	A	Greenville	384	77	95	14	64	247	349	464	813	14	71	0.55	20	6	51	216	6.01
2012	A+	Salem	437	60	109	9	63	249	296	391	687	6	73	0.25	16	0	39	142	3.94

Short, muscular INF who had poor season. Ks increased, BB decreased, and power not as evident. Young for level and still possesses instincts and quickness. Good pop for frame with above avg bat speed and quick load. Has been more patient in past and needs to make more contact. Has good speed and hands.

Cozens, Dylan

9 | **Philadelphia** | EXP MLB DEBUT: 2016 | POTENTIAL: Starting RF | **7D**

Bats L Age 19
2012 (2) HS, AZ
Pwr + + +
BAvg +
Spd + +
Def + +

Year	Lev	Team	AB	R	H	HR	RBI	Avg	OB	Slg	OPS	bb%	ct%	Eye	SB	CS	x/h%	Iso	RC/G
2012	Rk	GCL Phillies	161	24	41	5	24	255	341	441	782	12	73	0.48	8	2	44	186	5.46

Huge 6-6, 245 OF has plus physical tools, but is still very raw. Hit 19 home runs his senior season and notched 5 in his pro debut, but his swing can be a bit long, though he does have good bat speed. Phillies see him as an OF for now, but he likely profiles better at 1B down the road.

Crocker, Bobby

789 | **Oakland** | EXP MLB DEBUT: 2015 | POTENTIAL: Starting OF | **7D**

Bats R Age 23
2011 (4) Cal Poly
Pwr + + +
BAvg + + +
Spd + + + +
Def + +

Year	Lev	Team	AB	R	H	HR	RBI	Avg	OB	Slg	OPS	bb%	ct%	Eye	SB	CS	x/h%	Iso	RC/G
2010	NCAA	Cal Poly	67	10	21	1	20	313	352	418	770	6	70	0.20	9	0	24	104	5.09
2011	NCAA	Cal Poly	189	37	64	5	20	339	396	497	893	9	79	0.46	9	2	30	159	6.61
2011	Rk	Athletics	88	14	23	0	4	261	301	375	676	5	75	0.23	2	2	30	114	3.88
2011	A-	Vermont	118	19	38	3	15	322	365	441	806	6	81	0.36	6	1	21	119	5.28
2012	A	Burlington	406	56	109	6	53	268	333	369	702	9	73	0.36	17	10	25	101	4.24

Tall, strong OF who hasn't tapped into raw power, but has good tools and instincts. Crushed LHP (.350) with line drive approach. Sees a lot of pitches, though has holes in swing. Flat swing path may mute power. Has above avg speed for SB and offers sufficient range, though likely to end up in OF corner.

Cron, C.J.

3 | **Los Angeles (A)** | EXP MLB DEBUT: 2014 | POTENTIAL: Starting 1B | **8B**

Bats R Age 23
2011 (1) Utah
Pwr + + + +
BAvg + + +
Spd +
Def + +

Year	Lev	Team	AB	R	H	HR	RBI	Avg	OB	Slg	OPS	bb%	ct%	Eye	SB	CS	x/h%	Iso	RC/G
2009	NCAA	Utah	246	39	83	11	58	337	373	557	930	5	87	0.45	1	2	37	220	6.63
2010	NCAA	Utah	197	55	85	20	81	431	477	817	1294	8	88	0.74	0	0	42	386	10.68
2011	NCAA	Utah	198	51	86	15	59	434	511	803	1314	14	89	1.48	1	1	49	369	11.52
2011	Rk	Orem	143	30	44	13	41	308	353	629	982	7	76	0.29	1	0	43	322	7.40
2012	A+	Inland Empire	525	73	154	27	123	293	315	516	832	3	86	0.24	3	4	40	223	5.32

Thick-framed natural hitter who showed plus power before undergoing surgery for torn labrum. Should be back early and could knock on door to big leagues. Makes great contact for plus power stroke and can hit breaking balls. Bat speed is ideal, though he rarely walks. Bat will have to carry him.

Crumbliss, Conner

47 | **Oakland** | EXP MLB DEBUT: 2014 | POTENTIAL: Utility player | **6B**

Bats L Age 26
2009 (28) Emporia State
Pwr + +
BAvg + +
Spd + + +
Def + +

Year	Lev	Team	AB	R	H	HR	RBI	Avg	OB	Slg	OPS	bb%	ct%	Eye	SB	CS	x/h%	Iso	RC/G
2009	A	Kane County	50	11	14	0	3	280	410	400	810	18	82	1.22	2	1	36	120	6.29
2009	A-	Vancouver	205	40	60	2	25	293	429	405	834	19	86	1.75	11	2	25	112	6.61
2010	A	Kane County	491	95	133	5	56	271	420	371	790	20	81	1.37	24	8	28	100	6.05
2011	A+	Stockton	426	75	114	7	52	268	402	378	780	18	80	1.13	24	7	25	110	5.75
2012	AA	Midland	470	94	121	10	45	257	408	391	800	20	79	1.22	24	8	31	134	6.09

Short, selective INF who led TL in BB. Tough out due to batting eye and selectivity. Uses short swing to make decent contact and is proficient bunter. Bat speed and power are below avg and offers little with bat other than BB. Played mostly LF after 2B in past and has fringy range, passable speed, and avg arm.

Culberson, Charlie

4 | **Colorado** | EXP MLB DEBUT: 2012 | POTENTIAL: Starting 2B | **6B**

Bats R Age 24
2007 (1-S) HS (GA)
Pwr + +
BAvg + + +
Spd + +
Def + + + +

Year	Lev	Team	AB	R	H	HR	RBI	Avg	OB	Slg	OPS	bb%	ct%	Eye	SB	CS	x/h%	Iso	RC/G
2010	A+	San Jose	503	80	146	16	71	290	334	457	791	6	80	0.33	25	7	33	167	5.14
2011	AA	Richmond	553	69	143	10	56	259	287	382	669	4	77	0.17	14	4	32	123	3.53
2012	AAA	Fresno	351	53	83	10	53	236	278	396	674	5	78	0.26	8	2	36	160	3.66
2012	MLB	San Francisco	22	0	3	0	1	136	136	136	273	0	68	0.00	0	0	0	0	
2012	AAA	Col Springs	125	17	42	2	12	336	341	488	829	1	86	0.06	6	2	33	152	5.29

Offensive minded 2B with a nice power and speed mix. Good bat speed, quick hands, and a willingness to use the whole field. Can be overly aggressive, leading to poor plate discipline. Has decent speed, but inconsistent defense means he will likely be a UT player.

Culver, Cito

6 | **New York (A)** | EXP MLB DEBUT: 2015 | POTENTIAL: Starting SS | **7D**

Bats B Age 20
2010 (1) HS (NY)
Pwr + +
BAvg + +
Spd + + +
Def + + + +

Year	Lev	Team	AB	R	H	HR	RBI	Avg	OB	Slg	OPS	bb%	ct%	Eye	SB	CS	x/h%	Iso	RC/G
2010	Rk	GCL Yankees	160	21	43	2	18	269	324	363	686	8	74	0.32	6	3	23	94	3.96
2010	A-	Staten Island	43	2	8	0	0	186	314	209	523	16	77	0.80	1	1	13	23	2.20
2011	A-	Staten Island	276	40	69	2	33	250	324	337	660	10	79	0.53	10	0	26	87	3.81
2012	A	Charleston (Sc)	466	66	100	2	40	215	318	283	602	13	78	0.68	22	11	22	69	3.19

Smooth, quick INF who struggled in first full season. Known for plus defense where he exhibits range and clean, quick hands. Strong arm enhances defense and should stick at SS long-term. Has good head on shoulders and differentiates between balls and strikes. Too many Ks despite little power and below avg bat control mutes BA potential.

Cunningham, Todd | 8 | Atlanta | EXP MLB DEBUT: 2013 | POTENTIAL: Starting CF | 7C

Bats B Age 24
2010 (2) Jacksonville State
Pwr + +
BAvg + + +
3.90 Spd + + +
Def + +

Year	Lev	Team	AB	R	H	HR	RBI	Avg	OB	Slg	OPS	bb%	ct%	Eye	SB	CS	x/h%	Iso	RC/G
2010	NCAA	Jacksonville St	237	61	85	11	42	359	449	603	1053	14	86	1.18	21	2	38	245	8.72
2010	A	Rome	231	32	60	1	20	260	302	338	640	6	87	0.47	7	4	22	78	3.49
2011	Rk	GCL Braves	11	2	2	0	4	182	250	364	614	8	55	0.20	1	0	50	182	3.98
2011	A+	Lynchburg	334	59	86	4	20	257	324	353	678	9	86	0.70	14	6	23	96	4.06
2012	AA	Mississippi	466	77	144	3	51	309	361	403	765	8	89	0.75	24	8	22	94	5.06

Switch-hitter lacks a standout tool, but has a professional approach. Makes consistent contact with a short, compact stroke and has a solid understanding of the strike zone. Has the strength and bat speed for moderate power, but is more content with putting the ball in play. Runs well, but range is a little short for CF.

Curry, Matt | 3 | Pittsburgh | EXP MLB DEBUT: 2013 | POTENTIAL: Backup 1B | 6B

Bats L Age 24
2010 (16) TCU
Pwr + + +
BAvg + + +
Spd +
Def + +

Year	Lev	Team	AB	R	H	HR	RBI	Avg	OB	Slg	OPS	bb%	ct%	Eye	SB	CS	x/h%	Iso	RC/G
2010	A-	State College	197	36	59	7	29	299	415	477	892	17	76	0.83	7	5	36	178	7.08
2011	A	West Virginia	155	39	56	9	34	361	479	671	1150	18	81	1.21	6	2	48	310	10.36
2011	AA	Altoona	302	38	73	6	39	242	316	374	691	10	70	0.37	1	1	34	132	4.17
2012	AA	Altoona	396	53	113	11	76	285	357	480	837	10	73	0.41	4	4	44	194	6.18
2012	AAA	Indianapolis	5	0	2	0	2	400	500	400	900	17	80	1.00	0	1	0	0	7.22

Proto-typical bad body, good bat 1B regressed as he moved up. Has a good understanding of the strike zone and a short LH stroke. When he is going well, he drives the ball into the gaps, but doesn't make consistent contact and gets beat by breaking balls. Solid glove defensively, but the bat is the key and it looked less dynamic in '12.

Custodio, Claudio | 6 | New York (A) | EXP MLB DEBUT: 2015 | POTENTIAL: Starting SS | 7C

Bats R Age 22
2010 FA (DR)
Pwr +
BAvg + + +
Spd + + +
Def + + + +

Year	Lev	Team	AB	R	H	HR	RBI	Avg	OB	Slg	OPS	bb%	ct%	Eye	SB	CS	x/h%	Iso	RC/G
2011	Rk	GCL Yankees	157	46	51	1	19	325	408	414	822	12	75	0.55	26	2	22	89	6.09
2012	A-	Staten Island	241	33	61	1	22	253	294	349	643	5	76	0.24	13	1	26	95	3.37

Wiry strong INF who has yet to play full-season ball, but could advance quickly due to keen instincts. Could develop small ball skills with loose, fast bat. Power not evident, but should be able to hit gaps and leg out infield hits. Owns plus arm and range at SS. Needs to shorten swing and make better contact.

Cuthbert, Cheslor | 5 | Kansas City | EXP MLB DEBUT: 2015 | POTENTIAL: Starting 3B | 8D

Bats R Age 20
2009 FA (Nicaragua)
Pwr + + + +
BAvg + +
Spd + +
Def + + +

Year	Lev	Team	AB	R	H	HR	RBI	Avg	OB	Slg	OPS	bb%	ct%	Eye	SB	CS	x/h%	Iso	RC/G
2010	Rk	Idaho Falls	60	10	14	2	10	233	270	433	703	5	73	0.19	1	0	50	200	4.08
2010	Rk	Royals	68	14	18	1	5	265	324	412	736	8	72	0.32	1	1	33	147	4.78
2011	A	Kane County	300	33	80	8	51	267	345	397	742	11	78	0.55	2	0	28	130	4.77
2012	A+	Wilmington	475	47	114	7	59	240	295	322	617	7	83	0.46	6	3	22	82	3.13

Strong INF who was poor all season, but was among youngest regulars in league. Upside predicated on offensive potential. Drives balls to all fields with leverage and strength. Expanding strike zone was big problem and bat control needs to improve. Doesn't run well, though has soft hands and strong arm.

Dahl, David | 8 | Colorado | EXP MLB DEBUT: 2015 | POTENTIAL: Starting CF | 9C

Bats L Age 19
2012 (1) HS, AL
Pwr + + + +
BAvg + + + +
Spd + + +
Def + + +

Year	Lev	Team	AB	R	H	HR	RBI	Avg	OB	Slg	OPS	bb%	ct%	Eye	SB	CS	x/h%	Iso	RC/G
2012	Rk	Grand Junction	280	62	106	9	57	379	422	625	1047	7	85	0.50	12	7	39	246	8.28

Athletic hitter had a great pro debut. Should hit for average due to disciplined approach. Swing plane produces more line drives, but clearly has over the fence power as well. He is a solid-average CF with plus speed and a good arm. Has all of the tools needed to star and just needs time to fine-tune his approach.

Danks, Jordan | 789 | Chicago (A) | EXP MLB DEBUT: 2012 | POTENTIAL: Starting OF | 7C

Bats L Age 26
2008 (7) Texas
Pwr + + +
BAvg + + +
Spd + + +
Def + + + +

Year	Lev	Team	AB	R	H	HR	RBI	Avg	OB	Slg	OPS	bb%	ct%	Eye	SB	CS	x/h%	Iso	RC/G
2009	AA	Birmingham	284	50	69	6	20	243	330	356	686	12	74	0.51	7	3	28	113	4.10
2010	AAA	Charlotte	445	62	109	8	42	245	309	373	682	8	66	0.27	15	6	35	128	4.11
2011	AAA	Charlotte	463	65	119	14	65	257	338	425	764	11	67	0.37	18	4	37	168	5.36
2012	AAA	Charlotte	218	37	69	8	30	317	431	514	945	17	70	0.67	6	3	38	197	8.12
2012	MLB	Chicago (A)	67	12	15	1	4	224	288	284	571	8	76	0.38	3	1	13	60	2.41

Tall, speedy OF who spent 3rd year in AAA before earning time with CHW. Reduced K rate and is adept at working counts and drawing BB. Power is only avg at best despite size and still has tendency to chase pitches out of zone. Can hit LHP with smooth stroke, but defense is best quality. Exhibits plus range and instincts.

d'Arnaud, Travis | 2 | New York (N) | EXP MLB DEBUT: 2013 | POTENTIAL: Starting C | 8A

Bats R Age 24
2007 (1-S) HS (CA)
Pwr + + + +
BAvg + + + +
Spd + +
Def + + +

Year	Lev	Team	AB	R	H	HR	RBI	Avg	OB	Slg	OPS	bb%	ct%	Eye	SB	CS	x/h%	Iso	RC/G
2008	A-	Williamsport	175	21	54	4	25	309	373	463	836	9	83	0.62	1	2	33	154	5.92
2009	A	Lakewood	482	71	123	13	71	255	314	419	733	8	84	0.55	8	4	42	164	4.59
2010	A+	Dunedin	263	36	68	6	38	259	311	411	722	7	76	0.32	3	1	40	152	4.40
2011	AA	New Hampshire	424	72	132	21	78	311	361	542	904	7	76	0.33	4	2	42	231	6.65
2012	AAA	Las Vegas	279	45	93	16	52	333	376	595	971	6	79	0.32	1	1	42	262	7.34

Agile, athletic C who was having standout season before knee injury. Offers all-around tools that could lead to All Star campaigns. Controls bat and has avg to plus power to all fields, though can sell out for pop. Quick hands and bat speed offer BA potential. Improved blocker with plus, accurate arm.

Darnell, James | 5 | San Diego | EXP MLB DEBUT: 2011 | POTENTIAL: Starting LF/3B | 7D

Bats R Age 26
2008 (2) South Carolina
Pwr + + +
BAvg + + +
4.30 Spd + +
Def + +

Year	Lev	Team	AB	R	H	HR	RBI	Avg	OB	Slg	OPS	bb%	ct%	Eye	SB	CS	x/h%	Iso	RC/G
2011	AA	San Antonio	288	62	96	17	62	333	435	604	1039	15	83	1.08	2	1	45	271	8.63
2011	AAA	Tucson	134	20	35	6	17	261	340	425	765	11	78	0.53	0	0	29	164	4.95
2011	MLB	San Diego	45	2	10	1	7	222	300	333	633	10	84	0.71	1	0	30	111	3.50
2012	AAA	Tucson	116	22	31	7	21	267	356	500	856	12	78	0.64	1	1	42	233	6.16
2012	MLB	San Diego	17	1	4	1	1	235	316	471	786	11	88	1.00	0	0	50	235	5.27

For the 2nd straight season, failed to carve out a role with the Padres, this time due to injury. Should be 100% by spring, but is running out of time. Still has nice offenisve potential with good plate discipline and above-average power. The move off 3B seems permanent and might not have the range to play corner OF.

Davidson, Matt | 5 | Arizona | EXP MLB DEBUT: 2013 | POTENTIAL: Starting 3B | 7B

Bats R Age 22
2009 (1) HS, CA
Pwr + + + +
BAvg +
Spd + +
Def + +

Year	Lev	Team	AB	R	H	HR	RBI	Avg	OB	Slg	OPS	bb%	ct%	Eye	SB	CS	x/h%	Iso	RC/G
2009	A-	Yakima	270	29	65	2	28	241	296	319	614	7	72	0.28	0	2	26	78	3.00
2010	A	South Bend	415	58	120	16	79	289	356	504	860	9	74	0.39	0	2	45	214	6.36
2010	A+	Visalia	71	6	12	2	11	169	289	268	557	14	65	0.48	0	0	25	99	2.18
2011	A+	Visalia	535	93	148	20	106	277	341	465	806	9	73	0.35	0	1	41	189	5.61
2012	AA	Mobile	486	81	127	23	76	261	353	469	822	12	74	0.55	3	4	42	208	5.90

Strong 3B has the best power in the system and hit 23 HR at AA. Has good bat speed and reduced his K rate, but still has work to do. Played all year at 3B after splitting time the past two seasons. Made 28 errors, but has good hands and a strong arm. If he can make more consistent contact, he has good poential.

Davis, D.J. | 8 | Toronto | EXP MLB DEBUT: 2016 | POTENTIAL: Starting OF | 8C

Bats L Age 18
2012 (1) HS (MS)
Pwr + + +
BAvg + +
Spd + + + + +
Def + +

Year	Lev	Team	AB	R	H	HR	RBI	Avg	OB	Slg	OPS	bb%	ct%	Eye	SB	CS	x/h%	Iso	RC/G
2012	Rk	GCL Blue Jays	163	30	38	4	12	233	309	374	684	10	67	0.33	18	7	34	141	4.12
2012	Rk	Bluefield	47	9	16	1	6	340	392	511	903	8	79	0.40	6	2	31	170	6.76
2012	A-	Vancouver	18	3	3	0	0	167	348	167	514	22	67	0.83	1	1	0	0	1.84

Raw, yet exciting prospect who has among best speed in baseball. Has strength and above avg bat speed to project power, but not a natural hitter due to lots of swing and miss and inconsistent mechanics. Pitch recognition needs work. Could become plus CF, but has crude instincts and limited arm strength.

Davis, Glynn | 8 | Baltimore | EXP MLB DEBUT: 2014 | POTENTIAL: Starting OF | 7B

Bats R Age 21
2010 FA (Catonsville CC)
Pwr +
BAvg + + +
Spd + + + +
Def + + +

Year	Lev	Team	AB	R	H	HR	RBI	Avg	OB	Slg	OPS	bb%	ct%	Eye	SB	CS	x/h%	Iso	RC/G
2011	Rk	GCL Orioles	23	4	10	1	2	435	519	652	1171	15	87	1.33	1	1	30	217	10.14
2011	A+	Frederick	4	0	1	0	0	250	250	250	500	0	75	0.00	0	0	0	0	1.07
2011	A-	Aberdeen	255	34	69	1	14	271	336	337	673	9	79	0.47	23	9	22	67	3.91
2012	A	Delmarva	397	53	100	0	25	252	337	302	639	11	77	0.56	29	9	18	50	3.59
2012	A+	Frederick	82	11	21	0	4	256	351	293	644	13	70	0.48	8	1	10	37	3.66

Tall, slender OF with only 2 HR in career. OBP and speed are main assets along with CF defense. Disciplined approach, OBP and plus-plus speed equate to plentiful SB. Keeps ball on ground, but may need to add leverage to keep defense honest. Routes and reads are raw, but has plus range and arm strength.

Davis, Kentrail — 8 — Milwaukee

EXP MLB DEBUT: 2013 **POTENTIAL:** Starting CF **8D**

Bats L Age 25
2009 (1-S) Tennessee

	Pwr	++
4.10	BAvg	+++
	Spd	+++
	Def	+++

Year	Lev	Team	AB	R	H	HR	RBI	Avg	OB	Slg	OPS	bb%	ct%	Eye	SB	CS	x/h%	Iso	RC/G
2009	NCAA	Tennessee	214	58	66	9	30	308	401	528	929	13	78	0.69	4	1	38	220	7.35
2010	A	Wisconsin	245	44	82	3	46	335	409	518	928	11	85	0.86	3	1	41	184	7.27
2010	A+	Brevard County	123	20	30	0	17	244	336	341	677	12	77	0.61	8	2	23	98	4.21
2011	A+	Brevard County	507	76	124	8	46	245	296	361	657	7	81	0.38	33	8	28	116	3.59
2012	AA	Huntsville	438	55	120	7	41	274	354	404	758	11	72	0.45	19	11	30	130	5.16

Short, athletic speedster had a solid season at AA. Runs wells, controls the strike zone, and has a compact stroke with moderate power. Can be overly aggressive and strikes out too much. Will need to be more patient to be effective. His defense is solid in CF, but he sometimes gets bad jumps and is undersized.

Davis, Khris — 7 — Milwaukee

EXP MLB DEBUT: 2013 **POTENTIAL:** Backup OF **6C**

Bats R Age 25
2009 (7) Cal State Fullerton

	Pwr	++
	BAvg	++
	Spd	++
	Def	++

Year	Lev	Team	AB	R	H	HR	RBI	Avg	OB	Slg	OPS	bb%	ct%	Eye	SB	CS	x/h%	Iso	RC/G
2011	A+	Brevard County	304	50	94	15	68	309	408	533	941	14	77	0.73	10	5	39	224	7.52
2011	AA	Huntsville	124	10	26	2	16	210	269	331	599	7	81	0.43	0	0	38	121	2.95
2012	Rk	Brewers	19	7	7	3	5	368	429	842	1271	10	63	0.29	1	1	43	474	12.64
2012	AA	Huntsville	128	23	49	8	23	383	466	641	1107	14	74	0.61	2	2	35	258	9.77
2012	AAA	Nashville	113	23	35	4	24	310	414	522	936	15	76	0.74	1	0	46	212	7.64

Strong OF continues to show ability to hit for power and average, but doesn't get much respect. Has solid strike zone judgment and makes consistent contact. Swing can get long and does not have plus bat speed. Defensively he is limited to 1B or LF. Struggled when sent to the AFL.

de la Cruz, Keury — 78 — Boston

EXP MLB DEBUT: 2015 **POTENTIAL:** Starting OF **7B**

Bats L Age 21
2009 FA (DR)

	Pwr	+++
	BAvg	+++
	Spd	+++
	Def	+++

Year	Lev	Team	AB	R	H	HR	RBI	Avg	OB	Slg	OPS	bb%	ct%	Eye	SB	CS	x/h%	Iso	RC/G
2010	Rk	GCL Red Sox	198	35	52	6	31	263	321	475	796	8	75	0.34	9	6	44	212	5.48
2011	A-	Lowell	300	31	79	4	24	263	287	390	677	3	81	0.18	15	11	30	127	3.67
2012	A	Greenville	474	71	146	19	81	308	344	536	880	5	79	0.26	19	7	42	228	6.24
2012	A+	Salem	25	1	7	1	6	280	308	480	788	4	92	0.50	1	1	43	200	5.00

Fundamentally-sound, steady OF who owns good tools. Set career high in HR with improved swing, though still is free swinger. Could be more discerning at plate and can be pull-conscious. Hits LHP (.320) and owns solid-avg bat speed and developing pop. Profiles well in LF with average arm, speed, and arm.

de la Cruz, Vicmal — 79 — Oakland

EXP MLB DEBUT: 2016 **POTENTIAL:** Starting OF **8E**

Bats L Age 19
2010 FA (DR)

	Pwr	+++
	BAvg	+++
	Spd	+++
	Def	+++

Year	Lev	Team	AB	R	H	HR	RBI	Avg	OB	Slg	OPS	bb%	ct%	Eye	SB	CS	x/h%	Iso	RC/G
2012	Rk	Athletics	135	25	31	3	17	230	288	378	665	8	68	0.26	2	1	35	148	3.77

Strong, athletic OF who struggled in 1st yr in US, but has upside and tools. Has fast bat and power potential with strength in arms and wrists. Can be overly aggressive, but generally has strong batting eye. Needs to firm up approach against breaking balls and can be pull-conscious. Likely to end up in OF corner.

de la Rosa, Bryan — 2 — Atlanta

EXP MLB DEBUT: 2016 **POTENTIAL:** Backup C **6C**

Bats R Age 19
2012 (3) HS, FL

	Pwr	++
	BAvg	+
	Spd	+
	Def	+++

Year	Lev	Team	AB	R	H	HR	RBI	Avg	OB	Slg	OPS	bb%	ct%	Eye	SB	CS	x/h%	Iso	RC/G
2012	Rk	GCL Braves	68	5	11	1	3	162	186	221	406	3	56	0.07	0	1	18	59	

Short, compact backstop was one of the better defenders in the '12 draft class. Features a strong, accurate throwing arm and good receiving and blocking skills. Serious concerns about ability to hit raise doubts about long-term potential, but does have good power potential and has a decent approach at the plate.

Dean, Matt — 5 — Toronto

EXP MLB DEBUT: 2016 **POTENTIAL:** Starting 3B **8D**

Bats R Age 20
2011 (13) HS (TX)

	Pwr	++++
	BAvg	+++
	Spd	++
	Def	++

Year	Lev	Team	AB	R	H	HR	RBI	Avg	OB	Slg	OPS	bb%	ct%	Eye	SB	CS	x/h%	Iso	RC/G
2012	Rk	Bluefield	167	22	37	2	24	222	274	353	627	7	64	0.20	3	2	38	132	3.37

Tall, strong INF with raw ingredients to become special. Has projectable frame that could allow him to hit for plus power once strength is added. Crude pitch recognition hampers contact. Possesses positive tools with exception of speed and could become a quality defender with strong arm.

DeCarlo, Joe — 5 — Seattle

EXP MLB DEBUT: 2016 **POTENTIAL:** Starting 3B **7C**

Bats R Age 19
2012 (2) HS (PA)

	Pwr	+++
	BAvg	+++
	Spd	++
	Def	+++

Year	Lev	Team	AB	R	H	HR	RBI	Avg	OB	Slg	OPS	bb%	ct%	Eye	SB	CS	x/h%	Iso	RC/G
2012	Rk	Mariners	182	29	43	4	31	236	347	401	749	15	74	0.66	0	2	44	165	5.17

Short, compact INF with above avg strength and potential to hit for moderate BA and power. Features bat control, but has trouble with good breaking balls and high hard stuff. Power generated more from strength than bat speed. Not a threat for SB with below avg speed, though is good defender with strong arm.

Decker, Jaff — 7 — San Diego

EXP MLB DEBUT: 2014 **POTENTIAL:** Backup RF **6C**

Bats L Age 23
2008 (1) HS, AZ

	Pwr	+++
	BAvg	++
	Spd	++
	Def	++

Year	Lev	Team	AB	R	H	HR	RBI	Avg	OB	Slg	OPS	bb%	ct%	Eye	SB	CS	x/h%	Iso	RC/G
2009	A	Fort Wayne	358	78	107	16	64	299	433	514	947	19	74	0.92	10	6	40	215	7.99
2010	A+	Lake Elsinore	290	53	76	17	58	262	365	500	865	14	72	0.59	5	4	43	238	6.54
2011	AA	San Antonio	496	90	117	19	92	236	367	417	785	17	71	0.71	15	5	43	181	5.69
2012	Rk	Padres	27	5	8	1	7	296	387	593	980	13	89	1.33	0	0	50	296	7.90
2012	AA	San Antonio	147	30	27	3	9	184	358	293	651	21	75	1.08	6	2	30	109	4.00

Another lost season as he hit the DL with a foot injury. The Padres are trying to rework his swing so that it has less uppercut and is in the zone longer. Is a strong player with good plate discipline, but needs to make more consistent contact. Look for a rebound in 2013, but time is running out.

Deglan, Kellin — 2 — Texas

EXP MLB DEBUT: 2015 **POTENTIAL:** Reserve C **7D**

Bats L Age 21
2010 (1) HS (CAN)

	Pwr	+++
	BAvg	+
	Spd	++
	Def	++++

Year	Lev	Team	AB	R	H	HR	RBI	Avg	OB	Slg	OPS	bb%	ct%	Eye	SB	CS	x/h%	Iso	RC/G
2010	Rk	Rangers	28	5	8	0	5	286	333	357	690	7	75	0.29	0	0	13	71	4.05
2010	A-	Spokane	82	7	13	1	4	159	225	220	444	8	74	0.33	0	0	23	61	0.70
2011	A	Hickory	291	39	66	6	39	227	308	347	655	10	69	0.37	2	0	33	120	3.67
2012	A	Hickory	320	46	75	12	41	234	304	438	741	9	70	0.33	4	4	52	203	4.83

Athletic C who repeated Low-A and doubled HR output. Low BA despite clean swing. Ks pile up when selling out for power and lunging at unhittable breaking balls. Only hit .198 against LHP and could use more mature approach. Owns strong, accurate arm with quick release and offers above avg defense potential.

Delmonico, Nick — 34 — Baltimore

EXP MLB DEBUT: 2015 **POTENTIAL:** Starting 1B **8C**

Bats L Age 20
2011 (6) HS (TN)

	Pwr	++++
	BAvg	++
	Spd	++
	Def	++

Year	Lev	Team	AB	R	H	HR	RBI	Avg	OB	Slg	OPS	bb%	ct%	Eye	SB	CS	x/h%	Iso	RC/G
2012	A	Delmarva	338	49	84	11	54	249	340	411	752	12	78	0.64	8	1	39	163	4.97

Pure swinging INF with hand-eye coordination to hit for BA and potential power. Understands K zone and exhibits keen contact ability. Below avg speed plays up due to intellect and baserunning acumen. Struggled against LHP and future defensive position is question. Lacks first step quickness, though arm is playable.

DeMichele, Joey — 4 — Chicago (A)

EXP MLB DEBUT: 2015 **POTENTIAL:** Starting 2B **7C**

Bats L Age 22
2012 (3) Arizona State

	Pwr	++
	BAvg	+++
	Spd	++
	Def	++

Year	Lev	Team	AB	R	H	HR	RBI	Avg	OB	Slg	OPS	bb%	ct%	Eye	SB	CS	x/h%	Iso	RC/G
2010	NCAA	Arizona State	9	1	1	0	1	111	200	111	311	10	78	0.50	0	0	0	0	
2011	NCAA	Arizona State	182	37	67	9	48	368	413	665	1078	7	86	0.54	6	2	45	297	8.57
2012	NCAA	Arizona State	209	47	70	6	44	335	390	550	941	8	85	0.61	10	4	37	215	7.12
2012	Rk	Bristol	46	7	16	2	9	348	388	696	1083	6	83	0.38	3	0	56	348	8.83
2012	A	Kannapolis	234	30	61	5	29	261	316	436	752	8	77	0.35	5	4	39	175	4.87

Short INF who hit immediately upon signing. Doesn't look part of prospect, but maximizes tools with instincts and bat control. Uses entire field and laces line drives to gaps. Could grow into avg power despite limited size and has plus hand-eye coordination. Lacks footwork and quickness, though has enough arm.

den Dekker, Matt

8 | New York (N) | EXP MLB DEBUT: 2013 | POTENTIAL: Starting CF | 6B

Bats L Age 25	Year	Lev	Team	AB	R	H	HR	RBI	Avg	OB	Slg	OPS	bb%	ct%	Eye	SB	CS	x/h%	Iso	RC/G
2010 (5) Florida	2010	A	Savannah	104	21	36	0	15	346	398	471	869	8	73	0.32	3	0	36	125	6.66
Pwr +++	2011	A+	St. Lucie	267	54	79	6	36	296	354	494	848	8	76	0.37	12	5	42	199	6.22
BAvg ++	2011	AA	Binghamton	272	49	64	11	32	235	304	426	731	9	67	0.30	12	5	42	191	4.73
4.10 Spd +++	2012	AA	Binghamton	238	47	81	8	29	340	391	563	954	8	73	0.31	10	7	41	223	7.65
Def ++++	2012	AAA	Buffalo	295	37	65	9	47	220	256	373	629	5	69	0.16	11	2	35	153	3.03

Speedy CF runs well and has a short line-drive stroke. Started the season on fire, hitting .340 at AA, but struggled when promoted. Continues to show solid power, but might have to decide between hitting for average or power. Runs well and can handle all three OF positions, making him a likely 4th OF.

DeShields, Delino

4 | Houston | EXP MLB DEBUT: 2014 | POTENTIAL: Starting 2B/OF | 8C

Bats R Age 20	Year	Lev	Team	AB	R	H	HR	RBI	Avg	OB	Slg	OPS	bb%	ct%	Eye	SB	CS	x/h%	Iso	RC/G
2010 (1) HS (GA)	2010	Rk	GCL Astros	9	3	1	0	0	111	200	111	311	10	78	0.50	0	0	0	0	
Pwr +++	2010	Rk	Greeneville	67	11	21	0	8	313	361	433	794	7	73	0.28	5	1	33	119	5.57
BAvg +++	2011	A	Lexington	469	73	103	9	48	220	298	322	619	10	75	0.44	30	11	27	102	3.14
Spd ++++	2012	A	Lexington	440	96	131	10	52	298	394	439	833	14	75	0.65	83	14	28	141	6.21
Def ++	2012	A+	Lancaster	97	17	23	2	9	237	327	381	709	12	76	0.57	18	5	30	144	4.48

Short, quick INF who was HOU minor league POY after leading SAL in SB. Set career highs in BA, HR, and SB while drawing BB. Plus-plus speed is best attribute, but also offers power projection. Too many Ks and can get himself out by swinging at bad pitches. May move to CF where speed is more suitable, though arm is below avg.

DeVoss, Zeke

4 | Chicago (N) | EXP MLB DEBUT: 2014 | POTENTIAL: Backup 2B | 6C

Bats B Age 22	Year	Lev	Team	AB	R	H	HR	RBI	Avg	OB	Slg	OPS	bb%	ct%	Eye	SB	CS	x/h%	Iso	RC/G
2011 (3) Miami	2010	NCAA	Miami	211	49	53	9	33	251	336	450	786	11	76	0.54	24	4	40	199	5.35
Pwr ++	2011	NCAA	Miami	215	59	73	2	27	340	478	456	934	21	86	1.90	32	10	25	116	7.94
BAvg +++	2011	Rk	Cubs	17	4	5	0	3	294	333	353	686	6	76	0.25	2	0	20	59	3.90
Spd +++	2011	A-	Boise	132	28	41	0	14	311	445	386	831	20	79	1.14	14	4	22	76	6.61
Def +++	2012	A	Peoria	465	88	116	6	38	249	362	370	732	15	75	0.69	35	16	32	120	4.98

Another Cubs prospect who struggled when in the MWL. Has plus speed and is willing to take a walk, but also struck out 118 times and needs to make more consistent contact so that he can use his speed. Doesn't have much power, but is a good defender with solid athleticism.

Dickerson, Alex

3 | Pittsburgh | EXP MLB DEBUT: 2015 | POTENTIAL: Starting 1B | 8D

Bats L Age 23	Year	Lev	Team	AB	R	H	HR	RBI	Avg	OB	Slg	OPS	bb%	ct%	Eye	SB	CS	x/h%	Iso	RC/G
2011 (3) Indiana	2009	NCAA	Indiana	238	45	88	14	57	370	414	618	1032	7	80	0.38	2	4	34	248	8.04
Pwr ++++	2010	NCAA	Indiana	236	62	99	24	75	419	465	805	1270	8	85	0.57	3	2	43	386	10.56
BAvg +++	2011	NCAA	Indiana	215	33	79	9	49	367	431	540	970	10	90	1.14	2	1	24	172	7.36
Spd ++	2011	A-	State College	150	25	47	3	19	313	380	493	873	10	81	0.57	0	0	43	180	6.48
Def ++	2012	A+	Bradenton	488	65	144	13	90	295	347	451	798	7	81	0.42	12	7	33	156	5.32

Tall, athletic OF put up respectable numbers in the FSL. Has better power than the 13 HR suggests and slugged .507 after the 2nd month. He has a smooth LH stroke, but needs to make more consistent contact. Still struggles with quality breaking balls and can be overly pull conscious. Has the tools to be an above-average defender.

Dickerson, Corey

7 | Colorado | EXP MLB DEBUT: 2014 | POTENTIAL: Backup OF | 6B

Bats L Age 24	Year	Lev	Team	AB	R	H	HR	RBI	Avg	OB	Slg	OPS	bb%	ct%	Eye	SB	CS	x/h%	Iso	RC/G
2010 (8) Meridian CC																				
Pwr +++	2010	Rk	Casper	276	54	96	13	61	348	408	634	1042	9	82	0.55	12	6	46	286	8.44
BAvg +++	2011	A	Asheville	383	78	108	32	87	282	348	629	978	9	74	0.39	9	6	59	347	7.72
Spd ++	2012	A+	Modesto	240	43	81	9	43	338	400	583	983	9	83	0.60	9	5	46	246	7.73
Def ++	2012	AA	Tulsa	266	40	73	13	38	274	320	504	824	6	81	0.35	7	3	44	229	5.50

Tall, athletic OF has above-average power, but is limited in other aspects. Held his own when moved up to Double-A and hit .364 in the AFL. The Rockies tried him in CF, but spent most of the season in RF/LF where his speed fits better. Below-average arm could limit his playing time despite good power.

Dickson, O'Koyea

3 | Los Angeles (N) | EXP MLB DEBUT: 2014 | POTENTIAL: Backup 1B | 7C

Bats R Age 23	Year	Lev	Team	AB	R	H	HR	RBI	Avg	OB	Slg	OPS	bb%	ct%	Eye	SB	CS	x/h%	Iso	RC/G
2011 (12) Sonoma St																				
Pwr +++																				
BAvg ++																				
Spd ++	2011	Rk	Ogden	189	33	63	13	38	333	394	603	997	9	77	0.43	1	1	38	270	7.85
Def ++	2012	A	Great Lakes	386	63	105	17	48	272	350	479	829	11	83	0.71	11	6	43	207	5.81

Short, strong-bodied 1B has plus power and good strike zone judgment. He was a bit old for Low-A, but had a fine season. Drives the ball well with good bat speed and is a decent runner. Played mostly 1B though he did see some action in LF. Will turn 23 and needs to continue to move up quickly.

Diekroeger, Kenny

46 | Kansas City | EXP MLB DEBUT: 2015 | POTENTIAL: Reserve INF | 7D

Bats R Age 22	Year	Lev	Team	AB	R	H	HR	RBI	Avg	OB	Slg	OPS	bb%	ct%	Eye	SB	CS	x/h%	Iso	RC/G
2012 (4) Stanford																				
Pwr +++																				
BAvg ++																				
Spd +++																				
Def ++	2012	Rk	Burlington	202	21	42	8	33	208	273	366	639	8	70	0.30	5	0	36	158	3.22

Tall, versatile INF who hasn't lived up to expectations in college or short stint as pro. Provides pop generated from strong wrists and moderate bat speed. Has work to do to close holes in stroke. Can adequately play both middle infield spots, but 2B may be best bet due to iffy range. Hands and arm could also work at 3B.

Dietrich, Derek

46 | Miami | EXP MLB DEBUT: 2014 | POTENTIAL: Starting 3B | 7A

Bats L Age 23	Year	Lev	Team	AB	R	H	HR	RBI	Avg	OB	Slg	OPS	bb%	ct%	Eye	SB	CS	x/h%	Iso	RC/G
2010 (2) Georgia Tech	2010	NCAA	Georgia Tech	240	68	84	17	61	350	418	650	1068	10	85	0.76	8	4	42	300	8.54
Pwr +++	2010	A-	Hudson Valley	179	33	50	3	20	279	321	419	740	6	77	0.26	2	2	34	140	4.60
BAvg +++	2011	A	Bowling Green	480	73	133	22	81	277	330	502	832	7	73	0.30	5	7	45	225	5.85
Spd ++	2012	A+	Charlotte	372	49	105	10	58	282	327	468	795	6	79	0.32	4	2	38	185	5.29
Def ++	2012	AA	Montgomery	133	22	36	4	17	271	307	429	736	5	73	0.19	0	1	33	158	4.47

Offensive INF who was promoted to AA in July and moved to 2B. Smokes hard line drives with quick hands and smooth, level stroke. Possesses bat control, though can be overzealous. Ks a lot and needs to improve against LHP. Lack of range and quickness may lead to 2B or 3B, but arm strength is asset.

Domoromo, Luis

8 | San Diego | EXP MLB DEBUT: 2014 | POTENTIAL: Backup CF | 6D

Bats L Age 21	Year	Lev	Team	AB	R	H	HR	RBI	Avg	OB	Slg	OPS	bb%	ct%	Eye	SB	CS	x/h%	Iso	RC/G
2008 NDFA, Venezuela																				
Pwr ++																				
BAvg ++	2010	A-	Eugene	113	12	31	1	8	274	311	345	656	5	80	0.26	0	0	19	71	3.44
Spd +++	2011	A	Fort Wayne	435	66	123	9	68	283	338	405	742	8	81	0.43	7	7	26	122	4.64
Def ++	2012	A+	Lake Elsinore	351	34	77	3	36	219	265	302	567	6	75	0.25	9	2	27	83	2.33

Took a huge step back when he floundered in the hitter-friendly CAL. Has good speed, raw power, athleticism and plus bat speed, but has made little progress. Started his career playing CF, but has average speed and split time between LF and RF in '12. Will need to show something in '13, but time is running out.

Drury, Brandon

35 | Atlanta | EXP MLB DEBUT: 2015 | POTENTIAL: Starting 3B | 7D

Bats R Age 20	Year	Lev	Team	AB	R	H	HR	RBI	Avg	OB	Slg	OPS	bb%	ct%	Eye	SB	CS	x/h%	Iso	RC/G
2010 (13) HS, OR																				
Pwr ++																				
BAvg ++	2010	Rk	GCL Braves	192	20	38	3	17	198	234	292	525	4	74	0.18	2	2	29	94	1.66
Spd ++	2011	Rk	Danville	265	40	92	8	54	347	362	525	886	2	87	0.17	3	0	34	177	5.95
Def ++	2012	A	Rome	445	47	102	6	51	229	262	333	595	4	84	0.27	3	4	30	103	2.76

Hard working 1B/3B took a huge step backwards after a nice breakout in '11. Struggled to make consistent contact. Uses his hands too much in his swing and continues to be overly aggressive. Is a solid defender with good hands. Will need to prove that '12 was a fluke.

Dugan, Kelly

379 | Philadelphia | EXP MLB DEBUT: 2015 | POTENTIAL: Backup OF | 6D

Bats B Age 22	Year	Lev	Team	AB	R	H	HR	RBI	Avg	OB	Slg	OPS	bb%	ct%	Eye	SB	CS	x/h%	Iso	RC/G
2009 (2) HS, CA	2009	Rk	GCL Phillies	150	18	35	0	8	233	290	300	590	7	80	0.40	9	5	26	67	2.85
Pwr ++	2010	Rk	GCL Phillies	33	12	19	1	4	576	622	848	1470	11	88	1.00	2	2	32	273	13.39
BAvg ++	2010	A-	Williamsport	60	6	15	0	4	250	308	350	658	8	72	0.29	0	0	40	100	3.75
Spd ++	2011	A-	Williamsport	176	25	50	2	21	284	337	386	723	7	81	0.41	6	0	20	102	4.45
Def +++	2012	A	Lakewood	430	83	129	12	60	300	370	470	840	10	72	0.39	5	1	36	170	6.23

Tall, switch-hitting OF had a mini breakout. Good raw power finally starting to show up in game action with 33 2B and 12 HR. Swing can still get long and can be too aggressive at the plate. Poor contact rate does not support a .300 average going forward, but there was at least some progress for this 2nd rounder.

Dunston Jr, Shawon — 8 — Chicago (N)

EXP MLB DEBUT: 2015 — POTENTIAL: Starting CF — 7D

Bats L Age 20 — 2011 (11) HS, CA

Pwr + + | BAvg + + + | Spd + + + | Def + + +

Year	Lev	Team	AB	R	H	HR	RBI	Avg	OB	Slg	OPS	bb%	ct%	Eye	SB	CS	x/h%	Iso	RC/G
2012	Rk	Cubs	161	30	46	2	24	286	358	410	767	10	80	0.55	4	2	26	124	5.18
2012	A-	Boise	65	10	12	1	2	185	232	323	555	6	78	0.29	1	2	50	138	2.29

Tall, projectable CF struggled in the NWL, but looked more comfortable when demoted. Remains raw both on offense and defense. He has plus speed and good raw power, though there was limited evidence of either in his debut. Showed surprising patience at the plate and should continue to develop as he matures.

Duran, Juan — 7 — Cincinnati

EXP MLB DEBUT: 2014 — POTENTIAL: Backup LF — 6D

Bats R Age 21 — 2008 NDFA, D.R.

Pwr + + + | BAvg + | Spd + | Def + +

Year	Lev	Team	AB	R	H	HR	RBI	Avg	OB	Slg	OPS	bb%	ct%	Eye	SB	CS	x/h%	Iso	RC/G
2009	Rk	GCL Reds	164	15	29	0	17	177	215	268	483	5	68	0.15	0	0	38	91	1.18
2010	Rk	Billings	201	23	49	6	25	244	309	393	702	9	65	0.27	2	3	35	149	4.38
2011	A	Dayton	367	48	97	16	71	264	327	463	790	8	59	0.22	1	4	40	199	6.16
2012	A+	Bakersfield	422	47	100	12	57	237	281	370	651	6	64	0.17	3	2	30	133	3.51

Athletic OF took a step back in the CAL. Bat speed provides power to all fields, but poor pitch recognition and an overly aggressive approach results in horrible contact rate. Decent range with a strong arm, but continued poor plate discipline undercuts potential. Hard to see how he turns things around anytime soon.

Dykstra, Cutter — 4 — Washington

EXP MLB DEBUT: 2014 — POTENTIAL: Backup 2B — 6C

Bats R Age 24 — 2008 (2) HS, CA

Pwr + + | BAvg + + + | 4.15 Spd + + + + | Def + + +

Year	Lev	Team	AB	R	H	HR	RBI	Avg	OB	Slg	OPS	bb%	ct%	Eye	SB	CS	x/h%	Iso	RC/G
2009	Rk	Helena	209	35	51	5	26	244	331	349	680	11	76	0.54	14	4	22	105	3.98
2009	A	Wisconsin	99	16	21	1	7	212	297	303	600	11	73	0.44	4	2	29	91	2.96
2010	A	Wisconsin	353	66	110	5	39	312	404	411	815	13	80	0.76	27	8	18	99	5.93
2011	A+	Potomac	306	26	65	1	27	212	263	265	528	6	73	0.26	12	4	20	52	1.80
2012	A	Hagerstown	436	62	127	7	64	291	355	408	763	9	81	0.52	32	3	28	117	5.02

Dykstra is the son of former player Lenny Dykstra. Attempted to make the transition from CF to 2B and had a nice offensive season. Moderate bat speed produces line-drive power. Contact rate and plate discipline returned to acceptable levels and he could still carve out a nice role as a high-energy utility player.

Eaton, Adam — 9 — Arizona

EXP MLB DEBUT: 2012 — POTENTIAL: Starting LF — 8B

Bats L Age 24 — 2010 (19) Miami (OH)

Pwr + | BAvg + + + | Spd + + + | Def + + +

Year	Lev	Team	AB	R	H	HR	RBI	Avg	OB	Slg	OPS	bb%	ct%	Eye	SB	CS	x/h%	Iso	RC/G
2011	A+	Visalia	244	54	81	6	39	332	430	492	922	15	83	1.02	24	8	30	160	7.31
2011	AA	Mobile	212	31	64	4	28	302	388	429	818	12	83	0.86	10	6	23	127	5.89
2012	AA	Mobile	40	11	12	0	3	300	391	325	716	13	80	0.75	6	1	8	25	4.67
2012	AAA	Reno	488	119	186	7	45	381	442	539	981	10	86	0.78	38	10	31	158	7.71
2012	MLB	Arizona	85	19	22	2	5	259	364	412	775	14	82	0.93	2	3	32	153	5.47

Short, high-energy OF who continues to be an offensive sparkplug. The trade of C. Young removes one competitor for playing time and should insure that he makes the opening day roster. Doesn't have much power, but draws walks and has above-average speed. His career minor league line is now .355/.456/.510.

Edwards, Spencer — 6 — Tampa Bay

EXP MLB DEBUT: 2016 — POTENTIAL: Starting SS/CF — 8E

Bats R Age 20 — 2012 (2) HS (TX)

Pwr + + | BAvg + + | Spd + + + + | Def + +

Year	Lev	Team	AB	R	H	HR	RBI	Avg	OB	Slg	OPS	bb%	ct%	Eye	SB	CS	x/h%	Iso	RC/G
2012	Rk	GCL Rays	128	14	24	1	7	188	241	281	522	7	67	0.21	8	4	33	94	1.70

Lean, athletic prospect who is among fastest players in org. Needs to add strength to wiry frame and swing mechanics may need overhaul. Swings fast bat with quick wrists and could hit for moderate BA if he keeps ball on ground. Exhibits pure arm strength and could move to CF to take advantage of speed.

Eibner, Brett — 89 — Kansas City

EXP MLB DEBUT: 2015 — POTENTIAL: Starting OF — 8E

Bats R Age 24 — 2010 (2) Arkansas

Pwr + + + + | BAvg + + | Spd + + + | Def + + +

Year	Lev	Team	AB	R	H	HR	RBI	Avg	OB	Slg	OPS	bb%	ct%	Eye	SB	CS	x/h%	Iso	RC/G
2008	NCAA	Arkansas	191	36	57	8	48	298	388	497	886	13	76	0.61	3	3	35	199	6.76
2009	NCAA	Arkansas	147	34	34	12	34	231	365	510	875	17	59	0.52	3	5	47	279	7.42
2010	NCAA	Arkansas	216	66	72	22	71	333	435	718	1153	15	75	0.71	3	0	54	384	10.28
2011	A	Kane County	272	46	58	12	31	213	331	408	739	15	67	0.53	2	3	47	195	4.99
2012	A+	Wilmington	423	60	83	15	53	196	292	388	679	12	61	0.35	5	2	55	191	4.29

Athletic, strong OF who may move back to pitching after substandard campaign. Career .203 BA despite patient approach and well above avg bat speed. Sells out for power and chases pitches. May always have high Ks as he has too much swing and miss. Good defender and runs well. Plus-plus arm is best tool.

Elander, Josh — 2 — Atlanta

EXP MLB DEBUT: 2016 — POTENTIAL: Starting C — 7D

Bats R Age 22 — 2012 (6) TCU

Pwr + + + | BAvg + + + | Spd + + | Def + +

Year	Lev	Team	AB	R	H	HR	RBI	Avg	OB	Slg	OPS	bb%	ct%	Eye	SB	CS	x/h%	Iso	RC/G
2012	Rk	Danville	123	19	32	4	19	260	345	439	784	12	85	0.84	3	1	38	179	5.40

Strong, agile backstop had a solid pro debut, showing good pop with solid plate discipline. Saw limited action behind the plate at TCU so his blocking and receiving skills are raw. He will need to work hard to stay behind the plate. His bat speed is only average, but he squares the ball up well and doesn't expand the strike zone.

Erickson, Gorman — 2 — Los Angeles (N)

EXP MLB DEBUT: 2014 — POTENTIAL: Backup C — 6D

Bats B Age 25 — 2006 (15) HS, CA

Pwr + | BAvg + + | Spd + + | Def + + +

Year	Lev	Team	AB	R	H	HR	RBI	Avg	OB	Slg	OPS	bb%	ct%	Eye	SB	CS	x/h%	Iso	RC/G
2009	Rk	Ogden	197	40	60	5	36	305	380	482	862	11	82	0.67	0	0	40	178	6.36
2010	A	Great Lakes	261	32	56	2	27	215	305	310	615	12	83	0.76	3	0	32	96	3.43
2011	A+	Rancho Cuc	226	37	69	6	40	305	412	491	903	15	81	0.98	3	2	38	186	7.15
2011	AA	Chattanooga	142	18	39	7	26	275	327	479	806	7	85	0.50	1	0	38	204	5.27
2012	AA	Chattanooga	274	25	64	3	25	234	340	328	668	14	80	0.79	1	2	30	95	4.09

Tall, strong switch-hitting catcher struggled in repeat of AA. Has a decent approach at the plate with good plate discipline, but limited power. Should continue to hit for average due to ability to make consistent contact. Is one of the better defensive backstop in the organization so he continues to have value.

Esposito, Jason — 5 — Baltimore

EXP MLB DEBUT: 2015 — POTENTIAL: Starting 3B — 7B

Bats R Age 22 — 2011 (2) Vanderbilt

Pwr + + | BAvg + + | Spd + + + | Def + + + +

Year	Lev	Team	AB	R	H	HR	RBI	Avg	OB	Slg	OPS	bb%	ct%	Eye	SB	CS	x/h%	Iso	RC/G
2009	NCAA	Vanderbilt	237	39	68	4	42	287	332	401	733	6	80	0.33	20	5	26	114	4.47
2010	NCAA	Vanderbilt	262	65	94	12	64	359	432	599	1032	11	87	0.97	31	4	40	240	8.27
2011	NCAA	Vanderbilt	268	55	91	9	59	340	379	530	909	6	83	0.38	15	10	35	190	6.52
2012	A	Delmarva	473	52	99	5	51	209	251	277	527	5	76	0.23	8	3	20	68	1.76

Tall, athletic INF suffered thru miserable season at plate. Struggled with BA and lacked punch. Owns BA potential despite fringy bat speed and swing mechanics need to be smoother. Can be impact defender with strong arm and clean, quick hands. Glovework keeps him prospect while bat develops.

Evans, Phillip — 6 — New York (N)

EXP MLB DEBUT: 2015 — POTENTIAL: Backup SS — 6C

Bats R Age 20 — 2011 (15) HS, CA

Pwr + | BAvg + + | Spd + + + | Def + + +

Year	Lev	Team	AB	R	H	HR	RBI	Avg	OB	Slg	OPS	bb%	ct%	Eye	SB	CS	x/h%	Iso	RC/G
2011	Rk	Kingsport	11	3	4	0	3	364	417	545	962	8	82	0.50	0	0	50	182	7.65
2011	Rk	GCL Mets	15	3	5	0	1	333	412	467	878	12	80	0.67	0	1	40	133	6.81
2011	A-	Brooklyn	8	1	1	0	0	125	125	125	250	0	100		0	0	0	0	-0.29
2012	A-	Brooklyn	294	32	74	5	29	252	323	337	660	10	84	0.65	2	0	19	85	3.77

Short, but strong INF was considered a possible 1st rounder, but fell due to concerns about signability. Has a good approach at the plate and makes consistent contact with good plate discipline. Improved defense gives him the chance to stick. He has solid range with a strong arm and good instincts.

Fairley, Wendell — 8 — San Francisco

EXP MLB DEBUT: 2014 — POTENTIAL: Platoon CF — 6D

Bats L Age 25 — 2007 (1-S) HS, MS

Pwr + + | BAvg + + | Spd + + + + | Def + + +

Year	Lev	Team	AB	R	H	HR	RBI	Avg	OB	Slg	OPS	bb%	ct%	Eye	SB	CS	x/h%	Iso	RC/G
2010	A+	San Jose	391	42	114	1	46	292	340	343	683	7	78	0.34	10	6	15	51	3.90
2011	A+	San Jose	208	28	51	2	21	245	311	317	629	9	81	0.51	3	1	20	72	3.34
2011	AA	Richmond	98	11	26	0	7	265	321	337	657	8	72	0.30	2	2	19	71	3.67
2012	Rk	Giants	52	7	10	0	7	192	236	308	544	5	73	0.21	1	0	50	115	2.15
2012	AA	Richmond	109	6	24	0	9	220	303	266	569	11	70	0.39	1	1	21	46	2.52

Former 1st round pick has been a complete bust so far. He is a plus athlete with good speed, but simply can't hit and has shown little power as a professional. Possesses good bat speed and plate discipline, but has not translated that into game action and he remains raw in many aspects of the game.

Federowicz, Tim — 2 — Los Angeles (N)

EXP MLB DEBUT: 2011 | POTENTIAL: Starting C | 7D

Bats R Age 25
2008 (7) UNC
Pwr ++
BAvg +++
Spd +
Def ++++

Year	Lev	Team	AB	R	H	HR	RBI	Avg	OB	Slg	OPS	bb%	ct%	Eye	SB	CS	x/h%	Iso	RC/G
2011	AA	Portland	339	46	94	8	52	277	340	407	747	9	81	0.51	1	0	30	130	4.75
2011	AAA	Albuquerque	83	17	27	6	17	325	429	627	1055	15	76	0.75	0	0	48	301	9.04
2011	MLB	Dodgers	13	0	2	0	1	154	267	154	421	13	69	0.50	0	0	0	0	0.34
2012	AAA	Albuquerque	412	71	121	11	76	294	373	461	834	11	78	0.57	0	1	38	167	6.05
2012	MLB	Dodgers	3	0	1	0	0	333	500	333	833	25	33	0.50	0	0	0	0	13.10

Strong, stocky backstop is the best defender in the system. He blocks and receives well, calls a good game, and has a strong arm. Put up solid numbers at AAA, but also struck out a career high 91 times. Could compete for a back-up role with the Dodgers and has good long-term potential.

Fields, Daniel — 8 — Detroit

EXP MLB DEBUT: 2014 | POTENTIAL: Starting OF | 7E

Bats R Age 22
2009 (6) HS (MI)
Pwr ++
BAvg ++
Spd +++
Def ++++

Year	Lev	Team	AB	R	H	HR	RBI	Avg	OB	Slg	OPS	bb%	ct%	Eye	SB	CS	x/h%	Iso	RC/G
2010	A+	Lakeland	375	33	90	8	47	240	337	371	708	13	68	0.46	8	9	30	131	4.56
2011	A+	Lakeland	432	57	95	8	46	220	299	326	626	10	69	0.37	4	4	27	106	3.23
2012	A+	Lakeland	244	31	65	1	26	266	319	357	676	7	77	0.35	14	7	25	90	3.88
2012	AA	Erie	106	13	28	2	7	264	345	358	703	11	80	0.62	9	1	21	94	4.31

Athletic, strong OF who began 3rd stint in High-A before move to AA. Saw drastic increase in SB, but didn't hit for much power and BB dropped. Made better contact as he tweaked approach and started to use entire field. Goes gap to gap, but inability to master LHP mutes BA potential. Owns good range and OK arm.

Flores, Ramon — 789 — New York (A)

EXP MLB DEBUT: 2015 | POTENTIAL: Starting OF | 8C

Bats L Age 21
2008 FA (Venezuela)
Pwr ++
BAvg ++++
Spd +++
Def ++

Year	Lev	Team	AB	R	H	HR	RBI	Avg	OB	Slg	OPS	bb%	ct%	Eye	SB	CS	x/h%	Iso	RC/G
2010	A	Charleston (Sc)	48	3	12	0	2	250	294	313	607	6	69	0.20	1	0	25	63	2.90
2010	A+	Tampa	28	0	7	0	2	250	250	250	500	0	82	0.00	0	0	0	0	1.26
2011	A	Charleston (Sc)	468	59	124	11	59	265	350	400	749	12	80	0.66	13	2	31	135	4.95
2012	A+	Tampa	517	83	156	6	39	302	368	420	788	9	84	0.64	24	9	27	118	5.39
2012	AA	Trenton	5	2	2	1	2	400	400	1000	1400	0	100		0	0	50	600	10.25

Pure-hitting OF with myriad offensive tools. May only project to 10-15 HR, but has potential to hit for high BA. Advanced approach and shrewd K zone judgment give him high OBP. Profiles as top of order hitter with enough speed, but keen instincts, to be threat on base. Limited defensively with fringy arm strength.

Flores, Wilmer — 5 — New York (N)

EXP MLB DEBUT: 2014 | POTENTIAL: Starting 3B | 9D

Bats R Age 21
2007 NDFA, Venezuela
Pwr ++++
BAvg ++++
Spd ++
Def ++

Year	Lev	Team	AB	R	H	HR	RBI	Avg	OB	Slg	OPS	bb%	ct%	Eye	SB	CS	x/h%	Iso	RC/G
2010	A	Savannah	277	30	77	7	44	278	333	433	767	8	87	0.62	2	1	35	155	5.00
2010	A+	St. Lucie	277	32	83	4	40	300	322	415	737	3	86	0.23	2	4	28	116	4.36
2011	A+	St. Lucie	516	52	139	9	81	269	306	380	686	5	87	0.40	2	2	27	110	3.89
2012	A+	St. Lucie	242	31	70	10	42	289	338	463	801	7	88	0.60	3	2	31	174	5.24
2012	AA	Binghamton	251	37	78	8	33	311	362	494	856	7	88	0.67	0	0	36	183	5.99

Finally mastered High-A in his 3rd stint. An improved approach at the plate resulted in more consistent contact and a spike in power. Adjustments carried over after being promoted. Transition to 3B is a work in progress, but he does have good hands and a strong throwing arm. Will need to prove he can do it again.

Fontana, Nolan — 6 — Houston

EXP MLB DEBUT: 2015 | POTENTIAL: Starting SS | 7C

Bats L Age 22
2012 (2) Florida
Pwr ++
BAvg +++
Spd +++
Def +++

Year	Lev	Team	AB	R	H	HR	RBI	Avg	OB	Slg	OPS	bb%	ct%	Eye	SB	CS	x/h%	Iso	RC/G
2010	NCAA	Florida	216	56	62	3	23	287	428	417	844	20	87	1.83	11	5	32	130	6.74
2011	NCAA	Florida	256	57	74	5	49	289	409	434	843	17	88	1.73	6	4	30	145	6.54
2012	NCAA	Florida	243	59	69	9	30	284	402	444	847	16	89	1.78	13	1	29	160	6.43
2012	A	Lexington	151	37	34	2	25	225	458	338	796	30	71	1.48	12	2	35	113	6.47

Smart, efficient INF who showed plate patience in debut. Works counts and waits for good pitches to hit. Could stand to be more aggressive to take advantage of clean, level swing. Has enough power to keep defense honest and runs very well. Has defensive tools with OK range and arm. Hands work well.

Ford, Fred — 9 — Kansas City

EXP MLB DEBUT: 2017 | POTENTIAL: Starting OF | 8E

Bats R Age 21
2012 (7) Jefferson CC
Pwr ++++
BAvg ++
Spd ++
Def ++

Year	Lev	Team	AB	R	H	HR	RBI	Avg	OB	Slg	OPS	bb%	ct%	Eye	SB	CS	x/h%	Iso	RC/G
2012	Rk	Burlington	214	38	53	13	35	248	356	491	847	14	61	0.43	5	5	47	243	6.89

Long, lean OF with crude game, but intriguing upside. Must make more contact and could be more aggressive at plate. Has uppercut stroke and will work on keeping bat head in zone longer. Owns lots of power and athleticism. Range and arm suitable for OF corner, but bat will determine status.

Forsythe, Blake — 2 — New York (N)

EXP MLB DEBUT: 2014 | POTENTIAL: Backup C | 6C

Bats R Age 23
2010 (3) Tennessee
Pwr ++
BAvg ++
Spd ++
Def +++

Year	Lev	Team	AB	R	H	HR	RBI	Avg	OB	Slg	OPS	bb%	ct%	Eye	SB	CS	x/h%	Iso	RC/G
2010	NCAA	Tennessee	199	40	57	15	57	286	383	583	966	13	73	0.57	0	1	47	296	7.83
2010	Rk	GCL Mets	10	0	2	0	0	200	273	200	473	9	80	0.50	0	0	0	0	1.36
2010	A-	Brooklyn	101	14	24	3	8	238	313	396	709	10	59	0.27	1	1	38	158	4.83
2011	A	Savannah	370	44	87	9	43	235	336	395	730	13	67	0.46	0	1	43	159	4.97
2012	A+	St. Lucie	295	32	72	8	42	244	334	397	731	12	70	0.45	0	0	38	153	4.80

Big, strong-bodied backstop has failed to hit as anticipated. Has good raw power, but has yet to reach double-digit HR since turning pro and now has a career .238 avg. Defensively he moves well and has a strong arm and has a chance to stay behind the plate. Could develop into a reliable 2nd string catcher.

Franco, Maikel — 5 — Philadelphia

EXP MLB DEBUT: 2015 | POTENTIAL: Starting 3B | 9D

Bats R Age 20
2010 NDFA, D.R.
Pwr ++++
BAvg +++
Spd ++
Def +++

Year	Lev	Team	AB	R	H	HR	RBI	Avg	OB	Slg	OPS	bb%	ct%	Eye	SB	CS	x/h%	Iso	RC/G
2010	Rk	GCL Phillies	194	23	43	2	29	222	281	330	611	8	76	0.35	0	0	35	108	3.03
2011	A	Lakewood	65	6	8	1	6	123	136	200	336	2	77	0.07	0	0	38	77	
2011	A-	Williamsport	202	19	58	2	38	287	366	411	777	11	85	0.83	0	0	34	124	5.40
2012	A	Lakewood	503	70	141	14	84	280	331	439	770	7	84	0.48	3	1	35	159	4.96

Strong, agile 3B continues to make progress. Has good bat speed, decent plate discipline, and good hand-eye coordination. Has good raw power and exciting potential. He can be overly aggressive and sometimes tries to pull everything. He is a below average runner, but fields his position well and should stick at 3B.

Franklin, Nick — 46 — Seattle

EXP MLB DEBUT: 2013 | POTENTIAL: Starting SS/2B | 8B

Bats B Age 22
2009 (1) HS (FL)
Pwr +++
BAvg ++++
Spd +++
Def +++

Year	Lev	Team	AB	R	H	HR	RBI	Avg	OB	Slg	OPS	bb%	ct%	Eye	SB	CS	x/h%	Iso	RC/G
2011	Rk	Mariners	11	1	1	0	0	91	91	91	182	0	45	0.00	0	0	0	0	
2011	A+	High Desert	258	50	71	5	20	275	353	411	764	11	78	0.55	13	1	28	136	5.13
2011	AA	Jackson	83	13	27	2	6	325	371	482	853	7	78	0.33	5	3	26	157	6.02
2012	AA	Jackson	205	25	66	4	26	322	393	502	895	10	81	0.63	9	2	38	180	6.81
2012	AAA	Tacoma	267	39	65	7	29	243	306	416	722	8	75	0.35	3	2	42	172	4.48

Instinctual, natural INF who split time between SS and 2B, but solely played 2B in AFL. Has good feel for hitting with line drive stroke to gaps. Above avg bat speed with moderate power potential. Has understanding of K zone and should hit for BA with improved patience. Fits better at 2B with average speed and arm.

Freeman, Ronnie — 2 — Arizona

EXP MLB DEBUT: 2015 | POTENTIAL: Backup C | 6C

Bats R Age 22
2012 (5) Kennesaw St
Pwr ++
BAvg ++
Spd +
Def ++

Year	Lev	Team	AB	R	H	HR	RBI	Avg	OB	Slg	OPS	bb%	ct%	Eye	SB	CS	x/h%	Iso	RC/G
2010	NCAA	Kennesaw St	211	27	77	9	47	365	394	531	924	5	85	0.32	2	0	22	166	6.44
2011	NCAA	Kennesaw St	217	49	85	10	51	392	480	622	1102	15	86	1.19	1	0	35	230	9.34
2012	NCAA	Kennesaw St	230	42	80	6	54	348	419	483	901	11	84	0.76	0	0	24	135	6.74
2012	A-	Yakima	165	13	45	0	16	273	310	333	644	5	85	0.36	0	0	22	61	3.45

Strong, offensive-minded backstop has good size and raw power. Needs to make more consistent contact and improve his plate discipline. Below-average defensively, and the Diamondbacks have more skilled catchers in Trahan and Perez, so a move to a new position is possible.

Fuentes, Reymond — 8 — San Diego

EXP MLB DEBUT: 2014 | POTENTIAL: Backup CF | 6C

Bats L Age 22
2009 (1) HS, P.R.
Pwr ++
BAvg ++
Spd ++++
Def ++

Year	Lev	Team	AB	R	H	HR	RBI	Avg	OB	Slg	OPS	bb%	ct%	Eye	SB	CS	x/h%	Iso	RC/G
2009	Rk	GCL Red Sox	145	16	42	1	14	290	322	379	702	5	83	0.29	9	5	21	90	4.05
2010	A	Greenville	374	59	101	5	41	270	316	377	693	6	77	0.29	42	5	25	107	3.99
2011	A+	Lake Elsinore	510	84	140	5	45	275	332	369	701	8	77	0.38	41	14	21	94	4.19
2012	AA	San Antonio	473	53	103	4	34	218	295	302	598	10	72	0.39	35	9	27	85	2.89

Fuentes came over as part of the A. Gonzalez deal and has not lived up to expectations. Is fast and athletic, but hasn't figured out how to hit. Can hit hard line drives to gaps, but doesn't make contact. Struggles with pitch recognition and doesn't look like he will hit enough to have value.

Galindo, Jesus — 8 — San Francisco

EXP MLB DEBUT: 2015 | **POTENTIAL:** Starting CF | **7C**

Bats B | Age 22 | 2009 NDFA, D.R.

Pwr + | BAvg + + | Spd + + + + | Def + + + +

Year	Lev	Team	AB	R	H	HR	RBI	Avg	OB	Slg	OPS	bb%	ct%	Eye	SB	CS	x/h%	Iso	RC/G
2011	A-	Salem-Keizer	239	49	66	2	20	276	345	364	709	9	81	0.54	47	8	21	88	4.40
2012	A	Augusta	250	39	63	0	23	252	318	308	626	9	80	0.49	40	11	17	56	3.34

Is one of the faster players in the system and now has 152 career SB. Has good strike zone judgment and is willing to take a walk, but doesn't make hard contact. Covers ground in CF and has enough arm strength for the position. Will need to be more dangerous at the plate.

Gallagher, Austin — 53 — Los Angeles (N)

EXP MLB DEBUT: 2014 | **POTENTIAL:** Platoon 1B | **6C**

Bats L | Age 24 | 2007 (3) HS, PA

Pwr + + | BAvg + + | Spd + + | Def + +

Year	Lev	Team	AB	R	H	HR	RBI	Avg	OB	Slg	OPS	bb%	ct%	Eye	SB	CS	x/h%	Iso	RC/G
2008	A+	Inland Empire	307	36	90	5	55	293	354	456	810	9	76	0.40	1	4	43	163	5.72
2009	A	Great Lakes	226	28	58	3	30	257	320	345	665	9	81	0.49	1	1	24	88	3.76
2010	A+	Inland Empire	422	47	123	6	64	291	350	405	755	8	82	0.49	0	2	28	114	4.89
2011	A+	Rancho Cuc	390	73	114	13	62	292	389	451	841	14	82	0.89	0	1	30	159	6.17
2012	A+	Rancho Cuc	374	58	106	15	74	283	380	481	861	13	78	0.71	2	5	41	198	6.44

Tall, athletic hitter with bat speed and plate discipline has been stuck at High-A for three years despite decent results. Swing can get long, but has ability to adjust. Has good arm strength and soft hands but lacks first-step quickness and so is limited to 1B, though he did see a few games in LF.

Gallagher, Cameron — 2 — Kansas City

EXP MLB DEBUT: 2017 | **POTENTIAL:** Starting C | **7C**

Bats R | Age 20 | 2011 (2) HS (PA)

Pwr + + | BAvg + + + | Spd + | Def + + +

Year	Lev	Team	AB	R	H	HR	RBI	Avg	OB	Slg	OPS	bb%	ct%	Eye	SB	CS	x/h%	Iso	RC/G
2011	Rk	Idaho Falls	30	2	6	1	2	200	273	300	573	9	87	0.75	0	0	17	100	2.70
2011	Rk	Royals	78	6	11	1	7	141	212	179	391	8	81	0.47	0	0	9	38	0.30
2012	Rk	Burlington	127	13	35	3	15	276	328	425	754	7	87	0.63	1	3	37	150	4.84

Tall, natural-hitting C who has overcome variety of minor injuries. Controls bat and K zone well for age and makes easy contact. Should hit for BA and present pull power could develop into plus pop. Defensive instincts are sound and has proven to be capable receiver. Throws with strong, accurate arm and keeps SB in check.

Gallo, Joey — 5 — Texas

EXP MLB DEBUT: 2016 | **POTENTIAL:** Starting 3B | **8C**

Bats L | Age 19 | 2012 (1-S) HS (NV)

Pwr + + + + + | BAvg + + | Spd + + | Def + +

Year	Lev	Team	AB	R	H	HR	RBI	Avg	OB	Slg	OPS	bb%	ct%	Eye	SB	CS	x/h%	Iso	RC/G
2012	Rk	Rangers	150	44	44	18	43	293	433	733	1166	20	65	0.71	6	0	66	440	11.47
2012	A-	Spokane	56	9	12	4	9	214	343	464	808	16	54	0.42	0	0	50	250	6.85

Big, strong INF who was MVP of AZL after league HR record. Power potential may be best of any prospect. Owns vicious uppercut stroke with quickness and leverage. Power enhanced by disciplined eye. Swings and misses too often and can get long. Has plus arm and runs OK for size, but power is ticket to majors.

Galvez, Jonathan — 4 — San Diego

EXP MLB DEBUT: 2014 | **POTENTIAL:** Starting 2B | **8D**

Bats R | Age 22 | 2007 NDFA, D.R.

Pwr + + | BAvg + + + | Spd + + + | Def + +

Year	Lev	Team	AB	R	H	HR	RBI	Avg	OB	Slg	OPS	bb%	ct%	Eye	SB	CS	x/h%	Iso	RC/G
2009	Rk	Padres	193	45	57	6	27	295	390	503	893	13	77	0.68	14	6	44	207	6.98
2010	A	Fort Wayne	398	64	103	10	49	259	353	397	750	13	70	0.48	18	7	31	138	5.11
2011	A+	Lake Elsinore	488	84	142	13	86	291	346	465	811	8	75	0.33	37	9	38	174	5.64
2012	AA	San Antonio	312	47	91	6	35	292	356	426	782	9	78	0.44	12	3	31	135	5.27

Wiry, athletic INF was a consistent peformer in '12 after getting a late start due to an ankle injury. Still needs to make more consistent contact, but he does draw a good number of walks. Moves well defensively, but below-average arm caused him to shift from SS to 2B where he profiles better.

Garcia, Anthony — 7 — St. Louis

EXP MLB DEBUT: 2014 | **POTENTIAL:** Backup OF | **6C**

Bats R | Age 21 | 2009 (18) HS, P.R.

Pwr + + + | BAvg + + | Spd + + | Def + +

Year	Lev	Team	AB	R	H	HR	RBI	Avg	OB	Slg	OPS	bb%	ct%	Eye	SB	CS	x/h%	Iso	RC/G
2009	Rk	GCL Cardinals	51	12	12	0	3	235	291	333	624	7	80	0.40	2	1	33	98	3.33
2010	Rk	Johnson City	3	1	1	0	1	333	500	667	1167	25	67	1.00	0	0	100	333	12.77
2010	Rk	GCL Cardinals	116	20	33	5	20	284	385	457	842	14	85	1.12	2	0	27	172	6.15
2011	Rk	Johnson City	182	38	56	6	31	308	379	527	907	10	80	0.58	4	1	43	220	6.91
2012	A	Quad Cities	396	63	111	19	74	280	337	525	862	8	73	0.32	3	6	50	245	6.32

Strong, professional hitter doesn't get as much attention as he should. Has a nice compact swing and the ball jumps off his bat. Is a below-average runner and is questionable on defense, but his bat is good enough to get him to the next level.

Garcia, Avisail — 9 — Detroit

EXP MLB DEBUT: 2012 | **POTENTIAL:** Starting OF | **9D**

Bats R | Age 22 | 2007 FA (Venezuela)

Pwr + + + + | BAvg + + + | Spd + + + | Def + + +

Year	Lev	Team	AB	R	H	HR	RBI	Avg	OB	Slg	OPS	bb%	ct%	Eye	SB	CS	x/h%	Iso	RC/G
2010	A	West Michigan	494	58	139	4	63	281	309	356	666	4	77	0.18	20	4	18	75	3.49
2011	A+	Lakeland	488	53	129	11	56	264	291	389	680	4	73	0.14	14	5	26	125	3.65
2012	A+	Lakeland	266	47	77	8	36	289	318	447	765	4	79	0.19	14	4	27	158	4.69
2012	AA	Erie	215	31	67	6	22	312	333	465	798	3	82	0.18	9	4	27	153	5.02
2012	MLB	Detroit	47	7	15	0	3	319	360	319	679	6	79	0.30	0	2	0	0	3.71

Athletic, strong OF who leveraged career year into platoon role in MLB playoffs. Has boatload of tools, led by above avg raw power. Cut down on Ks while setting career high in HR and SB. Hits LHP and RHP with quick swing. Rarely works counts and can expand strike zone. Solid-avg RF with avg speed and strong arm.

Garcia, Jonathan — 8 — Los Angeles (N)

EXP MLB DEBUT: 2015 | **POTENTIAL:** Backup OF | **6D**

Bats R | Age 21 | 2009 (8) HS, P.R.

Pwr + + + | BAvg + | Spd + | Def + +

Year	Lev	Team	AB	R	H	HR	RBI	Avg	OB	Slg	OPS	bb%	ct%	Eye	SB	CS	x/h%	Iso	RC/G
2009	Rk	Dodgers	138	22	42	3	21	304	351	500	851	7	73	0.27	4	0	48	196	6.27
2010	Rk	Ogden	239	45	73	10	40	305	357	527	884	7	75	0.32	4	1	42	222	6.50
2011	A	Great Lakes	464	58	106	19	63	228	281	420	701	7	71	0.26	2	1	46	192	4.08
2012	A+	Rancho Cuc	378	54	88	12	41	233	262	386	648	4	65	0.11	2	3	36	153	3.40

Short, toolsy OF failed to bounce-back in the CAL, leaving his future very much in doubt. Has good power for his size, runs well, and can drive the ball, but hit just .233. Defensively he covers lots of ground and has a strong throwing arm. Still young but struck out 134 times while walking just 15.

Garcia, Leury — 46 — Texas

EXP MLB DEBUT: 2014 | **POTENTIAL:** Starting 2B/SS | **7B**

Bats B | Age 22 | 2007 FA (DR)

Pwr + + | BAvg + + + | Spd + + + + | Def + + + +

Year	Lev	Team	AB	R	H	HR	RBI	Avg	OB	Slg	OPS	bb%	ct%	Eye	SB	CS	x/h%	Iso	RC/G
2009	A	Hickory	276	28	64	1	18	232	279	286	565	6	77	0.28	19	6	16	54	2.34
2010	Rk	Rangers	18	5	9	0	2	500	591	611	1202	18	78	1.00	4	2	22	111	11.55
2010	A	Hickory	359	57	94	3	22	262	306	323	629	6	84	0.40	47	9	13	61	3.25
2011	A+	Myrtle Beach	442	65	113	3	38	256	300	342	642	6	77	0.28	30	12	24	86	3.34
2012	AA	Frisco	377	55	110	2	30	292	331	398	729	6	79	0.28	31	7	23	106	4.47

Short, compact INF who has advanced one level per year, but shows improvement. Speed and defense stand out. Exhibits plus speed with range to both sides and strong arm. Makes tough plays look easy with nimble actions. Flat swing path and below avg strength limit power, but has good feel and can play small ball.

Garcia, Willy — 7 — Pittsburgh

EXP MLB DEBUT: 2015 | **POTENTIAL:** Starting OF | **7D**

Bats R | Age 20 | 2010 NDFA, D.R.

Pwr + + + | BAvg + + | Spd + + + | Def + + +

Year	Lev	Team	AB	R	H	HR	RBI	Avg	OB	Slg	OPS	bb%	ct%	Eye	SB	CS	x/h%	Iso	RC/G
2011	Rk	GCL Pirates	177	26	47	5	35	266	309	446	755	6	72	0.22	7	5	38	181	4.85
2011	A-	State College	7	1	2	0	0	286	286	286	571	0	100	1.00	0	0	0	0	2.76
2012	A	West Virginia	459	57	110	18	77	240	289	403	692	7	71	0.24	10	8	34	163	3.90

Tall, lean OF has lots of potential, but is still very raw. Is already tapping into his raw power as a 19-year-old. Has above-average speed, but isn't a burner. Struggled with breaking balls and will need to tone down his approach (131 K with 33 BB) and make more consistent contact.

Garfield, Cameron — 2 — Milwaukee

EXP MLB DEBUT: 2014 | **POTENTIAL:** Backup C | **6C**

Bats R | Age 22 | 2009 (2) HS, CA

Pwr + + | BAvg + + | Spd + + | Def + + +

Year	Lev	Team	AB	R	H	HR	RBI	Avg	OB	Slg	OPS	bb%	ct%	Eye	SB	CS	x/h%	Iso	RC/G
2009	Rk	Helena	218	26	54	4	21	248	281	353	634	4	72	0.16	3	4	28	106	3.09
2010	A	Wisconsin	384	41	94	3	46	245	286	318	603	5	81	0.30	2	4	23	73	2.85
2011	Rk	Brewers	36	7	13	2	10	361	395	667	1061	5	75	0.22	0	0	46	306	8.74
2011	A	Wisconsin	17	3	2	0	2	118	167	176	343	6	82	0.33	0	1	50	59	-0.14
2012	A	Wisconsin	225	33	67	11	33	298	373	524	897	11	81	0.64	3	1	43	227	6.66

Strong defensive-minded backstop finally mastered Low-A, but can't seem to stay healthy. Was limited to just 225 AB with a knee injury. When he did return, he showed nice power and good plate discipline. Has a strong arm, but does not have a quick release and sometimes struggles blocking balls.

Gelalich, Jeff

9 | Cincinnati | EXP MLB DEBUT: 2015 | POTENTIAL: Starting RF | 7C

Bats L Age 22
2012 (1-S) UCLA
Pwr ++
BAvg +++
Spd +++
Def +++

Year	Lev	Team	AB	R	H	HR	RBI	Avg	OB	Slg	OPS	bb%	ct%	Eye	SB	CS	x/h%	Iso	RC/G
2012	Rk	Billings	127	27	31	2	9	244	319	378	697	10	67	0.33	4	1	35	134	4.40

Solid OF showed a good all-around approach, hitting for average and power at UCLA. Runs well and has the potential for power and speed. Simple, compact swing with good bat speed and strike zone judgment allows him to barrel the ball. Arm is likely a bit short for RF so CF or LF are the most likely destinations.

Gennett, Scooter

4 | Milwaukee | EXP MLB DEBUT: 2014 | POTENTIAL: Starting 2B | 7C

Bats L Age 23
2009 (16) HS, FL
Pwr ++
BAvg +++
Spd ++
Def ++++

Year	Lev	Team	AB	R	H	HR	RBI	Avg	OB	Slg	OPS	bb%	ct%	Eye	SB	CS	x/h%	Iso	RC/G
2010	A	Wisconsin	482	87	149	9	55	309	351	463	814	6	81	0.34	14	4	35	154	5.49
2011	A+	Brevard County	556	74	167	9	51	300	333	406	739	5	88	0.39	11	10	21	106	4.49
2012	AA	Huntsville	533	66	156	5	44	293	328	385	713	5	87	0.39	11	5	24	92	4.23

Short, athletic INF plays the game with intensity. Has a compact, line-drive approach and puts the ball into play. Generates a bit of pop, with above-average speed, but only average plate discipline. Solid defender with good range and soft hands. Has a chance because of his bat and work ethic.

Gillaspie, Conor

5 | San Francisco | EXP MLB DEBUT: 2008 | POTENTIAL: Backup 3B | 6C

Bats L Age 25
2008 (1-S) Wichita St
Pwr ++
BAvg ++
4.35 Spd ++
Def ++

Year	Lev	Team	AB	R	H	HR	RBI	Avg	OB	Slg	OPS	bb%	ct%	Eye	SB	CS	x/h%	Iso	RC/G
2010	AA	Richmond	491	57	141	8	67	287	337	420	757	7	86	0.55	0	4	29	132	4.88
2011	AAA	Fresno	428	63	127	11	61	297	391	453	844	13	82	0.84	9	9	31	157	6.26
2011	MLB	San Francisco	19	2	5	1	2	263	333	421	754	10	95	2.00	0	0	20	158	4.95
2012	AAA	Fresno	413	60	116	14	49	281	346	441	786	9	87	0.76	0	0	30	160	5.25
2012	MLB	San Francisco	20	2	3	0	2	150	150	200	350	0	90	0.00	0	0	33	50	0.10

Continues to work hard and had three stints with the Giants. Has decent athleticism, but is not a burner. Has good bat speed and extension through the zone and makes consistent, hard contact. Showed improved power with a career high in HR and has plus strike zone judgment. Continues to improve defensively and split time at 3B, 1B, and DH.

Gillies, Tyson

7 | Philadelphia | EXP MLB DEBUT: 2013 | POTENTIAL: Starting LF | 7C

Bats L Age 24
2005 (26) HS, Canada
Pwr ++
BAvg +++
Spd ++++
Def +++

Year	Lev	Team	AB	R	H	HR	RBI	Avg	OB	Slg	OPS	bb%	ct%	Eye	SB	CS	x/h%	Iso	RC/G
2010	AA	Reading	105	15	25	2	6	238	273	333	606	5	77	0.21	2	2	20	95	2.72
2011	A+	Clearwater	13	1	2	0	0	154	154	308	462	0	92	0.00	0	0	100	154	1.60
2012	A	Lakewood	5	2	2	0	0	400	571	400	971	29	100	1.00	0	0	0	0	9.16
2012	A+	Clearwater	17	1	3	0	0	176	176	235	412	0	59	0.00	1	0	33	59	
2012	AA	Reading	276	59	84	4	24	304	347	453	800	6	81	0.35	8	6	30	149	5.36

Strong, athletic, OF continues to have issues. This year was suspended for arguing with the team bus driver. In the past he's had legal problems and a series of injuries. When he's on the field, he continues to look dynamic. Can play all three OF slots and has a plus arm. Just needs to stay healthy and out of trouble.

Gindl, Caleb

9 | Milwaukee | EXP MLB DEBUT: 2013 | POTENTIAL: Platoon LF/RF | 6C

Bats L Age 24
2007 (5) HS, FL
Pwr ++
BAvg ++
Spd +++
Def ++

Year	Lev	Team	AB	R	H	HR	RBI	Avg	OB	Slg	OPS	bb%	ct%	Eye	SB	CS	x/h%	Iso	RC/G
2008	A	West Virginia	508	86	156	13	81	307	384	474	858	11	72	0.44	14	5	35	167	6.55
2009	A+	Brevard County	394	61	109	17	71	277	368	459	827	13	77	0.62	18	4	32	183	5.93
2010	AA	Huntsville	463	61	126	9	60	272	349	406	755	11	83	0.71	10	5	34	134	5.03
2011	AAA	Nashville	472	84	145	15	60	307	389	472	861	12	80	0.68	6	5	30	165	6.34
2012	AAA	Nashville	452	54	118	12	50	261	317	423	740	8	78	0.38	4	1	37	162	4.63

Short OF has a decent offensive game, but looked less dynamic in repeat of PCL. Regressed across the board and now looks more like a 4th OF. Plate discipline dropped off noticably as pitchers got ahead of him. Speed is an asset on the bases, but doesn't translate to SB or range in the OF.

Glaesmann, Todd

89 | Tampa Bay | EXP MLB DEBUT: 2015 | POTENTIAL: Starting OF | 8D

Bats R Age 22
2009 (3) HS (TX)
Pwr ++++
BAvg ++
Spd +++
Def +++

Year	Lev	Team	AB	R	H	HR	RBI	Avg	OB	Slg	OPS	bb%	ct%	Eye	SB	CS	x/h%	Iso	RC/G
2010	Rk	Princeton	236	41	55	4	24	233	273	398	671	5	70	0.19	13	6	47	165	3.82
2011	Rk	GCL Rays	37	7	8	0	0	216	310	243	553	12	73	0.50	6	1	13	27	2.34
2011	A	Bowling Green	210	28	48	4	21	229	277	343	620	6	60	0.16	6	0	29	114	3.30
2012	A	Bowling Green	352	57	99	13	53	281	324	469	792	6	75	0.25	8	3	35	188	5.21
2012	A+	Charlotte	139	20	41	8	22	295	333	554	887	5	75	0.23	0	0	44	259	6.37

Strong, natural-hitting OF who set easy career high in HR by focusing on driving hittable pitches. Learned to swing with more authority, but can be overzealous. Showed improved pitch recognition. Ideal tools to project as big league RF with plus arm strength and power profile. Can play CF with good speed and terrific range.

Goeddel, Tyler

5 | Tampa Bay | EXP MLB DEBUT: 2015 | POTENTIAL: Starting 3B | 8D

Bats R Age 20
2011 (1-S) HS (CA)
Pwr ++
BAvg +++
Spd ++++
Def ++

Year	Lev	Team	AB	R	H	HR	RBI	Avg	OB	Slg	OPS	bb%	ct%	Eye	SB	CS	x/h%	Iso	RC/G
2012	A	Bowling Green	329	52	81	6	46	246	324	371	695	10	71	0.40	30	5	33	125	4.24

Tall, athletic player who oozes projection with loose, quick swing. Uses level swing path and will need leverage to realize plus power. Focuses on contact, though aggressive approach needs to be tamed. Runs extremely well and should maintain speed when body fills out. Needs to improve first-step quickness, but arm strength and hands are positives.

Goetzman, Granden

79 | Tampa Bay | EXP MLB DEBUT: 2016 | POTENTIAL: Starting OF | 8D

Bats R Age 20
2011 (2) HS (FL)
Pwr ++++
BAvg ++
Spd +++
Def ++

Year	Lev	Team	AB	R	H	HR	RBI	Avg	OB	Slg	OPS	bb%	ct%	Eye	SB	CS	x/h%	Iso	RC/G
2011	Rk	GCL Rays	75	8	13	0	8	173	253	213	466	10	77	0.47	6	1	23	40	1.26
2012	Rk	Princeton	47	10	14	1	8	298	353	468	821	8	85	0.57	7	1	43	170	5.69

Tall, strong OF whose season ended after 47 AB due to stress fracture in back. Has pure tools with above avg raw power and solid-avg speed. Could put together 20/20 seasons. Tweaked swing to create leverage and has impressive bat speed. Long swing could lead to low BA. Also has trouble staying healthy.

Golden, Reggie

8 | Chicago (N) | EXP MLB DEBUT: 2015 | POTENTIAL: Starting CF | 7D

Bats R Age 21
2010 (2) HS, AL
Pwr +++
BAvg ++
Spd ++
Def ++

Year	Lev	Team	AB	R	H	HR	RBI	Avg	OB	Slg	OPS	bb%	ct%	Eye	SB	CS	x/h%	Iso	RC/G
2010	Rk	Cubs	15	3	5	0	1	333	375	400	775	6	53	0.14	1	0	20	67	6.71
2011	A-	Boise	231	36	56	7	39	242	324	420	744	11	71	0.41	5	2	39	177	4.94
2012	A	Peoria	26	1	5	0	0	192	222	192	415	4	65	0.11	1	0	0	0	

Short, muscular, OF suffered torn ACL and was limited to just 26 AB. Prior to the injury was a legit 5-tool player, but he's had just 272 AB since being drafted. Has good power and bat speed and runs well with a strong arm. Still has the potential to develop into an exciting player, but needs to prove he can stay healthy.

Gomes, Yan

235 | Cleveland | EXP MLB DEBUT: 2012 | POTENTIAL: Utility player | 6B

Bats R Age 25
2009 (10) Barry
Pwr ++++
BAvg +++
Spd +
Def ++

Year	Lev	Team	AB	R	H	HR	RBI	Avg	OB	Slg	OPS	bb%	ct%	Eye	SB	CS	x/h%	Iso	RC/G
2010	A+	Dunedin	233	37	64	9	40	275	302	489	791	4	73	0.14	0	0	48	215	5.19
2011	AA	New Hampshire	276	34	69	13	51	250	312	464	776	8	73	0.33	0	0	46	214	5.12
2011	AAA	Las Vegas	14	1	3	0	1	214	267	286	552	7	71	0.25	0	0	33	71	2.19
2012	AAA	Las Vegas	305	44	100	13	59	328	379	557	936	8	76	0.35	4	0	43	230	7.16
2012	MLB	Toronto	98	9	20	4	13	204	250	367	617	6	67	0.19	0	0	40	163	2.86

Versatile prospect who reached big leagues on basis of strong offense and showed enough with glove to profile as utility player. Has big and strong frame that produces above avg pop. Hit for nice BA, though needs to improve selectivity and pitch recognition. Quick behind plate with strong arm, but lacks instincts.

Gomez, Hector

6 | Milwaukee | EXP MLB DEBUT: 2011 | POTENTIAL: Starting SS | 7C

Bats R Age 25
2005 NDFA, D.R.
Pwr +
BAvg +++
Spd +++
Def +++

Year	Lev	Team	AB	R	H	HR	RBI	Avg	OB	Slg	OPS	bb%	ct%	Eye	SB	CS	x/h%	Iso	RC/G
2010	A-	Tri-City	69	8	17	2	7	246	297	391	689	7	78	0.33	0	3	29	145	3.89
2011	AA	Tulsa	425	46	100	14	50	235	268	416	684	4	78	0.20	16	4	43	181	3.74
2011	MLB	Colorado	6	1	2	0	0	333	429	333	762	14	67	0.50	0	0	0	0	5.49
2012	A+	Modesto	8	2	3	0	3	375	500	625	1125	20	50	0.50	1	0	33	250	15.04
2012	A+	Brevard County	76	9	8	1	8	105	150	211	361	5	75	0.21	0	0	63	105	

Wiry, athletic INF with plus defensive skills was picked up on waivers from the Rockies. Suffered a serious groin injury and was re-injured in the off-season. Prior to that, he had disappointed due to poor plate discipline and low contact rate. When healthy he has plus range with a strong arm.

Gonzalez, Elevys — 5 — Los Angeles (N)

EXP MLB DEBUT: 2014 | POTENTIAL: Backup 3B | 6C

Bats B Age 23 | 2008 NDFA, Venezuela | Pwr ++ | BAvg ++ | Spd +++ | Def +++

Year	Lev	Team	AB	R	H	HR	RBI	Avg	OB	Slg	OPS	bb%	ct%	Eye	SB	CS	x/h%	Iso	RC/G
2009	A-	State College	51	5	11	0	3	216	231	333	564	2	73	0.07	2	1	36	118	2.26
2010	A	West Virginia	236	30	65	6	31	275	360	424	783	12	80	0.65	8	11	29	148	5.39
2011	A+	Bradenton	454	63	146	6	83	322	375	467	842	8	80	0.42	7	5	33	145	6.02
2012	A+	Bradenton	148	17	32	4	20	216	329	372	701	14	72	0.60	3	3	44	155	4.45
2012	AA	Altoona	148	10	29	2	15	196	265	291	556	9	72	0.33	1	3	31	95	2.23

Short, switch-hitting 3B was taken by the Dodgers in the Rule 5 Draft. Has played a variety of positions, but seems to have settled in at 3B. Put up impressive numbers in '11, but struggled to repeat. Has below-average power for the position, but is a capable defender. This might be his last chance to make an impact.

Goodwin, Brian — 8 — Washington

EXP MLB DEBUT: 2015 | POTENTIAL: Starting CF | 9D

Bats L Age 22 | 2011 (1-S) Miami Dade JC | Pwr ++++ | BAvg +++ | Spd +++ | Def ++++

Year	Lev	Team	AB	R	H	HR	RBI	Avg	OB	Slg	OPS	bb%	ct%	Eye	SB	CS	x/h%	Iso	RC/G
2010	NCAA	North Carolina	227	47	66	7	63	291	408	511	919	17	78	0.92	7	2	42	220	7.49
2012	A	Hagerstown	216	47	70	9	38	324	436	542	978	17	82	1.10	15	4	40	218	8.07
2012	AA	Harrisburg	166	17	37	5	14	223	299	373	672	10	70	0.36	3	3	38	151	3.84

Athletic OF can do a bit of everything. Missed 5 weeks with an injury, but then hit .319 at Low-A. Has plus speed, solid strike zone judgment, and a compact LH stroke. He has good raw power and should hit for average. Defensively he covers ground well with a strong arm. Has the potential to be a 20/20 guy.

Green, Dean — 3 — Detroit

EXP MLB DEBUT: 2014 | POTENTIAL: Reserve 1B | 6B

Bats L Age 24 | 2011 (11) Barry | Pwr +++ | BAvg ++ | Spd + | Def ++

Year	Lev	Team	AB	R	H	HR	RBI	Avg	OB	Slg	OPS	bb%	ct%	Eye	SB	CS	x/h%	Iso	RC/G
2010	NCAA	Oklahoma St	166	34	44	6	23	265	326	452	778	8	86	0.63	0	0	43	187	5.11
2011	A-	Connecticut	246	33	84	7	44	341	386	520	907	7	86	0.51	1	0	33	179	6.55
2012	Rk	GCL Tigers	32	1	3	0	5	94	194	94	288	11	84	0.80	0	0	0	0	
2012	A	West Michigan	219	34	67	9	38	306	372	502	874	10	82	0.59	0	3	37	196	6.30
2012	A+	Lakeland	141	16	49	3	36	348	378	518	896	5	82	0.28	2	0	33	170	6.38

Muscular 1B who brings imposing figure and patient approach to plate. Game is all about bat as he has ability to battle LHP and makes good contact for power profile. Rarely swings at bad pitches, but is solely a FB hitter who struggles to recognize breaking balls. Speed and defense are well below avg.

Green, Grant — 4578 — Oakland

EXP MLB DEBUT: 2013 | POTENTIAL: Starting 2B | 8B

Bats R Age 25 | 2009 (1) USC | Pwr +++ | BAvg ++++ | Spd +++ | Def +++

Year	Lev	Team	AB	R	H	HR	RBI	Avg	OB	Slg	OPS	bb%	ct%	Eye	SB	CS	x/h%	Iso	RC/G
2009	NCAA	USC	211	46	79	4	32	374	429	569	997	9	82	0.53	16	8	35	194	7.94
2009	A+	Stockton	19	2	6	0	3	316	350	368	718	5	74	0.20	1	0	17	53	4.30
2010	A+	Stockton	548	107	174	20	87	318	362	520	882	6	79	0.32	9	5	37	203	6.33
2011	AA	Midland	530	76	154	9	62	291	339	408	747	7	78	0.33	6	8	28	117	4.69
2012	AAA	Sacramento	524	73	155	15	75	296	338	458	796	6	86	0.44	13	9	32	162	5.19

Natural hitter who has moved all over diamond and being moved to 2B after 3B and CF in '12. Made much better contact and reduced K rate while hitting for high BA. Possesses smooth swing and tapping into moderate pop potential. Has defensive skills despite new positions and plays with good range and avg arm.

Green, Taylor — 54 — Milwaukee

EXP MLB DEBUT: 2011 | POTENTIAL: Backup 3B | 7D

Bats L Age 26 | 2005 (26) Cypress JC | Pwr +++ | BAvg +++ | 4.40 Spd ++ | Def ++

Year	Lev	Team	AB	R	H	HR	RBI	Avg	OB	Slg	OPS	bb%	ct%	Eye	SB	CS	x/h%	Iso	RC/G
2011	AA	Huntsville	11	2	4	0	3	364	364	455	818	0	73	0.00	0	0	25	91	5.42
2011	AAA	Nashville	420	74	141	22	88	336	413	583	996	12	83	0.76	1	0	42	248	7.89
2011	MLB	Milwaukee	37	2	10	0	1	270	270	351	622	0	84	0.00	0	0	30	81	2.88
2012	AAA	Nashville	282	24	77	7	29	273	339	408	747	9	80	0.49	1	3	31	135	4.76
2012	MLB	Milwaukee	103	8	19	3	14	184	257	340	596	9	77	0.42	0	0	53	155	2.81

Strong 3B with above-average power and a plus bat. Finally got a chance to see extended action in the majors and fell flat. Makes consistent, hard contact and has solid bat speed, giving him the potential to hit for average and power. He has soft hands with a decent arm, but is below-average defensively and needs to crush the ball to have value.

Green, Zach — 6 — Philadelphia

EXP MLB DEBUT: 2016 | POTENTIAL: Starting SS | 7C

Bats R Age 19 | 2012 (3) HS, CA | Pwr +++ | BAvg ++ | Spd ++ | Def ++

Year	Lev	Team	AB	R	H	HR	RBI	Avg	OB	Slg	OPS	bb%	ct%	Eye	SB	CS	x/h%	Iso	RC/G
2012	Rk	GCL Phillies	169	20	48	3	21	284	316	426	742	5	75	0.19	2	2	35	142	4.59

A tall, strong INF who has good bat speed and raw power. Needs to polish his game on both sides of the ball. His swing can get complicated and he needs to be more patient and make better contact. He is young and has time to develop, but also a long way to go.

Greene, Larry — 7 — Philadelphia

EXP MLB DEBUT: 2015 | POTENTIAL: Starting 1B | 8D

Bats L Age 20 | 2011 (1) HS, GA | Pwr ++++ | BAvg ++ | Spd ++ | Def ++

Year	Lev	Team	AB	R	H	HR	RBI	Avg	OB	Slg	OPS	bb%	ct%	Eye	SB	CS	x/h%	Iso	RC/G
2012	A-	Williamsport	257	36	70	2	26	272	372	381	754	14	70	0.53	1	2	34	109	5.35

Strong, athletic 1st rounder had an rough debut. Arrived in camp out of shape and didn't make his debut until June. Has strength and a strong arm, but poor conditioning will likely cause him to move to 1B. Continues to show plus power, but struggled to hit in game action. Still young, but will need to show more in '13.

Gregorius, Didi — 6 — Arizona

EXP MLB DEBUT: 2012 | POTENTIAL: Starting SS | 8C

Bats L Age 23 | 2008 NDFA, Netherlands | Pwr ++ | BAvg ++ | Spd +++ | Def ++++

Year	Lev	Team	AB	R	H	HR	RBI	Avg	OB	Slg	OPS	bb%	ct%	Eye	SB	CS	x/h%	Iso	RC/G
2011	A+	Bakersfield	188	30	57	5	28	303	338	457	796	5	87	0.40	8	8	32	154	5.14
2011	AA	Carolina	148	18	40	2	16	270	312	392	704	6	83	0.36	3	2	28	122	4.15
2012	AA	Pensacola	316	45	88	1	31	278	339	373	713	8	84	0.59	3	4	23	95	4.48
2012	AAA	Louisville	185	25	45	6	23	243	289	427	716	6	83	0.39	0	2	42	184	4.27
2012	MLB	Cincinnati	20	1	6	0	2	300	300	300	600	0	75	0.00	0	0	0	0	2.34

Slick fielding INF has developed into one of the better all-around SS in the minors. Has good range, a great glove, and a strong arm. Has just moderate bat speed and minimal power. Can be overly aggressive and will need a better approach to hit for average in the majors, but the defense is major league ready right now.

Grichuk, Randal — 89 — Los Angeles (A)

EXP MLB DEBUT: 2015 | POTENTIAL: Starting OF | 8C

Bats R Age 21 | 2009 (1) HS (TX) | Pwr ++++ | BAvg +++ | Spd +++ | Def +++

Year	Lev	Team	AB	R	H	HR	RBI	Avg	OB	Slg	OPS	bb%	ct%	Eye	SB	CS	x/h%	Iso	RC/G
2010	A	Cedar Rapids	202	41	59	7	36	292	322	530	852	4	75	0.18	4	0	51	238	6.02
2011	Rk	Angels	24	2	8	0	6	333	385	458	843	8	83	0.50	0	0	25	125	6.05
2011	A	Cedar Rapids	122	12	28	2	13	230	266	402	667	5	76	0.21	0	1	46	172	3.69
2011	A+	Inland Empire	53	13	15	1	6	283	283	491	774	0	75	0.00	0	0	47	208	4.85
2012	A+	Inland Empire	537	79	160	18	71	298	327	488	815	4	83	0.25	16	6	36	190	5.30

Pure athlete who stayed healthy and was especially hot last three months (.330, 15 HR). Set career highs in HR and SB while crushing LHP (.353). Plus bat speed suggests more pop to come and has good speed for SB. Pitch selection needs work and could use better plate coverage. Plays solid RF defense with avg arm and range.

Grossman, Robbie — 78 — Houston

EXP MLB DEBUT: 2014 | POTENTIAL: Starting CF | 7C

Bats B Age 23 | 2008 (6) HS (TX) | Pwr ++ | BAvg +++ | Spd +++ | Def +++

Year	Lev	Team	AB	R	H	HR	RBI	Avg	OB	Slg	OPS	bb%	ct%	Eye	SB	CS	x/h%	Iso	RC/G
2009	A	West Virginia	451	83	120	5	42	266	371	355	725	14	64	0.46	35	12	23	89	5.07
2010	A+	Bradenton	470	84	115	4	50	245	338	345	682	12	75	0.56	15	8	31	100	4.19
2011	A+	Bradenton	490	127	144	13	56	294	418	451	869	18	77	0.94	24	10	34	157	6.85
2012	AA	Altoona	350	59	93	7	36	266	372	406	777	14	78	0.76	9	10	33	140	5.51
2012	AA	Corpus Christi	135	22	36	3	11	267	353	422	775	12	68	0.42	4	1	36	156	5.55

Patient hitter who has keen understanding of K zone. Covers plate well with bat control. Better hitter from right side with more pop, though won't jerk too many out of park. Ks a lot despite fringy power, but runs well and is a good baserunner. Good range in CF and may be better in LF, though he'll need more pop.

Guerrero, Gabriel — 9 — Seattle

EXP MLB DEBUT: 2017 | POTENTIAL: Starting OF | 9E

Bats R Age 19 | 2011 FA (DR) | Pwr ++++ | BAvg +++ | Spd ++ | Def ++

Year	Lev	Team	AB	R	H	HR	RBI	Avg	OB	Slg	OPS	bb%	ct%	Eye	SB	CS	x/h%	Iso	RC/G
2012	Rk	Arizona Mariners	75	17	25	4	18	333	359	560	919	4	83	0.23	0	0	36	227	6.40

Tall, very projectable OF who had outstanding debut. Covers plate with long arms and makes easy, hard contact. Exhibits bat speed and should grow into plus power. Destroys LHP, but free-swinging ways could get him in trouble. Secondary skills lag and lack of speed relegates him to OF corner. Strong arm is asset.

Gumbs, Angelo

4 | **New York (A)** | EXP MLB DEBUT: 2015 | POTENTIAL: Starting 2B | **8C**

Bats R Age 20
2010 (2) HS (CA)

- Pwr + + -
- BAvg + + -
- Spd + + -
- Def + +

Year	Lev	Team	AB	R	H	HR	RBI	Avg	OB	Slg	OPS	bb%	ct%	Eye	SB	CS	x/h%	Iso	RC/G
2010	Rk	GCL Yankees	26	1	5	0	0	192	222	231	453	4	88	0.33	3	0	20	38	1.31
2011	A-	Staten Island	197	32	52	3	29	264	332	406	738	9	71	0.35	11	7	35	142	4.87
2012	A	Charleston (Sc)	257	40	70	7	36	272	320	432	752	7	77	0.30	26	3	34	160	4.73

Athletic, strong INF who ended season after torn elbow ligament. Will be healthy for ST and should continue to hit. Drives ball with plus bat speed, but struggles with long swing. Exhibits more line drive pop at present, but has avg power potential. Not an agile defender, but has improved glovework and good quickness.

Guyer, Brandon

789 | **Tampa Bay** | EXP MLB DEBUT: 2011 | POTENTIAL: Starting OF | **8D**

Bats R Age 27
2007 (5) Virginia

- Pwr + + -
- BAvg + + -
- Spd + + -
- Def + + -

Year	Lev	Team	AB	R	H	HR	RBI	Avg	OB	Slg	OPS	bb%	ct%	Eye	SB	CS	x/h%	Iso	RC/G
2010	AA	Tennessee	369	76	127	13	58	344	389	588	977	7	86	0.53	30	3	46	244	7.41
2011	AAA	Durham	388	78	121	14	61	312	369	521	889	8	80	0.44	16	6	40	209	6.53
2011	MLB	Tampa Bay	41	7	8	2	3	195	214	366	580	2	78	0.11	0	0	38	171	2.18
2012	AAA	Durham	85	9	25	3	13	294	348	459	807	8	82	0.47	2	0	28	165	5.37
2012	MLB	Tampa Bay	7	2	1	1	1	143	143	571	714	0	86	0.00	0	0	100	429	3.45

Fluid, well-rounded OF has been on verge of winning big league job, but tore labrum in shoulder and season ended in May. Exhibits nice tools and could develop into everyday player despite age. Fluid, quick swing with strength and leverage. Owns plus speed and solid defensive instincts with strong arm.

Guzman, Ronald

3 | **Texas** | EXP MLB DEBUT: 2016 | POTENTIAL: Starting OF | **8D**

Bats L Age 18
2011 FA (DR)

- Pwr + + -
- BAvg + + -
- Spd + +
- Def + +

Year	Lev	Team	AB	R	H	HR	RBI	Avg	OB	Slg	OPS	bb%	ct%	Eye	SB	CS	x/h%	Iso	RC/G
2012	Rk	Rangers	212	29	68	1	33	321	377	434	811	8	80	0.45	7	1	28	113	5.66

Long, lean OF who was high profile international sign and exceeded expectations. Shows ability to hit LHP (.358) with feel for contact. Swings effortlessly with moderate bat speed and has advanced approach for OBP. May only hit for avg pop, but should hit lots of 2B. Lacks speed and has work to do at 1B.

Gyorko, Jedd

5 | **San Diego** | EXP MLB DEBUT: 2013 | POTENTIAL: Starting 3B | **8B**

Bats R Age 24
2010 (2) West Virginia

- Pwr + + -
- BAvg + + -
- Spd + + -
- Def + +

Year	Lev	Team	AB	R	H	HR	RBI	Avg	OB	Slg	OPS	bb%	ct%	Eye	SB	CS	x/h%	Iso	RC/G
2010	A-	Eugene	106	16	35	5	18	330	383	528	911	8	75	0.35	1	1	31	198	6.77
2011	A+	Lake Elsinore	340	78	124	18	74	365	429	638	1067	10	81	0.59	11	3	44	274	8.74
2011	AA	San Antonio	236	41	68	7	40	288	359	428	787	10	79	0.52	1	0	28	140	5.28
2012	AA	San Antonio	130	18	34	6	17	262	347	431	778	12	79	0.63	1	1	29	169	5.15
2012	AAA	Tucson	369	62	121	24	83	328	385	588	973	8	82	0.50	4	3	40	260	7.33

Has quick hands, plus power, and is one of the better pure hitters in the minors. Hit .311 with 30 HR in '12. Remains steady on defense with good hands and a strong arm, but a thick lower half. The emergence of Chase Headley likely means he will have to move to a new position, but the bat is plus and should play somewhere.

Hager, Jake

6 | **Tampa Bay** | EXP MLB DEBUT: 2015 | POTENTIAL: Starting SS | **7B**

Bats R Age 20
2011 (1) HS (NV)

- Pwr + +
- BAvg + + -
- Spd + + -
- Def + +

Year	Lev	Team	AB	R	H	HR	RBI	Avg	OB	Slg	OPS	bb%	ct%	Eye	SB	CS	x/h%	Iso	RC/G
2011	Rk	Princeton	193	29	52	4	17	269	302	399	701	4	87	0.35	5	7	31	130	4.03
2012	A	Bowling Green	442	63	124	10	72	281	340	412	752	8	86	0.67	17	11	28	131	4.85

Instinctual, quick INF who maximizes avg tools with grinding nature. Makes consistent contact with short, compact stroke and offers good power. Makes adjustments and is tough out. Lacks standout tool and may eventually move to 2B where avg range is more appropriate. Owns soft hands with very strong arm.

Hague, Rick

6 | **Washington** | EXP MLB DEBUT: 2014 | POTENTIAL: Reserve SS/2B | **6C**

Bats R Age 24
2010 (3) Rice

- Pwr + +
- BAvg + +
- Spd + +
- Def + + -

Year	Lev	Team	AB	R	H	HR	RBI	Avg	OB	Slg	OPS	bb%	ct%	Eye	SB	CS	x/h%	Iso	RC/G
2010	NCAA	Rice	259	71	88	15	55	340	408	591	999	10	80	0.57	10	2	40	251	7.90
2010	Rk	GCL Nationals	40	7	11	0	6	275	396	300	696	17	78	0.89	3	0	9	25	4.58
2010	A	Hagerstown	159	26	52	3	27	327	382	522	904	8	79	0.41	3	2	38	195	6.86
2011	A+	Potomac	14	4	5	1	4	357	438	714	1152	13	93	2.00	1	0	60	357	9.55
2012	A+	Potomac	395	58	102	6	48	258	307	370	677	7	76	0.30	20	5	28	111	3.80

Missed most all of '11 with an injury. When he returned to action, he wasn't nearly as effective, but did manage to steal 20 bases. He has quick hands and a good approach, but his plate discipline regressesd. Defensively, he doesn't have the range for SS and split time at SS, 2B, and DH. Has a chance to become a UT player.

Hamilton, Billy

8 | **Cincinnati** | EXP MLB DEBUT: 2013 | POTENTIAL: Starting CF | **9D**

Bats R Age 22
2009 (2) HS, MS

- Pwr +
- BAvg + + -
- 3.60 Spd + + -
- Def + + -

Year	Lev	Team	AB	R	H	HR	RBI	Avg	OB	Slg	OPS	bb%	ct%	Eye	SB	CS	x/h%	Iso	RC/G
2009	Rk	GCL Reds	166	19	34	0	11	205	254	277	531	6	72	0.23	14	3	26	72	1.89
2010	Rk	Billings	283	61	90	2	24	318	379	456	835	9	80	0.50	48	9	28	138	6.03
2011	A	Dayton	550	99	153	3	50	278	341	360	701	9	76	0.39	103	20	20	82	4.25
2012	A+	Bakersfield	337	79	109	1	30	323	411	439	850	13	79	0.71	104	21	26	116	6.48
2012	AA	Pensacola	175	33	50	1	15	286	408	383	790	17	75	0.84	51	16	20	97	5.91

Had a season for the ages, stealing 155 bases. Has game changing speed and continues to improve at the plate. Managed to walk 86 times and ability to bunt and beat out infield hits should allow him to get on base. Struggled at SS due to a below-average arm. Saw action in CF in the AFL where he looked comfortable.

Haniger, Mitch

8 | **Milwaukee** | EXP MLB DEBUT: 2015 | POTENTIAL: Starting CF | **7C**

Bats R Age 22
2012 (1-S) Cal Poly

- Pwr + + -
- BAvg + +
- Spd + +
- Def + + -

Year	Lev	Team	AB	R	H	HR	RBI	Avg	OB	Slg	OPS	bb%	ct%	Eye	SB	CS	x/h%	Iso	RC/G
2010	NCAA	Cal Poly	68	15	24	2	11	353	421	515	936	11	75	0.47	3	4	29	162	7.39
2011	NCAA	Cal Poly	189	33	52	6	27	275	372	466	837	13	84	0.94	4	3	42	190	6.16
2012	NCAA	Cal Poly	211	48	73	13	64	346	441	626	1067	15	85	1.13	6	6	44	280	8.87
2012	A	Wisconsin	49	9	14	1	8	286	375	429	804	13	73	0.54	1	0	36	143	5.82

Strong OF was the 38th pick in the draft. Has good raw power but other tools are average. Avg bat speed and long swing could leave him in between the ability to hit for power and average. Doesn't have a ton of speed so sticking in CF seems unlikely. Saw limited action in his pro debut, but looked OK in the MWL

Hanson, Alen

6 | **Pittsburgh** | EXP MLB DEBUT: 2015 | POTENTIAL: Starting SS/2B | **8B**

Bats B Age 20
2009 NDFA, D.R.

- Pwr + + -
- BAvg + + -
- Spd + + -
- Def + +

Year	Lev	Team	AB	R	H	HR	RBI	Avg	OB	Slg	OPS	bb%	ct%	Eye	SB	CS	x/h%	Iso	RC/G
2011	Rk	GCL Pirates	198	42	52	2	35	263	333	429	763	10	83	0.62	24	6	42	167	5.19
2011	A-	State College	10	1	2	0	0	200	273	200	473	9	80	0.50	0	0	0	0	1.36
2012	A	West Virginia	489	99	151	16	62	309	379	528	906	10	79	0.52	35	19	41	219	6.93

Impressive breakout seasons and has an exciting mix of speed and power. Has an aggressive approach and can put a charge into the ball, but makes enough contact that he should be able to hit. Is below-average defensively and could be moved to 2B, but has the potential to be a 20/20 middle infielder.

Harrison, Travis

5 | **Minnesota** | EXP MLB DEBUT: 2015 | POTENTIAL: Starting 3B | **8D**

Bats R Age 20
2011 (1-S) HS (CA)

- Pwr + + -
- BAvg + + -
- Spd +
- Def + +

Year	Lev	Team	AB	R	H	HR	RBI	Avg	OB	Slg	OPS	bb%	ct%	Eye	SB	CS	x/h%	Iso	RC/G
2012	Rk	Elizabethton	219	39	66	5	27	301	370	461	832	10	77	0.47	3	0	32	160	5.99

Natural hitting INF who exhibited power in first season. Possesses strength in wrists and arms to make powerful contact. Should add more pop as he adds loft and leverage to stroke and advanced bat control allows for BA. Lacks athleticism or speed and suspect agility at 3B is concern. Could slide over to 1B.

Havens, Reese

6 | **New York (N)** | EXP MLB DEBUT: 2013 | POTENTIAL: Starting 2B | **7C**

Bats L Age 26
2008 (1) South Carolina

- Pwr + + -
- BAvg + + -
- 4.40 Spd + +
- Def + + -

Year	Lev	Team	AB	R	H	HR	RBI	Avg	OB	Slg	OPS	bb%	ct%	Eye	SB	CS	x/h%	Iso	RC/G
2010	A+	St. Lucie	57	9	16	3	7	281	369	509	878	12	68	0.44	0	1	38	228	6.88
2010	AA	Binghamton	68	12	23	6	12	338	392	662	1054	8	78	0.40	0	2	39	324	8.36
2011	A+	St. Lucie	11	1	3	0	2	273	385	455	839	15	55	0.40	0	0	67	182	8.19
2011	AA	Binghamton	211	37	61	6	26	289	370	455	825	11	72	0.46	2	0	36	166	6.06
2012	AA	Binghamton	325	41	70	10	39	215	334	351	685	15	65	0.51	1	1	34	135	4.25

Can't seem to stay healthy and bad back once again limited him to just 325 AB. When healthy, has shown the ability to hit for power and average. Has strong hands, good bat speed, and a solid understanding of the strike zone. Defensively he moves well, has soft hands, and strong throwing arm. Will need to prove he can stay healthy.

Hawkins, Christopher

79 | **Toronto** | EXP MLB DEBUT: 2015 | POTENTIAL: Starting OF | **7B**

Bats L Age 21
2010 (3) HS (GA)
Pwr +++
BAvg +++
Spd +++
Def ++

Year	Lev	Team	AB	R	H	HR	RBI	Avg	OB	Slg	OPS	bb%	ct%	Eye	SB	CS	x/h%	Iso	RC/G
2010	Rk	GCL Blue Jays	157	29	40	0	15	255	320	350	670	9	76	0.41	8	3	30	96	3.94
2011	Rk	Bluefield	242	49	77	5	52	318	375	492	867	8	81	0.48	14	4	34	174	6.30
2011	A+	Dunedin	4	0	0	0	0	0	0	0	0	0	50	0.00	0	0	0	0	
2012	A	Lansing	491	67	132	2	43	269	331	332	663	9	84	0.59	11	0	17	63	3.84

Big, projectable prospect who had inconsistent season. Stats don't tell entire story as he makes consistent, hard contact and works counts. Possesses ample power potential due to strong, quick wrists and has mature ability to hit LHP. Runs well for size. Defensive instincts are raw and arm strength subpar.

Hawkins, Courtney

789 | **Chicago (A)** | EXP MLB DEBUT: 2015 | POTENTIAL: Starting OF | **9C**

Bats R Age 19
2012 (1) HS (TX)
Pwr +++
BAvg +++
Spd +++
Def +++

Year	Lev	Team	AB	R	H	HR	RBI	Avg	OB	Slg	OPS	bb%	ct%	Eye	SB	CS	x/h%	Iso	RC/G
2012	Rk	Bristol	147	25	40	3	16	272	305	401	707	5	75	0.19	8	2	30	129	4.06
2012	A	Kannapolis	65	11	20	4	15	308	348	631	979	6	74	0.24	3	2	55	323	7.74
2012	A+	Winston-Salem	17	3	5	1	2	294	294	588	882	0	88	0.00	0	1	60	294	5.74

Athletic, gifted OF who reached High-A at age 18. Swings fast bat and profiles as middle of order producer with plus-plus power. Swings with authority and may need to shorten stroke to produce better contact. Can be pull-conscious, but hits breaking balls. Runs well and offers avg range with strong, RF arm.

Hazelbaker, Jeremy

79 | **Boston** | EXP MLB DEBUT: 2013 | POTENTIAL: Starting OF | **7C**

Bats L Age 25
2009 (4) Ball State
Pwr +++
BAvg ++
Spd +++
Def ++

Year	Lev	Team	AB	R	H	HR	RBI	Avg	OB	Slg	OPS	bb%	ct%	Eye	SB	CS	x/h%	Iso	RC/G
2010	A	Greenville	442	78	118	12	62	267	353	455	808	12	69	0.44	63	17	42	188	5.99
2011	A+	Salem	122	26	34	5	14	279	380	475	856	14	72	0.59	12	6	41	197	6.54
2011	AA	Portland	354	60	94	12	41	266	343	435	778	11	70	0.40	35	8	35	169	5.38
2012	AA	Portland	436	77	119	19	64	273	327	479	806	7	74	0.31	33	11	39	206	5.48
2012	AAA	Pawtucket	30	2	8	0	3	267	267	367	633	0	73	0.00	3	0	38	100	3.03

Very athletic OF who could make impact with above avg speed and improving power. SB totals have declined over last 3 years, but runs well while showcasing nice pop to pull side. Long swing can be exploited and aggressive approach needs to be tamed. Good range, but arm strength is below avg.

Head, Miles

35 | **Oakland** | EXP MLB DEBUT: 2014 | POTENTIAL: Starting 1B | **8D**

Bats R Age 22
2009 (26) HS (GA)
Pwr +++
BAvg +++
Spd +
Def ++

Year	Lev	Team	AB	R	H	HR	RBI	Avg	OB	Slg	OPS	bb%	ct%	Eye	SB	CS	x/h%	Iso	RC/G
2010	A-	Lowell	229	21	55	1	35	240	328	341	669	12	84	0.83	1	1	35	100	4.15
2011	A	Greenville	263	61	89	15	53	338	406	612	1018	10	80	0.57	4	2	46	274	8.17
2011	A+	Salem	232	27	59	7	29	254	313	405	719	8	76	0.36	0	2	34	151	4.34
2012	A+	Stockton	267	57	102	18	56	382	431	715	1146	8	79	0.42	3	0	46	333	9.64
2012	AA	Midland	213	25	58	5	28	272	323	404	727	7	65	0.21	0	1	28	131	4.73

Powerful, compact INF who played 3B and could move to 1B. Dominated High-A and established career high in HR with strong, quick swing. Consistent run producer, but has limited athleticism and speed. Swings and misses often and may struggle to hit for BA. Lacks range, though hands and arm work well.

Heathcott, Slade

78 | **New York (A)** | EXP MLB DEBUT: 2015 | POTENTIAL: Starting OF | **8C**

Bats L Age 22
2009 (1) HS (TX)
Pwr +++
BAvg +++
Spd +++
Def +++

Year	Lev	Team	AB	R	H	HR	RBI	Avg	OB	Slg	OPS	bb%	ct%	Eye	SB	CS	x/h%	Iso	RC/G
2010	A	Charleston (Sc)	298	48	77	2	30	258	350	352	702	12	66	0.42	15	10	27	94	4.61
2011	A	Charleston (Sc)	210	36	57	4	16	271	332	419	751	8	73	0.33	6	7	33	148	4.93
2011	A+	Tampa	5	2	3	1	1	600	600	1200	1800	0	80	0.00	0	0	33	600	16.14
2012	Rk	GCL Yankees	17	3	4	0	2	235	409	353	762	23	76	1.25	2	0	50	118	5.86
2012	A+	Tampa	215	38	66	5	27	307	366	470	836	9	69	0.30	17	4	35	163	6.24

Athletic, toolsy OF who returned after second shoulder surgery. Has been injury prone, but now healthy. Skills showed improvement and bat has chance to be special. Has strength and swing path for above avg pop and plus speed enhances value. Needs to make more contact. Can be above avg defender with strong arm.

Hechavarria, Adeiny

6 | **Miami** | EXP MLB DEBUT: 2012 | POTENTIAL: Starting SS | **8D**

Bats R Age 24
2010 NDFA, Cuba
Pwr +
BAvg +++
Spd +++
Def +++

Year	Lev	Team	AB	R	H	HR	RBI	Avg	OB	Slg	OPS	bb%	ct%	Eye	SB	CS	x/h%	Iso	RC/G
2010	AA	New Hampshire	253	36	69	3	34	273	306	360	665	5	84	0.30	6	3	22	87	3.59
2011	AA	New Hampshire	464	58	109	6	46	235	274	347	621	5	83	0.32	19	13	31	112	3.13
2011	AAA	Las Vegas	108	16	42	2	11	389	431	537	968	7	81	0.38	1	2	24	148	7.43
2012	AAA	Las Vegas	443	78	138	6	63	312	366	424	790	8	81	0.44	8	2	23	113	5.30
2012	MLB	Toronto	126	10	32	2	15	254	277	365	642	3	75	0.13	0	0	31	111	3.16

Short, quick INF who took advantage of home environs and hit .300 in every month. Reached TOR and held his own, though will likely hit at bottom of order unless he improves power and patience. Owns quick bat and can shoot gaps. Runs well, but SB opps are limited given low OBP. Gifted defender with plus range and arm.

Hedges, Austin

2 | **San Diego** | EXP MLB DEBUT: 2015 | POTENTIAL: Starting C | **8C**

Bats R Age 20
2011 (2) HS, CA
Pwr ++
BAvg +++
Spd +++
Def +++

Year	Lev	Team	AB	R	H	HR	RBI	Avg	OB	Slg	OPS	bb%	ct%	Eye	SB	CS	x/h%	Iso	RC/G
2011	Rk	Padres	16	3	5	1	4	313	476	500	976	24	94	5.00	1	0	20	188	8.32
2011	A-	Eugene	10	0	1	0	0	100	250	200	450	17	70	0.67	0	0	100	100	1.03
2012	A	Fort Wayne	337	44	94	10	56	279	325	451	776	6	82	0.37	14	9	40	172	4.99

Quickly developing into one of the best defensive backstops in the minors. He blocks and receives well with a strong, accurate arm and nailed 32% of baserunners. More surprising was his performance at the plate in the MWL. Improved contact rate and developing power give him exciting offenisve potential.

Hefflinger, Robby

7 | **Atlanta** | EXP MLB DEBUT: 2015 | POTENTIAL: Backup OF | **6D**

Bats R Age 23
2009 (7) Georgia Perimeter CC
Pwr ++
BAvg ++
Spd ++
Def ++

Year	Lev	Team	AB	R	H	HR	RBI	Avg	OB	Slg	OPS	bb%	ct%	Eye	SB	CS	x/h%	Iso	RC/G
2010	A	Rome	282	28	69	6	53	245	306	376	682	8	70	0.29	2	5	36	131	3.97
2011	A	Rome	425	55	109	8	56	256	296	407	703	5	71	0.20	1	1	41	151	4.19
2011	A+	Lynchburg	44	2	5	0	2	114	170	159	329	6	57	0.16	0	0	40	45	
2012	A	Rome	296	44	84	12	58	284	365	483	848	11	73	0.47	7	1	40	199	6.30
2012	A+	Lynchburg	123	14	28	4	11	228	326	390	716	13	62	0.38	1	1	43	163	4.85

Tall, athletic OF made nice progress in '12. At 6-5, 225 he has good size and plus raw strength. Needs to make more consistent contact and be more disciplined in his approach at the plate. HIs contact rate was just 62% at Double-A and he has some work to do to realize his untapped potential.

Hernandez, Cesar

4 | **Philadelphia** | EXP MLB DEBUT: 2013 | POTENTIAL: Backup 2B | **6B**

Bats B Age 23
2006 NDFA, Venezuela
Pwr +
BAvg +++
Spd +++
Def +++

Year	Lev	Team	AB	R	H	HR	RBI	Avg	OB	Slg	OPS	bb%	ct%	Eye	SB	CS	x/h%	Iso	RC/G
2009	Rk	GCL Phillies	150	21	40	0	18	267	341	313	655	10	87	0.85	13	5	15	47	3.92
2010	A-	Williamsport	255	36	83	0	23	325	388	392	780	9	89	0.96	32	6	18	67	5.37
2011	A+	Clearwater	421	47	113	4	37	268	306	333	639	5	81	0.29	23	10	13	64	3.24
2012	AA	Reading	411	50	125	2	51	304	347	436	783	6	84	0.40	16	12	31	131	5.20
2012	AAA	Lehigh Valley	121	13	30	0	6	248	272	298	570	3	91	0.36	5	3	17	50	2.67

Short, quick 2B makes consistent contact with above-average speed. Nice breakout at Double-A, hitting .304 with 16 SB, earning him a late-season promotion to Triple-A. Solid defender with good hands and above-average range. Not much power, but his game is to put the bat on the ball and use his speed.

Hernandez, Elier

9 | **Kansas City** | EXP MLB DEBUT: 2017 | POTENTIAL: Starting OF | **9E**

Bats R Age 18
2011 FA (DR)
Pwr ++
BAvg +++
Spd +++
Def +++

Year	Lev	Team	AB	R	H	HR	RBI	Avg	OB	Slg	OPS	bb%	ct%	Eye	SB	CS	x/h%	Iso	RC/G
2012	Rk	Idaho Falls	250	30	52	0	34	208	250	280	530	5	74	0.21	2	0	27	72	1.86

High-ceiling OF who has work to do, but has tantalizing upside. Possesses ideal, athletic frame with projection and natural, raw power. Plus bat speed produces hard line drives to gaps, but can swing thru pitches as he doesn't recognize breaking balls. RF profile due to very strong arm and average speed.

Hernandez, Marco

4 | **Chicago (N)** | EXP MLB DEBUT: 2015 | POTENTIAL: Starting SS/2B | **7D**

Bats L Age 20
2008 NDFA, D.R.
Pwr +++
BAvg ++
Spd +++
Def +++

Year	Lev	Team	AB	R	H	HR	RBI	Avg	OB	Slg	OPS	bb%	ct%	Eye	SB	CS	x/h%	Iso	RC/G
2011	Rk	Cubs	210	39	70	2	42	333	381	486	866	7	86	0.55	9	7	33	152	6.22
2012	A	Peoria	157	18	33	2	12	210	253	299	552	5	75	0.23	2	1	21	89	2.08
2012	A-	Boise	269	39	77	5	38	286	312	416	728	4	87	0.28	8	3	27	130	4.30

Lean, athletic INF struggled in the MWL, earning him a demotion to Boise where he looked better. Switch-hitter with moderate, gap power and the ability to make contact. Needs to be more patient, but made progress throughout season and does have a nice line-drive stroke. Is a capable defender with good range, soft hands, and a strong arm.

Herrera, Dilson

4 | **Pittsburgh** | EXP MLB DEBUT: 2016 | POTENTIAL: Starting 2B | **8D**

Bats R Age 19
2011 NDFA, Colombia

- Pwr +++
- BAvg +++
- Spd +++
- Def ++

Year	Lev	Team	AB	R	H	HR	RBI	Avg	OB	Slg	OPS	bb%	ct%	Eye	SB	CS	x/h%	Iso	RC/G
2012	Rk	GCL Pirates	199	41	56	7	27	281	341	482	823	8	79	0.44	11	4	39	201	5.70
2012	A-	State College	28	7	9	1	2	321	345	536	881	3	79	0.17	1	0	33	214	6.15

Had a nice breakout season with good bat speed and power to all fields. Can be overly aggressive and strikes out too much, but also draws plenty of walks. Is a below-average defender for now, but shows decent instincts and has the raw tools to be average at 2B.

Herrera, Odubel

46 | **Texas** | EXP MLB DEBUT: 2015 | POTENTIAL: Utility player | **6A**

Bats L Age 21
2008 FA (Venezuela)

- Pwr ++
- BAvg +++
- Spd ++++
- Def +++

Year	Lev	Team	AB	R	H	HR	RBI	Avg	OB	Slg	OPS	bb%	ct%	Eye	SB	CS	x/h%	Iso	RC/G
2010	Rk	Rangers	178	33	60	0	31	337	392	421	813	8	85	0.59	8	5	18	84	5.66
2010	A-	Spokane	9	0	2	0	0	222	222	333	556	0	89	0.00	0	0	50	111	2.36
2011	A	Hickory	464	72	142	3	56	306	340	394	735	5	83	0.31	34	11	23	88	4.46
2012	A+	Myrtle Beach	500	72	142	5	46	284	328	382	710	6	80	0.33	27	7	23	98	4.22

Small, quick INF with athleticism and easy actions. Has nose for game with intelligence. Makes consistent contact, though needs to make more given lack of power. Stays in against LHP and sprays balls to all fields. Posseses above avg wheels and SB potential. Can play either middle spot with smooth hands. Has enough arm and can turn DP.

Herrera, Rosell

6 | **Colorado** | EXP MLB DEBUT: 2015 | POTENTIAL: Starting SS | **8E**

Bats R Age 20
2009 NDFA, D.R.

- Pwr ++
- BAvg +++
- Spd ++
- Def ++

Year	Lev	Team	AB	R	H	HR	RBI	Avg	OB	Slg	OPS	bb%	ct%	Eye	SB	CS	x/h%	Iso	RC/G
2011	Rk	Casper	243	38	69	6	34	284	356	449	804	10	74	0.44	5	4	29	165	5.67
2012	A	Asheville	213	22	43	1	26	202	274	272	546	9	77	0.43	6	3	26	70	2.25
2012	A-	Tri-City	194	30	55	1	30	284	332	351	682	7	82	0.41	7	3	16	67	3.92

Switch-hitting SS from the D.R. struggled in the SAL, but found his form when sent down. Power should continue to develop as he matures but could be undermined by an overly aggressive approach and fringy plate discipline. For now, scouts are mixed on whether he can stick at short, but he does have smooth actions, with good range, and a strong arm.

Herrmann, Chris

2 | **Minnesota** | EXP MLB DEBUT: 2012 | POTENTIAL: Backup C | **6B**

Bats L Age 25
2009 (6) Miami (FL)

- Pwr ++
- BAvg +++
- Spd ++
- Def +++

Year	Lev	Team	AB	R	H	HR	RBI	Avg	OB	Slg	OPS	bb%	ct%	Eye	SB	CS	x/h%	Iso	RC/G
2010	A+	Fort Myers	356	34	78	2	30	219	300	301	600	10	79	0.55	3	2	28	81	3.08
2011	A+	Fort Myers	87	14	27	1	16	310	412	425	837	15	93	2.50	1	0	26	115	6.44
2011	AA	New Britain	337	53	87	7	46	258	377	392	768	16	80	0.94	9	3	30	134	5.46
2012	AA	New Britain	490	91	135	10	61	276	352	392	744	11	82	0.65	2	1	27	116	4.84
2012	MLB	Minnesota	18	0	1	0	1	56	105	56	161	5	72	0.20	0	0	0	0	

Versatile and athletic player who set career high in HR while reaching MIN for first time. Uses advanced approach for OBP and can hit LHP with short, direct path. Flat swing path limits power. Improved receiver and should be able to stick there in MIN. Has quick release with nice arm and just needs a little polish.

Hicks, Aaron

8 | **Minnesota** | EXP MLB DEBUT: 2013 | POTENTIAL: Starting OF | **8C**

Bats B Age 23
2008 (1) HS (CA)

- Pwr +++
- BAvg +++
- Spd ++++
- Def ++++

Year	Lev	Team	AB	R	H	HR	RBI	Avg	OB	Slg	OPS	bb%	ct%	Eye	SB	CS	x/h%	Iso	RC/G
2008	Rk	GCL Twins	173	32	55	4	27	318	413	491	904	14	82	0.88	12	2	33	173	7.09
2009	A	Beloit	251	43	63	4	29	251	354	382	736	14	78	0.73	10	8	35	131	4.96
2010	A	Beloit	423	86	118	8	49	279	403	428	831	17	74	0.79	21	11	35	149	6.46
2011	A+	Fort Myers	443	79	107	5	38	242	355	368	723	15	75	0.71	17	9	38	126	4.88
2012	AA	New Britain	472	100	135	13	61	286	388	460	848	14	75	0.68	32	11	33	174	6.46

Toolsy, athletic OF who had best season and led EL in BB. Set career high in HR and SB while maintaining high OBP. Uses plus speed on base and in CF. Range is exemplary and arm strength continues to be plus. Hits well from both sides with improved swing and has tapped into avg raw power. Still Ks too much.

Hicks, John

2 | **Seattle** | EXP MLB DEBUT: 2015 | POTENTIAL: Starting C | **7D**

Bats R Age 23
2011 (4) Virginia

- Pwr ++
- BAvg +++
- Spd ++
- Def +++

Year	Lev	Team	AB	R	H	HR	RBI	Avg	OB	Slg	OPS	bb%	ct%	Eye	SB	CS	x/h%	Iso	RC/G
2009	NCAA	Virginia	254	51	78	8	39	307	333	476	810	4	84	0.25	6	5	31	169	5.19
2010	NCAA	Virginia	244	59	75	8	48	307	350	488	838	6	88	0.55	9	1	37	180	5.69
2011	NCAA	Virginia	277	52	92	8	59	332	373	502	875	6	93	0.95	5	4	33	170	6.14
2011	A	Clinton	139	21	43	2	26	309	333	446	779	3	88	0.29	2	3	30	137	4.92
2012	A+	High Desert	506	87	158	15	79	312	348	472	821	5	86	0.38	22	8	31	160	5.41

Athletic, fundamentally-sound C who hit at least .299 each month. Benefited from home park for power, but makes easy contact with controlled swing and strong hand-eye coordination. Lacks bat speed and strength to hit consistent HRs. Doesn't run well, but not a clogger. Avg receiver with OK catch-and-throw skills.

Hoes, L.J.

789 | **Baltimore** | EXP MLB DEBUT: 2012 | POTENTIAL: Starting LF | **7B**

Bats R Age 23
2008 (3) HS (MD)

- Pwr ++
- BAvg +++
- Spd +++
- Def +++

Year	Lev	Team	AB	R	H	HR	RBI	Avg	OB	Slg	OPS	bb%	ct%	Eye	SB	CS	x/h%	Iso	RC/G
2011	A+	Frederick	158	23	38	3	17	241	286	342	627	6	84	0.40	4	2	26	101	3.20
2011	AA	Bowie	344	47	105	6	54	305	382	413	795	11	84	0.77	16	7	23	108	5.52
2012	AA	Bowie	196	25	52	2	16	265	366	372	738	14	83	0.94	12	5	27	107	5.04
2012	AAA	Norfolk	317	54	95	3	38	300	368	397	765	10	86	0.79	8	7	22	98	5.15
2012	MLB	Baltimore	1	0	0	0	0	0	0	0	0	0	100	0.00	0	0	0	0	

Pure-hitting prospect who earned September callup. Owns solid approach at plate and ability to make contact with balanced, level stroke. Hits line drives and has some pop. Power development is paramount for future starting role and will need to upgrade OF defense. Has avg wheels and arm, but still learning reads.

Holt, Brock

6 | **Boston** | EXP MLB DEBUT: 2012 | POTENTIAL: Utility INF | **6B**

Bats L Age 25
2009 (9) Rice

- Pwr +
- BAvg +++
- Spd ++
- Def ++

Year	Lev	Team	AB	R	H	HR	RBI	Avg	OB	Slg	OPS	bb%	ct%	Eye	SB	CS	x/h%	Iso	RC/G
2010	A+	Bradenton	194	31	68	1	27	351	408	438	847	9	85	0.63	6	6	21	88	6.06
2011	AA	Altoona	511	62	147	1	40	288	351	387	739	9	83	0.59	18	10	27	100	4.83
2012	AA	Altoona	382	52	123	2	43	322	386	432	818	9	87	0.78	11	11	26	110	5.81
2012	AAA	Indianapolis	95	13	41	1	7	432	481	537	1018	9	91	1.00	5	2	20	105	7.92
2012	MLB	Pittsburgh	65	6	19	0	3	292	333	354	687	6	78	0.29	0	0	16	62	3.93

Short, scrappy INF raked the ball in '12 and looked at home when making his MLB debut. Has a short, compact stroke with plus strike zone judgment and contact ability. Is a below-average defender and does not have the range or arm to play short in the big leagues, but could do just fine if he gets a chance at 2B.

Hood, Destin

8 | **Washington** | EXP MLB DEBUT: 2013 | POTENTIAL: Starting CF | **8D**

Bats R Age 23
2008 (2) HS, AL

- Pwr +++
- BAvg ++
- 4.25 Spd ++++
- Def +++

Year	Lev	Team	AB	R	H	HR	RBI	Avg	OB	Slg	OPS	bb%	ct%	Eye	SB	CS	x/h%	Iso	RC/G
2009	A-	Vermont	138	12	34	2	24	246	302	333	635	7	67	0.24	2	1	21	87	3.29
2010	A	Hagerstown	492	56	140	5	65	285	330	388	718	6	76	0.28	5	7	27	104	4.34
2011	A+	Potomac	463	61	128	13	83	276	357	445	802	11	79	0.60	21	6	37	168	5.61
2012	AA	Harrisburg	355	45	87	3	45	245	293	344	637	6	75	0.27	6	1	30	99	3.30
2012	A-	Auburn	17	3	3	0	0	176	263	235	498	11	59	0.29	0	0	33	59	1.46

Raw, toolsy OF scuffled in '12. Erosion of contact rate cut into gains made over the past two years. A wrist and groin injury partially explain the decline and he still has plus bat speed and the potential to hit for power and average. Good range in CF, but only fringe-average arm strength. Still has some work to do, but there is some upside.

Iglesias, Jose

6 | **Boston** | EXP MLB DEBUT: 2011 | POTENTIAL: Starting SS | **8C**

Bats R Age 23
2009 FA (Cuba)

- Pwr +
- BAvg +++
- Spd ++++
- Def +++++

Year	Lev	Team	AB	R	H	HR	RBI	Avg	OB	Slg	OPS	bb%	ct%	Eye	SB	CS	x/h%	Iso	RC/G
2010	A-	Lowell	40	8	14	0	7	350	447	500	947	15	80	0.88	2	1	29	150	7.91
2011	AAA	Pawtucket	357	35	84	1	31	235	278	269	547	6	84	0.36	12	4	12	34	2.24
2012	AAA	Pawtucket	353	46	94	1	23	266	318	306	624	7	87	0.59	12	3	12	40	3.35
2012	MLB	Boston	68	5	8	1	2	118	167	191	358	6	76	0.25	1	0	38	74	
2012	A-	Lowell	8	1	3	0	0	375	444	500	944	11	88	1.00	1	0	33	125	7.45

Short and quick INF could be top defensive SS in baseball, but bat hasn't shown much growth. Has decent bat speed and keeps ball on ground consistently to use average speed. Can be aggressive at plate and lacks strength for pop. Hands, feet, arm, instincts, and range are all well above average.

Jackson, Bralin

8 | **Tampa Bay** | EXP MLB DEBUT: 2016 | POTENTIAL: Starting OF | **8E**

Bats R Age 19
2012 (5) HS (MO)

- Pwr ++
- BAvg ++
- Spd ++++
- Def ++

Year	Lev	Team	AB	R	H	HR	RBI	Avg	OB	Slg	OPS	bb%	ct%	Eye	SB	CS	x/h%	Iso	RC/G
2012	Rk	GCL Rays	146	16	37	0	11	253	283	342	625	4	73	0.15	5	3	24	89	3.10

Toolsy, athletic OF with muscular frame and exciting projection. Could take time to develop skills and may not realize power until he learns to recognize breaking balls. Can expand K zone and flail at pitches. Strong arm highlights raw defensive attributes, but has good speed to track down balls. Routes and reads are raw.

Jackson, Brett | 8 | Chicago (N) | EXP MLB DEBUT: 2012 | POTENTIAL: Starting CF | 8C

Bats L Age 24
2009 (1) UC Berkeley
Pwr + + +
BAvg + +
4.15 Spd + + + +
Def + + +

Year	Lev	Team	AB	R	H	HR	RBI	Avg	OB	Slg	OPS	bb%	ct%	Eye	SB	CS	x/h%	Iso	RC/G
2010	AA	Tennessee	228	47	63	6	28	276	360	465	825	12	72	0.48	18	4	40	189	6.13
2011	AA	Tennessee	246	45	63	10	32	256	371	443	814	15	70	0.61	15	6	37	187	6.06
2011	AAA	Iowa	185	39	55	10	26	297	390	551	941	13	65	0.44	6	1	45	254	8.12
2012	AAA	Iowa	407	66	104	15	47	256	333	479	812	10	61	0.30	27	5	47	224	6.48
2012	MLB	Chicago (N)	120	14	21	4	9	175	303	342	644	15	51	0.37	0	3	52	167	4.30

Athletic OF took a step backwards, struggling at AAA and then looking overmatched with the Cubs. Speed and power remain plus tools, but abysmal contact rate is a red flag and struck out 207 times. Is a plus defender and has the potential to be a 20/20 CF, but if he hits .220 it doesn't have much value. Look for a rebound.

Jackson, Ryan | 6 | St. Louis | EXP MLB DEBUT: 2012 | POTENTIAL: Starting SS | 7C

Bats R Age 25
2009 (5) Miami
Pwr + +
BAvg + +
Spd + +
Def + + + +

Year	Lev	Team	AB	R	H	HR	RBI	Avg	OB	Slg	OPS	bb%	ct%	Eye	SB	CS	x/h%	Iso	RC/G
2010	A	Quad Cities	302	47	82	2	27	272	371	348	719	14	79	0.76	6	7	21	76	4.75
2010	A+	Palm Beach	148	14	43	1	8	291	340	392	732	7	86	0.52	3	2	28	101	4.60
2011	AA	Springfield	533	65	148	11	73	278	333	415	747	8	83	0.48	2	0	32	137	4.74
2012	AAA	Memphis	445	60	121	10	47	272	336	396	732	9	83	0.57	2	0	28	124	4.59
2012	MLB	St. Louis	17	2	2	0	0	118	167	118	284	6	82	0.33	0	0	0	0	

Athletic INF with good speed and plus defense. Questions about offensive potential have been answered with two solid seasons. Makes consistent contact with a nice line-drive stroke and hit double-digit home runs again. Has plus range, soft hands, and a strong arm. Played 2B when called up to the majors where he struggled in limited action.

Jacobs, Brandon | 7 | Boston | EXP MLB DEBUT: 2014 | POTENTIAL: Starting OF | 8D

Bats R Age 22
2009 (10) HS (GA)
Pwr + + + +
BAvg + +
Spd + + +
Def + +

Year	Lev	Team	AB	R	H	HR	RBI	Avg	OB	Slg	OPS	bb%	ct%	Eye	SB	CS	x/h%	Iso	RC/G
2009	Rk	GCL Red Sox	24	1	6	0	0	250	308	333	641	8	67	0.25	0	0	33	83	3.56
2010	A-	Lowell	236	30	57	6	31	242	304	411	715	8	75	0.36	4	1	46	169	4.38
2011	A	Greenville	442	75	134	17	80	303	365	505	869	9	72	0.35	30	7	39	201	6.51
2012	A+	Salem	437	62	110	13	61	252	313	410	723	8	71	0.30	17	9	39	158	4.49

Athletic, muscular OF who regressed after breakout '11 season. HR and SB both fell, but exhibits good hitting skills with bat speed and strength. Ability to make adjustments could lead to BA improvement while plus power remains. Chases pitches and will have trouble with Ks. Can play CF, but avg speed and range more suited for LF.

James, Jiwan | 8 | Philadelphia | EXP MLB DEBUT: 2014 | POTENTIAL: Starting CF | 7D

Bats B Age 24
2007 (22) HS, FL
Pwr + +
BAvg + +
Spd + + + +
Def + + + +

Year	Lev	Team	AB	R	H	HR	RBI	Avg	OB	Slg	OPS	bb%	ct%	Eye	SB	CS	x/h%	Iso	RC/G
2009	A-	Williamsport	121	15	32	1	13	264	326	372	698	8	82	0.50	7	4	25	107	4.24
2010	A	Lakewood	556	85	150	5	64	270	313	365	678	6	76	0.27	33	20	25	95	3.80
2011	A+	Clearwater	526	76	141	4	38	268	320	363	683	7	77	0.33	31	16	26	95	3.94
2012	AA	Reading	381	55	95	6	31	249	289	360	648	5	70	0.18	8	8	26	110	3.39

Switch-hitting OF has some exciting tools, highlighted by plus speed. Has good bat speed and nice power potential, but struggles with breaking balls and has yet to tap into power. Covers ground well with a strong throwing arm. Plate discipline and pitch recognition will need to improve for him to realize his potential.

Jankowski, Travis | 8 | San Diego | EXP MLB DEBUT: 2015 | POTENTIAL: Starting CF | 8D

Bats L Age 22
2012 (1-S) Stony Brook
Pwr + +
BAvg + + +
Spd + + + +
Def + + + +

Year	Lev	Team	AB	R	H	HR	RBI	Avg	OB	Slg	OPS	bb%	ct%	Eye	SB	CS	x/h%	Iso	RC/G
2010	NCAA	Stony Brook	103	20	27	0	9	262	327	301	628	9	76	0.40	13	1	7	39	3.29
2011	NCAA	Stony Brook	186	39	66	2	38	355	417	457	874	10	88	0.91	30	4	18	102	6.42
2012	NCAA	Stony Brook	266	79	110	5	46	414	462	620	1082	8	92	1.09	36	6	31	207	8.68
2012	Rk	Padres	8	1	2	0	4	250	250	250	500	0	88	0.00	0	0	0	0	1.47
2012	A	Fort Wayne	238	32	67	1	23	282	319	370	688	5	82	0.30	17	7	22	88	3.94

LH hitting collegiate OF was the 44th overall pick. Has good bat speed, but uses hands a lot and doesn't generate much power. Runs well and should be able to stick in CF where he has an average arm. Showed good strike zone judgment in college and should be able to hit for average with 20+ SB.

Jensen, Kyle | 79 | Miami | EXP MLB DEBUT: 2013 | POTENTIAL: Backup OF | 6B

Bats R Age 25
2009 (12) St. Mary's
Pwr + + + +
BAvg +
Spd + +
Def + +

Year	Lev	Team	AB	R	H	HR	RBI	Avg	OB	Slg	OPS	bb%	ct%	Eye	SB	CS	x/h%	Iso	RC/G
2009	A-	Jamestown	182	24	51	4	24	280	345	456	801	9	75	0.39	3	0	37	176	5.62
2010	A	Greensboro	470	61	128	18	86	272	336	447	783	9	75	0.38	5	1	35	174	5.20
2011	A+	Jupiter	391	53	121	22	66	309	382	535	917	11	71	0.40	0	0	36	225	7.18
2011	AA	Jacksonville	80	14	20	5	10	250	310	475	785	8	71	0.30	1	0	35	225	5.14
2012	AA	Jacksonville	445	70	104	24	84	234	337	452	788	13	64	0.43	1	1	45	218	5.78

Strong OF has stalled since hitting AA. Has good power, but struck out 162 times. Has average bat speed that leaves him late on fastballs and in-between on breaking balls. Defensively has the speed and arm strength to be an above-average OF. At 24, will need to move quickly if he hopes to carve out a full-time role.

Jhang, Jin-De | 2 | Pittsburgh | EXP MLB DEBUT: 2016 | POTENTIAL: Starting C | 7D

Bats L Age 20
2012 NDFA, Taiwan
Pwr + +
BAvg + + +
Spd + +
Def + +

Year	Lev	Team	AB	R	H	HR	RBI	Avg	OB	Slg	OPS	bb%	ct%	Eye	SB	CS	x/h%	Iso	RC/G
2012	Rk	GCL Pirates	128	12	39	1	23	305	373	398	772	10	88	0.88	1	1	21	94	5.26

Stocky Taiwanese backstop has good hands, a quick bat, and makes consistent contact. Nice approach at the plate with good strike zone judgment. Has decent raw power, but it didn't show in game action and will be key to his development. Is raw behind the plate and slow due to size, but does have a good arm and nailed 28% of runners.

Jimenez, A.J. | 2 | Toronto | EXP MLB DEBUT: 2014 | POTENTIAL: Starting C | 7C

Bats R Age 23
2008 (9) HS (PR)
Pwr + +
BAvg + + +
Spd + +
Def + + + +

Year	Lev	Team	AB	R	H	HR	RBI	Avg	OB	Slg	OPS	bb%	ct%	Eye	SB	CS	x/h%	Iso	RC/G
2009	A	Lansing	278	30	73	3	31	263	281	356	637	2	74	0.10	5	2	26	94	3.07
2010	A	Lansing	262	35	80	4	54	305	350	435	785	6	79	0.32	17	4	33	130	5.18
2010	A+	Dunedin	9	1	1	1	1	111	111	444	556	0	44	0.00	0	0	100	333	2.96
2011	A+	Dunedin	379	49	115	4	52	303	351	417	768	7	84	0.47	11	2	30	113	5.00
2012	AA	New Hampshire	105	14	27	2	10	257	291	371	662	5	87	0.36	2	3	26	114	3.60

Strong C who underwent TJ surgery in May. Has nice overall skill set and stands out with solid defensive attributes. Moves well and offers advanced blocking and receiving. Keeps SB low with above avg, accurate arm. Line drive stroke produces contact and has enough speed to leg out doubles to gaps.

Jimenez, Luis | 5 | Los Angeles (A) | EXP MLB DEBUT: 2013 | POTENTIAL: Starting 3B | 7B

Bats R Age 25
2006 FA (Venezuela)
Pwr + + +
BAvg + + +
Spd + + +
Def + +

Year	Lev	Team	AB	R	H	HR	RBI	Avg	OB	Slg	OPS	bb%	ct%	Eye	SB	CS	x/h%	Iso	RC/G
2008	Rk	Orem	284	57	94	15	65	331	356	630	986	4	84	0.24	6	2	52	299	7.29
2010	A	Cedar Rapids	168	32	49	2	38	292	335	476	811	6	84	0.41	6	2	45	185	5.57
2010	A+	Rancho Cuc	318	52	91	12	43	286	314	522	836	4	86	0.30	15	8	52	236	5.57
2011	AA	Arkansas	490	62	142	18	94	290	327	486	813	5	85	0.38	15	6	42	196	5.32
2012	AAA	Salt Lake	485	78	150	16	85	309	335	495	830	4	86	0.27	17	7	37	186	5.44

Consistent INF who hits for BA and avg pop despite free swinging approach and poor K zone control. Rarely takes BB, but has smooth stroke and ability to hit any pitch. Makes good contact due to hand-eye coordination. Has avg speed, though likely to slow down. Plays passable defense with avg arm.

Jones, Duanel | 5 | San Diego | EXP MLB DEBUT: 2015 | POTENTIAL: Starting 3B | 6C

Bats R Age 20
2010 NDFA, D.R.
Pwr + +
BAvg + +
Spd + +
Def + + +

Year	Lev	Team	AB	R	H	HR	RBI	Avg	OB	Slg	OPS	bb%	ct%	Eye	SB	CS	x/h%	Iso	RC/G
2011	Rk	Padres	150	38	40	8	23	267	337	500	837	10	71	0.37	1	1	43	233	6.04
2011	A-	Eugene	68	7	14	0	5	206	260	279	540	7	63	0.20	3	0	36	74	2.04
2012	A	Fort Wayne	394	51	89	5	41	226	292	330	622	9	75	0.37	4	4	35	104	3.18

Strong 3B prospect has exciting potential, but has yet to prove he can hit. Is overly aggressive and struck out 99 times in 394 AB. Missed 50 games for substance abuse violation in '10, but hasn't had a problem since. Has good size and raw power, but needs to make more consistent contact and improve defensively.

Jones, James | 89 | Seattle | EXP MLB DEBUT: 2014 | POTENTIAL: Starting OF | 8E

Bats R Age 24
2009 (4) Long Island
Pwr + + +
BAvg + +
Spd + +
Def + + +

Year	Lev	Team	AB	R	H	HR	RBI	Avg	OB	Slg	OPS	bb%	ct%	Eye	SB	CS	x/h%	Iso	RC/G
2009	NCAA	Long Island	173	47	63	9	32	364	450	618	1068	14	86	1.13	20	3	37	254	8.83
2009	A-	Everett	164	28	51	3	24	311	383	463	846	10	76	0.48	0	3	33	152	6.26
2010	A	Clinton	491	87	132	12	65	269	351	432	783	11	75	0.51	24	10	35	163	5.43
2011	A+	High Desert	296	42	73	5	29	247	340	378	719	12	69	0.46	16	3	34	132	4.74
2012	A+	High Desert	493	109	151	14	76	306	375	497	872	10	75	0.44	26	17	36	191	6.57

Lean, athletic OF who repeated High-A and improved. Works counts with honed approach, though struggles with pitch recognition and breaking balls. Needs to firm up swing against LHP and shorten with two strikes. Owns raw power that projects well. Below avg range likely to limit him to corner, but has plus-plus arm.

Jones, Mycal

89 | Atlanta | EXP MLB DEBUT: 2014 | POTENTIAL: Backup CF | 6D

Bats R Age 26
2009 (4) Miami Dade JC
- Pwr + +
- BAvg + +
- 6.4/60 Spd + + + +
- Def + + + +

Year	Lev	Team	AB	R	H	HR	RBI	Avg	OB	Slg	OPS	bb%	ct%	Eye	SB	CS	x/h%	Iso	RC/G
2010	A+	Myrtle Beach	275	51	74	7	22	269	343	422	765	10	76	0.47	15	4	36	153	5.10
2010	AA	Mississippi	30	5	6	2	5	200	226	467	692	3	70	0.11	1	0	50	267	3.74
2011	AA	Mississippi	373	63	94	7	36	252	350	381	730	13	76	0.62	17	6	35	129	4.82
2012	A+	Lynchburg	383	45	97	3	30	253	314	363	677	8	83	0.53	22	8	34	110	4.01
2012	AA	Mississippi	85	11	12	0	0	141	223	141	365	10	71	0.36	7	5	0	0	

Athletic player has bounced around since being drafted, playing SS, 2B, and now CF. Has plus speed, good range, and a a strong arm. Stole 23 bases, but power has not developed. Has plus bat speed and makes decent contact, but doesn't drive the ball well. Can handle CF due to plus speed and a strong arm.

Joseph, Corban

4 | New York (A) | EXP MLB DEBUT: 2013 | POTENTIAL: Reserve 2B | 7D

Bats L Age 24
2008 (4) HS (TN)
- Pwr + + +
- BAvg + + + +
- Spd +
- Def + +

Year	Lev	Team	AB	R	H	HR	RBI	Avg	OB	Slg	OPS	bb%	ct%	Eye	SB	CS	x/h%	Iso	RC/G
2010	A+	Tampa	381	52	115	6	52	302	373	436	808	10	81	0.58	5	8	31	134	5.68
2010	AA	Trenton	111	11	24	0	13	216	310	342	652	12	70	0.45	1	0	42	126	3.90
2011	AA	Trenton	499	75	138	5	58	277	353	415	768	11	79	0.57	4	3	37	138	5.27
2012	AA	Trenton	86	9	27	2	6	314	416	430	846	15	85	1.15	0	0	22	116	6.34
2012	AAA	Scranton/W-B	327	50	87	13	56	266	368	474	842	14	83	0.93	0	1	46	208	6.21

Consistent, aggressive INF who set career high in HR while continuing to possess ideal plate discipline. Despite increase in power, still has more doubles-oriented pop with clean, line drive stroke to gaps. Makes consistent contact with fine swing mechanics. Secondary skills – speed, arm, quickness – are well below avg.

Joseph, Tommy

2 | Philadelphia | EXP MLB DEBUT: 2013 | POTENTIAL: Starting C | 8D

Bats R Age 21
2009 (2) HS, AZ
- Pwr + + + +
- BAvg + +
- Spd + +
- Def + +

Year	Lev	Team	AB	R	H	HR	RBI	Avg	OB	Slg	OPS	bb%	ct%	Eye	SB	CS	x/h%	Iso	RC/G
2010	A	Augusta	436	46	103	16	68	236	279	401	681	6	73	0.22	0	0	38	165	3.70
2011	A+	San Jose	514	80	139	22	95	270	309	471	780	5	80	0.28	1	0	41	200	4.92
2012	AA	Richmond	304	32	79	8	38	260	316	391	708	8	79	0.39	0	3	30	132	4.17
2012	AA	Reading	100	12	25	3	10	250	312	420	732	8	68	0.28	0	1	44	170	4.73

Strong C saw his HR total cut in half, but does have solid bat speed and should be able to hit for power in the majors. Has worked hard to improve on defense and is better at blocking balls with a quick release. Will need to show improved plate discipline if he is going to hit at higher levels, but should be able to stick behind the plate.

Kelly, Carson

5 | St. Louis | EXP MLB DEBUT: 2016 | POTENTIAL: Starting 3B | 8D

Bats R Age 18
2012 (2) HS, OR
- Pwr + + +
- BAvg + +
- Spd + +
- Def + +

Year	Lev	Team	AB	R	H	HR	RBI	Avg	OB	Slg	OPS	bb%	ct%	Eye	SB	CS	x/h%	Iso	RC/G
2012	Rk	Johnson City	213	24	48	9	25	225	260	399	659	4	85	0.30	0	0	40	174	3.42

Strong, agile 3B is already physically strong and has athleticism. Has good hands a plus arm. Has good raw power and makes consistent contact. Could be more selective in his approach, which would enable him to drive the ball more effectively. He is an average runner, but should be able to stick at 3B.

Kelly, Ty

457 | Baltimore | EXP MLB DEBUT: 2013 | POTENTIAL: Utility player | 7D

Bats L Age 24
2009 (13) UC-Davis
- Pwr + +
- BAvg + + +
- Spd + +
- Def + + +

Year	Lev	Team	AB	R	H	HR	RBI	Avg	OB	Slg	OPS	bb%	ct%	Eye	SB	CS	x/h%	Iso	RC/G
2010	A	Delmarva	487	68	126	4	58	259	350	370	719	12	83	0.84	5	4	32	111	4.76
2011	A	Delmarva	457	63	125	4	46	274	366	328	695	13	86	1.06	11	4	14	55	4.47
2012	A+	Frederick	263	47	91	9	41	346	457	513	971	17	84	1.32	2	3	29	167	7.97
2012	AA	Bowie	172	24	53	1	27	308	383	413	796	11	84	0.75	1	0	26	105	5.62
2012	AAA	Norfolk	36	3	10	1	2	278	350	389	739	10	92	1.33	1	0	20	111	4.86

Versatile, consistent prospect who posted career high in HR. Draws BB with disciplined approach and puts bat to ball with ease. Power more of gap variety and lacks bat speed for pop. Runs OK, though not a threat, and has enough quickness and arm to play number of positions. Lacks range for full time INF.

Kepler, Max

789 | Minnesota | EXP MLB DEBUT: 2016 | POTENTIAL: Starting OF | 8D

Bats L Age 20
2009 FA (Germany)
- Pwr + + +
- BAvg + + +
- Spd + + +
- Def + +

Year	Lev	Team	AB	R	H	HR	RBI	Avg	OB	Slg	OPS	bb%	ct%	Eye	SB	CS	x/h%	Iso	RC/G
2010	Rk	GCL Twins	140	15	40	0	11	286	346	343	689	8	81	0.48	6	1	18	57	4.12
2011	Rk	Elizabethton	191	29	50	1	24	262	341	366	708	11	72	0.43	1	1	30	105	4.53
2012	Rk	Elizabethton	232	40	69	10	49	297	371	539	909	10	86	0.82	7	0	45	241	6.81

Tall, lean OF who continues to show promising improvement. Added strength to slender frame and hit for more consistent power. Controls strike zone and uses whole field. Hits LHP well and should hit for avg BA and pop. Relegated to LF due to questionable arm, but has improved range with avg speed.

Keyes, Kevin

7 | Washington | EXP MLB DEBUT: 2015 | POTENTIAL: Reserve OF | 6C

Bats R Age 24
2010 (7) Texas
- Pwr + + + +
- BAvg +
- Spd + +
- Def + +

Year	Lev	Team	AB	R	H	HR	RBI	Avg	OB	Slg	OPS	bb%	ct%	Eye	SB	CS	x/h%	Iso	RC/G
2009	NCAA	Texas	213	46	65	9	46	305	393	521	915	13	74	0.56	9	3	42	216	7.23
2010	NCAA	Texas	238	49	74	15	59	311	381	550	932	10	81	0.59	14	3	36	239	6.95
2010	A-	Vermont	126	13	22	3	23	175	307	278	584	16	71	0.67	1	2	32	103	2.78
2011	A	Hagerstown	304	49	80	17	65	263	333	510	843	10	74	0.40	6	0	50	247	6.03
2012	A+	Potomac	390	47	87	21	78	223	284	459	743	8	72	0.31	4	2	56	236	4.63

Has tremendous raw power but is fairly one-dimensional. Does not run well and has all-or-nothing swing that leads to high K totals. Hit a career high in home runs, but also struck out 108 times. Has an average arm and and at 23 it would be surprising for him to turn into an everyday regular.

Kieschnick, Roger

8 | San Francisco | EXP MLB DEBUT: 2013 | POTENTIAL: Backup CF | 7C

Bats L Age 26
2008 (3) Texas Tech
- Pwr + + + +
- BAvg + +
- 4.15 Spd + +
- Def + + +

Year	Lev	Team	AB	R	H	HR	RBI	Avg	OB	Slg	OPS	bb%	ct%	Eye	SB	CS	x/h%	Iso	RC/G
2009	A+	San Jose	517	86	153	23	110	296	342	532	874	7	75	0.28	9	1	44	236	6.34
2010	AA	Richmond	223	21	56	4	23	251	307	368	675	7	75	0.33	2	3	27	117	3.79
2011	AA	Richmond	459	71	117	16	65	255	306	429	735	7	74	0.28	13	7	37	174	4.53
2012	Rk	Giants	12	0	1	0	4	83	83	167	250	0	58	0.00	0	0	100	83	
2012	AAA	Fresno	222	49	68	15	40	306	374	604	978	10	69	0.35	0	2	47	297	8.13

Had his best season at AAA, but an injury limited him to 55 games. Has good bat speed and power to all fields. Swing is long and he can be overly aggressive. Plus arm and good range make him an above average fielder in CF. Has a chance to work himself into the better half of a platoon.

Kivlehan, Patrick

5 | Seattle | EXP MLB DEBUT: 2015 | POTENTIAL: Starting 3B | 7C

Bats R Age 23
2012 (4) Rutgers
- Pwr + + + +
- BAvg + +
- Spd + + +
- Def + + +

Year	Lev	Team	AB	R	H	HR	RBI	Avg	OB	Slg	OPS	bb%	ct%	Eye	SB	CS	x/h%	Iso	RC/G
2012	NCAA	Rutgers	189	47	74	14	50	392	455	693	1148	10	79	0.55	24	4	36	302	9.76
2012	A-	Everett	282	46	85	12	52	301	346	511	856	6	67	0.20	14	1	38	209	6.46

Strong, athletic INF who was NWL MVP with hard contact and above avg power. Owns quick bat and vicious stroke. K totals are concern and needs to tone down approach as he advances. Secondary skills have good potential. Has good speed and soft hands. Lack of arm strength could move him to LF.

Kobernus, Jeff

4 | Detroit | EXP MLB DEBUT: 2013 | POTENTIAL: Starting 2B | 7D

Bats R Age 25
2009 (2) UC Berkeley
- Pwr +
- BAvg + + +
- Spd + + +
- Def + + +

Year	Lev	Team	AB	R	H	HR	RBI	Avg	OB	Slg	OPS	bb%	ct%	Eye	SB	CS	x/h%	Iso	RC/G
2009	NCAA	California	217	43	74	8	40	341	389	544	933	7	88	0.68	20	4	34	203	6.83
2009	A-	Vermont	41	8	9	0	2	220	256	244	500	5	88	0.40	4	0	11	24	1.82
2010	A	Hagerstown	312	40	87	1	42	279	316	346	662	5	81	0.29	21	10	22	67	3.59
2011	A+	Potomac	489	67	138	7	52	282	312	387	698	4	82	0.24	53	8	24	104	3.93
2012	AA	Harrisburg	330	41	93	1	19	282	321	333	654	5	83	0.33	42	11	14	52	3.50

Speedy INF saw limited action due to injury, but managed to swipe 42 bases. A quick bat and plus speed give him the ability to hit and make things happen. Pitch recognition and BB rate could be better and has no power. Plays above-average defense with good range, soft hands, and good footwork.

Komatsu, Eric

7 | Washington | EXP MLB DEBUT: 2012 | POTENTIAL: Backup OF | 6B

Bats L Age 25
2008 (8) Cal St. Fullerton
- Pwr + +
- BAvg + + +
- Spd + + + +
- Def + + +

Year	Lev	Team	AB	R	H	HR	RBI	Avg	OB	Slg	OPS	bb%	ct%	Eye	SB	CS	x/h%	Iso	RC/G
2011	AA	Huntsville	320	48	94	6	40	294	394	416	810	14	86	1.20	13	6	28	122	5.93
2011	AA	Harrisburg	128	12	30	1	8	234	295	297	592	8	83	0.50	8	3	20	63	2.89
2012	AAA	Syracuse	104	16	28	3	14	269	350	394	745	11	88	1.00	2	5	25	125	4.90
2012	MLB	Minnesota	32	2	7	0	1	219	306	219	524	11	91	1.33	0	0	0	0	2.59
2012	MLB	St. Louis	19	3	4	0	0	211	286	211	496	10	89	1.00	0	0	0	0	2.12

4th OF type is a professional hitter who bounced around in 2012, playing for the Cardinals and Twins before coming back to the Nationals. Has above-average plate discipline and good speed, but also limited power. Can play all three OF positions, but doesn't offer much as none of his tools are plus.

Kozma, Peter
6 | St. Louis | EXP MLB DEBUT: 2011 | POTENTIAL: Starting SS | 7A

Bats R Age 25 — 2007 (1) HS, OK

	Year	Lev	Team	AB	R	H	HR	RBI	Avg	OB	Slg	OPS	bb%	ct%	Eye	SB	CS	x/h%	Iso	RC/G
Pwr +	2010	AA	Springfield	503	69	122	13	72	243	318	384	702	10	78	0.50	13	2	35	141	4.25
BAvg +++	2011	AAA	Memphis	398	48	85	3	47	214	279	289	568	8	77	0.40	2	2	26	75	2.49
	2011	MLB	St. Louis	17	2	3	0	1	176	333	235	569	19	76	1.00	0	0	33	59	2.97
4.10 Spd +++	2012	AAA	Memphis	448	61	104	11	63	232	297	355	651	8	83	0.55	7	4	29	123	3.60
Def ++++	2012	MLB	St. Louis	72	11	24	2	14	333	392	569	962	9	74	0.37	2	0	42	236	7.87

Provided the Cards with a spark down the stretch and in playoffs when Furcal hit the DL. Is a plus defender with good range, soft hands, and a strong arm. Can also play 2B and could fill a utility role in '13. Looked good at the plate, but track record does not support this level of production, so look for some regression.

Krauss, Marc
379 | Houston | EXP MLB DEBUT: 2013 | POTENTIAL: Starting LF | 8E

Bats L Age 25 — 2009 (2) Ohio

	Year	Lev	Team	AB	R	H	HR	RBI	Avg	OB	Slg	OPS	bb%	ct%	Eye	SB	CS	x/h%	Iso	RC/G
	2010	A+	Visalia	530	107	160	25	87	302	370	509	879	10	73	0.40	1	3	35	208	6.56
Pwr ++++	2011	AA	Mobile	433	69	105	16	65	242	340	439	779	13	72	0.52	3	3	45	196	5.46
BAvg ++	2012	AA	Mobile	346	75	98	15	61	283	408	509	917	17	74	0.80	6	4	47	225	7.52
Spd ++	2012	AA	Corpus Christi	29	11	12	5	16	414	514	1000	1514	17	83	1.20	1	0	58	586	14.06
Def ++	2012	AAA	Oklahoma City	57	3	7	0	2	123	206	123	329	10	65	0.30	1	1	0	0	

Solidly-built prospect who repeated AA and posted better numbers. Hits for power to all fields and draws BB leading to high OBP. Power predicated more on strength than bat speed and struggles to catch up to quick FB. Could be platoon option as he hits RHP well. Lacks speed and limited to LF or 1B with poor range.

Kubitza, Kyle
5 | Atlanta | EXP MLB DEBUT: 2015 | POTENTIAL: Backup 3B | 6C

Bats L Age 22 — 2011 (3) Texas State

	Year	Lev	Team	AB	R	H	HR	RBI	Avg	OB	Slg	OPS	bb%	ct%	Eye	SB	CS	x/h%	Iso	RC/G
	2009	NCAA	Texas State	97	23	29	6	21	299	477	515	992	25	77	1.50	7	1	28	216	8.67
Pwr ++	2010	NCAA	Texas State	229	59	82	11	58	358	447	607	1054	14	82	0.88	7	2	40	249	8.84
BAvg +++	2011	NCAA	Texas State	226	59	70	10	66	310	443	558	1000	19	79	1.13	16	3	41	248	8.61
Spd +++	2011	Rk	Danville	162	36	52	1	34	321	409	475	884	13	77	0.63	9	3	38	154	7.01
Def ++	2012	A	Rome	448	68	107	9	59	239	345	393	738	14	72	0.57	18	11	39	154	5.03

Took a step back after an impressive debut. Does have above-average raw power and is patient at the plate, but he can be too passive and struck out 127 times. Has above-average speed and stole 18 bases. Is solid defensively with soft hands, range, and a strong arm. He is a better player than he showed in '12.

Lagares, Juan
7 | New York (N) | EXP MLB DEBUT: 2013 | POTENTIAL: Backup LF | 6B

Bats R Age 24 — 2006 NDFA, D.R.

	Year	Lev	Team	AB	R	H	HR	RBI	Avg	OB	Slg	OPS	bb%	ct%	Eye	SB	CS	x/h%	Iso	RC/G
	2010	A	Savannah	290	42	87	5	39	300	316	459	775	2	85	0.16	18	2	31	159	4.80
Pwr ++	2010	A+	St. Lucie	133	16	31	2	16	233	244	316	560	1	86	0.11	7	3	23	83	2.23
BAvg +++	2011	A+	St. Lucie	308	51	104	7	49	338	380	494	873	6	85	0.45	5	6	27	156	6.15
Spd ++	2011	AA	Binghamton	162	21	60	2	22	370	389	512	902	3	82	0.17	10	2	27	142	6.34
Def ++	2012	AA	Binghamton	499	69	141	4	48	283	332	389	721	7	81	0.40	21	10	28	106	4.43

Athletic OF makes hard contact and drives the ball into the gaps. Has above-average speed and the ability to hit for average despite marginal strike zone judgment. Has nice athleticism and did steal 21 bags, but his below-average power and struggles with pitch recognition make him more of a 4th OF type.

Laird, Brandon
35 | Houston | EXP MLB DEBUT: 2011 | POTENTIAL: Starting 3B | 7D

Bats R Age 25 — 2007 (27) Cypress JC

	Year	Lev	Team	AB	R	H	HR	RBI	Avg	OB	Slg	OPS	bb%	ct%	Eye	SB	CS	x/h%	Iso	RC/G
	2010	AAA	Scranton/W-B	122	13	30	2	12	246	270	344	614	3	78	0.15	0	0	27	98	2.79
Pwr ++++	2011	AAA	Scranton/W-B	462	51	120	16	69	260	286	422	708	4	82	0.20	0	0	36	162	3.94
BAvg ++	2011	MLB	New York (A)	21	3	4	0	1	190	292	190	482	13	81	0.75	0	0	0	0	1.68
Spd ++	2012	AAA	Scranton/W-B	503	54	128	15	77	254	302	414	715	6	80	0.33	1	0	38	159	4.22
Def +++	2012	MLB	Houston	35	2	9	1	4	257	297	371	669	5	77	0.25	0	0	22	114	3.50

Aggressive hitter who was acquired from NYY and promoted to big league roster. Impressive bat speed and leverage produces power to all fields and has success against LHP. Free-swinging has led to high Ks and poor OBP. Flails at breaking balls and needs to close holes in swing. Solid defender with good hands and arm.

Lake, Junior
6 | Chicago (N) | EXP MLB DEBUT: 2013 | POTENTIAL: Starting SS/3B | 8D

Bats R Age 23 — 2008 NDFA, D.R.

	Year	Lev	Team	AB	R	H	HR	RBI	Avg	OB	Slg	OPS	bb%	ct%	Eye	SB	CS	x/h%	Iso	RC/G
	2009	A	Peoria	463	71	115	7	42	248	277	365	642	4	70	0.13	10	7	29	117	3.25
Pwr ++	2010	A+	Daytona	394	56	104	9	46	264	324	398	722	8	75	0.35	13	9	30	135	4.45
BAvg ++	2011	A+	Daytona	203	39	64	6	34	315	335	498	832	3	76	0.12	19	4	33	182	5.59
Spd +++	2011	AA	Tennessee	242	41	60	6	17	248	286	380	666	5	75	0.22	19	2	30	132	3.53
Def ++++	2012	AA	Tennessee	405	56	113	10	50	279	336	432	768	8	74	0.33	21	12	35	153	5.08

Athletic player runs well and has a strong arm. Good power potential, but not in game action. Is overly aggressive with a long swing. When he does make contact, the ball jumps but poor contact limits his ability to hit. Good range, but his actions are long with poor footwork and a move to a new position still seems likely.

LaMarre, Ryan
8 | Cincinnati | EXP MLB DEBUT: 2014 | POTENTIAL: Backup CF | 6C

Bats R Age 24 — 2010 (2) Michigan

	Year	Lev	Team	AB	R	H	HR	RBI	Avg	OB	Slg	OPS	bb%	ct%	Eye	SB	CS	x/h%	Iso	RC/G
	2010	A	Dayton	227	44	64	5	29	282	343	396	739	8	77	0.40	18	7	25	115	4.64
Pwr +	2010	A+	Lynchburg	27	2	6	1	3	222	276	407	683	7	85	0.50	1	1	50	185	3.92
BAvg ++	2011	A+	Bakersfield	445	78	124	6	47	279	341	371	712	9	78	0.43	52	14	21	92	4.33
Spd +++	2011	AA	Carolina	15	3	4	0	0	267	389	333	722	17	80	1.00	3	0	25	67	5.01
Def ++++	2012	AA	Pensacola	482	68	127	5	32	263	345	353	698	11	75	0.50	30	10	24	89	4.30

Speed is his best tool and gives him value if he can figure out how to hit. Has moderate gap power and a nice line-drive stroke, but isn't likely to have much HR power. Draws walks, but needs to make more consistent contact. Has plenty of range in CF, but probably not enough power for a corner OF slot.

Lambo, Andrew
7 | Pittsburgh | EXP MLB DEBUT: 2013 | POTENTIAL: Backup 1B | 6D

Bats L Age 24 — 2007 (4) HS, CA

	Year	Lev	Team	AB	R	H	HR	RBI	Avg	OB	Slg	OPS	bb%	ct%	Eye	SB	CS	x/h%	Iso	RC/G
	2010	AA	Altoona	91	12	25	2	10	275	340	352	692	9	67	0.30	0	0	12	77	4.09
Pwr ++	2011	AA	Altoona	252	35	69	8	41	274	342	437	778	9	77	0.44	4	3	36	163	5.18
BAvg ++	2011	AAA	Indianapolis	185	19	34	3	17	184	252	292	544	8	74	0.35	1	0	41	108	2.10
4.35 Spd ++	2012	Rk	GCL Pirates	33	10	16	1	6	485	553	697	1250	13	85	1.00	1	0	31	212	11.14
Def ++	2012	AA	Altoona	92	13	23	4	16	250	349	435	784	13	79	0.74	0	1	35	185	5.37

Has seen his stock fall steadily since being serving a 50-game suspension in '10. Does have good raw strength, but his long-ball power has regressed and injuries limited him in '12. Improved strike zone judgment and the fact that he is still just 23 give him a chance, but the clock is ticking.

Landry, Leon
78 | Seattle | EXP MLB DEBUT: 2014 | POTENTIAL: Starting OF | 7B

Bats L Age 23 — 2010 (3) Louisiana State

	Year	Lev	Team	AB	R	H	HR	RBI	Avg	OB	Slg	OPS	bb%	ct%	Eye	SB	CS	x/h%	Iso	RC/G
	2010	NCAA	Louisiana State	240	55	81	6	45	338	411	513	924	11	90	1.20	16	4	30	175	7.07
Pwr +++	2010	Rk	Ogden	249	46	87	4	38	349	398	510	908	7	86	0.56	13	9	32	161	6.69
BAvg +++	2011	A	Great Lakes	500	59	125	4	41	250	302	360	662	7	87	0.55	28	12	29	110	3.83
Spd +++	2012	A+	Rancho Cuca	345	63	113	8	51	328	354	559	913	4	85	0.27	20	9	43	232	6.58
Def +++	2012	A+	High Desert	104	25	40	5	25	385	413	663	1076	5	87	0.36	7	2	40	279	8.31

Short, athletic OF who hit at least .310 each month and led CAL in BA. Showed ability to hit RHP and LHP while improving power stroke. Exhibits clean, quick swing, but raw approach doesn't lead to OBP. Can be free swinger and needs to improve pitch recognition. Has good speed with solid range, but limited arm.

LaStella, Tommy
4 | Atlanta | EXP MLB DEBUT: 2014 | POTENTIAL: Starting 2B | 7D

Bats L Age 24 — 2011 (8) Coastal Carolina

	Year	Lev	Team	AB	R	H	HR	RBI	Avg	OB	Slg	OPS	bb%	ct%	Eye	SB	CS	x/h%	Iso	RC/G
	2010	NCAA	Coastal Carolina	246	63	93	14	66	378	450	622	1072	12	94	2.13	6	0	32	244	8.55
Pwr ++	2011	NCAA	Coastal Carolina	231	59	92	14	70	398	471	680	1151	12	92	1.78	7	4	36	281	9.51
BAvg +++	2011	A	Rome	232	46	76	9	40	328	395	543	938	10	88	0.93	2	2	36	216	7.11
Spd ++	2012	Rk	GCL Braves	13	4	3	1	3	231	412	615	1027	24	92	4.00	0	0	67	385	8.88
Def ++	2012	A+	Lynchburg	298	43	90	5	56	302	377	460	837	11	92	1.50	13	2	36	158	6.15

Is one of the better pure hitters in the system with a polished approach at the plate. Has decent power for 2B and shoots balls into the gap with a quick stroke. Has average speed and runs the bases well. Is below average defensively but if defense holds up, he has enough offense to make him a regular.

Lee, Hak-Ju
6 | Tampa Bay | EXP MLB DEBUT: 2013 | POTENTIAL: Starting SS | 8B

Bats L Age 22 — 2008 FA (South Korea)

	Year	Lev	Team	AB	R	H	HR	RBI	Avg	OB	Slg	OPS	bb%	ct%	Eye	SB	CS	x/h%	Iso	RC/G
	2009	A-	Boise	264	56	87	2	33	330	400	420	820	11	81	0.62	25	8	21	91	5.85
Pwr ++	2010	A	Peoria	485	85	137	1	40	282	348	351	699	9	82	0.57	32	7	20	68	4.30
BAvg +++	2011	A+	Charlotte	400	82	127	4	23	318	382	443	825	10	82	0.58	28	14	24	125	5.87
Spd ++++	2011	AA	Montgomery	100	16	19	1	7	190	270	310	580	10	78	0.50	5	2	32	120	2.80
Def ++++	2012	AA	Montgomery	475	68	124	4	37	261	333	360	693	10	79	0.50	37	9	23	99	4.21

Tall, thin INF who has better glove than bat. Two-time Futures Game participant has range, hands, and arm requisite of plus defender in middle infield. Set career high in SB and plus speed is best attribute. Short swing allows for line drives to gaps, but often resorts to slap approach. Should hit for BA with limited pop.

Lemmerman, Jake — 6 — St. Louis

EXP MLB DEBUT: 2014 | POTENTIAL: Utility INF | 6D

Bats R Age 24	Year	Lev	Team	AB	R	H	HR	RBI	Avg	OB	Slg	OPS	bb%	ct%	Eye	SB	CS	x/h%	Iso	RC/G
2010 (5) Duke	2010	NCAA	Duke	218	47	73	11	45	335	411	569	979	11	85	0.85	9	3	36	234	7.63
Pwr + +	2010	Rk	Ogden	259	69	94	12	47	363	431	610	1041	11	78	0.55	5	4	40	247	8.61
BAvg +	2011	A+	Rancho Cuca	400	71	117	8	54	293	367	420	787	11	78	0.52	9	3	28	128	5.40
Spd + +	2011	AA	Chattanooga	77	11	18	2	11	234	306	390	695	9	71	0.36	1	0	44	156	4.19
Def + + +	2012	AA	Chattanooga	373	52	87	7	46	233	329	378	707	12	75	0.56	8	0	44	145	4.50

Smart INF gets the most of abilities, but doesn't have great tools. Cardinals will look to try and make some adjustments after offseason trade. Showed moderate power for position and squares the ball up consistently. Speed is a tick below average, but he's a plus defender.

Leon, Sandy — 2 — Washington

EXP MLB DEBUT: 2012 | POTENTIAL: Backup C | 6B

Bats B Age 24	Year	Lev	Team	AB	R	H	HR	RBI	Avg	OB	Slg	OPS	bb%	ct%	Eye	SB	CS	x/h%	Iso	RC/G
2007 NDFA, Venezuela	2011	A+	Potomac	370	36	93	6	43	251	313	362	675	8	81	0.48	1	3	30	111	3.88
Pwr +	2012	AA	Harrisburg	135	15	42	1	19	311	354	422	776	6	88	0.56	1	0	31	111	5.11
BAvg + + +	2012	AAA	Syracuse	52	8	18	2	4	346	469	558	1026	19	77	1.00	0	0	39	212	9.01
Spd +	2012	MLB	Washington	30	2	8	0	2	267	353	333	686	12	63	0.36	0	0	25	67	4.47
Def + + + +	2012	A-	Auburn	15	3	5	0	3	333	444	467	911	17	87	1.50	0	0	40	133	7.48

Stocky backstop had a nice breakout, hitting .322 and then made his MLB debut. Good defensive catcher with blocking skills, a quick release and a strong arm. Struggled to hit for average or power in the past, but something seemed to click this year. Still likely a backup, but worth watching in 2013.

Leonard, Patrick — 5 — Tampa Bay

EXP MLB DEBUT: 2016 | POTENTIAL: Starting 3B | 8D

Bats R Age 20	Year	Lev	Team	AB	R	H	HR	RBI	Avg	OB	Slg	OPS	bb%	ct%	Eye	SB	CS	x/h%	Iso	RC/G
2011 (5) HS (TX)																				
Pwr + + + +																				
BAvg + +																				
Spd + +																				
Def + +	2012	Rk	Burlington	235	37	59	14	46	251	336	494	829	11	77	0.55	6	2	44	243	5.82

Big, strong INF who led APPY in HR. Quick wrists generate bat speed and ideal power for 3B. Has good idea of K zone and makes surprising contact. Can be pull happy and should focus on going opposite way at times. Limited range and speed, but has soft hands and strong arm that could work in OF corner.

Lin, Che-Hsuan — 89 — Houston

EXP MLB DEBUT: 2012 | POTENTIAL: Starting OF | 7C

Bats R Age 24	Year	Lev	Team	AB	R	H	HR	RBI	Avg	OB	Slg	OPS	bb%	ct%	Eye	SB	CS	x/h%	Iso	RC/G
2007 FA (Taiwan)	2010	AA	Portland	458	88	126	2	34	275	374	343	716	14	86	1.14	26	12	18	68	4.83
Pwr + +	2011	AA	Portland	138	23	37	0	11	268	361	333	694	13	90	1.43	12	3	19	65	4.65
BAvg + +	2011	AAA	Pawtucket	328	49	77	2	25	235	314	293	607	10	84	0.75	16	4	18	58	3.27
Spd + + + +	2012	AAA	Pawtucket	396	42	98	2	30	247	320	316	635	10	84	0.65	15	4	18	68	3.56
Def + + + +	2012	MLB	Boston	12	1	3	0	0	250	250	250	500	0	58	0.00	0	0	0	0	1.15

Natural hitting OF who was acquired off waivers from BOS. Power hasn't developed and fringy bat speed and flat swing path limit pop potential. Control K zone with contact approach. Has intellect for game and runs bases with plus speed. Can play any OF position due to instincts. Plus arm is asset.

Lin, Tzu-Wei — 6 — Boston

EXP MLB DEBUT: 2016 | POTENTIAL: Starting SS | 8E

Bats L Age 19	Year	Lev	Team	AB	R	H	HR	RBI	Avg	OB	Slg	OPS	bb%	ct%	Eye	SB	CS	x/h%	Iso	RC/G
2012 FA (Taiwan)																				
Pwr +																				
BAvg + + +																				
Spd + + + +																				
Def + + +	2012	Rk	GCL Red Sox	110	21	28	0	16	255	349	318	667	13	75	0.57	4	2	21	64	4.03

Natural hitting INF who signed in June and immediately produced. Has offensive ability with quick, simple stroke and should hit for BA with all-fields approach. Differentiates between balls and strikes and contact should improve once he reads breaking balls better. Exhibits plus speed and has range and arm to stick at SS.

Linares, Juan Carlos — 789 — Boston

EXP MLB DEBUT: 2013 | POTENTIAL: Reserve OF | 6B

Bats R Age 28	Year	Lev	Team	AB	R	H	HR	RBI	Avg	OB	Slg	OPS	bb%	ct%	Eye	SB	CS	x/h%	Iso	RC/G
2010 FA (Cuba)	2010	Rk	GCL Red Sox	15	2	4	0	1	267	313	333	646	6	87	0.50	0	0	25	67	3.60
Pwr + + +	2010	AA	Portland	46	3	11	1	4	239	239	391	630	0	72	0.00	1	1	45	152	2.92
BAvg + + +	2011	AAA	Pawtucket	60	8	14	3	12	233	281	500	781	6	80	0.33	0	1	64	267	5.05
Spd + +	2012	AA	Portland	210	34	70	8	33	333	397	538	935	9	86	0.73	0	1	37	205	7.03
Def + + +	2012	AAA	Pawtucket	202	24	60	8	29	297	321	480	801	3	82	0.19	0	0	33	183	5.02

Steady prospect who makes such easy contact that he rarely draws BB. Has short swing for extreme bat-to-ball ability and uses entire field with avg pop. Breaking balls have been problematic and could pull ball more. Owns fringy speed and rarely steals bases. Can play any OF spot with avg range and arm.

Lindor, Francisco — 6 — Cleveland

EXP MLB DEBUT: 2015 | POTENTIAL: Starting SS | 9B

Bats B Age 19	Year	Lev	Team	AB	R	H	HR	RBI	Avg	OB	Slg	OPS	bb%	ct%	Eye	SB	CS	x/h%	Iso	RC/G
2011 (1) HS (PR)																				
Pwr + + +																				
BAvg + + + +																				
Spd + + + +	2011	A-	Mahoning Val	19	4	6	0	2	316	350	316	666	5	74	0.20	1	0	0	0	3.48
Def + + + +	2012	A	Lake County	490	83	126	6	42	257	339	355	694	11	84	0.78	27	12	26	98	4.35

Athletic, fundamentally-sound INF who was youngest regular in MWL. Has tools and actions requisite of All-Star MIF. Possesses polish, plus range, quickness and strong arm at SS. Bat control allows for easy contact and has enough pop for double digit HR. Knows strike zone and should hit for very high BA at peak

Lindsey, Taylor — 4 — Los Angeles (A)

EXP MLB DEBUT: 2014 | POTENTIAL: Starting 2B | 7A

Bats L Age 21	Year	Lev	Team	AB	R	H	HR	RBI	Avg	OB	Slg	OPS	bb%	ct%	Eye	SB	CS	x/h%	Iso	RC/G
2010 (1-S) HS (AZ)																				
Pwr + + +																				
BAvg + + + +	2010	Rk	Angels	194	26	55	0	18	284	325	407	732	6	83	0.36	8	3	33	124	4.62
Spd + +	2011	Rk	Orem	290	64	105	9	46	362	389	593	983	4	84	0.28	10	4	41	231	7.34
Def + + +	2012	A+	Inland Empire	547	79	158	9	58	289	325	408	732	5	88	0.44	8	6	26	119	4.46

Pure hitting INF who bypassed Low-A and was star in a weak system. Combines contact approach with plus hand-eye coordination. Will never hit for much pop because of bat path, but can reach seats. Needs to improve against LHP to play every day in majors. Defense is OK and has sufficient range.

Lipka, Matt — 8 — Atlanta

EXP MLB DEBUT: 2014 | POTENTIAL: Starting CF | 7C

Bats R Age 21	Year	Lev	Team	AB	R	H	HR	RBI	Avg	OB	Slg	OPS	bb%	ct%	Eye	SB	CS	x/h%	Iso	RC/G
2010 (1-S) HS, TX																				
Pwr + +	2010	Rk	GCL Braves	192	33	58	1	24	302	350	401	751	7	89	0.64	20	3	22	99	4.86
BAvg + +	2010	Rk	Danville	16	1	2	0	1	125	176	125	301	6	88	0.50	1	0	0	0	
6.3/60 Spd + + + +	2011	A	Rome	530	78	131	1	37	247	302	304	606	7	84	0.51	28	14	19	57	3.11
Def + +	2012	A+	Lynchburg	199	32	54	2	13	271	338	337	675	9	84	0.63	12	6	15	65	3.96

Toolsy former 1st rounder who was moved from SS to CF. He has plus speed with an ability to get on base and create havoc, but is not likely to hit for power. Does have bat speed, but prefers to spray line drives with good strike zone judgment. A hamstring injury in June limited him and has been slow to develop.

Liriano, Rymer — 9 — San Diego

EXP MLB DEBUT: 2014 | POTENTIAL: Starting CF | 9D

Bats R Age 22	Year	Lev	Team	AB	R	H	HR	RBI	Avg	OB	Slg	OPS	bb%	ct%	Eye	SB	CS	x/h%	Iso	RC/G
2007 NDFA, D.R.	2010	A-	Eugene	203	35	55	0	12	271	327	394	721	8	74	0.32	17	7	35	123	4.63
Pwr + + + +	2011	A	Fort Wayne	455	81	145	12	62	319	382	499	881	9	79	0.49	65	20	34	180	6.54
BAvg + + +	2011	A+	Lake Elsinore	55	8	7	0	6	127	213	182	395	10	76	0.46	1	1	29	55	0.32
Spd + + + +	2012	A+	Lake Elsinore	282	41	84	5	41	298	347	443	790	7	76	0.30	22	7	35	145	5.33
Def + + +	2012	AA	San Antonio	183	24	46	3	20	251	325	377	702	10	73	0.40	10	1	33	126	4.33

Has plus power and speed potential. Plate discipline and pitch recognition continue to be an issue and he struck out 119 times. That shortcoming is holding him back from being an elite prospect, as he does everything else well. Covers ground well with a strong throwing arm and has enough speed to stay in CF.

Lohman, Devin — 5 — Cincinnati

EXP MLB DEBUT: 2014 | POTENTIAL: Starting 2B | 7C

Bats R Age 24	Year	Lev	Team	AB	R	H	HR	RBI	Avg	OB	Slg	OPS	bb%	ct%	Eye	SB	CS	x/h%	Iso	RC/G
2010 (3) Long Beach St	2010	Rk	Billings	230	33	55	1	31	239	311	322	633	9	80	0.51	2	5	27	83	3.46
Pwr + +	2011	Rk	Billings	115	23	37	4	21	322	405	461	865	12	81	0.73	6	2	22	139	6.35
BAvg + + +	2011	A	Dayton	207	14	43	1	31	208	268	256	524	8	77	0.36	9	2	16	48	1.87
Spd + + +	2011	A+	Bakersfield	130	25	43	5	17	331	392	554	945	9	82	0.57	4	2	40	223	7.21
Def + + +	2012	A+	Bakersfield	494	80	127	14	70	257	338	401	738	11	78	0.56	34	9	31	144	4.74

Strong athletic INF has not developed as anticipated. Failed to duplicate breakout of '11 in a repeat of the CAL. Does have moderate power hit 14 HR with 34 SB, but hit just .257. Defensively has good hands and range. Arm and actions are better suited at 2B where he saw the bulk of action in '12.

Lopes, Timothy — 4 — Seattle

EXP MLB DEBUT: 2016 | POTENTIAL: Starting 2B | 7C

Bats R Age 19 | 2012 (6) HS (CA) | Pwr ++ | BAvg +++ | Spd +++ | Def +++

Year	Lev	Team	AB	R	H	HR	RBI	Avg	OB	Slg	OPS	bb%	ct%	Eye	SB	CS	x/h%	Iso	RC/G
2012	Rk	Mariners	215	42	68	0	32	316	385	479	864	10	87	0.83	7	3	34	163	6.51
2012	A+	High Desert	12	2	3	0	1	250	250	417	667	0	92	0.00	0	0	33	167	3.72

Short, instinctual INF who has simple approach and focuses on consistent contact to all fields. Should hit for moderate BA as he owns good hand-eye coordination and level swing. Power isn't in cards, though. Exhibits solid quickiness which benefits range at 2B. Could play SS, though arm and actions suitable for 2B.

Lough, David — 789 — Kansas City

EXP MLB DEBUT: 2012 | POTENTIAL: Reserve OF | 6B

Bats L Age 27 | 2007 (11) Mercyhurst | Pwr ++ | BAvg +++ | Spd +++ | Def +++

Year	Lev	Team	AB	R	H	HR	RBI	Avg	OB	Slg	OPS	bb%	ct%	Eye	SB	CS	x/h%	Iso	RC/G
2009	AA	NW Arkansas	236	41	78	9	31	331	363	517	880	5	87	0.40	13	4	31	186	6.02
2010	AAA	Omaha	460	65	129	11	58	280	338	437	775	8	84	0.56	14	5	29	157	5.11
2011	AAA	Omaha	456	87	145	9	65	318	368	482	850	7	89	0.73	14	8	32	164	6.00
2012	AAA	Omaha	491	69	135	10	69	275	310	420	730	5	87	0.38	26	4	30	145	4.42
2012	MLB	Kansas City	59	9	14	0	2	237	286	305	591	6	85	0.44	1	0	21	68	2.92

Fundamentally-sound OF who made it to KC after 3 yrs in AAA. Doesn't own plus tool and does everything relatively well. Has polish, though limited upside. Can play all OF spots, but arm is on short side and better in LF. Consistent performer who can hit for BA and avg pop. Uses direct swing to make extreme contact.

Lowery, Jake — 2 — Cleveland

EXP MLB DEBUT: 2015 | POTENTIAL: Backup C | 6B

Bats L Age 22 | 2011 (4) James Madison | Pwr +++ | BAvg ++ | Spd + | Def ++

Year	Lev	Team	AB	R	H	HR	RBI	Avg	OB	Slg	OPS	bb%	ct%	Eye	SB	CS	x/h%	Iso	RC/G
2010	NCAA	James Madison	186	32	53	8	41	285	361	505	866	11	78	0.54	1	7	42	220	6.36
2011	NCAA	James Madison	251	80	90	24	91	359	443	797	1240	13	81	0.81	9	3	60	438	10.96
2011	A-	Mahoning Val	253	43	62	6	43	245	378	415	793	18	78	0.96	3	2	48	170	5.88
2012	A	Lake County	137	25	34	7	28	248	360	504	864	15	72	0.62	1	0	56	255	6.70
2012	A+	Carolina	203	20	45	2	25	222	316	325	641	12	65	0.39	0	1	38	103	3.67

Strong. compact C who regressed as season progressed and demoted to Low-A. Can be too patient and let hittable pitches pass. Has keen eye, but limited contact and BA as a result. Has punch in strong swing. Possesses avg power potential to whole field. Catching skills still developing, though arm is very strong.

Lutz, Zach — 5 — New York (N)

EXP MLB DEBUT: 2012 | POTENTIAL: Reserve 3B/1B | 6C

Bats R Age 27 | 2007 (5) Alvernia | Pwr +++ | BAvg ++ | Spd ++ | Def ++

Year	Lev	Team	AB	R	H	HR	RBI	Avg	OB	Slg	OPS	bb%	ct%	Eye	SB	CS	x/h%	Iso	RC/G
2011	A+	St. Lucie	8	0	0	0	1	0	111	0	111	11	75	0.50	0	0			
2011	AAA	Buffalo	220	38	65	11	31	295	372	500	872	11	68	0.39	0	0	35	205	6.74
2012	A+	St. Lucie	20	2	5	1	8	250	375	500	875	17	75	0.80	0	0	60	250	6.83
2012	AAA	Buffalo	244	34	73	10	35	299	402	496	898	15	69	0.56	0	0	37	197	7.31
2012	MLB	New York (N)	11	1	1	0	0	91	91	91	182	0	55	0.00	0	0	0	0	

Former 5th rounder made his MLB debut after a solid season at AAA. Strong, stocky 3B has solid power, but can't seem to stay healthy. Broken ankle in '09, and broken foot in '10, two concusions in '11, and a broken hand in '12. When healthy has a nice bat and good power. but is below-average defensively.

Mahoney, Joseph — 3 — Miami

EXP MLB DEBUT: 2012 | POTENTIAL: Starting 1B | 8E

Bats L Age 26 | 2007 (6) Richmond | Pwr +++ | BAvg +++ | Spd ++ | Def +++

Year	Lev	Team	AB	R	H	HR	RBI	Avg	OB	Slg	OPS	bb%	ct%	Eye	SB	CS	x/h%	Iso	RC/G
2010	AA	Bowie	191	30	61	9	29	319	375	545	920	8	80	0.44	8	1	38	225	6.82
2011	A+	Frederick	8	0	4	0	2	500	667	750	1417	33	88	4.00	0	0	50	250	15.08
2011	AA	Bowie	315	43	91	11	67	289	341	502	843	7	73	0.30	7	2	44	213	6.08
2012	AAA	Norfolk	491	54	130	10	56	265	314	389	703	7	81	0.37	4	2	31	124	4.11
2012	MLB	Baltimore	4	0	0	0	0	0	0	0	0	0	100	0.00	0	0	0	0	

Tall, strong INF who reached BAL despite lack of power growth. Doesn't hit for as much pop as frame suggests as he owns level stroke and focuses on using entire field. Can be jammed inside and has trouble catching up to good FB. Doesn't draw many BB and swing can be exploited. Secondary skills are avg at best.

Mahtook, Mikie — 89 — Tampa Bay

EXP MLB DEBUT: 2014 | POTENTIAL: Starting OF | 8C

Bats R Age 23 | 2011 (1) LSU | Pwr +++ | BAvg +++ | Spd +++ | Def +++

Year	Lev	Team	AB	R	H	HR	RBI	Avg	OB	Slg	OPS	bb%	ct%	Eye	SB	CS	x/h%	Iso	RC/G
2009	NCAA	Louisiana State	196	41	62	7	38	316	362	495	857	7	79	0.34	9	4	29	179	5.98
2010	NCAA	Louisiana State	239	68	80	14	50	335	426	623	1049	14	77	0.70	22	10	46	289	8.91
2011	NCAA	Louisiana State	196	61	75	14	56	383	489	709	1199	17	84	1.28	29	9	41	327	10.68
2012	A+	Charlotte	341	44	99	5	37	290	346	419	765	8	79	0.41	19	6	27	129	5.01
2012	AA	Montgomery	153	17	38	4	25	248	299	405	704	7	80	0.35	4	3	39	157	4.13

Athletic, advanced OF who had solid pro debut. Makes consistent, hard contact to all fields with short stroke and offers mature approach. Can overswing and flail at breaking pitches, but is complete hitter when focused. Runs well and SB totals enhanced by instincts. Lacks true plus tool, but does everything relatively well.

Marder, Jack — 24 — Seattle

EXP MLB DEBUT: 2015 | POTENTIAL: Reserve C/2B | 7D

Bats R Age 23 | 2011 (16) Oregon | Pwr ++ | BAvg +++ | Spd ++ | Def ++

Year	Lev	Team	AB	R	H	HR	RBI	Avg	OB	Slg	OPS	bb%	ct%	Eye	SB	CS	x/h%	Iso	RC/G
2010	NCAA	Oregon	197	38	49	5	33	249	299	391	689	7	86	0.52	7	0	35	142	4.02
2011	NCAA	Oregon	139	19	29	2	19	209	295	295	590	11	81	0.63	10	3	28	86	2.94
2011	A+	High Desert	71	11	23	2	12	324	342	493	835	3	83	0.17	3	1	35	169	5.45
2012	A+	High Desert	278	68	100	10	56	360	405	583	987	7	84	0.48	16	6	38	223	7.54

Athletic, natural hitting prospect who split time between C and 2B in solid offensive season. Doesn't have typical profile of C as he runs well and has quick actions. Still relatively raw behind plate, but possesses strong arm with quick release. Uses level swing path for gap power, but lacks leverage and load for pop.

Marin, Adrian — 6 — Baltimore

EXP MLB DEBUT: 2015 | POTENTIAL: Starting SS | 8D

Bats R Age 19 | 2012 (3) HS (FL) | Pwr ++ | BAvg +++ | Spd +++ | Def +++

Year	Lev	Team	AB	R	H	HR	RBI	Avg	OB	Slg	OPS	bb%	ct%	Eye	SB	CS	x/h%	Iso	RC/G
2012	Rk	GCL Orioles	178	24	51	0	13	287	328	360	688	6	81	0.32	6	1	20	73	3.97
2012	A	Delmarva	21	5	6	0	2	286	318	286	604	5	90	0.50	2	0	0	0	3.02

Thin, athletic INF who started slow upon signing, but finished hot. Exceptional instincts and feel for game allow tools to play up. Runs well and owns nimble feet and hands. Ranges well to both sides and avg arm is sufficient. Swing can get long and may struggle with breaking balls, but has potential for 5 tools.

Marisnick, Jake — 8 — Miami

EXP MLB DEBUT: 2014 | POTENTIAL: Starting OF | 9C

Bats R Age 22 | 2009 (3) HS (CA) | Pwr ++++ | BAvg +++ | Spd ++++ | Def ++++

Year	Lev	Team	AB	R	H	HR	RBI	Avg	OB	Slg	OPS	bb%	ct%	Eye	SB	CS	x/h%	Iso	RC/G
2010	Rk	GCL Blue Jays	122	17	35	3	14	287	356	459	815	10	85	0.72	14	1	43	172	5.70
2010	A	Lansing	127	16	28	1	12	220	272	339	611	7	71	0.24	9	2	39	118	3.01
2011	A	Lansing	462	68	148	14	77	320	378	496	874	9	80	0.47	37	8	32	175	6.33
2012	A+	Dunedin	266	41	70	6	35	263	329	451	780	9	79	0.47	10	5	44	188	5.29
2012	AA	New Hampshire	223	25	52	2	15	233	269	336	606	5	80	0.24	14	4	31	103	2.87

Tall, instinctual OF with athleticism and power potential. Struggled in first AA trial, but still has high ceiling. Chases breaking balls out of zone, though has ability to catch up to good fastballs. Drives balls to all fields and power still developing. Runs very well and has enough speed for 20+ SB. Has plus range and arm.

Marlette, Tyler — 2 — Seattle

EXP MLB DEBUT: 2016 | POTENTIAL: Starting C | 8D

Bats R Age 20 | 2011 (5) HS (FL) | Pwr ++++ | BAvg ++ | Spd ++ | Def ++

Year	Lev	Team	AB	R	H	HR	RBI	Avg	OB	Slg	OPS	bb%	ct%	Eye	SB	CS	x/h%	Iso	RC/G
2011	Rk	Pulaski	45	4	7	0	2	156	156	200	356	0	71	0.00	0	0	29	44	-0.80
2012	Rk	Pulaski	208	23	59	5	23	284	304	423	727	3	78	0.13	3	1	32	139	4.18
2012	A-	Everett	5	0	2	0	0	400	400	600	1000	0	80	0.00	0	1	50	200	7.60

Short, strong C who could leverage plus power into high ceiling. Doesn't work counts, but puts charge into ball due to excellent bat speed. Swings aggressively and can be fooled by offspeed stuff. Has strong arm and good catch and throw skills, but receiving and blocking need work. Could be solid offense-first catcher.

Marrero, Chris — 3 — Washington

EXP MLB DEBUT: 2013 | POTENTIAL: Starting 1B | 7D

Bats R Age 25 | 2006 (1) HS, FL | Pwr +++ | BAvg +++ | 4.40 Spd ++ | Def +++

Year	Lev	Team	AB	R	H	HR	RBI	Avg	OB	Slg	OPS	bb%	ct%	Eye	SB	CS	x/h%	Iso	RC/G
2012	A	Hagerstown	4	1	1	0	0	250	400	500	900	20	50	0.50	0	0	100	250	10.30
2012	A+	Potomac	13	1	6	1	4	462	462	769	1231	0	85	0.00	0	0	33	308	9.55
2012	AA	Harrisburg	22	2	6	1	3	273	273	500	773	0	86	0.00	0	0	50	227	4.52
2012	AAA	Syracuse	127	13	31	0	12	244	329	307	636	11	78	0.57	0	0	23	63	3.57
2012	A-	Auburn	14	4	5	1	3	357	438	643	1080	13	57	0.33	0	0	40	286	11.35

Former 1st rounder had another injury-filled season. Hamstring injury kept him out of action until June and he looked sluggish when he returned. Has good bat speed and the ability to make adjustments, but swings aggressively and struggled to make contact. Remains an average defender with below-average speed.

Marrero, Deven | 6 | Boston | EXP MLB DEBUT: 2014 | POTENTIAL: Starting SS | 7B

Bats R Age 22	Year	Lev	Team	AB	R	H	HR	RBI	Avg	OB	Slg	OPS	bb%	ct%	Eye	SB	CS	x/h%	Iso	RC/G
2012 (1) Arizona State																				
Pwr ++	2010	NCAA	Arizona State	156	31	62	6	42	397	444	628	1072	8	85	0.54	11	1	34	231	8.56
BAvg +++	2011	NCAA	Arizona State	207	30	66	2	20	319	359	444	804	6	86	0.45	10	5	29	126	5.38
Spd +++	2012	NCAA	Arizona State	208	36	58	4	32	279	333	438	771	8	92	1.06	10	3	34	159	5.19
Def ++++	2012	A-	Lowell	246	45	66	2	24	268	357	374	731	12	80	0.71	24	6	29	106	4.86

Athletic, instinctual INF who impressed upon signing. Won't wow with power, but offers gap ability and works counts. Compact stroke helpful in making contact, but can be beaten with good FB. A true plus defender with quick feet and above average range and could win hardware in future. Instincts are off the charts.

Marte, Alfredo | 8 | Arizona | EXP MLB DEBUT: 2014 | POTENTIAL: Starting LF | 7D

Bats R Age 24	Year	Lev	Team	AB	R	H	HR	RBI	Avg	OB	Slg	OPS	bb%	ct%	Eye	SB	CS	x/h%	Iso	RC/G
2005 NDFA, D.R.	2009	A	South Bend	475	49	119	7	71	251	288	364	652	5	84	0.32	5	2	31	114	3.48
Pwr +++	2010	A+	Visalia	516	76	134	9	61	260	305	374	679	6	79	0.32	9	5	28	114	3.80
BAvg ++	2011	A+	Visalia	234	35	70	7	33	299	339	479	817	6	82	0.33	5	0	36	179	5.45
Spd ++	2011	AA	Mobile	43	4	10	1	6	233	298	326	623	9	77	0.40	1	0	20	93	3.09
Def ++	2012	AA	Mobile	398	68	117	20	75	294	350	523	872	8	82	0.47	6	6	41	229	6.15

Nice breakout season, hitting a career-high 20 HR and making an appearance in the Futures Game. Can be overly aggressive at the plate but improved contact rate at the same time he showed improved power. Looks to be a late bloomer. Solid defender with good range, but the raw power is going to be his calling card.

Marte, Jefry | 5 | Oakland | EXP MLB DEBUT: 2014 | POTENTIAL: Starting 3B | 8E

Bats R Age 22	Year	Lev	Team	AB	R	H	HR	RBI	Avg	OB	Slg	OPS	bb%	ct%	Eye	SB	CS	x/h%	Iso	RC/G
2007 NDFA, D.R.	2008	Rk	GCL Mets	154	29	50	4	24	325	377	532	910	8	81	0.43	2	0	42	208	6.82
Pwr +++	2009	A	Savannah	485	58	113	6	41	233	271	338	609	5	76	0.21	5	5	29	105	2.84
BAvg ++	2010	A	Savannah	329	40	87	6	44	264	326	401	727	8	80	0.46	4	5	33	137	4.55
4.30 Spd ++	2011	A+	St. Lucie	483	56	120	7	55	248	307	346	653	8	82	0.48	14	2	26	97	3.60
Def ++	2012	AA	Binghamton	462	61	116	9	58	251	315	366	681	9	84	0.57	9	5	28	115	3.98

Has been slow to develop and was traded this off-season. Has moderate plate discipline and quick hands that give him the potential to hit for average, but that hasn't happened yet. Below average defense with limited range and stiff hands. He has been young for every level, but will need to prove he can hit eventually.

Marte, Ketel | 46 | Seattle | EXP MLB DEBUT: 2017 | POTENTIAL: Starting 2B/SS | 8E

Bats B Age 19	Year	Lev	Team	AB	R	H	HR	RBI	Avg	OB	Slg	OPS	bb%	ct%	Eye	SB	CS	x/h%	Iso	RC/G
2010 FA (DR)																				
Pwr +																				
BAvg ++																				
Spd ++++	2012	A	Clinton	14	3	4	0	2	286	375	286	661	13	79	0.67	1	0	0	0	3.87
Def ++++	2012	A-	Everett	251	36	62	0	22	247	281	279	560	5	86	0.34	14	4	10	32	2.44

Aggressive, quick INF who plays above avg defense with plus instincts. Has advanced feel with great quickness. Makes routine and spectacular plays with soft hands. Offensive game could come around, though has little power and is more of singles hitter. Aggressive approach needs to be tamed, but controls bat.

Martin, Brandon | 6 | Tampa Bay | EXP MLB DEBUT: 2015 | POTENTIAL: Starting SS | 8D

Bats R Age 19	Year	Lev	Team	AB	R	H	HR	RBI	Avg	OB	Slg	OPS	bb%	ct%	Eye	SB	CS	x/h%	Iso	RC/G
2011 (1-S) HS (CA)																				
Pwr +++																				
BAvg ++																				
Spd +++	2011	Rk	GCL Rays	47	10	12	1	3	255	352	340	692	13	74	0.58	5	3	17	85	4.20
Def +++	2012	Rk	Princeton	254	46	53	10	32	209	269	402	671	8	71	0.29	8	1	47	193	3.71

Short, quick INF who had impressive power display. Exhibits bat speed due to quick wrists and natural strength and can catch up to any FB. Crude pitch recognition could hinder BA and will likely have plenty of Ks. Possesses avg speed, but defense plays up due to instincts. Has strong, accurate arm.

Martin, Leonys | 8 | Texas | EXP MLB DEBUT: 2011 | POTENTIAL: Starting OF | 8C

Bats L Age 25	Year	Lev	Team	AB	R	H	HR	RBI	Avg	OB	Slg	OPS	bb%	ct%	Eye	SB	CS	x/h%	Iso	RC/G
2011 FA (Cuba)	2011	AA	Frisco	112	24	39	4	24	348	425	571	997	12	93	1.88	10	8	38	223	7.91
Pwr +++	2011	AAA	Round Rock	175	27	46	0	17	263	306	314	621	6	86	0.46	9	2	17	51	3.25
BAvg ++++	2011	MLB	Texas	8	2	3	0	0	375	375	500	875	0	88	0.00	0	0	33	125	5.80
Spd ++++	2012	AAA	Round Rock	231	48	83	12	42	359	420	610	1030	9	83	0.62	10	9	39	251	8.15
Def ++++	2012	MLB	Texas	46	6	8	0	6	174	240	370	610	8	74	0.33	3	0	88	196	3.30

Tall, lean OF with natural hitting skills. Has leadoff potential due to quick, level swing, and easy contact. Has plus raw power, but focuses more on line drives. Can lengthen swing at times and get himself out by swinging at bad pitches. Has ideal speed for SB and plays CF with plus range and arm.

Martin, Trey | 8 | Chicago (N) | EXP MLB DEBUT: 2016 | POTENTIAL: Starting CF | 7C

Bats R Age 20	Year	Lev	Team	AB	R	H	HR	RBI	Avg	OB	Slg	OPS	bb%	ct%	Eye	SB	CS	x/h%	Iso	RC/G
2011 (13) HS, GA																				
Pwr +++																				
BAvg ++	2011	Rk	Cubs	70	10	17	0	8	243	284	357	641	5	76	0.24	3	2	24	114	3.43
Spd +++	2012	Rk	Cubs	29	5	13	0	6	448	484	690	1174	6	90	0.67	2	0	46	241	9.78
Def +++	2012	A-	Boise	204	26	55	3	23	270	313	377	691	6	76	0.27	6	5	22	108	3.94

Lean, wiry OF had a solid season. Has exciting tools with above-average speed and good raw power. Makes consistent contact, but needs to be more selective and shorten his swing. He is a plus defender in CF who takes good routes and has a strong, accurate arm. Still has some work to do, but the raw tools give him potential.

Martinez, Alberth | 8 | San Diego | EXP MLB DEBUT: 2014 | POTENTIAL: Starting CF | 8C

Bats R Age 22	Year	Lev	Team	AB	R	H	HR	RBI	Avg	OB	Slg	OPS	bb%	ct%	Eye	SB	CS	x/h%	Iso	RC/G
2009 NDFA, D.R.	2011	A	Fort Wayne	13	0	0	0	0	0	71	0	71	7	54	0.17	0	1			
Pwr +++	2011	AAA	Tucson	17	0	2	0	0	118	118	118	235	0	59	0.00	0	0	0	0	
BAvg +++	2011	A-	Eugene	44	3	8	0	3	182	217	273	490	4	82	0.25	4	0	38	91	1.58
Spd ++++	2012	A	Fort Wayne	62	8	8	0	3	129	182	194	375	6	77	0.29	3	0	50	65	0.01
Def ++++	2012	A-	Eugene	232	37	59	0	20	254	322	310	632	9	84	0.61	9	4	20	56	3.51

Lean, athletic OF has an exciting package of tools, but struggled to duplicate his breakout of '11. Was overmatched in the MWL before being sent down to short-season in the NWL. Has plus bat speed and the potential to hit for average and power while playing good defense. Will need to rebound in '13, but has time.

Martinez, Francisco | 5 | Seattle | EXP MLB DEBUT: 2013 | POTENTIAL: Starting 3B | 7B

Bats R Age 22	Year	Lev	Team	AB	R	H	HR	RBI	Avg	OB	Slg	OPS	bb%	ct%	Eye	SB	CS	x/h%	Iso	RC/G
2007 FA (Venezuela)	2010	A+	Lakeland	340	47	92	3	29	271	326	353	679	8	79	0.39	12	5	23	82	3.89
Pwr +++	2011	AA	Erie	348	63	98	7	46	282	319	405	724	5	77	0.24	7	8	26	124	4.29
BAvg +++	2011	AA	Jackson	129	20	40	3	23	310	331	481	811	3	81	0.17	3	2	33	171	5.25
Spd +++	2012	Rk	Mariners	28	7	8	0	7	286	310	500	810	3	79	0.17	1	0	50	214	5.63
Def +++	2012	AA	Jackson	352	55	80	2	23	227	311	295	607	11	76	0.51	27	7	24	68	3.10

Athletic, strong INF who repeated AA and regressed in many areas. BA and HR dropped and power not developing as expected. Owns extremely fast bat, but intent on going to opposite field has negated natural strength in wrists. Has trouble controlling K zone. Has excellent speed and quickness. Could play CF.

Martinez, Jorge | 5 | Cleveland | EXP MLB DEBUT: 2016 | POTENTIAL: Starting 3B | 8E

Bats B Age 20	Year	Lev	Team	AB	R	H	HR	RBI	Avg	OB	Slg	OPS	bb%	ct%	Eye	SB	CS	x/h%	Iso	RC/G
2009 FA (DR)																				
Pwr +++	2010	Rk	Indians	190	23	41	2	21	216	255	274	529	5	78	0.24	3	4	17	58	1.80
BAvg +++	2011	Rk	Indians	180	25	46	4	30	256	316	400	716	8	81	0.47	4	3	35	144	4.39
Spd ++	2012	Rk	Indians	190	31	66	7	39	347	398	563	961	8	77	0.36	4	0	36	216	7.50
Def ++	2012	A-	Mahoning Val	32	4	6	1	6	188	235	375	610	6	72	0.22	0	0	67	188	2.88

Long, lean INF who has spent last 3 years in short-season, but has made improvement. Nice upside predicated on ability to make loud contact with line drive stroke. Possesses avg power from both sides, but avg swing mechanics may not work in upper levels. Can be nimble defender, but is sloppy at times.

Martinson, Jason | 6 | Washington | EXP MLB DEBUT: 2014 | POTENTIAL: Utility INF | 6C

Bats R Age 24	Year	Lev	Team	AB	R	H	HR	RBI	Avg	OB	Slg	OPS	bb%	ct%	Eye	SB	CS	x/h%	Iso	RC/G
2010 (5) Texas State	2010	NCAA	Texas State	234	44	75	4	55	321	398	479	876	11	82	0.73	10	3	35	158	6.61
Pwr ++	2010	A-	Vermont	253	38	61	2	36	241	340	344	684	13	71	0.51	4	2	26	103	4.28
BAvg ++	2011	A	Hagerstown	433	64	109	19	64	252	351	448	799	13	67	0.46	26	6	40	196	5.86
Spd +++	2012	A	Hagerstown	265	68	72	10	63	272	381	449	830	15	67	0.53	23	3	33	177	6.44
Def +++	2012	A+	Potomac	237	36	51	12	43	215	279	409	688	8	67	0.27	7	2	35	194	3.95

Strong-bodied SS started the season well, but scuffled when promoted. Can be aggressive at the plate and does have good power with 22 HR, but also struck out 167 times and eeds to develop better pitch recognition. Defensively he has a plus arm, but range and speed are better suited for 3B.

Mathisen, Wyatt — 2 — Pittsburgh

EXP MLB DEBUT: 2016 | POTENTIAL: Starting C | 8D

Bats R Age 19
2012 (2) HS, TX

Pwr ++
BAvg +++
Spd +++
Def ++

Year	Lev	Team	AB	R	H	HR	RBI	Avg	OB	Slg	OPS	bb%	ct%	Eye	SB	CS	x/h%	Iso	RC/G
2012	Rk	GCL Pirates	139	24	41	1	15	295	368	374	742	10	86	0.84	10	8	22	79	4.92

Athletic, versatile backstop. Is raw behind the plate, but has good strength, bat speed, and solid plate discipline, so could hit for both average and power. Had a solid pro debut in the GCL where he threw out 36% of baserunners, though he is still learning the fine details of game calling, blocking, and receiving.

Matthes, Kent — 9 — Colorado

EXP MLB DEBUT: 2013 | POTENTIAL: Backup OF | 6B

Bats R Age 26
2009 (4) Alabama

Pwr ++++
BAvg ++
Spd +
Def +

Year	Lev	Team	AB	R	H	HR	RBI	Avg	OB	Slg	OPS	bb%	ct%	Eye	SB	CS	x/h%	Iso	RC/G
2009	NCAA	Alabama	204	67	73	28	81	358	445	858	1303	14	77	0.70	13	2	60	500	11.78
2009	A-	Tri-City	239	39	69	5	35	289	346	456	802	8	68	0.27	6	4	42	167	5.85
2010	A	Asheville	81	9	15	1	11	185	233	333	566	6	60	0.16	0	0	60	148	2.54
2011	A+	Modesto	371	70	124	23	95	334	372	642	1013	6	78	0.28	7	4	52	307	7.88
2012	AA	Tulsa	336	44	72	17	40	214	263	432	694	6	76	0.28	6	2	51	217	3.86

Power hitting OF took a huge step back at AA. Still has good power, blasting 17 HR, but fringy contact rate and poor strike zone judgment took their toll and give a more accurate picture of his future. He looks more like a 4th OF-type with nice power, but not much else.

Maxwell, Bruce — 2 — Oakland

EXP MLB DEBUT: 2015 | POTENTIAL: Reserve C | 7E

Bats L Age 22
2012 (2) Birmingham So.

Pwr ++
BAvg +++
Spd +
Def ++

Year	Lev	Team	AB	R	H	HR	RBI	Avg	OB	Slg	OPS	bb%	ct%	Eye	SB	CS	x/h%	Iso	RC/G
2012	Rk	Athletics	21	8	11	0	4	524	615	714	1330	19	86	1.67	0	0	36	190	12.83
2012	A-	Vermont	228	22	58	0	22	254	331	316	646	10	85	0.74	1	0	24	61	3.79

Tall, durable C who makes up for lack of athleticism and agility with solid hitting skills. May move to 1B where defensive attributes could be hidden better and will have to hit for more power. Hits to gaps with level swing path and has good plate coverage. Draws BB, but lacks foot speed and quickness.

Maynard, Pratt — 2 — Los Angeles (N)

EXP MLB DEBUT: 2014 | POTENTIAL: Backup C | 6D

Bats L Age 23
2011 (3) North Carolina State

Pwr ++
BAvg ++
Spd ++
Def ++

Year	Lev	Team	AB	R	H	HR	RBI	Avg	OB	Slg	OPS	bb%	ct%	Eye	SB	CS	x/h%	Iso	RC/G
2010	NCAA	North Carolina St	209	55	57	11	49	273	443	493	936	23	80	1.52	2	3	40	220	7.84
2011	NCAA	North Carolina St	251	46	81	5	41	323	412	474	886	13	82	0.84	1	0	33	151	6.81
2011	Rk	Ogden	88	16	21	2	11	239	337	341	678	13	73	0.54	0	0	24	102	4.01
2012	A	Great Lakes	282	34	71	3	34	252	324	348	671	10	83	0.63	6	2	30	96	3.97
2012	A+	Rancho Cuc	28	1	6	0	3	214	313	214	527	13	79	0.67	1	0	0	0	2.14

Strong, physical backstop has yet to prove he can hit for average. Has good raw strength, but it hasn't translated into home run power. Below average defensively and might not stick at the position. Solid plate discipline and makes good contact, but former 3rd round pick has been a disappointment.

Mazara, Nomar — 9 — Texas

EXP MLB DEBUT: 2017 | POTENTIAL: Starting OF | 9E

Bats L Age 18
2011 FA (DR)

Pwr ++++
BAvg ++
Spd +++
Def ++

Year	Lev	Team	AB	R	H	HR	RBI	Avg	OB	Slg	OPS	bb%	ct%	Eye	SB	CS	x/h%	Iso	RC/G
2012	Rk	Rangers	201	40	53	6	39	264	378	448	826	16	65	0.53	5	2	42	184	6.58

Projectable, lanky OF with a patient approach and natural strength. Should grow into frame and add more power to nice palette of tools. LHP have given him problems and has holes in long swing. OF play is raw and will need to time to develop instincts. Has high ceiling with potential to hit for plus power with avg speed.

McCann, James — 2 — Detroit

EXP MLB DEBUT: 2013 | POTENTIAL: Starting C | 7D

Bats R Age 23
2011 (2) Arkansas

Pwr ++
BAvg ++
Spd ++
Def ++++

Year	Lev	Team	AB	R	H	HR	RBI	Avg	OB	Slg	OPS	bb%	ct%	Eye	SB	CS	x/h%	Iso	RC/G
2011	NCAA	Arkansas	209	35	64	6	38	306	378	469	847	10	88	0.92	11	6	33	163	6.08
2011	Rk	GCL Tigers	14	1	5	1	6	357	400	643	1043	7	93	1.00	0	0	40	286	7.81
2011	A	West Michigan	34	0	2	0	1	59	111	88	199	6	65	0.17	0	0	50	29	
2012	A+	Lakeland	160	24	46	0	20	288	329	350	679	6	82	0.34	3	0	22	63	3.86
2012	AA	Erie	220	15	44	2	19	200	228	282	510	4	80	0.18	2	2	32	82	1.61

Defense-first C who swung nice bat in High-A before struggling upon move to AA. Has solid frame and strong, accurate arm. Has agility for solid blocking and receiving. May struggle to hit for BA as he is a free-swinger with no eye for balls and strikes. Bat speed may not be good enough, though has avg pull pop.

McClure, D'Vone — 78 — Cleveland

EXP MLB DEBUT: 2017 | POTENTIAL: Starting OF | 8E

Bats R Age 19
2012 (4) HS (AR)

Pwr +++
BAvg ++
Spd +++
Def ++

Year	Lev	Team	AB	R	H	HR	RBI	Avg	OB	Slg	OPS	bb%	ct%	Eye	SB	CS	x/h%	Iso	RC/G
2012	Rk	Indians	90	15	19	1	12	211	297	289	586	11	79	0.58	2	1	26	78	2.86

Raw, athletic OF with tools aplenty, but will likely need years to develop. Tall and muscular frame provides projection and plus bat speed should lead to power. Swings with authority and has loose stroke to make adjustments. Ks could be problem due to long, uppercut swing. Runs well, but OF defense is work in progress.

McDade, Mike — 3 — Cleveland

EXP MLB DEBUT: 2013 | POTENTIAL: Reserve 1B | 6B

Bats B Age 24
2007 (6) HS (NV)

Pwr ++++
BAvg ++
Spd +
Def ++

Year	Lev	Team	AB	R	H	HR	RBI	Avg	OB	Slg	OPS	bb%	ct%	Eye	SB	CS	x/h%	Iso	RC/G
2009	A	Lansing	408	50	113	16	57	277	330	466	795	7	73	0.29	0	0	39	189	5.34
2010	A+	Dunedin	480	60	128	21	64	267	306	448	754	5	71	0.19	2	0	34	181	4.70
2011	AA	New Hampshire	484	71	136	16	74	281	320	457	777	5	79	0.27	0	1	39	176	4.94
2012	AA	New Hampshire	378	44	104	15	49	275	349	437	786	10	78	0.51	1	0	30	161	5.24
2012	AAA	Las Vegas	71	9	24	2	18	338	397	493	890	9	85	0.64	0	0	25	155	6.49

Large-framed prospect who has vastly improved approach over last 2 seasons. Has reduced Ks while also becoming more patient and increasing BB. Natural strength produces consistent, above avg power, but long swing hinders BA. Lacks secondary skills. Owns poor speed and limited defensive value.

McElroy, C.J. — 8 — St. Louis

EXP MLB DEBUT: 2016 | POTENTIAL: Starting CF | 7D

Bats R Age 20
2011 (3) HS, TX

Pwr +
BAvg ++
Spd ++++
Def +++

Year	Lev	Team	AB	R	H	HR	RBI	Avg	OB	Slg	OPS	bb%	ct%	Eye	SB	CS	x/h%	Iso	RC/G
2011	Rk	GCL Cardinals	79	10	18	0	7	228	291	278	569	8	81	0.47	8	2	17	51	2.62
2012	Rk	Johnson City	247	40	67	0	22	271	313	332	645	6	83	0.36	24	5	19	61	3.46

Fleet-footed CF with nice athleticism. Has a solid line-drive stroke and can occasionally drive the ball, but is not going to hit for power and has yet to hit home run as a professional. Uses his plus speed well on the bases on in the field. Stole 24 bases and needs to get on base to have value.

Medrano, Kevin — 4 — Arizona

EXP MLB DEBUT: 2016 | POTENTIAL: Backup 2B | 6C

Bats L Age 23
2012 (18) Missouri State

Pwr +
BAvg ++
Spd +++
Def ++

Year	Lev	Team	AB	R	H	HR	RBI	Avg	OB	Slg	OPS	bb%	ct%	Eye	SB	CS	x/h%	Iso	RC/G
2009	NCAA	Missouri State	231	38	76	3	40	329	382	442	824	8	85	0.57	0	0	24	113	5.70
2010	NCAA	Missouri State	210	44	86	4	29	410	483	571	1055	13	88	1.20	16	2	28	162	8.71
2011	NCAA	Missouri State	206	34	67	0	34	325	388	383	771	9	93	1.50	13	2	12	58	5.34
2012	NCAA	Missouri State	248	39	81	0	24	327	377	403	780	7	88	0.69	12	5	23	77	5.24
2012	A-	Yakima	264	33	90	0	24	341	374	402	776	5	89	0.47	13	5	13	61	4.98

18th round pick had an impressive pro debut, hitting .341 with 13 SB in the NWL. Has a quick, compact left-handed stroke and shoots line drives to all fields. He doesn't have much power, but does make consistent contact and should hit for average. Is a solid defender with good hands, but lack of range limits him to 2B.

Mejias-Brean, Seth — 5 — Cincinnati

EXP MLB DEBUT: 2016 | POTENTIAL: Starting 3B | 7C

Bats R Age 22
2012 (8) Arizona

Pwr +++
BAvg ++
Spd +++
Def ++++

Year	Lev	Team	AB	R	H	HR	RBI	Avg	OB	Slg	OPS	bb%	ct%	Eye	SB	CS	x/h%	Iso	RC/G
2012	Rk	Billings	179	35	56	8	40	313	385	536	921	11	84	0.72	6	0	39	223	6.93

Strong collegiate 3B has good power and solid plate discipline and fared well in his pro debut. Plus defender at 3B with good hands, range, and a strong arm. Doesn't run well, but is not a base-clogger and could be a steal this late in the draft.

Mercedes, Alexander — 478 — Baltimore

EXP MLB DEBUT: 2016 | POTENTIAL: Starting 2B/SS | 8E

Bats R Age 21 — 2009 FA (DR)

Pwr +
BAvg +++
Spd ++++
Def

Year	Lev	Team	AB	R	H	HR	RBI	Avg	OB	Slg	OPS	bb%	ct%	Eye	SB	CS	x/h%	Iso	RC/G
2012	Rk	GCL Orioles	27	3	5	0	0	185	241	185	427	7	93	1.00	3	1	0	0	1.39
2012	A-	Aberdeen	15	0	4	0	0	267	267	333	600	0	80	0.00	0	0	25	67	2.54

Lean, athletic prospect who spent first year in US after 3 yrs in Dominican. Best present tool is speed which results in plus range in OF. Laces line drives to gaps with consistent, level swing and will need to add strength and loft to have any power. Controls bat and should hit for BA with solid OBP due to discerning eye.

Mercer, Jordy — 6 — Pittsburgh

EXP MLB DEBUT: 2012 | POTENTIAL: Utility INF | 6B

Bats R Age 26 — 2008 (3) Oklahoma St

Pwr +
BAvg ++
Spd +++
Def +++

Year	Lev	Team	AB	R	H	HR	RBI	Avg	OB	Slg	OPS	bb%	ct%	Eye	SB	CS	x/h%	Iso	RC/G
2010	AA	Altoona	485	67	137	3	65	282	326	373	699	6	86	0.45	7	1	26	91	4.15
2011	AA	Altoona	265	40	71	13	48	268	326	487	813	8	87	0.66	6	3	44	219	5.45
2011	AAA	Indianapolis	226	39	54	6	21	239	280	385	665	5	81	0.30	3	3	37	146	3.58
2012	AAA	Indianapolis	209	28	60	4	27	287	349	421	770	9	78	0.44	3	5	32	134	5.10
2012	MLB	Pittsburgh	62	7	13	1	5	210	258	371	629	6	77	0.29	0	1	54	161	3.25

Tall, oversized INF made big league debut, but at 25 profiles as a utility player. Has shown an ability to hit for average, but without power. Solid understanding of the strike zone and an ability to make contact. Slightly above-average speed, but not a SB threat. Split time between SS, 2B, and 3B to give him positional flexibility.

Mesa, Melky — 789 — New York (A)

EXP MLB DEBUT: 2012 | POTENTIAL: Reserve OF | 6B

Bats R Age 26 — 2003 FA (DR)

Pwr ++++
BAvg ++
Spd +++
Def +++

Year	Lev	Team	AB	R	H	HR	RBI	Avg	OB	Slg	OPS	bb%	ct%	Eye	SB	CS	x/h%	Iso	RC/G
2011	A+	Tampa	12	1	2	0	1	167	333	250	583	20	67	0.75	1	0	50	83	3.01
2011	AA	Trenton	386	58	97	9	46	251	315	404	719	9	67	0.28	18	13	38	153	4.65
2012	AA	Trenton	332	60	92	14	46	277	335	464	799	8	77	0.39	17	3	36	187	5.31
2012	AAA	Scranton/W-B	126	19	29	9	23	230	271	524	794	5	66	0.16	5	1	62	294	5.46
2012	MLB	New York (A)	2	0	1	0	1	500	500	500	1000	0	100	1.00	0	0	0	0	6.83

Very athletic OF who posted career high in HR. Produced 20-20 season and finally taking advantage of tools. Offers strength and speed with plus raw power to all fields. Doesn't control K zone and free-swinging can be exploited. Likely to hit for below average BA. Possesses strong arm and range for OF corner.

Michael, Levi — 46 — Minnesota

EXP MLB DEBUT: 2014 | POTENTIAL: Starting SS | 7D

Bats B Age 22 — 2011 (1) North Carolina

Pwr ++
BAvg ++
Spd +++
Def +++

Year	Lev	Team	AB	R	H	HR	RBI	Avg	OB	Slg	OPS	bb%	ct%	Eye	SB	CS	x/h%	Iso	RC/G
2009	NCAA	North Carolina	262	54	76	13	57	290	354	527	881	9	79	0.46	5	4	42	237	6.41
2010	NCAA	North Carolina	214	76	74	9	54	346	457	575	1032	17	88	1.69	20	2	36	229	8.68
2011	NCAA	North Carolina	242	53	70	5	48	289	409	434	843	17	81	1.04	15	1	31	145	6.48
2012	A+	Fort Myers	431	58	106	2	38	246	333	311	644	11	81	0.68	6	0	19	65	3.70

Short, instinctual INF who had disappointing season with bat. Doesn't profile as slugger, but can reach seats with strong wrists and moderate bat speed. Owns discerning eye and can read breaking pitches. Key is staying consistent and not expanding K zone. Can be smooth defender with good arm and range.

Mier, Jio — 6 — Houston

EXP MLB DEBUT: 2014 | POTENTIAL: Starting SS | 7D

Bats R Age 22 — 2009 (1) HS (CA)

Pwr ++
BAvg +++
Spd +++
Def +++

Year	Lev	Team	AB	R	H	HR	RBI	Avg	OB	Slg	OPS	bb%	ct%	Eye	SB	CS	x/h%	Iso	RC/G
2010	A	Lexington	493	63	116	2	53	235	322	314	636	11	78	0.59	15	7	29	79	3.58
2011	A	Lexington	216	39	53	5	29	245	354	380	734	15	73	0.64	6	2	36	135	
2011	A+	Lancaster	206	35	48	2	23	233	335	306	641	12	74	0.54	5	3	21	73	
2012	Rk	GCL Astros	14	1	3	0	2	214	250	286	536	7	100		0	0	33	72	
2012	A+	Lancaster	171	28	50	3	25	292	396	409	805	15	80	0.85	6	3	26	117	

Tall, lean INF who missed time due to hamstring injury. Had solid season by becoming less aggressive at plate and improving. Uses both gaps with balanced swing, but lack of premium bat speed limits power. Isn't burner on base, but is a good baserunner. Owns soft, quick hands and avg range.

Mikolas, Nathan — 79 — New York (A)

EXP MLB DEBUT: 2016 | POTENTIAL: Starting OF | 7E

Bats L Age 19 — 2012 (3) HS (WI)

Pwr +++
BAvg ++
Spd ++
Def ++

Year	Lev	Team	AB	R	H	HR	RBI	Avg	OB	Slg	OPS	bb%	ct%	Eye	SB	CS	x/h%	Iso	RC/G
2012	Rk	GCL Yankees	87	7	13	1	5	149	253	184	436	12	60	0.34	1	1	8	34	0.22

Short, muscular OF who has impressive raw tools. Swings with authority and has good bat speed and hitting instincts. Recognizes pitches and offers at least avg power potential. Needs to add loft to swing to realize pop, though has swing path to hit for BA. Poor athlete with limited speed and defensive ability.

Miller, Brad — 6 — Seattle

EXP MLB DEBUT: 2013 | POTENTIAL: Starting SS | 7A

Bats L Age 23 — 2011 (2) Clemson

Pwr ++
BAvg ++++
Spd ++++
Def +++

Year	Lev	Team	AB	R	H	HR	RBI	Avg	OB	Slg	OPS	bb%	ct%	Eye	SB	CS	x/h%	Iso	RC/G
2010	NCAA	Clemson	252	71	90	8	49	357	464	560	1023	17	83	1.16	9	2	34	202	8.68
2011	NCAA	Clemson	195	53	77	5	50	395	498	559	1057	17	83	1.18	21	5	25	164	9.16
2011	A	Clinton	53	9	22	0	7	415	456	528	984	7	83	0.44	1	0	23	113	7.66
2012	A+	High Desert	410	89	139	11	56	339	413	524	938	11	80	0.66	19	6	35	185	7.34
2012	AA	Jackson	147	21	47	4	12	320	408	476	884	13	82	0.85	4	1	28	156	6.72

Tall, lean INF who finished 2nd in CAL in BA. Has simple swing and makes consistent contact. Has line drive power and polished approach could lead to leadoff opportunities. Uses entire field and has speed for XBH and SB. Dependable defender with arm strength, range, and quickness and should stick at SS.

Miller, Brandon — 9 — Washington

EXP MLB DEBUT: 2015 | POTENTIAL: Starting RF | 7C

Bats R Age 23 — 2012 (4) Samford

Pwr +++
BAvg ++
Spd ++
Def ++

Year	Lev	Team	AB	R	H	HR	RBI	Avg	OB	Slg	OPS	bb%	ct%	Eye	SB	CS	x/h%	Iso	RC/G
2011	NCAA	Samford	196	40	53	16	43	270	376	582	957	14	74	0.66	3	1	51	311	7.64
2012	A-	Auburn	113	20	33	4	21	292	350	549	898	8	68	0.28	0	0	55	257	7.27

Was moved from behind the plate fo RF and has a strong arm and good raw power. Is overly aggressive and struggles to make contact, but puts a charge into the ball when he does. Was drafted as a college senior, so will need to move quickly.

Milligan, Adam — 7 — Atlanta

EXP MLB DEBUT: 2013 | POTENTIAL: Backup OF | 6C

Bats L Age 25 — 2008 (8) Walters State CC

Pwr +++
BAvg ++
Spd +
Def ++

Year	Lev	Team	AB	R	H	HR	RBI	Avg	OB	Slg	OPS	bb%	ct%	Eye	SB	CS	x/h%	Iso	RC/G
2009	A+	Myrtle Beach	24	2	4	1	6	167	167	333	500	0	67	0.00	0	0	50	167	1.00
2010	A+	Myrtle Beach	85	13	17	4	8	200	277	376	653	10	59	0.26	2	0	41	176	3.75
2011	A+	Lynchburg	237	35	69	12	40	291	336	557	893	6	68	0.21	1	0	51	266	6.97
2012	A+	Lynchburg	337	45	86	15	49	255	297	463	760	6	60	0.15	3	0	44	208	5.45
2012	AA	Mississippi	102	4	18	1	9	176	236	255	491	7	63	0.21	0	0	33	78	1.19

Strong bodied OF was overmatched at AA. Partially regained his form when demoted, but he's been stuck at High-A since '09. Has good raw power, but poor plate discipline and contact rate limit his ability to hit for average. Has average speed and arm strength and is is competent on defense.

Mitchell, Jared — 8 — Chicago (A)

EXP MLB DEBUT: 2013 | POTENTIAL: Starting CF | 8D

Bats L Age 24 — 2009 (1) LSU

Pwr +++
BAvg ++
Spd +++
Def +++

Year	Lev	Team	AB	R	H	HR	RBI	Avg	OB	Slg	OPS	bb%	ct%	Eye	SB	CS	x/h%	Iso	RC/G
2009	NCAA	Louisiana State	226	64	74	11	50	327	463	580	1043	20	72	0.89	36	9	41	252	9.54
2009	A	Kannapolis	115	13	34	0	10	296	413	435	848	17	65	0.58	5	3	41	139	7.23
2011	A+	Winston-Salem	477	74	106	9	58	222	299	377	676	10	62	0.28	14	6	45	155	4.29
2012	AA	Birmingham	334	50	80	10	54	240	359	440	799	16	62	0.49	20	5	44	201	6.35
2012	AAA	Charlotte	121	18	28	1	13	231	321	364	685	12	56	0.30	1	1	46	132	4.91

Muscular, athletic OF who finished 3rd in minors in K, but offers solid tools. Hit .341 in April, but .214 rest of way. Set career high in HR and SB, though Ks due to tendency to chase pitches. May need to be more aggressive early in count. Exhibits average pop with above avg bat speed. Can play CF with avg arm.

Mondesi, Adalberto — 6 — Kansas City

EXP MLB DEBUT: 2017 | POTENTIAL: Starting SS | 9D

Bats B Age 17 — 2011 FA (DR)

Pwr +++
BAvg +++
Spd ++++
Def ++++

Year	Lev	Team	AB	R	H	HR	RBI	Avg	OB	Slg	OPS	bb%	ct%	Eye	SB	CS	x/h%	Iso	RC/G
2012	Rk	Idaho Falls	207	35	60	3	30	290	350	386	736	8	69	0.29	11	2	20	97	4.79

Athletic, lean INF who was youngest player in league. Has instincts and potential for plus offensive and defensive attributes. Swings quick bat with authority, but lack of plate discipline needs to be addressed. Has gap power and could grow into above avg pop. Runs well and has plus range and arm.

Monsalve, Alex — 2 — Cleveland

EXP MLB DEBUT: 2015 | POTENTIAL: Starting C | 7C

Bats R Age 21
2008 FA (Venezuela)
- Pwr + + +
- BAvg + +
- Spd + +
- Def + +

Year	Lev	Team	AB	R	H	HR	RBI	Avg	OB	Slg	OPS	bb%	ct%	Eye	SB	CS	x/h%	Iso	RC/G
2010	Rk	Indians	182	18	40	1	18	220	237	313	550	2	71	0.08	0	0	30	93	1.96
2011	A	Lake County	458	55	121	5	44	264	311	356	667	6	79	0.32	7	6	24	92	3.66
2012	A	Lake County	283	36	75	7	36	265	320	406	727	8	88	0.66	1	2	33	141	4.53
2012	A+	Carolina	116	10	27	1	6	233	276	293	570	6	85	0.41	1	0	19	60	2.57

Big, strong C who repeated Low-A before promotion. Made much better contact as swing mechanics improved and set career high in HR. Still struggles with pitch recognition. Exhibits decent athleticism and quickness and has potential to be above avg behind plate. Owns good arm with quick release, but still raw.

Moore, Jeremy — 89 — Los Angeles (N)

EXP MLB DEBUT: 2011 | POTENTIAL: Starting OF | 8E

Bats L Age 26
2005 (6) HS (LA)
- Pwr + + +
- BAvg + + +
- Spd + + + +
- Def + + +

Year	Lev	Team	AB	R	H	HR	RBI	Avg	OB	Slg	OPS	bb%	ct%	Eye	SB	CS	x/h%	Iso	RC/G
2008	A	Cedar Rapids	362	47	87	17	48	240	282	478	760	5	65	0.17	28	10	46	238	5.12
2009	A+	Rancho Cuc	470	61	131	11	58	279	327	443	770	7	69	0.24	17	13	33	164	5.22
2009	AA	Arkansas	21	5	7	2	10	333	417	714	1131	13	67	0.43	1	1	43	381	10.64
2010	AA	Arkansas	456	72	138	13	61	303	358	463	820	8	73	0.32	24	10	27	160	5.77
2011	AAA	Salt Lake	426	76	127	15	66	298	331	545	876	5	73	0.18	21	10	45	246	6.45

Aggressive, athletic OF who missed entire season after hip surgery. When healthy, has plus speed and plays quality CF defense with solid instincts and plenty of range. Owns average pop, though has tendency to lengthen swing. Could steal loads of bases with higher OBP. Signed with LA in offseason.

Morales, Angel — 789 — Minnesota

EXP MLB DEBUT: 2015 | POTENTIAL: Reserve OF | 7E

Bats R Age 23
2007 (3) HS (PR)
- Pwr + + +
- BAvg + +
- Spd + + +
- Def + + +

Year	Lev	Team	AB	R	H	HR	RBI	Avg	OB	Slg	OPS	bb%	ct%	Eye	SB	CS	x/h%	Iso	RC/G
2010	A	Beloit	211	34	61	4	36	289	362	474	836	10	69	0.37	18	7	39	185	6.42
2010	A+	Fort Myers	261	35	71	1	19	272	343	349	691	10	71	0.37	11	5	21	77	4.22
2011	Rk	GCL Twins	14	2	3	1	4	214	214	500	714	0	93	0.00	0	0	67	286	3.90
2011	A+	Fort Myers	121	17	32	3	13	264	336	388	724	10	70	0.36	3	2	28	124	4.58
2012	A+	Fort Myers	363	56	80	7	35	220	306	328	634	11	68	0.39	12	3	25	107	3.38

Strong, aggressive hitter who performed poorly in repeat trip to High-A. Prospect status has fallen as he hasn't realized plus power potential. Can overswing leading to high Ks. Struggles with offspeed stuff and lacks instincts to hit for BA. Owns good speed, but needs to get on. Strong arm profiles well in OF corner.

Morban, Julio — 789 — Seattle

EXP MLB DEBUT: 2014 | POTENTIAL: Starting OF | 8D

Bats L Age 21
2008 FA (DR)
- Pwr + + +
- BAvg + + +
- Spd + + +
- Def + + +

Year	Lev	Team	AB	R	H	HR	RBI	Avg	OB	Slg	OPS	bb%	ct%	Eye	SB	CS	x/h%	Iso	RC/G
2010	A+	High Desert	6	0	2	0	1	333	333	333	667	0	67	0.00	0	0	0	0	3.37
2010	A-	Everett	4	0	1	0	0	250	250	250	500	0	50	0.00	0	0	0	0	1.64
2011	A	Clinton	301	44	77	4	28	256	315	382	697	8	67	0.26	10	5	30	126	4.33
2012	Rk	Mariners	21	2	5	0	3	238	238	238	476	0	86	0.00	0	0	0	0	1.13
2012	A+	High Desert	300	56	94	17	52	313	358	550	908	7	78	0.31	5	1	37	237	6.56

Strong OF who improved power output while reducing K rate. Shows mature feel for hitting despite limited action in past due to injuries. Has inconsistent approach, but bat speed is sound and puts ball in play. Exhibits avg speed, but generally doesn't run often. Defense is adequate with strong arm and range.

Morris, Hunter — 3 — Milwaukee

EXP MLB DEBUT: 2014 | POTENTIAL: Starting 1B | 8D

Bats L Age 24
2010 (4) Auburn
- Pwr + + + +
- BAvg + + +
- Spd + +
- Def + +

Year	Lev	Team	AB	R	H	HR	RBI	Avg	OB	Slg	OPS	bb%	ct%	Eye	SB	CS	x/h%	Iso	RC/G
2010	NCAA	Auburn	272	66	105	23	76	386	440	743	1182	9	82	0.52	6	2	44	357	9.89
2010	A	Wisconsin	291	38	73	9	44	251	299	436	735	6	80	0.34	7	2	44	186	4.52
2011	A+	Brevard County	501	75	136	19	67	271	297	461	758	3	83	0.21	7	3	38	190	4.55
2011	AA	Huntsville	17	6	6	1	2	353	353	706	1059	0	94	0.00	0	0	50	353	7.64
2012	AA	Huntsville	522	77	158	28	113	303	352	563	916	7	78	0.34	2	1	47	261	6.77

Strong-bodied 1B with offensive potential had a nice breakout season. Makes consistent contact with fringy plate discipline. Is a below-average runner but does have good hands and range. Is limited to 1B and will have to mash to earn full-time AB. Proto-typical bad body, good bat 1B.

Moya, Steven — 9 — Detroit

EXP MLB DEBUT: 2016 | POTENTIAL: Starting OF | 8D

Bats L Age 21
2008 FA (PR)
- Pwr + + + +
- BAvg + +
- Spd + +
- Def + +

Year	Lev	Team	AB	R	H	HR	RBI	Avg	OB	Slg	OPS	bb%	ct%	Eye	SB	CS	x/h%	Iso	RC/G
2010	Rk	GCL Tigers	137	12	26	2	11	190	224	299	523	4	53	0.09	0	0	35	109	2.00
2011	A	West Michigan	323	38	66	13	39	204	233	362	595	4	61	0.09	1	1	36	158	2.64
2012	A	West Michigan	243	28	70	9	47	288	319	481	800	4	76	0.19	5	3	37	193	5.22

Tall, rangy OF who repeated Low-A and saw season end after TJ surgery. Should be ready early in season to build upon successful '12. Cut down on Ks by shortening stroke and polishing approach. Struggles with selectivity, but covers plate well. Projects to plus power and would make ideal RF with good arm.

Muncy, Max — 3 — Oakland

EXP MLB DEBUT: 2015 | POTENTIAL: Starting 1B | 7D

Bats L Age 22
2012 (5) Baylor
- Pwr + +
- BAvg + + +
- Spd + + +
- Def + +

Year	Lev	Team	AB	R	H	HR	RBI	Avg	OB	Slg	OPS	bb%	ct%	Eye	SB	CS	x/h%	Iso	RC/G
2010	NCAA	Baylor	230	47	69	11	53	300	366	500	866	9	79	0.50	5	0	35	200	6.19
2011	NCAA	Baylor	227	40	73	9	44	322	417	511	928	14	84	1.03	6	3	30	189	7.23
2012	NCAA	Baylor	255	55	82	7	56	322	416	494	910	14	87	1.28	7	5	33	173	7.08
2012	A	Burlington	229	34	63	4	23	275	385	432	817	15	84	1.11	3	1	41	157	6.12

Athletic INF who fits OAK mold by having disciplined eye and high OBP. Makes hard contact with short, direct swing path and can make adjustments from AB to AB. Has present pull power and may not have bat speed or leverage for anything more than gap power. Limited defensively at 1B, but works hard.

Muno, Danny — 6 — New York (N)

EXP MLB DEBUT: 2014 | POTENTIAL: Starting 2B | 7C

Bats B Age 24
2011 (8) Fresno State
- Pwr + +
- BAvg + + +
- Spd + + +
- Def + + +

Year	Lev	Team	AB	R	H	HR	RBI	Avg	OB	Slg	OPS	bb%	ct%	Eye	SB	CS	x/h%	Iso	RC/G
2009	NCAA	Fresno State	224	74	85	3	41	379	517	540	1058	22	87	2.21	13	3	34	161	9.55
2010	NCAA	Fresno State	246	68	81	7	33	329	439	500	939	16	87	1.45	10	3	32	171	7.58
2011	NCAA	Fresno State	204	47	71	3	52	348	468	471	939	18	87	1.70	14	6	25	123	7.78
2011	A-	Brooklyn	220	45	78	2	24	355	460	514	974	16	82	1.10	9	4	36	159	8.22
2012	A+	St. Lucie	289	36	81	6	39	280	386	412	798	15	82	0.94	19	3	30	131	5.78

Stocky INF had another solid season at the plate. Professional hitter with a quick bat who sprays the ball to all fields. Plus plate discipline means he should continue to hit and get on base as he moves up. After two years, he has as .422 OB%. Average runner with decent range and actions.

Munoz, Jose — 6 — Arizona

EXP MLB DEBUT: 2016 | POTENTIAL: Starting 3B | 7D

Bats R Age 19
2012 (2) HS, CA
- Pwr + +
- BAvg + +
- Spd +
- Def + +

Year	Lev	Team	AB	R	H	HR	RBI	Avg	OB	Slg	OPS	bb%	ct%	Eye	SB	CS	x/h%	Iso	RC/G
2012	Rk	Diamondbacks	173	25	45	2	20	260	326	341	667	8	66	0.24	4	4	17	81	

2nd round pick is a bit of a project. Showed the ability to hit in HS with good power potential, but also swings and misses frequently. Played SS in high school, but most evaluators see him at 3B as a professional, though he played exclusively at SS in his debut. An average runner whose bat will need to carry him.

Murphy, J.R. — 2 — New York (A)

EXP MLB DEBUT: 2014 | POTENTIAL: Starting C | 7C

Bats B Age 22
2009 (2) HS (FL)
- Pwr + + +
- BAvg + + +
- Spd + +
- Def + +

Year	Lev	Team	AB	R	H	HR	RBI	Avg	OB	Slg	OPS	bb%	ct%	Eye	SB	CS	x/h%	Iso	RC/G
2010	A	Charleston (Sc)	330	46	84	7	54	255	328	376	704	10	81	0.56	4	5	29	121	4.29
2011	A	Charleston (Sc)	256	31	76	6	32	297	345	457	802	7	85	0.50	2	0	38	160	5.37
2011	A+	Tampa	85	8	22	1	14	259	276	365	641	2	89	0.22	0	0	32	106	3.32
2012	A+	Tampa	265	39	68	5	28	257	323	374	697	9	85	0.63	4	3	29	117	4.23
2012	AA	Trenton	147	23	34	4	16	231	307	408	715	10	78	0.50	0	0	50	177	4.46

Short, athletic C who set career high in HR. Likes to use entire field, particularly gaps, and runs well for C. Long swing and fringe bat speed need tweaking, but is good enough athlete to make adjustments. Receiving and blocking are still developing while avg arm with quick release are solid assets.

Murphy, Tom — 2 — Colorado

EXP MLB DEBUT: 2016 | POTENTIAL: Starting C | 8D

Bats R Age 22
2012 (3) Buffalo
- Pwr + + +
- BAvg + + +
- Spd + +
- Def + + +

Year	Lev	Team	AB	R	H	HR	RBI	Avg	OB	Slg	OPS	bb%	ct%	Eye	SB	CS	x/h%	Iso	RC/G
2010	NCAA	Buffalo	131	23	41	4	25	313	392	489	880	11	75	0.52	5	1	37	176	6.73
2011	NCAA	Buffalo	190	34	73	10	44	384	445	626	1072	10	87	0.84	7	4	36	242	8.56
2012	NCAA	Buffalo	219	46	68	13	51	311	398	616	1015	13	79	0.70	6	3	54	306	8.35
2012	A-	Tri-City	212	26	61	6	38	288	332	462	794	6	75	0.27	1	1	36	175	5.30

Strong collegiate C was a 3rd round pick. Balanced approach at the plate generates power to all fields. Has good bat speed and made consistent contact, but struggled in pro debut. Moves well behind the plate with a strong arm. Should be able to stick behind the plate, but offense will be ticket to the majors.

Myers, Wil — 589 — Tampa Bay

EXP MLB DEBUT: 2013 | POTENTIAL: Starting OF | 9B

Bats R Age 22
2009 (3) HS (NC)
Pwr ++++
BAvg ++++
Spd ++
Def +++

Year	Lev	Team	AB	R	H	HR	RBI	Avg	OB	Slg	OPS	bb%	ct%	Eye	SB	CS	x/h%	Iso	RC/G
2010	A	Burlington	242	42	70	10	45	289	407	500	907	17	77	0.87	10	3	43	211	7.24
2010	A+	Wilmington	205	28	71	4	38	346	446	512	958	15	81	0.95	2	3	34	166	7.90
2011	AA	NW Arkansas	354	50	90	8	49	254	350	393	742	13	75	0.60	9	2	36	138	4.95
2012	AA	NW Arkansas	134	32	46	13	30	343	413	731	1145	11	69	0.38	4	1	54	388	10.52
2012	AAA	Omaha	388	66	118	24	79	304	376	554	931	10	75	0.46	2	2	37	250	7.16

Natural-hitting prospect who finished 2nd in minors in HR. Profiles as ideal middle-of-order run producer with exceptional bat speed and strength. Should hit for both BA and power due to pitch recognition and plus hand-eye coordination. Offers slightly below avg wheels, but has plus arm strength and instincts.

Myles, Bryson — 789 — Cleveland

EXP MLB DEBUT: 2015 | POTENTIAL: Fourth OF | 7D

Bats R Age 23
2011 (6) Stephen F Austin
Pwr ++
BAvg +++
Spd ++++
Def ++

Year	Lev	Team	AB	R	H	HR	RBI	Avg	OB	Slg	OPS	bb%	ct%	Eye	SB	CS	x/h%	Iso	RC/G
2011	NCAA	StphenFAustin	241	69	99	8	36	411	462	581	1043	9	85	0.64	53	15	22	170	8.23
2011	A-	Mahoning Val	192	36	58	1	15	302	380	401	781	11	83	0.75	20	7	24	99	5.44
2012	A	Lake County	369	40	107	3	59	290	348	379	728	8	77	0.39	20	12	23	89	4.56

Short, thick OF who has impressive skill set that projects to reserve role in big leagues. Speed is only above avg tool and he steals bases while exemplifying range in OF. Still raw with routes and reads and has below avg arm. Needs to develop more power for corner OF, though has good strength and quick stroke.

Naquin, Tyler — 8 — Cleveland

EXP MLB DEBUT: 2015 | POTENTIAL: Starting CF | 7A

Bats L Age 22
2012 (1-S) Texas A&M
Pwr ++
BAvg ++++
Spd +++
Def +++

Year	Lev	Team	AB	R	H	HR	RBI	Avg	OB	Slg	OPS	bb%	ct%	Eye	SB	CS	x/h%	Iso	RC/G
2010	NCAA	Texas A&M	172	29	42	2	19	244	305	326	630	8	78	0.41	6	2	24	81	3.27
2011	NCAA	Texas A&M	273	68	104	2	44	381	440	538	979	10	87	0.83	6	7	31	158	7.72
2012	NCAA	Texas A&M	242	56	92	3	49	380	438	541	980	9	85	0.68	21	5	29	161	7.71
2012	A-	Mahoning Val	137	22	37	0	13	270	351	380	730	11	81	0.65	4	3	35	109	4.87

Athletic, quick OF with solid all-around game. Has natural, line drive swing that produces gap power and has approach and bat control to hit breaking balls. Is adept at bunting and making defense work thanks to solid speed. May not have enough pop for corner OF, but owns strong arm. Still raw in CF, but is likely his future home.

Nash, Telvin — 379 — Houston

EXP MLB DEBUT: 2014 | POTENTIAL: Reserve OF | 7D

Bats R Age 22
2009 (3) HS (GA)
Pwr ++++
BAvg ++
Spd +
Def ++

Year	Lev	Team	AB	R	H	HR	RBI	Avg	OB	Slg	OPS	bb%	ct%	Eye	SB	CS	x/h%	Iso	RC/G
2010	Rk	Greeneville	200	30	53	12	39	265	347	515	862	11	68	0.39	1	1	47	250	6.58
2010	A-	Tri City	13	2	4	1	1	308	308	769	1077	0	46	0.00	0	1	75	462	14.53
2011	Rk	GCL Astros	13	5	5	0	0	385	500	538	1038	19	85	1.50	0	0	40	154	9.22
2011	A	Lexington	268	41	72	14	37	269	364	485	849	13	62	0.39	2	0	42	216	6.92
2012	A+	Lancaster	393	61	88	29	75	224	307	494	800	11	50	0.24	0	1	55	270	7.32

Big, strong prospect who doubled career high in HR, but led all of minors in Ks. Exhibits top of line bat speed, but choppy swing mechanics and uppercut stroke lead to easy outs. Can be too passive at plate and swing at bad pitches. Well below avg speed doesn't help and suspect arm leaves him without defensive home.

Nay, Mitch — 5 — Toronto

EXP MLB DEBUT: 2016 | POTENTIAL: Starting 3B | 8E

Bats R Age 19
2012 (1-S) HS (AZ)
Pwr +++
BAvg ++
Spd ++
Def ++

Year	Lev	Team	AB	R	H	HR	RBI	Avg	OB	Slg	OPS	bb%	ct%	Eye	SB	CS	x/h%	Iso	RC/G

Tall, projectable INF who will make pro debut in '13. Very rough around edges with hitting tool and pitch recognition is far from polished. Can be pull-conscious, but raw, power potential is unquestioned. Moves well at 3B with first-step quickness. Possesses extremely strong arm and should be able to stick.

Neal, Thomas — 79 — Cleveland

EXP MLB DEBUT: 2012 | POTENTIAL: Reserve OF | 7D

Bats R Age 25
2005 (36) Riverside JC
Pwr +++
BAvg +++
Spd ++
Def ++

Year	Lev	Team	AB	R	H	HR	RBI	Avg	OB	Slg	OPS	bb%	ct%	Eye	SB	CS	x/h%	Iso	RC/G
2010	AA	Richmond	525	69	153	12	69	291	349	440	789	8	82	0.49	11	5	35	149	5.26
2011	AAA	Fresno	220	35	65	2	25	295	335	409	744	6	77	0.26	7	6	28	114	4.65
2011	AAA	Columbus	36	5	9	0	1	250	270	278	548	3	81	0.14	1	0	11	28	2.00
2012	AA	Akron	405	77	127	12	51	314	384	467	850	10	82	0.65	11	8	29	153	6.09
2012	MLB	Cleveland	23	2	5	0	2	217	217	261	478	0	74	0.00	0	0	20	43	0.88

Tall, strong OF who dropped a level in '12, but still reached CLE for cup of coffee. Hasn't developed offensively due to avg bat speed and greater focus on contact. Puts bat to ball and can hit for BA with emphasis on drives to gaps. Recognizes pitches and willing to draw BB. Doesn't run well and has avg range.

Nessy, Santiago — 2 — Toronto

EXP MLB DEBUT: 2016 | POTENTIAL: Starting C | 7C

Bats R Age 20
2009 FA (Venezuela)
Pwr +++
BAvg ++
Spd +
Def ++++

Year	Lev	Team	AB	R	H	HR	RBI	Avg	OB	Slg	OPS	bb%	ct%	Eye	SB	CS	x/h%	Iso	RC/G
2011	Rk	GCL Blue Jays	134	12	41	3	19	306	345	425	770	6	78	0.28	0	2	24	119	4.86
2012	Rk	Bluefield	160	26	41	8	23	256	312	456	768	8	71	0.28	0	0	39	200	4.98
2012	A-	Vancouver	22	4	2	1	3	91	200	273	473	12	68	0.43	0	0	100	182	0.88

Tall, strong C who is advanced defender. Has excellent agility while maintaining outstanding catch-and-throw skills. Should be even better once footwork improves. Generates solid bat speed with quick wrists and profiles as moderate to plus pop. Lacks speed and BA potential lags behind due to poor contact.

Nick, David — 46 — Arizona

EXP MLB DEBUT: 2014 | POTENTIAL: Backup 2B | 6C

Bats R Age 23
2009 (4) HS, CA
Pwr ++
BAvg ++
6.5/60 Spd ++
Def ++

Year	Lev	Team	AB	R	H	HR	RBI	Avg	OB	Slg	OPS	bb%	ct%	Eye	SB	CS	x/h%	Iso	RC/G
2009	Rk	Missoula	273	46	78	6	35	286	339	440	779	7	82	0.45	16	8	35	154	5.12
2010	A	South Bend	495	66	124	7	49	251	308	366	673	8	80	0.42	12	7	29	115	3.85
2011	A+	Visalia	564	99	169	13	68	300	335	449	784	5	86	0.38	5	5	31	149	5.02
2012	AA	Mobile	458	49	114	5	43	249	292	341	633	6	81	0.33	13	5	26	92	3.25

Took a huge step back in his first taste of Double-A, hitting just .240 with 5 HR and doesn't have any standout tools. Unorthodox approach at the plate limits ability to hit for average. Defensively has good hands but limited speed and range forced a shift to 2B where he is now above-average.

Nimmo, Brandon — 7 — New York (N)

EXP MLB DEBUT: 2015 | POTENTIAL: Starting CF | 9D

Bats L Age 20
2011 (1) HS, WY
Pwr +++
BAvg ++++
Spd +++
Def +++

Year	Lev	Team	AB	R	H	HR	RBI	Avg	OB	Slg	OPS	bb%	ct%	Eye	SB	CS	x/h%	Iso	RC/G
2011	Rk	Kingsport	9	0	1	0	0	111	333	111	444	25	44	0.60	0	0	0	0	0.02
2011	Rk	GCL Mets	29	5	7	2	4	241	313	448	761	9	69	0.33	0	0	29	207	4.81
2012	A-	Brooklyn	266	41	66	6	40	248	359	406	765	15	71	0.59	1	5	42	158	5.44

Raw OF held his own against older competition in the NYPL. Power should develop once his approach is refined. Compact LH stroke and solid plate discipline should allow him to hit for average. Is a good runner with a strong throwing arm and has the raw tools to develop into a stud CF, but also a long way to go.

Nunez, Renato — 5 — Oakland

EXP MLB DEBUT: 2016 | POTENTIAL: Starting 3B | 9E

Bats R Age 19
2010 FA (Venezuela)
Pwr ++++
BAvg +++
Spd ++
Def ++

Year	Lev	Team	AB	R	H	HR	RBI	Avg	OB	Slg	OPS	bb%	ct%	Eye	SB	CS	x/h%	Iso	RC/G
2012	Rk	Athletics	160	31	52	4	42	325	390	550	940	10	80	0.53	4	0	48	225	7.36

Projectable INF who has upside with plus, raw power to all fields. Shows advanced bat control and covers plate well. Bat speed is borderline plus with loft and leverage. Still raw in overall game and can be too aggressive at times. Glovework must improve, but likely to get better as he gains experience. Arm strength is asset.

O'Brien, Peter — 2 — New York (A)

EXP MLB DEBUT: 2015 | POTENTIAL: Starting C/1B | 8E

Bats R Age 22
2012 (2) Miami (FL)
Pwr ++++
BAvg ++
Spd +
Def ++

Year	Lev	Team	AB	R	H	HR	RBI	Avg	OB	Slg	OPS	bb%	ct%	Eye	SB	CS	x/h%	Iso	RC/G
2010	NCAA	Bethune-Ckman	202	51	78	20	56	386	436	748	1184	8	81	0.46	0	3	42	361	9.80
2011	NCAA	Bethune-Ckman	230	41	70	14	69	304	375	557	932	10	77	0.50	3	2	41	252	7.07
2012	NCAA	Miami	147	31	50	10	40	340	429	626	1055	14	84	1.00	1	2	44	286	8.62
2012	Rk	GCL Yankees	14	2	5	0	2	357	357	500	857	0	93	0.00	0	0	40	143	5.65
2012	A-	Staten Island	198	27	40	10	32	202	240	394	634	5	69	0.16	0	1	45	192	3.00

Tall, strong C whose power and arm strength are above avg tools. Rest of game is questionable. Produces power to all fields with impressive bat speed and powerful wrists. Can be jammed inside and struggles to hit breaking balls. Plus arm neutralizes running game, but lacks agility and mobility.

Odor, Rougned — 46 — Texas

EXP MLB DEBUT: 2015 | POTENTIAL: Starting 2B | 7B

Bats L Age 19
2011 FA (Venezuela)

Pwr + + +
BAvg + +
Spd + + + +
Def + + + +

Year	Lev	Team	AB	R	H	HR	RBI	Avg	OB	Slg	OPS	bb%	ct%	Eye	SB	CS	x/h%	Iso	RC/G
2011	A-	Spokane	233	33	61	2	29	262	301	352	653	5	84	0.35	10	4	23	90	3.52
2012	A	Hickory	432	60	112	10	47	259	300	400	700	5	85	0.38	19	10	33	141	4.07

Smooth, strong INF who was youngest regular in league and stood out for speed and defense. Possesses excellent tools with bat, including controlled stroke and surprising pop for size. Has quick hands, but swing mechanics can get choppy. Runs well and could be outstanding defender at 2B with great hands and arm.

Olson, Matt — 3 — Oakland

EXP MLB DEBUT: 2016 | POTENTIAL: Starting 1B | 8C

Bats L Age 19
2012 (1-S) HS (GA)

Pwr + + + +
BAvg + + + +
Spd +
Def + + +

Year	Lev	Team	AB	R	H	HR	RBI	Avg	OB	Slg	OPS	bb%	ct%	Eye	SB	CS	x/h%	Iso	RC/G
2012	Rk	Athletics	177	29	50	8	41	282	342	520	862	8	74	0.35	0	0	50	237	6.30
2012	A-	Vermont	11	3	3	1	4	273	429	545	974	21	64	0.75	0	0	33	273	8.67

Tall, advanced prospect who could develop into middle of order run producer. Though swing can get long and has struggles with Ks, has potential for plus BA and power. Owns bat speed and leverage while drives balls against LHP and RHP. Fits profile of slugging 1B and is nimble defender with strong arm.

Olt, Mike — 35 — Texas

EXP MLB DEBUT: 2012 | POTENTIAL: Starting 3B | 9C

Bats R Age 24
2010 (1-S) Connecticut

Pwr + + + +
BAvg + + +
Spd + +
Def + + + +

Year	Lev	Team	AB	R	H	HR	RBI	Avg	OB	Slg	OPS	bb%	ct%	Eye	SB	CS	x/h%	Iso	RC/G
2010	A-	Spokane	263	57	77	9	43	293	386	464	850	13	71	0.52	6	0	34	171	6.50
2011	Rk	Rangers	14	2	3	1	4	214	267	429	695	7	64	0.20	0	0	33	214	3.90
2011	A+	Myrtle Beach	240	39	64	14	42	267	389	504	893	17	71	0.69	0	1	45	238	7.12
2012	AA	Frisco	354	65	102	28	82	288	393	579	972	15	71	0.60	4	0	45	291	8.00
2012	MLB	Texas	33	2	5	0	5	152	263	182	445	13	61	0.38	1	1	20	30	0.51

Big, strong INF who leveraged huge power output to big leagues. Led TL in HR and Slg while playing plus defense at 3B. Moved over to 1B at times and will be asset at either position. Has strong arm and good range. Uses selective approach to attack balls. Has below avg speed and won't steal many bases.

Oropesa, Ricky — 3 — San Francisco

EXP MLB DEBUT: 2015 | POTENTIAL: Backup 1B | 6C

Bats L Age 23
2011 (3) USC

Pwr + + +
BAvg + +
Spd +
Def + +

Year	Lev	Team	AB	R	H	HR	RBI	Avg	OB	Slg	OPS	bb%	ct%	Eye	SB	CS	x/h%	Iso	RC/G
2009	NCAA	USC	185	35	58	13	48	314	389	578	968	11	75	0.50	3	4	38	265	7.62
2010	NCAA	USC	235	53	83	20	67	353	433	711	1143	12	78	0.65	7	5	52	357	9.85
2011	NCAA	USC	208	35	67	7	44	322	405	481	886	12	78	0.63	4	2	27	159	6.70
2012	A+	San Jose	518	70	136	16	98	263	338	425	763	10	71	0.39	1	1	36	162	5.13

Strong 1B with plus power mashed 16 HR in pro debut. Is overly aggressive and struggles with breaking balls. Will need to make more contact to hit for average. Played 3B at USC and does have a good arm, but lack of speed and range limit him to 1B. Works hard, but power-hitting 1B are not scarce.

Ortega, Angel — 6 — Milwaukee

EXP MLB DEBUT: 2016 | POTENTIAL: Backup SS | 6D

Bats R Age 19
2012 (6) P.R.

Pwr +
BAvg + +
Spd + +
Def + + +

Year	Lev	Team	AB	R	H	HR	RBI	Avg	OB	Slg	OPS	bb%	ct%	Eye	SB	CS	x/h%	Iso	RC/G
2012	Rk	Brewers	178	26	43	1	16	242	286	315	600	6	87	0.46	9	4	21	73	3.01

Athletic SS is a plus defender with good range and a strong arm. Could add power as he matures and fills out, but for now is below average can be beat by quality fastballs. Does have a good appraoch and decent strike zone judgment. Struggled in his pro debut, but still has value due to plus defense.

Ortega, Rafael — 8 — Colorado

EXP MLB DEBUT: 2012 | POTENTIAL: Starting CF | 8D

Bats L Age 22
2008 NDFA, Venezuela

Pwr + +
BAvg + + +
Spd + + +
Def + + +

Year	Lev	Team	AB	R	H	HR	RBI	Avg	OB	Slg	OPS	bb%	ct%	Eye	SB	CS	x/h%	Iso	RC/G
2010	Rk	Casper	288	69	103	7	45	358	415	510	925	9	85	0.67	23	9	26	153	6.91
2011	A	Asheville	479	77	141	9	66	294	333	438	772	6	81	0.31	32	19	30	144	4.93
2012	A+	Modesto	495	81	140	8	60	283	344	410	754	9	81	0.49	36	18	28	127	4.89
2012	MLB	Colorado	4	0	2	0	0	500	600	500	1100	20	50	0.50	1	0	0	0	14.09

Toolsy OF continues to make steady progress. Has plus speed on the bases, good raw power, and a quick bat. Solid plate discipline gives him a chance to hit for average and utilize his speed. Plus defender in CF with good range, good routes, and a strong, accurate arm. Still raw, but starting to realize his potential.

Osuna, Jose — 3 — Pittsburgh

EXP MLB DEBUT: 2015 | POTENTIAL: Starting 1B | 7D

Bats R Age 20
2009 NDFA, Venezuela

Pwr + + + +
BAvg + +
Spd + +
Def + +

Year	Lev	Team	AB	R	H	HR	RBI	Avg	OB	Slg	OPS	bb%	ct%	Eye	SB	CS	x/h%	Iso	RC/G
2011	Rk	GCL Pirates	178	28	59	4	32	331	393	511	904	9	88	0.86	3	2	36	180	6.74
2011	A-	State College	8	2	2	0	1	250	333	375	708	11	100	1.00	0	0	50	125	5.15
2012	A	West Virginia	482	68	135	16	72	280	324	454	778	6	83	0.38	4	4	39	174	4.96

Was moved from the OF to 1B and has plus power potential. Had a nice season as a 19-year-old in the SAL. Drives the ball well and has power to all fields. Plate discipline and walk rate regressed as he was more aggressive in search for power. Has a strong arm, but is still learning the position.

Ovando, Ariel — 9 — Houston

EXP MLB DEBUT: 2016 | POTENTIAL: Starting OF | 9E

Bats L Age 19
2010 FA (DR)

Pwr + + + +
BAvg + + +
Spd + +
Def + +

Year	Lev	Team	AB	R	H	HR	RBI	Avg	OB	Slg	OPS	bb%	ct%	Eye	SB	CS	x/h%	Iso	RC/G
2011	Rk	Greeneville	170	16	40	2	30	235	286	365	650	7	70	0.24	0	0	38	129	3.56
2012	Rk	Greeneville	223	34	64	6	35	287	351	444	795	9	70	0.33	0	0	33	157	5.60

Tall, projectable OF who is progressing nicely despite repeat performance in short season. Uses leverage in loose swing to produce plus raw power. Exhibits athleticism, but is raw and secondary skills need time. Overall defense is crude, though arm strength is ideal for RF. Needs to add strength.

Owings, Chris — 6 — Arizona

EXP MLB DEBUT: 2014 | POTENTIAL: Starting SS | 8D

Bats R Age 21
2009 (1) HS, SC

Pwr + + +
BAvg + + +
4.15 Spd + + +
Def + + +

Year	Lev	Team	AB	R	H	HR	RBI	Avg	OB	Slg	OPS	bb%	ct%	Eye	SB	CS	x/h%	Iso	RC/G
2009	Rk	Missoula	108	20	33	2	10	306	324	426	750	3	77	0.12	3	0	24	120	4.48
2010	A	South Bend	255	39	76	5	28	298	322	447	769	3	80	0.18	1	3	34	149	4.77
2011	A+	Visalia	521	67	128	11	50	246	267	388	655	3	75	0.12	10	4	36	142	3.32
2012	A+	Visalia	241	51	78	11	24	324	358	544	902	5	74	0.21	8	3	37	220	6.62
2012	AA	Mobile	297	35	78	6	28	263	289	377	666	4	77	0.16	4	3	24	114	3.45

Finally had the breakout many had been waiting for. Has a short, compact stroke and showed improved power. Plate discipline remains well below average and could limit his ability to hit. He has the tools to make all of the plays defensively and reduced his errors from 32 down to 23, but still has work to do.

Ozuna, Marcell — 9 — Miami

EXP MLB DEBUT: 2013 | POTENTIAL: Starting RF | 8D

Bats R Age 22
2008 NDFA, D.R.

Pwr + + + +
BAvg + +
Spd + +
Def + +

Year	Lev	Team	AB	R	H	HR	RBI	Avg	OB	Slg	OPS	bb%	ct%	Eye	SB	CS	x/h%	Iso	RC/G
2009	Rk	GCL Marlins	214	32	67	5	39	313	377	486	863	9	76	0.42	4	2	40	173	6.41
2010	A	Greensboro	25	3	4	1	2	160	222	280	502	7	60	0.20	0	0	25	120	1.12
2010	A-	Jamestown	270	53	72	21	60	267	310	556	866	6	65	0.18	3	1	47	289	6.51
2011	A	Greensboro	496	87	132	23	71	266	328	482	810	8	76	0.38	17	2	42	216	5.53
2012	A+	Jupiter	489	89	130	24	95	266	326	476	803	8	76	0.38	8	3	41	211	5.37

Has some of the best power in the minors. Far from a one-dimensional slugger, has above-average speed but continues to strikeout too much. Showed solid growth in the 2nd half and has good range and a strong arm. Swing can get long at times and he remains a bit raw, but the power upside is substantial.

Pan, Chih-Fang — 4 — Oakland

EXP MLB DEBUT: 2014 | POTENTIAL: Starting 2B | 6B

Bats L Age 22
2010 FA (Taiwan)

Pwr +
BAvg + + +
Spd + + +
Def + + +

Year	Lev	Team	AB	R	H	HR	RBI	Avg	OB	Slg	OPS	bb%	ct%	Eye	SB	CS	x/h%	Iso	RC/G
2011	A-	Vermont	143	22	48	1	22	336	387	385	772	8	81	0.44	8	4	10	49	5.00
2012	A	Burlington	296	36	72	2	37	243	293	324	618	7	81	0.38	8	3	25	81	3.13

Lean, athletic INF who profiles as top of order hitter with small ball game. Beats out grounders with speed and instincts. Can slash line drives to gaps with quick, compact stroke. Hits much better from left and uses entire field. No power, but could hit for BA. Good defender with sufficient range and arm strength.

Panik, Joe — 4 — San Francisco

EXP MLB DEBUT: 2014 | POTENTIAL: Starting 2B | **8D**

Bats L Age 22
2011 (1) St. Johns

- Pwr ++
- BAvg +++
- Spd +++
- Def +++

Year	Lev	Team	AB	R	H	HR	RBI	Avg	OB	Slg	OPS	bb%	ct%	Eye	SB	CS	x/h%	Iso	RC/G
2009	NCAA	St. John's	187	38	62	5	47	332	421	513	935	13	91	1.81	6	1	32	182	7.36
2010	NCAA	St. John's	227	66	85	10	53	374	464	621	1085	14	93	2.24	6	3	38	247	9.04
2011	NCAA	St. John's	226	60	90	10	57	398	496	642	1138	16	89	1.83	21	6	36	243	9.83
2011	A-	Salem-Keizer	270	49	92	6	54	341	403	467	869	9	91	1.12	13	5	21	126	6.29
2012	A+	San Jose	535	93	159	7	76	297	366	402	768	10	90	1.07	10	4	24	105	5.23

Athletic grinder gets the most of his abilities. Has good bat speed and uses a short, compact stroke to barrell the ball. Battles every AB and doesn't give anything away. Has moderate gap-to-gap power and could hit double-digit home runs. Is an average runner and doesn't have great range or a strong arm.

Parker, Jarrett — 7 — San Francisco

EXP MLB DEBUT: 2015 | POTENTIAL: Starting RF | **7D**

Bats L Age 24
2010 (2) Virginia

- Pwr +++
- BAvg ++
- Spd +++
- Def +++

Year	Lev	Team	AB	R	H	HR	RBI	Avg	OB	Slg	OPS	bb%	ct%	Eye	SB	CS	x/h%	Iso	RC/G
2008	NCAA	Virginia	148	29	39	0	16	264	347	331	678	11	72	0.46	14	2	18	68	4.13
2009	NCAA	Virginia	265	76	94	16	65	355	438	664	1102	13	70	0.49	20	5	46	309	10.14
2010	NCAA	Virginia	243	56	81	10	56	333	413	593	1006	12	77	0.59	12	2	43	259	8.37
2011	A+	San Jose	486	81	123	13	61	253	352	397	749	13	70	0.51	20	5	33	144	5.09
2012	A+	San Jose	409	71	101	15	67	247	357	443	800	15	57	0.40	28	6	43	196	6.66

Tall OF has yet to have breakout. Can be patient, but also struck out 175 times. Has good speed and athleticism, but swing can get long and will need to make better contact. He runs well, is a good defender, and has the tools to be a 20/20 player, but might not make enough contact to have an impact.

Parker, Kyle — 9 — Colorado

EXP MLB DEBUT: 2014 | POTENTIAL: Starting RF | **8C**

Bats R Age 23
2010 (1) Clemson

- Pwr ++++
- BAvg +++
- Spd ++
- Def ++

Year	Lev	Team	AB	R	H	HR	RBI	Avg	OB	Slg	OPS	bb%	ct%	Eye	SB	CS	x/h%	Iso	RC/G
2008	NCAA	Clemson	211	44	64	14	50	303	395	559	954	13	77	0.67	2	1	41	256	7.50
2009	NCAA	Clemson	231	48	59	12	52	255	338	442	780	11	77	0.56	6	0	32	186	5.14
2010	NCAA	Clemson	247	85	85	20	64	344	465	656	1121	18	76	0.93	4	2	42	312	10.06
2011	A	Asheville	445	75	127	21	95	285	355	483	838	10	70	0.36	2	0	35	198	6.11
2012	A+	Modesto	390	86	120	23	73	308	408	562	969	14	77	0.75	1	2	39	254	7.84

Strong hitter who continues to show plus power. Improved pitch recognition and ct% are positive signs and suggest he should hit for average. Good bat speed with a short stroke and raw strength. Is below average defensively but does have a strong arm. Will need to prove himself at AA, but the bat could be special.

Parker, Stephen — 5 — Oakland

EXP MLB DEBUT: 2013 | POTENTIAL: Starting 3B | **7D**

Bats L Age 25
2009 (5) BYU

- Pwr +++
- BAvg +++
- Spd ++
- Def +++

Year	Lev	Team	AB	R	H	HR	RBI	Avg	OB	Slg	OPS	bb%	ct%	Eye	SB	CS	x/h%	Iso	RC/G
2009	A	Kane County	254	27	62	5	39	244	312	362	674	9	78	0.45	1	4	29	118	3.86
2010	A+	Stockton	524	102	155	21	98	296	393	508	901	14	80	0.80	3	1	41	212	6.96
2011	AA	Midland	504	72	144	10	74	286	372	413	784	12	79	0.64	1	1	29	127	5.45
2011	AAA	Sacramento	25	4	8	0	2	320	370	320	690	7	76	0.33	0	0	0	0	3.94
2012	AAA	Sacramento	328	43	84	7	47	256	322	390	712	9	72	0.34	5	1	30	134	4.40

Natural hitting INF with feel for bat control. Understands K zone and brings mature approach to plate. Has moderate power and should have enough pop to stick at 3B. Can be too passive and swing can get long when selling out for power. Has improved defense, but hands are stiff. On verge of big leagues, but needs polish.

Paulino, Dorssys — 6 — Cleveland

EXP MLB DEBUT: 2016 | POTENTIAL: Starting SS | **8B**

Bats R Age 18
2011 FA (DR)

- Pwr +++
- BAvg ++++
- Spd +++
- Def ++

Year	Lev	Team	AB	R	H	HR	RBI	Avg	OB	Slg	OPS	bb%	ct%	Eye	SB	CS	x/h%	Iso	RC/G
2012	Rk	Indians	172	42	61	6	30	355	406	610	1017	8	82	0.48	9	1	43	256	8.10
2012	A-	Mahoning Val	59	5	16	1	8	271	306	407	713	5	76	0.21	2	1	38	136	4.20

Quick, mature INF with potential for above avg offensive output. Exhibits plus hand-eye coordination for maximum contact and has quick hands and bat speed for both BA and power. Swing can lengthen at times and can flail at breaking balls. Solid defender with good quickness, but has mental lapses.

Payne, Shawn — 7 — San Francisco

EXP MLB DEBUT: 2015 | POTENTIAL: Starting OF | **7D**

Bats R Age 23
2011 (35) Georgia Southern

- Pwr ++
- BAvg +++
- Spd ++++
- Def +++

Year	Lev	Team	AB	R	H	HR	RBI	Avg	OB	Slg	OPS	bb%	ct%	Eye	SB	CS	x/h%	Iso	RC/G
2010	NCAA	GA Southern	206	68	71	5	33	345	440	500	940	15	77	0.73	43	2	30	155	7.67
2011	NCAA	GA Southern	242	70	76	6	39	314	407	504	911	14	75	0.63	33	3	37	190	7.33
2011	A-	Salem-Keizer	160	37	49	0	19	306	413	394	806	15	80	0.91	21	6	22	88	6.05
2012	A	Augusta	405	66	125	6	57	309	399	430	829	13	82	0.86	53	3	25	121	6.10
2012	A+	San Jose	9	1	3	0	2	333	333	444	778	0	78	0.00	0	0	33	111	4.79

35th round pick continues to impress in pro career, but gets little attention. Has good size, speed, and surprising pop. Makes hard contact with solid strike zone judgment. Was not young for this level and will need to prove himself as he moves up, but is worth keeping an eye on.

Pederson, Joc — 7 — Los Angeles (N)

EXP MLB DEBUT: 2014 | POTENTIAL: Starting CF | **9D**

Bats L Age 21
2010 (11) HS, CA

4.20

- Pwr +++
- BAvg ++++
- Spd +++
- Def +++

Year	Lev	Team	AB	R	H	HR	RBI	Avg	OB	Slg	OPS	bb%	ct%	Eye	SB	CS	x/h%	Iso	RC/G
2010	Rk	Dodgers	7	1	0	0	0	0	364	0	364	36	29	0.80	0	0			
2011	Rk	Ogden	266	54	94	11	64	353	430	568	998	12	80	0.67	24	5	35	214	8.08
2011	A	Great Lakes	50	4	8	0	1	160	263	160	423	12	82	0.78	2	0	0	0	0.99
2012	A+	Rancho Cuc	434	96	136	18	70	313	386	516	902	11	81	0.63	26	14	35	203	6.72

Athletic OF was impressive in the CA. Can do a bit of everything and continues to develop. Hit 16 HR in the 2nd half. Solid approach from the LH side with good strike zone judgment and plus bat speed. Makes solid and consistent contact with above-average power. Runs well and has good range in CF

Peguero, Francisco — 7 — San Francisco

EXP MLB DEBUT: 2012 | POTENTIAL: Starting LF | **8D**

Bats R Age 25
2006 NDFA, D.R.

4.00

- Pwr ++
- BAvg +++
- Spd +++
- Def ++++

Year	Lev	Team	AB	R	H	HR	RBI	Avg	OB	Slg	OPS	bb%	ct%	Eye	SB	CS	x/h%	Iso	RC/G
2010	A+	San Jose	510	78	168	10	77	329	352	488	841	3	83	0.20	40	22	27	159	5.62
2011	A+	San Jose	68	12	22	2	9	324	387	441	828	9	88	0.88	4	0	18	118	5.73
2011	AA	Richmond	285	34	88	5	37	309	321	446	766	2	84	0.11	8	1	26	137	4.61
2012	AAA	Fresno	449	46	122	5	68	272	295	394	689	3	82	0.18	1	0	29	122	3.84
2012	MLB	Giants	16	6	3	0	0	188	188	188	375	0	56	0.00	3	0	0	0	

Short, athletic OF made his MLB debut after six years in the minors. Sqaures the ball well and has a bit of pop, but is not disciplined. Was healthy after missing half of '11 with a knee injury. Plus defender in CF with good range above-average arm. Will need to be more selective as he moves up, but is fun to watch.

Penalvar, Carlos — 6 — Chicago (N)

EXP MLB DEBUT: 2016 | POTENTIAL: Starting SS | **7D**

Bats R Age
2011 NDFA, Venezuela

- Pwr ++
- BAvg ++
- Spd +++
- Def +++

Year	Lev	Team	AB	R	H	HR	RBI	Avg	OB	Slg	OPS	bb%	ct%	Eye	SB	CS	x/h%	Iso	RC/G
2012	Rk	Cubs	183	27	50	0	20	273	342	322	664	9	83	0.61	7	4	16	49	3.89

Lean, athletic 2B prospect continues to put up solid offensive numbers. Has plus speed and an advanced approach at the plate, but very little power. Showed some contact ability and puts the ball onto the ball regularly. Decent defender and should be able to stick at SS with good range and a strong arm.

Peraza, Jose — 6 — Atlanta

EXP MLB DEBUT: 2016 | POTENTIAL: Starting 2B | **7B**

Bats R Age 19
2010 NDFA, Venezuela

- Pwr +
- BAvg +++
- Spd +++
- Def +++

Year	Lev	Team	AB	R	H	HR	RBI	Avg	OB	Slg	OPS	bb%	ct%	Eye	SB	CS	x/h%	Iso	RC/G
2012	Rk	GCL Braves	85	17	27	0	10	318	348	424	772	4	93	0.67	10	3	22	106	5.06
2012	Rk	Danville	121	21	34	1	18	281	331	339	670	7	85	0.50	15	2	15	58	3.79

Dynamic player has true top-of-the-order potential with plus speed and the ability to hit. Handles the bat well with a short compact stroke and makes consistent contact. Needs to walk more, but is a threat once on base. Not likely to hit for much power, but is a plus defender with good range and a strong arm.

Perez, Carlos — 2 — Houston

EXP MLB DEBUT: 2014 | POTENTIAL: Starting C | **7B**

Bats R Age 22
2007 FA (DR)

- Pwr ++
- BAvg +++
- Spd ++
- Def ++++

Year	Lev	Team	AB	R	H	HR	RBI	Avg	OB	Slg	OPS	bb%	ct%	Eye	SB	CS	x/h%	Iso	RC/G
2009	Rk	GCL Blue Jays	141	17	41	1	21	291	363	433	796	10	84	0.70	2	5	37	142	5.62
2010	A-	Auburn	235	44	70	2	41	298	387	438	825	13	83	0.83	7	3	30	140	6.11
2011	A	Lansing	383	58	98	3	41	256	321	355	677	9	81	0.50	6	2	27	99	3.99
2012	A	Lansing	273	48	75	5	40	275	357	447	804	11	86	0.92	3	2	43	172	5.75
2012	A+	Lancaster	88	11	28	0	10	318	362	409	771	6	81	0.35	0	1	25	91	5.05

Strong-armed C who is quickly evolving into two-way prospect. Owns strong arm with quick release and controls running game. Raw with receiving, but getting better. Possesses natural hitting skills with bat control and coverage. Doesn't K often and knows how to read pitches. Power is emerging, but needs more.

Perez, Eury

8 | **Washington** | EXP MLB DEBUT: 2012 | POTENTIAL: Starting CF | **7C**

	Year	Lev	Team	AB	R	H	HR	RBI	Avg	OB	Slg	OPS	bb%	ct%	Eye	SB	CS	x/h%	Iso	RC/G
Bats R Age 23																				
2007 NDFA, D.R.	2011	A+	Potomac	424	54	120	1	41	283	318	321	639	5	85	0.35	45	15	10	38	3.32
Pwr +	2012	Rk	GCL Nationals	22	4	9	0	2	409	435	455	889	4	100	1.00	5	0	11	45	6.27
BAvg ++++	2012	AA	Harrisburg	351	34	105	0	30	299	313	342	655	2	85	0.13	26	10	12	43	3.32
Spd ++++	2012	AAA	Syracuse	159	21	53	0	10	333	365	390	755	5	84	0.31	20	5	15	57	4.69
Def +++	2012	MLB	Washington	5	3	1	0	0	200	200	200	400	0	100	1.00	3	0	0	0	1.14

Speedy Dominican OF uses his plus, plus speed to wreak havoc on the bases. Has a quick bat and puts the ball into play. Covers ground well and has a strong, accurate throwing arm, so should be able to stay in CF. Power is not part of his game, but the stolen base ability gives him plenty of fantasy value.

Perez, Hernan

4 | **Detroit** | EXP MLB DEBUT: 2012 | POTENTIAL: Reserve INF | **6B**

	Year	Lev	Team	AB	R	H	HR	RBI	Avg	OB	Slg	OPS	bb%	ct%	Eye	SB	CS	x/h%	Iso	RC/G
Bats R Age 22																				
2007 FA (Venezuela)	2009	A+	Lakeland	72	7	19	0	10	264	293	347	641	4	71	0.14	0	0	26	83	3.32
Pwr ++	2010	A	West Michigan	473	45	111	5	50	235	273	298	571	5	79	0.26	5	1	18	63	2.36
BAvg ++	2011	A	West Michigan	503	69	130	8	42	258	311	364	674	7	83	0.44	23	6	26	105	3.82
Spd +++	2012	A+	Lakeland	441	50	115	5	44	261	299	338	637	5	84	0.34	27	4	17	77	3.28
Def +++	2012	MLB	Detroit	2	1	1	0	0	500	500	500	1000	0	100	1.00	0	0	0	0	6.83

Lean, athletic INF who is developing slowly, yet earned brief callup. Good defensive instincts with nice footwork and quick actions. Hands work well and strong arm is asset, but range best served at 2B. Improved with bat, but needs to up OBP in order to utilize speed. Can play gap to gap, but won't hit many HR.

Perez, Michael

2 | **Arizona** | EXP MLB DEBUT: 2016 | POTENTIAL: Starting C | **8D**

	Year	Lev	Team	AB	R	H	HR	RBI	Avg	OB	Slg	OPS	bb%	ct%	Eye	SB	CS	x/h%	Iso	RC/G
Bats L Age 20																				
2011 (5) HS, PR																				
Pwr +++																				
BAvg ++																				
Spd +	2011	Rk	Diamondbacks	23	5	5	2	3	217	280	565	845	8	57	0.20	1	0	80	348	7.15
Def ++++	2012	Rk	Missoula	225	43	66	10	60	293	351	542	893	8	68	0.28	0	1	47	249	7.09

Strong, offensive-minded catcher put up good numbers this year in the PIO. Has good bat speed and can drive the ball out of any park. Needs to be more selective at the plate and make more consistent contact, but he does show solid offensive potential. Is raw behind the plate, but has a very strong arm and most observers believe in him as catcher.

Perio, Noah

4 | **Miami** | EXP MLB DEBUT: 2015 | POTENTIAL: Starting 2B | **7D**

	Year	Lev	Team	AB	R	H	HR	RBI	Avg	OB	Slg	OPS	bb%	ct%	Eye	SB	CS	x/h%	Iso	RC/G
Bats L Age 21																				
2009 (39) HS, CA																				
Pwr ++	2009	Rk	GCL Marlins	14	2	6	0	5	429	429	643	1071	0	100	1.00	1	0	33	214	7.91
BAvg +++	2010	A-	Jamestown	225	30	58	0	31	258	310	302	612	7	89	0.68	7	0	17	44	3.30
Spd ++	2011	A	Greensboro	488	76	144	6	52	295	321	406	727	4	87	0.30	15	6	27	111	4.32
Def ++	2012	A+	Jupiter	463	50	115	1	40	248	290	311	601	6	85	0.40	6	4	22	63	2.97

Wiry, athletic 2B took a step back in '12. Has good bat speed and makes solid contact, but does not have over the fence power. Below average strike zone judgment and pitch recognition limits offensive upside. Fringy defender was moved from SS to 2B where his average speed plays better. The FSL can be a tough environment. Look for more in '13.

Peterson, Jace

6 | **San Diego** | EXP MLB DEBUT: 2015 | POTENTIAL: Starting SS/CF | **8C**

	Year	Lev	Team	AB	R	H	HR	RBI	Avg	OB	Slg	OPS	bb%	ct%	Eye	SB	CS	x/h%	Iso	RC/G
Bats L Age 23																				
2011 (1-S) McNeese State	2009	NCAA	McNeese State	71	14	26	0	9	366	438	437	874	11	92	1.50	13	1	15	70	6.60
Pwr ++	2010	NCAA	McNeese State	232	68	82	4	49	353	451	491	942	15	85	1.17	35	5	26	138	7.59
BAvg +++	2011	NCAA	McNeese State	224	67	75	2	34	335	442	473	915	16	88	1.54	30	10	25	138	7.41
Spd ++++	2011	A-	Eugene	276	48	67	2	27	243	359	333	692	15	81	0.94	39	10	24	91	4.53
Def ++++	2012	A	Fort Wayne	444	78	127	2	48	286	374	392	765	12	86	0.98	51	13	27	106	5.37

Strong, athletic SS looks to be a true top-of-the-order hitter with plus speed, the ability to make good contact, and solid strike zone judgment. Has plus speed and gets on base, so should be a stolen base threat regardless of position. Has good range, but is raw defensively and will need to work hard to stay at SS.

Pham, Tommy

8 | **St. Louis** | EXP MLB DEBUT: 2013 | POTENTIAL: Backup OF | **7D**

	Year	Lev	Team	AB	R	H	HR	RBI	Avg	OB	Slg	OPS	bb%	ct%	Eye	SB	CS	x/h%	Iso	RC/G
Bats R Age 25																				
2006 (16) HS, NV	2009	A+	Palm Beach	336	47	78	8	44	232	306	378	684	10	70	0.35	18	6	36	146	4.07
Pwr ++	2010	A+	Palm Beach	237	42	62	3	27	262	373	392	765	15	75	0.71	13	4	34	131	5.45
BAvg ++	2010	AA	Springfield	121	19	41	3	18	339	424	537	962	13	77	0.64	4	2	41	198	7.92
Spd +++	2011	AA	Springfield	143	31	42	5	16	294	373	517	890	11	72	0.45	3	3	45	224	7.00
Def ++++	2012	AA	Springfield	39	3	6	1	3	154	233	282	515	9	51	0.21	0	0	50	128	1.82

Lean, toolsy OF can't seem to stay healthy. A broken hand limited him to 40 games in '11 and a shoulder injury in '12 cost him all but 12 games. Still raw, but has a nice swing and potential power. Also has a good arm, solid speed, and covers ground well in CF. Still has some work to do, but if everything comes together could have a nice career.

Phegley, Josh

2 | **Chicago (A)** | EXP MLB DEBUT: 2013 | POTENTIAL: Backup C | **6A**

	Year	Lev	Team	AB	R	H	HR	RBI	Avg	OB	Slg	OPS	bb%	ct%	Eye	SB	CS	x/h%	Iso	RC/G
Bats R Age 25																				
2009 (1-S) Indiana	2010	A+	Winston-Salem	89	16	26	3	12	292	344	427	771	7	75	0.32	0	0	23	135	4.92
Pwr +++	2010	AA	Birmingham	72	7	21	2	13	292	311	431	741	3	69	0.09	0	0	29	139	4.51
BAvg ++	2011	AA	Birmingham	364	43	88	7	50	242	287	368	655	6	83	0.38	1	2	34	126	3.55
Spd ++	2011	AAA	Charlotte	79	9	19	2	6	241	310	367	677	9	77	0.44	0	0	32	127	3.87
Def +++	2012	AAA	Charlotte	394	40	105	6	48	266	302	373	675	5	85	0.33	3	0	28	107	3.74

Short C who could compete for backup job in Spring Training. Was inconsistent all season, but has level swing path and plus raw power to provide offense. Lacks eye and selectivity to get on base and lacks bat speed to catch up to good FB. Not the best athlete, but has strong arm and is grinder.

Phelps, Cord

45 | **Cleveland** | EXP MLB DEBUT: 2011 | POTENTIAL: Utility player | **6B**

	Year	Lev	Team	AB	R	H	HR	RBI	Avg	OB	Slg	OPS	bb%	ct%	Eye	SB	CS	x/h%	Iso	RC/G
Bats B Age 26																				
2008 (3) Stanford	2010	AAA	Columbus	243	41	77	6	31	317	378	506	884	9	84	0.62	3	2	39	189	6.51
Pwr ++	2011	AAA	Columbus	378	51	111	14	63	294	378	492	870	12	76	0.57	3	6	39	198	6.53
BAvg +++	2011	MLB	Cleveland	71	10	11	1	6	155	241	254	494	10	76	0.47	1	0	36	99	1.56
Spd ++	2012	AAA	Columbus	503	82	139	16	62	276	366	451	817	12	81	0.76	9	4	38	175	5.84
Def ++	2012	MLB	Cleveland	33	2	7	1	5	212	235	303	538	3	70	0.10	0	0	14	91	1.56

Instinctual, tall, and versatile INF who lacks skill set of regular, but has talent to win role. Set career-high in HR, but power isn't his game. Makes good contact with nice bat control and sense of K zone. Limited ceiling with bat and offers little speed. Ordinary glove and quickness leave him without home.

Phillips, Dane

2 | **San Diego** | EXP MLB DEBUT: 2015 | POTENTIAL: Starting C | **7D**

	Year	Lev	Team	AB	R	H	HR	RBI	Avg	OB	Slg	OPS	bb%	ct%	Eye	SB	CS	x/h%	Iso	RC/G
Bats L Age 22																				
2012 (2) Oklahoma City																				
Pwr ++																				
BAvg +++	2010	NCAA	Oklahoma St	193	33	65	3	34	337	410	477	887	11	79	0.59	1	2	29	140	6.76
Spd ++	2011	NCAA	Oklahoma St	245	44	83	4	32	339	389	518	907	8	79	0.38	2	0	34	180	6.86
Def ++	2012	A-	Eugene	234	33	53	4	30	226	335	350	685	14	77	0.72	4	2	40	124	4.27

Strong, offensive-minded catcher was the Padres 2nd round pick. Has a good approach at the plate with a solid understanding of the strike zone. Swing can get long due to slow hands and weight transfer, but he does have good power and a quick bat. Split time at C, 1B, and DH and is below-average defensively.

Pillar, Kevin

789 | **Toronto** | EXP MLB DEBUT: 2014 | POTENTIAL: Reserve OF | **6A**

	Year	Lev	Team	AB	R	H	HR	RBI	Avg	OB	Slg	OPS	bb%	ct%	Eye	SB	CS	x/h%	Iso	RC/G
Bats R Age 24																				
2011 (32) Cal State DH																				
Pwr ++																				
BAvg ++++	2011	Rk	Bluefield	236	44	82	7	37	347	374	534	908	4	85	0.28	8	4	33	186	6.38
Spd +++	2012	A	Lansing	335	49	108	5	57	322	386	451	837	9	84	0.66	35	6	27	128	5.97
Def ++	2012	A+	Dunedin	164	16	53	1	34	323	343	415	758	3	90	0.29	16	3	21	91	4.66

Instinctual, natural-hitting OF who won MWL MVP. Has mature sense of K zone and swings only at hittable pitches. Level, balanced swing and bat control should continue to result in BA while power is more of doubles variety. Not gifted defensively, but has avg speed to provide range in outfield corner.

Pimentel, Guillermo

7 | **Seattle** | EXP MLB DEBUT: 2015 | POTENTIAL: Starting OF | **9E**

	Year	Lev	Team	AB	R	H	HR	RBI	Avg	OB	Slg	OPS	bb%	ct%	Eye	SB	CS	x/h%	Iso	RC/G
Bats L Age 20																				
2009 FA (DR)	2010	A	Hickory	149	20	34	3	14	228	290	329	619	8	64	0.25	1	2	24	101	3.10
Pwr ++++	2010	A-	Spokane	32	3	11	1	6	344	364	469	832	3	69	0.10	1	2	18	125	5.76
BAvg ++	2011	A-	Spokane	220	30	61	1	15	277	356	314	670	11	74	0.47	7	6	8	36	3.88
Spd ++	2011	Rk	Pulaski	245	33	65	11	46	265	308	441	749	6	70	0.21	4	1	32	176	4.64
Def ++	2012	A	Clinton	372	37	91	9	51	245	281	366	647	5	69	0.17	5	2	30	121	3.30

Free swinging OF with as much power potential as any prospect, but struggles to make contact and hit LHP. Natural loft and leverage in swing produce plus-plus pop. Kills FB, but gets himself out easily by expanding K zone. Defense is below aveg as he doesn't run well and has limited range and arm strength.

Pinto, Josmil

2 | **Minnesota** | EXP MLB DEBUT: 2015 | POTENTIAL: Backup C | **7E**

Bats R Age 24
2006 FA (Venezuela)
Pwr +++
BAvg +++
Spd +
Def +

Year	Lev	Team	AB	R	H	HR	RBI	Avg	OB	Slg	OPS	bb%	ct%	Eye	SB	CS	x/h%	Iso	RC/G
2010	A	Beloit	347	60	78	10	54	225	290	378	668	8	81	0.48	2	3	41	153	3.76
2011	A	Beloit	32	4	8	1	9	250	294	438	732	6	69	0.20	0	0	50	188	4.63
2011	A+	Fort Myers	221	21	58	5	32	262	300	389	690	5	84	0.33	1	0	29	127	3.88
2012	A+	Fort Myers	349	45	103	12	51	295	366	473	839	10	82	0.62	0	0	35	178	5.94
2012	AA	New Britain	47	8	14	2	9	298	353	553	906	8	79	0.40	0	0	50	255	6.76

Short, big-bodied C who had career year at plate while showing incremental improvement behind it. Lacks tools requisite of everyday C, but has value with bat. Makes good, solid contact and set career high in HR by laying off bad pitches and using strong swing. Defense is still below avg, but no longer liability.

Pirela, Jose

4567 | **New York (A)** | EXP MLB DEBUT: 2014 | POTENTIAL: Utility player | **6B**

Bats B Age 23
2006 FA (Venezuela)
Pwr ++
BAvg +++
Spd +++
Def +++

Year	Lev	Team	AB	R	H	HR	RBI	Avg	OB	Slg	OPS	bb%	ct%	Eye	SB	CS	x/h%	Iso	RC/G
2008	Rk	GCL Yankees	141	19	33	0	10	234	275	277	552	5	87	0.42	4	2	15	43	2.43
2009	A	Charleston (Sc)	404	65	119	0	46	295	354	381	735	8	84	0.57	9	8	24	87	4.75
2010	A+	Tampa	497	68	125	5	61	252	329	364	693	10	82	0.66	30	7	26	113	4.30
2011	AA	Trenton	468	50	112	8	45	239	278	353	630	5	81	0.28	9	7	29	113	3.16
2012	AA	Trenton	317	55	93	8	33	293	347	448	795	8	85	0.54	9	3	32	155	5.30

Short, versatile prospect who repeated AA and played variety of positions. Showed ability to put bat to ball with solid bat control and approach allows him to drive balls. Goes gap to gap and has decent strength to hit occasional HR. Only has avg speed, but has good instincts. Quick hands and arm strength are assets at any position.

Piscotty, Stephen

5 | **St. Louis** | EXP MLB DEBUT: 2015 | POTENTIAL: Starting 3B | **8C**

Bats R Age 22
2012 (1) HS, CA
Pwr +++
BAvg +++
Spd +++
Def +++

Year	Lev	Team	AB	R	H	HR	RBI	Avg	OB	Slg	OPS	bb%	ct%	Eye	SB	CS	x/h%	Iso	RC/G
2010	NCAA	Stanford	227	45	74	4	36	326	368	454	822	6	92	0.83	5	1	28	128	5.59
2011	NCAA	Stanford	216	34	80	3	39	370	416	477	893	7	88	0.63	2	3	20	106	6.42
2012	NCAA	Stanford	246	44	81	5	56	329	402	467	870	11	91	1.30	4	0	26	138	6.44
2012	A	Quad Cities	210	29	62	4	27	295	351	448	798	8	88	0.72	3	0	37	152	5.44

36th overall pick in the draft after a standout career at Stanford. Big bodied player makes consistent contact, but moderate bat speed and line-drive approach project to avg power at best. Moves well at 3B but needs to be more consistent, though he does have a plus arm. Makes frequent contact, but needs to be more selective to maximize power.

Plawecki, Kevin

2 | **New York (N)** | EXP MLB DEBUT: 2015 | POTENTIAL: Backup C | **7D**

Bats R Age 22
2012 (1-S) Purdue
Pwr ++
BAvg +++
Spd +
Def ++

Year	Lev	Team	AB	R	H	HR	RBI	Avg	OB	Slg	OPS	bb%	ct%	Eye	SB	CS	x/h%	Iso	RC/G
2010	NCAA	Purdue	204	36	70	8	53	343	368	529	897	4	95	0.73	2	3	30	186	6.15
2011	NCAA	Purdue	211	46	72	2	39	341	393	436	829	8	95	1.80	3	2	22	95	5.87
2012	NCAA	Purdue	223	54	80	7	47	359	426	578	1004	10	96	3.25	3	3	39	220	7.92
2012	A-	Brooklyn	216	26	54	7	27	250	328	384	712	10	89	1.04	0	0	28	134	4.50

Tall, collegiate backstop showed offensive potential in the Big Ten. Makes consistent contact with good plate discipline and solid power. Is a bit fringy behind the plate with average arm strength but solid blocking and game calling skills. Abiility to consistently put the ball into play with decent power, should be enough to get him to the majors.

Polanco, Gregory

8 | **Pittsburgh** | EXP MLB DEBUT: 2014 | POTENTIAL: Starting CF | **9D**

Bats L Age 21
2009 NDFA, D.R.
Pwr ++++
BAvg +++
Spd ++++
Def +++

Year	Lev	Team	AB	R	H	HR	RBI	Avg	OB	Slg	OPS	bb%	ct%	Eye	SB	CS	x/h%	Iso	RC/G
2010	Rk	GCL Pirates	188	21	38	3	23	202	239	287	526	5	78	0.22	19	2	24	85	1.74
2011	Rk	GCL Pirates	169	34	40	3	34	237	332	361	693	12	80	0.73	18	0	28	124	4.33
2011	A-	State College	10	0	1	0	1	100	100	100	200	0	80	0.00	0	0	0	0	
2012	A	West Virginia	437	84	142	16	85	325	387	522	908	9	85	0.69	40	15	34	197	6.70

Things came together in a significant way in '12 and he simply dominated the SAL. Has good plate discipline and contact ability, which fueled the breakout. Is a plus runner just beginning to tap into his power. Improved defensively and has the range and arm strength to stick in CF.

Polanco, Jorge

46 | **Minnesota** | EXP MLB DEBUT: 2016 | POTENTIAL: Starting SS | **8D**

Bats B Age 19
2009 FA (DR)
Pwr ++
BAvg +++
Spd +++
Def ++++

Year	Lev	Team	AB	R	H	HR	RBI	Avg	OB	Slg	OPS	bb%	ct%	Eye	SB	CS	x/h%	Iso	RC/G
2010	Rk	GCL Twins	103	12	23	1	12	223	304	301	605	10	91	1.33	2	4	26	78	3.51
2011	Rk	GCL Twins	172	21	43	1	16	250	310	349	659	8	86	0.63	6	4	28	99	3.85
2012	Rk	Elizabethton	173	35	55	5	27	318	389	514	903	10	85	0.77	6	3	40	197	6.79

Versatile, athletic INF with quick actions, hands, and instincts. Offense shows potential, though full season ball will be test. Lacks present strength and power potential lags behind. Makes consistent contact with excellent barrel control and has good sense of strike zone. Uses avg speed to his advantage.

Pollock, A.J.

8 | **Arizona** | EXP MLB DEBUT: 2012 | POTENTIAL: Backup OF | **7C**

Bats R Age 25
2009 (1) Notre Dame
Pwr ++
BAvg ++
Spd +++
Def +++

Year	Lev	Team	AB	R	H	HR	RBI	Avg	OB	Slg	OPS	bb%	ct%	Eye	SB	CS	x/h%	Iso	RC/G
2009	NCAA	Notre Dame	241	69	88	10	52	365	435	610	1045	11	90	1.25	21	4	39	245	8.39
2009	A	South Bend	255	36	69	3	22	271	314	376	690	6	86	0.44	10	4	26	106	4.03
2011	AA	Mobile	550	103	169	8	73	307	359	444	802	7	84	0.51	36	7	32	136	5.44
2012	AAA	Reno	428	65	136	3	52	318	365	411	776	7	88	0.62	21	8	23	93	5.13
2012	MLB	Arizona	81	8	20	2	8	247	322	395	717	10	86	0.82	1	2	35	148	4.57

Solid all-around performer. Has a smooth, level swing and good bat speed that produces doubles power and has moderate long ball potential. Pollock has good speed to go along with mature instincts and a strong arm. Was among league-leaders in all offensive categories except HR.

Poythress, Rich

3 | **Seattle** | EXP MLB DEBUT: 2013 | POTENTIAL: Reserve 1B | **6B**

Bats R Age 25
2009 (2) Georgia
Pwr ++
BAvg +++
Spd +
Def ++

Year	Lev	Team	AB	R	H	HR	RBI	Avg	OB	Slg	OPS	bb%	ct%	Eye	SB	CS	x/h%	Iso	RC/G
2009	AA	W Tennessee	87	11	20	1	9	230	343	287	630	15	72	0.63	1	0	15	57	3.46
2010	A+	High Desert	476	88	150	31	130	315	383	580	962	10	79	0.52	3	2	43	265	7.38
2011	AA	Jackson	450	50	120	11	64	267	340	416	756	10	82	0.61	2	3	35	149	4.97
2012	Rk	Mariners	13	7	5	3	7	385	600	1154	1754	35	77	2.33	0	0	80	769	18.73
2012	AA	Jackson	303	39	92	6	45	304	402	439	841	14	89	1.52	4	0	30	135	6.34

Large-framed INF who repeated AA and had solid season. Puts bat to ball and draws BB with professional approach. Hit 31 HR in '10, but lacks load and trigger in inside-out swing. Hits line drives to gaps with natural strength. Plays passable defense at 1B with nice footwork and avg arm, but has no agility.

Profar, Jurickson

46 | **Texas** | EXP MLB DEBUT: 2012 | POTENTIAL: Starting SS | **9A**

Bats B Age 20
2009 FA (Curacao)
Pwr ++++
BAvg ++++
Spd ++++
Def ++++

Year	Lev	Team	AB	R	H	HR	RBI	Avg	OB	Slg	OPS	bb%	ct%	Eye	SB	CS	x/h%	Iso	RC/G
2010	A-	Spokane	252	42	63	4	23	250	325	373	698	10	82	0.61	8	3	37	123	4.30
2011	A	Hickory	430	86	123	12	65	286	380	493	873	13	85	1.03	23	9	46	207	6.64
2012	AA	Frisco	480	76	135	14	62	281	368	452	820	12	84	0.84	16	4	35	171	5.88
2012	MLB	Texas	17	2	3	1	2	176	176	471	647	0	76	0.00	0	0	100	294	3.07

Young, advanced INF who has myriad skills and talent and projects as perennial All-Star. Mostly plays SS, but can slide over to 2B. Possesses excellent range and a strong arm. Owns incredible bat speed, control, and pitch recognition. Could grow into plus power and seems destined to be .300+ hitter.

Proscia, Steve

345 | **Seattle** | EXP MLB DEBUT: 2014 | POTENTIAL: Starting 1B/3B | **8D**

Bats R Age 23
2011 (7) Virginia
Pwr ++++
BAvg +++
Spd ++
Def ++

Year	Lev	Team	AB	R	H	HR	RBI	Avg	OB	Slg	OPS	bb%	ct%	Eye	SB	CS	x/h%	Iso	RC/G
2010	NCAA	Virginia	255	52	80	10	65	314	364	533	897	7	82	0.44	8	0	40	220	6.49
2011	NCAA	Virginia	275	52	88	8	59	320	366	484	850	7	86	0.53	11	5	32	164	5.86
2011	A+	High Desert	185	28	56	12	42	303	317	568	885	2	82	0.12	3	3	43	265	5.87
2012	A+	High Desert	436	88	145	24	94	333	369	567	935	5	78	0.26	12	2	35	234	6.84
2012	AA	Jackson	76	10	16	4	9	211	250	395	645	5	79	0.25	0	2	38	184	3.11

Big, strong INF who finished 3rd in CAL in BA. Took advantage of friendly home environs to produce offense, but should carry over to AA due to strength, bat speed, and above avg pop. Should also hit for BA, but needs to clean up approach. Lacks ideal foot speed, quickness, and instincts, but solid arm works well.

Puello, Cesar

9 | **New York (N)** | EXP MLB DEBUT: 2015 | POTENTIAL: Starting RF | **8E**

Bats R Age 22
2007 NDFA, D.R.
Pwr +++
BAvg ++
Spd ++++
Def +++

Year	Lev	Team	AB	R	H	HR	RBI	Avg	OB	Slg	OPS	bb%	ct%	Eye	SB	CS	x/h%	Iso	RC/G
2008	Rk	GCL Mets	151	24	46	1	17	305	327	364	691	3	79	0.16	14	5	15	60	3.75
2009	Rk	Kingsport	196	37	58	5	23	296	330	423	754	5	74	0.20	15	5	26	128	4.65
2010	A	Savannah	404	80	118	1	34	292	344	359	703	7	80	0.39	45	10	20	67	4.21
2011	A+	St. Lucie	441	67	114	10	50	259	288	397	684	4	77	0.17	19	9	32	138	3.73
2012	A+	St. Lucie	227	36	59	4	21	260	282	423	705	3	74	0.12	19	2	42	163	4.07

Athletic OF struggled in his 2nd stint in the FSL. Has above-average speed and stole 19 bases in 21 tries. Covers ground well and might have the best OF arm in the system, but lacks power. Still young but he needs to make more consistent contact and the clock is ticking.

Puig, Yasiel — 8 — Los Angeles (N)

Bats R Age 22
2012 NDFA, Cuba
Pwr +++
BAvg +++
Spd +++
Def +++

EXP MLB DEBUT: 2014 — POTENTIAL: Starting CF — 9D

Year	Lev	Team	AB	R	H	HR	RBI	Avg	OB	Slg	OPS	bb%	ct%	Eye	SB	CS	x/h%	Iso	RC/G
2012	Rk	Dodgers	30	10	12	4	11	400	500	1000	1500	17	77	0.86	1	1	58	600	14.88
2012	A+	Rancho Cuc	52	10	17	1	4	327	397	423	820	10	85	0.75	7	4	18	96	5.73

Athletic Cuban defector landed a $42 million deal. Has easy raw power and good bat speed that should translate well to pro game. Good pitch recognition and plate discipline give him the chance to hit for power and average. Also has plus speed and covers ground well in the OF with a strong arm. Impressive debut.

Quinn, Roman — 6 — Philadelphia

Bats R Age 20
2011 (2) HS, FL
Pwr ++
BAvg +++
Spd +++
Def +++

EXP MLB DEBUT: 2015 — POTENTIAL: Starting SS — 7B

Year	Lev	Team	AB	R	H	HR	RBI	Avg	OB	Slg	OPS	bb%	ct%	Eye	SB	CS	x/h%	Iso	RC/G
2012	A-	Williamsport	267	56	75	1	23	281	349	408	757	9	77	0.46	30	6	28	127	5.13

Was one of the more exciting players in the NYPL. Has decent plate discipline and battles to put the ball into play where he can use his 80-grade speed. He has moderate pop for his size, but power is not part of his game. Defenisvely he has a strong arm and good range, but has stiff hands and made 27 errors in 66 games.

Rahier, Tanner — 5 — Cincinnati

Bats R Age 19
2012 (2) HS, CA
Pwr ++
BAvg ++
Spd ++
Def +++

EXP MLB DEBUT: 2016 — POTENTIAL: Starting 3B — 7D

Year	Lev	Team	AB	R	H	HR	RBI	Avg	OB	Slg	OPS	bb%	ct%	Eye	SB	CS	x/h%	Iso	RC/G
2012	Rk	Reds	193	21	37	4	30	192	271	311	582	10	78	0.49	5	2	38	119	2.71

Aggressive OF prospect scuffled in his pro debut. Has decent bat speed and showed good plate discipline in HS, but didn't make much contact as a pro. Was moved from SS to 3B and has the potential to hit for enough power to stick. Has good hands and a strong throwing arm, but needs time to master 3B.

Ramirez, Jose — 4 — Cleveland

Bats B Age 20
2009 FA (DR)
Pwr +
BAvg +++
Spd +++
Def +++

EXP MLB DEBUT: 2016 — POTENTIAL: Reserve INF — 6B

Year	Lev	Team	AB	R	H	HR	RBI	Avg	OB	Slg	OPS	bb%	ct%	Eye	SB	CS	x/h%	Iso	RC/G
2011	Rk	Indians	194	30	63	1	20	325	348	448	797	3	91	0.41	12	6	29	124	5.20
2012	A	Lake County	277	54	98	3	27	354	405	462	867	8	91	0.92	15	6	20	108	6.23
2012	A-	Mahoning Val	11	2	4	0	0	364	417	545	962	8	100	0.00	2	1	50	182	7.55

Short, lithe INF who hits well from both sides of plate. Makes such easy contact with plus hand-eye coordination and bat control that he doesn't walk much. Swing and strength aren't conducive to HR and lacks power projection. Can get on base via bunts and infield hits. Plays excellent defense with sure hands and strong arm.

Ramirez, Nick — 3 — Milwaukee

Bats L Age 23
2011 (4) Cal State Fullerton
Pwr +++
BAvg ++
Spd +
Def ++

EXP MLB DEBUT: 2015 — POTENTIAL: Backup 1B — 6D

Year	Lev	Team	AB	R	H	HR	RBI	Avg	OB	Slg	OPS	bb%	ct%	Eye	SB	CS	x/h%	Iso	RC/G
2010	NCAA	CalSt Fullerton	260	62	90	16	75	346	391	646	1037	7	81	0.38	6	0	50	300	8.14
2011	NCAA	CalSt Fullerton	200	39	57	9	45	285	384	505	889	14	79	0.76	4	5	44	220	6.79
2011	Rk	Helena	103	23	38	8	30	369	381	689	1070	2	79	0.09	0	1	45	320	8.20
2011	A	Wisconsin	137	11	27	3	23	197	247	350	597	6	74	0.25	0	0	56	153	2.74
2012	A	Wisconsin	383	46	95	16	70	248	296	446	742	6	62	0.18	0	0	46	198	5.04

Physically mature 1B has good power, but failed to impress in repeat of Low-A. Has quick hands and raw strength, but tends to pull everything and needs to make more consistent contact. Average defender with good hands and a strong arm and was a two-way player in college. Needs to prove he can hit for average.

Ramsey, James — 8 — St. Louis

Bats L Age 23
2012 (1) Florida State
Pwr ++
BAvg +++
Spd +++
Def +++

EXP MLB DEBUT: 2015 — POTENTIAL: Starting CF — 8D

Year	Lev	Team	AB	R	H	HR	RBI	Avg	OB	Slg	OPS	bb%	ct%	Eye	SB	CS	x/h%	Iso	RC/G
2009	NCAA	Florida State	68	19	20	2	14	294	407	426	834	16	74	0.72	0	0	25	132	6.31
2010	NCAA	Florida State	230	57	66	9	63	287	414	517	932	18	79	1.04	11	1	44	230	7.64
2011	NCAA	Florida State	236	56	86	10	66	364	438	593	1031	12	80	0.65	11	3	36	229	8.50
2012	NCAA	Florida State	233	78	88	13	58	378	510	652	1162	21	82	1.50	11	5	36	275	10.66
2012	A+	Palm Beach	210	36	48	1	14	229	333	314	648	14	72	0.56	10	2	27	86	3.78

Athletic OF with good speed, but none of his other tools stand out. Exhibits average pop to the pull side and has a disciplined approach at the plate. Has a simple swing that makes consistent contact. The Cards gambled on this polished college senior. but he might end up without enough power for a corner or enough speed for CF.

Realmuto, Jacob — 2 — Miami

Bats R Age 22
2010 (3) HS, OK
Pwr ++
BAvg +++
Spd +++
Def ++

EXP MLB DEBUT: 2015 — POTENTIAL: Starting C — 7C

Year	Lev	Team	AB	R	H	HR	RBI	Avg	OB	Slg	OPS	bb%	ct%	Eye	SB	CS	x/h%	Iso	RC/G
2010	Rk	GCL Marlins	40	2	7	0	4	175	298	175	473	15	73	0.64	0	1	0	0	1.27
2011	A	Greensboro	348	46	100	12	49	287	337	454	791	7	78	0.33	13	6	31	167	5.18
2012	A+	Jupiter	446	63	114	8	46	256	313	345	658	8	86	0.58	13	5	21	90	3.68

Strong catcher struggled in the pitcher-friendly FSL and production was down across the board. Has good bat speed, power potential, and offensive upside. Runs well for a catcher and is agile behind the plate with a strong arm. Should be able to stick at catcher and has nice offensive upside despite a down season in '12.

Renda, Tony — 4 — Washington

Bats R Age 22
2012 (2) California
Pwr +
BAvg +++
Spd +++
Def +++

EXP MLB DEBUT: 2015 — POTENTIAL: Starting 2B — 7D

Year	Lev	Team	AB	R	H	HR	RBI	Avg	OB	Slg	OPS	bb%	ct%	Eye	SB	CS	x/h%	Iso	RC/G
2010	NCAA	California	217	55	81	3	37	373	421	548	970	8	84	0.53	13	2	35	175	7.49
2011	NCAA	California	265	38	88	3	44	332	363	434	797	5	89	0.46	9	2	22	102	5.18
2012	NCAA	California	219	41	75	5	27	342	419	484	903	12	92	1.61	16	3	28	142	6.87
2012	A-	Auburn	295	47	78	0	32	264	334	295	629	10	89	0.94	15	3	12	31	3.63

Small, hard-nosed player doesn't have one standout tool, but gets the job done. Above-average runner with good baserunning skills. Short, compact RH stroke with solid strike zone judgment and occasional gap power. Good range and hands at 2B and should be able to get on base to use his speed.

Rendon, Anthony — 5 — Washington

Bats R Age 23
2011 (1) Rice
Pwr ++++
BAvg ++++
Spd +++
Def ++++

EXP MLB DEBUT: 2013 — POTENTIAL: Starting 3B/2B — 9B

Year	Lev	Team	AB	R	H	HR	RBI	Avg	OB	Slg	OPS	bb%	ct%	Eye	SB	CS	x/h%	Iso	RC/G
2011	NCAA	Rice	214	37	70	6	37	327	510	523	1034	27	85	2.42	13	5	40	196	9.50
2012	Rk	GCL Nationals	11	2	4	2	6	364	500	1000	1500	21	73	1.00	0	0	75	636	15.24
2012	A+	Potomac	27	5	9	0	0	333	438	630	1067	16	85	1.25	0	0	56	296	9.50
2012	AA	Harrisburg	68	14	11	3	3	162	278	368	646	14	76	0.69	0	0	64	206	3.60
2012	A-	Auburn	27	7	7	1	3	259	355	444	799	13	78	0.67	0	0	43	185	5.62

Missed most of the season with a broken ankle, his third ankle injury. Has bat speed, above-average power, and is a pure hitter. Good plate discipline and a short, compact stroke enables him to square the ball up. Solid defender at 3B with a good glove and a strong arm. A move to 2B is possible, but the range and footwork could be problematic.

Reynolds, Matt — 6 — New York (N)

Bats R Age 22
2012 (2) Arkansas
Pwr ++
BAvg ++
Spd ++
Def ++

EXP MLB DEBUT: 2016 — POTENTIAL: Backup 3B — 6C

Year	Lev	Team	AB	R	H	HR	RBI	Avg	OB	Slg	OPS	bb%	ct%	Eye	SB	CS	x/h%	Iso	RC/G
2010	NCAA	Arkansas	64	13	13	1	5	203	261	297	558	7	78	0.36	0	2	31	94	2.29
2011	NCAA	Arkansas	202	36	49	3	22	243	346	351	698	14	79	0.76	16	2	31	109	4.44
2012	NCAA	Arkansas	235	48	76	7	45	323	422	498	920	15	86	1.21	16	5	36	174	7.23
2012	A	Savannah	158	18	41	3	13	259	312	367	679	7	84	0.46	5	1	27	108	3.87

Played both SS and 3B in college, though serious thumb injury helped push him to 3B. The Mets moved him back to SS in his debut. Solid approach at the plate with good contact ability and a line-drive approach. Willing to use the whole field, but isn't likely to develop more than average power.

Rincon, Edinson — 5 — San Diego

Bats R Age 22
2007 NDFA, D.R.
Pwr +++
BAvg +++
Spd +++
Def ++

EXP MLB DEBUT: 2014 — POTENTIAL: Starting 3B — 8D

Year	Lev	Team	AB	R	H	HR	RBI	Avg	OB	Slg	OPS	bb%	ct%	Eye	SB	CS	x/h%	Iso	RC/G
2009	A-	Eugene	267	47	80	7	47	300	403	468	871	15	78	0.77	5	0	35	169	6.74
2010	A	Fort Wayne	511	72	128	13	69	250	310	399	709	8	81	0.46	1	2	38	149	4.27
2011	Rk	Padres	10	0	3	0	1	300	364	300	664	9	90	1.00	0	0	0	0	3.98
2011	A+	Lake Elsinore	298	54	98	8	50	329	394	497	891	10	80	0.54	1	1	34	168	6.63
2012	AA	San Antonio	494	45	144	10	48	291	322	413	735	4	84	0.28	1	6	28	121	4.36

Aggressive hitter with good power continues to progress. Makes consistent contact, but needs to be more patient and selective. Is only average defensively and at the end of the season he moved to LF. If that move is permanent it hurts his long-term value. SB and power have not developed, but he is still young.

Rivera, Alexis — 79 — Kansas City

EXP MLB DEBUT: 2016 — POTENTIAL: Starting OF — 8C

Bats L — Age 19 — 2012 (10) HS (FL)

	Rating
Pwr	++++
BAvg	++++
Spd	+++
Def	++

Year	Lev	Team	AB	R	H	HR	RBI	Avg	OB	Slg	OPS	bb%	ct%	Eye	SB	CS	x/h%	Iso	RC/G
2012	Rk	Royals	176	35	60	3	34	341	417	477	894	12	84	0.79	9	3	23	136	6.79

Physical OF who generates plus bat speed with loose mechanics and quick wrists. Recognizes pitches and has plenty of strength for above avg raw power. Controls strike zone well and willing to draw BB. Limitations abound in OF where arm strength isn't up to snuff and avg speed and range will limit him to corner.

Rivera, Yadiel — 6 — Milwaukee

EXP MLB DEBUT: 2014 — POTENTIAL: Backup SS — 6C

Bats R — Age 21 — 2010 (9) HS, P.R.

	Rating
Pwr	++
BAvg	+++
Spd	+++
Def	++++

Year	Lev	Team	AB	R	H	HR	RBI	Avg	OB	Slg	OPS	bb%	ct%	Eye	SB	CS	x/h%	Iso	RC/G
2010	Rk	Brewers	206	22	43	0	23	209	242	257	499	4	65	0.13	6	2	21	49	1.27
2011	Rk	Helena	330	47	82	8	38	248	279	406	685	4	72	0.15	7	3	35	158	3.82
2011	A	Wisconsin	103	6	20	1	5	194	224	262	486	4	67	0.12	0	0	20	68	1.01
2012	A	Wisconsin	465	60	115	12	49	247	287	402	689	5	74	0.22	7	3	37	155	3.88

Tall, but skinny SS has developed into a plus defender. Doesn't provide much in the way of home runs, but also struck out 119 times while walking just 26. Has good SS actions and nice range with good speed, but will need to hit to have value.

Roache, Victor — 7 — Milwaukee

EXP MLB DEBUT: 2015 — POTENTIAL: Starting LF — 8D

Bats R — Age 21 — 2012 (1) Georgia Southern

	Rating
Pwr	++++
BAvg	++
Spd	++
Def	++

Year	Lev	Team	AB	R	H	HR	RBI	Avg	OB	Slg	OPS	bb%	ct%	Eye	SB	CS	x/h%	Iso	RC/G
2010	NCAA	GA Southern	151	38	38	8	38	252	379	464	843	17	72	0.74	7	2	39	212	6.38
2011	NCAA	GA Southern	230	58	75	30	84	326	419	778	1198	14	82	0.88	3	4	56	452	10.16
2012	NCAA	GA Southern	17	6	7	2	5	412	583	765	1348	29	94	7.00	0	0	29	353	12.67

Was considered the top college power prospect coming into '12, but a borken wrist sidelined him and he slipped to 28th overall. Is solidly built with a quick bat and plus raw power. Makes consistent contact and has at least average plate discipline. Is only an average runner but does have a strong arm and profiles as a power-hitting corner OF.

Robertson, Daniel — 56 — Oakland

EXP MLB DEBUT: 2016 — POTENTIAL: Starting 3B — 8D

Bats R — Age 19 — 2012 (1-S) HS (CA)

	Rating
Pwr	+++
BAvg	+++
Spd	++
Def	+++

Year	Lev	Team	AB	R	H	HR	RBI	Avg	OB	Slg	OPS	bb%	ct%	Eye	SB	CS	x/h%	Iso	RC/G
2012	Rk	Athletics	101	25	30	4	22	297	393	554	948	14	85	1.07	2	0	53	257	7.53
2012	A-	Vermont	94	9	17	1	8	181	238	234	472	7	67	0.23	1	1	18	53	0.85

Polished INF who was hot in rookie ball, but struggled at short season. Owns clean swing with plus bat speed and power potential. Mostly gap power now, but should grow into more as he learns to read pitches better. Profiles as above avg defender at 3B, but can play SS with quick hands and strong arm.

Robinson, Clint — 3 — Pittsburgh

EXP MLB DEBUT: 2012 — POTENTIAL: Reserve 1B — 6B

Bats L — Age 28 — 2007 (25) Troy

	Rating
Pwr	+++
BAvg	+++
Spd	+
Def	+

Year	Lev	Team	AB	R	H	HR	RBI	Avg	OB	Slg	OPS	bb%	ct%	Eye	SB	CS	x/h%	Iso	RC/G
2009	A+	Wilmington	436	65	130	13	57	298	350	463	814	7	82	0.44	4	3	35	165	5.49
2010	AA	NW Arkansas	477	90	160	29	98	335	407	625	1032	11	82	0.67	4	3	47	289	8.30
2011	AAA	Omaha	503	86	164	23	100	326	396	533	929	10	83	0.66	2	1	35	207	6.99
2012	AAA	Omaha	487	70	142	13	67	292	390	452	842	14	87	1.22	1	0	36	160	6.28
2012	MLB	Kansas City	4	0	0	0	0	0	0	0	0	0	50	0.00	0	0	0	0	

Big, burly hitter who was acquired from KC in Nov and has shot for big league action. Works counts and posted more BB than Ks while polishing approach. Produced less power by shortening swing and focusing on using entire field. Secondary skills aren't up to snuff—well below avg speed and no defensive value.

Rodriguez, Aderlin — 5 — New York (N)

EXP MLB DEBUT: 2014 — POTENTIAL: Starting 3B — 7D

Bats R — Age 21 — 2008 NDFA, D.R.

	Rating
Pwr	++++
BAvg	++
Spd	++
Def	++

Year	Lev	Team	AB	R	H	HR	RBI	Avg	OB	Slg	OPS	bb%	ct%	Eye	SB	CS	x/h%	Iso	RC/G
2010	Rk	Kingsport	250	44	78	13	48	312	351	556	907	6	83	0.35	3	1	45	244	6.42
2010	A	Savannah	30	3	6	1	11	200	333	333	667	17	67	0.60	0	0	33	133	3.94
2011	A	Savannah	516	59	114	17	78	221	262	372	634	5	79	0.27	2	1	37	151	3.12
2012	A	Savannah	318	41	87	16	59	274	334	497	831	8	78	0.41	1	0	44	223	5.73
2012	A+	St. Lucie	153	19	37	8	24	242	280	431	711	5	80	0.27	1	0	35	190	3.94

Strong, solidly built 3B has good power. Has plus bat speed, but can be overly-aggressive at the plate and needs to make more consistent contact. Struggled when promoted to AA, but continues to improve defensively where he has a strong arm but limited range. Saw some time at 1B where he likely profiles better

Rodriguez, Henry — 4 — Cincinnati

EXP MLB DEBUT: 2012 — POTENTIAL: Backup 3B — 6C

Bats B — Age 23 — 2007 NDFA, Venezuela

	Rating
Pwr	++
BAvg	+++
Spd	++
Def	++

Year	Lev	Team	AB	R	H	HR	RBI	Avg	OB	Slg	OPS	bb%	ct%	Eye	SB	CS	x/h%	Iso	RC/G
2011	AA	Carolina	278	39	84	5	37	302	360	432	791	8	85	0.58	18	3	30	129	5.32
2012	Rk	Reds	17	1	4	0	1	235	278	294	572	6	88	0.50	0	0	25	59	2.76
2012	AA	Pensacola	132	19	46	2	15	348	390	439	829	6	86	0.50	3	0	17	91	5.59
2012	AAA	Louisville	213	23	52	3	20	244	265	333	598	3	84	0.17	5	4	25	89	2.67
2012	MLB	Cincinnati	14	0	3	0	2	214	313	286	598	13	86	1.00	0	0	33	71	3.40

Athletic INF moved from 2B to 3B and played at four levels. Switch-hitter makes consistent contact and puts the ball into play. Doesn't walk very much, but does have moderate power. Has been young at every level and is a player to keep an eye on. Move to 3B was necessitated by the presence of B. Phillips.

Rodriguez, Luigi — 8 — Cleveland

EXP MLB DEBUT: 2015 — POTENTIAL: Starting OF — 8D

Bats B — Age 20 — 2009 FA (DR)

	Rating
Pwr	+++
BAvg	++
Spd	++++
Def	++

Year	Lev	Team	AB	R	H	HR	RBI	Avg	OB	Slg	OPS	bb%	ct%	Eye	SB	CS	x/h%	Iso	RC/G
2011	Rk	Indians	95	18	36	3	14	379	410	579	989	5	80	0.26	12	5	31	200	7.54
2011	A	Lake County	132	10	33	0	5	250	322	311	633	10	73	0.39	6	5	18	61	3.40
2012	A	Lake County	463	75	124	11	48	268	339	406	745	10	71	0.38	24	9	30	138	4.89

Short, quick OF with surprising strength and pop in wiry frame. Showed improved power while swinging fast bat from both sides. Owns keen eye and willing to work counts. Will need to shorten swing with two strikes and make more consistent contact. Has exceptional speed which aids CF defense with plus range.

Rodriguez, Rafael — 8 — San Francisco

EXP MLB DEBUT: 2015 — POTENTIAL: Backup OF — 7D

Bats R — Age 20 — 2008 NDFA, D.R.

	Rating
Pwr	++
BAvg	+
Spd	+++
Def	++++

Year	Lev	Team	AB	R	H	HR	RBI	Avg	OB	Slg	OPS	bb%	ct%	Eye	SB	CS	x/h%	Iso	RC/G
2009	Rk	Giants	127	25	38	0	19	299	378	362	740	11	82	0.70	5	4	21	63	4.93
2010	Rk	Giants	123	20	37	2	14	301	328	398	726	4	81	0.22	4	2	22	98	4.21
2010	A-	Salem-Keizer	43	3	7	0	4	163	217	209	427	7	72	0.25	1	0	14	47	0.43
2011	A	Augusta	364	39	86	1	30	236	284	297	580	6	81	0.35	1	6	21	60	2.65
2012	A-	Salem-Keizer	162	9	38	3	20	235	275	364	639	5	81	0.29	7	7	37	130	3.29

Tall Dominican OF signed for $2.55 million and has been largely a bust. Has good hand-eye cooridnation, but is not patient enough to wait for strikes and does not make much hard contact. Does have decent speed and a strong arm, but is only an average defender.

Rodriguez, Ronny — 46 — Cleveland

EXP MLB DEBUT: 2015 — POTENTIAL: Starting 2B/SS — 8D

Bats R — Age 21 — 2010 FA (DR)

	Rating
Pwr	+++
BAvg	++
Spd	+++
Def	+++

Year	Lev	Team	AB	R	H	HR	RBI	Avg	OB	Slg	OPS	bb%	ct%	Eye	SB	CS	x/h%	Iso	RC/G
2011	A	Lake County	370	41	91	11	42	246	272	449	720	3	78	0.16	10	7	51	203	4.22
2012	A+	Carolina	454	67	120	19	66	264	294	452	745	4	81	0.22	7	7	36	187	4.40

Raw prospect who can adeptly play both MIF spots with plus range and strong, accurate arm. Needs to be more selective in order to fully realize offensive potential. Has above avg bat speed and good strength, but free-swinging ways need to be tamed. Struggles with breaking balls, but crushes LHP.

Rodriguez, Wilfredo — 2 — Colorado

EXP MLB DEBUT: 2016 — POTENTIAL: Backup C — 7E

Bats R — Age 19 — 2012 (7) HS, P.R.

	Rating
Pwr	++
BAvg	+++
Spd	++
Def	++

Year	Lev	Team	AB	R	H	HR	RBI	Avg	OB	Slg	OPS	bb%	ct%	Eye	SB	CS	x/h%	Iso	RC/G
2012	Rk	Grand Junction	166	26	53	2	27	319	369	452	821	7	86	0.57	1	1	32	133	5.66

Nice athleticism and moves well, but has an average arm and threw out just 21% of runners. Will have to work hard to stick behind the plate. Does have a good approach at the plate with a short, balanced stroke. Shoots balls into the gap and could develop average power with decent plate discipline. Solid debut.

Rodriguez, Yorman — 8 — Cincinnati

EXP MLB DEBUT: 2015 | POTENTIAL: Starting CF | 8E

Bats R Age 20
2008 NDFA, Venezuela
Pwr ++
BAvg ++
Spd ++++
Def ++++

Year	Lev	Team	AB	R	H	HR	RBI	Avg	OB	Slg	OPS	bb%	ct%	Eye	SB	CS	x/h%	Iso	RC/G
2009	Rk	Billings	183	21	40	3	17	219	255	344	599	5	67	0.15	5	2	38	126	2.76
2010	Rk	Billings	171	25	58	2	39	339	369	456	825	4	82	0.27	12	2	22	117	5.50
2011	A	Dayton	280	38	71	7	40	254	315	393	708	8	70	0.30	20	8	30	139	4.31
2012	A	Dayton	258	35	70	6	44	271	304	430	734	4	76	0.20	7	5	37	159	4.43
2012	A+	Bakersfield	90	7	14	0	7	156	183	200	383	3	57	0.08	4	0	29	44	

Has all kinds of tools, but remains raw in all aspects of the game. Has raw power and bat speed, but below-average plate discipline and contact rate limit his potential and power has yet to develop. Plus speed should allow him to steal bases and plays solid defense with plus arm strength and range.

Rojas, Mel Jr. — 7 — Pittsburgh

EXP MLB DEBUT: 2014 | POTENTIAL: Starting OF | 7E

Bats B Age 23
2010 (3) Wabash Valley CC
Pwr ++
BAvg ++
6.6/60 Spd +++
Def +++

Year	Lev	Team	AB	R	H	HR	RBI	Avg	OB	Slg	OPS	bb%	ct%	Eye	SB	CS	x/h%	Iso	RC/G
2010	A-	State College	164	19	34	0	14	207	297	250	547	11	74	0.50	7	3	21	43	2.31
2011	A	West Virginia	508	66	125	5	46	246	309	335	643	8	77	0.39	23	14	22	89	3.46
2012	A+	Bradenton	497	61	122	6	51	245	295	354	649	7	78	0.33	16	8	25	109	3.48

Fleet-footed switch-hitting CF continues to struggle with pitch recognition and plate discipline. Flat, slashing stroke makes it unlikely he will hit for much power though he does have good speed. Will stick in CF for now and continues to show a strong, accurate arm and solid range.

Romero, Avery — 5 — Miami

EXP MLB DEBUT: 2016 | POTENTIAL: Utility INF | 7C

Bats R Age 20
2012 (3) HS, FL
Pwr ++
BAvg +++
Spd +
Def ++

Year	Lev	Team	AB	R	H	HR	RBI	Avg	OB	Slg	OPS	bb%	ct%	Eye	SB	CS	x/h%	Iso	RC/G
2012	Rk	GCL Marlins	121	8	27	3	15	223	282	347	630	8	83	0.48	0	1	33	124	3.27
2012	A-	Jamestown	21	3	8	0	4	381	458	381	839	13	100	0.00	1	0	0	0	6.42

Small, but strong SS has some nice offensive upside. Has a short stroke with above-average strength and good strike zone judgment. Is a bit stocky and doesn't have great speed or range, so a move to 2B is likely. Struggled in a limited pro debut but then looked better in the NYPL.

Romero, Stefen — 4 — Seattle

EXP MLB DEBUT: 2014 | POTENTIAL: Starting 2B | 7B

Bats R Age 24
2010 (12) Oregon State
Pwr +++
BAvg ++++
Spd ++
Def ++

Year	Lev	Team	AB	R	H	HR	RBI	Avg	OB	Slg	OPS	bb%	ct%	Eye	SB	CS	x/h%	Iso	RC/G
2009	NCAA	Oregon State	223	44	65	5	51	291	342	466	808	7	86	0.53	1	0	40	175	5.49
2010	NCAA	Oregon State	184	39	60	13	41	326	395	603	998	10	82	0.64	5	1	40	277	7.73
2011	A	Clinton	429	62	120	16	65	280	330	462	791	7	84	0.46	16	9	35	182	5.16
2012	A+	High Desert	258	47	92	11	51	357	387	581	969	5	86	0.37	6	2	36	225	7.06
2012	AA	Jackson	216	38	75	12	50	347	387	620	1007	6	83	0.38	6	3	41	273	7.66

Natural hitting INF who was SEA minor league POY. Short, compact stroke produces easy contact along with solid pop to pull side. Bat speed is avg at best, but has strength and trigger. Has instincts and feel for game. Needs to improve defensively as he lacks quickness and range, but should become offensive 2B.

Romine, Andrew — 456 — Los Angeles (A)

EXP MLB DEBUT: 2010 | POTENTIAL: Reserve 2B/SS | 6B

Bats B Age 27
2007 (5) Arizona State
Pwr ++
BAvg +++
Spd +++
Def ++++

Year	Lev	Team	AB	R	H	HR	RBI	Avg	OB	Slg	OPS	bb%	ct%	Eye	SB	CS	x/h%	Iso	RC/G
2010	MLB	Angels	11	0	1	0	0	91	91	91	182	0	64	0.00	0	0	0	0	
2011	AAA	Salt Lake	381	67	107	4	35	281	357	346	703	11	77	0.52	23	6	14	66	4.31
2011	MLB	Angels	16	2	2	0	0	125	176	125	301	6	63	0.17	1	0	0	0	
2012	AAA	Salt Lake	351	57	100	4	39	285	331	390	721	6	87	0.52	23	10	22	105	4.43
2012	MLB	Angels	17	2	7	0	1	412	500	412	912	15	82	1.00	1	0	0	0	7.22

Athletic, versatile INF who is terrific defender with quick and nimble hands and feet. Owns strong arm while possessing honed instincts. Will draw BB in and makes easy contact with a short stroke. Lacks bat speed and strength to hit for power and profiles as solid #2 hitter for his situational hitting and ability to make contact.

Romine, Austin — 2 — New York (A)

EXP MLB DEBUT: 2011 | POTENTIAL: Starting C | 7B

Bats R Age 24
2007 (2) HS (CA)
Pwr +++
BAvg +++
Spd ++
Def +++

Year	Lev	Team	AB	R	H	HR	RBI	Avg	OB	Slg	OPS	bb%	ct%	Eye	SB	CS	x/h%	Iso	RC/G
2011	AAA	Scranton/W-B	15	1	2	0	1	133	133	133	267	0	80	0.00	0	0	0	0	
2011	MLB	Yankees	19	2	3	0	0	158	200	158	358	5	74	0.20	0	0	0	0	
2012	Rk	GCL Yankees	24	3	5	0	5	208	345	333	678	17	88	1.67	0	0	60	125	4.74
2012	A+	Tampa	18	2	7	1	1	389	421	556	977	5	83	0.33	0	0	14	167	7.02
2012	AAA	Scranton/W-B	61	6	13	3	9	213	304	393	698	12	84	0.80	0	0	38	180	4.20

Athletic C who returned to action after missing time with back injury. When healthy, exhibits above avg raw power and keen ability to make hard contact. Power more evident in BP than games and will need to hit in order to win big league job. Doesn't run well and still working on footwork and release behind plate.

Rosa, Gabriel — 5 — Cincinnati

EXP MLB DEBUT: 2015 | POTENTIAL: Starting 3B | 8E

Bats R Age 20
2011 (2) HS, P.R
Pwr +++
BAvg ++
Spd +++
Def +++

Year	Lev	Team	AB	R	H	HR	RBI	Avg	OB	Slg	OPS	bb%	ct%	Eye	SB	CS	x/h%	Iso	RC/G
2011	Rk	Reds	106	17	26	2	10	245	298	406	704	7	74	0.29	6	3	38	160	4.25
2012	Rk	Billings	78	8	14	0	5	179	190	256	446	1	68	0.04	2	0	43	77	0.50

Was moved from OF to 3B in '12, but continues to flounder at the plate. Inability to make consistent contact as professional raises doubts about his future development and he walked just once in 80 AB. Does have good power with plus bat speed, but is still very raw. Swing needs refinement and is all or nothing.

Rosario, Eddie — 48 — Minnesota

EXP MLB DEBUT: 2015 | POTENTIAL: Starting 2B | 8C

Bats L Age 21
2010 (4) HS (PR)
Pwr +++
BAvg ++++
Spd +++
Def ++

Year	Lev	Team	AB	R	H	HR	RBI	Avg	OB	Slg	OPS	bb%	ct%	Eye	SB	CS	x/h%	Iso	RC/G
2010	Rk	GCL Twins	194	34	57	5	26	294	348	438	786	8	86	0.57	22	5	28	144	5.18
2011	Rk	Elizabethton	270	71	91	21	60	337	397	670	1068	9	78	0.45	17	6	43	333	8.73
2012	Rk	GCL Twins	19	2	7	1	4	368	400	684	1084	5	89	0.50	0	0	57	316	8.38
2012	A	Beloit	392	60	116	12	70	296	348	490	837	7	82	0.45	11	11	41	194	5.81

Advanced hitter who missed two months after breaking bone in face. Shows natural batting skills with level swing path, and bat control. Works counts and has ability to hit for good pop to whole field. Should evolve into doubles machine with avg HR output. Lacks defensive position after mediocre 2B debut.

Ruf, Darin — 3 — Philadelphia

EXP MLB DEBUT: 2012 | POTENTIAL: Backup 1B | 7C

Bats R Age 26
2009 (20) Creighton
Pwr ++++
BAvg +++
Spd +
Def ++

Year	Lev	Team	AB	R	H	HR	RBI	Avg	OB	Slg	OPS	bb%	ct%	Eye	SB	CS	x/h%	Iso	RC/G
2010	A	Lakewood	115	25	38	4	17	330	434	548	982	15	80	0.91	3	2	37	217	8.15
2010	A+	Clearwater	368	45	102	5	50	277	325	421	746	7	76	0.30	2	2	40	144	4.77
2011	A+	Clearwater	484	72	149	17	82	308	380	506	886	10	80	0.59	0	1	41	198	6.59
2012	AA	Reading	489	93	155	38	104	317	397	620	1017	12	79	0.64	2	0	46	303	8.12
2012	MLB	Phillies	33	4	11	3	10	333	371	727	1099	6	64	0.17	0	0	55	394	10.32

Monster season included a 20-HR August. Power is legit and is partially supported by contact rate and plate discipline, but has to be put into context vs. age and level. He's a below average defender though he did see time at both 1B and LF.

Ruiz, Rio — 5 — Houston

EXP MLB DEBUT: 2016 | POTENTIAL: Starting 3B | 8C

Bats L Age 19
2012 (4) HS (CA)
Pwr +++
BAvg ++++
Spd ++
Def +++

Year	Lev	Team	AB	R	H	HR	RBI	Avg	OB	Slg	OPS	bb%	ct%	Eye	SB	CS	x/h%	Iso	RC/G
2012	Rk	GCL Astros	85	13	23	0	11	271	361	412	773	12	74	0.55	2	0	43	141	5.58
2012	Rk	Greeneville	50	8	11	1	7	220	278	380	658	7	80	0.40	0	0	45	160	3.67

Advanced INF who has exciting offensive potential. Has fast bat that produces gap power and potential for significantly more pop. Should be able to maintain high BA due to short stroke and disciplined approach. Hands and arm strength work well and should be able to stay at 3B. Only apparent weakness is speed.

Rupp, Cameron — 2 — Philadelphia

EXP MLB DEBUT: 2014 | POTENTIAL: Backup C | 6C

Bats R Age 24
2010 (3) Texas
Pwr ++++
BAvg ++
Spd ++
Def ++++

Year	Lev	Team	AB	R	H	HR	RBI	Avg	OB	Slg	OPS	bb%	ct%	Eye	SB	CS	x/h%	Iso	RC/G
2009	NCAA	Texas	216	46	63	11	46	292	381	505	885	13	75	0.58	0	1	38	213	6.69
2010	NCAA	Texas	240	50	73	10	54	304	386	483	869	12	75	0.52	0	0	32	179	6.50
2010	A-	Williamsport	193	20	42	5	28	218	307	378	686	11	74	0.49	0	0	50	161	4.13
2011	A	Lakewood	324	33	88	4	44	272	335	373	709	9	70	0.32	0	0	27	102	4.40
2012	A+	Clearwater	344	32	92	10	49	267	344	424	768	10	78	0.52	0	0	36	157	5.12

Strong C doesn't really have a plus tool, but is average across the board. Swing mechanics are not great and plate discipline leaves something to be desired, though he did show improvement. Solid defensively with a strong throwing arm, but is not quick and struggles limiting the running game.

Russell, Addison — 6 — Oakland

EXP MLB DEBUT: 2015 | POTENTIAL: Starting SS | 9D

Bats R Age 19
2012 (1) HS (FL)
Pwr +++
BAvg ++++
Spd ++++
Def +++

Year	Lev	Team	AB	R	H	HR	RBI	Avg	OB	Slg	OPS	bb%	ct%	Eye	SB	CS	x/h%	Iso	RC/G
2012	Rk	Athletics	106	29	44	6	29	415	483	717	1200	12	78	0.61	9	1	34	302	10.72
2012	A	Burlington	58	8	18	0	9	310	365	448	813	8	79	0.42	5	1	33	138	5.78
2012	A-	Vermont	53	9	18	1	7	340	386	509	895	7	75	0.31	2	0	28	170	6.75

Athletic INF who had unbelievable debut; ended the season in Low-A at 18. Has exciting power/speed combo and keen ability to hit for BA. Hit .300 at every level and should continue as he advances. Tools are off charts, led by plus speed and has positive defensive attributes that should allow him to stick at SS.

Russell, Kyle — 9 — Los Angeles (N)

EXP MLB DEBUT: 2013 | POTENTIAL: Starting RF | 6C

Bats L Age 27
2008 (3) Texas
Pwr ++++
BAvg ++
Spd ++
Def +++

Year	Lev	Team	AB	R	H	HR	RBI	Avg	OB	Slg	OPS	bb%	ct%	Eye	SB	CS	x/h%	Iso	RC/G
2010	AA	Chattanooga	273	36	67	10	28	245	318	462	779	10	59	0.26	3	2	54	216	6.14
2011	AA	Chattanooga	394	61	102	19	69	259	335	497	832	10	63	0.31	5	1	51	239	6.51
2011	AAA	Albuquerque	38	6	8	1	3	211	348	395	743	17	74	0.80	1	0	50	184	5.18
2012	AA	Chattanooga	229	38	60	11	44	262	374	493	868	15	70	0.59	4	2	50	231	6.83
2012	AAA	Albuquerque	18	4	2	0	0	111	200	111	311	10	78	0.50	0	0	0	0	-0.77

Hasn't looked the same since his CAL-induced breakout in '10. Still has plus power, but long swing has been exploited at higher levels. Missed the 2nd half of the season with an injury, but still had an .872 OPS. He is a below-average runner and doesn't do much defensively. At 26 this might be his last chance.

Saladino, Tyler — 46 — Chicago (A)

EXP MLB DEBUT: 2014 | POTENTIAL: Starting SS | 7D

Bats R Age 23
2010 (7) Oral Roberts
Pwr ++
BAvg +++
Spd ++
Def +++

Year	Lev	Team	AB	R	H	HR	RBI	Avg	OB	Slg	OPS	bb%	ct%	Eye	SB	CS	x/h%	Iso	RC/G
2010	Rk	Bristol	48	7	14	1	6	292	358	417	775	9	75	0.42	1	2	29	125	5.21
2010	A	Kannapolis	165	40	51	2	18	309	390	442	833	12	73	0.50	4	2	33	133	6.26
2011	A+	Winston-Salem	397	75	107	16	55	270	353	501	854	11	77	0.57	7	7	48	232	6.31
2012	AA	Birmingham	418	71	99	4	39	237	353	321	674	15	78	0.82	38	8	23	84	4.21
2012	AAA	Charlotte	49	9	11	0	6	224	283	265	548	8	67	0.25	1	0	18	41	2.09

Well-rounded INF who finished 3rd in SL in BB and SB. Had strange season where SB and BB drastically increased while BA and HR dropped dramatically. Steady defender with above average instincts, average range, and strong arm. Should hit for BA due to line drive approach and keen knowledge of strike zone.

Salcedo, Edward — 5 — Atlanta

EXP MLB DEBUT: 2013 | POTENTIAL: Starting 3B | 8E

Bats R Age 21
2010 NDFA, D.R.
Pwr ++++
BAvg ++
Spd ++
Def +

Year	Lev	Team	AB	R	H	HR	RBI	Avg	OB	Slg	OPS	bb%	ct%	Eye	SB	CS	x/h%	Iso	RC/G
2010	A	Rome	193	23	38	2	16	197	240	295	536	5	71	0.20	6	5	29	98	1.86
2011	A	Rome	508	83	126	12	68	248	304	396	700	7	79	0.39	23	10	36	148	4.13
2012	A+	Lynchburg	471	65	113	17	61	240	290	412	702	7	72	0.25	23	14	40	172	4.06

Strong bodied 3B has plenty of power but continues to struggle defensively and doesn't make enough contact. Good bat speed and can drive the ball out of the park, but struck out 130 times. Has decent speed and a strong arm, but his glove and footwork are well below average (42 errors in '12) and a move to a corner OF spot seems likely.

Sale, Josh — 7 — Tampa Bay

EXP MLB DEBUT: 2015 | POTENTIAL: Starting OF | 8D

Bats L Age 22
2010 (1) HS (WA)
Pwr ++++
BAvg ++
Spd ++
Def ++

Year	Lev	Team	AB	R	H	HR	RBI	Avg	OB	Slg	OPS	bb%	ct%	Eye	SB	CS	x/h%	Iso	RC/G
2011	Rk	Princeton	214	24	45	4	15	210	287	346	633	10	81	0.56	4	3	40	136	3.46
2012	A	Bowling Green	239	35	63	10	44	264	393	464	858	18	74	0.82	7	6	38	201	6.67

Improving OF whose season was derailed after 50 game suspension for PED. Showed skill growth across board and offers nice upside as hitter. Packs plenty of power in compact frame and works counts. Understands K zone, though swing mechanics can get choppy and may K a bit. Defense and speed are below avg.

Sanchez, Carlos — 46 — Chicago (A)

EXP MLB DEBUT: 2013 | POTENTIAL: Starting 2B/SS | 8C

Bats R Age 21
2009 FA (Venezuela)
Pwr ++
BAvg ++++
Spd +++
Def ++++

Year	Lev	Team	AB	R	H	HR	RBI	Avg	OB	Slg	OPS	bb%	ct%	Eye	SB	CS	x/h%	Iso	RC/G
2011	Rk	Bristol	16	4	4	0	3	250	429	313	741	24	88	2.50	1	2	25	63	5.80
2011	A	Kannapolis	264	44	76	1	27	288	326	345	671	5	81	0.31	7	8	16	57	3.68
2012	A+	Winston-Salem	365	58	115	1	42	315	369	395	763	8	82	0.48	19	10	18	79	5.00
2012	AA	Birmingham	119	17	44	0	13	370	419	462	881	8	82	0.45	7	5	23	92	6.47
2012	AAA	Charlotte	39	4	10	0	1	256	256	308	564	0	85	0.00	0	0	20	51	2.18

Steady INF who led CAR in BA. Performed well at three levels on both sides of ball. Should advance quickly due to mature game—balanced approach and line drive focus. Won't hit many HR and basestealing needs work, but has other strengths. Owns great hands and strong, accurate arm. Plus defender.

Sanchez, Gary — 2 — New York (A)

EXP MLB DEBUT: 2015 | POTENTIAL: Starting C | 9C

Bats R Age 20
2009 FA (DR)
Pwr ++++
BAvg ++++
Spd ++
Def ++

Year	Lev	Team	AB	R	H	HR	RBI	Avg	OB	Slg	OPS	bb%	ct%	Eye	SB	CS	x/h%	Iso	RC/G
2010	Rk	GCL Yankees	119	25	42	6	36	353	408	597	1004	8	76	0.39	1	1	40	244	8.04
2010	A-	Staten Island	54	8	15	2	7	278	316	426	742	5	70	0.19	1	1	27	148	4.53
2011	A	Charleston (Sc)	301	49	77	17	52	256	335	485	820	11	69	0.39	2	1	44	229	5.90
2012	A	Charleston (Sc)	263	44	78	13	56	297	351	517	868	8	75	0.34	11	4	41	221	6.23
2012	A+	Tampa	172	21	48	5	29	279	319	436	755	5	76	0.24	4	0	33	157	4.69

Big, strong C thriving in power department while showing improved defense. Continues to mature offensively with powerful stroke and has shown quick bat capable of crushing FB. Exhibits plus power and demolishes LHP. Receiving and blocking getting better while strong arm remains.

Sanchez, Tony — 2 — Pittsburgh

EXP MLB DEBUT: 2013 | POTENTIAL: Backup C | 6C

Bats R Age 25
2009 (1) Boston College
Pwr ++
BAvg ++
Spd ++
Def +++

Year	Lev	Team	AB	R	H	HR	RBI	Avg	OB	Slg	OPS	bb%	ct%	Eye	SB	CS	x/h%	Iso	RC/G
2009	A-	State College	13	2	4	0	1	308	357	385	742	7	85	0.50	0	0	25	77	4.74
2010	A+	Bradenton	207	31	65	4	35	314	396	454	850	12	80	0.68	2	1	32	140	6.29
2011	AA	Altoona	402	46	97	5	44	241	321	318	639	10	81	0.62	5	5	21	77	3.54
2012	AA	Altoona	141	22	39	0	17	277	358	390	749	11	77	0.55	1	1	38	113	5.13
2012	AAA	Indianapolis	206	21	48	8	26	233	310	408	718	10	78	0.50	0	0	42	175	4.39

4th overall pick '09 looks like a bust. Moderate bat speed limits power and he hit a career high 8 HR. Does have decent pitch recognition and will take a walk, but doesn't make great contact. Remains a solid defender with a good arm and threw out 31% of runners. Should get a chance to win the backup job in '13.

Sano, Miguel — 5 — Minnesota

EXP MLB DEBUT: 2015 | POTENTIAL: Starting 3B | 9B

Bats R Age 20
2009 FA (DR)
Pwr ++++
BAvg ++++
Spd ++
Def ++

Year	Lev	Team	AB	R	H	HR	RBI	Avg	OB	Slg	OPS	bb%	ct%	Eye	SB	CS	x/h%	Iso	RC/G
2010	Rk	GCL Twins	148	23	43	4	19	291	335	466	802	6	71	0.23	2	2	42	176	5.56
2011	Rk	Elizabethton	267	58	78	20	59	292	348	637	985	8	71	0.30	5	4	58	345	8.03
2012	A	Beloit	457	75	118	28	100	258	369	521	890	15	68	0.56	8	3	51	263	7.12

Big, powerful INF who led MWL in HR and 2nd in BB. Has produced consistent plus-plus power since signing. Selective and disciplined approach could eventually lead to higher BA, but vicious swing has holes. Runs fairly well for size, but not much of SB threat. Exhibits agility at 3B with cannon for arm.

Santana, Alex — 5 — Los Angeles (N)

EXP MLB DEBUT: 2015 | POTENTIAL: Starting 3B | 8D

Bats R Age 19
2011 (2) HS, FL
Pwr +++
BAvg +++
Spd +++
Def +++

Year	Lev	Team	AB	R	H	HR	RBI	Avg	OB	Slg	OPS	bb%	ct%	Eye	SB	CS	x/h%	Iso	RC/G
2011	Rk	Dodgers	189	30	45	1	19	238	276	339	615	5	66	0.16	8	1	31	101	3.07
2012	Rk	Ogden	93	14	25	1	19	269	299	409	708	4	69	0.14	1	2	40	140	4.32
2012	Rk	Dodgers	96	12	23	1	12	240	318	323	641	10	57	0.27	4	1	22	83	3.88

Has plus bat speed, strong hands, and a quick bat, but is overly aggressive and struggles to make contact, striking out 41 times in 96 PIO League AB. Moves well at 3B with soft hands, good range, and a strong arm. He is still young, but needs to prove he can make some adjustments and soon.

Santana, Daniel — 46 — Minnesota

EXP MLB DEBUT: 2015 | POTENTIAL: Utility player | 6A

Bats B Age 22
2007 FA (DR)
Pwr ++
BAvg +++
Spd ++++
Def ++++

Year	Lev	Team	AB	R	H	HR	RBI	Avg	OB	Slg	OPS	bb%	ct%	Eye	SB	CS	x/h%	Iso	RC/G
2009	Rk	GCL Twins	170	30	45	3	25	265	298	418	715	4	84	0.30	12	1	33	153	4.24
2010	Rk	Elizabethton	140	23	37	4	16	264	280	421	701	2	79	0.10	5	4	35	157	3.81
2010	A	Beloit	130	14	31	0	11	238	277	315	593	5	69	0.18	10	4	23	77	2.71
2011	A	Beloit	365	55	90	7	41	247	295	373	667	6	73	0.26	24	15	30	126	3.66
2012	A+	Fort Myers	507	70	145	8	60	286	325	410	735	5	85	0.38	17	11	26	124	4.49

Quick INF who is one of best defensive players in system. Plays both MIF spots with aplomb and gets to balls deep in hole. Quick hands and strong arm can make any play. Exhibits good speed, but could stand to increase OBP. Drives balls and set career high in HR. Can be overly aggressive at plate and be easy out.

Santana, Domingo — 9 — Houston

Bats R Age 20
2009 NDFA D.R.
Pwr ++++ BAvg ++++ Spd ++ Def ++

EXP MLB DEBUT: 2014 POTENTIAL: Starting RF 9D

Year	Lev	Team	AB	R	H	HR	RBI	Avg	OB	Slg	OPS	bb%	ct%	Eye	SB	CS	x/h%	Iso	RC/G
2010	A	Lakewood	165	27	30	3	16	182	304	297	601	15	54	0.38	5	6	43	115	3.35
2010	A-	Williamsport	186	28	44	5	20	237	321	366	686	11	61	0.32	4	4	32	129	4.37
2011	A	Lakewood	350	45	94	7	32	269	319	434	753	7	66	0.22	4	1	43	166	5.20
2011	A	Lexington	68	13	26	5	21	382	432	662	1094	8	78	0.40	1	0	35	279	8.93
2012	A+	Lancaster	457	87	138	23	97	302	377	536	913	11	68	0.37	7	1	40	234	7.42

Tall, physical OF who set career high in HR and was helped by improved plate discipline. Some of output was enhanced by CAL ballparks, but he made more consistent, hard contact and showed an ability to make adjustments. Has potential for plus power though Ks will always be there. Raw defensively and needs to add polish.

Santana, Ravel — 8 — New York (A)

Bats R Age 21
2008 FA (DR)
Pwr +++ BAvg +++ Spd ++++ Def ++++

EXP MLB DEBUT: 2016 POTENTIAL: Starting OF 8C

Year	Lev	Team	AB	R	H	HR	RBI	Avg	OB	Slg	OPS	bb%	ct%	Eye	SB	CS	x/h%	Iso	RC/G
2011	Rk	GCL Yankees	162	43	48	9	29	296	363	568	931	9	75	0.43	10	3	48	272	7.20
2012	A-	Staten Island	218	22	47	3	19	216	296	289	585	10	69	0.37	3	1	21	73	2.64

Tall, lean OF who has yet to play full season ball. Severe ankle injury in Aug '11 set him back and didn't perform well in '12. Has excellent tools across board. Exemplary bat speed gives him BA potential and avg power, though swings and misses too often. Range and arm are ideal for any OF position.

Santander, Anthony — 79 — Cleveland

Bats B Age 18
2011 FA (Venezuela)
Pwr +++ BAvg +++ Spd +++ Def ++

EXP MLB DEBUT: 2017 POTENTIAL: Starting OF 8E

Year	Lev	Team	AB	R	H	HR	RBI	Avg	OB	Slg	OPS	bb%	ct%	Eye	SB	CS	x/h%	Iso	RC/G
2012	Rk	Indians	154	27	47	4	32	305	359	494	853	8	76	0.35	6	3	43	188	6.19

Tall, projectable OF who showed off impressive skills in first season as pro. Hits well from both sides, though has more potential from left. Has good athleticism to repeat swing mechanics and could eventually add loft to realize avg power potential. Overswings, but has time to make corrections. Below avg arm limits him to OF corner.

Sardinas, Luis — 46 — Texas

Bats B Age 20
2009 FA (Venezuela)
Pwr ++ BAvg +++ Spd ++++ Def ++++

EXP MLB DEBUT: 2015 POTENTIAL: Starting SS 8D

Year	Lev	Team	AB	R	H	HR	RBI	Avg	OB	Slg	OPS	bb%	ct%	Eye	SB	CS	x/h%	Iso	RC/G
2010	Rk	Rangers	103	22	32	0	8	311	355	350	704	6	85	0.47	8	2	13	39	4.19
2011	Rk	Rangers	52	11	16	0	7	308	357	385	742	7	81	0.40	2	1	19	77	4.72
2012	A	Hickory	374	65	109	2	30	291	342	356	698	7	86	0.56	32	9	17	64	4.19

Smooth, agile INF who has been injury prone, but shows feel for game when healthy. Speed is best tool and could contend for SB titles with improved baserunning. Has good hand-eye coordination to make consistent contact. Lacks strength and can make weak contact with slashing swing. Owns strong arm and soft hands.

Schafer, Logan — 8 — Milwaukee

Bats L Age 26
2008 (3) Cal Poly
Pwr ++ BAvg +++ Spd +++ Def +++

EXP MLB DEBUT: 2011 POTENTIAL: Starting CF 7B

Year	Lev	Team	AB	R	H	HR	RBI	Avg	OB	Slg	OPS	bb%	ct%	Eye	SB	CS	x/h%	Iso	RC/G
2011	AA	Huntsville	189	31	57	0	19	302	359	392	751	8	87	0.68	10	5	23	90	4.97
2011	AAA	Nashville	169	31	56	5	23	331	392	521	913	9	89	0.94	5	3	36	189	6.79
2011	MLB	Brewers	3	1	1	0	0	333	500	333	833	25	67	1.00	0	0	0	0	7.07
2012	AAA	Nashville	464	72	129	11	40	278	320	438	758	6	84	0.40	16	7	33	159	4.78
2012	MLB	Brewers	23	3	7	0	5	304	333	522	855	4	87	0.33	0	1	43	217	6.09

Lean, athletic CF with plus defense. Has shown good plate discipline in the past, but was more aggressive in '12. The result was a bit more power, but also fewer walks. Uses a line-drive approach to make consistent contact, but power is more of the gap variety. Uses his speed well but will have decide if he is going to hit for average or moderate power.

Schoop, Jonathan — 456 — Baltimore

Bats R Age 21
2008 FA (Curacao)
Pwr +++ BAvg +++ Spd +++ Def +++

EXP MLB DEBUT: 2014 POTENTIAL: Starting 3B 8B

Year	Lev	Team	AB	R	H	HR	RBI	Avg	OB	Slg	OPS	bb%	ct%	Eye	SB	CS	x/h%	Iso	RC/G
2010	Rk	Bluefield	133	16	42	2	16	316	372	459	831	8	89	0.86	1	1	33	143	5.86
2010	A+	Frederick	21	5	5	0	3	238	273	381	654	5	81	0.25	0	0	60	143	3.63
2011	A	Delmarva	212	45	67	8	34	316	375	514	889	9	85	0.63	6	4	34	198	6.43
2011	A+	Frederick	299	37	81	5	37	271	321	375	695	7	85	0.50	6	3	23	104	4.09
2012	AA	Bowie	485	68	119	14	56	245	316	386	701	9	79	0.49	5	3	33	140	4.18

Advanced natural hitter who produced career high in HR despite being young for level. Makes consistent contact and crushes LHP with bat speed and strength. Exhibits above avg power potential, but needs better pitch recognition to succeed at higher levels. Has hands and arm to play any infield position, but likely 2B or 3B.

Schotts, Austin — 8 — Detroit

Bats R Age 19
2012 (3) HS (TX)
Pwr ++ BAvg ++++ Spd ++++ Def +++

EXP MLB DEBUT: 2016 POTENTIAL: Starting OF 8C

Year	Lev	Team	AB	R	H	HR	RBI	Avg	OB	Slg	OPS	bb%	ct%	Eye	SB	CS	x/h%	Iso	RC/G
2012	Rk	GCL Tigers	155	31	48	3	21	310	359	452	811	7	74	0.29	15	4	31	142	5.65
2012	A+	Lakeland	3	1	1	0	0	333	333	333	667	0	67	0.00	1	0	0	0	3.37

Ultra-athletic OF who converted to CF from SS upon signing. Uses aggressive approach and makes consistent, hard contact to gaps. Offers moderate power potential and will need to add strength and leverage to short, level swing. Can swing and miss often. Possesses incredible speed and has plus range in CF.

Seager, Corey — 6 — Los Angeles (N)

Bats R Age 19
2012 (1) HS, NC
Pwr ++++ BAvg +++ Spd ++ Def +++

EXP MLB DEBUT: 2016 POTENTIAL: Starting 3B 9D

Year	Lev	Team	AB	R	H	HR	RBI	Avg	OB	Slg	OPS	bb%	ct%	Eye	SB	CS	x/h%	Iso	RC/G
2012	Rk	Ogden	175	34	54	8	33	309	383	520	903	11	81	0.64	8	2	35	211	6.73

Lean and lanky prepster will likely be moving over to 3B soon. Has plus bat speed and is just starting to tap into his raw power. Short, simple swing generates plenty of loft and good power. Has an advanced understanding of the strike zone and hit well in pro debut. Has good hands and a strong arm, but limited range.

Semien, Marcus — 46 — Chicago (A)

Bats R Age 22
2011 (6) California
Pwr ++ BAvg +++ Spd +++ Def +++

EXP MLB DEBUT: 2015 POTENTIAL: Starting 2B/SS 7D

Year	Lev	Team	AB	R	H	HR	RBI	Avg	OB	Slg	OPS	bb%	ct%	Eye	SB	CS	x/h%	Iso	RC/G
2009	NCAA	California	71	10	14	1	7	197	305	282	587	13	85	1.00	0	3	21	85	3.16
2010	NCAA	California	195	40	64	4	34	328	402	497	899	11	81	0.65	5	2	36	169	6.87
2011	NCAA	California	229	41	63	5	35	275	364	415	779	12	83	0.80	9	5	30	140	5.40
2011	A	Kannapolis	229	35	58	3	26	253	319	376	694	9	77	0.42	3	4	34	122	4.17
2012	A+	Winston-Salem	418	80	114	14	59	273	357	471	829	12	77	0.57	11	5	44	199	6.01

Athletic INF who set career high in HR while exhibiting more polished batting eye. Learned to lay off breaking balls out of zone and instead focused on putting ball in play. Has strength to reach fences, but uses line drive stroke for 2B. Has soft hands and average arm. May not have range for SS and projects better as 2B.

Shaffer, Richie — 5 — Tampa Bay

Bats R Age 22
2012 (1) Clemson
Pwr ++++ BAvg ++++ Spd + Def ++

EXP MLB DEBUT: 2014 POTENTIAL: Starting 3B/1B 8B

Year	Lev	Team	AB	R	H	HR	RBI	Avg	OB	Slg	OPS	bb%	ct%	Eye	SB	CS	x/h%	Iso	RC/G
2010	NCAA	Clemson	158	45	51	7	36	323	392	525	917	10	77	0.50	2	0	35	203	6.98
2011	NCAA	Clemson	222	62	70	13	55	315	429	577	1005	17	76	0.83	8	1	43	261	8.50
2012	NCAA	Clemson	232	49	78	10	46	336	478	573	1051	21	77	1.19	8	2	42	237	9.48
2012	A-	Hudson Valley	117	25	36	4	26	308	391	487	878	12	74	0.52	0	0	31	179	6.74

Polished, pure-hitting INF who leveraged collegiate pedigree into plus pro debut. Uses whole field with simple swing and mature eye to get on base and hit for high BA. Recognizes pitches and understands strike zone while hitting for plus power. Range limited and could see possible move to 1B or RF where arm strength would play up.

Shaw, Travis — 35 — Boston

Bats L Age 23
2011 (9) Kent State
Pwr ++++ BAvg ++ Spd ++ Def +++

EXP MLB DEBUT: 2014 POTENTIAL: Starting 1B 8E

Year	Lev	Team	AB	R	H	HR	RBI	Avg	OB	Slg	OPS	bb%	ct%	Eye	SB	CS	x/h%	Iso	RC/G
2011	NCAA	Kent State	244	48	75	14	51	307	405	553	958	14	84	1.00	0	1	40	246	7.53
2011	A	Greenville	9	1	3	0	1	333	400	444	844	10	100	1.00	0	0	33	111	6.41
2011	A-	Lowell	202	30	53	8	36	262	369	446	814	14	77	0.72	3	0	40	183	5.88
2012	A+	Salem	354	69	108	16	73	305	404	545	950	14	77	0.73	11	2	46	240	7.69
2012	AA	Portland	110	13	25	3	12	227	351	427	778	16	69	0.62	1	1	64	200	5.75

Tall, strong INF who finished 3rd in CAR in BA and BB before struggling in AA. Played mostly 1B, but also saw time at 3B. Has good glove at 1B with soft hands and nice arm. Offensive production enhanced by power stroke and instinctual swing. Controls bat well. Power based on strength and can get pull happy.

Shipman, Aaron — 78 — Oakland

EXP MLB DEBUT: 2016 | POTENTIAL: Starting OF | 8E

Bats L Age 21
2010 (3) HS (GA)
Pwr ++
BAvg ++
Spd ++++
Def ++++

Year	Lev	Team	AB	R	H	HR	RBI	Avg	OB	Slg	OPS	bb%	ct%	Eye	SB	CS	x/h%	Iso	RC/G
2010	Rk	Athletics	17	2	2	0	2	118	118	118	235	0	65	0.00	3	0	0	0	
2011	A-	Vermont	201	34	51	0	19	254	383	303	686	17	81	1.08	17	3	18	50	4.56
2012	A	Burlington	360	40	74	0	32	206	319	261	580	14	76	0.70	11	11	22	56	2.93

Athletic OF with multitude of tools, but little performance. Draws BB with mature approach and has plus speed, but isn't a very good hitter and swings passively. Makes weak contact and hasn't yet hit a HR as pro. Could be leadoff hitter. Gets good jumps and takes nice routes in CF while possessing strong, accurate arm.

Short, Brandon — 789 — Chicago (A)

EXP MLB DEBUT: 2013 | POTENTIAL: Reserve OF | 7D

Bats R Age 24
2008 (28) St. John's River CC
Pwr +++
BAvg ++
Spd +++
Def +++

Year	Lev	Team	AB	R	H	HR	RBI	Avg	OB	Slg	OPS	bb%	ct%	Eye	SB	CS	x/h%	Iso	RC/G
2010	A+	Winston-Salem	491	77	155	15	79	316	353	491	843	5	78	0.26	7	10	33	175	5.79
2011	AA	Birmingham	526	75	138	13	60	262	310	411	720	6	76	0.29	21	9	34	148	4.32
2012	A+	Winston-Salem	37	4	11	0	7	297	422	351	774	18	65	0.62	0	1	18	54	5.97
2012	AA	Birmingham	42	5	9	0	1	214	250	262	512	5	83	0.29	1	0	22	48	1.81
2012	AAA	Charlotte	6	0	2	0	2	333	333	333	667	0	83	0.00	0	0	0	0	3.20

Multi-tooled OF who underwent surgery to repair torn labrum in shoulder after running into fence. Returned in Aug and showed good skills. Possesses clean swing, but has trouble controlling K zone. Lacks standout tool, but has avg raw power and good speed. Can play any OF position with avg arm and range.

Shuck, JB — 789 — Los Angeles (A)

EXP MLB DEBUT: 2011 | POTENTIAL: Reserve OF | 6B

Bats L Age 26
2008 (6) Ohio St
Pwr +
BAvg +++
Spd +++
Def +++

Year	Lev	Team	AB	R	H	HR	RBI	Avg	OB	Slg	OPS	bb%	ct%	Eye	SB	CS	x/h%	Iso	RC/G
2010	AA	Corpus Christi	389	52	116	2	28	298	372	360	732	11	86	0.82	9	9	16	62	4.80
2010	AAA	Round Rock	139	15	38	0	7	273	348	317	665	10	89	1.07	7	3	11	43	4.12
2011	AAA	Oklahoma City	354	60	105	0	30	297	393	367	760	14	92	1.87	20	11	17	71	5.51
2011	MLB	Houston	81	9	22	0	3	272	359	321	680	12	91	1.57	2	0	14	49	4.47
2012	AAA	Oklahoma City	315	49	94	0	33	298	376	352	728	11	94	1.95	12	8	15	54	5.02

Short, compact OF who hasn't hit HR in three seasons, but is among toughest outs. Has more BB than K in every pro season except one. Easy contact, but slashing approach limits him to singles. Released by HOU in Nov '12, he has good speed, but few SB. OF instincts are iffy and arm relegates him to LF.

Silva, Juan — 7 — Cincinnati

EXP MLB DEBUT: 2014 | POTENTIAL: Starting LF | 7D

Bats L Age 22
2009 (8) HS, P.R.
Pwr ++
BAvg ++
Spd +++
Def +++

Year	Lev	Team	AB	R	H	HR	RBI	Avg	OB	Slg	OPS	bb%	ct%	Eye	SB	CS	x/h%	Iso	RC/G
2009	Rk	GCL Reds	143	26	40	1	16	280	372	462	833	13	69	0.47	7	4	43	182	6.66
2010	Rk	Arizona Reds	178	26	41	3	24	230	318	371	689	11	73	0.48	4	1	34	140	4.24
2011	Rk	Billings	150	30	44	4	21	293	404	413	818	16	71	0.65	4	6	18	120	6.13
2012	A	Dayton	380	58	103	8	42	271	383	413	796	15	71	0.63	25	12	34	142	5.90

Has enough speed and athleticism to play all three positions, though LF is the most likely destination. Struggles to make contact, but is able to draw walks. He runs well and stole a career high 25 bases, but was also caught 12 times. There is some potential, but also a long way to go.

Silverio, Alfredo — 7 — Miami

EXP MLB DEBUT: 2013 | POTENTIAL: Starting RF/LF | 8D

Bats R Age 26
2003 NDFA D.R.
Pwr ++++
BAvg +++
Spd ++++
Def +++

Year	Lev	Team	AB	R	H	HR	RBI	Avg	OB	Slg	OPS	bb%	ct%	Eye	SB	CS	x/h%	Iso	RC/G
2008	A	Great Lakes	376	37	99	10	45	263	277	404	681	2	78	0.08	6	3	29	141	3.53
2009	A	Great Lakes	490	75	139	13	61	284	320	457	777	5	79	0.25	2	5	38	173	4.97
2010	A+	Inland Empire	387	66	113	12	43	292	323	486	809	4	84	0.29	17	7	40	194	5.28
2010	AA	Chattanooga	16	1	1	0	0	63	63	63	125	0	81	0.00	0	0	0	0	
2011	AA	Chattanooga	533	90	163	16	85	306	343	542	885	5	83	0.33	11	12	47	236	6.33

Missed most of the '12 following a car accident that left him with multiple injuries. Prior to the accident, had shown nice tools. Has plus bat speed and drives the ball with authority. Has moderate plate discipline and good pitch recognition and should be able to hit for average with moderate power. He moves well defensively and can play all three OF positions.

Silverio, Juan — 5 — Chicago (A)

EXP MLB DEBUT: 2015 | POTENTIAL: Utility player | 6B

Bats R Age 22
2007 FA (DR)
Pwr ++
BAvg ++
Spd +++
Def ++++

Year	Lev	Team	AB	R	H	HR	RBI	Avg	OB	Slg	OPS	bb%	ct%	Eye	SB	CS	x/h%	Iso	RC/G
2010	Rk	Great Falls	87	11	26	3	16	299	344	506	850	6	77	0.30	3	1	46	207	5.99
2010	A	Kannapolis	220	20	44	4	24	200	221	336	558	3	74	0.11	3	4	43	136	2.08
2011	A	Kannapolis	329	48	95	5	58	289	326	459	785	5	75	0.22	4	7	42	170	5.24
2011	A+	Winston-Salem	170	28	47	4	27	276	317	441	758	6	76	0.24	2	1	36	165	4.81
2012	A+	Winston-Salem	263	36	64	8	51	243	284	433	718	5	75	0.22	4	4	48	190	4.29

Tall, athletic INF who hasn't developed with bat as much as hoped. Owns excellent bat speed, but poor plate discipline negates upside. Continues to make easy outs with weak contact. Could grow into gap power as he gains experience. Incredible arm is tops in org and possesses quick actions at 3B.

Singleton, Jonathan — 3 — Houston

EXP MLB DEBUT: 2013 | POTENTIAL: Starting 1B | 9B

Bats L Age 21
2009 (8) HS (CA)
Pwr ++++
BAvg ++++
Spd ++
Def +++

Year	Lev	Team	AB	R	H	HR	RBI	Avg	OB	Slg	OPS	bb%	ct%	Eye	SB	CS	x/h%	Iso	RC/G
2009	Rk	GCL Phillies	100	12	29	2	12	290	398	440	838	15	87	1.38	1	0	38	150	6.37
2010	A	Lakewood	376	64	109	14	77	290	390	479	869	14	80	0.84	9	7	38	189	6.57
2011	A+	Clearwater	320	48	91	9	47	284	391	413	803	15	74	0.67	3	3	25	128	5.82
2011	A+	Lancaster	129	20	43	4	16	333	399	512	910	10	69	0.35	0	0	33	178	7.34
2012	AA	Corpus Christi	461	94	131	21	79	284	399	497	896	16	72	0.67	7	2	40	213	7.20

Smooth swinging prospect with All-Star potential has innate feel for strike zone, excellent plate coverage and plus bat speed. Makes explosive contact with simple swing, but could improve against LHP. Defense is passable at 1B, but needs more reps. Won't get them early, as he will miss the first 50 games of 2013 due to drug suspension.

Skipworth, Kyle — 2 — Miami

EXP MLB DEBUT: 2013 | POTENTIAL: Backup C | 6C

Bats L Age 23
2008 (1) HS, CA
Pwr ++++
BAvg +
Spd ++
Def ++

Year	Lev	Team	AB	R	H	HR	RBI	Avg	OB	Slg	OPS	bb%	ct%	Eye	SB	CS	x/h%	Iso	RC/G
2009	A	Greensboro	264	28	55	7	37	208	259	348	607	6	66	0.20	1	2	40	140	2.87
2010	A	Greensboro	397	55	99	17	59	249	305	426	731	7	67	0.24	1	2	35	176	4.61
2010	AA	Jacksonville	7	1	0	0	0	0	125	0	125	13	57	0.33	0	0		0	
2011	AA	Jacksonville	396	35	82	11	49	207	270	331	601	8	64	0.24	0	4	30	124	2.79
2012	AA	Jacksonville	420	59	91	21	63	217	279	414	693	8	66	0.25	1	1	43	198	4.05

6th overall pick in '08 draft has not lived up to expectations. Still has plus power and did hit 21 HR, but continues to be overly aggressive and is not able to make consistent contact. Plus power and ability to stick behind the plate gives him the potential as a backup C, but that isn't what you expect from the 6th pick.

Skole, Matt — 5 — Washington

EXP MLB DEBUT: 2015 | POTENTIAL: Starting 3B | 8D

Bats L Age 23
2011 (5) Georgia Tech
Pwr ++++
BAvg +++
Spd ++
Def +

Year	Lev	Team	AB	R	H	HR	RBI	Avg	OB	Slg	OPS	bb%	ct%	Eye	SB	CS	x/h%	Iso	RC/G
2010	NCAA	Georgia Tech	233	62	78	20	63	335	442	682	1125	16	85	1.32	1	1	49	348	9.53
2011	NCAA	Georgia Tech	233	56	81	10	58	348	451	545	996	16	86	1.33	1	3	32	197	8.15
2011	A-	Auburn	272	43	79	5	48	290	385	438	823	13	81	0.81	2	1	37	147	6.05
2012	A	Hagerstown	343	73	98	27	92	286	439	574	1014	22	66	0.81	10	0	46	289	9.27
2012	A+	Potomac	70	11	22	0	12	314	360	486	846	7	76	0.29	1	0	50	171	6.26

Has nice power from the LH side and led the SAL in HR and BB. Solid plate discipline means the ability to hit for power and average are legit. Below-average defender with stiff hands and limited range. Was moved to 1B in the Arizona Fall League, where he continues to look suspect. He will need to continue to hit to have value.

Smith, Dwight — 78 — Toronto

EXP MLB DEBUT: 2016 | POTENTIAL: Starting OF | 8D

Bats L Age 20
2011 (1-S) HS (GA)
Pwr +++
BAvg +++
Spd +++
Def +++

Year	Lev	Team	AB	R	H	HR	RBI	Avg	OB	Slg	OPS	bb%	ct%	Eye	SB	CS	x/h%	Iso	RC/G
2012	Rk	Bluefield	159	20	36	4	21	226	276	340	616	6	86	0.50	1	1	28	113	3.12
2012	A-	Vancouver	63	5	11	0	8	175	246	254	500	9	83	0.55	0	0	36	79	1.93

Short, instinctual OF who struggled to hit for BA. Possesses simple swing with exemplary bat speed and ability to use entire field. Should hit for higher BA with better pitch recognition and improvement against LHP. Power is mostly gap and will need strength to realize avg pop. Speed, defense, and arm are avg at best.

Smith, Jordan — 9 — Cleveland

EXP MLB DEBUT: 2015 | POTENTIAL: Fourth OF | 6B

Bats L Age 23
2011 (9) St. Cloud State
Pwr +++
BAvg +++
Spd ++
Def ++

Year	Lev	Team	AB	R	H	HR	RBI	Avg	OB	Slg	OPS	bb%	ct%	Eye	SB	CS	x/h%	Iso	RC/G
2011	A-	Mahoning Val	243	36	73	0	47	300	388	391	779	13	88	1.17	3	1	29	91	5.60
2012	A	Lake County	468	70	148	9	74	316	364	453	817	7	89	0.67	9	3	26	137	5.56

Advanced, balanced OF who is sleeper. Was a little old for Low-A, but added polish and could still advance quickly. Very difficult to K with short swing and bat control. Can hit LHP and has good, discerning eye. Power is fringe-avg and could grow into more if he swings harder. Doesn't run well and has strong arm.

Smith, Kevan

2 | Chicago (A) | EXP MLB DEBUT: 2015 | POTENTIAL: Starting C | 7D

Bats R Age 25
2011 (7) Pittsburgh
- Pwr +++
- BAvg +++
- Spd ++
- Def ++

Year	Lev	Team	AB	R	H	HR	RBI	Avg	OB	Slg	OPS	bb%	ct%	Eye	SB	CS	x/h%	Iso	RC/G
2011	NCAA	Pittsburgh	209	59	83	11	56	397	455	675	1129	10	90	1.10	10	1	39	278	9.15
2011	Rk	Great Falls	107	22	34	2	16	318	397	523	920	12	85	0.88	1	0	47	206	7.18
2011	Rk	Bristol	96	24	38	7	32	396	473	740	1212	13	85	1.00	1	2	47	344	10.44
2012	A	Kannapolis	340	48	96	7	60	282	332	421	752	7	82	0.40	0	1	34	138	4.75
2012	A+	Winston-Salem	77	8	21	3	23	273	317	494	811	6	78	0.29	0	0	43	221	5.44

Athletic C who was old for level, but continues to show skills. Has quickness and agility for large frame, though still working on receiving. Exhibits average arm with fringy accuracy. Recognizes pitches in contact approach and has avg power to all fields. Could also hit for moderate BA, but could be more patient.

Smolinski, Jake

7 | Miami | EXP MLB DEBUT: 2013 | POTENTIAL: Backup OF | 6C

Bats R Age 24
2007 (2) HS, IL
- Pwr ++
- BAvg ++
- Spd ++
- Def +++

Year	Lev	Team	AB	R	H	HR	RBI	Avg	OB	Slg	OPS	bb%	ct%	Eye	SB	CS	x/h%	Iso	RC/G
2008	A-	Vermont	98	17	30	0	9	306	364	408	773	8	83	0.53	4	0	30	102	5.22
2009	A	Greensboro	279	50	79	7	31	283	369	448	817	12	84	0.84	2	5	41	165	5.86
2010	A+	Jupiter	405	45	107	5	51	264	317	383	699	7	85	0.50	8	5	33	119	4.21
2011	AA	Jacksonville	396	42	97	7	36	245	343	364	706	13	86	1.04	6	5	34	119	4.62
2012	AA	Jacksonville	408	71	105	7	42	257	377	382	759	16	82	1.05	9	4	32	125	5.38

Short, athletic OF with solid plate discipline, but not much else. Has stalled since hitting Double-A and his power has yet to develop. Defense at 3B was below-average and was moved to LF. Does have a good arm and average speed, but without the ability to hit for average or power he is unlikely to be more than a 4th OF.

Soler, Jorge

9 | Chicago (N) | EXP MLB DEBUT: 2015 | POTENTIAL: Starting RF | 8C

Bats R Age 21
2012 NDFA, Cuba
- Pwr +++
- BAvg +++
- Spd ++
- Def +++

Year	Lev	Team	AB	R	H	HR	RBI	Avg	OB	Slg	OPS	bb%	ct%	Eye	SB	CS	x/h%	Iso	RC/G
2012	Rk	Cubs	54	14	13	2	10	241	317	389	706	10	76	0.46	8	0	31	148	4.19
2012	A	Peoria	80	14	27	3	15	338	384	513	896	7	93	1.00	4	1	30	175	6.37

Cuban defector agreed to a 9-year, $30 million deal. Has good power, but is far from a one-dimensional. Has plus bat speed and showed solid plate discipline and contact ability in debut. Has above-average speed, but needs to improve his routes to stick in CF. Young and somewhat raw, but with tremendous potential.

Solorzano, Jesus

8 | Miami | EXP MLB DEBUT: 2015 | POTENTIAL: Starting CF | 8D

Bats R Age 22
2009 NDFA, Venezuela
- Pwr ++
- BAvg +++
- Spd ++++
- Def +++

Year	Lev	Team	AB	R	H	HR	RBI	Avg	OB	Slg	OPS	bb%	ct%	Eye	SB	CS	x/h%	Iso	RC/G
2011	Rk	GCL Marlins	194	34	58	3	31	299	343	454	797	6	85	0.43	18	7	34	155	5.32
2012	A-	Jamestown	210	36	66	8	27	314	366	519	885	7	77	0.35	7	6	36	205	6.47

Toolsy, athletic OF from Venezuela had nice U.S. debut. Runs very well with a strong throwing arm and has the potential to hit for average/moderate power. Has the tools to stick in CF, but will be more of a leadoff hitter who gets on base and not a run producer.

Songco, Angelo

7 | Los Angeles (N) | EXP MLB DEBUT: 2014 | POTENTIAL: Starting LF | 7D

Bats L Age 24
2009 (5) Loyola
- Pwr +++
- BAvg ++
- Spd ++
- Def ++

Year	Lev	Team	AB	R	H	HR	RBI	Avg	OB	Slg	OPS	bb%	ct%	Eye	SB	CS	x/h%	Iso	RC/G
2009	A	Great Lakes	120	8	18	1	16	150	215	258	474	8	77	0.36	1	0	50	108	1.30
2010	A	Great Lakes	507	87	139	15	71	274	341	446	786	9	82	0.56	6	1	37	172	5.28
2011	A+	Rancho Cuc	534	110	167	29	114	313	363	581	943	7	77	0.35	4	3	49	268	7.15
2012	A	Great Lakes	120	15	21	6	20	175	261	367	628	10	78	0.54	0	0	52	192	3.18
2012	A+	Rancho Cuc	188	20	41	6	20	218	269	351	620	6	73	0.26	1	1	32	133	2.91

Strong, aggressive hitter floundered after a breakout season in the CAL, hitting .201 and is now 24 years old. HR production dropped from 26 to 12 and he simply didn't make very consistent contact. Dead pull hitter who swings and misses a lot and his swing can get long. Might be too late to make the adjustments he needs.

Soto, Neftali

3 | Cincinnati | EXP MLB DEBUT: 2013 | POTENTIAL: Starting 1B | 8D

Bats R Age 24
2007 (3) HS, P.R.
- Pwr ++++
- BAvg ++
- 4.30 Spd +++
- Def +++

Year	Lev	Team	AB	R	H	HR	RBI	Avg	OB	Slg	OPS	bb%	ct%	Eye	SB	CS	x/h%	Iso	RC/G
2009	A+	Sarasota	505	53	125	11	57	248	280	362	643	4	81	0.24	1	3	27	115	3.23
2010	A+	Lynchburg	522	73	140	21	73	268	310	460	770	6	80	0.30	0	0	40	192	4.83
2011	AA	Carolina	379	70	103	30	76	272	317	575	892	6	75	0.26	0	1	50	303	6.36
2011	AAA	Louisville	17	1	7	1	4	412	444	588	1033	6	88	0.50	0	0	14	176	7.57
2012	AAA	Louisville	465	55	114	14	59	245	306	400	706	8	75	0.35	2	1	39	155	4.20

Lean, athletic hitter has a lightning quick bat and plus raw power, but lack of plate discipline cuts into BA ability and HR total fell from 31 to 14. Good bad-ball hitter with solid power. Has a strong arm and soft hands, but limited range and poor footwork and was moved to 1B. The move hurts his long-term value as he is now stuck behind Votto.

Soto, Wendell

6 | Los Angeles (A) | EXP MLB DEBUT: 2016 | POTENTIAL: Starting SS | 7C

Bats B Age 21
2010 (3) HS (FL)
- Pwr +++
- BAvg +++
- Spd +++
- Def +++

Year	Lev	Team	AB	R	H	HR	RBI	Avg	OB	Slg	OPS	bb%	ct%	Eye	SB	CS	x/h%	Iso	RC/G
2010	Rk	Angels	127	14	33	0	16	260	314	307	621	7	72	0.28	13	4	12	47	3.11
2011	Rk	Angels	132	21	30	2	13	227	306	356	662	10	71	0.39	6	5	33	129	3.82
2012	Rk	Orem	234	45	77	4	37	329	382	500	882	8	78	0.39	8	1	35	171	6.55
2012	A	Cedar Rapids	167	20	36	5	23	216	276	347	624	8	75	0.33	4	4	33	132	3.04

Diminutive, strong INF who fields his position with plus range and avg arm. Has yet to make impact above short season and could be breakout candidate with line drive approach and avg power potential. Owns long swing and needs to make more contact. Isn't a burner on base, but can swipe a bag.

Spangenberg, Cory

4 | San Diego | EXP MLB DEBUT: 2013 | POTENTIAL: Starting 2B | 7B

Bats L Age 22
2011 (1) Indian River JC
- Pwr +
- BAvg +++
- Spd +++
- Def +++

Year	Lev	Team	AB	R	H	HR	RBI	Avg	OB	Slg	OPS	bb%	ct%	Eye	SB	CS	x/h%	Iso	RC/G
2010	NCAA	Virginia MI	235	62	87	11	49	370	406	596	1001	6	81	0.31	24	5	32	226	7.61
2011	A	Fort Wayne	189	35	54	2	24	286	335	365	700	7	78	0.33	15	4	19	79	4.09
2011	A-	Eugene	86	20	33	1	20	384	547	535	1082	26	83	2.07	10	4	33	151	10.25
2012	A+	Lake Elsinore	384	53	104	1	40	271	317	352	669	6	81	0.36	27	9	20	81	3.77

Athletic 2B suffered a serious concussion in June that stalled his development. Has a patient approach at the plate that allows him to get on base and use his speed. Has a textbook swing and can put bat to ball consistently. Uses the entire field, but has little power. Solid defender at 2B with impressive all-around skills. Look for a rebound in '13.

Springer, George

8 | Houston | EXP MLB DEBUT: 2014 | POTENTIAL: Starting OF | 8A

Bats R Age 23
2011 (1) Connecticut
- Pwr ++++
- BAvg +++
- Spd ++++
- Def ++++

Year	Lev	Team	AB	R	H	HR	RBI	Avg	OB	Slg	OPS	bb%	ct%	Eye	SB	CS	x/h%	Iso	RC/G
2010	NCAA	Connecticut	243	84	82	18	62	337	469	658	1127	20	71	0.86	33	2	46	321	10.62
2011	NCAA	Connecticut	237	60	83	12	77	350	436	624	1060	13	84	0.95	31	7	46	274	8.81
2011	A-	Tri City	28	8	5	1	3	179	233	393	626	7	93	1.00	4	0	80	214	3.57
2012	A+	Lancaster	433	101	137	22	82	316	395	557	951	11	70	0.43	28	6	36	240	7.87
2012	AA	Corpus Christi	73	8	16	2	5	219	278	342	621	8	66	0.24	4	2	31	123	3.06

Tall, athletic OF who has upside with both power and speed and should consistently achieve 20 HR/20 SB seasons in majors. Tools are best in system and has great quickness and speed. Can play legitimate CF defense with instincts and strong arm. Needs to close holes in swing and reduce Ks to make impact.

Stanley, Cody

2 | St. Louis | EXP MLB DEBUT: 2015 | POTENTIAL: Platoon C | 7D

Bats L Age 24
2010 (4) NC - Willimgton
- Pwr +++
- BAvg +++
- Spd ++
- Def ++

Year	Lev	Team	AB	R	H	HR	RBI	Avg	OB	Slg	OPS	bb%	ct%	Eye	SB	CS	x/h%	Iso	RC/G
2010	Rk	Johnson City	209	34	67	5	39	321	383	498	880	9	86	0.70	8	1	33	177	6.45
2010	A	Quad Cities	4	1	1	1	2	250	250	1000	1250	0	50	0.00	0	0	100	750	14.93
2011	A	Quad Cities	379	54	100	11	66	264	313	425	738	7	76	0.29	4	2	37	161	4.55
2012	Rk	GCL Cardinals	10	1	3	0	0	300	300	500	800	0	60	0.00	0	0	67	200	6.47
2012	A+	Palm Beach	157	11	44	3	35	280	307	401	708	4	80	0.19	1	0	27	121	4.00

LH catcher was suspended for 50 games for testing positive for a banned substance. Barrels the ball well, but below-average plate discpline will limit BA potential. Is an average defender who can make all of the plays, but has a below-average arm and at this point the offense is ahead of the defense. Struggled in the AFL, hitting just .208.

Starling, Bubba

8 | Kansas City | EXP MLB DEBUT: 2015 | POTENTIAL: Starting OF | 9C

Bats R Age 20
2011 (1) HS (KS)
- Pwr ++++
- BAvg +++
- Spd ++++
- Def ++++

Year	Lev	Team	AB	R	H	HR	RBI	Avg	OB	Slg	OPS	bb%	ct%	Eye	SB	CS	x/h%	Iso	RC/G
2012	Rk	Burlington	200	35	55	10	33	275	364	485	849	12	65	0.40	10	1	36	210	6.65

Ultra-athletic OF with great set of skills, but may need time to develop intellect for game. Power, speed, range, and arm are well above avg and he could evolve into offensive behemoth. High K totals are concern due to rigid swing mechanics and needs to close holes in swing and recognize pitches better.

Stassi, Max — 2 — Oakland

EXP MLB DEBUT: 2014 | POTENTIAL: Starting C | **8C**

Bats R Age 22 | 2009 (4) HS (CA)
Pwr ++++ | BAvg +++ | Spd ++ | Def +++

Year	Lev	Team	AB	R	H	HR	RBI	Avg	OB	Slg	OPS	bb%	ct%	Eye	SB	CS	x/h%	Iso	RC/G
2009	Rk	Athletics	1	0	0	0	0	0	500	0	500	50	0	1.00	0	0	-	0	--
2009	A-	Vancouver	49	3	14	0	8	286	314	367	681	4	78	0.18	0	0	29	82	3.78
2010	A	Kane County	411	54	94	13	51	229	305	380	684	10	66	0.32	3	3	37	151	4.10
2011	A+	Stockton	121	22	28	2	19	231	321	331	652	12	82	0.73	1	1	29	99	3.78
2012	A+	Stockton	314	48	84	15	45	268	326	468	794	8	74	0.33	3	1	39	201	5.28

Short, compact C who returned from shoulder surgery and set career high in HR with natural feel for bat. Has bat speed and showed better eye, though still needs work. Needs to shorten swing with two strikes. Had solid arm prior to surgery and regaining strength. Has good receiving skills with fine agility.

Story, Trevor — 6 — Colorado

EXP MLB DEBUT: 2014 | POTENTIAL: Starting SS | **9D**

Bats R Age 20 | 2011 (2) HS, TX
Pwr +++ | BAvg +++ | Spd +++ | Def +++

Year	Lev	Team	AB	R	H	HR	RBI	Avg	OB	Slg	OPS	bb%	ct%	Eye	SB	CS	x/h%	Iso	RC/G
2011	Rk	Casper	179	37	48	6	28	268	361	436	797	13	77	0.63	13	1	33	168	5.59
2012	A	Asheville	477	96	132	18	63	277	358	505	863	11	75	0.50	15	3	51	229	6.50

Continues to emerge as one of the better SS prospects. Professional approach at the plate with a quick stroke and good strike zone judgment. Isn't the biggest player, but has good bat speed and is stronger than he looks with the potential to hit 20+ HR. Runs well and can make all of the plays on defense with good range and a plus arm.

Suarez, Eugenio — 46 — Detroit

EXP MLB DEBUT: 2015 | POTENTIAL: Starting SS/2B | **7B**

Bats B Age 21 | 2008 FA (Venezuela)
Pwr ++ | BAvg +++ | Spd +++ | Def +++

Year	Lev	Team	AB	R	H	HR	RBI	Avg	OB	Slg	OPS	bb%	ct%	Eye	SB	CS	x/h%	Iso	RC/G
2011	Rk	GCL Tigers	44	11	15	2	9	341	383	636	1019	6	91	0.75	2	0	60	295	7.78
2011	A-	Connecticut	204	37	51	5	24	250	311	426	737	8	79	0.42	9	5	41	176	4.68
2012	A	West Michigan	511	82	147	6	67	288	368	409	777	11	77	0.56	21	9	31	121	5.39

Quick, instinctual INF who had breakout season with bat and glove. Consistently good hitter from both sides and should hit for BA with gap power. Uses short, quick stroke to drive balls and exhibits discerning eye at plate. Fine defender with quick hands and sufficient range, though can be lazy with throws.

Susac, Andrew — 2 — San Francisco

EXP MLB DEBUT: 2015 | POTENTIAL: Starting C | **7C**

Bats R Age 23 | 2011 (2) Oregon State
Pwr ++ | BAvg ++ | Spd ++ | Def ++++

Year	Lev	Team	AB	R	H	HR	RBI	Avg	OB	Slg	OPS	bb%	ct%	Eye	SB	CS	x/h%	Iso	RC/G
2010	NCAA	Oregon State	96	15	25	2	13	260	360	365	725	14	76	0.65	0	1	24	104	4.71
2011	NCAA	Oregon State	134	31	42	5	32	313	429	552	981	17	76	0.84	0	1	43	239	8.36
2012	A+	San Jose	361	58	88	9	52	244	344	380	723	13	72	0.55	1	1	32	136	4.70

Good athlete and a solid defender with a strong, accurate arm. The Giants pushed him to High-A for his debut and he wasn't ready. Does have moderate power and a track record of hitting for average, but might have to alter his approach to use a better timing mechanism. Should be able to stay behind the plate and is better than he showed in '12.

Swanner, Will — 2 — Colorado

EXP MLB DEBUT: 2015 | POTENTIAL: Starting C | **8D**

Bats R Age 21 | 2010 (15) HS, CA
Pwr +++ | BAvg +++ | Spd ++ | Def ++

Year	Lev	Team	AB	R	H	HR	RBI	Avg	OB	Slg	OPS	bb%	ct%	Eye	SB	CS	x/h%	Iso	RC/G
2010	Rk	Casper	76	14	23	7	13	303	303	632	934	0	57	0.00	0	1	48	329	8.37
2011	Rk	Casper	159	33	42	10	24	264	346	553	900	11	62	0.33	1	2	60	289	7.65
2012	A	Asheville	325	60	98	16	61	302	375	529	904	10	69	0.38	3	2	42	228	7.19

Strong and athletic with good power. Swing can be long and contact rate and pitch recognition are problematic. Can be overly aggressive in his approach. Still very raw behind the plate, so there is work to do. Needs to improve on signal calling and blocking to remain behind the plate. Should have enough pop in his bat to survive a move to the OF.

Swihart, Blake — 2 — Boston

EXP MLB DEBUT: 2015 | POTENTIAL: Starting C | **8C**

Bats B Age 21 | 2011 (1) HS (NM)
Pwr +++ | BAvg +++ | Spd ++ | Def +++

Year	Lev	Team	AB	R	H	HR	RBI	Avg	OB	Slg	OPS	bb%	ct%	Eye	SB	CS	x/h%	Iso	RC/G
2011	Rk	GCL Red Sox	6	0	0	0	0	0	0	0	0	0	67	0.00	0	0		0	
2012	A	Greenville	344	44	90	7	53	262	314	395	709	7	80	0.38	6	2	31	134	4.22

Offensive-minded backstop who got off to slow start, but finished well. Very athletic with simple, quick swing that could lead to high BA with avg power. Aggressive approach could be toned down and pitch recognition needs work. Exhibits smooth actions and strong arm, but lacks ideal size for durability behind plate.

Szczur, Matt — 8 — Chicago (N)

EXP MLB DEBUT: 2014 | POTENTIAL: Starting CF | **7B**

Bats R Age 23 | 2010 (5) Villanova
Pwr ++ | BAvg +++ | 6.4/60 Spd ++++ | Def +++

Year	Lev	Team	AB	R	H	HR	RBI	Avg	OB	Slg	OPS	bb%	ct%	Eye	SB	CS	x/h%	Iso	RC/G
2010	A-	Boise	73	17	29	0	8	397	443	521	964	8	85	0.55	1	0	31	123	7.43
2011	A	Peoria	274	55	86	5	27	314	363	431	793	7	90	0.75	17	5	24	117	5.30
2011	A+	Daytona	173	20	45	5	19	260	281	410	691	3	88	0.25	7	0	31	150	3.83
2012	A+	Daytona	295	68	87	2	34	295	392	407	799	14	83	0.94	38	12	29	112	5.83
2012	AA	Tennessee	143	24	30	2	6	210	280	357	637	9	80	0.48	4	2	43	147	3.51

Has blazing speed and continues to draw walks and demonstrate solid strike zone judgment. Isn't going to develop much power due to a slashing swing, but should be able to hit for average. Worked hard on improving routes in CF and has the speed and arm-strength. Still raw, but has the tools to develop into a top-of-the-order hitter.

Tate, Donavan — 8 — San Diego

EXP MLB DEBUT: 2014 | POTENTIAL: Starting CF | **7D**

Bats R Age 22 | 2009 (1) HS, GA
Pwr + | BAvg ++ | 6.3/60 Spd ++++ | Def +++

Year	Lev	Team	AB	R	H	HR	RBI	Avg	OB	Slg	OPS	bb%	ct%	Eye	SB	CS	x/h%	Iso	RC/G
2010	Rk	Padres	90	19	20	2	10	222	333	344	678	14	54	0.37	7	1	35	122	4.72
2011	A	Fort Wayne	19	3	6	0	2	316	435	421	856	17	84	1.33	2	2	33	105	6.82
2011	A-	Eugene	127	24	36	0	20	283	401	409	811	16	75	0.78	17	5	33	126	6.27
2012	A	Fort Wayne	193	26	40	1	21	207	288	254	542	10	68	0.35	10	5	18	47	2.04
2012	A+	Lake Elsinore	178	28	44	0	7	247	380	303	683	18	69	0.68	11	9	18	56	4.46

Former 3rd overall pick has yet to pan out. Still has exciting raw tools, but has been injury-prone and power has not developed. Had two drug-related suspensions and a variety of ailments. Was healthy in '12, but didn't hit. Covers tons of ground and has a strong arm, but looks more and more like a bust.

Taveras, Oscar — 9 — St. Louis

EXP MLB DEBUT: 2013 | POTENTIAL: Starting CF | **9B**

Bats L Age 21 | 2008 NDFA, D.R.
Pwr ++++ | BAvg ++++ | Spd +++ | Def ++++

Year	Lev	Team	AB	R	H	HR	RBI	Avg	OB	Slg	OPS	bb%	ct%	Eye	SB	CS	x/h%	Iso	RC/G
2010	Rk	Johnson City	211	39	68	8	43	322	359	526	885	5	81	0.29	8	5	35	204	6.24
2010	Rk	GCL Cardinals	30	1	5	0	2	167	194	200	394	3	83	0.20	1	0	20	33	0.34
2011	A	Quad Cities	308	52	119	8	62	386	444	584	1029	9	83	0.62	1	4	34	198	8.28
2012	AA	Springfield	477	83	153	23	94	321	376	572	948	8	88	0.75	10	1	44	252	7.05

Has developed into one of the top prospects in baseball. Has an aggressive approach and takes a vicious hack, but makes consistent contact and has good balance. Plus bat speed, excellent hand-eye coordination, and good strike zone judgment enable him to hit for power and average. Solid speed and a strong arm allow him to play all three OF positions.

Taylor, Chris — 46 — Seattle

EXP MLB DEBUT: 2015 | POTENTIAL: Utility player | **6A**

Bats R Age 22 | 2012 (5) Virginia
Pwr + | BAvg +++ | Spd ++++ | Def ++++

Year	Lev	Team	AB	R	H	HR	RBI	Avg	OB	Slg	OPS	bb%	ct%	Eye	SB	CS	x/h%	Iso	RC/G
2010	NCAA	Virginia	59	19	18	0	7	305	453	390	843	21	81	1.45	0	0	22	85	6.87
2011	NCAA	Virginia	285	63	87	2	49	305	365	404	769	9	84	0.60	15	6	25	98	5.13
2012	NCAA	Virginia	236	57	67	5	47	284	376	445	821	13	84	0.92	12	2	34	161	6.00
2012	A	Clinton	46	5	14	0	4	304	333	304	638	4	91	0.50	4	1	0	0	3.38
2012	A-	Everett	137	26	45	2	18	328	418	474	892	13	87	1.17	13	5	33	146	6.91

Quick INF who may not project well with bat, but owns outstanding defensive attributes. Game revolves around glove and legs. Has clean, quick hands at SS along with plus, accurate arm, and range. Is a SB threat with above average wheels. Focuses on going to opp field and could stand to swing harder.

Taylor, Michael — 9 — Oakland

EXP MLB DEBUT: 2011 | POTENTIAL: Starting OF | **8D**

Bats R Age 27 | 2007 (5) Stanford
Pwr +++ | BAvg +++ | Spd +++ | Def +++

Year	Lev	Team	AB	R	H	HR	RBI	Avg	OB	Slg	OPS	bb%	ct%	Eye	SB	CS	x/h%	Iso	RC/G
2010	AAA	Sacramento	464	79	126	6	51	272	344	392	736	10	80	0.55	16	5	30	121	4.77
2011	AAA	Sacramento	349	51	95	16	46	272	357	456	813	12	77	0.58	14	5	34	183	5.65
2011	MLB	Oakland	30	4	6	1	5	200	314	300	614	14	63	0.45	0	0	17	100	3.04
2012	AAA	Sacramento	449	81	129	12	67	287	402	441	843	16	77	0.82	18	4	34	154	6.43
2012	MLB	Oakland	21	2	3	0	0	143	143	190	333	0	52	0.00	0	0	33	48	

Tall, strong OF who spent his third season in AAA. Controls strike zone with disciplined eye, but may not realize plus power potential without being more aggressive at plate. Content with using entire field and using avg speed effectively. Plays solid defense in RF with average arm strength and sufficient range.

Taylor, Michael

8 | **Washington** | EXP MLB DEBUT: 2014 | POTENTIAL: Starting CF | **8D**

Bats R Age 22
2009 (6) HS, FL

- Pwr +++
- BAvg ++
- Spd +++
- Def +++

Year	Lev	Team	AB	R	H	HR	RBI	Avg	OB	Slg	OPS	bb%	ct%	Eye	SB	CS	x/h%	Iso	RC/G
2010	Rk	GCL Nationals	128	14	25	1	12	195	275	297	572	10	76	0.45	1	2	32	102	2.63
2011	A	Hagerstown	442	64	112	13	68	253	304	432	736	7	73	0.27	23	12	41	179	4.61
2012	A+	Potomac	384	51	93	3	37	242	314	362	676	9	71	0.35	19	9	41	120	4.05

Raw, athletic player was moved from SS to CF where his speed and strong arm play well. Has the tools to hit for power and average, though he struggled to do so. Has plus bat speed that generates gap power, but will need to improve his strike zone judgment and make more contact to hit for average.

Taylor, Tyrone

8 | **Milwaukee** | EXP MLB DEBUT: 2016 | POTENTIAL: Starting CF | **7C**

Bats R Age 19
2012 (2) HS, CA

- Pwr ++
- BAvg +++
- Spd +++
- Def +++

Year	Lev	Team	AB	R	H	HR	RBI	Avg	OB	Slg	OPS	bb%	ct%	Eye	SB	CS	x/h%	Iso	RC/G
2012	Rk	Helena	39	11	15	2	5	385	455	641	1096	11	79	0.63	3	2	40	256	9.26
2012	Rk	Brewers	36	11	14	0	6	389	405	694	1100	3	92	0.33	3	1	57	306	8.72

Strong, athletic two-sport start in high school was a 2nd round pick in '12. Has plus speed with some bat speed and good raw power. Has a slightly unorthodox swing and can be overly aggressive at times. Had a very nice debut, hitting .387 in 75 AB. Will get a good test in full-season ball in '13 and has some interesting upside.

Terdoslavich, Joey

3 | **Atlanta** | EXP MLB DEBUT: 2013 | POTENTIAL: Backup 1B | **7C**

Bats B Age 24
2010 (6) Long Beach State

- Pwr +++
- BAvg ++
- Spd +
- Def ++

Year	Lev	Team	AB	R	H	HR	RBI	Avg	OB	Slg	OPS	bb%	ct%	Eye	SB	CS	x/h%	Iso	RC/G
2010	Rk	Danville	189	27	56	2	24	296	348	402	750	7	86	0.56	3	3	25	106	4.82
2010	A	Rome	79	7	25	0	10	316	357	430	788	6	77	0.28	0	0	36	114	5.32
2011	A+	Lynchburg	483	72	138	20	82	286	342	526	867	8	78	0.38	2	0	54	240	6.27
2012	AA	Mississippi	298	43	94	5	51	315	372	480	852	8	79	0.44	4	0	36	164	6.17
2012	AAA	Gwinnett	194	19	35	4	20	180	254	263	516	9	74	0.38	3	0	23	82	1.65

Undersized switch-hitting 1B failed to duplicate breakout. The Braves skipped him from High-A to Triple-A, but he struggled. Recovered after being demoted to AA, but without the long-ball power. Has a simple, compact swing and drives the ball. Moderate plate discipline will likely limit his average, but he handles the bat well.

Thompson, Trayce

8 | **Chicago (A)** | EXP MLB DEBUT: 2014 | POTENTIAL: Starting CF | **9D**

Bats R Age 22
2009 (2) HS (CA)

- Pwr ++++
- BAvg ++
- Spd ++++
- Def ++++

Year	Lev	Team	AB	R	H	HR	RBI	Avg	OB	Slg	OPS	bb%	ct%	Eye	SB	CS	x/h%	Iso	RC/G
2010	A	Kannapolis	210	28	48	8	31	229	299	433	732	9	67	0.30	6	4	50	205	4.78
2011	A	Kannapolis	519	95	125	24	87	241	320	457	776	10	67	0.35	8	4	50	216	5.42
2012	A+	Winston-Salem	449	77	114	22	90	254	322	486	807	9	68	0.31	18	3	48	232	5.79
2012	AA	Birmingham	50	10	14	3	6	280	379	520	899	14	68	0.50	2	0	36	240	7.23
2012	AAA	Charlotte	18	1	3	0	0	167	250	278	528	10	67	0.33	1	0	67	111	2.00

Tall, lean OF who led CAR in HR, but also finished 2nd in K. Had 20/20 season. Focused on using entire field and shortening swing, but has inconsistent stroke and below avg pitch recognition. Too many Ks and hitting for BA is question. Can play CF with range due to plus speed and owns strong, accurate arm.

Tilson, Charlie

8 | **St. Louis** | EXP MLB DEBUT: 2015 | POTENTIAL: Starting CF | **7C**

Bats L Age 20
2011 (2) HS, IL

- Pwr ++
- BAvg +++
- Spd +++
- Def +++

Year	Lev	Team	AB	R	H	HR	RBI	Avg	OB	Slg	OPS	bb%	ct%	Eye	SB	CS	x/h%	Iso	RC/G
2011	Rk	Johnson City	15	2	7	0	4	467	500	600	1100	6	93	1.00	0	0	29	133	8.69
2011	Rk	GCL Cardinals	12	2	2	0	1	167	286	167	452	14	75	0.67	1	0	0	0	1.08

Had shoulder surgery and missed all of the season. Prior to the injury the 2nd rounder had gotten off to a nice start. High-energy CF with a smooth compact LH stroke and is willing to drive the ball the opposite way. Has gap power, above-average speed, and good plate discipline. If healthy, look for a breakout in '13.

Toles, Andrew

8 | **Tampa Bay** | EXP MLB DEBUT: 2015 | POTENTIAL: Starting OF | **7B**

Bats L Age 21
2012 (3) Chipola JC

- Pwr +++
- BAvg +++
- Spd +++
- Def +++

Year	Lev	Team	AB	R	H	HR	RBI	Avg	OB	Slg	OPS	bb%	ct%	Eye	SB	CS	x/h%	Iso	RC/G
2012	Rk	Princeton	199	31	56	7	33	281	322	482	805	6	82	0.33	14	5	41	201	5.29

Athletic, quick OF with solid skill set and could be sleeper. Does everything relatively well, though no tool stands out other than speed. Bat speed is incredibly quick for size and could develop solid power. Can be pitched inside and plate coverage needs attention. Owns plus CF range with strong arm and decent instincts.

Torreyes, Ronald

5 | **Chicago (N)** | EXP MLB DEBUT: 2014 | POTENTIAL: Backup 2B | **6B**

Bats R Age 20
2010 NDFA, Venezuela

- Pwr ++
- BAvg +++
- Spd +++
- Def ++

Year	Lev	Team	AB	R	H	HR	RBI	Avg	OB	Slg	OPS	bb%	ct%	Eye	SB	CS	x/h%	Iso	RC/G
2010	Rk	Reds	83	13	29	1	11	349	357	494	851	1	94	0.20	2	2	31	145	5.60
2010	A	Dayton	25	3	6	0	2	240	240	400	640	0	88	0.00	0	0	50	160	3.34
2011	A	Dayton	278	53	99	3	41	356	387	457	844	5	93	0.74	12	7	17	101	5.74
2012	A+	Daytona	421	62	111	6	47	264	316	385	700	7	93	1.10	13	4	31	121	4.41

Short, speedy 2B struggled in the pitcher-friendly FSL. Listed at 5-7, 140 he has surprising pop, solid strike zone judgment, and a bit of speed. He squares the ball up consistently and struck out just 29 times in 421 AB. Range and arm strength limit him to 2B and give him a profile similar to Jose Altuve.

Tovar, Wilfredo

6 | **New York (N)** | EXP MLB DEBUT: 2014 | POTENTIAL: Backup SS | **6C**

Bats R Age 21
2007 NDFA, Venezuela

- Pwr +
- BAvg ++
- Spd +++
- Def ++++

Year	Lev	Team	AB	R	H	HR	RBI	Avg	OB	Slg	OPS	bb%	ct%	Eye	SB	CS	x/h%	Iso	RC/G
2010	A+	St. Lucie	118	14	29	0	6	246	264	305	570	2	81	0.14	4	3	21	59	2.34
2010	A-	Brooklyn	68	11	18	0	6	265	286	324	609	3	87	0.22	4	3	17	59	2.95
2011	A	Savannah	491	70	123	2	41	251	312	318	630	8	89	0.83	15	9	21	67	3.59
2012	A+	St. Lucie	218	31	62	1	23	284	368	385	754	12	92	1.71	12	7	31	101	5.33
2012	AA	Binghamton	193	20	49	0	27	254	294	332	626	5	89	0.50	2	1	27	78	3.39

Slick-fielding, light-hitting SS. Runs well and has good range with a strong arm. Defense is major league ready right now. Makes consistent contact, but hit just .254 in 193 AB. Does have decent speed and stole 14 bases. Defense will get him to the majors, but his bat might keep him from being a starter.

Townsend, Tyler

3 | **Baltimore** | EXP MLB DEBUT: 2014 | POTENTIAL: Starting 1B | **8D**

Bats L Age 25
2009 (3) Florida Int'l

- Pwr ++++
- BAvg +++
- Spd +
- Def ++

Year	Lev	Team	AB	R	H	HR	RBI	Avg	OB	Slg	OPS	bb%	ct%	Eye	SB	CS	x/h%	Iso	RC/G
2011	A+	Frederick	252	43	80	13	50	317	346	583	929	4	75	0.17	2	2	49	266	6.93
2012	Rk	GCL Orioles	33	3	5	3	8	152	222	455	677	8	64	0.25	0	0	80	303	3.66
2012	A+	Frederick	118	14	30	3	18	254	338	373	711	11	74	0.48	0	1	27	119	4.40
2012	AA	Bowie	73	11	18	6	13	247	337	521	858	12	67	0.42	0	0	44	274	6.40
2012	A-	Aberdeen	14	3	6	0	0	429	467	571	1038	7	93	1.00	0	0	33	143	8.10

Smart, powerful hitter who has missed time with injuries. When healthy, has a smooth, power stroke that should allow him to hit for BA and above avg pop. Is menace against LHP and covers plate well. Purely a bat-only prospect with few secondary skills. Lacks agility and speed to be anything more than 1B.

Trahan, Stryker

2 | **Arizona** | EXP MLB DEBUT: 2016 | POTENTIAL: Starting C | **8D**

Bats L Age 19
2012 (1) HS, LA

- Pwr +++
- BAvg +++
- Spd ++
- Def ++

Year	Lev	Team	AB	R	H	HR	RBI	Avg	OB	Slg	OPS	bb%	ct%	Eye	SB	CS	x/h%	Iso	RC/G
2012	Rk	Diamondbacks	167	29	47	5	25	281	420	473	893	19	71	0.83	8	1	40	192	7.46

Offensive-minded catcher had a solid pro debut. The18-year-old has good bat speed, raw power, and good strike zone judgment. Trahan has a strong throwing arm, but nailed just 24% of base-runners and will likely be moved to either 1B or RF down the road, but his bat could be very good.

Triunfel, Carlos

46 | **Seattle** | EXP MLB DEBUT: 2012 | POTENTIAL: Starting INF | **8E**

Bats R Age 23
2006 FA (DR)

- Pwr +++
- BAvg +++
- Spd ++
- Def +++

Year	Lev	Team	AB	R	H	HR	RBI	Avg	OB	Slg	OPS	bb%	ct%	Eye	SB	CS	x/h%	Iso	RC/G
2010	AA	W Tennessee	470	51	121	7	42	257	277	332	609	3	89	0.24	2	8	17	74	2.90
2011	AA	Jackson	395	45	111	6	35	281	324	392	716	6	82	0.35	5	7	27	111	4.26
2011	AAA	Tacoma	111	7	31	0	10	279	292	351	643	2	85	0.12	1	0	23	72	3.24
2012	AAA	Tacoma	496	74	129	10	62	260	293	391	684	4	82	0.26	3	2	33	131	3.78
2012	MLB	Seattle	22	2	5	0	3	227	261	318	579	4	82	0.25	0	0	40	91	2.63

Strong, compact INF who posted career high in HR and more power could come once he polishes approach. Has taken a while to develop as injuries have been issue. Owns excellent bat speed and ideal hand-eye coordination for good contact. Could stick at SS with cannon of an arm and passable range.

Tucker, Preston — 79 — Houston

EXP MLB DEBUT: 2015 | POTENTIAL: Reserve OF | 6B

Bats L | Age 22 | 2012 (7) Florida
Pwr ++++ | BAvg ++ | Spd + | Def ++

Year	Lev	Team	AB	R	H	HR	RBI	Avg	OB	Slg	OPS	bb%	ct%	Eye	SB	CS	x/h%	Iso	RC/G
2009	NCAA	Florida	242	48	88	15	85	364	414	628	1043	8	91	0.95	5	2	35	264	7.97
2010	NCAA	Florida	245	50	81	11	49	331	431	551	982	15	88	1.48	8	0	37	220	7.90
2011	NCAA	Florida	286	55	88	15	74	308	369	545	915	9	90	0.97	5	3	43	238	6.68
2012	NCAA	Florida	262	57	84	16	50	321	401	584	985	12	90	1.30	6	3	42	263	7.63
2012	A-	Tri City	165	32	53	8	38	321	388	509	897	10	90	1.13	1	2	28	188	6.50

Strong, big-bodied OF who has plenty of bat to make impact, but needs improvement with rest of game. Has slow foot speed and lacks mobility and instincts for OF. Has excellent feel for hitting, particularly with plus, raw power. Combination of avg bat speed and strength give him pop potential, though swing can get long.

Urrutia, Henry — 79 — Baltimore

EXP MLB DEBUT: 2013 | POTENTIAL: Starting OF | 7C

Bats B | Age 26 | 2012 FA (Cuba)
Pwr ++ | BAvg +++ | Spd +++ | Def +++

Year	Lev	Team	AB	R	H	HR	RBI	Avg	OB	Slg	OPS	bb%	ct%	Eye	SB	CS	x/h%	Iso	RC/G
2012		Did not play																	

OF who played 3 years in Cuba's top league and owns athleticism and solid hitting skills. Smokes line drives to gaps and makes consistent, hard contact with fluid and balanced stroke. Has strength for over-the-fence power, but goes gap-to gap instead. Has avg speed and range along with a strong arm.

Urshela, Giovanny — 5 — Cleveland

EXP MLB DEBUT: 2015 | POTENTIAL: Starting 3B | 8D

Bats R | Age 21 | 2008 FA (Colombia)
Pwr +++ | BAvg ++ | Spd ++ | Def ++++

Year	Lev	Team	AB	R	H	HR	RBI	Avg	OB	Slg	OPS	bb%	ct%	Eye	SB	CS	x/h%	Iso	RC/G
2009	Rk	Indians	105	10	27	0	11	257	322	276	598	9	89	0.83	3	0	7	19	3.20
2010	A-	Mahoning Val	221	22	64	3	35	290	326	367	693	5	86	0.38	5	3	17	77	3.93
2011	A	Lake County	505	57	120	9	46	238	258	347	605	3	86	0.20	3	0	29	109	2.82
2012	A+	Carolina	439	50	122	14	59	278	303	446	750	4	86	0.27	1	1	37	169	4.49

Unheralded INF who has progressed one level per year, but had breakout at end of season. Improved tools across board, including defense that borders on Gold Glove. Instinctual on both sides of ball, but often expands K zone with long swing. Rarely walks, but can put a charge into ball. Power is best offensive skill.

Valera, Breyvic — 4 — St. Louis

EXP MLB DEBUT: 2015 | POTENTIAL: Starting SS | 7C

Bats B | Age 20 | 2010 NDFA, Venezuela
Pwr + | BAvg +++ | Spd +++ | Def ++++

Year	Lev	Team	AB	R	H	HR	RBI	Avg	OB	Slg	OPS	bb%	ct%	Eye	SB	CS	x/h%	Iso	RC/G
2011	Rk	Johnson City	73	16	29	0	8	397	436	479	915	6	88	0.56	7	5	17	82	6.68
2011	Rk	GCL Cardinals	110	23	28	1	13	255	317	364	680	8	85	0.59	7	1	29	109	4.07
2012	AA	Springfield	5	2	1	0	1	200	200	200	400	0	100		0	0	0	0	1.14
2012	A-	Batavia	282	39	89	1	33	316	357	418	775	6	90	0.67	10	6	26	103	5.12

Short, athletic Dominican infielder continues to surpass exceptations. Has a nice approach at the plate, making solid contact and showing gap power. He has good speed and should be able to get on base consistently. He is a good defender and split time between 2B and SS. He has good range, soft hands, and a strong arm.

Valle, Sebastian — 2 — Philadelphia

EXP MLB DEBUT: 2013 | POTENTIAL: Starting CA | 8D

Bats R | Age 23 | 2006 NDFA, Mexico
Pwr +++ | BAvg +++ | Spd + | Def +++

Year	Lev	Team	AB	R	H	HR	RBI	Avg	OB	Slg	OPS	bb%	ct%	Eye	SB	CS	x/h%	Iso	RC/G
2009	A-	Williamsport	192	25	59	6	40	307	342	531	873	5	79	0.24	0	0	44	224	6.21
2010	A	Lakewood	447	51	114	16	74	255	297	430	727	6	77	0.27	3	2	39	174	4.31
2011	A+	Clearwater	348	34	99	5	40	284	310	394	704	4	76	0.15	0	0	26	109	3.98
2012	AA	Reading	310	31	81	13	45	261	287	435	722	3	73	0.13	0	2	33	174	4.12
2012	AAA	Lehigh Valley	78	7	17	4	13	218	238	397	635	3	60	0.06	0	1	35	179	3.20

Best defensive catcher in the system has a good arm, soft hands, and nice agility. Struggled offensively and can be overly aggressive with poor pitch recognition. The results were troubling—13 BB/114 K. Does have good power, but doesn't make enough contact and without an adjustment, his upside is limited.

Van Slyke, Scott — 9 — Los Angeles (N)

EXP MLB DEBUT: 2012 | POTENTIAL: Backup RF | 6C

Bats R | Age 26 | 2005 (14) HS, MO
Pwr +++ | BAvg +++ | Spd ++ | Def ++

Year	Lev	Team	AB	R	H	HR	RBI	Avg	OB	Slg	OPS	bb%	ct%	Eye	SB	CS	x/h%	Iso	RC/G
2010	AA	Chattanooga	217	28	51	4	29	235	294	350	644	8	83	0.49	4	2	27	115	3.50
2010	AAA	Albuquerque	38	5	11	1	5	289	289	474	763	0	82	0.00	0	0	45	184	4.49
2011	AA	Chattanooga	457	81	159	20	92	348	429	595	1024	12	78	0.65	6	5	43	247	8.55
2012	AAA	Albuquerque	358	68	117	18	67	327	403	578	982	11	82	0.72	5	3	45	251	7.75
2012	MLB	Dodgers	54	4	9	2	7	167	196	315	511	4	74	0.14	1	0	44	148	1.35

Floundered in limited MLB action, but was good at AAA. Has raw power and can punish mistakes. Has good strike zone judgment, but can be beat by more advanced pitching. Is an average defender with a nice bat. The Dodgers removed him from their 40-man roster, but he should latch on with another team.

Vargas, Kennys — 3 — Minnesota

EXP MLB DEBUT: 2015 | POTENTIAL: Reserve 1B | 6B

Bats B | Age 22 | 2009 FA (PR)
Pwr ++++ | BAvg +++ | Spd + | Def +

Year	Lev	Team	AB	R	H	HR	RBI	Avg	OB	Slg	OPS	bb%	ct%	Eye	SB	CS	x/h%	Iso	RC/G
2009	Rk	GCL Twins	109	12	28	3	18	257	357	404	761	13	69	0.50	2	0	36	147	5.31
2010	Rk	GCL Twins	142	24	46	3	26	324	381	507	888	8	72	0.33	1	0	41	183	6.90
2011	Rk	Elizabethton	174	27	56	6	33	322	376	489	864	8	71	0.30	0	0	30	167	6.40
2012	A	Beloit	154	22	49	11	36	318	423	610	1033	15	73	0.68	0	0	45	292	8.88

Big-bodied INF who was suspended 50 games for positive PED test, but returned with outstanding power. Works counts with patient approach and is learning to swing at good pitches. Still struggles with offspeed stuff. Speed, agility, and defense are very poor and needs to work hard to become adequate at 1B.

Vasquez, Danry — 7 — Detroit

EXP MLB DEBUT: 2016 | POTENTIAL: Starting OF | 9E

Bats L | Age 19 | 2010 FA (Venezuela)
Pwr ++++ | BAvg ++ | Spd ++ | Def ++

Year	Lev	Team	AB	R	H	HR	RBI	Avg	OB	Slg	OPS	bb%	ct%	Eye	SB	CS	x/h%	Iso	RC/G
2011	Rk	GCL Tigers	206	25	56	2	30	272	296	350	645	3	83	0.21	3	2	20	78	3.26
2012	A	West Michigan	99	5	16	1	7	162	217	222	439	7	80	0.35	0	0	25	61	0.83
2012	A-	Connecticut	289	36	90	2	35	311	341	401	742	4	84	0.29	6	4	22	90	4.51

Tall, wiry strong OF who was demoted to short-season ball, but rebounded in major way and showed high ceiling tools. Uses both gaps with plus bat speed and should reach seats with more strength. Needs to be more selective at plate and learn to hit LHP. Defense and speed are subpar, but arm is asset.

Vaughn, Cory — 7 — New York (N)

EXP MLB DEBUT: 2014 | POTENTIAL: Starting RF/LF | 8D

Bats R | Age 24 | 2010 (4) San Diego State
Pwr ++++ | BAvg ++ | Spd +++ | Def +++

Year	Lev	Team	AB	R	H	HR	RBI	Avg	OB	Slg	OPS	bb%	ct%	Eye	SB	CS	x/h%	Iso	RC/G
2010	NCAA	San Diego St	188	42	71	9	55	378	440	606	1047	10	71	0.38	15	1	34	229	9.09
2010	A-	Brooklyn	264	45	81	14	56	307	386	557	943	11	76	0.54	12	5	41	250	7.41
2011	A	Savannah	245	33	70	4	30	286	377	408	785	13	74	0.56	8	5	29	122	5.59
2011	A+	St. Lucie	210	29	46	9	29	219	296	395	691	10	75	0.43	2	3	39	176	3.99
2012	A+	St. Lucie	456	73	111	23	69	243	338	463	801	12	75	0.57	21	4	46	219	5.57

Strong, powerful player has the best raw power in the system, but struggles with pitch recognition and consistent contact. Did make some improvements and walked 65 times, but still has work to do. Has good speed and covers ground well in the OF with a strong arm. Did manage a 20/20 season but hit just .243.

Vazquez, Christian — 2 — Boston

EXP MLB DEBUT: 2014 | POTENTIAL: Backup C | 6B

Bats R | Age 22 | 2008 (9) HS (PR)
Pwr +++ | BAvg ++ | Spd ++ | Def +++

Year	Lev	Team	AB	R	H	HR	RBI	Avg	OB	Slg	OPS	bb%	ct%	Eye	SB	CS	x/h%	Iso	RC/G
2009	A-	Lowell	65	4	8	2	9	123	250	246	496	14	75	0.69	0	0	50	123	1.58
2010	A	Greenville	270	34	71	3	32	263	321	337	658	8	77	0.37	3	1	20	74	3.58
2011	A	Greenville	392	71	111	18	84	283	354	505	859	10	79	0.51	1	1	43	222	6.19
2012	A+	Salem	293	43	78	7	41	266	354	396	750	12	76	0.57	2	2	31	130	4.98
2012	AA	Portland	73	11	15	0	5	205	284	260	544	10	88	0.89	0	0	27	55	2.68

Short, stocky C who has excellent tools behind plate. Owns strong arm with quick release and neutralizes running game. Textbook footwork enhances overall package and is solid blocker. Offensive production is in question. Didn't hit for much pop and inconsistent approach hinders BA potential. Needs better bat control.

Vettleson, Drew — 9 — Tampa Bay

EXP MLB DEBUT: 2015 | POTENTIAL: Starting OF | 9D

Bats L | Age 21 | 2010 (1-S) HS (WA)
Pwr +++ | BAvg +++ | Spd +++ | Def ++

Year	Lev	Team	AB	R	H	HR	RBI	Avg	OB	Slg	OPS	bb%	ct%	Eye	SB	CS	x/h%	Iso	RC/G
2011	Rk	Princeton	234	33	66	7	40	282	356	462	818	10	77	0.51	20	6	36	179	5.79
2012	A	Bowling Green	505	80	139	15	69	275	342	432	773	9	77	0.44	20	11	32	156	5.12

Steady, consistent OF who has shown proclivity for hitting with mature approach and ability to hit LHP. Works counts and should develop above avg pop when he trusts hands in repeatable stroke. Likes to use whole field and has speed to be asset. Needs polish in RF where routes and jumps could improve.

Villanueva, Christian — 5 — Chicago (N)

EXP MLB DEBUT: 2014 | POTENTIAL: Starting 3B | 8C

Bats R Age 22
2009 NDFA, Mexico
Pwr +++
BAvg +++
Spd ++
Def ++++

Year	Lev	Team	AB	R	H	HR	RBI	Avg	OB	Slg	OPS	bb%	ct%	Eye	SB	CS	x/h%	Iso	RC/G
2010	Rk	Rangers	188	30	59	2	35	314	358	431	789	6	78	0.31	6	2	29	117	5.26
2011	A	Hickory	467	78	130	17	84	278	331	465	796	7	82	0.43	32	6	38	186	5.25
2012	A+	Myrtle Beach	375	45	107	10	59	285	328	421	750	6	78	0.29	9	9	28	136	4.62
2012	A+	Daytona	84	14	21	4	9	250	330	452	782	11	71	0.42	5	2	43	202	5.31

Short, strong-bodied 3B continues to emerge. Came over as part of the Dempster trade. Short, compact stroke and good bat speed results in above-average power, but aggressive approach cuts into batting average. Plus defender with good hands, range, and strong, accurate arm. Is surprisingly quick for his size.

Villar, Jonathan — 6 — Houston

EXP MLB DEBUT: 2014 | POTENTIAL: Starting SS | 7B

Bats B Age 22
2008 FA (DR)
Pwr +++
BAvg +++
Spd ++++
Def +++

Year	Lev	Team	AB	R	H	HR	RBI	Avg	OB	Slg	OPS	bb%	ct%	Eye	SB	CS	x/h%	Iso	RC/G
2010	A	Lakewood	371	61	101	2	36	272	320	358	678	7	72	0.25	38	13	24	86	3.88
2010	A+	Lancaster	129	18	29	3	19	225	291	372	663	9	61	0.24	7	2	38	147	4.00
2011	A+	Lancaster	174	26	45	4	26	259	352	414	766	13	68	0.45	20	6	33	155	5.45
2011	AA	Corpus Christi	324	52	75	10	26	231	295	386	680	8	69	0.29	14	6	37	154	3.91
2012	AA	Corpus Christi	326	54	85	11	50	261	332	396	728	10	73	0.40	39	8	24	135	4.50

Quick, toolsy SS who ended season after breaking hand. Still led TL in SB. Exhibits plus speed while possessing well above avg range and arm strength. Racks up errors, mostly due to poor concentration. Offensive upside with solid gap power, but needs to tame aggressive approach and see more pitches.

Vinicio, Jose — 6 — Boston

EXP MLB DEBUT: 2015 | POTENTIAL: Starting SS | 7D

Bats B Age 19
2009 FA (DR)
Pwr ++
BAvg ++
Spd ++++
Def ++++

Year	Lev	Team	AB	R	H	HR	RBI	Avg	OB	Slg	OPS	bb%	ct%	Eye	SB	CS	x/h%	Iso	RC/G
2010	Rk	GCL Red Sox	158	23	40	1	22	253	285	373	658	4	84	0.27	13	1	28	120	3.59
2011	Rk	GCL Red Sox	179	22	52	2	18	291	317	419	736	4	82	0.21	19	10	27	128	4.43
2012	A	Greenville	256	37	71	3	32	277	312	371	683	5	78	0.23	24	11	21	94	3.78
2012	A-	Lowell	8	0	0	0	0	0	0	0	0	0	75	0.00	0	0	--	0	

Light-framed INF with smooth actions to be potent defender. Possesses exemplary range and soft, quick hands. Swings better from left side and hand-eye coordination and bat control allow for BA potential. Needs to work counts more and frame has room to add strength. Doesn't project for much power.

Vitters, Josh — 5 — Chicago (N)

EXP MLB DEBUT: 2012 | POTENTIAL: Starting 3B | 7D

Bats R Age 23
2007 (1) HS, CA
Pwr +++
BAvg ++
Spd ++
Def ++

Year	Lev	Team	AB	R	H	HR	RBI	Avg	OB	Slg	OPS	bb%	ct%	Eye	SB	CS	x/h%	Iso	RC/G
2010	A+	Daytona	110	16	32	3	13	291	339	445	784	7	80	0.36	4	1	34	155	5.11
2010	AA	Tennessee	206	28	46	7	26	223	269	383	653	6	80	0.32	2	0	41	160	3.40
2011	AA	Tennessee	449	56	127	14	81	283	316	448	764	5	88	0.41	4	10	35	165	4.75
2012	AAA	Iowa	415	54	126	17	68	304	351	513	864	7	81	0.39	6	3	40	210	6.04
2012	MLB	Chicago	99	7	12	2	5	121	179	202	381	7	67	0.21	2	0	33	81	

Was having his best season since '08, but looked abysmal when called up. Continued to put the bat on the ball in the minors, but does not walk enough. Uses a short, compact stroke and can drive the ball when he squares it up, but needs to be more selective. Is still just 22 years old and should get another chance.

Vogelbach, Dan — 3 — Chicago (N)

EXP MLB DEBUT: 2015 | POTENTIAL: Starting 1B | 9D

Bats R Age 20
2011 (2) HS, FL
Pwr ++++
BAvg ++++
Spd +
Def ++

Year	Lev	Team	AB	R	H	HR	RBI	Avg	OB	Slg	OPS	bb%	ct%	Eye	SB	CS	x/h%	Iso	RC/G
2011	Rk	Cubs	24	4	7	1	6	292	346	542	888	8	92	1.00	1	0	57	250	6.41
2012	Rk	Cubs	102	16	33	7	31	324	395	686	1081	11	86	0.86	1	0	64	363	8.78
2012	A-	Boise	143	23	46	10	31	322	416	608	1024	14	76	0.68	0	1	43	287	8.52

Lost 40 pounds in the off-season and came into camp hitting the ball all over the place. Has the best raw power in the system and showed better than anticipated plate discipline. Quick left-handed stroke allows him to make hard and consistent contact. Size and lack of speed limit him to 1B but the bat is for real.

Vollmuth, B.A. — 5 — Oakland

EXP MLB DEBUT: 2014 | POTENTIAL: Starting 3B | 7C

Bats R Age 23
2011 (3) Southern Miss
Pwr ++++
BAvg ++
Spd ++
Def ++

Year	Lev	Team	AB	R	H	HR	RBI	Avg	OB	Slg	OPS	bb%	ct%	Eye	SB	CS	x/h%	Iso	RC/G
2011	NCAA	So Mississippi	219	48	66	12	49	301	402	548	950	14	73	0.62	2	0	41	247	7.81
2011	Rk	Athletics	27	3	4	1	2	148	233	259	493	10	78	0.50	0	0	25	111	1.39
2011	A-	Vermont	14	8	7	0	6	500	563	929	1491	13	79	0.67	0	1	71	429	15.26
2012	A	Burlington	265	37	69	7	44	260	333	411	745	10	72	0.39	7	1	36	151	4.87
2012	A+	Stockton	264	45	69	7	29	261	330	398	728	9	73	0.39	0	2	32	136	4.55

Tall, strong INF who consistently produced on two levels in solid overall season. Lack of contact hinders BA development and he doesn't run well. Best tool is power. Has lots of loft and leverage in strong swing to produce above avg pop to all fields. Has good instincts for game and bat should get him to majors.

Walding, Mitch — 6 — Philadelphia

EXP MLB DEBUT: 2015 | POTENTIAL: Backup 3B | 6D

Bats L Age 20
2011 (5) HS, CA
Pwr ++
BAvg ++
Spd ++
Def ++

Year	Lev	Team	AB	R	H	HR	RBI	Avg	OB	Slg	OPS	bb%	ct%	Eye	SB	CS	x/h%	Iso	RC/G
2012	A-	Williamsport	253	33	59	1	31	233	317	308	625	11	74	0.47	5	2	24	75	3.35

Athletic, two-sport start in HS did not make his pro debut until this year. Struggled with the long lay-off, but was considered a pure hitter when drafted. Played 3B in his debut and has good bat speed and makes solid contact so he should develop at least moderate power as he matures. Will need to show more in '13.

Waldrop, Kyle — 9 — Cincinnati

EXP MLB DEBUT: 2015 | POTENTIAL: Backup RF | 7D

Bats L Age 21
2010 (12) HS, FL
Pwr ++
BAvg ++
Spd +++
Def +++

Year	Lev	Team	AB	R	H	HR	RBI	Avg	OB	Slg	OPS	bb%	ct%	Eye	SB	CS	x/h%	Iso	RC/G
2010	Rk	Reds	28	1	6	0	1	214	241	250	491	3	68	0.11	0	0	17	36	1.11
2011	Rk	Billings	278	38	76	5	29	273	299	471	770	3	77	0.15	4	4	47	198	4.96
2012	A	Dayton	416	59	118	8	50	284	344	421	764	8	81	0.49	10	6	30	137	5.00

Good all-around prospect has a smooth LH stroke, makes decent contact, and has the potential to develop moderate power. Has good speed, plays solid defense, and has a strong throwing arm. Needs better plate discipline and might not stick in CF, but should have the power needed to play a corner slot.

Walker, Adam — 9 — Minnesota

EXP MLB DEBUT: 2015 | POTENTIAL: Starting OF | 8E

Bats R Age 21
2012 (3) Jacksonville
Pwr ++++
BAvg ++
Spd +++
Def ++

Year	Lev	Team	AB	R	H	HR	RBI	Avg	OB	Slg	OPS	bb%	ct%	Eye	SB	CS	x/h%	Iso	RC/G
2012	Rk	Elizabethton	232	44	58	14	45	250	307	496	802	8	67	0.25	4	0	43	246	5.60

Tall, powerful OF with very exciting power potential and decent athleticism for size. Runs well and should be able to stick in RF despite fringe-avg arm. BA doesn't project as he chases breaking pitches out of zone. Could become middle of order run producer with better approach and will likely advance steadily.

Walker, Christian — 3 — Baltimore

EXP MLB DEBUT: 2014 | POTENTIAL: Starting 1B | 8D

Bats R Age 22
2012 (4) South Carolina
Pwr +++
BAvg ++++
Spd +
Def ++

Year	Lev	Team	AB	R	H	HR	RBI	Avg	OB	Slg	OPS	bb%	ct%	Eye	SB	CS	x/h%	Iso	RC/G
2010	NCAA	South Carolina	226	35	74	9	51	327	377	518	895	7	92	1.00	2	1	31	190	6.38
2011	NCAA	South Carolina	271	64	97	10	62	358	433	554	987	12	89	1.20	4	3	33	196	7.76
2012	NCAA	South Carolina	240	48	77	11	55	321	440	525	965	18	90	2.13	3	2	32	204	7.86
2012	A-	Aberdeen	81	12	23	2	9	284	363	420	782	11	83	0.71	2	1	30	136	5.33

Strong, instinctual hitter who focuses on hard line drives to gaps. Strike zone awareness is strength and controls bat for above avg contact. Should hit for BA while avg, raw power develops. Limited to 1B where stiff hands and feet can be hidden. Lacks speed to steal bases, but hitting tool enough to give him value.

Walker, Keenyn — 78 — Chicago (A)

EXP MLB DEBUT: 2015 | POTENTIAL: Starting OF | 8C

Bats B Age 22
2011 (1-S) Central AZ JC
Pwr ++
BAvg +++
Spd ++++
Def ++++

Year	Lev	Team	AB	R	H	HR	RBI	Avg	OB	Slg	OPS	bb%	ct%	Eye	SB	CS	x/h%	Iso	RC/G
2011	NCAA	Central AZ	53	9	22	0	13	415	466	547	1013	9	85	0.63	1	0	27	132	8.10
2011	Rk	Great Falls	60	16	20	0	9	333	403	483	886	10	72	0.41	11	5	40	150	7.16
2011	A	Kannapolis	162	25	37	0	15	228	290	259	549	8	60	0.22	10	4	8	31	2.16
2012	A	Kannapolis	266	53	75	1	39	282	396	387	783	16	65	0.54	39	11	28	105	6.08
2012	A+	Winston-Salem	143	31	34	3	16	238	347	364	711	14	65	0.48	17	4	32	126	4.74

Exciting OF with terrific plus speed and ability to impact game with legs. Works counts and draws BB which bodes well for high SB totals while BA positively affected by infield hits. Keeps ball on ground and offers gap power. Profiles as leadoff hitter, but swings and misses often. Offers plus range and arm in CF.

Walsh, Colin

4 | **St. Louis** | EXP MLB DEBUT: 2015 | POTENTIAL: Starting 3B | **7C**

Bats B Age 23
2010 (13) Stanford
Pwr + + +
BAvg + + +
Spd + +
Def + +

Year	Lev	Team	AB	R	H	HR	RBI	Avg	OB	Slg	OPS	bb%	ct%	Eye	SB	CS	x/h%	Iso	RC/G
2010	A	Quad Cities	98	15	21	2	6	214	347	337	684	17	80	1.00	5	1	29	122	4.40
2010	A-	Batavia	90	20	27	2	12	300	411	433	845	16	84	1.21	2	1	26	133	6.42
2011	A	Quad Cities	230	36	55	4	29	239	359	378	737	16	81	1.00	6	2	42	139	5.10
2012	Rk	GCL Cardinals	8	1	1	0	1	125	125	125	250	0	88	0.00	0	0	0	0	
2012	A	Quad Cities	353	69	111	16	68	314	414	530	944	15	82	0.92	4	3	35	215	7.48

22-year-old switch hitter had a nice breakout, including a career best 16 HR. Was a bit old for the MWL and spent time at a variety of positions, including LF, DH, 1B, 3B, and 2B. Has good bat speed and controls the strike zone well. Has below-average speed and defense, but he can definitely hit.

Washington, LeVon

78 | **Cleveland** | EXP MLB DEBUT: 2015 | POTENTIAL: Starting CF | **7D**

Bats L Age 21
2010 (2) Chipola JC
Pwr +
BAvg + +
Spd + + + +
Def + + +

Year	Lev	Team	AB	R	H	HR	RBI	Avg	OB	Slg	OPS	bb%	ct%	Eye	SB	CS	x/h%	Iso	RC/G
2010	Rk	Indians	9	0	4	0	3	444	583	444	1028	25	89	3.00	1	0	0	0	9.38
2011	A	Lake County	298	35	65	4	20	218	329	315	644	14	70	0.55	15	6	26	97	3.67
2012	Rk	Indians	9	3	4	0	2	444	500	444	944	10	78	0.50	1	0	0	0	7.36
2012	A	Lake County	25	8	11	0	1	440	548	480	1028	19	68	0.75	0	3	9	40	9.84
2012	A+	Carolina	14	2	1	0	1	71	133	71	205	7	79	0.33	0	0	0	0	-2.17

Ultra athletic OF who missed most of season after undergoing hip surgery. Injuries have limited him in three seasons, though has exciting package of tools. Above avg bat speed could allow him to hit for BA if he closes holes in swing. Will likely never hit for much power. Has range due to plus speed, but a below avg arm.

Wates, Austin

78 | **Houston** | EXP MLB DEBUT: 2013 | POTENTIAL: Starting CF | **7C**

Bats R Age 24
2010 (3) Virginia Tech
Pwr + +
BAvg + + +
Spd + + + +
Def + + +

Year	Lev	Team	AB	R	H	HR	RBI	Avg	OB	Slg	OPS	bb%	ct%	Eye	SB	CS	x/h%	Iso	RC/G
2010	Rk	GCL Astros	3	1	0	0	0	0	0	0	0	0	33	0.00	0	0	--	0	
2010	A-	Tri City	38	11	12	1	6	316	435	500	935	17	84	1.33	9	0	33	184	7.65
2011	A+	Lancaster	526	85	158	6	75	300	358	413	770	8	84	0.55	26	7	24	112	5.10
2012	Rk	GCL Astros	9	2	5	1	2	556	556	889	1444	0	78	0.00	0	0	20	333	12.39
2012	AA	Corpus Christi	359	58	109	7	48	304	359	429	788	8	80	0.44	17	11	25	125	5.24

Athletic OF who profiles as top of order hitter with feel for hitting. Lacks leverage and loft in simple, compact stroke and likely won't hit for much power. Goes to opp field frequently and uses speed to leg out 2B Can swing passively and make weak contact. Should be able to stick in CF due to good speed and range.

Wessinger, Matt

4 | **Colorado** | EXP MLB DEBUT: 2015 | POTENTIAL: Backup 2B | **6C**

Bats R Age 22
2012 (5) St. Johns
Pwr + +
BAvg + + +
Spd + +
Def + +

Year	Lev	Team	AB	R	H	HR	RBI	Avg	OB	Slg	OPS	bb%	ct%	Eye	SB	CS	x/h%	Iso	RC/G
2012	Rk	Grand Junction	248	53	68	4	27	274	348	379	727	10	77	0.49	22	8	22	105	4.61

Strong, offensive-minded collegiate INF has a nice bat and had a solid pro debut. Has above-average speed and a nice swing that generates decent power. Is well below average defensively and made 22 errors at short as a senior. Most likely he ends up moving to 2B and he saw action at SS, 3B, and 2B in '12.

Westlake, Aaron

3 | **Detroit** | EXP MLB DEBUT: 2015 | POTENTIAL: Starting 1B | **7C**

Bats L Age 24
2011 (3) Vanderbilt
Pwr + + +
BAvg + + +
Spd +
Def + +

Year	Lev	Team	AB	R	H	HR	RBI	Avg	OB	Slg	OPS	bb%	ct%	Eye	SB	CS	x/h%	Iso	RC/G
2010	NCAA	Vanderbilt	260	66	80	14	61	308	384	538	922	11	82	0.68	6	0	39	231	6.92
2011	NCAA	Vanderbilt	250	59	86	18	56	344	448	640	1088	16	78	0.87	2	5	43	296	9.37
2011	Rk	GCL Tigers	18	2	3	1	4	167	250	389	639	10	67	0.33	0	0	67	222	3.27
2011	A-	Connecticut	106	14	28	2	15	264	328	377	705	9	78	0.43	1	0	25	113	4.23
2012	A	West Michigan	465	56	116	9	69	249	318	391	710	9	77	0.45	4	1	40	142	4.37

Large-frame INF who lacks consistency, but continues to show potential. Hits 2B, but long ball power has been slow to develop. Uses level swing and could add loft for additional pop. Draws BB with disciplined eye, but can be too passive. Hits LHP (.333), but struggled with RHP (.219). OK defender with good hands.

Wheeler, Ryan

3 | **Colorado** | EXP MLB DEBUT: 2012 | POTENTIAL: Starting 1B | **8D**

Bats L Age 24
2009 (5) Loyola
Pwr + + + +
BAvg + +
Spd + +
Def +

Year	Lev	Team	AB	R	H	HR	RBI	Avg	OB	Slg	OPS	bb%	ct%	Eye	SB	CS	x/h%	Iso	RC/G
2010	A+	Visalia	465	62	132	9	57	284	334	404	738	7	79	0.36	3	1	27	120	4.57
2010	AA	Mobile	67	8	17	3	10	254	306	433	738	7	76	0.31	0	0	35	179	4.45
2011	AA	Mobile	480	69	141	16	89	294	354	465	819	9	79	0.44	3	4	34	171	5.63
2012	AAA	Reno	362	56	127	15	90	351	394	572	966	7	81	0.39	3	1	36	221	7.28
2012	MLB	Diamondbacks	109	11	26	1	10	239	297	339	636	8	80	0.41	1	0	31	101	3.40

Offensive-minded player showed solid progress. Worked hard to shorten his stroke and can hit breaking balls to all parts of the field. Not clear that his approach will allow him to hit for both average and power. Stiff and slow on defense with limited range, but the trade creates an opportunity.

Wheeler, Tim

8 | **Colorado** | EXP MLB DEBUT: 2013 | POTENTIAL: Starting CF | **8D**

Bats L Age 25
2009 (1) Cal State
Pwr + + +
BAvg + + +
Spd + + +
Def + + +

Year	Lev	Team	AB	R	H	HR	RBI	Avg	OB	Slg	OPS	bb%	ct%	Eye	SB	CS	x/h%	Iso	RC/G
2009	NCAA	Sacramento St	200	59	77	18	72	385	463	765	1228	13	86	1.04	15	2	48	380	10.50
2009	A-	Tri-City	273	44	70	5	35	256	328	381	709	10	78	0.48	10	4	30	125	4.36
2010	A+	Modesto	510	88	127	12	63	249	328	384	712	11	78	0.53	22	8	31	135	4.42
2011	AA	Tulsa	561	105	161	33	86	287	355	535	890	10	75	0.42	21	12	42	248	6.59
2012	AAA	Colo Springs	379	67	115	2	37	303	353	412	765	7	82	0.42	7	7	29	108	5.00

Had an odd season. Suffered a hand injury in April and missed two months of action. When he returned, he hit the ball well, but without any power. After hitting 33 home runs in '11, he hit just 2 in '12. Has good size and moderate speed, but is unlikely to be able to stick in CF so power needs to return to have value.

White, Max

8 | **Colorado** | EXP MLB DEBUT: 2016 | POTENTIAL: Backup CF | **7D**

Bats L Age 19
2012 (2) HS, FL
Pwr +
BAvg + +
Spd + + +
Def + + +

Year	Lev	Team	AB	R	H	HR	RBI	Avg	OB	Slg	OPS	bb%	ct%	Eye	SB	CS	x/h%	Iso	RC/G
2012	Rk	Grand Junction	170	30	34	4	18	200	317	335	652	15	58	0.40	6	5	35	135	4.05

Lean, athletic CF with a nice LH stroke. Has above-average speed, but stole just 6 bases. Has good bat speed and should develop at least average power once he matures. Has good raw tools, but is very much a work in progress and struggled in his debut, hitting just .200 with 72 strikeouts in 170 AB.

Wilkins, Andy

3 | **Chicago (A)** | EXP MLB DEBUT: 2013 | POTENTIAL: Backup 1B | **7C**

Bats L Age 24
2010 (5) Arkansas
Pwr + + + +
BAvg + +
Spd +
Def + +

Year	Lev	Team	AB	R	H	HR	RBI	Avg	OB	Slg	OPS	bb%	ct%	Eye	SB	CS	x/h%	Iso	RC/G
2009	NCAA	Arkansas	235	53	75	19	58	319	435	638	1073	17	78	0.94	8	1	49	319	9.19
2010	NCAA	Arkansas	235	49	66	15	69	281	394	540	935	16	81	1.00	4	1	45	260	7.33
2010	Rk	Great Falls	218	37	67	6	40	307	398	463	862	13	86	1.06	7	2	31	156	6.44
2011	A+	Winston-Salem	493	72	137	23	89	278	352	485	836	10	82	0.62	2	2	41	207	5.86
2012	AA	Birmingham	435	68	104	17	69	239	335	425	761	13	78	0.67	6	4	44	186	5.09

Power-hitting INF who continues to fly under radar despite strength and plus power to all fields. Pop generated by pure strength as opposed to avg bat speed. Makes good contact for profile and has discerning eye. Struggles against LHP (.223) may make platoon an option, but has below avg secondary skills.

Williams, Everett

8 | **San Diego** | EXP MLB DEBUT: 2013 | POTENTIAL: Starting CF | **7D**

Bats L Age 22
2009 (2) HS, TX
Pwr + +
BAvg + +
Spd + + + +
Def + + + +

Year	Lev	Team	AB	R	H	HR	RBI	Avg	OB	Slg	OPS	bb%	ct%	Eye	SB	CS	x/h%	Iso	RC/G
2009	Rk	Padres	18	1	7	0	6	389	421	611	1032	5	61	0.14	2	1	43	222	10.30
2009	A-	Eugene	25	1	5	1	3	200	310	400	710	14	56	0.36	0	0	60	200	5.12
2010	A	Fort Wayne	390	53	95	5	59	244	331	372	703	12	66	0.39	10	5	37	128	4.58
2011	A	Fort Wayne	20	5	6	0	1	300	364	300	664	9	85	0.67	3	0	0	0	3.83
2012	A+	Lake Elsinore	397	38	96	5	50	242	292	363	654	7	72	0.25	9	4	35	121	3.57

Was fully recovered from ACL tear, but struggled to hit in the CAL. Does have some nice tools, highlighted by plus speed and raw power. Can be overly aggressive and needs to make more contact. Has the potential to develop into one of the better power/speed prospects in the NL, but has some work to do.

Williams, Mason

8 | **New York (A)** | EXP MLB DEBUT: 2015 | POTENTIAL: Starting OF | **8B**

Bats L Age 21
2010 (4) HS (FL)
Pwr + + +
BAvg + + + +
Spd + + + +
Def + + + +

Year	Lev	Team	AB	R	H	HR	RBI	Avg	OB	Slg	OPS	bb%	ct%	Eye	SB	CS	x/h%	Iso	RC/G
2010	Rk	GCL Yankees	18	0	4	0	0	222	263	222	485	5	78	0.25	1	2	0	0	1.24
2011	A-	Staten Island	269	42	94	3	31	349	394	468	863	7	85	0.49	28	12	21	119	6.11
2012	A	Charleston (Sc)	276	55	84	8	28	304	354	489	843	7	88	0.64	19	9	37	185	5.85
2012	A+	Tampa	83	13	23	3	7	277	302	422	724	3	83	0.21	1	4	26	145	4.08

Athletic OF whose season ended after surgery to repair torn labrum. Injury doesn't diminish prospect status because of excellent tools. Offers strength in lean frame and has plus bat speed and BA potential. Makes easy contact with short, quick swing and can reach fences. Plus-plus speed enhances defense.

Williams, Nick — 7 — Texas

EXP MLB DEBUT: 2017 | POTENTIAL: Starting OF | 7C

Bats L Age 19 — 2012 (2) HS (TX)
Pwr +++ | BAvg ++ | Spd +++ | Def ++

Year	Lev	Team	AB	R	H	HR	RBI	Avg	OB	Slg	OPS	bb%	ct%	Eye	SB	CS	x/h%	Iso	RC/G
2012	Rk	Rangers	201	34	63	2	27	313	364	448	812	7	75	0.32	15	2	27	134	5.70

Tall, raw OF who exceeded expectations. Very crude defensively and he'll need time to develop instincts for routes and reads. Has good speed for range, though arm limits him to LF. Showed advanced ability to hit LHP (.370) with plus bat speed and natural strength. Needs to hang in against good breaking pitches.

Williamson, Mac — 9 — San Francisco

EXP MLB DEBUT: 2015 | POTENTIAL: Starting RF | 7C

Bats R Age 22 — 2012 (3) Wake Forest
Pwr +++ | BAvg +++ | Spd ++ | Def ++

Year	Lev	Team	AB	R	H	HR	RBI	Avg	OB	Slg	OPS	bb%	ct%	Eye	SB	CS	x/h%	Iso	RC/G
2010	NCAA	Wake Forest	179	29	50	7	37	279	335	464	799	8	70	0.28	12	6	36	184	5.53
2011	NCAA	Wake Forest	205	33	56	12	49	273	352	493	845	11	72	0.43	11	3	38	220	6.11
2012	NCAA	Wake Forest	192	42	55	17	52	286	363	589	951	11	79	0.56	12	3	44	302	7.14
2012	Rk	Giants	17	4	3	2	7	176	263	529	793	11	71	0.40	0	0	67	353	5.02
2012	A-	Salem-Keizer	114	22	39	7	25	342	375	596	971	5	83	0.32	0	0	38	254	7.06

Tall, strong collegiate OF had an impressive debut. Has a quick bat, raw power, and good speed. Can be overly aggressive at the plate, but showed decent pitch recognition and has the potential to hit for power and average with a bit of speed. He is a good defender with a plus arm and covers ground well in RF.

Winker, Jesse — 7 — Cincinnati

EXP MLB DEBUT: 2016 | POTENTIAL: Starting LF | 8D

Bats L Age 19 — 2012 (1-S) HS, FL
Pwr +++ | BAvg +++ | Spd ++ | Def ++

Year	Lev	Team	AB	R	H	HR	RBI	Avg	OB	Slg	OPS	bb%	ct%	Eye	SB	CS	x/h%	Iso	RC/G
2012	Rk	Billings	228	42	77	5	35	338	437	500	937	15	78	0.80	1	3	31	162	7.64

Has good size and a feel for squaring the ball up. Uses good bat speed and plus strike zone judgment to hunt for pitches he can drive. Has a nice, balanced swing that generates good loft and carry and he should add power as he matures. Is a below average runner with an average arm. Had an excellent pro debut.

Wisdom, Patrick — 5 — St. Louis

EXP MLB DEBUT: 2015 | POTENTIAL: Starting 3B | 8D

Bats R Age 21 — 2012 (1) St. Marys
Pwr +++ | BAvg ++ | Spd ++ | Def +++

Year	Lev	Team	AB	R	H	HR	RBI	Avg	OB	Slg	OPS	bb%	ct%	Eye	SB	CS	x/h%	Iso	RC/G
2010	NCAA	St. Mary's (CA)	186	37	54	12	39	290	359	543	902	10	77	0.48	3	2	43	253	6.64
2011	NCAA	St. Mary's (CA)	208	33	73	8	46	351	416	553	968	10	80	0.56	5	2	34	202	7.57
2012	NCAA	St. Mary's (CA)	191	39	50	9	24	262	382	476	858	16	77	0.86	4	2	44	215	6.51
2012	A-	Batavia	241	40	68	6	32	282	364	465	829	11	76	0.53	2	1	40	183	6.07

Works hard to get the most of his tools and looked just fine in his debut. A supplemental 1st round pick in '12 out of St. Mary's, he has a good all-around game. Has average bat speed, moderate power, and decent plate discipline. Has good athleticism, but is a below-average runner and is limited to a corner OF slot.

Witherspoon, Travis — 8 — Los Angeles (A)

EXP MLB DEBUT: 2014 | POTENTIAL: Starting OF | 8D

Bats R Age 24 — 2009 (12) Spartanburg
Pwr +++ | BAvg ++ | Spd ++++ | Def ++++

Year	Lev	Team	AB	R	H	HR	RBI	Avg	OB	Slg	OPS	bb%	ct%	Eye	SB	CS	x/h%	Iso	RC/G
2010	Rk	Orem	288	57	89	10	45	309	362	472	834	8	75	0.33	20	0	27	163	5.84
2011	A	Cedar Rapids	404	60	99	12	42	245	307	394	700	8	75	0.35	44	9	32	149	4.12
2011	A+	Inland Empire	68	15	19	1	10	279	329	382	711	7	79	0.36	2	2	26	103	4.23
2012	A+	Inland Empire	270	52	86	7	27	319	393	470	863	11	81	0.63	25	7	26	152	6.34
2012	AA	Arkansas	208	28	42	6	21	202	284	351	635	10	74	0.44	9	4	40	149	3.35

Athletic, quick OF with multitude of tools, led by plus CF defense and above average speed. Tied career high in HR, though doesn't project as middle of order threat. Showed improved selectivity and OBP with smoother stroke. Still some length in swing and can be pull-conscious when trying to hit HR.

Wolters, Tony — 46 — Cleveland

EXP MLB DEBUT: 2015 | POTENTIAL: Starting 2B | 7C

Bats L Age 21 — 2010 (3) HS (CA)
Pwr ++ | BAvg +++ | Spd ++ | Def +++

Year	Lev	Team	AB	R	H	HR	RBI	Avg	OB	Slg	OPS	bb%	ct%	Eye	SB	CS	x/h%	Iso	RC/G
2010	Rk	Indians	19	2	4	0	3	211	286	211	496	10	74	0.40	2	0	0	0	1.44
2011	A-	Mahoning Val	267	50	78	1	20	292	364	363	727	10	82	0.61	19	4	18	71	4.68
2012	A+	Carolina	485	66	126	8	58	260	311	404	715	7	79	0.35	5	9	37	144	4.35

Short, polished INF who bypassed Low-A. Set career high in HR and shows advanced approach by working counts and focusing on line drives to all fields. Puts bat to ball with ease, but below avg power limits upside. Played both SS and 2B with quick hands and strong, accurate arm, but likely targeted for 2B.

Wong, Kolten — 4 — St. Louis

EXP MLB DEBUT: 2014 | POTENTIAL: Starting 2B | 8B

Bats L Age 22 — 2011 (1) Hawaii
Pwr ++ | BAvg +++ | Spd +++ | Def +++

Year	Lev	Team	AB	R	H	HR	RBI	Avg	OB	Slg	OPS	bb%	ct%	Eye	SB	CS	x/h%	Iso	RC/G
2009	NCAA	Hawaii	226	46	77	11	52	341	406	597	1004	10	90	1.09	11	4	44	257	7.80
2010	NCAA	Hawaii	249	57	89	7	40	357	439	534	973	13	92	1.80	19	7	29	177	7.71
2011	NCAA	Hawaii	209	48	79	7	53	378	482	560	1042	17	90	2.10	23	7	27	182	8.77
2011	A	Quad Cities	194	39	65	5	25	335	400	510	910	10	88	0.88	9	5	34	175	6.81
2012	AA	Springfield	523	79	150	9	52	287	342	405	748	8	86	0.59	21	11	25	119	4.78

Has quickly developed into one of the best 2B prospects. Skipped over High-A and he responded with a solid season. Uses a short, compact LH stroke to get surprising power. He has a disciplined eye and is a good situational hitter. Is a passable defender with a good arm and average speed.

Wright, Ryan — 4 — Cincinnati

EXP MLB DEBUT: 2014 | POTENTIAL: Starting 2B | 7C

Bats R Age 23 — 2011 (5) Louisville
Pwr ++ | BAvg ++ | Spd +++ | Def +++

Year	Lev	Team	AB	R	H	HR	RBI	Avg	OB	Slg	OPS	bb%	ct%	Eye	SB	CS	x/h%	Iso	RC/G
2011	NCAA	Louisville	234	49	81	12	52	346	427	598	1025	12	86	1.03	16	2	38	252	8.24
2011	Rk	Billings	161	28	48	7	32	298	335	522	857	5	83	0.33	6	1	42	224	5.84
2011	Rk	Reds	22	4	7	1	5	318	318	636	955	0	77	0.00	1	2	57	318	7.04
2012	A	Dayton	389	53	111	5	50	285	340	424	764	8	87	0.63	14	1	34	139	5.04
2012	A+	Bakersfield	96	17	26	5	16	271	286	521	807	2	82	0.12	3	1	46	250	5.03

Offensive-minded 2B continues to hit and gets the most of his abilities. Does not have a ton of raw power, but did hit 32 2B and 10 home runs. Has good strike zone judgment and a short, compact stroke. Puts the ball into play and uses his average speed well. Has good instincts on defense.

Yarbrough, Alex — 4 — Los Angeles (A)

EXP MLB DEBUT: 2015 | POTENTIAL: Starting 2B | 7B

Bats B Age 21 — 2012 (4) Mississippi
Pwr ++ | BAvg +++ | Spd ++ | Def +++

Year	Lev	Team	AB	R	H	HR	RBI	Avg	OB	Slg	OPS	bb%	ct%	Eye	SB	CS	x/h%	Iso	RC/G
2010	NCAA	Mississippi	240	39	68	4	41	283	333	413	746	7	78	0.35	4	4	29	129	4.71
2011	NCAA	Mississippi	214	49	75	7	38	350	409	542	951	9	87	0.78	4	1	32	192	7.18
2012	NCAA	Mississippi	250	43	95	3	43	380	430	508	938	8	90	0.92	4	0	24	128	7.03
2012	A	Cedar Rapids	244	35	70	0	27	287	315	410	725	4	92	0.50	9	2	30	123	4.53
2012	AA	Arkansas	18	1	2	0	0	111	111	167	278	0	83	0.00	0	0	50	56	

Patient, versatile INF with limited ceiling, but is safe bet. Plays game with intelligence and maximizes tools. Profiles to doubles power, but has plus bat control and above average hand-eye coordination. Level swing makes ideal contact and has professional approach. Makes plays at 2B with quick hands and avg arm.

Yelich, Christian — 8 — Miami

EXP MLB DEBUT: 2013 | POTENTIAL: Starting CF | 9C

Bats L Age 21 — 2010 (1) HS, CA
Pwr +++ | BAvg ++++ | Spd +++ | Def ++++

Year	Lev	Team	AB	R	H	HR	RBI	Avg	OB	Slg	OPS	bb%	ct%	Eye	SB	CS	x/h%	Iso	RC/G
2010	Rk	GCL Marlins	24	3	9	0	3	375	423	500	923	8	71	0.29	1	0	22	125	7.51
2010	A	Greensboro	23	2	8	0	2	348	375	435	810	4	74	0.17	0	0	25	87	5.52
2011	A	Greensboro	461	73	144	15	77	312	386	484	869	11	78	0.54	32	5	33	171	6.42
2012	Rk	GCL Marlins	4	0	1	0	0	250	250	250	500	0	100	0.00	0	0	0	0	2.09
2012	A+	Jupiter	397	76	131	12	48	330	404	519	922	11	79	0.58	20	6	35	189	7.16

Projectable CF is quickly developing into an elite prospect. Makes consistent, hard contact with lots of line drives and emerging power. Advanced approach at the plate and short compact LH stroke fueled his breakout. Plus speed gives him above-average range in CF and the potential to develop into a 20/20 player.

Zunino, Mike — 2 — Seattle

EXP MLB DEBUT: 2013 | POTENTIAL: Starting C | 9B

Bats R Age 22 — 2012 (1) Florida
Pwr ++++ | BAvg ++++ | Spd ++ | Def +++

Year	Lev	Team	AB	R	H	HR	RBI	Avg	OB	Slg	OPS	bb%	ct%	Eye	SB	CS	x/h%	Iso	RC/G
2010	NCAA	Florida	176	31	47	9	41	267	303	472	774	5	78	0.24	8	3	36	205	4.76
2011	NCAA	Florida	264	75	98	19	67	371	439	674	1113	11	80	0.62	7	2	43	303	9.29
2012	NCAA	Florida	245	53	79	19	67	322	399	669	1068	11	81	0.66	9	1	59	347	8.75
2012	AA	Jackson	51	6	17	3	8	333	393	588	981	9	86	0.71	0	0	41	255	7.42
2012	A-	Everett	110	29	41	10	35	373	461	736	1197	14	76	0.69	1	0	49	364	10.75

Big, strong C who could reach SEA early in '13. Has potential to become middle of order run producer with plus power and high BA. Has excellent feel for hitting with above avg bat speed. Can shorten swing when needed and go to opp field. Has improved receiving to go along with above avg catch-and-throw skills.

PITCHERS

Pitchers are classified as Starters (SP) or Relievers (RP).

THROWS: Handedness — right (RH) or left (LH).

AGE: Pitcher's age, as of April 1, 2013.

DRAFTED: The year, round, and school that the pitcher performed at as an amateur if drafted, or the year and country where the player was signed from, if a free agent.

EXP MLB DEBUT: The year a player is expected to debut in the major leagues.

PROJ ROLE: The role that the pitcher is expected to have for the majority of his major league career, not necessarily his greatest upside.

PITCHES: Each pitch that a pitcher throws is graded and designated with a "+", indicating the quality of the pitch, taking into context the pitcher's age and level pitched. Pitches are graded for their velocity, movement, and command. An average pitch will receive three "+" marks. If known, a pitcher's velocity for each pitch is indicated.

FB	fastball
CB	curveball
SP	split-fingered fastball
SL	slider
CU	change-up
CT	cut-fastball
KC	knuckle-curve
KB	knuckle-ball
SC	screwball
SU	slurve

PLAYER STAT LINES: Pitchers receive statistics for the last five teams that they played for (if applicable), including college and the major leagues.

TEAM DESIGNATIONS: Each team that the pitcher performed for during a given year is included.

LEVEL DESIGNATIONS: The level for each team a player performed is included. "AAA" means Triple-A, "AA" means Double-A, "A+" means high Class-A, "A-" means low Class-A and "Rk" means rookie level.

SABERMETRIC CATEGORIES: Descriptions of all the sabermetric categories appear in the glossary.

CAPSULE COMMENTARIES: For each pitcher, a brief analysis of their skills/statistics, and their future potential is provided.

ELIGIBILITY: Eligibility for inclusion is the standard for which Major League Baseball adheres to; 50 innings pitched or 45 days on the 25-man roster, not including the month of September.

POTENTIAL RATINGS: The Potential Ratings are a two-part system in which a player is assigned a number rating based on his upside potential (1-10) and a letter rating based on the probability of reaching that potential (A-E).

Potential

10:	Hall of Famer	5:	MLB reserve
9:	Elite player	4:	Top minor leaguer
8:	Solid regular	3:	Average minor leaguer
7:	Average regular	2:	Minor league reserve
6:	Platoon player	1:	Minor league roster filler

Probability Rating

A: 90% probability of reaching potential
B: 70% probability of reaching potential
C: 50% probability of reaching potential
D: 30% probability of reaching potential
E: 10% probability of reaching potential

FASTBALL: Scouts grade a fastball in terms of both velocity and movement. Movement of a pitch is purely subjective, but one can always watch the hitter to see how he reacts to a pitch or if he swings and misses. Pitchers throw four types of fastballs with varying movement. A two-seam fastball is often referred to as a sinker. A four-seam fastball appears to maintain its plane at high velocities. A cutter can move in different directions and is caused by the pitcher both cutting-off his extension out front and by varying the grip. A split-fingered fastball (forkball) is thrown with the fingers spread apart against the seams and demonstrates violent downward movement. Velocity is often graded on the 20-80 scale and is indicated by the chart below.

Scout Grade	Velocity (mph)
80	96+
70	94-95
60	92-93
50 (avg)	89-91
40	87-88
30	85-86
20	82-84

PITCHER RELEASE TIMES: The speed (in seconds) that a pitcher releases a pitch from the stretch is extremely important in terms of halting the running game and establishing good pitching mechanics. Pitchers are timed from the movement of the front leg until the baseball reaches the catcher's mitt. The phrases "slow to the plate" or "quick to the plate" may often appear in the capsule commentary box.

1.0-1.2	+
1.3-1.4	MLB average
1.5+	−

Adam, Jason — SP — Kansas City
EXP MLB DEBUT: 2014 | POTENTIAL: #3 starter | 8D

Thrws R Age 21
2010 (5) HS (KS)

88-94	FB	+ + +
76-81	CB	+ + +
80-84	CU	+ +

Year	Lev	Team	W	L	Sv	IP	K	ERA	WHIP	BF/G	OBA	H%	S%	xERA	Ctl	Dom	Cmd	hr/9	BPV
2011	A	Kane County	6	9	0	104	76	4.23	1.14	19.7	242	28	64	3.16	2.2	6.6	3.0	0.8	78
2012	A+	Wilmington	7	12	0	158	123	3.53	1.16	23.3	249	29	73	3.55	2.1	7.0	3.4	1.0	89

Tall, powerful SP who finished 3rd in CAR in Ks. Has ideal frame and arm action, but pitches to contact and throws quality strikes. Velocity varies and needs to repeat arm speed to improve CU. Commands FB to both sides of plate and can drop good CB into zone. Could grow into more velocity in time.

Adams, Austin — SP — Cleveland
EXP MLB DEBUT: 2014 | POTENTIAL: #4 starter/Setup reliever | 7C

Thrws R Age 26
2009 (5) Faulkner

90-98	FB	+ + + +
81-83	SL	+ +
80-82	CB	+ + +
	CU	+ +

Year	Lev	Team	W	L	Sv	IP	K	ERA	WHIP	BF/G	OBA	H%	S%	xERA	Ctl	Dom	Cmd	hr/9	BPV
2009	A-	Mahoning Val	3	1	1	37	29	4.86	1.46	9.3	272	32	68	4.55	3.6	7.1	1.9	1.0	46
2010	A	Lake County	2	4	1	53	61	3.54	1.14	16.3	210	27	74	3.11	3.5	10.3	2.9	1.2	108
2010	A+	Kinston	6	1	0	59	51	1.53	1.11	17.7	232	28	92	2.93	2.3	7.8	3.4	0.8	97
2011	AA	Akron	11	10	0	136	131	3.77	1.54	22.8	277	36	75	4.28	4.2	8.7	2.1	0.4	61
2012		Did not pitch																	

Small, power-armed pitcher who did not pitch all season due to shoulder surgery. May take time for plus FB to return. Throws with compact delivery and arm speed and may slow down tempo. Exhibits athleticism, but has tendency to overthrow. CB is best secondary and CU needs to develop to stick as starter.

Agosta, Martin — SP — San Francisco
EXP MLB DEBUT: 2016 | POTENTIAL: #5 starter | 7C

Thrws R Age 22
2012 (2) St. Mary's

90-93	FB	+ + +
	SL	+ +
83-85	CT	+ + +
	CU	+

Year	Lev	Team	W	L	Sv	IP	K	ERA	WHIP	BF/G	OBA	H%	S%	xERA	Ctl	Dom	Cmd	hr/9	BPV
2012	Rk	Giants	0	0	0	11	19	4.22	1.59	9.4	210	42	71	3.08	7.6	16.0	2.1	0.0	102

Short, collegiate right-hander has a 90-92 mph fastball that tops out at 96 mph. Best offering is a mid-80s cutter and mixes in a decent breaking ball and a show-me change-up. Had mixed results in pro debut, striking out 16 per nine, but also walking 7.6 per nine. Small stature and inconsistent velocity make a move to the pen likely down the road.

Alcantara, Raul — SP — Oakland
EXP MLB DEBUT: 2015 | POTENTIAL: #3 starter | 8D

Thrws R Age 20
2009 FA (DR)

88-95	FB	+ + +
77-80	SL	+ + +
81-84	CU	+ +

Year	Lev	Team	W	L	Sv	IP	K	ERA	WHIP	BF/G	OBA	H%	S%	xERA	Ctl	Dom	Cmd	hr/9	BPV
2011	Rk	GCL Red Sox	1	1	0	48	36	0.75	0.60	18.3	145	19	86	0.04	1.1	6.8	6.0	0.0	109
2011	A-	Lowell	0	3	0	17	14	6.23	1.79	20.0	338	42	61	5.50	3.1	7.3	2.3	0.0	65
2012	A	Burlington	6	11	0	103	57	5.08	1.53	16.5	291	32	68	5.10	3.3	5.0	1.5	1.1	18

Tall, lean SP who moved to pen to iron out mechanical difficulties, but will return to rotation. Has high ceiling based upon power arsenal and approach. FB has potential for more velo and hard SL can register Ks. Needs to refine CU and FB command. Low K rate is concern, though has natural stuff.

Alderson, Tim — SP — Pittsburgh
EXP MLB DEBUT: 2013 | POTENTIAL: #5 starter | 6D

Thrws R Age 24
2007 (1-C) HS, AZ

88-92	FB	+ +
78-81	CB	+ +
80-82	CU	+ +

Year	Lev	Team	W	L	Sv	IP	K	ERA	WHIP	BF/G	OBA	H%	S%	xERA	Ctl	Dom	Cmd	hr/9	BPV
2010	A+	Bradenton	4	3	0	39	25	6.98	1.55	18.8	301	33	55	5.40	3.0	5.8	1.9	1.2	41
2010	AA	Altoona	7	6	0	90	59	5.62	1.55	21.8	307	34	64	5.34	2.7	5.9	2.2	1.0	51
2011	AA	Altoona	0	4	0	74	57	4.12	1.30	7.3	250	30	69	3.63	3.3	6.9	2.1	0.7	54
2012	AA	Altoona	5	4	3	85	62	4.25	1.36	13.6	272	32	69	4.08	2.8	6.6	2.4	0.7	62
2012	AAA	Indianapolis	0	0	0	4	4	4.50	1.75	9.1	307	35	83	6.98	4.5	9.0	2.0	2.3	59

Tall, thin hurler has not lived up to his 1st round status. Had fringy fastball when drafted and loss of velocity since then doomed him as a starter. Showed decent control at AA, but struck out just 6.6 per nine while making 11 starts and 15 relief appearances. Is still just 23 and could make his MLB debut in 2013, but looks like nothing more than a reliever now.

Allen, Cody — RP — Cleveland
EXP MLB DEBUT: 2012 | POTENTIAL: Closer | 7B

Thrws R Age 24
2011 (23) High Point

91-97	FB	+ + + +
82-86	CB	+ + +
82-85	CU	+

Year	Lev	Team	W	L	Sv	IP	K	ERA	WHIP	BF/G	OBA	H%	S%	xERA	Ctl	Dom	Cmd	hr/9	BPV
2011	AA	Akron	0	0	0	1	2	18.00	3.00	5.8	515	79	33	12.58	0.0	18.0		0.0	342
2012	A+	Carolina	0	0	0	4	8	0.00	0.25	6.1	81	23	100	0.00	0.0	18.0		0.0	342
2012	AA	Akron	0	0	1	8	10	1.17	0.26	4.7	85	8	100	0.00	0.0	11.7		1.2	229
2012	AAA	Columbus	3	2	2	32	35	2.27	0.98	5.0	198	26	82	2.24	2.6	9.9	3.9	0.9	128
2012	MLB	Cleveland	0	1	0	29	27	3.72	1.52	4.7	262	33	76	4.21	4.7	8.4	1.8	0.6	43

Overpowering, athletic RP who reached majors after less than 100 IP. Pitches aggressively with clean arm and electric FB can be imposing. Complements heater with hard CB that can be nasty. Shows little feel for changing speeds and may not get away with elevated FB in big leagues. Has stuff and tenacity to battle LHH and RHH alike.

Almonte, Miguel — SP — Kansas City
EXP MLB DEBUT: 2016 | POTENTIAL: #2 starter | 9E

Thrws R Age 20
2010 FA (DR)

89-96	FB	+ + +
77-79	CB	+ + +
83-85	CU	+ + +

Year	Lev	Team	W	L	Sv	IP	K	ERA	WHIP	BF/G	OBA	H%	S%	xERA	Ctl	Dom	Cmd	hr/9	BPV
2012	Rk	Royals	2	1	0	27	28	2.33	1.00	17.2	224	31	74	1.82	1.7	9.3	5.6	0.0	141

Tall, slender SP who is major sleeper with very high ceiling. Dominated in limited action with loose arm and clean delivery. Shows advanced feel and confidence with three potent offerings. Repeats athletic delivery that allows FB to play up, but needs to fine-tune CB. Solid-average CU is weapon against LHH.

Alvarez, R.J. — RP — Los Angeles (A)
EXP MLB DEBUT: 2014 | POTENTIAL: Closer | 8D

Thrws R Age 22
2012 (3) Florida Atlantic

91-97	FB	+ + + +
82-84	SL	+ + +
80-82	CU	+

Year	Lev	Team	W	L	Sv	IP	K	ERA	WHIP	BF/G	OBA	H%	S%	xERA	Ctl	Dom	Cmd	hr/9	BPV
2010	NCAA	Florida Atlantic	3	1	0	60	49	5.10	1.50	16.2	284	34	67	4.75	3.5	7.4	2.1	0.9	57
2011	NCAA	Florida Atlantic	6	6	0	74	72	5.23	1.64	20.6	292	37	67	4.92	4.3	8.8	2.1	0.6	61
2012	NCAA	Florida Atlantic	5	0	8	38	47	0.72	0.80	6.2	158	24	93	0.76	2.4	11.2	4.7	0.2	156
2012	A	Cedar Rapids	3	2	0	27	38	3.29	1.21	4.8	222	34	74	2.90	3.6	12.5	3.5	0.7	145

Power-armed righty who was immediately placed at Low-A and could reach big leagues quickly. Can dominate hitters with plus velocity and hard SL that can wipe out batters from both sides. Has tenacity to fit at back end of bullpen, though needs better offspeed pitch to limit LHH. Throws with max effort.

Ames, Jeff — SP — Tampa Bay
EXP MLB DEBUT: 2015 | POTENTIAL: #3 starter | 8D

Thrws R Age 22
2011 (1-S) Lower Columbia JC

89-95	FB	+ + + +
82-87	SL	+ + +
80-83	CU	+

Year	Lev	Team	W	L	Sv	IP	K	ERA	WHIP	BF/G	OBA	H%	S%	xERA	Ctl	Dom	Cmd	hr/9	BPV
2011	Rk	Princeton	4	2	1	30	39	7.12	1.55	12.0	319	44	53	5.64	2.1	11.6	5.6	1.2	170
2012	A-	Hudson Valley	6	1	0	64	70	1.96	0.99	17.5	195	28	79	1.59	2.8	9.8	3.5	0.1	119

Tall, durable SP who was difficult to hit in short-season. Improved mechanics in offseason and started to use height to throw downhill. FB exhibits late run and sink. Can rear back and add velocity when needed and complements heater with solid-avg hard SL. To last as SP, needs to upgrade CU. Can slow arm speed.

Ames, Steven — RP — Los Angeles (N)
EXP MLB DEBUT: 2013 | POTENTIAL: Setup reliever | 6B

Thrws R Age 25
2009 (17) Gonzaga

90-93	FB	+ + +
81-83	SL	+ + +

Year	Lev	Team	W	L	Sv	IP	K	ERA	WHIP	BF/G	OBA	H%	S%	xERA	Ctl	Dom	Cmd	hr/9	BPV
2010	Rk	Arizona Dodgers	0	0	0	3	4	0.00	0.67	3.5	191	31	100	0.56	0.0	12.0		0.0	234
2010	A	Great Lakes	0	2	16	28	44	2.54	0.85	4.5	208	37	67	1.19	1.0	14.0	14.7	0.0	244
2011	A+	Rancho Cuc	0	0	9	15	28	1.17	0.78	3.7	188	37	91	1.32	1.2	16.4	14.0	0.6	282
2011	AA	Chattanooga	2	2	5	33	41	2.48	1.32	4.8	258	36	85	3.81	3.0	11.3	3.7	0.8	139
2012	AA	Chattanooga	3	3	18	63	72	1.56	1.03	4.5	226	32	86	2.16	1.8	10.2	5.5	0.3	152

Short, strong-armed reliever continues to dominate hitters with his fastball/slider mix. FB sits in the 90-93 range and low-80s slider gets plenty of swings and misses. Doesn't have the highest upside, but career ERA now stands at 1.93 with 35 BB/236 K in 172.2 IP. Doesn't get a lot of attention, but should make his MLB debut in 2013.

Anderson, Chase — SP — Arizona
EXP MLB DEBUT: 2013 | POTENTIAL: #4 starter | 7C

Thrws R Age 25
2009 (9) Oklahoma

88-92	FB	+ +
	SL	+ +
	CB	+ +
	CU	+ + + +

Year	Lev	Team	W	L	Sv	IP	K	ERA	WHIP	BF/G	OBA	H%	S%	xERA	Ctl	Dom	Cmd	hr/9	BPV
2009	Rk	Missoula	3	1	0	45	48	2.38	1.06	9.8	215	30	77	2.04	2.6	9.5	3.7	0.2	120
2010	A	South Bend	2	4	0	38	31	2.82	1.17	21.9	250	31	75	2.83	2.1	7.3	3.4	0.2	92
2010	A+	Visalia	5	3	3	70	83	3.60	1.06	14.3	227	31	69	2.83	2.1	10.7	5.2	0.9	155
2011	A+	Visalia	1	1	0	13	20	5.40	1.13	17.5	271	42	50	3.35	0.7	13.5	20.0	0.7	243
2012	AA	Mobile	5	4	0	104	97	2.86	1.12	19.5	237	29	78	3.01	2.2	8.4	3.9	0.8	111

Smallish right-hander from Oklahoma had a nice comeback after missing most of the '11 season with an elbow injury. Attacks hitters with an 88-92 mph fastball, a plus change-up, and a decent breaking ball. Anderson isn't overpowering, but has some of the best control in the system and could emerge as a solid back-end starter and looked good in the AFL.

Anderson, Tyler — SP — Colorado

EXP MLB DEBUT: 2014 | POTENTIAL: #3 starter | 7C

Thrws L Age 23
2011 (1) Oregon

Velo	Pitch	Grade
88-93	FB	+++
77-80	SL	+++
74-77	CB	++
81-83	CU	+++

Year	Lev	Team	W	L	Sv	IP	K	ERA	WHIP	BF/G	OBA	H%	S%	xERA	Ctl	Dom	Cmd	hr/9	BPV
2009	NCAA	Oregon	2	9	0	82	66	6.26	1.67	24.5	298	35	63	5.47	4.3	7.2	1.7	1.0	33
2010	NCAA	Oregon	7	5	0	103	105	2.98	1.14	23.9	225	28	78	3.09	2.9	9.2	3.2	1.0	106
2011	NCAA	Oregon	8	3	0	108	114	2.34	1.02	27.6	198	28	76	1.72	2.9	9.5	3.3	0.2	111
2012	A	Asheville	12	3	0	120	81	2.47	1.08	23.5	231	27	78	2.49	2.1	6.1	2.9	0.4	71

Soft-tossing lefty carved up hitters in the SAL, going 12-3 with a 2.47 ERA. Has a decent 89-93 mph FB and complements it with a SL, CB, and an above-average CU. Has good command of all of pitches and has nice deception. Dominated due to FB/CU combination, but lack of dominance is a concern as he moves up.

Andriese, Matt — SP — San Diego

EXP MLB DEBUT: 2015 | POTENTIAL: #3 starter | 8D

Thrws R Age 23
2011 (3) UC-Riverside

Velo	Pitch	Grade
91-94	FB	+++
85-86	SP	++++
	SL	++

Year	Lev	Team	W	L	Sv	IP	K	ERA	WHIP	BF/G	OBA	H%	S%	xERA	Ctl	Dom	Cmd	hr/9	BPV
2009	NCAA	Cal-Riverside	5	4	0	66	37	3.93	1.28	19.4	258	30	67	3.27	2.7	5.0	1.9	0.3	35
2010	NCAA	Cal-Riverside	5	5	0	104	69	4.95	1.43	29.4	308	36	63	4.42	1.6	6.0	3.8	0.3	84
2011	NCAA	Cal-Riverside	4	5	0	96	74	2.63	1.22	27.6	254	32	76	2.80	2.4	7.0	3.0	0.0	80
2011	A-	Eugene	5	1	0	42	42	1.51	0.94	13.0	198	28	82	1.35	2.2	9.1	4.2	0.0	123
2012	A+	Lake Elsinore	10	8	0	146	131	3.58	1.22	21.8	254	32	71	3.29	2.3	8.1	3.4	0.6	100

Surived a full season in the CAL, going 10-8 with a 3.58 ERA. Has a nice three-pitch mix that includes a 90-94 mph sinking FB, a power CB, and a decent CU. He commands all three offerings well and walked just 38 in 146 IP. Made 26 starts in '12 and questions about his durability seem to have been answered. He should head to Double-A in 2013.

Aquino, Jayson — SP — Colorado

EXP MLB DEBUT: 2016 | POTENTIAL: #3 starter | 8D

Thrws L Age 20
2009 NDFA, D.R.

Velo	Pitch	Grade
88-92	FB	+++
	CB	+
	CU	++++

Year	Lev	Team	W	L	Sv	IP	K	ERA	WHIP	BF/G	OBA	H%	S%	xERA	Ctl	Dom	Cmd	hr/9	BPV
2012	Rk	Grand Junction	4	0	0	43	36	1.87	0.99	23.6	208	26	83	2.01	2.3	7.5	3.3	0.4	91

Short Dominican lefty finally made his state-side debut after spending three years in the DSL. Already has a good 88-92 mph FB with room for more as he matures. Possesses an above-average CU that allows him to keep hitters off-balance and an inconsistent CB. He controls the strike zone well and gave up just 2 HR in 43.1 IP.

Araujo, Elvis — SP — Cleveland

EXP MLB DEBUT: 2015 | POTENTIAL: #3 starter | 8E

Thrws L Age 21
2007 FA (Venezuela)

Velo	Pitch	Grade
90-96	FB	++++
82-85	SL	++
81-83	CU	++

Year	Lev	Team	W	L	Sv	IP	K	ERA	WHIP	BF/G	OBA	H%	S%	xERA	Ctl	Dom	Cmd	hr/9	BPV
2011	Rk	Indians	9	1	0	63	58	2.86	1.14	19.2	233	30	74	2.57	2.6	8.3	3.2	0.3	98
2011	A-	Mahoning Val	0	0	0	7	5	8.10	2.70	18.4	369	44	67	8.34	9.4	6.7	0.7	0.0	-116
2012	A	Lake County	7	10	0	135	111	5.00	1.50	20.8	270	33	65	4.14	4.1	7.4	1.8	0.5	41

Tall, lanky SP who struggled in first full season. Has tendency to overthrow and struggles with RHH due to below avg CU. Inconsistent arm slot has led to command issues. Core stuff is good with quick arm able to produce velo and hard SL that can be dominant. Uses height to throw downhill and keep ball low.

Archer, Chris — SP — Tampa Bay

EXP MLB DEBUT: 2012 | POTENTIAL: #3 starter / Setup reliever | 8B

Thrws R Age 24
2006 (5) HS (NC)

Velo	Pitch	Grade
92-97	FB	++++
83-88	SL	++++
85-86	CU	+++

Year	Lev	Team	W	L	Sv	IP	K	ERA	WHIP	BF/G	OBA	H%	S%	xERA	Ctl	Dom	Cmd	hr/9	BPV
2010	AA	Tennessee	8	2	0	70	67	1.80	1.24	21.9	196	26	86	2.34	5.0	8.6	1.7	0.3	38
2011	AA	Montgomery	8	7	0	134	118	4.42	1.61	23.8	264	32	73	4.58	5.4	7.9	1.5	0.7	16
2011	AAA	Durham	1	0	0	13	12	0.69	1.31	26.8	231	31	94	2.69	4.2	8.3	2.0	0.0	55
2012	AAA	Durham	7	9	0	128	139	3.66	1.26	20.9	215	30	70	2.75	4.4	9.8	2.2	0.4	76
2012	MLB	Tampa Bay	1	3	0	29	36	4.60	1.23	19.8	218	30	64	3.16	4.0	11.0	2.8	0.9	109

Athletic, strong pitcher who led IL in Ks. Earned trip to big leagues due to improved control and more consistent velocity.Pitches aggressively to both sides of plate. Induces groundballs due to delivery on downhill plane and punches out hitters with SL. CU showing improvement, but still needs polish along with overall command.

Arnett, Eric — RP — Milwaukee

EXP MLB DEBUT: 2013 | POTENTIAL: Reliever | 6D

Thrws R Age 25
2009 (1) Indiana

Velo	Pitch	Grade
88-92	FB	+++
80-82	SL	++
	CU	++

Year	Lev	Team	W	L	Sv	IP	K	ERA	WHIP	BF/G	OBA	H%	S%	xERA	Ctl	Dom	Cmd	hr/9	BPV
2010	Rk	Brewers	2	0	1	16	19	7.31	1.69	14.4	307	42	54	5.22	3.9	10.7	2.7	0.6	104
2010	A	Wisconsin	1	9	1	85	60	6.70	1.62	18.8	291	32	60	5.72	4.1	6.4	1.5	1.5	21
2011	Rk	Helena	4	2	0	52	49	5.19	1.40	24.4	304	37	65	5.09	1.6	8.5	5.4	1.2	129
2011	A	Wisconsin	0	4	0	27	25	5.00	1.44	23.0	289	37	63	4.15	2.7	8.3	3.1	0.3	96
2012	A+	Brevard County	1	0	1	61	61	3.56	1.40	7.8	240	31	75	3.59	4.6	9.0	2.0	0.6	57

Tall, strong-bodied RH was moved from starter to reliever with improved results. When going well he can dominate with a solid FB and hard SL. Velocity on FB jumped back into the low-90s with move to the pen and SL can be tough to hit, but remains inconsistent. Showed improved Dom but continues to struggle with control.

Aumont, Phillippe — RP — Philadelphia

EXP MLB DEBUT: 2012 | POTENTIAL: Potential Closer | 8C

Thrws R Age 24
2007 (1) HS, Canada

Velo	Pitch	Grade
95-97	FB	++++
78-80	CB	+++
84-86	CU	+

Year	Lev	Team	W	L	Sv	IP	K	ERA	WHIP	BF/G	OBA	H%	S%	xERA	Ctl	Dom	Cmd	hr/9	BPV
2010	AA	Reading	1	6	0	50	38	7.43	1.87	21.2	282	33	58	5.50	6.9	6.9	1.0	0.7	-44
2011	AA	Reading	1	5	4	31	41	2.32	1.10	4.9	208	31	81	2.39	3.2	11.9	3.7	0.6	146
2011	AAA	Lehigh Valley	1	0	3	23	37	3.18	1.54	5.5	247	44	77	3.43	5.6	14.7	2.6	0.0	132
2012	AAA	Lehigh Valley	3	1	15	44	59	4.26	1.53	4.7	214	32	72	3.58	6.9	12.0	1.7	0.6	47
2012	MLB	Phillies	0	1	2	15	14	3.68	1.30	3.4	195	27	68	2.22	5.5	8.6	1.6	0.0	24

Former 1st rounder moved into relief and made his MLB debut. Attacks hitters with a 95-97 mph FB and a plus power CB. Command of FB and breaking ball continue to hold him back though he can dominate and misses bats. Front-side mechanics remain weak, which explains the inconsistent command. Has the stuff to close in the majors and did notch 15 saves.

Bandilla, Bryce — SP — San Francisco

EXP MLB DEBUT: 2014 | POTENTIAL: #4 starter/reliever | 7D

Thrws L Age 23
2011 (4) Arizona

Velo	Pitch	Grade
92-96	FB	+++
	SL	++
	CU	+++

Year	Lev	Team	W	L	Sv	IP	K	ERA	WHIP	BF/G	OBA	H%	S%	xERA	Ctl	Dom	Cmd	hr/9	BPV
2009	NCAA	Arizona	3	3	0	49	30	6.20	1.68	8.5	268	31	60	4.50	5.8	5.5	0.9	0.4	-41
2010	NCAA	Arizona	6	4	1	77	70	4.07	1.60	11.8	292	37	74	4.72	4.0	8.1	2.1	0.5	58
2011	NCAA	Arizona	5	3	1	47	48	3.66	1.50	6.3	205	28	74	3.03	6.9	9.3	1.3	0.2	-3
2012	Rk	Giants	0	0	0	14	20	1.93	0.64	12.1	151	24	75	0.65	1.3	12.9	10.0	0.6	215
2012	A	Augusta	2	4	0	44	48	3.05	1.62	17.9	260	36	80	4.05	5.7	9.7	1.7	0.2	40

Athletic lefty had an impressive pro debut, going 2-4 with a 2.78 ERA. Attacks hitters with a mid-90s FB that tops out at 97 mph. Struggled with control in college and in his debut, walking 4.6 per nine, but also struck out 10.5. Complements the FB with a good SL and an improved CU. Will need to show better control to remain a starter, but has a live arm.

Banuelos, Manny — SP — New York (A)

EXP MLB DEBUT: 2015 | POTENTIAL: #2 starter | 8B

Thrws L Age 22
2008 FA (Mexico)

Velo	Pitch	Grade
88-95	FB	++++
79-82	CB	+++
80-83	CU	+++

Year	Lev	Team	W	L	Sv	IP	K	ERA	WHIP	BF/G	OBA	H%	S%	xERA	Ctl	Dom	Cmd	hr/9	BPV
2010	A+	Tampa	0	3	0	44	62	2.23	1.17	17.7	233	37	80	2.53	2.8	12.6	4.4	0.2	168
2010	AA	Trenton	0	1	0	15	17	3.52	1.50	22.1	258	33	81	4.61	4.7	10.0	2.1	1.2	71
2011	AA	Trenton	4	5	0	95	94	3.59	1.53	20.7	259	33	78	4.24	4.9	8.9	1.8	0.7	45
2011	AAA	Scranton/W-B	2	2	0	34	31	4.19	1.60	21.7	271	34	74	4.46	5.0	8.1	1.6	0.5	30
2012	AAA	Scranton/W-B	0	2	0	24	22	4.50	1.63	17.8	300	37	73	5.16	3.8	8.3	2.2	0.8	65

Short, powerful SP who will miss entire '13 campaign after TJ surgery. Has youth and pitchability on his side. Secondary offerings are inconsistent, but has arm strength and quick arm. Possesses swing and miss stuff and pitches exhibit impressive movement. Repeats arm speed on nice CU, but will need to improve strikethrowing to reach ceiling.

Barbato, John — SP — San Diego

EXP MLB DEBUT: 2015 | POTENTIAL: #4 starter | 7D

Thrws R Age 20
2010 (6) HS, FL

Velo	Pitch	Grade
92-95	FB	+++
	SL	++
	CU	+

Year	Lev	Team	W	L	Sv	IP	K	ERA	WHIP	BF/G	OBA	H%	S%	xERA	Ctl	Dom	Cmd	hr/9	BPV
2011	A-	Eugene	1	4	0	57	50	4.89	1.46	16.2	244	30	66	3.84	4.9	7.9	1.6	0.6	28
2012	A	Fort Wayne	6	1	3	73	84	1.84	1.13	6.0	201	28	86	2.32	3.8	10.3	2.7	0.5	101

Strong, athletic right-hander was moved to relief and put up impressive numbers in the MWL. Has a nice 90-94 mph FB and a good overhand CB. He lacked a 3rd offering so the move to relief was a logical one. Still struggles with control and command, but did strikeout a ton and has a bright future.

Bard, Luke — SP — Minnesota

EXP MLB DEBUT: 2015 | POTENTIAL: #3 starter | 8D

Thrws R Age 22
2012 (1-S) Georgia Tech

Velo	Pitch	Grade
89-95	FB	++++
82-86	SL	+++
80-83	CU	++

Year	Lev	Team	W	L	Sv	IP	K	ERA	WHIP	BF/G	OBA	H%	S%	xERA	Ctl	Dom	Cmd	hr/9	BPV
2012	Rk	GCL Twins	0	0	0	4	3	6.75	2.00	6.4	210	27	63	4.19	11.3	6.8	0.6	0.0	-164
2012	Rk	Elizabethton	0	0	1	3	4	0.00	1.33	3.1	191	31	100	2.24	6.0	12.0	2.0	0.0	72

Strong-armed SP with power arsenal that should be solid in any role. Generates FB with clean, quick arm and has repeatable delivery. Can dominate in stretches with FB/SL combo and will need to hone CU to reach ceiling. FB has tendency to be straight at higher velocities and he struggles with SL consistency.

Barnes, Matt — SP — Boston

EXP MLB DEBUT: 2014 | POTENTIAL: #2 starter | 9C

Thrws R Age 23 | 2011 (1) Connecticut | 90-97 FB ++++ | 77-81 CB +++ | 83-86 CU +++

Year	Lev	Team	W	L	Sv	IP	K	ERA	WHIP	BF/G	OBA	H%	S%	xERA	Ctl	Dom	Cmd	hr/9	BPV
2009	NCAA	Connecticut	5	3	1	53	55	5.43	1.45	17.4	265	36	60	3.82	3.9	9.3	2.4	0.3	81
2010	NCAA	Connecticut	8	3	0	83	75	3.92	1.26	22.5	253	32	69	3.47	2.7	8.2	3.0	0.7	91
2011	NCAA	Connecticut	11	4	0	117	111	1.70	0.87	26.9	177	24	82	1.25	2.4	8.6	3.6	0.3	108
2012	A	Greenville	2	0	0	27	42	0.34	0.60	18.2	138	27	94	0.00	1.3	14.2	10.5	0.0	237
2012	A+	Salem	5	5	0	93	91	3.58	1.18	18.6	245	32	70	3.10	2.4	8.8	3.6	0.6	111

Aggressive SP who generates plus velocity with easy arm action and loose delivery. Challenges hitters by peppering strike zone consistently with variety of offerings, including hard CB and solid CU. Has tendency to elevate ball when overthrowing, but has makings of high K starter.

Barnes, Scott — RP — Cleveland

EXP MLB DEBUT: 2012 | POTENTIAL: Setup reliever | 7B

Thrws L Age 25 | 2008 (8) St. John's | 88-94 FB +++ | 80-83 SL +++ | 81-84 CU +++

Year	Lev	Team	W	L	Sv	IP	K	ERA	WHIP	BF/G	OBA	H%	S%	xERA	Ctl	Dom	Cmd	hr/9	BPV
2010	AA	Akron	6	11	0	138	127	5.22	1.33	22.0	245	30	62	3.85	3.8	8.3	2.2	1.0	65
2011	AA	Akron	1	0	0	11	17	1.64	0.64	19.0	139	26	71	0.00	1.6	13.9	8.5	0.0	224
2011	AAA	Columbus	7	4	0	88	90	3.68	1.30	22.6	244	30	76	3.97	3.5	9.2	2.6	1.2	90
2012	AAA	Columbus	2	3	2	52	67	3.98	1.15	6.7	201	31	63	2.07	4.0	11.6	2.9	0.2	119
2012	MLB	Indians	0	0	0	19	16	4.26	1.26	4.8	241	30	65	3.16	3.3	7.6	2.3	0.5	65

Tall, dependable pitcher who was converted to RP. Repeats athletic delivery despite moving parts. Doesn't possess overpowering stuff, but keeps ball in ballpark. Solid, tight SL can be good offering and changes speeds effectively. K rate increased in bullpen and could be situational reliever as he dominates LHH.

Barrett, Jake — RP — Arizona

EXP MLB DEBUT: 2014 | POTENTIAL: Setup reliever | 7D

Thrws R Age 21 | 2012 (3) Arizona State | 93-95 FB ++++ | 83-86 SL +++ | SP ++ | CU +

Year	Lev	Team	W	L	Sv	IP	K	ERA	WHIP	BF/G	OBA	H%	S%	xERA	Ctl	Dom	Cmd	hr/9	BPV
2010	NCAA	Arizona State	2	0	2	29	43	3.41	1.24	4.2	241	38	74	3.19	3.1	13.3	4.3	0.6	174
2011	NCAA	Arizona State	7	4	0	76	72	4.14	1.26	22.2	259	34	66	3.28	2.5	8.5	3.4	0.4	104
2012	NCAA	Arizona State	2	4	11	32	35	1.39	0.80	3.9	172	24	84	0.98	1.9	9.7	5.0	0.3	141
2012	A	South Bend	0	3	6	25	25	5.84	1.66	4.4	287	37	64	5.03	4.7	9.1	1.9	0.7	54

3rd round pick out of ASU where he was a dominant reliever. Comes after hitters with a mid-90s FB that tops out at 98 mph, a SP, and an above-average SL. Struggled with command and control in his debut, but also struck out 25 in 24.2 IP. Concerns about durability, control, and max-effort delivery will keep him in relief role.

Bauer, Trevor — SP — Cleveland

EXP MLB DEBUT: 2012 | POTENTIAL: #1 starter | 9B

Thrws R Age 22 | 2011 (1) UCLA | 92-96 FB ++++ | 85-86 SL ++++ | 77-79 CB +++ | 82-85 CU +++

Year	Lev	Team	W	L	Sv	IP	K	ERA	WHIP	BF/G	OBA	H%	S%	xERA	Ctl	Dom	Cmd	hr/9	BPV
2011	A+	Visalia	0	1	0	9	17	3.00	1.22	12.1	216	42	80	3.15	4.0	17.0	4.3	1.0	216
2011	AA	Mobile	1	1	0	17	26	7.56	1.68	18.8	298	46	54	5.52	4.3	14.0	3.3	1.1	154
2012	AA	Mobile	7	1	0	48	60	1.68	1.22	24.4	195	30	86	2.18	4.8	11.2	2.3	0.2	88
2012	AAA	Reno	5	1	0	82	97	2.85	1.33	24.3	242	33	82	3.69	3.8	10.6	2.8	0.9	106
2012	MLB	Arizona	1	2	0	16	17	6.06	1.65	18.3	233	29	64	4.62	7.2	9.4	1.3	1.1	-7

Right-hander has a deep arsenal of offerings, but struggled with control. Features a 90-95 mph FB, a SL, splitter, CU, and plus CB. Has a complicated over the top delivery, leading some to worry about durability. Struggled with a consistent release point, but did make his MLB debut. Still has tremendous long-term potential.

Beck, Chris — SP — Chicago (A)

EXP MLB DEBUT: 2015 | POTENTIAL: #3 starter | 8D

Thrws R Age 22 | 2012 (2) Georgia Southern | 89-95 FB +++ | 83-86 SL +++ | 80-82 CU ++

Year	Lev	Team	W	L	Sv	IP	K	ERA	WHIP	BF/G	OBA	H%	S%	xERA	Ctl	Dom	Cmd	hr/9	BPV
2012	Rk	Great Falls	4	3	0	40	36	4.69	1.56	11.8	310	38	70	5.07	2.7	8.0	3.0	0.7	90

Tall, durable SP who had middling pro debut, but offers potential for 3 avg to plus pitches. Struggled with LHH (.347 oppBA) while SL and CU appeared flat. SL has chance to become plus offering. Velocity is sufficient and could throw harder with tweaks, though has tendency to overthrow.

Bedrosian, Cam — SP — Los Angeles (A)

EXP MLB DEBUT: 2015 | POTENTIAL: #3 starter | 8D

Thrws R Age 21 | 2010 (1) HS (GA) | 89-96 FB +++ | 80-83 SL +++ | 77-80 CB ++ | 78-80 CU ++

Year	Lev	Team	W	L	Sv	IP	K	ERA	WHIP	BF/G	OBA	H%	S%	xERA	Ctl	Dom	Cmd	hr/9	BPV
2010	Rk	Angels	0	2	0	12	10	4.50	1.67	10.8	278	35	70	4.23	5.3	7.5	1.4	0.0	11
2012	A	Cedar Rapids	3	11	0	83	48	6.31	1.73	17.9	281	32	62	4.97	5.7	5.2	0.9	0.5	-41

Short, strong SP who had difficulty returning from TJS. Velo hasn't yet returned and hard SL doesn't show as much bite. Still hopeful that stuff will return to normal upon repetition. When healthy, can have explosive FB and mix in SL that is tough on RHH. Repeats delivery well and will need to enhance CU.

Belfiore, Michael — RP — Baltimore

EXP MLB DEBUT: 2013 | POTENTIAL: Setup reliever | 6A

Thrws L Age 24 | 2009 (1-S) Boston College | 89-93 FB +++ | 80-83 SL ++ | 79-82 CU +++

Year	Lev	Team	W	L	Sv	IP	K	ERA	WHIP	BF/G	OBA	H%	S%	xERA	Ctl	Dom	Cmd	hr/9	BPV
2009	Rk	Missoula	2	2	0	58	55	2.17	1.24	16.8	265	34	83	3.27	2.0	8.5	4.2	0.3	117
2010	A	South Bend	3	10	0	126	105	3.99	1.43	21.5	281	35	71	4.09	3.0	7.5	2.5	0.4	72
2011	A+	Visalia	4	4	0	79	79	5.92	1.81	10.5	279	32	72	6.41	6.5	9.0	1.4	1.9	5
2012	A+	Visalia	0	0	1	19	28	2.37	0.95	6.0	195	30	81	2.19	2.4	13.3	5.6	0.9	193
2012	AA	Bowie	5	1	2	47	50	2.85	1.35	7.1	244	33	79	3.31	4.0	9.5	2.4	0.4	81

Tall, deceptive RP who was promoted to AA upon trade from ARI. Best offerings include sneaky quick FB and solid-avg CU. Projects as situational lefty and held LHH to .157 oppBA. Throws with quick, easy arm and generates good velocity. Doesn't have swing and miss or dependable breaking ball.

Bergman, Christian — SP — Colorado

EXP MLB DEBUT: 2015 | POTENTIAL: #5 starter | 6C

Thrws R Age 25 | 2010 (24) UC Irvine | 87-90 FB ++ | CU +++

Year	Lev	Team	W	L	Sv	IP	K	ERA	WHIP	BF/G	OBA	H%	S%	xERA	Ctl	Dom	Cmd	hr/9	BPV
2009	NCAA	Cal-Irvine	9	3	0	98	66	3.50	1.30	26.8	287	33	75	4.24	1.5	6.1	4.1	0.8	88
2010	NCAA	Cal-Irvine	9	3	1	102	78	3.72	1.23	20.6	275	33	70	3.60	1.4	6.9	4.9	0.5	104
2010	Rk	Casper	1	4	0	48	37	5.96	1.51	14.9	313	36	60	5.25	2.0	6.9	3.4	0.9	87
2011	A-	Tri-City	7	5	0	97	68	2.59	0.97	24.6	232	28	73	2.21	1.0	6.3	6.2	0.4	104
2012	A+	Modesto	16	5	0	163	121	3.65	1.22	24.3	260	30	73	3.69	2.0	6.7	3.3	0.9	83

Finesse RH put up impressive numbers despite pedestrian stuff. Rarely breaks 90 with his FB, but complements it with a plus CU that keeps hitters off-balance. Is an extreme strike-thrower, but was not young for this level. If he can duplicate these results, he will get more attention.

Berrios, J.O. — SP — Minnesota

EXP MLB DEBUT: 2016 | POTENTIAL: #2 starter | 9D

Thrws R Age 19 | 2012 (1-S) HS (PR) | 91-96 FB ++++ | 79-83 SL +++ | 80-82 CU +++

Year	Lev	Team	W	L	Sv	IP	K	ERA	WHIP	BF/G	OBA	H%	S%	xERA	Ctl	Dom	Cmd	hr/9	BPV
2012	Rk	GCL Twins	1	0	4	17	27	1.08	0.60	7.1	130	26	80	0.00	1.6	14.6	9.0	0.0	237
2012	Rk	Elizabethton	2	0	0	14	22	1.29	0.64	16.2	168	29	88	0.83	0.6	14.1	22.0	0.6	255

Short, athletic SP with two out pitches in FB and hard SL. Advanced feel and should dominate lower levels with solid three pitch mix. Lacks projection in strong frame, but changes speeds well. CU features good movement and can move FB all over K zone. Needs experience with pitch sequencing.

Berry, Tim — SP — Baltimore

EXP MLB DEBUT: 2014 | POTENTIAL: #3 starter | 8D

Thrws L Age 22 | 2009 (50) HS (CA) | 88-93 FB +++ | 79-82 CB ++++ | 80-82 CU ++

Year	Lev	Team	W	L	Sv	IP	K	ERA	WHIP	BF/G	OBA	H%	S%	xERA	Ctl	Dom	Cmd	hr/9	BPV
2010	Rk	GCL Orioles	0	1	0	20	23	1.35	1.35	6.0	187	28	89	2.25	6.3	10.4	1.6	0.0	34
2011	A	Delmarva	3	7	0	117	96	5.17	1.44	19.1	245	29	64	4.02	4.7	7.4	1.6	0.8	24
2012	A	Delmarva	2	7	0	52	44	5.02	1.48	22.4	290	36	65	4.44	2.9	7.6	2.6	0.5	76
2012	A+	Frederick	5	5	0	75	61	4.32	1.37	21.0	282	34	69	4.23	2.4	7.3	3.1	0.7	85
2012	AA	Bowie	0	1	0	2	4	37.72	5.39	13.7	598	91	22	21.72	10.8	21.6	2.0	0.0	115

Lean, athletic SP showed improvement despite subpar numbers. Hit hard as he peppered fat part of plate often. Upgraded control, but struggled to get pitches to work in tandem. Best pitch is CB while sinker keeps ball on ground. Offers projection and potential for three avg to plus pitches.

Betances, Dellin — SP — New York (A)

EXP MLB DEBUT: 2011 | POTENTIAL: #3 starter | 8D

Thrws R Age 25 | 2006 (8) HS (NJ) | 89-97 FB ++++ | 80-82 CB +++ | 84-88 CU ++

Year	Lev	Team	W	L	Sv	IP	K	ERA	WHIP	BF/G	OBA	H%	S%	xERA	Ctl	Dom	Cmd	hr/9	BPV
2011	AA	Trenton	4	6	0	105	115	3.42	1.34	20.9	225	30	75	3.24	4.7	9.8	2.1	0.6	68
2011	AAA	Scranton/W-B	0	3	0	21	27	5.14	1.48	22.6	213	30	66	3.66	6.4	11.6	1.8	0.9	53
2011	MLB	New York (A)	0	0	0	3	2	6.74	2.62	7.3	117	15	71	4.76	20.2	6.7	0.3	0.0	-407
2012	AA	Trenton	3	4	0	57	53	6.51	1.82	23.9	314	39	63	5.74	4.8	8.4	1.8	0.6	41
2012	AAA	Scranton/W-B	3	5	0	75	71	6.39	1.87	21.9	252	31	66	5.41	8.3	8.6	1.0	1.1	-53

Big, physical pitcher who suffered thru miserable season and was demoted to AA. Owns big league stuff, but lacks consistency and mechanics may need overhaul. Has difficulty throwing strikes and repeating delivery. Lively FB thrown downhill along with hard CB that can get swings and misses.

Bettis, Chad
SP | Colorado | EXP MLB DEBUT: 2015 | POTENTIAL: #2 starter/reliever | 9E

Thrws R Age 24
2010 (3) Texas Tech

Velo	Pitch	Grade
88-94	FB	++++
81-84	SL	+++
		++

Year	Lev	Team	W	L	Sv	IP	K	ERA	WHIP	BF/G	OBA	H%	S%	xERA	Ctl	Dom	Cmd	hr/9	BPV
2010	A	Asheville	2	0	0	19	17	0.96	0.91	23.2	210	27	94	1.89	1.4	8.2	5.7	0.5	126
2010	A-	Tri-City	4	1	0	48	39	1.12	1.12	19.0	244	31	89	2.39	1.9	7.3	3.9	0.0	98
2011	A+	Modesto	12	5	0	170	184	3.34	1.10	24.6	229	31	70	2.63	2.4	9.8	4.1	0.5	129

Strong-armed RHP missed season with tricep injury. Prior to the injury, featured a 89-94 mph FB that topped out around 98 mph and had good late movement. Also has a good hard 81-84 mph SL and an inconsistent CU. If healthy, he has the best arm in a pitching-thin system.

Biddle, Jesse
SP | Philadelphia | EXP MLB DEBUT: 2014 | POTENTIAL: #2 starter | 8C

Thrws L Age 21
2010 (1) HS, PA

Velo	Pitch	Grade
90-93	FB	++++
70-73	CB	+++
77-80	CU	+++

Year	Lev	Team	W	L	Sv	IP	K	ERA	WHIP	BF/G	OBA	H%	S%	xERA	Ctl	Dom	Cmd	hr/9	BPV
2010	Rk	GCL Phillies	3	1	0	33	41	4.32	1.32	15.3	271	38	67	3.74	2.4	11.1	4.6	0.5	152
2010	A-	Williamsport	1	0	0	10	9	2.61	1.55	15.0	146	20	81	2.34	9.6	7.8	0.8	0.0	-100
2011	A	Lakewood	7	8	0	133	124	2.98	1.28	21.8	217	28	76	2.76	4.5	8.4	1.9	0.3	48
2012	A+	Clearwater	10	6	0	143	151	3.22	1.28	22.5	243	32	76	3.36	3.4	9.5	2.8	0.6	97

Durable LH continues to dominate. FB sits at 90-93 and tops out around 94 mph. Locates the FB well and works both sides of the plate. FB command is plus and CB has become more consistent. CU also showed progress, giving him three good pitches. Was 2nd youngest in the FSL and yet led with 151 K.

Bird, Zach
SP | Los Angeles (N) | EXP MLB DEBUT: 2016 | POTENTIAL: #3 starter | 8D

Thrws R Age 18
2012 (9) HS, MS

Velo	Pitch	Grade
88-92	FB	+++
70-73	CB	++
	CU	+

Year	Lev	Team	W	L	Sv	IP	K	ERA	WHIP	BF/G	OBA	H%	S%	xERA	Ctl	Dom	Cmd	hr/9	BPV
2012	Rk	Dodgers	1	2	0	40	46	4.54	1.34	16.5	243	34	65	3.33	3.9	10.4	2.7	0.5	102

Tall RH is long and lean and throws from a high 3/4 slot. Pitches off an 88-92 mph FB and also has a big, looping CB, and a CU that has some potential. CB will need to tighten up and needs to refine his approach, but the upside is substantial.

Black, Corey
SP | New York (A) | EXP MLB DEBUT: 2015 | POTENTIAL: #3 starter | 8C

Thrws R Age 21
2012 (4) Faulkner

Velo	Pitch	Grade
90-98	FB	++++
82-85	SL	++
80-83	CU	++

Year	Lev	Team	W	L	Sv	IP	K	ERA	WHIP	BF/G	OBA	H%	S%	xERA	Ctl	Dom	Cmd	hr/9	BPV
2010	NCAA	San Diego St	2	2	2	47	50	7.04	1.86	15.8	314	41	61	5.96	5.1	9.5	1.9	0.8	51
2011	NCAA	San Diego St	4	5	0	73	78	3.56	1.49	16.6	245	33	76	3.77	5.2	9.6	1.9	0.5	51
2012	Rk	GCL Yankees	0	0	0	1	0	6.77	3.01	7.8	348	35	75	8.80	13.5	0.0	0.0	0.0	-347
2012	A	Charleston (Sc)	2	2	0	24	29	3.80	0.97	17.9	212	32	57	1.59	1.9	11.0	5.8	0.0	165
2012	A-	Staten Island	0	0	0	28	21	2.28	1.08	18.0	220	27	79	2.31	2.6	6.8	2.6	0.3	71

Short and quick-armed SP who impressed with huge FB and K ability. Slight frame is deceptive, but durability not concern. May head to bullpen where he could hit triple digits regularly. Keeps ball down and induces high number of GB. Needs better secondary pitch to match effectiveness of plus FB.

Black, Victor
RP | Pittsburgh | EXP MLB DEBUT: 2013 | POTENTIAL: Reliever | 7C

Thrws R Age 25
2009 (1-S) Dallas Baptist

Velo	Pitch	Grade
92-94	FB	+++
82-84	SL	++
	CU	++

Year	Lev	Team	W	L	Sv	IP	K	ERA	WHIP	BF/G	OBA	H%	S%	xERA	Ctl	Dom	Cmd	hr/9	BPV
2009	A-	State College	1	2	1	31	33	3.45	1.31	10.0	227	32	71	2.64	4.3	9.5	2.2	0.0	72
2010	A	West Virginia	0	0	0	5	8	9.64	1.71	10.6	186	28	43	4.91	9.6	15.4	1.6	1.9	35
2011	A	West Virginia	2	1	1	29	23	5.28	1.59	5.8	268	34	63	3.90	5.0	7.1	1.4	0.0	12
2011	A+	Bradenton	1	0	0	7	5	4.05	1.80	6.2	298	34	82	6.15	5.4	6.7	1.3	1.3	-6
2012	AA	Altoona	2	3	13	60	85	1.65	1.15	4.7	191	31	87	2.05	4.4	12.8	2.9	0.3	130

Strong armed hurler pitches off a 92-94 mph sinking FB that tops out at 97 mph. Also has a SL and an average CU. Uses a low 3/4 arm slot to get movement, but inconsistent mechanics results in poor control. Was finally healthy and move to relief worked. Struck out 85 in 60 IP and posted a 1.65 ERA.

Blackburn, Clayton
SP | San Francisco | EXP MLB DEBUT: 2015 | POTENTIAL: #2 starter | 9D

Thrws R Age 20
2011 (16) HS, OK

Velo	Pitch	Grade
90-93	FB	++++
	CB	++
	SL	+++
	CU	++

Year	Lev	Team	W	L	Sv	IP	K	ERA	WHIP	BF/G	OBA	H%	S%	xERA	Ctl	Dom	Cmd	hr/9	BPV
2011	Rk	Giants	3	1	0	33	30	1.08	0.57	9.4	145	18	88	0.37	0.8	8.1	10.0	0.5	142
2012	A	Augusta	8	4	0	131	143	2.54	1.02	22.9	239	33	74	2.24	1.2	9.8	7.9	0.2	161

Polished RH with a nice four-pitch mix that includes a 92-94 mph sinking FB, a SL, CB, and CU. Locates all of them well and knows how to pitch. Gave up 3 HR in 131.1 IP and had a 4.3 GB/FB ratio. Low 3/4 delivery is repeatable and provides good deception. Doesn't profile as a #1 starter, but is low risk.

Blackburn, Paul
SP | Chicago (N) | EXP MLB DEBUT: 2016 | POTENTIAL: #3 starter | 7D

Thrws R Age 19
2012 (1-S) HS, CA

Velo	Pitch	Grade
90-92	FB	+++
	CB	++
	CU	++

Year	Lev	Team	W	L	Sv	IP	K	ERA	WHIP	BF/G	OBA	H%	S%	xERA	Ctl	Dom	Cmd	hr/9	BPV
2012	Rk	Cubs	2	0	0	21	13	3.48	1.45	9.8	283	32	79	4.60	3.0	5.7	1.9	0.9	38

Lean, athletic RH was the 56th overal pick in the draft. FB isn't overpowering and sits in the 90-92 mph range, topping out at 94 mph. Secondary offerings include a CB and CU that have potential. Tends to be around the strike zone and is fairly polished, but doesn't have tremendous long-term upside.

Blair, Seth
SP | St. Louis | EXP MLB DEBUT: 2014 | POTENTIAL: #5 starter | 6D

Thrws R Age 24
2010 (1-S) Arizona State

Velo	Pitch	Grade
88-92	FB	+++
78-81	CB	+++
80-82	CU	+
	CU	

Year	Lev	Team	W	L	Sv	IP	K	ERA	WHIP	BF/G	OBA	H%	S%	xERA	Ctl	Dom	Cmd	hr/9	BPV
2009	NCAA	Arizona State	7	2	1	77	78	3.39	1.30	18.7	244	32	75	3.37	3.5	9.1	2.6	0.6	87
2010	NCAA	Arizona State	12	1	0	106	108	3.64	1.33	24.5	272	34	75	4.15	2.5	9.1	3.7	0.9	116
2011	A	Quad Cities	6	3	0	82	70	5.29	1.73	17.7	255	30	70	5.00	6.8	7.7	1.1	1.0	-28
2012	Rk	GCL Cardinals	0	0	0	3	1	0.00	1.00	5.7	106	12	100	0.61	6.0	3.0	0.5	0.0	-90
2012	A+	Palm Beach	1	3	0	17	12	5.40	1.92	15.8	277	33	71	5.38	7.6	6.5	0.9	0.5	-69

Hand injury cut season short, but looked fine in the AFL. He has a nice four pitch mix featuring a 92-94 mph sinking FB, a good 12-6 CB, a slurvy SL, and a CU. Both of the breaking balls need work but they do have potential. Does have some recoil on his low 3/4 delivery and an inconsistent arm slot.

Boer, Madison
SP | Minnesota | EXP MLB DEBUT: 2014 | POTENTIAL: #4 starter | 7D

Thrws R Age 23
2011 (2) Oregon

Velo	Pitch	Grade
89-94	FB	+++
83-87	SL	+++
79-84	CU	++

Year	Lev	Team	W	L	Sv	IP	K	ERA	WHIP	BF/G	OBA	H%	S%	xERA	Ctl	Dom	Cmd	hr/9	BPV
2011	NCAA	Oregon	3	6	3	99	74	2.27	1.17	22.0	225	28	80	2.46	3.2	6.7	2.1	0.2	53
2011	Rk	Elizabethton	2	1	9	17	31	2.60	0.87	4.3	210	40	71	1.73	1.0	16.1	15.5	0.5	280
2011	A	Beloit	0	0	2	8	12	6.75	1.63	4.4	347	53	54	5.17	1.1	13.5	12.0	0.0	231
2012	A	Beloit	2	2	0	28	20	3.58	1.30	22.8	250	30	71	3.24	3.3	6.5	2.0	0.3	47
2012	A+	Fort Myers	7	10	0	111	66	6.41	1.61	22.4	320	35	61	5.90	2.6	5.4	2.1	1.2	44

Tall, projectable SP who showed some progress late. Exhibits plus control with three pitches and has strong, durable arm capable of maintaining velocity. Drastic decline in K rate is concerning, but doesn't throw as hard as SP. Could return to bullpen where velocity jumps and would make SL look even better.

Bonilla, Lisalverto
RP | Texas | EXP MLB DEBUT: 2013 | POTENTIAL: Potential Closer | 8C

Thrws R Age 23
2008 NDFA, D.R.

Velo	Pitch	Grade
91-95	FB	++++
78-81	SL	+++
82-84	CU	+++

Year	Lev	Team	W	L	Sv	IP	K	ERA	WHIP	BF/G	OBA	H%	S%	xERA	Ctl	Dom	Cmd	hr/9	BPV
2010	Rk	GCL Phillies	2	1	0	32	38	1.95	1.14	21.4	260	35	88	3.42	1.4	10.6	7.6	0.8	171
2010	A-	Williamsport	1	3	0	26	18	6.49	1.71	11.9	308	33	65	6.41	4.1	6.2	1.5	1.7	18
2011	A	Lakewood	4	5	4	106	95	2.80	1.13	16.1	233	29	78	2.92	2.5	8.1	3.3	0.7	97
2012	A+	Clearwater	1	1	1	13	18	1.35	0.98	5.1	193	31	85	1.36	2.7	12.2	4.5	0.0	164
2012	AA	Reading	2	1	3	33	46	1.64	1.18	6.3	191	31	87	2.11	4.6	12.5	2.7	0.3	119

Strong-armed hurler was moved to relief and was lights-out. Attacks hitters with a 91-94 mph FB, SL, and a plus CU. Is lean and athletic and has easy arm action, though he does have some recoil on his follow-through so the move to relief makes sense. Not your typical failed starter turned to relief.

Bowman, Josh
SP | Oakland | EXP MLB DEBUT: 2014 | POTENTIAL: #4 starter | 7C

Thrws R Age 24
2010 (10) Tampa

Velo	Pitch	Grade
87-93	FB	+++
84-87	SL	+++
75-78	CB	+++
	CU	++

Year	Lev	Team	W	L	Sv	IP	K	ERA	WHIP	BF/G	OBA	H%	S%	xERA	Ctl	Dom	Cmd	hr/9	BPV
2010	Rk	Athletics	0	0	0	1	2	0.00	0.00	2.8	0	0	1	0.00	0.0	18.0		0.0	342
2010	A-	Vancouver	0	2	0	22	23	3.74	1.57	6.8	322	41	78	5.42	2.1	9.6	4.6	0.8	134
2011	A	Burlington	8	6	0	155	98	3.55	1.24	22.4	253	29	72	3.33	2.6	5.7	2.2	0.5	52
2012	A+	Stockton	6	10	0	147	127	3.62	1.30	24.1	275	33	74	4.07	2.0	7.8	3.8	0.9	104
2012	AA	Midland	0	1	0	5	3	5.40	1.80	23.1	332	39	67	5.43	3.6	5.4	1.5	0.0	18

Tall, athletic SP who got hot midseason. Uses darting FB to get ahead of hitters and follows up with hard SL, avg CB, and developing CU. Both breaking balls thrown for strikes and CB used as chase pitch. Higher K rate due to better pitch sequencing and could slot in at back end of rotation.

Boxberger, Brad — RP — San Diego

EXP MLB DEBUT: 2012 — POTENTIAL: Closer — 8C

Thrws R Age 25
2009 (2) USC

Velo	Pitch	Grade
92-95	FB	+ + + +
84-86	SL	+ + +
74-76	CB	+ + +
	CU	+ +

Year	Lev	Team	W	L	Sv	IP	K	ERA	WHIP	BF/G	OBA	H%	S%	xERA	Ctl	Dom	Cmd	hr/9	BPV
2010	AA	Carolina	1	4	0	30	40	8.49	1.92	6.4	295	42	55	6.22	6.7	12.1	1.8	1.2	56
2011	AA	Carolina	1	2	4	34	57	1.31	0.84	4.2	142	26	89	0.94	3.4	14.9	4.4	0.5	195
2011	AAA	Louisville	1	2	7	28	36	2.93	1.12	4.4	170	25	76	2.08	4.9	11.7	2.4	0.7	97
2012	AAA	Tucson	2	2	5	43	62	2.70	1.29	4.8	232	38	77	2.63	3.9	12.9	3.3	0.0	143
2012	MLB	Padres	0	0	0	28	33	2.60	1.45	4.9	220	30	86	3.79	5.9	10.7	1.8	1.0	53

Was up and down between the Padres and AAA all year, but was effective in both places. Has a plus 90-95 mph FB and above-average SL. A deceptive delivery enhances his stuff. He continues to struggle with control, but struck out a bunch at AAA and has one of the best FB/SL combinations going.

Boyd, Hudson — SP — Minnesota

EXP MLB DEBUT: 2016 — POTENTIAL: #3 starter — 8E

Thrws R Age 20
2011 (1-S) HS (FL)

Velo	Pitch	Grade
90-94	FB	+ + +
77-80	CB	+ + +
81-83	CU	+

Year	Lev	Team	W	L	Sv	IP	K	ERA	WHIP	BF/G	OBA	H%	S%	xERA	Ctl	Dom	Cmd	hr/9	BPV
2012	Rk	Elizabethton	2	5	0	58	36	2.95	1.48	19.2	278	31	85	4.82	3.6	5.6	1.6	1.1	22

Large, durable SP with excellent pure stuff, but needs IP. Can pitch tentatively with FB, but throws with clean, quick arm and smooth mechanics. Throws from high arm slot and downward trajectory to induce gb. CB can be plus pitch, but CU in development phase. Struggles with LHH (.348 oppBA).

Bradley, Archie — SP — Arizona

EXP MLB DEBUT: 2014 — POTENTIAL: #1 Starter — 9D

Thrws R Age 20
2011 (1) HS (OK)

Velo	Pitch	Grade
93-95	FB	+ + + +
80-83	CB	+ + +
83-85	CU	+ +

Year	Lev	Team	W	L	Sv	IP	K	ERA	WHIP	BF/G	OBA	H%	S%	xERA	Ctl	Dom	Cmd	hr/9	BPV
2011	Rk	Missoula	0	0	0	2	4	0.00	0.50	3.3	151	38	100	0.00	0.0	18.0		0.0	342
2012	A	South Bend	12	6	0	136	152	3.84	1.26	20.5	185	26	68	2.37	5.6	10.1	1.8	0.4	49

Tall hurler has one of the best arms in the system. Is physically mature and generates easy velocity. Plus 93-96 mph FB is his best offering and reached triple digits in the past. Improved CB and CU with potential. Limited opposition to a .181 oppBAA. Has the arm to be a #1 starter and struck out 152 in 136 IP.

Bradley, J.R. — RP — Arizona

EXP MLB DEBUT: 2015 — POTENTIAL: Reliever — 6D

Thrws R Age 21
2010 (2) HS (WV)

Velo	Pitch	Grade
88-92	FB	+ + +
77-80	CU	+ +
73-75	CB	+ +
	SL	+ +

Year	Lev	Team	W	L	Sv	IP	K	ERA	WHIP	BF/G	OBA	H%	S%	xERA	Ctl	Dom	Cmd	hr/9	BPV
2010	Rk	Missoula	1	7	0	55	40	5.93	1.65	17.4	300	34	65	5.60	4.0	6.6	1.7	1.2	30
2011	A	South Bend	6	16	0	143	88	4.98	1.54	23.0	296	33	69	5.15	3.2	5.6	1.7	1.0	31
2012	A	South Bend	7	8	0	117	60	5.98	1.65	18.7	311	33	65	5.80	3.5	4.6	1.3	1.2	8

Fomer 2nd round pick has yet to figure things out. FB is now very pedestrian and sits in the 88-92 mph range. Also has a CU, CB, and SL, but none of them are effective. Struggled in repeat of MWL where the league hit over .300 against him. Will need to make significant strides soon.

Bradley, Jed — SP — Milwaukee

EXP MLB DEBUT: 2015 — POTENTIAL: #2 starter — 8D

Thrws L Age 23
2011 (1) Georgia Tech

Velo	Pitch	Grade
90-93	FB	+ + +
80-83	SL	+ + +
78-80	CB	+ + +
	CU	+ + +

Year	Lev	Team	W	L	Sv	IP	K	ERA	WHIP	BF/G	OBA	H%	S%	xERA	Ctl	Dom	Cmd	hr/9	BPV
2009	NCAA	Georgia Tech	2	3	0	45	49	6.65	1.59	16.4	300	37	61	6.05	3.4	9.9	2.9	1.8	103
2010	NCAA	Georgia Tech	9	5	0	91	99	4.83	1.45	24.3	294	39	66	4.44	2.5	9.8	4.0	0.6	127
2011	NCAA	Georgia Tech	7	3	0	98	106	3.49	1.22	24.8	244	34	69	2.72	2.8	9.7	3.4	0.1	116
2012	A+	Brevard County	5	10	0	107	60	5.53	1.67	24.1	310	34	66	5.46	3.6	5.0	1.4	0.8	11

15th overall pick in '11 didn't look like the same player. In college, showed a four-pitch mix with control and the ability to dominate. Has struggled with control since and doesn't miss many bats. Still has a good 90-93 mph FB, a SL, a CB, and a CU. Too early to call this a bust, but he must show more in '13.

Brasier, Ryan — RP — Los Angeles (A)

EXP MLB DEBUT: 2013 — POTENTIAL: Middle reliever — 7D

Thrws R Age 25
2007 (6) Weatherford JC

Velo	Pitch	Grade
89-96	FB	+ + +
79-84	SL	+ + +
81-82	CU	+

Year	Lev	Team	W	L	Sv	IP	K	ERA	WHIP	BF/G	OBA	H%	S%	xERA	Ctl	Dom	Cmd	hr/9	BPV
2009	AA	Arkansas	2	1	2	11	6	5.56	1.77	6.5	289	32	68	5.42	5.6	4.8	0.9	0.8	-46
2010	AA	Arkansas	7	12	0	142	94	5.07	1.37	21.3	241	24	69	4.67	4.3	6.0	1.4	1.8	9
2011	AA	Arkansas	0	1	16	25	26	0.71	1.26	4.1	201	27	97	2.54	5.0	9.2	1.9	0.4	50
2011	AAA	Salt Lake	2	1	3	27	26	5.00	1.30	4.4	255	32	61	3.59	3.0	8.7	2.9	0.7	93
2012	AAA	Salt Lake	7	3	13	60	54	4.37	1.51	4.7	282	36	69	4.03	3.6	8.1	2.3	0.2	67

Aggressive RHP who has found stride since moving to RP. K rate has jumped and he uses short, quick arm to generate good FB with tail and sink. Mixes in power SL with short, late break. Has stocky and powerful frame with some effort in delivery. Lives up in zone, but hasn't fallen victim to HR. Lacks touch for CU.

Brennan, Brandon — SP — Chicago (A)

EXP MLB DEBUT: 2015 — POTENTIAL: #4 starter — 7C

Thrws R Age 21
2012 (4) Orange Coast CC

Velo	Pitch	Grade
89-93	FB	+ + +
81-83	SL	+ + +
82-84	CU	+ +

Year	Lev	Team	W	L	Sv	IP	K	ERA	WHIP	BF/G	OBA	H%	S%	xERA	Ctl	Dom	Cmd	hr/9	BPV
2012	Rk	Great Falls	3	2	0	37	31	4.34	1.61	11.8	295	36	72	4.79	3.9	7.5	1.9	0.5	48

Tall, durable SP who relies on sinker to induce GB and keep defense active. Doesn't project to many Ks, but moves ball around plate and keeps hitters off-guard. Uses effective sinker and has hard SL that could develop into plus pitch. Enough separation between FB and CU, but can slow arm speed.

Brewer, Charles — SP — Arizona

EXP MLB DEBUT: 2013 — POTENTIAL: #4 starter — 7D

Thrws R Age 25
2009 (12) UCLA

Velo	Pitch	Grade
90-93	FB	+ + +
72-74	CB	+ + +
78-80	CU	+ + +
	SL	+ +

Year	Lev	Team	W	L	Sv	IP	K	ERA	WHIP	BF/G	OBA	H%	S%	xERA	Ctl	Dom	Cmd	hr/9	BPV
2010	A+	Visalia	7	3	0	82	75	2.98	1.09	22.8	243	31	74	2.82	1.7	8.3	5.0	0.6	122
2011	Rk	Diamondbacks	0	0	0	3	4	0.00	1.00	11.5	262	40	100	2.29	0.0	12.0		0.0	234
2011	AA	Mobile	5	1	0	52	48	2.58	1.28	19.5	245	32	80	3.13	3.3	8.3	2.5	0.3	78
2012	AA	Mobile	0	0	0	17	13	4.15	1.21	23.3	280	32	68	4.10	1.0	6.8	6.5	1.0	111
2012	AAA	Reno	11	7	0	134	104	5.99	1.58	24.5	320	36	66	6.30	2.3	7.0	3.1	1.8	82

Tall righty has a nice four-pitch mix. Best offering is an average 90-93 mph FB that has nice late movement. Also throws a tight 72-74 mph CB and a decent CU. Is a strike-thrower and walked only 34 in 133.2 IP, but lacks the FB velocity to get more advanced hitters out and the PCL hit .312 against him.

Brice, Austin — SP — Miami

EXP MLB DEBUT: 2015 — POTENTIAL: #3 starter — 7D

Thrws R Age 21
2010 (9) HS, NC

Velo	Pitch	Grade
92-94	FB	+ + + +
80-82	CB	+ +
	CU	+

Year	Lev	Team	W	L	Sv	IP	K	ERA	WHIP	BF/G	OBA	H%	S%	xERA	Ctl	Dom	Cmd	hr/9	BPV
2010	Rk	GCL Marlins	0	1	0	8	8	4.32	1.68	6.2	230	31	71	3.61	7.6	8.6	1.1	0.0	-31
2011	Rk	GCL Marlins	6	0	0	49	55	2.96	1.34	18.4	189	27	78	2.59	6.1	10.2	1.7	0.4	36
2012	A	Greensboro	8	6	3	110	122	4.35	1.50	18.9	237	31	74	4.23	5.6	10.0	1.8	1.1	48

Projectable righty had an impressive showing in the SAL. Attacks hitters with a lively 92-94 mph FB. Also has the makings of an above-average CB and CU, but both currently need work. Poor front-side mechanics leads to problems with control. Needs significant improvement, but there is some potential here.

Brickhouse, Bryan — SP — Kansas City

EXP MLB DEBUT: 2016 — POTENTIAL: #3 starter — 8E

Thrws R Age 21
2011 (3) HS (TX)

Velo	Pitch	Grade
90-96	FB	+ + +
75-79	CB	+ + +
81-83	SL	+ +
82-83	CU	+ +

Year	Lev	Team	W	L	Sv	IP	K	ERA	WHIP	BF/G	OBA	H%	S%	xERA	Ctl	Dom	Cmd	hr/9	BPV
2012	Rk	Idaho Falls	0	0	0	2	1	37.72	4.79	12.7	515	52	14	22.26	16.2	5.4	0.3	5.4	-322
2012	A	Kane County	3	3	0	51	40	5.61	1.42	21.8	257	31	59	3.82	4.0	7.0	1.7	0.5	35

Short, strong SP who pitches aggressively with some effort in delivery and could profile as late-innings RP. Keeps ball down in zone with hard sinker and tight CB can generate swings and misses. Delivery could use refinement as it affects FB command. CU needs work and stamina is in question.

Bridwell, Parker — SP — Baltimore

EXP MLB DEBUT: 2015 — POTENTIAL: #3 starter — 8D

Thrws R Age 21
2010 (9) HS (TX)

Velo	Pitch	Grade
87-95	FB	+ + + +
80-82	CB	+ + +
79-83	CU	+ +

Year	Lev	Team	W	L	Sv	IP	K	ERA	WHIP	BF/G	OBA	H%	S%	xERA	Ctl	Dom	Cmd	hr/9	BPV
2010	Rk	GCL Orioles	0	0	0	2	4	5.39	2.40	4.4	175	59	75	4.64	16.2	21.6	1.3	0.0	-31
2010	A-	Aberdeen	0	0	0	4	2	0.00	1.00	7.6	210	24	100	1.70	2.3	4.5	2.0	0.0	38
2011	A	Delmarva	0	3	0	22	13	7.06	1.66	19.4	273	32	53	4.18	5.4	5.4	1.0	0.0	-31
2011	A-	Aberdeen	2	5	0	54	57	4.53	1.45	19.1	270	36	67	3.88	3.7	9.6	2.6	0.3	90
2012	A	Delmarva	5	9	0	114	71	5.98	1.62	22.1	275	30	64	5.19	5.0	5.6	1.1	1.2	-15

Tall, quick-armed SP is all about projection as performance hasn't lived up to potential. Had trouble keeping ball in park while mechanical problems led to poor command. Smooth arm generates good velocity and has some feel for CU. CB is K pitch, but tough to fan hitters when behind in count.

Brigham, Jake — SP — Texas

EXP MLB DEBUT: 2013 | POTENTIAL: #4 starter / Setup reliever | **7C**

Thrws R Age 25

Profile	Year	Lev	Team	W	L	Sv	IP	K	ERA	WHIP	BF/G	OBA	H%	S%	xERA	Ctl	Dom	Cmd	hr/9	BPV
2006 (6) HS (FL)	2010	A	Hickory	6	5	0	83	67	3.36	1.08	23.1	220	27	69	2.51	2.6	7.3	2.8	0.5	79
88-94 FB +++	2010	A+	Bakersfield	1	5	0	49	39	6.93	1.89	21.1	325	38	63	6.37	4.7	7.1	1.5	0.9	18
80-82 CB +++	2011	AA	Frisco	6	6	0	114	114	4.49	1.42	13.8	249	31	70	4.16	4.3	9.0	2.1	1.0	63
82-84 CU ++	2012	AA	Tennessee	0	2	0	4	3	19.62	4.09	12.7	515	58	50	17.72	9.8	7.4	0.8	2.5	-114
	2012	AA	Frisco	5	5	0	124	116	4.28	1.35	24.7	259	31	73	4.47	3.3	8.4	2.5	1.4	79

Tall SP who repeated AA and was re-acquired by TEX after July trade to CHC. Numbers haven't matched pure, power stuff, though repeats simple delivery and keeps FB low in zone for GB. Has solid durability and stamina to hold velocity. Hard CB is nice secondary, though lacks deception and has subpar CU.

Britton, Drake — SP — Boston

EXP MLB DEBUT: 2014 | POTENTIAL: #3 starter | **8E**

Thrws L Age 24

Profile	Year	Lev	Team	W	L	Sv	IP	K	ERA	WHIP	BF/G	OBA	H%	S%	xERA	Ctl	Dom	Cmd	hr/9	BPV
2007 (23) HS (TX)	2009	A-	Lowell	0	0	0	5	8	1.93	1.50	6.7	233	44	86	3.13	5.8	15.4	2.7	0.0	139
88-94 FB +++	2010	A	Greenville	2	3	0	76	78	2.97	1.22	14.5	244	32	77	3.18	2.7	9.3	3.4	0.6	111
74-78 CB +++	2011	A+	Salem	1	13	0	98	89	6.91	1.70	17.0	287	35	59	5.49	5.1	8.2	1.6	1.1	29
80-83 SL ++	2012	A+	Salem	3	5	0	45	42	5.80	1.36	18.8	249	30	57	3.98	3.8	8.4	2.2	1.0	67
82-85 CU +++	2012	AA	Portland	4	7	0	85	76	3.72	1.46	22.7	265	34	74	3.84	4.0	8.1	2.0	0.3	54

High-ceiling pitcher who was promoted to AA despite shaky start. Ended year strong with improvement in command. Induces GB with sinking FB and can knockout hitters with CB. Possesses nice touch on CU and next step is to polish inconsistent SL. Victim of reverse splits and release point needs to be firm.

Brown, Mitch — SP — Cleveland

EXP MLB DEBUT: 2016 | POTENTIAL: #2 starter | **8C**

Thrws R Age 19

Profile	Year	Lev	Team	W	L	Sv	IP	K	ERA	WHIP	BF/G	OBA	H%	S%	xERA	Ctl	Dom	Cmd	hr/9	BPV
2012 (2) HS (MN)																				
90-94 FB ++++																				
84-86 SL ++																				
77-79 CB ++																				
81-84 CU +++	2012	Rk	Indians	2	0	0	28	26	3.58	1.08	13.5	204	25	70	2.71	3.3	8.5	2.6	1.0	82

Durable, strong SP features solid pitchability. Produces easy velocity with clean, repeatable mechanics and plus FB is top current offering. Has feel for two breaking balls, but both need refinement and consistency. Deceptive CU thrown with similar arm speed and slot is good enough to get swings and misses or GB.

Bucci, Nick — SP — Milwaukee

EXP MLB DEBUT: 2014 | POTENTIAL: #4 starter | **6C**

Thrws R Age 22

Profile	Year	Lev	Team	W	L	Sv	IP	K	ERA	WHIP	BF/G	OBA	H%	S%	xERA	Ctl	Dom	Cmd	hr/9	BPV
2008 (18) Ontario, CAN	2009	AA	Huntsville	1	0	0	4	3	6.75	1.25	5.4	210	11	67	6.53	4.5	6.8	1.5	4.5	18
87-91 FB +++	2010	A	Wisconsin	6	7	1	121	100	3.51	1.36	19.4	220	26	77	3.53	5.1	7.5	1.5	0.9	15
78-82 SL ++	2011	A+	Brevard County	8	11	0	150	119	3.84	1.29	23.7	253	30	71	3.63	3.1	7.1	2.3	0.7	64
72-74 CB ++	2012	Rk	Brewers	1	1	0	11	7	1.64	0.64	9.5	184	20	83	1.24	0.0	5.7		0.8	121
CU ++	2012	A+	Brevard County	2	2	0	32	37	1.99	1.26	21.6	219	30	89	3.20	4.3	10.5	2.5	0.9	92

Athletic righty has pitchability and knows how to keep hitters off-balance. Features an 88-92 mph FB, a CB, and a solid CU. Shoulder injury limited him to just 10 starts in '12, but looked good in limited action. Throws strikes and isn't afraid to pitch to contact. Was healthy in the AFL, but his FB was 86-90 mph.

Buckel, Cody — SP — Texas

EXP MLB DEBUT: 2014 | POTENTIAL: #3 starter | **8B**

Thrws R Age 21

Profile	Year	Lev	Team	W	L	Sv	IP	K	ERA	WHIP	BF/G	OBA	H%	S%	xERA	Ctl	Dom	Cmd	hr/9	BPV
2010 (2) HS (CA)																				
89-94 FB ++++	2010	Rk	Rangers	0	0	0	5	9	0.00	0.60	4.3	124	28	100	0.00	1.8	16.2	9.0	0.0	261
77-80 CB +++	2011	A	Hickory	8	3	0	97	120	2.61	1.14	16.6	233	33	80	2.88	2.5	11.2	4.4	0.7	151
86-89 SL ++	2012	A+	Myrtle Beach	5	3	0	76	91	1.31	0.98	22.1	187	28	88	1.53	3.0	10.8	3.6	0.2	133
82-84 CU +++	2012	AA	Frisco	5	5	0	69	68	3.78	1.14	21.0	223	28	69	3.04	3.0	8.9	3.0	0.9	97

Deceptive SP who mixes four pitches with precision and must continue that in order to succeed at higher levels. Lively FB is plus pitch and both CB and CU can get swings and misses. Induces weak contact by fooling hitters with ability to hide ball in delivery. Throws consistent strikes.

Bullock, Billy — RP — Atlanta

EXP MLB DEBUT: 2013 | POTENTIAL: Reliever | **6D**

Thrws R Age 25

Profile	Year	Lev	Team	W	L	Sv	IP	K	ERA	WHIP	BF/G	OBA	H%	S%	xERA	Ctl	Dom	Cmd	hr/9	BPV
2009 (2) Florida	2010	AA	New Britain	2	4	13	37	60	3.44	1.58	5.4	247	42	80	4.22	5.9	14.7	2.5	0.7	124
92-94 FB +++	2011	AA	Mississippi	3	1	11	50	65	4.53	1.39	4.2	200	31	66	2.82	6.2	11.8	1.9	0.4	64
80-82 SL +	2011	AAA	Gwinnett	1	0	0	1	1	0.00	2.00	4.8	415	52	100	7.49	0.0	9.0		0.0	180
CU +	2012	AA	Mississippi	1	2	1	39	41	3.89	1.60	6.7	213	28	77	3.84	7.6	9.4	1.2	0.7	-17
	2012	AAA	Gwinnett	0	0	0	20	26	11.07	2.75	8.1	365	48	60	10.03	10.2	11.5	1.1	1.8	-50

Tall, lanky reliever has a good 92-94 mph FB, but will miss the first 50 games of '13 for failing a drug test. Has power stuff, but also struggles with control, walking 6 per nine. Also mixes in a hard low-80s SL and has had success as a minor league closer. If control improves, could develop as a quality reliever.

Bundy, Bobby — SP — Baltimore

EXP MLB DEBUT: 2013 | POTENTIAL: #4 starter | **7C**

Thrws R Age 23

Profile	Year	Lev	Team	W	L	Sv	IP	K	ERA	WHIP	BF/G	OBA	H%	S%	xERA	Ctl	Dom	Cmd	hr/9	BPV
2008 (8) HS (OK)	2009	Rk	Bluefield	2	7	0	55	38	5.10	1.21	18.3	234	26	58	3.42	3.1	6.3	2.0	1.0	46
88-94 FB +++	2010	A	Delmarva	4	6	0	116	91	3.65	1.22	16.8	234	27	73	3.41	3.3	7.1	2.2	0.9	57
75-79 CB ++	2011	A+	Frederick	11	5	0	121	100	2.75	1.10	23.7	230	28	77	2.72	2.3	7.4	3.2	0.6	90
80-83 SL ++	2011	AA	Bowie	1	3	0	15	13	9.60	2.40	15.7	371	43	61	9.32	6.6	7.8	1.2	1.8	-20
82-85 CU ++	2012	AA	Bowie	2	11	0	81	64	6.25	1.65	21.2	301	36	61	5.27	3.9	7.1	1.8	0.8	41

Aggressive, strong SP whose season ended after surgery to remove bone spurs in elbow. Has solid build and ability to mix 4 pitches. FB is top offering with low location. Has tendency to leave CB and SL up and subject to HR. Power CB shows potential, though lacks feel for CU and slows arm speed.

Bundy, Dylan — SP — Baltimore

EXP MLB DEBUT: 2012 | POTENTIAL: #1 starter | **10C**

Thrws R Age 20

Profile	Year	Lev	Team	W	L	Sv	IP	K	ERA	WHIP	BF/G	OBA	H%	S%	xERA	Ctl	Dom	Cmd	hr/9	BPV
2011 (1) HS (OK)																				
93-99 FB +++++	2012	A	Delmarva	1	0	0	30	40	0.00	0.23	11.5	56	10	100	0.00	0.6	12.0	20.0	0.0	218
77-82 CB ++++	2012	A+	Frederick	6	3	0	57	66	2.84	1.16	18.9	230	31	79	3.02	2.8	10.4	3.7	0.8	129
79-84 CU +++	2012	AA	Bowie	2	0	0	17	13	3.24	1.32	23.0	229	28	76	3.22	4.3	7.0	1.6	0.5	28
	2012	MLB	Baltimore	0	0	0	2	0	0.00	1.20	3.4	175	18	100	1.84	5.4	0.0	0.0	0.0	-128

Advanced SP reached BAL at 19. Few prospects can match upside and dominant ability. Despite strict IP limit, easily worked way thru minors due to repertoire. Plus-plus FB thrown with effortless delivery while CB and CU also elicit swings and misses. Should be annual Cy Young contender.

Burgoon, Tyler — RP — Seattle

EXP MLB DEBUT: 2014 | POTENTIAL: Setup reliever | **6B**

Thrws R Age 24

Profile	Year	Lev	Team	W	L	Sv	IP	K	ERA	WHIP	BF/G	OBA	H%	S%	xERA	Ctl	Dom	Cmd	hr/9	BPV
2010 (10) Michigan	2009	NCAA	Michigan	4	2	4	37	32	4.86	1.73	8.0	301	37	72	5.43	4.6	7.8	1.7	0.7	33
90-93 FB +++	2010	NCAA	Michigan	6	4	10	61	72	3.71	1.29	10.8	256	36	71	3.36	2.8	10.7	3.8	0.4	134
80-85 SL +++	2010	A-	Everett	1	1	1	14	15	4.40	0.98	6.8	198	24	58	2.63	2.5	9.4	3.8	1.3	120
82-84 CU ++	2011	A	Clinton	5	5	14	63	66	2.30	1.12	5.9	237	33	78	2.42	2.2	9.5	4.4	0.1	130
	2012	A+	High Desert	8	2	3	64	80	3.25	1.34	5.0	231	33	78	3.40	4.4	11.3	2.6	0.7	103

Short RP who has spent career in bullpen. Increased K rate as velocity slightly increased and learned to trust SL earlier in count. Induces GB with FB and registers Ks with hard SL. Has been menace to RHH (.208), but needs to throw more strikes to win role in SEA bullpen. Size hasn't been concern.

Burgos, Alex — SP — Detroit

EXP MLB DEBUT: 2015 | POTENTIAL: #4 starter | **7E**

Thrws L Age 22

Profile	Year	Lev	Team	W	L	Sv	IP	K	ERA	WHIP	BF/G	OBA	H%	S%	xERA	Ctl	Dom	Cmd	hr/9	BPV
2010 (5) State JC of Florida																				
87-93 FB +++																				
74-77 CB +++	2010	Rk	GCL Tigers	0	0	1	12	15	1.54	1.11	5.7	233	33	92	2.92	2.3	11.6	5.0	0.8	164
81-82 SL ++	2011	A	West Michigan	6	5	0	95	89	2.19	1.01	22.7	191	25	79	1.83	3.1	8.5	2.7	0.4	86
CU +++	2012	A+	Lakeland	8	10	0	121	78	4.90	1.67	21.8	252	29	70	4.32	6.5	5.8	0.9	0.4	-54

Short, deceptive SP whose command and control fell apart. BB rate more than doubled while K rate drastically fell. Had trouble commanding sinking FB and fringy breaking balls. Doesn't have ideal size, though arm works well and has advanced sequencing. Needs to throw strikes early.

Burgos, Hiram — SP — Milwaukee

EXP MLB DEBUT: 2013 | POTENTIAL: #5 starter | **6B**

Thrws R Age 25

Profile	Year	Lev	Team	W	L	Sv	IP	K	ERA	WHIP	BF/G	OBA	H%	S%	xERA	Ctl	Dom	Cmd	hr/9	BPV
2009 (6) HS, P.R.	2010	A	Wisconsin	5	7	0	74	62	4.48	1.32	16.2	269	33	66	3.80	2.5	7.5	3.0	0.6	84
89-91 FB ++	2011	A+	Brevard County	6	8	0	120	80	4.89	1.48	21.4	296	33	68	4.97	2.6	6.0	2.3	1.0	55
CB +++	2012	A+	Brevard County	2	1	0	41	41	0.87	0.65	20.5	153	21	88	0.34	1.3	8.9	6.8	0.2	143
SL +	2012	AA	Huntsville	6	1	0	83	77	1.94	1.15	25.5	224	29	84	2.52	3.0	8.3	2.8	0.3	86
CU ++	2012	AAA	Nashville	2	2	0	46	35	2.91	1.17	23.1	230	27	78	3.06	2.9	6.8	2.3	0.8	62

Lacks dominant stuff, but hard to argue with the results. FB sits in the upper 80 topping out at 91 mph, but he throws five solid offerings, including a FB, SL, CU, CT, and CB. He locates all of them well and has clean, simple mechanics and for the year was 10-4 with a 1.95 ERA at three different levels.

Butler, Eddie — SP — Colorado

EXP MLB DEBUT: 2015 **POTENTIAL:** #2 starter **8D**

Thrws R Age 22
2012 (1-S) Radford

92-95	FB	++++
78-81	SL	++
71-74	CB	+
	CU	++

Year	Lev	Team	W	L	Sv	IP	K	ERA	WHIP	BF/G	OBA	H%	S%	xERA	Ctl	Dom	Cmd	hr/9	BPV
2012	Rk	Grand Junction	7	1	0	68	55	2.13	1.06	20.2	236	30	79	2.28	1.7	7.3	4.2	0.1	103

Comes after hitters with a heavy 92-95 mph sinking FB that can go as high as 98. Also has a hard SL and a below average CU. Showed good durability in college, working deep into games and maintaining his velocity. Clean, repeatable mechanics with a low 3/4 arm slot give him potential.

Buttrey, Ty — SP — Boston

EXP MLB DEBUT: 2016 **POTENTIAL:** #2 starter **9E**

Thrws R Age 20
2012 (4) HS (NC)

88-96	FB	++
77-80	CB	++
80-82	CU	+++

Year	Lev	Team	W	L	Sv	IP	K	ERA	WHIP	BF/G	OBA	H%	S%	xERA	Ctl	Dom	Cmd	hr/9	BPV
2012	Rk	GCL Red Sox	0	0	0	5	5	1.80	1.20	5.0	262	35	83	2.82	1.8	9.0	5.0	0.0	131

Lean, projectable SP with raw skills, but tantalizing upside. Generates decent velocity and occasionally pops 96 mph. Erratic mechanics result in inconsistency, but will be given time to smooth out delivery. Hard CB serves as put-away pitch, though he needs to stay on top of it. Best present pitch is CU.

Cabrera, Edwar — SP — Colorado

EXP MLB DEBUT: 2012 **POTENTIAL:** #4 starter **7C**

Thrws L Age 25
2008 NDFA, D.R.

88-92	FB	+++
	CU	++++
	SL	++

Year	Lev	Team	W	L	Sv	IP	K	ERA	WHIP	BF/G	OBA	H%	S%	xERA	Ctl	Dom	Cmd	hr/9	BPV
2011	A	Asheville	4	2	0	86	110	3.14	1.10	26.0	241	34	76	3.26	1.9	11.5	6.1	1.0	174
2011	A+	Modesto	4	1	0	81	107	3.56	1.25	25.3	255	37	74	3.65	2.6	11.9	4.7	0.9	163
2012	AA	Tulsa	8	4	0	98	82	2.94	0.90	24.3	190	20	77	2.47	2.1	7.5	3.6	1.4	97
2012	AAA	Col Springs	3	1	0	32	39	3.41	1.20	21.2	225	28	81	3.93	3.4	11.1	3.3	1.7	125
2012	MLB	Colorado	0	2	0	6	5	11.11	2.82	16.0	360	35	69	12.95	11.1	7.9	0.7	4.8	-139

Crafty lefty continues to thrive due to his plus, plus CU and ability to spot his sinking FB. Was not as dominant as a year ago, but still got the job done. Induces plenty of ground balls, but also gives up an alarming number of home runs. CU sets him apart, but Coors Field is a difficult place for soft-tossers.

Cabrera, Mauricio — SP — Atlanta

EXP MLB DEBUT: 2017 **POTENTIAL:** #3 starter **8D**

Thrws R Age 19
2010 NDFA, D.R.

93-95	FB	++++
80-82	SL	+
	CU	++

Year	Lev	Team	W	L	Sv	IP	K	ERA	WHIP	BF/G	OBA	H%	S%	xERA	Ctl	Dom	Cmd	hr/9	BPV
2012	Rk	Danville	2	2	0	58	48	2.97	1.18	19.2	217	27	74	2.49	3.6	7.5	2.1	0.3	56

Short Dominican hurler looked impressive in his state-side debut, posting a 2.97 ERA in 57.2 IP. Has a nice mid-90s sinking FB that generates plenty of ground ball outs and he mixes in an above-average CU and an inconsistent SL. Still learning how to pitch, but has the power stuff needed to succeed.

Cain, Colton — SP — Houston

EXP MLB DEBUT: 2015 **POTENTIAL:** #4 starter **7D**

Thrws L Age 22
2009 (8) HS (TX)

86-92	FB	+++
77-79	CB	+++
79-82	CU	+++

Year	Lev	Team	W	L	Sv	IP	K	ERA	WHIP	BF/G	OBA	H%	S%	xERA	Ctl	Dom	Cmd	hr/9	BPV
2010	Rk	GCL Pirates	0	1	0	14	15	3.77	1.19	14.4	229	30	69	2.94	3.1	9.4	3.0	0.6	103
2010	A-	State College	1	1	0	34	32	5.03	1.09	12.1	193	25	51	2.18	3.7	8.5	2.3	0.5	70
2011	A	West Virginia	6	8	0	106	81	3.64	1.16	17.6	235	28	68	2.85	2.6	6.9	2.6	0.5	71
2012	A+	Bradenton	3	5	0	75	51	4.20	1.24	19.0	248	27	70	3.83	3.0	6.1	2.0	1.2	47
2012	A+	Lancaster	2	2	0	36	25	5.55	1.65	22.8	290	33	67	5.34	4.5	6.3	1.4	1.0	9

Tall, durable SP who uses height and deceptive delivery to keep balls on ground and keep hitters off-balance. Doesn't own true put-away pitch, but mixes pitches and has confidence to use in any count. Arm action produces pitch movement, though needs to iron out delivery.

Callahan, Jamie — SP — Boston

EXP MLB DEBUT: 2016 **POTENTIAL:** #3 starter **8D**

Thrws R Age 18
2012 (2) HS (SC)

86-94	FB	+++
78-80	CB	+++
80-83	SL	++
80-83	CU	+

Year	Lev	Team	W	L	Sv	IP	K	ERA	WHIP	BF/G	OBA	H%	S%	xERA	Ctl	Dom	Cmd	hr/9	BPV
2012	Rk	GCL Red Sox	1	0	0	9	7	5.19	1.27	7.1	247	31	55	2.80	3.1	7.3	2.3	0.0	65

Durable pitcher who will likely be brought along slowly due to crude feel. Has big frame and projectable velocity to match. Could add a few ticks upon improving arm slot and mechanics. CB exhibits nice break and also has SL in arsenal. Lacks present command and feel for CU, though has avg potential.

Campos, Jose — SP — New York (A)

EXP MLB DEBUT: 2015 **POTENTIAL:** #2 starter **9D**

Thrws R Age 20
2009 FA (Venezuela)

91-96	FB	++++
79-83	CB	+++
80-83	CU	+++

Year	Lev	Team	W	L	Sv	IP	K	ERA	WHIP	BF/G	OBA	H%	S%	xERA	Ctl	Dom	Cmd	hr/9	BPV
2011	A-	Everett	5	5	0	81	85	2.32	0.97	22.0	223	30	77	2.15	1.4	9.4	6.5	0.4	148
2012	A	Charleston (Sc)	3	0	0	25	26	4.01	1.13	19.5	223	29	65	2.83	2.9	9.5	3.3	0.7	110

Tall, poised SP who started only 5 games due to elbow. Did not undergo surgery and questionable for beginning of '13. When healthy, has potential for three plus pitches, including quick FB and hard CB. Repeats athletic delivery and throws good strikes. Add in deceptive delivery and he has high ceiling.

Capps, Carter — RP — Seattle

EXP MLB DEBUT: 2012 **POTENTIAL:** Setup reliever/Closer **8C**

Thrws R Age 22
2011 (3-S) Mount Olive

92-99	FB	++++
79-83	CB	++
84-87	CU	+

Year	Lev	Team	W	L	Sv	IP	K	ERA	WHIP	BF/G	OBA	H%	S%	xERA	Ctl	Dom	Cmd	hr/9	BPV
2011	A	Clinton	1	1	0	18	21	6.00	1.61	19.9	272	38	61	4.46	5.0	10.5	2.1	0.5	72
2012	AA	Jackson	2	3	19	50	72	1.26	1.04	5.1	221	36	90	2.18	2.2	13.0	6.0	0.4	193
2012	AAA	Tacoma	0	0	0	1	3	0.00	0.00	3.8	0	0	100	0.00	0.0	20.3	0.0	0.0	383
2012	MLB	Seattle	0	0	0	25	28	3.96	1.44	5.9	262	37	69	3.41	4.0	10.1	2.5	0.0	93

Tall, powerful RP who reached SEA quickly. Pitches effectively with power arsenal highlighted by FB that can touch 100. Relies on FB to get ahead of hitters and wipe them out with high, hard heat or improving CB. Still needs offspeed pitch to counter LHH. Arm action will keep him in bullpen.

Cardona, Adonys — SP — Toronto

EXP MLB DEBUT: 2016 **POTENTIAL:** #3 starter **8D**

Thrws R Age 19
2010 FA (VZ)

89-93	FB	+++
77-80	CB	++
81-84	CU	+++

Year	Lev	Team	W	L	Sv	IP	K	ERA	WHIP	BF/G	OBA	H%	S%	xERA	Ctl	Dom	Cmd	hr/9	BPV
2011	Rk	GCL Blue Jays	1	3	0	32	35	4.55	1.36	13.2	258	35	66	3.69	3.4	9.9	2.9	0.6	105
2012	Rk	GCL Blue Jays	0	1	0	16	20	6.32	1.60	8.6	253	37	58	4.22	5.7	11.5	2.0	0.6	70

Lean, projectable SP who repeated rookie ball and ended season in July. Needs plenty of polish due to inexperience, but has ideal frame to add velocity. Repeats delivery and slot, but has effort in that impacts command and velo. Keeps ball down well and exhibits good arm speed on solid CU.

Carpenter, Chris — RP — Boston

EXP MLB DEBUT: 2011 **POTENTIAL:** Setup reliever **8E**

Thrws R Age 27
2008 (3) Kent State

92-98	FB	++++
84-88	SL	+++
80-83	CU	+

Year	Lev	Team	W	L	Sv	IP	K	ERA	WHIP	BF/G	OBA	H%	S%	xERA	Ctl	Dom	Cmd	hr/9	BPV
2012	Rk	GCL Red Sox	0	0	0	2	1	4.50	1.00	3.8	151	18	50	1.03	4.5	4.5	1.0	0.0	-23
2012	A	Greenville	0	0	0	2	4	4.50	1.00	3.8	151	38	50	0.90	4.5	18.0	4.0	0.0	221
2012	AA	Portland	0	0	0	2	3	4.50	1.00	7.6	262	43	50	2.27	0.0	13.5	0.0	0.0	261
2012	AAA	Pawtucket	1	0	4	16	17	1.15	0.96	3.7	137	18	93	1.27	4.6	9.8	2.1	0.6	70
2012	MLB	Boston	1	0	0	6	2	9.00	2.83	4.2	293	29	69	8.85	15.0	3.0	0.2	1.5	-333

Tall, athletic RP who returned in July after elbow surgery. Converted to pen to take advantage of power arsenal. Still overthrows and struggles with command, but wicked FB and hard SL work well in tandem. Both pitches can get Ks. Doesn't use CU much and likely won't need it.

Carreno, Marcelo — SP — Chicago (N)

EXP MLB DEBUT: 2015 **POTENTIAL:** #4 starter **7D**

Thrws R Age 22
2007 FA (Venezuela)

87-94	FB	+++
77-80	CB	++
81-83	CU	++

Year	Lev	Team	W	L	Sv	IP	K	ERA	WHIP	BF/G	OBA	H%	S%	xERA	Ctl	Dom	Cmd	hr/9	BPV
2010	A-	Connecticut	5	6	0	64	59	4.76	1.51	19.9	261	33	68	4.25	4.6	8.3	1.8	0.7	42
2011	A	West Michigan	7	10	1	125	115	4.55	1.39	22.8	273	35	66	3.93	3.0	8.3	2.8	0.5	88
2012	A	West Michigan	9	8	0	139	119	3.23	1.13	20.4	247	31	70	2.75	1.8	7.7	4.3	0.3	108

Command and control-oriented SP who was acquired from DET in Oct. Repeated Low-A and showcased lively FB thrown with smooth arm. Locates FB to both sides and induces high amount of gb. Lacks true put away pitch and will need to develop both CB and CU to be effective as he advances.

Carreras, Alexander — SP — Arizona — EXP MLB DEBUT: 2016 — POTENTIAL: #4 starter — 7D

Thrws L Age 23
2011 NDFA, Cuba

87-90	FB	+++
	CT	+
	CB	+
	CU	+

Year	Lev	Team	W	L	Sv	IP	K	ERA	WHIP	BF/G	OBA	H%	S%	xERA	Ctl	Dom	Cmd	hr/9	BPV
2012	A-	Yakima	8	5	0	82	55	2.96	1.40	23.1	255	30	80	3.78	4.0	6.0	1.5	0.5	20
2012	A+	Visalia	1	3	0	13	12	9.94	2.05	15.4	359	42	52	8.51	4.3	8.5	2.0	2.1	56

LH Cuban defector had mixed results in his pro debut, posting a 3.90 ERA, but walking 42 in 94.2 IP. FB sits in the 87-90 mph range and tops out at 93 mph. Mixes in a CT, a CB, and an average CU. Struggled in the CAL with a 9.95 ERA, but was better when demoted and made 15 starts with a sub-3.00 ERA.

Carroll, Damion — SP — Tampa Bay — EXP MLB DEBUT: 2017 — POTENTIAL: #3 starter — 8E

Thrws R Age 19
2012 (6) HS (VA)

87-95	FB	+++
80-81	CB	++
82-84	SL	++
	CU	++

Year	Lev	Team	W	L	Sv	IP	K	ERA	WHIP	BF/G	OBA	H%	S%	xERA	Ctl	Dom	Cmd	hr/9	BPV
2012	Rk	GCL Rays	1	0	0	19	20	2.33	1.66	8.7	193	27	84	3.09	8.8	9.3	1.1	0.0	-53

Athletic, physical SP whose crude mechanics keep command and control well below avg. Very strong and quick arm generates high-quality FB with late movement. Induces fair share of GB, and uses both SL and CB, but both need work. CB shows greater potential and CU in infancy stage.

Carson, Robert — RP — New York (N) — EXP MLB DEBUT: 2012 — POTENTIAL: Reliever — 6D

Thrws L Age 24
2007 (14) HS, MS

88-92	FB	+++
85-86	CT	++
78-81	SL	++
75-80	CU	++

Year	Lev	Team	W	L	Sv	IP	K	ERA	WHIP	BF/G	OBA	H%	S%	xERA	Ctl	Dom	Cmd	hr/9	BPV
2010	AA	Binghamton	1	6	0	49	30	8.32	1.87	22.8	331	36	55	6.81	4.3	5.5	1.3	1.3	3
2011	AA	Binghamton	4	11	0	128	91	5.05	1.63	22.8	299	34	70	5.38	3.9	6.4	1.7	1.0	29
2012	AA	Binghamton	1	2	9	36	37	4.79	1.68	5.2	309	40	71	5.20	3.8	9.3	2.5	0.5	84
2012	AAA	Buffalo	0	0	1	16	15	1.72	1.40	6.6	266	34	90	3.93	3.4	8.6	2.5	0.6	80
2012	MLB	New York Mets	0	0	0	13	5	4.73	1.28	3.2	257	25	67	4.27	2.7	3.4	1.3	1.4	6

Tall, strong lefty reliever with a power sinker got into 17 games with the Mets, but didn't do anything to stand out. Has a nice 88-92 power sinker to go along with a CT and a below-average CU. Average FB and none of his other offerings generate many swings-and-misses. Becoming a LOOGY might be his only hope.

Cash, Ralston — SP — Los Angeles (N) — EXP MLB DEBUT: 2014 — POTENTIAL: #4 starter — 7D

Thrws R Age 21
2010 (2) HS, GA

88-92	FB	+++
75-77	CB	++
	CU	++

Year	Lev	Team	W	L	Sv	IP	K	ERA	WHIP	BF/G	OBA	H%	S%	xERA	Ctl	Dom	Cmd	hr/9	BPV
2010	Rk	Ogden	0	0	0	6	5	12.00	2.33	15.5	394	43	50	10.72	4.5	7.5	1.7	3.0	32
2010	Rk	Dodgers	2	2	0	30	25	3.60	1.33	13.8	255	33	70	3.08	3.3	7.5	2.3	0.0	64
2012	A	Great Lakes	1	6	0	41	29	6.42	1.70	20.4	282	32	62	5.21	5.3	6.4	1.2	0.9	-10

Long, lean 2nd rounder missed all of '11 with a hip injury and looked rusty upon his return. Had shown solid FB control in the past, but walked 24 in 40.2 IP and was not effective. Showed a good CB and a useable CU so there is still some potential. Look for better things.

Castillo, Richard — SP — St. Louis — EXP MLB DEBUT: 2013 — POTENTIAL: Spot starter/reliever — 6C

Thrws R Age 23
2007 NDFA, Venezuela

87-92	FB	++
	CB	++
	CU	++

Year	Lev	Team	W	L	Sv	IP	K	ERA	WHIP	BF/G	OBA	H%	S%	xERA	Ctl	Dom	Cmd	hr/9	BPV
2010	A+	Palm Beach	7	12	0	133	75	5.20	1.72	22.4	310	35	69	5.51	4.1	5.1	1.3	0.7	0
2011	A+	Palm Beach	5	4	0	60	47	3.62	1.41	19.4	269	33	74	3.89	3.3	7.1	2.1	0.5	56
2011	AA	Springfield	1	1	0	44	42	4.30	1.86	8.6	330	41	78	6.29	4.3	8.6	2.0	0.8	57
2012	A+	Palm Beach	2	3	0	39	23	1.86	0.83	23.5	168	19	80	1.21	2.3	5.4	2.3	0.5	52
2012	AA	Springfield	7	5	0	110	65	3.76	1.44	24.6	289	32	75	4.45	2.6	5.3	2.0	0.7	43

Short, athletic pitcher doesn't have great stuff, but knows how to set up hitters and throw strikes. Generates good pitch movement with quick arm action and has decent control. Also has a CB and a CU, but neither is plus. Made 25 starts this year, going 9-8 with a 3.27 ERA, but most likely profiles as a reliever.

Castro, Simon — SP — Chicago (A) — EXP MLB DEBUT: 2013 — POTENTIAL: #3 starter — 8E

Thrws R Age 25
2006 FA (DR)

88-96	FB	++++
82-84	SL	+++
83-86	CU	++

Year	Lev	Team	W	L	Sv	IP	K	ERA	WHIP	BF/G	OBA	H%	S%	xERA	Ctl	Dom	Cmd	hr/9	BPV
2011	AA	San Antonio	5	6	0	89	73	4.33	1.24	22.7	274	32	67	3.96	1.6	7.4	4.6	0.9	107
2011	AAA	Tucson	2	2	0	26	21	10.17	2.14	21.2	338	38	52	8.03	6.3	7.4	1.2	1.8	-20
2012	Rk	Bristol	0	0	0	2	0	4.50	1.50	8.6	347	35	67	4.99	0.0	0.0		0.0	18
2012	AA	Birmingham	6	4	0	90	72	3.70	1.22	24.3	260	32	69	3.24	2.1	7.2	3.4	0.4	91
2012	AAA	Charlotte	1	1	0	25	16	4.32	1.52	21.7	312	36	72	5.08	2.2	5.8	2.7	0.7	63

Tall, thick SP with impressive FB and SL combo, but hasn't found success above AA. Has imposing figure on mound and effectively locates stuff in K zone. Works efficiently and gets batters to hit ball on ground. K rate has fallen and he struggles with LHH. Plus FB and hard SL could eventually lead him to bullpen.

Chaffee, Ryan — RP — Los Angeles (A) — EXP MLB DEBUT: 2014 — POTENTIAL: Setup reliever — 7C

Thrws R Age 25
2008 (3) Chipola JC

90-96	FB	+++
76-79	CB	+++
81-84	CU	++

Year	Lev	Team	W	L	Sv	IP	K	ERA	WHIP	BF/G	OBA	H%	S%	xERA	Ctl	Dom	Cmd	hr/9	BPV
2010	A+	Rancho Cuc	7	6	0	105	83	6.36	1.64	23.4	299	35	62	5.55	4.0	7.1	1.8	1.1	40
2011	A+	Inland Empire	2	10	0	97	87	7.26	1.68	14.5	295	36	56	5.47	4.5	8.1	1.8	1.0	43
2011	AAA	Salt Lake	1	1	0	10	8	6.51	1.76	11.1	323	34	71	7.78	3.7	7.4	2.0	2.8	52
2012	A+	Inland Empire	2	0	7	23	28	2.38	1.15	5.0	210	29	83	2.75	3.6	11.1	3.1	0.8	122
2012	AA	Arkansas	5	1	0	43	56	2.72	1.19	4.7	165	24	79	2.17	5.7	11.7	2.1	0.6	76

Tall, interesting RP who varies arm angles to deceive hitters. Moved to bullpen in mid '11 and has seen K rate increase. Throws hard in late innings with FB that features late, darting life. Changes arm angle depending on breaking ball and hitters can chase pitches out of zone. Command is below avg.

Chafin, Andrew — SP — Arizona — EXP MLB DEBUT: 2014 — POTENTIAL: #2 starter — 8D

Thrws L Age 23
2011 (1-S) Kent State

90-94	FB	+++
81-83	SL	++++
	CU	++

Year	Lev	Team	W	L	Sv	IP	K	ERA	WHIP	BF/G	OBA	H%	S%	xERA	Ctl	Dom	Cmd	hr/9	BPV
2009	NCAA	Kent State	4	1	8	36	55	1.26	1.15	8.3	199				4.0	13.9	3.4		159
2011	NCAA	Kent State	8	1	0	89	105	2.02	0.92	23.8	190	28	78	1.40	2.3	10.6	4.6	0.2	146
2011	Rk	Diamondbacks	0	0	0	1	2	0.00	1.00	3.8	262	55	100	2.23	0.0	18.0		0.0	342
2012	A+	Visalia	6	6	0	122	150	4.93	1.48	17.5	245	34	67	4.11	5.1	11.0	2.2	0.9	80

Chafin features a quality 90-95 mph FB, a plus SL, a CB, and a decent CU. Competes on the mound and has the stuff to dominate, but struggles with control. Concerns about durability are no longer an issue and if he can become more consistent he has the power stuff to star in the majors.

Chapman, Kevin — RP — Houston — EXP MLB DEBUT: 2013 — POTENTIAL: Setup reliever — 6A

Thrws L Age 25
2010 (4) Florida

90-95	FB	++++
79-83	SL	+++
	CU	+

Year	Lev	Team	W	L	Sv	IP	K	ERA	WHIP	BF/G	OBA	H%	S%	xERA	Ctl	Dom	Cmd	hr/9	BPV
2010	NCAA	Florida	3	0	11	44	44	1.65	0.85	5.2	196	25	88	1.87	1.4	9.1	6.3	0.8	142
2010	A+	Wilmington	1	1	1	18	20	5.50	1.56	5.6	283	38	63	4.47	4.0	10.0	2.5	0.5	90
2011	A+	Wilmington	0	2	7	22	40	4.84	1.39	6.3	276	50	63	3.80	2.8	16.1	5.7	0.4	232
2011	AA	NW Arkansas	1	2	3	40	50	4.99	1.46	6.8	249	34	68	4.34	4.8	11.3	2.4	1.1	94
2012	AA	Corpus Christi	6	3	2	58	59	2.64	1.40	5.0	231	31	81	3.19	5.0	9.2	1.8	0.3	49

Big-bodied RP who thrives on aggressively battling LHH, but has plus FB that could lead him to role more than lefty specialist. FB has late movement and cutting action and can be blown by hitters. Has difficulty locating FB due to sink/cut. Mixes in solid-avg SL, though CU hasn't developed.

Chargois, J.T. — RP — Minnesota — EXP MLB DEBUT: 2015 — POTENTIAL: Closer — 7C

Thrws R Age 22
2012 (2) Rice

92-97	FB	++++
80-82	CB	+++
81-83	CU	+

Year	Lev	Team	W	L	Sv	IP	K	ERA	WHIP	BF/G	OBA	H%	S%	xERA	Ctl	Dom	Cmd	hr/9	BPV
2012	Rk	Elizabethton	0	0	5	16	22	1.69	0.94	5.0	181	30	80	1.13	2.8	12.4	4.4	0.0	165

Big, powerful RP with electric FB that registers Ks. Pitches FB that features late movement and keeps ball on ground. Can also get hitters to chase CB that shows flashes of being plus. Slows arm on CU, but won't need in late innings role. Uses max effort delivery, but has deception.

Cingrani, Tony — SP — Cincinnati — EXP MLB DEBUT: 2012 — POTENTIAL: #3 starter/power reliever — 9D

Thrws L Age 24
2011 (3) Rice

92-95	FB	++++
80-82	SL	++
85-86	CU	++

Year	Lev	Team	W	L	Sv	IP	K	ERA	WHIP	BF/G	OBA	H%	S%	xERA	Ctl	Dom	Cmd	hr/9	BPV
2011	NCAA	Rice	4	2	12	57	66	1.74	1.00	6.4	226	33	81	1.84	1.6	10.4	6.6	0.0	163
2011	Rk	Billings	3	2	0	51	80	1.75	0.80	14.3	195	34	78	1.08	1.1	14.0	13.3	0.2	242
2012	A+	Bakersfield	5	1	0	57	71	1.11	0.92	21.2	196	29	90	1.56	2.1	11.3	5.5	0.3	165
2012	AA	Pensacola	5	3	0	89	101	2.12	1.10	21.9	190	26	85	2.31	3.9	10.2	2.6	0.7	95
2012	MLB	Cincinnati	0	0	0	5	9	1.80	1.20	6.7	221	37	100	3.91	3.6	16.2	4.5	1.8	212

Tall, lean LH does not get the attention he should. Can't seem to win over skeptics despite being lights-out. Goes after hitters with a plus mid-90 FB, SL and CU. He has a long arm action and a low 3/4 slot that gives nice deception. Gets nice arm-side run away from RH batters and makes his FB effective.

Cisco, Drew — SP — Cincinnati

EXP MLB DEBUT: 2015 | POTENTIAL: #4 starter | 7D

Thrws R Age 21
2010 (6) HS, SC

88-92	FB	+++
74-76	CB	++
75-78	CU	++

Year	Lev	Team	W	L	Sv	IP	K	ERA	WHIP	BF/G	OBA	H%	S%	xERA	Ctl	Dom	Cmd	hr/9	BPV
2012	Rk	Billings	4	1	0	58	45	3.39	1.15	15.4	267	32	71	3.37	1.1	6.9	6.4	0.6	114

Short RH is recovered from TJS and showed showed no ill effects. Isn't overpowering but controls FB well and has some nice late action. Also mixes in an above-average CB and a decent CU. He commands all three well and has the potential to develop into a nice back-end starter.

Cisnero, Jose — SP — Houston

EXP MLB DEBUT: 2013 | POTENTIAL: #4 starter | 7C

Thrws R Age 24
2007 FA (DR)

87-97	FB	++++
80-83	SL	++
81-84	CU	++

Year	Lev	Team	W	L	Sv	IP	K	ERA	WHIP	BF/G	OBA	H%	S%	xERA	Ctl	Dom	Cmd	hr/9	BPV
2009	Rk	Greeneville	4	2	0	56	64	3.56	1.11	16.8	169	23	70	2.22	4.9	10.3	2.1	0.8	73
2010	A	Lexington	8	6	0	133	126	3.65	1.29	21.0	220	28	73	3.20	4.4	8.5	1.9	0.7	53
2011	A+	Lancaster	8	11	0	123	152	6.06	1.54	19.9	248	34	60	4.37	5.5	11.1	2.0	0.9	70
2012	AA	Corpus Christi	9	6	0	109	116	3.40	1.28	22.3	233	31	74	3.17	3.8	9.6	2.5	0.6	88
2012	AAA	Oklahoma City	4	1	0	40	32	4.54	1.76	22.7	317	39	72	5.30	4.1	7.3	1.8	0.2	38

Lean, yet durable SP who has flown under radar. Establishes control early in count with 2-seamer and can blow 4-seamer by batters. Possesses natural stuff that plays up due to quick arm. Can be inefficient when going for K and long arm action provides little deception. Needs to find consistent secondary offering.

Clemens, Paul — SP — Houston

EXP MLB DEBUT: 2013 | POTENTIAL: #4 starter | 7C

Thrws R Age 25
2008 (7) Louisburg JC

91-96	FB	+++
83-86	SL	++
75-78	CB	+++
	CU	+++

Year	Lev	Team	W	L	Sv	IP	K	ERA	WHIP	BF/G	OBA	H%	S%	xERA	Ctl	Dom	Cmd	hr/9	BPV
2011	AA	Mississippi	6	5	0	109	93	3.73	1.35	22.7	252	31	73	3.70	3.6	7.7	2.1	0.7	58
2011	AA	Corpus Christi	2	1	0	31	26	2.35	1.14	24.3	210	25	84	2.85	3.5	7.6	2.2	0.9	60
2011	AAA	Oklahoma City	0	1	0	5	6	15.42	2.14	23.2	233	30	22	6.60	11.6	11.6	1.0	1.9	-86
2012	AA	Corpus Christi	3	2	0	42	37	3.46	1.25	24.2	259	30	80	4.33	2.4	8.0	3.4	1.5	98
2012	AAA	Oklahoma City	8	8	0	102	68	6.73	1.74	23.2	336	37	63	6.67	2.8	6.0	2.1	1.4	50

Long, lanky SP who was demoted to AA after miserable start to season. Generally pitches low in zone to induce GB, but fell victim to HR. Can be guilty of throwing too many strikes and could benefit from getting hitters to chase CB. Electric arm produces quality FB with heavy sink and mixes in CU.

Cleto, Maikel — RP — St. Louis

EXP MLB DEBUT: 2011 | POTENTIAL: Power reliever | 7C

Thrws R Age 24
2006 NDFA, Venezuela

94-97	FB	++++
78-81	SL	++
82-86	CU	++

Year	Lev	Team	W	L	Sv	IP	K	ERA	WHIP	BF/G	OBA	H%	S%	xERA	Ctl	Dom	Cmd	hr/9	BPV
2011	AA	Springfield	2	2	0	34	36	3.93	1.51	21.3	292	38	74	4.54	3.1	9.4	3.0	0.5	103
2011	AAA	Memphis	5	3	0	71	66	4.29	1.40	23.2	221	27	70	3.51	5.4	8.3	1.5	0.8	21
2011	MLB	Cardinals	0	0	0	4	6	12.47	2.54	7.7	364	45	56	11.71	8.3	12.5	1.5	4.2	18
2012	AAA	Memphis	3	2	2	54	66	5.37	1.36	5.0	252	36	59	3.70	3.7	11.1	3.0	0.7	118
2012	MLB	Cardinals	0	0	0	9	15	7.00	1.67	4.5	339	46	73	8.88	2.0	15.0	7.5	4.0	234

Stocky reliever has a live arm and FB sits at 94-97 topping out at 101, but has erractic control. Complements the FB with a CB and a CU, both of which are good but inconsistent. Throws strikes, but does not command his FB well and despite good velocity he got knocked around in '12.

Clevinger, Michael — SP — Los Angeles (A)

EXP MLB DEBUT: 2015 | POTENTIAL: #3 starter | 8E

Thrws R Age 22
2011 (4) Seminole State JC

91-96	FB	+++
81-83	SL	+++
81-84	CU	++

Year	Lev	Team	W	L	Sv	IP	K	ERA	WHIP	BF/G	OBA	H%	S%	xERA	Ctl	Dom	Cmd	hr/9	BPV
2010	NCAA	The Citadel	5	3	0	93	77	5.15	1.62	25.7	306	37	68	5.17	3.4	7.5	2.2	0.7	61
2011	Rk	Orem	0	0	0	4	5	2.25	1.25	5.4	210	32	80	2.26	4.5	11.3	2.5	0.0	99
2012	A	Cedar Rapids	1	1	0	41	34	3.73	1.22	20.7	242	29	70	3.24	2.9	7.5	2.6	0.7	75

Tall, powerful SP who underwent TJ surgery that will likely keep him out for most of '13. Turned heads when healthy by using solid-avg FB to get ahead in count and getting hitters to swing and miss at SL. Gets good movement with quick arm and CU has potential to be third average pitch. Has effort in delivery.

Cloyd, Tyler — SP — Philadelphia

EXP MLB DEBUT: 2012 | POTENTIAL: #5 starter/reliever | 6B

Thrws R Age 26
2008 (18) HS, NE

87-90	FB	++
73-75	CB	++
80-82	CU	++

Year	Lev	Team	W	L	Sv	IP	K	ERA	WHIP	BF/G	OBA	H%	S%	xERA	Ctl	Dom	Cmd	hr/9	BPV
2011	A+	Clearwater	3	1	0	39	39	2.75	0.97	11.5	218	28	74	2.31	1.6	8.9	5.6	0.7	135
2011	AA	Reading	6	3	0	107	99	2.78	1.09	23.2	251	32	76	2.96	1.3	8.4	6.6	0.6	134
2012	AA	Reading	3	0	0	25	20	1.80	1.00	23.9	238	29	83	2.35	1.1	7.2	6.7	0.4	118
2012	AAA	Lehigh Valley	12	1	0	142	93	2.35	1.01	24.7	208	23	82	2.51	2.4	5.9	2.4	0.9	59
2012	MLB	Phillies	2	2	0	33	30	4.91	1.21	22.2	262	28	69	4.91	1.9	8.2	4.3	2.2	114

Relies on throwing strikes and the results are hard to argue with. Locates 87-90 mph FB to both sides of the plate and mixes in a CB and CU. Walked only 41 in 167 IP and was 15-1 with a 2.26 ERA before being called up. Was shut down at the end of the season, but should get a chance to win the 5th spot.

Cohoon, Mark — SP — New York (N)

EXP MLB DEBUT: 2013 | POTENTIAL: #5 starter | 6C

Thrws L Age 25
2008 (12) North Central Texas JC

87-90	FB	+++
70-74	CB	++
81-83	CU	++

Year	Lev	Team	W	L	Sv	IP	K	ERA	WHIP	BF/G	OBA	H%	S%	xERA	Ctl	Dom	Cmd	hr/9	BPV
2010	AA	Binghamton	5	4	0	71	56	4.18	1.25	22.2	270	32	67	3.68	1.9	7.1	3.7	0.6	94
2011	AA	Binghamton	1	3	0	52	44	3.81	1.46	24.7	287	34	78	4.99	2.9	7.6	2.6	1.2	76
2011	AAA	Buffalo	4	11	0	94	51	6.11	1.67	23.6	311	34	64	5.77	3.6	4.9	1.3	1.0	8
2012	AA	Binghamton	8	11	0	147	83	3.62	1.21	25.7	262	29	72	3.57	1.8	5.1	2.8	0.7	60
2012	AAA	Buffalo	0	1	0	8	4	14.63	2.38	20.8	415	43	35	10.60	3.4	4.5	1.3	2.3	8

Finesse lefty struggled at AAA, but was better when sent back to AA. Has a decent 87-90 mph FB, a backdoor CB, and a nice CU, but none are plus. Struggles with control, which is a concern given his lack of dominance. Has good mound pressence and knows what he can do, but upside is limited.

Cole, A.J. — SP — Oakland

EXP MLB DEBUT: 2015 | POTENTIAL: #2 starter | 9D

Thrws R Age 21
2010 (4) HS (FL)

90-97	FB	++++
77-79	CB	+++
	CU	++

Year	Lev	Team	W	L	Sv	IP	K	ERA	WHIP	BF/G	OBA	H%	S%	xERA	Ctl	Dom	Cmd	hr/9	BPV
2010	A-	Vermont	0	0	0	1	1	0.00	2.00	4.8	262	35	100	4.84	9.0	9.0	1.0	0.0	-63
2011	A	Hagerstown	4	7	0	89	108	4.04	1.25	18.1	257	36	68	3.43	2.4	10.9	4.5	0.6	149
2012	A	Burlington	6	3	0	96	102	2.07	1.01	19.3	224	30	83	2.47	1.8	9.6	5.4	0.7	142
2012	A+	Stockton	0	7	0	38	31	7.82	1.84	22.1	359	41	59	7.55	2.4	7.3	3.1	1.7	86

Lean, projectable SP who got off to rough start, but stabilized in Low-A. Has high ceiling with mix of power and control. Repeats delivery and throws consistent strikes from low ¾ slot. Doesn't have much deception in delivery, but power stuff is good enough to get hitters out. CB could develop into plus pitch.

Cole, Gerrit — SP — Pittsburgh

EXP MLB DEBUT: 2013 | POTENTIAL: #1 starter | 9C

Thrws R Age 22
2011 (1) UCLA

93-97	FB	++++
86-88	SL	++++
83-85	CU	+++

Year	Lev	Team	W	L	Sv	IP	K	ERA	WHIP	BF/G	OBA	H%	S%	xERA	Ctl	Dom	Cmd	hr/9	BPV
2010	NCAA	UCLA	11	4	0	123	153	3.37	1.17	25.8	210	31	70	2.33	3.8	11.2	2.9	0.3	117
2011	NCAA	UCLA	6	8	0	114	119	3.31	1.11	28.1	242	32	71	2.92	1.9	9.4	5.0	0.6	136
2012	A+	Bradenton	5	1	0	67	69	2.55	1.10	20.2	219	29	80	2.65	2.8	9.3	3.3	0.7	109
2012	AA	Altoona	3	6	0	59	60	2.90	1.31	20.3	245	33	77	3.14	3.5	9.2	2.6	0.3	88
2012	AAA	Indianapolis	1	0	0	6	7	4.50	1.17	23.9	262	38	57	2.72	1.5	10.5	7.0	0.0	167

Quickly developing into one of the best pitchers in the minors. Comes after hitters with a plus FB that tops out at 100 mph. Also has a nasty SL, a good CU, and a CB. His command can be iffy and he will leave pitches up, but can get away with it. If command improves he has the stuff to be an ace.

Cole, Taylor — SP — Toronto

EXP MLB DEBUT: 2015 | POTENTIAL: #5 starter | 7C

Thrws R Age 23
2011 (29) Brigham Young

89-93	FB	+++
81-83	SL	+++
82-84	CU	+++

Year	Lev	Team	W	L	Sv	IP	K	ERA	WHIP	BF/G	OBA	H%	S%	xERA	Ctl	Dom	Cmd	hr/9	BPV
2011	NCAA	Brigham Young	5	5	0	93	67	2.99	1.29	23.9	240	29	76	3.04	3.6	6.5	1.8	0.3	38
2011	A-	Vancouver	1	3	0	34	25	5.88	1.54	13.4	269	31	61	4.57	4.5	6.7	1.5	0.8	16
2012	A-	Vancouver	6	0	0	66	57	0.81	0.80	20.0	161	22	89	0.61	2.3	7.7	3.4	0.0	95

Sinkerballer who repeated short-season and was unhittable (.161 oppBA). All about feel and moxie and has no plus pitch. Induces GB with sinker and locates well. Throws tight SL and has good CU with depth and fade as third pitch. Has profile of back-end starter and could advance quickly due to intellect.

Collier, Tommy — SP — Detroit

EXP MLB DEBUT: 2015 | POTENTIAL: #5 starter | 7D

Thrws R Age 23
2011 (22) San Jacinto JC

87-93	FB	+++
81-84	SL	++
80-82	CU	+++

Year	Lev	Team	W	L	Sv	IP	K	ERA	WHIP	BF/G	OBA	H%	S%	xERA	Ctl	Dom	Cmd	hr/9	BPV
2011	A-	Connecticut	4	1	0	39	35	1.85	0.97	21.1	203	26	81	1.73	2.3	8.1	3.5	0.2	101
2012	A	West Michigan	9	8	0	125	84	2.74	1.20	20.9	242	29	77	2.91	2.7	6.1	2.3	0.4	55

Consistent, durable SP who lacks upside, but has good size and exhibits control. Sinker induces plenty of GB and can sometimes get hitters to chase SL. Has good separation in velo between FB and CU which allows CU to play up. Focuses on pitching to contact early in count. Delivery lacks fluidity.

Colome, Alexander — SP — Tampa Bay — EXP MLB DEBUT: 2013 — POTENTIAL: #3 starter — 8C

Thrws R Age 24	Year	Lev	Team	W	L	Sv	IP	K	ERA	WHIP	BF/G	OBA	H%	S%	xERA	Ctl	Dom	Cmd	hr/9	BPV
2007 FA (DR)	2010	A+	Charlotte	0	0	0	4	8	2.25	1.25	16.3	307	60	80	3.52	0.0	18.0		0.0	342
89-97 FB ++++	2011	A+	Charlotte	9	5	0	106	92	3.66	1.15	22.1	207	25	69	2.66	3.7	7.8	2.1	0.7	58
79-83 CB +++	2011	AA	Montgomery	3	4	0	52	31	4.15	1.33	24.0	219	24	70	3.43	4.8	5.4	1.1	0.9	-16
81-86 SL ++	2012	AA	Montgomery	8	3	0	75	75	3.48	1.37	22.5	246	33	73	3.27	4.1	9.0	2.2	0.2	70
80-84 CU +++	2012	AAA	Durham	0	1	0	17	15	3.24	1.26	22.7	203	26	75	2.74	4.9	8.1	1.7	0.5	33

Athletic, quick-armed SP with electric arm that produces plus FB with late sink. Keeps ball on ground and has sharp CB that hitters chase out of zone. CU shows flashes of solid third offering. Also mixes in below avg SL that he might shelve. Lacks deception in delivery and overall command needs work.

Colvin, Brody — SP — Philadelphia — EXP MLB DEBUT: 2014 — POTENTIAL: #3 starter — 8E

Thrws R Age 22	Year	Lev	Team	W	L	Sv	IP	K	ERA	WHIP	BF/G	OBA	H%	S%	xERA	Ctl	Dom	Cmd	hr/9	BPV
2009 (7) HS, LA	2009	Rk	GCL Phillies	0	0	0	2	2	0.00	0.50	6.6	0	0	100	0.00	4.5	9.0	2.0	0.0	59
92-94 FB +++	2010	A	Lakewood	6	8	0	138	120	3.39	1.30	21.1	262	33	74	3.52	2.7	7.8	2.9	0.5	85
75-77 CU +++	2011	A+	Clearwater	3	8	0	117	78	4.71	1.48	22.8	285	33	69	4.61	3.2	6.0	1.9	0.8	39
CB ++	2012	A+	Clearwater	5	6	0	105	93	4.27	1.56	20.0	276	35	72	4.32	4.4	7.9	1.8	0.4	43
	2012	AA	Reading	1	4	0	33	16	11.02	2.02	22.6	318	33	43	7.33	6.3	4.4	0.7	1.7	-74

Power-armed RH struggles with control, but has a plus 92-94 mph FB with a sharp CB. Repeat of High-A was marginally better, but hit a wall at AA. Weak front-side mechanics and nagging back injury resulted in poor command. Still time for him to develop, but he needs to make adjustments soon.

Comer, Kevin — SP — Houston — EXP MLB DEBUT: 2016 — POTENTIAL: #3 starter — 8E

Thrws R Age 20	Year	Lev	Team	W	L	Sv	IP	K	ERA	WHIP	BF/G	OBA	H%	S%	xERA	Ctl	Dom	Cmd	hr/9	BPV
2011 (1-S) HS (NJ)																				
86-92 FB +++																				
74-78 CB +++																				
CU ++	2012	Rk	Greeneville	0	1	0	6	5	9.00	2.00	14.5	371	40	60	9.44	3.0	7.5	2.5	3.0	72
	2012	Rk	Bluefield	3	3	0	43	29	3.95	1.18	17.3	260	30	68	3.55	1.7	6.0	3.6	0.8	82

Projectable SP who benefits from athleticism and smooth mechanics. Throws with clean arm action and should be able to add a few ticks to lively FB. Uses height to pitch with good angle and also has CB that he throws for strikes. Has tendency to slow arm speed on CU and needs time to polish FB command and learn sequencing.

Conley, Adam — SP — Miami — EXP MLB DEBUT: 2014 — POTENTIAL: #3 starter — 8D

Thrws L Age 23	Year	Lev	Team	W	L	Sv	IP	K	ERA	WHIP	BF/G	OBA	H%	S%	xERA	Ctl	Dom	Cmd	hr/9	BPV
2011 (2) Washington State	2010	NCAA	Washington St	5	4	12	68	47	3.32	1.29	9.6	260	30	75	3.54	2.7	6.3	2.4	0.5	59
91-95 FB ++++	2011	NCAA	Washington St	6	7	0	108	83	3.50	1.30	27.8	271	33	72	3.44	2.3	6.9	3.1	0.3	82
SL ++	2011	Rk	GCL Marlins	0	0	0	2	2	0.00	0.50	3.3	151	22	100	0.00	0.0	9.0		0.0	180
CU +++	2012	A	Greensboro	7	3	0	74	84	2.78	1.10	20.8	217	30	76	2.44	2.9	10.2	3.5	0.5	123
	2012	A+	Jupiter	4	2	0	53	51	4.44	1.48	18.9	284	38	67	3.85	3.2	8.7	2.7	0.0	87

Lefty continues transition to a starting role. Has a nice 88-93 mph FB that can hit 95 mph. Also features an above-average CU and a good SL. Breaking ball will need to make progress and there are still concerns about his durability. Struggled at High-A, but overall numbers were encouraging.

Cooney, Tim — SP — St. Louis — EXP MLB DEBUT: 2015 — POTENTIAL: #4 starter — 7D

Thrws L Age 22	Year	Lev	Team	W	L	Sv	IP	K	ERA	WHIP	BF/G	OBA	H%	S%	xERA	Ctl	Dom	Cmd	hr/9	BPV
2012 (3) Wake Forest																				
88-92 FB ++	2010	NCAA	Wake Forest	4	6	0	80	54	5.49	1.34	23.9	271	29	62	4.70	2.7	6.1	2.3	1.5	54
75-77 CB ++	2011	NCAA	Wake Forest	7	3	0	99	91	3.01	1.23	28.5	270	33	79	3.87	1.6	8.3	5.1	0.9	123
82-85 SL +++	2012	NCAA	Wake Forest	6	7	0	99	90	3.82	1.38	27.7	262	33	72	3.72	3.5	8.2	2.4	0.5	72
	2012	A-	Batavia	3	3	0	56	43	3.40	1.15	17.0	263	31	72	3.34	1.3	7.0	5.4	0.6	108

Finesse left-hander from Wake Forest had a nice pro debut in the NYPL. Cooney has a decent 88-92 mph FB, SL, CB, and CU, but doesn't have a swing-and-miss offering. He gets plenty of ground ball outs and commands the strike zone well, but will have to work hard to remain a starter.

Corcino, Daniel — SP — Cincinnati — EXP MLB DEBUT: 2013 — POTENTIAL: #3 starter — 8C

Thrws R Age 22	Year	Lev	Team	W	L	Sv	IP	K	ERA	WHIP	BF/G	OBA	H%	S%	xERA	Ctl	Dom	Cmd	hr/9	BPV
2008 NDFA, D.R.	2009	Rk	Billings	1	4	3	26	30	4.91	1.48	5.5	241	33	67	3.89	5.3	10.5	2.0	0.7	65
91-95 FB ++++	2010	Rk	Billings	1	3	0	40	31	3.40	1.39	18.5	254	31	75	3.62	3.9	7.0	1.8	0.5	40
75-78 SL ++++	2010	A	Dayton	1	1	0	31	29	4.31	1.47	22.4	260	34	69	3.74	4.3	8.3	1.9	0.3	52
84-85 CU +++	2011	A	Dayton	11	7	0	139	156	3.42	1.16	21.3	246	33	72	3.11	2.2	10.1	4.6	0.6	140
	2012	AA	Pensacola	8	8	0	143	126	3.01	1.23	22.3	215	27	77	2.83	4.1	7.9	1.9	0.6	50

Short righty goes after hitters with a plus low-90s FB with good late life. Complements the FB with a good SL and a CU that sinks and fades. Can overthrow at times, which led to struggles with control. Questions about his size (5'11", 165 lb) and durability linger, but some compare him to Johnny Cueto.

Cosart, Jarred — SP — Houston — EXP MLB DEBUT: 2013 — POTENTIAL: #2 starter — 9C

Thrws R Age 23	Year	Lev	Team	W	L	Sv	IP	K	ERA	WHIP	BF/G	OBA	H%	S%	xERA	Ctl	Dom	Cmd	hr/9	BPV
2008 (38) HS (TX)	2010	A	Lakewood	7	3	0	71	77	3.79	1.07	19.8	230	31	63	2.41	2.0	9.7	4.8	0.4	138
92-98 FB ++++	2011	A+	Clearwater	9	8	0	108	79	3.92	1.31	22.3	243	29	70	3.41	3.6	6.6	1.8	0.6	40
78-81 CB +++	2011	AA	Corpus Christi	1	2	0	36	22	4.71	1.27	21.2	244	26	64	3.71	3.2	5.5	1.7	1.0	29
82-84 CU +++	2012	AA	Corpus Christi	5	5	0	87	68	3.52	1.39	24.4	253	31	74	3.49	3.9	7.0	1.8	0.3	38
	2012	AAA	Oklahoma City	1	2	0	28	24	2.60	1.41	19.5	250	32	79	3.20	4.2	7.8	1.8	0.0	44

Lean, power pitcher who has yet to put together standout season, but has all tools to become frontline starter. Produces easy velo with smooth arm action while FB exhibits natural sink. Big-breaking CB can serve as K pitch, but he doesn't throw for consistent strikes. Lacks overall command and control.

Cote, Jordan — SP — New York (A) — EXP MLB DEBUT: 2016 — POTENTIAL: #2 starter — 9E

Thrws R Age 20	Year	Lev	Team	W	L	Sv	IP	K	ERA	WHIP	BF/G	OBA	H%	S%	xERA	Ctl	Dom	Cmd	hr/9	BPV
2011 (3) HS (NH)																				
88-94 FB +++																				
77-80 CB ++																				
80-82 SL ++																				
CU +++	2012	Rk	GCL Yankees	3	0	0	28	25	0.98	0.90	17.2	212	28	88	1.44	1.3	8.1	6.3	0.0	129

Tall SP with clean delivery and ideal arm action. Could add a few mph to FB as he gains strength. Both breaking balls remain inconsistent, though has gotten hitters to chase CB. CU is best secondary offering with solid depth. Tends to rush delivery and needs to harness quick arm. Commands FB well.

Crabbe, Tim — SP — Cincinnati — EXP MLB DEBUT: 2015 — POTENTIAL: #4 starter — 7D

Thrws R Age 25	Year	Lev	Team	W	L	Sv	IP	K	ERA	WHIP	BF/G	OBA	H%	S%	xERA	Ctl	Dom	Cmd	hr/9	BPV
2009 (14) HS, AZ	2010	A	Dayton	3	7	0	82	76	4.26	1.63	20.3	254	32	75	4.52	6.0	8.3	1.4	0.8	5
90-95 FB +++	2011	A	Dayton	2	2	1	25	25	3.65	1.18	12.3	240	31	70	3.15	2.6	9.1	3.6	0.7	113
SL ++++	2011	A+	Bakersfield	5	5	0	111	123	3.41	1.29	21.7	237	32	75	3.38	3.7	10.0	2.7	0.7	97
CB +	2012	A+	Bakersfield	5	2	0	58	60	3.28	1.06	22.4	220	29	71	2.65	2.3	9.4	4.0	0.8	123
CU +	2012	AA	Pensacola	3	6	0	86	93	4.90	1.70	21.7	250	32	72	4.80	6.9	9.7	1.4	0.9	7

Former 14th rounder has exceeded expectations. Has a good 91-94 mph FB and a plus SL. Crabbe struggled at Double-A, going 3-6 with a 4.90 ERA, but corrected things when sent back to High-A in the CAL where he showed good command and the ability to dominate.

Crick, Kyle — SP — San Francisco — EXP MLB DEBUT: 2015 — POTENTIAL: #2 starter — 9D

Thrws R Age 20	Year	Lev	Team	W	L	Sv	IP	K	ERA	WHIP	BF/G	OBA	H%	S%	xERA	Ctl	Dom	Cmd	hr/9	BPV
2011 (2) HS, TX																				
94-98 FB ++++																				
72-74 CB +++																				
81-83 SL ++	2011	Rk	Giants	1	0	0	7	8	6.43	2.43	5.2	313	43	71	6.66	10.3	10.3	1.0	0.0	-75
78-82 CU ++	2012	A	Augusta	7	6	0	111	128	2.51	1.28	19.8	193	28	79	2.21	5.4	10.3	1.9	0.1	58

Big-bodied righty with a nice 90-94 FB that tops out at 97. Complements the FB with a CB, a SL, and a CU. SL improved and gives him a chance to be an elite stater, but he needs to show better command of his plus fastbal. He walked 75 in 118.1 IP, but also struck out 136.

Crosby, Casey — SP — Detroit — EXP MLB DEBUT: 2012 — POTENTIAL: #3 starter — 8C

Thrws L Age 24	Year	Lev	Team	W	L	Sv	IP	K	ERA	WHIP	BF/G	OBA	H%	S%	xERA	Ctl	Dom	Cmd	hr/9	BPV
2007 (5) HS (IL)	2009	A	West Michigan	10	4	0	105	117	2.41	1.13	17.2	192	27	78	1.99	4.1	10.1	2.4	0.3	88
90-95 FB ++++	2010	Rk	GCL Tigers	0	1	0	12	10	8.76	2.03	19.9	377	45	54	7.47	2.9	7.3	2.5	0.7	71
80-84 CB ++++	2011	AA	Erie	9	7	0	132	121	4.10	1.51	22.8	247	31	74	4.12	5.3	8.3	1.6	0.8	25
82-84 CU +++	2012	AAA	Toledo	7	9	0	126	112	4.01	1.41	24.2	240	29	73	3.87	4.7	8.0	1.7	0.9	37
	2012	MLB	Detroit	1	1	0	12	9	9.49	2.11	20.3	301	34	54	7.08	8.0	6.6	0.8	1.5	-81

Tall, athletic SP got knocked around in 3 starts with DET, but has put together back-to-back healthy campaigns with makings of three avg-to-plus offerings. Plus FB can register Ks with excellent downward angle. Matches with CB that has varying velo. Offers some deception, but needs to trust CU.

Dayton, Grant — RP — Miami

EXP MLB DEBUT: 2013 | POTENTIAL: Reliever | 7C

Thrws L Age 25
2010 (11) Auburn

- 91-94 FB +++
- 81-84 SL +++
- CU +

Year	Lev	Team	W	L	Sv	IP	K	ERA	WHIP	BF/G	OBA	H%	S%	xERA	Ctl	Dom	Cmd	hr/9	BPV
2010	Rk	GCL Marlins	0	0	1	1	1	0.00	0.00	2.8	0	0	100	0.00	0.0	9.0		0.0	180
2010	A-	Jamestown	1	1	1	29	23	1.26	1.15	6.7	182	24	88	1.73	4.7	7.2	1.5	0.0	21
2011	A	Greensboro	7	1	5	72	99	2.89	1.16	5.8	226	34	77	2.80	3.0	12.4	4.1	0.6	160
2012	A+	Jupiter	2	5	2	60	71	2.10	1.10	7.6	221	32	80	2.16	2.7	10.7	3.9	0.2	137
2012	AA	Jacksonville	2	1	0	13	19	4.15	1.23	7.5	247	36	71	3.95	2.8	13.2	4.8	1.4	180

Strong-armed reliever continues to put up impressive numbers. Has a good FB/SL combination and sets up hitters effectively. FB sits at 92-94 and goes as high as 96 mph. SL has good depth and late movement. Mixes in a few CUs to keep hitters off-balance. Walked 22 while striking out 90 in 73 IP.

De Fratus, Justin — RP — Philadelphia

EXP MLB DEBUT: 2011 | POTENTIAL: Potential closer | 8C

Thrws R Age 25
2007 (11) Ventura JC

- 89-93 FB ++++
- 79-82 SL +++
- 80-81 CU ++

Year	Lev	Team	W	L	Sv	IP	K	ERA	WHIP	BF/G	OBA	H%	S%	xERA	Ctl	Dom	Cmd	hr/9	BPV
2011	MLB	Phillies	1	0	0	4	3	2.25	1.00	3.1	81	11	75	0.35	6.8	6.8	1.0	0.0	-43
2012	Rk	GCL Phillies	0	0	0	2	3	0.00	0.50	3.3	151	27	100	0.00	0.0	13.5		0.0	261
2012	A+	Clearwater	0	0	0	2	1	0.00	1.00	3.8	262	30	100	2.36	0.0	4.5		0.0	99
2012	AAA	Lehigh Valley	0	1	3	22	22	2.49	0.83	4.7	197	25	75	1.85	1.2	9.1	7.3	0.8	149
2012	MLB	Phillies	0	0	0	11	8	3.37	1.12	3.2	189	24	67	1.74	4.2	6.7	1.6	0.0	26

RH reliever was slowed by an elbow injury, but is healthy and profiles as a future closer. Goes after hitters with a 92-95 FB that hits 98 mph. Also throws a nasty, late breaking SL. Keeps ball low with sinking action on FB and is tough on RH batters. Concerns about durability re-emerged despite move to relief.

De La Rosa, Dane — RP — Tampa Bay

EXP MLB DEBUT: 2011 | POTENTIAL: Setup reliever | 6B

Thrws R Age 30
2002 (24) Riverside CC

- 91-97 FB +++
- 81-83 CB +++

Year	Lev	Team	W	L	Sv	IP	K	ERA	WHIP	BF/G	OBA	H%	S%	xERA	Ctl	Dom	Cmd	hr/9	BPV
2010	AA	Montgomery	9	3	4	73	75	1.97	1.26	6.3	243	32	85	3.06	3.2	9.2	2.9	0.4	98
2011	AAA	Durham	6	5	6	70	83	3.20	1.27	5.5	241	32	79	3.65	3.3	10.6	3.2	1.0	119
2011	MLB	Tampa Bay	0	0	0	7	8	9.82	1.77	4.8	326	42	42	6.38	3.7	9.8	2.7	1.2	95
2012	AAA	Durham	0	4	20	68	87	2.79	1.15	5.0	159	25	75	1.68	5.6	11.6	2.1	0.3	75
2012	MLB	Tampa Bay	0	0	0	5	5	12.60	1.80	4.6	332	35	29	8.78	3.6	9.0	2.5	3.6	83

Tall, strong RP who limited opposing batters to .158 oppBA. Can dominate by challenging with FB and setting up CB to put away hitters. Doesn't have any feel for CU and has lots of moving parts in delivery. FB can be straight at higher velocities and will be subject to flyballs. Has to throw more strikes.

De Leon, Victor — SP — St. Louis

EXP MLB DEBUT: 2015 | POTENTIAL: #3 starter | 8D

Thrws R Age 21
2009 NDFA, D.R.

- 92-95 FB ++++
- 80-82 SL ++
- CU ++

Year	Lev	Team	W	L	Sv	IP	K	ERA	WHIP	BF/G	OBA	H%	S%	xERA	Ctl	Dom	Cmd	hr/9	BPV
2011	Rk	GCL Cardinals	0	6	0	50	30	4.47	1.59	22.2	283	33	71	4.47	4.3	5.4	1.3	0.4	-1
2012	Rk	Johnson City	3	0	0	44	42	3.25	1.33	18.4	238	31	74	3.03	4.1	8.5	2.1	0.2	62

Dominican hurler features a live 95-96 FB that tops out at 97 mph. Also has a CU and an improved SL, but all remain inconsistent. Struggles with command and control and frequently overthrows his FB causing it to flatten out. Has a long way to go, but is still young and has tons of potential.

DeJong, Chase — SP — Toronto

EXP MLB DEBUT: 2016 | POTENTIAL: #3 starter | 8E

Thrws R Age 19
2012 (2) HS (CA)

- 87-93 FB +++
- 77-80 CB +++
- 80-81 CU ++

Year	Lev	Team	W	L	Sv	IP	K	ERA	WHIP	BF/G	OBA	H%	S%	xERA	Ctl	Dom	Cmd	hr/9	BPV
2012	Rk	GCL Blue Jays	1	0	0	12	15	1.50	0.67	7.0	171	27	75	0.35	0.8	11.3	15.0	0.0	200

Athletic, physical SP with upside, though may take a while to develop, particularly with crude mechanics. Can rush delivery and negatively impact command. Spots FB well and has solid-avg CB and developing CU at disposal. Could grow into more velocity and would make enticing late reliever.

Delgado, Dimasther — SP — Atlanta

EXP MLB DEBUT: 2015 | POTENTIAL: #4 starter/reliever | 7D

Thrws L Age 24
2007 NDFA, Panama

- 85-90 FB +++
- 71-74 CB ++
- 76-78 CU +++

Year	Lev	Team	W	L	Sv	IP	K	ERA	WHIP	BF/G	OBA	H%	S%	xERA	Ctl	Dom	Cmd	hr/9	BPV
2008	Rk	GCL Braves	5	1	0	40	39	4.31	1.51	15.6	313	40	71	4.79	2.0	8.8	4.3	0.5	122
2009	A	Rome	5	7	0	100	104	3.61	1.15	23.3	240	32	68	2.75	2.3	9.4	4.0	0.4	124
2011	A+	Lynchburg	9	6	0	96	77	3.94	1.40	17.6	241	29	73	3.76	4.5	7.2	1.6	0.8	26
2012	A+	Lynchburg	7	7	0	129	80	3.92	1.42	22.7	284	33	72	4.19	2.7	5.6	2.1	0.5	45

Was fully recovered from a car accident in '10, but spent the entire season in a repeat of High-A. Fared well and has a nice low-90s FB and a good CU. Big, looping CB can be effective, but spin on needs to be tighter to be effective. Still some work to do and will get a good test when he reaches AA.

Dodson, Zack — SP — Pittsburgh

EXP MLB DEBUT: 2014 | POTENTIAL: #4 starter | 6D

Thrws L Age 22
2009 (4) HS, TX

- 90-93 FB ++
- CB +++
- CU ++

Year	Lev	Team	W	L	Sv	IP	K	ERA	WHIP	BF/G	OBA	H%	S%	xERA	Ctl	Dom	Cmd	hr/9	BPV
2010	A-	State College	2	6	0	58	41	4.84	1.46	16.4	260	31	65	3.75	4.2	6.4	1.5	0.3	19
2011	Rk	GCL Pirates	0	1	0	9	7	4.15	1.27	11.8	247	29	70	3.78	3.1	7.3	2.3	1.0	65
2011	A	West Virginia	6	4	0	67	46	2.56	1.14	20.3	245	29	78	2.85	2.0	6.2	3.1	0.4	75
2011	A-	State College	0	1	0	18	13	4.58	1.47	19.0	306	35	71	5.13	2.0	6.6	3.3	1.0	82
2012	A	West Virginia	6	6	0	100	67	4.86	1.51	20.6	282	32	70	4.94	3.6	6.0	1.7	1.1	29

Athletic lefty was less impressive in his 2nd stint in the SAL. Has a nice 89-92 FB, a 12-6 good CB, and a below average CU. Gets plenty of GB outs and works hard, but fringy FB resulted in just 6.0 K per nine. FB is not good enough to dominate, but does have good control and competes well.

Drake, Oliver — SP — Baltimore

EXP MLB DEBUT: 2013 | POTENTIAL: #5 starter | 7C

Thrws R Age 26
2008 (43) Navy

- 89-94 FB +++
- 82-85 SL +++
- 78-80 CB ++
- 78-80 CU ++

Year	Lev	Team	W	L	Sv	IP	K	ERA	WHIP	BF/G	OBA	H%	S%	xERA	Ctl	Dom	Cmd	hr/9	BPV
2010	A+	Frederick	6	6	0	128	100	4.36	1.34	22.2	272	31	72	4.60	2.6	7.0	2.7	1.3	74
2011	A+	Frederick	8	3	0	97	80	2.14	0.99	26.3	222	29	77	1.89	1.7	7.4	4.4	0.1	107
2011	AA	Bowie	3	5	0	64	47	5.20	1.58	23.5	299	34	69	5.39	3.4	6.6	2.0	1.1	46
2011	AAA	Norfolk	0	0	0	2	2	0.00	1.00	7.6	151	22	100	0.99	4.5	9.0	2.0	0.0	59
2012	AA	Bowie	1	1	0	18	15	1.50	0.67	20.9	136	16	82	0.48	2.0	7.5	3.8	0.5	99

Athletic, tall SP who saw season end shoulder tendinitis. Induces lots of GB with solid-avg sinking FB. Pitches off sinker and sets up hitters for hard SL that serves as put-away offering. Throws with clean arm, though could stand upgrade with CB and CU. Doesn't project to high K rates at upper levels.

Dwyer, Chris — SP — Kansas City

EXP MLB DEBUT: 2013 | POTENTIAL: #3 starter / Setup reliever | 8D

Thrws L Age 25
2009 (4) Clemson

- 88-94 FB +++
- 80-82 CB ++++
- 80-82 CU +++

Year	Lev	Team	W	L	Sv	IP	K	ERA	WHIP	BF/G	OBA	H%	S%	xERA	Ctl	Dom	Cmd	hr/9	BPV
2010	A+	Wilmington	6	3	0	84	93	2.99	1.33	23.3	249	34	77	3.27	3.5	9.9	2.8	0.3	102
2010	AA	NW Arkansas	2	1	0	18	20	3.06	1.19	17.7	181	23	79	2.73	5.1	10.2	2.0	1.0	64
2011	AA	NW Arkansas	8	10	0	141	126	5.60	1.43	22.2	237	29	61	3.92	5.0	8.0	1.6	0.9	28
2012	AA	NW Arkansas	5	8	0	86	71	5.25	1.44	21.4	246	28	66	4.51	4.6	7.5	1.6	1.4	27
2012	AAA	Omaha	3	4	0	50	33	6.97	1.93	26.5	340	37	67	7.56	4.3	5.9	1.4	1.8	8

Athletic, durable SP who hasn't been effective last two seasons despite intriguing repertoire. Generates quality FB with quick arm and above avg CB that registers Ks. Avg CU gives him three effective offerings to battle hitters from both sides. Throws across body and inability to locate pitches mutes arsenal.

Edwards, C.J. — SP — Texas

EXP MLB DEBUT: 2015 | POTENTIAL: #3 starter | 8C

Thrws R Age 21
2011 (48) HS (SC)

- 90-95 FB ++++
- 74-78 CB +++
- 81-84 CU ++

Year	Lev	Team	W	L	Sv	IP	K	ERA	WHIP	BF/G	OBA	H%	S%	xERA	Ctl	Dom	Cmd	hr/9	BPV
2012	Rk	Rangers	3	0	0	20	25	0.00	0.60	17.1	96	16	100	0.00	2.7	11.3	4.2	0.0	148
2012	A-	Spokane	2	3	0	47	60	2.11	0.96	17.8	164	26	76	1.00	3.6	11.5	3.2	0.0	127

Quick-armed SP who had breakout campaign. Didn't allow an ER in rookie ball. Locates plus FB despite nasty late movement and hitters don't elevate it. Slow CB has been effective and needs to stay on top of it. Has shown nice feel for improving CU and should eventually have three avg to plus offerings.

Eflin, Zach — SP — San Diego

EXP MLB DEBUT: 2016 | POTENTIAL: #3 starter | 8D

Thrws R Age 19
2012 (1-S) HS (FL)

- 92-94 FB +++
- CB +
- 81-83 CU +++

Year	Lev	Team	W	L	Sv	IP	K	ERA	WHIP	BF/G	OBA	H%	S%	xERA	Ctl	Dom	Cmd	hr/9	BPV
2012	Rk	Padres	0	1	0	7	4	7.71	1.71	7.9	313	36	50	4.91	3.9	5.1	1.3	0.0	6

Exciting RH has a nice 92-94 FB from a high 3/4 arm slot. Is already physical and should add more as he fills out. Gets downward tilt on his FB, but needs to be more consistent. Also has a good CU, but his breaking ball is less reliable. Did have triceps tendinitis and the Padres were careful with him.

Elias, Roenis

SP | **Seattle** | EXP MLB DEBUT: 2014 | POTENTIAL: #4 starter | **7D**

Thrws L Age 24
2011 FA (Cuba)

88-93	FB	+++
80-81	SL	+++
74-77	CB	++
	CU	+++

Year	Lev	Team	W	L	Sv	IP	K	ERA	WHIP	BF/G	OBA	H%	S%	xERA	Ctl	Dom	Cmd	hr/9	BPV
2011	Rk	Pulaski	1	0	0	11	8	0.82	1.27	15.0	262	32	93	3.03	2.5	6.5	2.7	0.0	70
2011	Rk	Mariners	0	0	0	1	0	0.00	1.00	3.8	262	26	100	2.41	0.0	0.0		0.0	18
2011	A	Clinton	4	2	0	36	33	5.45	1.62	23.1	286	33	71	5.87	4.5	8.2	1.8	1.7	45
2012	A+	High Desert	11	6	0	148	128	3.76	1.19	22.9	245	29	73	3.68	2.5	7.8	3.1	1.2	91

Tall, lean SP who was among few who succeeded in home environment. Improved control and retired LHH (.212). Works in bottom half of zone with sinker. Uses quick arm to produce avg velocity and late movement. SL exhibits sufficient break, though CB lacks consistency and bite.

Erlin, Robbie

SP | **San Diego** | EXP MLB DEBUT: 2013 | POTENTIAL: #3 starter | **8A**

Thrws L Age 22
2009 (3) HS, CA

88-93	FB	++++
72-75	CB	++++
71-72	CU	+++

Year	Lev	Team	W	L	Sv	IP	K	ERA	WHIP	BF/G	OBA	H%	S%	xERA	Ctl	Dom	Cmd	hr/9	BPV
2011	A+	Myrtle Beach	3	2	0	55	62	2.14	0.55	20.5	140	16	74	0.81	0.8	10.2	12.4	1.2	179
2011	AA	Frisco	5	2	0	67	61	4.32	1.20	24.4	280	34	68	4.22	0.9	8.2	8.7	1.2	141
2011	AA	San Antonio	1	0	0	26	31	1.38	1.15	17.2	262	36	93	3.34	1.4	10.7	7.8	0.7	174
2012	Rk	Arizona	0	2	0	8	8	2.16	1.08	10.8	230	31	78	2.10	2.2	8.6	4.0	0.0	115
2012	AA	San Antonio	3	1	0	52	72	2.92	1.28	19.5	264	38	82	3.99	2.4	12.4	5.1	1.0	176

Short lefty with extreme pitchability. Elbow injury caused him to miss three months. Gets ahead of hitters by locating 88-92 FB then expands the zone with a plus CB and a good CU. Locates everything well and can pitch to all four quadrants. Look at BPV and has a career 7.4 Cmd. Not flashy, but effective.

Espinosa, Abraham

SP | **Atlanta** | EXP MLB DEBUT: 2015 | POTENTIAL: #3 starter | **8D**

Thrws R Age 20
2010 NDFA, Panama

86-89	FB	+++
	CB	+++
	CU	++

Year	Lev	Team	W	L	Sv	IP	K	ERA	WHIP	BF/G	OBA	H%	S%	xERA	Ctl	Dom	Cmd	hr/9	BPV
2012	Rk	GCL Braves	3	6	0	47	37	3.80	1.27	17.6	252	30	71	3.59	2.9	7.0	2.5	0.8	68

Short RH from Panama held his own in his U.S. debut. Is still mostly about projectability. FB sits in the upper-80s topping out at 89 mph, but could add more velocity as he fills out. Showed good control in the GCL. Is still learning how to pitch, but shows an advanced for throwing strikes. Nice back end starter.

Familia, Jeurys

RP | **New York (N)** | EXP MLB DEBUT: 2012 | POTENTIAL: Setup reliever | **8E**

Thrws R Age 23
2007 NDFA, D.R.

94-96	FB	++++
83-85	SL	+++
	CU	++

Year	Lev	Team	W	L	Sv	IP	K	ERA	WHIP	BF/G	OBA	H%	S%	xERA	Ctl	Dom	Cmd	hr/9	BPV
2010	A+	St. Lucie	6	9	0	121	137	5.58	1.58	22.2	255	35	63	4.16	5.5	10.2	1.9	0.5	53
2011	A+	St. Lucie	1	1	0	36	36	1.49	0.80	21.9	170	23	82	0.92	2.0	8.9	4.5	0.2	125
2011	AA	Binghamton	4	4	0	88	96	3.49	1.37	21.6	256	33	78	4.12	3.6	9.9	2.7	1.0	98
2012	AAA	Buffalo	9	9	0	137	128	4.73	1.59	21.6	273	35	70	4.46	4.8	8.4	1.8	0.5	40
2012	MLB	New York (N)	0	0	0	12	10	5.84	1.54	6.7	223	29	58	3.19	6.6	7.3	1.1	0.0	-28

Athletic RH struggled with control and consistency, walking 73 in 137 IP. Has a plus 93-95 FB that tops at 97 mph. SL and CU can be plus, but remain inconsistent. Mechanical adjustments he made in '11 didn't stick. Fell behind and got pounded when he found too much of the plate. Profiles better in relief.

Faulk, Kenny

RP | **Detroit** | EXP MLB DEBUT: 2013 | POTENTIAL: Situational reliever | **6A**

Thrws L Age 26
2009 (16) Kennesaw State

87-93	FB	+++
78-80	CB	+++
	CU	++

Year	Lev	Team	W	L	Sv	IP	K	ERA	WHIP	BF/G	OBA	H%	S%	xERA	Ctl	Dom	Cmd	hr/9	BPV
2009	NCAA	Kennesaw St	7	4	4	43	56	3.16	1.20	6.6	215	28	84	3.76	3.8	11.8	3.1	1.7	128
2009	A-	Oneonta	2	2	9	29	28	2.83	1.29	4.7	214	26	82	3.32	4.7	8.8	1.9	0.9	49
2010	A	West Michigan	5	4	12	58	78	2.16	1.41	5.0	240	38	83	3.02	4.6	12.0	2.6	0.0	110
2011	A+	Lakeland	2	5	20	53	67	2.56	1.23	4.4	252	37	81	3.23	2.6	11.4	4.5	0.5	155
2012	AA	Erie	1	0	4	58	68	4.53	1.56	6.3	263	36	72	4.46	5.0	10.6	2.1	0.8	74

Short, compact RP who relies on retiring LHH and deception. Projects as solid situational RP with high K ability. None of offerings grade as above avg, but uses well in tandem. Arm action leads to sneaky quick FB and can drop in CB for strikes. Walk rate increasing and flyball tendencies could become issue.

Fernandez, Jose

SP | **Miami** | EXP MLB DEBUT: 2014 | POTENTIAL: #1 starter | **9C**

Thrws R Age 20
2011 (1) HS, FL

93-97	FB	++++
80-83	CB	++++
	CU	++

Year	Lev	Team	W	L	Sv	IP	K	ERA	WHIP	BF/G	OBA	H%	S%	xERA	Ctl	Dom	Cmd	hr/9	BPV
2011	Rk	GCL Marlins	0	0	0	2	3	0.00	1.00	7.6	151	27	100	0.94	4.5	13.5	3.0	0.0	140
2011	A-	Jamestown	0	1	0	2	4	19.31	3.00	13.6	378	61	29	9.20	11.6	15.5	1.3	0.0	-17
2012	A	Greensboro	7	0	0	79	99	1.59	0.87	20.8	186	28	82	1.25	2.1	11.3	5.5	0.2	166
2012	A+	Jupiter	7	1	0	55	59	1.96	1.00	19.1	197	28	78	1.49	2.8	9.7	3.5	0.0	117

Might have been the most impressive pitcher in the minors in '12. Has a plus, plus 93-97 sinking FB that tops out at 99 mph. Also throws a late-breaking SL, a slow CB, and an improved CU. Strong frame should allow him to work deep into games. Confidence and flair rub some the wrong way, but he backs it up.

Ferrara, Anthony

SP | **St. Louis** | EXP MLB DEBUT: 2015 | POTENTIAL: #5 starter | **6C**

Thrws L Age 23
2008 (7) HS, FL

88-91	FB	+++
75-78	CB	+++
77-79	CU	+++

Year	Lev	Team	W	L	Sv	IP	K	ERA	WHIP	BF/G	OBA	H%	S%	xERA	Ctl	Dom	Cmd	hr/9	BPV
2009	Rk	Johnson City	4	1	0	50	40	3.24	1.32	15.9	258	32	74	3.26	3.1	7.2	2.4	0.2	65
2010	A-	Batavia	1	0	2	18	17	6.00	1.50	9.7	312	38	60	5.26	2.0	8.5	4.3	1.0	117
2011	A	Quad Cities	13	7	0	128	93	3.03	1.22	22.4	222	26	76	2.85	3.7	6.6	1.8	0.5	35
2012	A+	Palm Beach	5	7	0	98	77	3.58	1.38	22.9	244	29	75	3.65	4.2	7.1	1.7	0.6	31
2012	AA	Springfield	0	0	0	10	10	4.50	1.70	15.1	175	25	71	3.02	9.9	9.0	0.9	0.0	-87

Athletic hurler features quick arm action that generates movement and allows him to miss bats without great velocity. CB breaks well, being thrown on and off plate, and does a nice job of mixing pitches. Missed several weeks with a groin strain. Lack of overpowering FB limits his upside and control is marginal.

Foltynewicz, Mike

SP | **Houston** | EXP MLB DEBUT: 2015 | POTENTIAL: #3 starter | **8C**

Thrws R Age 21
2010 (1) HS (SC)

91-96	FB	++++
75-77	CB	+++
80-82	CU	+++

Year	Lev	Team	W	L	Sv	IP	K	ERA	WHIP	BF/G	OBA	H%	S%	xERA	Ctl	Dom	Cmd	hr/9	BPV
2010	Rk	Greeneville	0	3	0	45	39	4.03	1.37	15.6	267	33	71	3.89	3.0	7.9	2.6	0.6	78
2011	A	Lexington	5	11	0	134	88	4.97	1.49	22.2	283	32	66	4.52	3.4	5.9	1.7	0.7	32
2012	A	Lexington	14	4	0	152	125	3.14	1.36	23.5	253	31	79	3.73	3.7	7.4	2.0	0.7	52

Tall, smooth SP had favorable return to Low-A and showed improved command. Uses clean arm to generate lively FB that he spots to both sides. CB and CU became firmer and had more confidence to use while behind in count. Lacks swing-and-miss stuff, though K rate could increase as he learns to mix.

Font, Wilmer

RP | **Texas** | EXP MLB DEBUT: 2012 | POTENTIAL: Setup reliever / Closer | **8D**

Thrws R Age 23
2006 FA (DR)

91-98	FB	++++
74-79	CB	++
80-82	CU	+++

Year	Lev	Team	W	L	Sv	IP	K	ERA	WHIP	BF/G	OBA	H%	S%	xERA	Ctl	Dom	Cmd	hr/9	BPV
2010	A	Hickory	4	1	0	30	33	5.16	1.62	18.8	295	39	69	5.19	3.9	10.0	2.5	0.9	92
2010	A+	Bakersfield	1	2	0	49	52	3.86	1.43	23.1	216	28	75	3.66	5.9	9.6	1.6	0.9	31
2012	A+	Myrtle Beach	2	5	0	83	109	4.21	1.14	14.3	198	28	66	2.85	4.0	11.8	2.9	1.1	122
2012	AA	Frisco	2	0	1	15	29	3.00	1.07	5.8	175	38	73	1.90	4.2	17.4	4.1	0.6	218
2012	MLB	Texas	0	0	0	2	1	9.00	2.00	3.2	0	0	50	2.23	18.0	4.5	0.3	0.0	-387

Overpowering RP who reached TEX after missing entire '11 season. Has explosive FB and ability to pitch up. FB features heavy life and throws on downhill angle. Can miss bats with solid-avg CU, though lacks feel for CB. Can be subject to HR when hangs breaking ball. Could become dominant, ace reliever.

Frazier, Parker

SP | **Colorado** | EXP MLB DEBUT: 2014 | POTENTIAL: #5 starer/reliever | **6C**

Thrws R Age 24
2007 (8) HS, OK

88-92	FB	++
79-84	SL	++
	CU	+

Year	Lev	Team	W	L	Sv	IP	K	ERA	WHIP	BF/G	OBA	H%	S%	xERA	Ctl	Dom	Cmd	hr/9	BPV
2009	A	Asheville	10	7	0	131	98	4.48	1.46	24.3	300	36	68	4.51	2.3	6.7	3.0	0.5	78
2010	A-	Tri-City	1	3	0	20	15	7.53	1.77	18.7	328	39	54	5.70	3.5	6.6	1.9	0.4	42
2010	A+	Modesto	2	2	0	46	38	4.70	1.30	21.1	274	34	61	3.45	2.2	7.4	3.5	0.2	94
2011	A+	Modesto	11	11	0	154	105	4.50	1.41	24.1	283	32	69	4.49	2.7	6.1	2.3	0.9	56
2012	AA	Tulsa	5	14	0	167	93	3.88	1.33	25.7	279	30	74	4.39	2.2	5.0	2.3	1.0	50

Tall, lean righty has good stuff, but the results are not great. Has a good feel for pitching and good control. Works off a low-90s FB to go along with a plus SL and a below-average CU. Held his own at Double-A, but saw his Dom drop to 5.0 and simply doesn't miss enough bats. A move to relief seems likely.

Fried, Max

SP | **San Diego** | EXP MLB DEBUT: 2016 | POTENTIAL: #2 starter | **9D**

Thrws L Age 19
2012 (1) HS, CA

90-94	FB	+++
74-78	CB	+++
80-83	CU	++

Year	Lev	Team	W	L	Sv	IP	K	ERA	WHIP	BF/G	OBA	H%	S%	xERA	Ctl	Dom	Cmd	hr/9	BPV
2012	Rk	Padres	0	1	0	18	17	3.57	1.13	7.0	219	28	68	2.58	3.1	8.7	2.8	0.5	91

LH was the 7th pick in the '12 draft and has a lean, projectable frame. Already has a good 90-95 mph FB with some late arm-side run and a plus CB. CU needs work, but has nice potential. Shows good command of FB and CB and has some good deception. If CU develops he has the stuff to be a true #1.

Fuesser, Zac
RP | Pittsburgh | EXP MLB DEBUT: 2014 | POTENTIAL: Reliever | 6C

Thrws L Age 22
2009 (34) HS, SC

Velo	Pitch	Grade
88-91	FB	++
	CB	+++
	CU	++

Year	Lev	Team	W	L	Sv	IP	K	ERA	WHIP	BF/G	OBA	H%	S%	xERA	Ctl	Dom	Cmd	hr/9	BPV
2009	Rk	GCL Pirates	1	1	0	14	12	1.26	1.12	11.3	129	17	88	1.08	6.3	7.5	1.2	0.0	-16
2010	A-	State College	0	4	1	54	47	3.64	1.49	15.6	261	32	76	4.02	4.5	7.8	1.7	0.5	37
2011	A	West Virginia	3	6	2	108	95	3.74	1.33	14.0	267	32	76	4.31	2.7	7.9	2.9	1.2	86
2012	A	West Virginia	3	7	0	112	93	4.09	1.43	15.4	266	32	73	4.24	3.7	7.5	2.0	0.8	53

Finesse lefty worked both as a starter and in relief in '12 and took a step back in repeat of Low-A. Has a decent 88-91 mph FB, a good CB, and an average CU. Throws strikes, controls the zone, and keeps hitters off balance. Was more effective working in relief and will likely stay in that role going forward.

Fulmer, Michael
SP | New York (N) | EXP MLB DEBUT: 2015 | POTENTIAL: #2 starter | 8D

Thrws R Age 20
2011 (1-S) HS, OK

Velo	Pitch	Grade
92-95	FB	++++
83-85	SL	++++
	CU	+

Year	Lev	Team	W	L	Sv	IP	K	ERA	WHIP	BF/G	OBA	H%	S%	xERA	Ctl	Dom	Cmd	hr/9	BPV
2011	Rk	GCL Mets	0	1	0	5	10	10.13	2.44	7.0	375	64	54	7.69	6.8	16.9	2.5	0.0	140
2012	A	Savannah	7	6	0	108	101	2.74	1.20	20.7	231	30	78	2.89	3.2	8.4	2.7	0.5	84

Stocky RH had an impressive full-season debut. Has a solid has a 92-95 FB that tops out at 97 mph. Also throws a SL that has good late break. His CU remains undeveloped and he is not overly athletic. Mechanics are not perfect as verges close to max-effort, but he knows how to pitch, keeps the ball down.

Gagnon, Drew
SP | Milwaukee | EXP MLB DEBUT: 2015 | POTENTIAL: #3 starter | 7C

Thrws R Age 23
2011 (3) Long Beach State

Velo	Pitch	Grade
90-93	FB	+++
78-81	CB	+++
	CU	++

Year	Lev	Team	W	L	Sv	IP	K	ERA	WHIP	BF/G	OBA	H%	S%	xERA	Ctl	Dom	Cmd	hr/9	BPV
2010	NCAA	Long Beach St	5	7	0	93	65	3.28	1.22	25.1	248	29	74	3.26	2.6	6.3	2.4	0.6	61
2011	NCAA	Long Beach St	4	10	0	99	84	2.81	1.18	26.5	220	28	76	2.57	3.4	7.6	2.2	0.4	62
2011	Rk	Helena	0	3	1	19	27	8.05	1.84	11.1	318	47	53	5.68	4.7	12.8	2.7	0.5	120
2012	A	Wisconsin	6	1	0	83	65	2.83	1.04	22.8	223	27	75	2.55	2.1	7.1	3.4	0.7	90
2012	A+	Brevard County	1	2	0	67	49	2.82	1.10	23.9	229	27	75	2.55	2.4	6.6	2.7	0.4	71

Gagnon is not an overpowering RH but has a solid 90-93 mph FB and had good results. Attacks both sides of the strike zone and complements the FB with an improved CB and a decent CU. Has good command of all three offerings and could develop into a solid back-end starter.

Gannon, Nolan
SP | Tampa Bay | EXP MLB DEBUT: 2016 | POTENTIAL: #3 starter | 8E

Thrws R Age 19
2012 (4) HS (CA)

Velo	Pitch	Grade
87-91	FB	+++
73-78	CB	++
81-83	CU	+++

Year	Lev	Team	W	L	Sv	IP	K	ERA	WHIP	BF/G	OBA	H%	S%	xERA	Ctl	Dom	Cmd	hr/9	BPV
2012	Rk	GCL Rays	2	2	0	27	29	3.00	1.11	9.6	183	24	75	2.23	4.3	9.7	2.2	0.7	75

Projectable SP who has potential and upside predicated on clean arm and loose delivery. Velo is slightly below avg at present, but has the arm action to add more with strength. CB and CU have avg potential and will need to throw CB with more conviction. May spend a few years in short-season ball.

Garcia, Onelki
SP | Los Angeles (N) | EXP MLB DEBUT: 2016 | POTENTIAL: #3 starter | 8D

Thrws L Age 23
2012 (3) Cuba

Velo	Pitch	Grade
92-94	FB	+++
	CB	++
	CU	+

Year	Lev	Team	W	L	Sv	IP	K	ERA	WHIP	BF/G	OBA	H%	S%	xERA	Ctl	Dom	Cmd	hr/9	BPV
2012	A+	Rancho Cuc	0	0	0	2	4	0.00	0.00	5.6	0	0			0.0	18.0		0.0	342

LH Cuban defector was eligible for the draft and the makings of a good FB that currently sits in the 90-93 mph range. He also has a good but inconsistent CB and a below-average CU. Logged just 2 innings in his pro debut, so we will get a better read on him in 2013.

Gardner, Joe
SP | Colorado | EXP MLB DEBUT: 2013 | POTENTIAL: #4 starter | 7C

Thrws R Age 25
2009 (3) UC Santa Barbara

Velo	Pitch	Grade
87-92	FB	+++
74-78	SL	++
78-82	CU	++

Year	Lev	Team	W	L	Sv	IP	K	ERA	WHIP	BF/G	OBA	H%	S%	xERA	Ctl	Dom	Cmd	hr/9	BPV
2010	A	Lake County	1	0	0	25	38	3.24	1.12	16.4	194	32	73	2.40	4.0	13.7	3.5	0.7	157
2010	A+	Kinston	12	6	0	122	104	2.65	1.11	21.9	198	25	76	2.08	3.8	7.7	2.0	0.3	54
2011	AA	Akron	7	8	0	97	60	4.99	1.59	22.6	282	32	68	4.66	4.3	5.5	1.3	0.6	1
2011	AA	Tulsa	3	3	0	36	22	2.48	1.07	23.6	232	27	76	2.38	2.0	5.5	2.8	0.2	63
2012	AA	Tulsa	8	8	1	138	99	3.97	1.21	19.9	249	28	69	3.50	2.5	6.4	2.5	0.8	65

Tall, strong hurler generates tons of GB outs with a plus 89-93 sinking FB. Throws sinker from low 3/4 slot and can spot it consistently. Had a 3.0 GB/FB ratio in '12. All of his offerings have good movement and he throws free and easy. Will need CU and SL to improve in order to remain a starter.

Garner, Perci
SP | Philadelphia | EXP MLB DEBUT: 2014 | POTENTIAL: #3 starter | 7D

Thrws R Age 24
2010 (2) Ball State

Velo	Pitch	Grade
92-94	FB	+++
83-85	CB	++
	CU	++
	SL	++

Year	Lev	Team	W	L	Sv	IP	K	ERA	WHIP	BF/G	OBA	H%	S%	xERA	Ctl	Dom	Cmd	hr/9	BPV
2009	NCAA	Ball State	1	0	1	20	24	4.95	1.80	5.4	262	38	69	4.31	7.2	10.8	1.5	0.0	18
2010	NCAA	Ball State	5	3	0	74	83	4.62	1.50	18.8	262	36	68	4.02	4.5	10.1	2.2	0.5	78
2010	A-	Williamsport	0	2	0	4	1	18.00	2.25	10.1	415	41	13	10.30	2.3	2.3	1.0	2.3	-2
2011	A-	Williamsport	1	1	1	30	30	1.20	1.27	15.3	255	35	89	2.90	2.7	9.0	3.3	0.0	107
2012	A+	Clearwater	7	9	0	134	91	4.84	1.48	22.1	263	31	67	4.14	4.2	6.1	1.4	0.6	14

Athletic RH is still figuring out how to pitch. Was a two-sport stand-out at Ball State and has a good 92-94 FB with good late life. Also throws a CB, SL, and a CU. While his CB and CU show potential, neither is a plus and command remains inconsistent. Will need to show progress to reach potential.

Garrett, Amir
SP | Cincinnati | EXP MLB DEBUT: 2015 | POTENTIAL: #3 starter | 8D

Thrws L Age 21
2011 (22) HS, NV

Velo	Pitch	Grade
90-94	FB	+++
	CB	+
	CU	+

Year	Lev	Team	W	L	Sv	IP	K	ERA	WHIP	BF/G	OBA	H%	S%	xERA	Ctl	Dom	Cmd	hr/9	BPV
2012	Rk	Billings	0	0	0	6	5	0.00	0.83	11.0	191	25	100	1.03	1.5	7.5	5.0	0.0	113
2012	Rk	Reds	0	2	0	14	13	5.79	1.86	9.4	262	33	68	5.09	7.7	8.4	1.1	0.6	-40

Tall, strong LH also plays power forward at St. Johns University. Already has a 92-95 mph FB and could see more velocity once he grows into his 6'6" frame. Is still very raw on the mound. but has the makings of a decent CU and CB. At this point he is a project, but has significant potential.

Gast, John
SP | St. Louis | EXP MLB DEBUT: 2014 | POTENTIAL: #5 starter/reliever | 6C

Thrws L Age 24
2010 (6) Florida State

Velo	Pitch	Grade
88-92	FB	+++
76-78	CB	++
	CU	++

Year	Lev	Team	W	L	Sv	IP	K	ERA	WHIP	BF/G	OBA	H%	S%	xERA	Ctl	Dom	Cmd	hr/9	BPV
2010	A-	Batavia	6	0	0	35	36	1.54	1.00	16.7	215	29	85	1.95	2.1	9.3	4.5	0.3	129
2011	A+	Palm Beach	5	4	0	82	59	3.95	1.38	26.5	269	31	73	4.11	3.1	6.5	2.1	0.8	52
2011	AA	Springfield	4	4	0	79	54	4.08	1.42	25.9	263	29	74	4.40	3.7	6.1	1.6	1.0	27
2012	AA	Springfield	4	2	0	51	41	1.93	0.99	24.5	208	24	87	2.45	2.3	7.2	3.2	0.9	86
2012	AAA	Memphis	9	5	0	109	86	5.10	1.52	23.7	287	34	67	4.77	3.5	7.1	2.0	0.8	52

Short, power lefty who works off a nice 90-93 mph FB. Also features a solid CB and a decent CU. Delivery is close to max-effort and has already had TJS. Managed to make 28 starts, so concerns about health and durability seem to have been answered, but his stuff might work better in relief.

Gausman, Kevin
SP | Baltimore | EXP MLB DEBUT: 2014 | POTENTIAL: #2 starter | 9D

Thrws R Age 22
2012 (1) Louisiana State

Velo	Pitch	Grade
92-98	FB	++++
77-79	CB	++
83-86	SL	++
82-86	CU	++++

Year	Lev	Team	W	L	Sv	IP	K	ERA	WHIP	BF/G	OBA	H%	S%	xERA	Ctl	Dom	Cmd	hr/9	BPV
2011	NCAA	Louisiana State	5	6	0	90	86	3.51	1.04	24.7	217	28	66	2.30	2.3	8.6	3.7	0.5	111
2012	NCAA	Louisiana State	12	2	0	124	135	2.77	1.08	26.8	233	33	73	2.34	2.0	9.8	4.8	0.2	140
2012	A-	Aberdeen	0	0	0	6	5	0.00	0.17	9.0	56	8	100	0.00	0.0	7.5		0.0	153
2012	A+	Frederick	0	1	0	9	8	6.00	1.22	12.1	283	29	63	6.00	1.0	8.0	8.0	3.0	135

Tall, lean SP who should get to bigs quickly due to power arsenal. Pitches off vicious FB with plus movement. Best secondary is CU that features depth and fade. Owns SL and CB, though high arm slot more conducive to SL. Can be tough to make hard contact against, but needs consistency in breaking balls.

Geltz, Steven
RP | Los Angeles (A) | EXP MLB DEBUT: 2012 | POTENTIAL: Setup reliever | 6B

Thrws R Age 25
2008 FA (Buffalo)

Velo	Pitch	Grade
90-96	FB	++++
77-80	CB	+++
	CU	+

Year	Lev	Team	W	L	Sv	IP	K	ERA	WHIP	BF/G	OBA	H%	S%	xERA	Ctl	Dom	Cmd	hr/9	BPV
2011	AA	Arkansas	3	3	0	47	67	3.09	0.96	5.5	191	29	73	2.20	2.7	12.9	4.8	1.0	178
2011	AAA	Salt Lake	0	0	0	2	1	21.56	3.59	5.4	459	52	33	12.59	10.8	5.4	0.5	0.0	-176
2012	AA	Arkansas	3	0	6	25	37	0.36	0.75	4.3	154	27	95	0.35	2.1	13.1	6.2	0.0	197
2012	AAA	Salt Lake	0	1	5	34	33	5.08	1.28	5.5	234	29	62	3.65	3.7	8.8	2.4	1.1	76
2012	MLB	Angels	0	0	0	2	1	4.50	2.50	5.3	262	30	80	6.14	13.5	4.5	0.3	0.0	-266

Short, aggressive RP who defied odds by becoming NDFA who reached bigs. Throws hard with sneaky quick FB and works it up and down in zone. Has plus arm speed to generate velocity with solid-avg CB. Can get Ks with FB and CB, but tends to leave balls up due to lack of height. Not much upside.

Gibson, Kyle — SP — Minnesota

EXP MLB DEBUT: 2013 | POTENTIAL: #3 starter | 8B

Thrws R Age 25
2009 (1) Missouri

89-94	FB	++++
80-84	SL	+++
81-82	CU	+++

Year	Lev	Team	W	L	Sv	IP	K	ERA	WHIP	BF/G	OBA	H%	S%	xERA	Ctl	Dom	Cmd	hr/9	BPV
2010	AAA	Rochester	0	0	0	16	9	1.72	1.08	20.4	214	25	82	1.95	2.9	5.2	1.8	0.0	34
2011	AAA	Rochester	3	8	0	95	91	4.81	1.43	22.5	288	36	68	4.75	2.5	8.6	3.4	1.0	104
2012	Rk	GCL Twins	0	0	0	15	16	2.45	0.89	6.0	179	24	75	1.57	2.5	9.8	4.0	0.6	128
2012	A+	Fort Myers	0	0	0	7	7	2.57	1.00	13.4	233	28	83	3.14	1.3	9.0	7.0	1.3	145
2012	AAA	Rochester	0	2	0	7	10	9.45	1.80	15.4	369	53	45	7.28	1.3	13.5	10.0	1.3	224

Tall pitcher who returned from TJ surgery and was solid in AFL. Uses height to throw downhill and keeps sinking FB low. Throws strikes with all pitches and can get Ks with both SL and CU. Locates FB, but can work in fat part of plate. May have limited workload in '13, but good bet to pitch meaningful IP.

Gilmartin, Sean — SP — Atlanta

EXP MLB DEBUT: 2013 | POTENTIAL: #3 starter | 8C

Thrws L Age 23
2011 (1) Florida St

88-91	FB	+++
75-77	CU	+++
78-80	SL	+++
70-72	CB	++

Year	Lev	Team	W	L	Sv	IP	K	ERA	WHIP	BF/G	OBA	H%	S%	xERA	Ctl	Dom	Cmd	hr/9	BPV
2011	NCAA	Florida State	12	1	0	113	122	1.83	0.94	25.0	212	29	82	1.88	1.6	9.7	6.1	0.4	150
2011	Rk	GCL Braves	0	1	0	2	1	9.00	1.50	8.6	347	39	33	4.95	0.0	4.5		0.0	99
2011	A	Rome	2	1	0	21	30	2.53	0.94	16.0	230	33	82	2.90	0.8	12.7	15.0	1.3	223
2012	AA	Mississippi	5	8	0	119	86	3.54	1.15	23.7	248	29	70	3.17	2.0	6.5	3.3	0.7	82
2012	AAA	Gwinnett	1	2	0	38	25	4.78	1.43	22.9	278	30	71	5.02	3.1	6.0	1.9	1.4	42

Polished collegiate lefty reached AAA in full-season debut. Lacks an overpowering FB, but does have good control of an 88-92 mph heater with a plus CU, a CB, and a good SL. He has smooth, repeatable mechanics and is a strike-throwing machine. Attacks both sides of the plate and knows how to pitch.

Giolito, Lucas — SP — Washington

EXP MLB DEBUT: 2016 | POTENTIAL: #1 starter | 9D

Thrws R Age 18
2012 (1) HS, CA

93-96	FB	+++++
82-86	CB	++++
82-84	CU	++

Year	Lev	Team	W	L	Sv	IP	K	ERA	WHIP	BF/G	OBA	H%	S%	xERA	Ctl	Dom	Cmd	hr/9	BPV
2012	Rk	GCL Nationals	0	0	0	2	1	4.50	1.00	7.6	262	30	50	2.36	0.0	4.5		0.0	99

16th overall pick in the draft had TJS in August and will miss '13. Prior to the injury, had one of the best HS arms in the country. FB sat at 93-96 and topped out at 98 mph. Also had a power CB and a decent CU with excellent command. Assuming a full recovery, he gives the Nats another power arm.

Glasnow, Tyler — SP — Pittsburgh

EXP MLB DEBUT: 2015 | POTENTIAL: #3 starter | 8D

Thrws R Age 19
2011 (5) HS, CA

91-94	FB	++++
75-78	CB	+++
	CU	+

Year	Lev	Team	W	L	Sv	IP	K	ERA	WHIP	BF/G	OBA	H%	S%	xERA	Ctl	Dom	Cmd	hr/9	BPV
2012	Rk	GCL Pirates	0	3	0	34	40	2.10	1.02	12.0	164	22	84	1.90	4.2	10.5	2.5	0.8	94
2012	A-	State College	0	0	0	4	4	0.00	1.25	16.3	262	35	100	2.95	2.3	9.0	4.0	0.0	119

Tall RH has a good 91-94 FB, but could add more velocity as he fills out his lanky 6'7" frame. Mixes in a SL, CB, and CU with the CB being his best secondary pitch. Struggles with control, but showed progress and was one of the more dynamic starters in the GCL limiting opposing hitters to a .154 oppBAA.

Goeddel, Erik — RP — New York (N)

EXP MLB DEBUT: 2014 | POTENTIAL: #3 starter | 7D

Thrws R Age 24
2010 (24) UCLA

90-93	FB	+++
84-86	SL	+++
	CU	++

Year	Lev	Team	W	L	Sv	IP	K	ERA	WHIP	BF/G	OBA	H%	S%	xERA	Ctl	Dom	Cmd	hr/9	BPV
2010	NCAA	UCLA	2	0	1	50	59	3.06	1.34	5.8	238	33	79	3.51	4.1	10.6	2.6	0.7	97
2010	Rk	GCL Mets	0	0	0	1	1	0.00	1.00	3.8	262	35	100	2.32	0.0	9.0		0.0	180
2011	Rk	GCL Mets	0	0	0	6	2	1.50	0.83	7.3	228	25	80	1.51	0.0	3.0		0.0	72
2011	A	Savannah	3	5	0	72	67	3.39	1.14	18.9	223	28	71	2.77	3.0	8.4	2.8	0.6	88
2012	A+	St. Lucie	5	6	0	108	98	3.41	1.41	20.8	265	34	75	3.72	3.6	8.1	2.3	0.3	68

Tall, strong armed hurler with a good sinking FB that sits in the 90-93 range and has good downward tilt. Uses the sinker effectively to get plenty of groundball outs and gave up just 4 home runs in 108.1 innings. Also throws a decent CU and a plus SL with good break. Not much upside, but he knows how to pitch.

Goforth, David — SP — Milwaukee

EXP MLB DEBUT: 2014 | POTENTIAL: #4 starter | 7D

Thrws R Age 24
2011 (7) Mississippi

95-98	FB	++++
90-93	CT	++
	SL	++

Year	Lev	Team	W	L	Sv	IP	K	ERA	WHIP	BF/G	OBA	H%	S%	xERA	Ctl	Dom	Cmd	hr/9	BPV
2009	NCAA	Mississippi	1	1	3	35	36	2.80	1.27	5.8	201	26	81	2.95	5.1	9.2	1.8	0.8	46
2010	NCAA	Mississippi	1	6	3	56	43	9.43	2.27	13.0	362	39	61	9.38	6.1	6.9	1.1	2.4	-22
2011	NCAA	Mississippi	4	8	0	83	63	4.88	1.37	24.9	271	32	63	3.92	2.9	6.8	2.3	0.5	62
2011	Rk	Helena	0	4	2	41	42	4.43	1.33	8.9	277	35	69	4.40	2.2	9.3	4.2	1.1	126
2012	A	Wisconsin	10	8	0	151	93	4.66	1.44	22.9	266	29	69	4.42	3.8	5.6	1.5	1.0	16

Short RH was moved from relief to starter and put up solid numbers in the MWL. FB sits at 90-94 with good movement. Developed a good CT and a below-average SL. Development of the SL and a CU will determine whether he sticks as a starter. Either way he has a power arm worth watching.

Gonzales, Tyler — SP — Toronto

EXP MLB DEBUT: 2016 | POTENTIAL: #4 starter | 7D

Thrws R Age 20
2012 (1-S) HS (TX)

90-96	FB	+++
82-86	SL	+++
79-81	CU	++

Year	Lev	Team	W	L	Sv	IP	K	ERA	WHIP	BF/G	OBA	H%	S%	xERA	Ctl	Dom	Cmd	hr/9	BPV
2012	Rk	GCL Blue Jays	1	1	0	15	7	8.40	1.60	7.4	321	35	43	5.32	2.4	4.2	1.8	0.6	29

Tall, slender SP whose stuff is much better than performance. Exhibits lots of moving parts in delivery, but has athleticism to clean up and repeat. Delivery offers deception, but telegraphs hard SL and CU by changing arm slot and speed. FB is potential plus-plus offering with late movement and he gets GB.

Gould, Garrett — SP — Los Angeles (N)

EXP MLB DEBUT: 2014 | POTENTIAL: #3 starter | 7C

Thrws R Age 21
2009 (2) HS, KS

88-91	FB	+++
80-83	CB	+++
80-82	CU	++

Year	Lev	Team	W	L	Sv	IP	K	ERA	WHIP	BF/G	OBA	H%	S%	xERA	Ctl	Dom	Cmd	hr/9	BPV
2009	Rk	Ogden	0	1	0	3	4	10.11	2.25	4.5	347	46	60	9.90	6.7	13.5	2.0	3.4	79
2010	Rk	Ogden	1	4	0	58	52	4.06	1.53	19.3	295	37	74	4.71	3.1	8.1	2.6	0.6	80
2011	A	Great Lakes	11	6	0	124	104	2.40	1.12	18.1	226	28	81	2.72	2.7	7.6	2.8	0.6	82
2012	A+	Rancho Cuc	5	10	0	130	123	5.75	1.49	20.8	276	33	63	5.00	3.7	8.5	2.3	1.3	70

Flyball pitcher gave up 19 HR in the CAL, but is better than that. Has a nice 88-93 mph sinking FB and a plus 12-6 CB. Locates well and throws strikes. Isn't overpowering and projects as a back-end starter, but he knows how to pitch and keeps hitters off-balance with one of the best CB in the minors.

Graham, J.R. — SP — Atlanta

EXP MLB DEBUT: 2013 | POTENTIAL: #2 starter/Power Reliever | 9D

Thrws R Age 23
2011 (4) Santa Clara

92-95	FB	++++
83-85	SL	+++
	CU	++

Year	Lev	Team	W	L	Sv	IP	K	ERA	WHIP	BF/G	OBA	H%	S%	xERA	Ctl	Dom	Cmd	hr/9	BPV
2010	NCAA	Santa Clara	1	1	4	27	21	5.27	2.01	5.7	369	44	72	6.91	3.3	6.9	2.1	0.3	54
2011	NCAA	Santa Clara	3	5	3	62	45	3.34	1.00	10.3	233	29	64	2.09	1.3	6.5	5.0	0.1	100
2011	Rk	Danville	5	2	0	58	52	1.72	1.13	17.5	242	32	83	2.38	2.0	8.1	4.0	0.0	109
2012	A+	Lynchburg	9	1	0	103	68	2.63	1.02	23.2	233	27	76	2.52	1.5	6.0	4.0	0.5	85
2012	AA	Mississippi	3	1	0	45	42	3.18	1.15	20.0	215	28	72	2.46	3.4	8.3	2.5	0.4	77

Doesn't get a lot of attention, but gets the job done. FB sits at 92-95 and tops out at 100 mph. Also features a nice SL and a below-average CU. Attacks hitters low in the strike zone, inducing plenty of ground balls. The conversion from college closer to pro starter is a work in progress.

Gray, Sonny — SP — Oakland

EXP MLB DEBUT: 2013 | POTENTIAL: #3 starter | 8C

Thrws R Age 23
2011 (1) Vanderbilt

89-95	FB	+++
82-84	CB	++++
	CU	++

Year	Lev	Team	W	L	Sv	IP	K	ERA	WHIP	BF/G	OBA	H%	S%	xERA	Ctl	Dom	Cmd	hr/9	BPV
2011	NCAA	Vanderbilt	12	4	0	126	132	2.43	1.17	26.5	214	29	79	2.41	3.6	9.4	2.6	0.3	89
2011	Rk	Athletics	0	1	0	2	2	4.50	2.00	9.6	415	52	75	7.49	0.0	9.0		0.0	180
2011	AA	Midland	1	0	0	20	18	0.45	1.05	15.5	210	28	95	1.79	2.7	8.1	3.0	0.0	91
2012	AA	Midland	6	9	0	148	97	4.14	1.39	23.9	262	30	70	3.77	3.5	5.9	1.7	0.5	31
2012	AAA	Sacramento	0	0	0	4	2	9.00	2.75	22.3	470	52	64	10.75	2.3	4.5	2.0	0.0	38

Smooth power pitcher with excellent pure pitch mix thrown with clean arm. Despite size, maintains velo and works in bottom half of K zone. Gets ahead of hitters with sinking FB and plus, hard CB is out pitch. Hasn't been K artist, but could improve if he develops CU and FB command.

Green, Tyler — SP — Arizona

EXP MLB DEBUT: 2015 | POTENTIAL: Reliever | 7D

Thrws R Age 21
2010 (8) HS (TX)

90-94	FB	++++
78-80	CB	++
80-81	SL	++
	CU	+

Year	Lev	Team	W	L	Sv	IP	K	ERA	WHIP	BF/G	OBA	H%	S%	xERA	Ctl	Dom	Cmd	hr/9	BPV
2011	A	South Bend	6	8	1	114	79	4.97	1.46	19.5	268	31	66	4.35	3.9	6.2	1.6	0.8	26
2012	A	South Bend	4	9	1	126	75	3.78	1.52	21.1	270	31	76	4.32	4.3	5.3	1.3	0.6	-1

Short, athletic right-hander struggled tremendously with control in a repeat of the MWL. Does have a good, lively 91-94 mph FB, a CB, SL, and a below-average CU. Breaking balls and off-speed stuff remain fringy. Mechanics are inconsistent and a move to relief seems likely.

Gregorio, Joan — SP — San Francisco
EXP MLB DEBUT: 2015 | POTENTIAL: #4 starter | 7D

Thrws R Age 21
2010 NDFA, D.R.
88-93 FB +++
SL ++
CU +

Year	Lev	Team	W	L	Sv	IP	K	ERA	WHIP	BF/G	OBA	H%	S%	xERA	Ctl	Dom	Cmd	hr/9	BPV
2011	Rk	Giants	3	0	0	50	43	2.32	1.17	16.7	233	30	79	2.54	2.9	7.7	2.7	0.2	79
2012	A-	Salem-Keizer	7	7	0	76	69	5.54	1.41	20.2	283	34	62	4.67	2.7	8.1	3.0	1.1	91

Tall, lean frame with a good low-90s FB, but struggled in the MWL with a 5.54 ERA. His BPIs were not as bad as the results suggest, though he was very hittable and gave up a .272 oppBAA. Breaking ball and CU are still raw, but the SL has shown potential. Will need to get things back on track in '13.

Grimm, Justin — SP — Texas
EXP MLB DEBUT: 2012 | POTENTIAL: #4 starter | 7B

Thrws R Age 24
2010 (5) Georgia
90-96 FB +++
80-82 CB +++
82-84 CU ++

Year	Lev	Team	W	L	Sv	IP	K	ERA	WHIP	BF/G	OBA	H%	S%	xERA	Ctl	Dom	Cmd	hr/9	BPV
2011	A	Hickory	2	1	0	50	54	3.40	1.25	22.8	241	31	76	3.50	3.2	9.7	3.0	0.9	105
2011	A+	Myrtle Beach	5	2	0	90	73	3.39	1.26	23.0	248	31	71	2.99	3.0	7.3	2.4	0.2	68
2012	AA	Frisco	9	3	0	84	73	1.72	1.00	20.0	229	29	84	2.21	1.5	7.9	5.2	0.3	119
2012	AAA	Round Rock	2	3	0	51	30	4.59	1.35	23.6	269	31	64	3.68	2.8	5.3	1.9	0.4	37
2012	MLB	Texas	1	1	0	14	13	9.00	1.79	12.9	358	44	46	6.42	1.9	8.4	4.3	0.6	116

Athletic SP who dominated AA. Has lots of life with plus FB and throws quality strikes to all quadrants of K zone. Power CB is solid offering and can get hitters to chase. Hasn't been strikeout pitcher and needs to refine CU to keep LHH at bay. Tends to rush delivery and has effort to it.

Gueller, Mitch — SP — Philadelphia
EXP MLB DEBUT: 2016 | POTENTIAL: #3 starter | 7C

Thrws R Age 19
2012 (1-S) HS, WA
90-93 FB +++
CB ++
CU +

Year	Lev	Team	W	L	Sv	IP	K	ERA	WHIP	BF/G	OBA	H%	S%	xERA	Ctl	Dom	Cmd	hr/9	BPV
2012	Rk	GCL Phillies	1	5	0	27	19	5.27	1.39	14.4	252	31	58	3.20	4.0	6.3	1.6	0.0	24

Lean and lanky RH has a good 90-93 mph heater and could get a bit more once he matures. Also has a decent slurvy CB and a CU with potential. Struggled with control in his limited debut and will need to refine his approach as he moves up, but his raw stuff gives him some long-term potential.

Guerra, Deolis — RP — Minnesota
EXP MLB DEBUT: 2013 | POTENTIAL: Setup reliever | 6B

Thrws R Age 24
2005 FA (Venezuela)
88-94 FB +++
70-74 CB ++
77-80 CU +++

Year	Lev	Team	W	L	Sv	IP	K	ERA	WHIP	BF/G	OBA	H%	S%	xERA	Ctl	Dom	Cmd	hr/9	BPV
2010	AA	New Britain	2	10	0	102	67	6.24	1.60	23.8	306	34	62	5.66	3.3	5.9	1.8	1.2	36
2010	AAA	Rochester	0	3	0	25	18	6.84	1.72	22.7	332	36	63	6.91	2.9	6.5	2.3	1.8	57
2011	AA	New Britain	8	7	1	95	95	5.59	1.37	10.8	276	34	60	4.42	2.7	9.0	3.4	1.0	108
2012	AA	New Britain	2	0	1	13	15	0.71	0.47	6.0	123	19	83	0.00	0.7	10.7	15.0	0.0	191
2012	AAA	Rochester	2	3	0	57	56	4.87	1.40	8.3	267	33	67	4.42	3.3	8.8	2.7	1.1	87

Tall, hefty RP who has found niche in pen. Pitches aggressively in short innings, yet can use sinking and fading CU to keep hitters off guard. FB exhibits late life and CB has been slow to develop and will need in order to keep K rate high. Has been in upper minors since '09 and needs to break through.

Guerrieri, Taylor — SP — Tampa Bay
EXP MLB DEBUT: 2015 | POTENTIAL: #2 starter | 9C

Thrws R Age 20
2011 (1) HS (SC)
90-95 FB ++++
77-81 CB ++++
80-83 CU +++

Year	Lev	Team	W	L	Sv	IP	K	ERA	WHIP	BF/G	OBA	H%	S%	xERA	Ctl	Dom	Cmd	hr/9	BPV
2012	A-	Hudson Valley	1	2	0	52	45	1.04	0.77	15.6	193	26	85	0.88	0.9	7.8	9.0	0.0	135

Tall, lean SP who dominated in first pro sason. Steady and consistent delivery and arm slot produce quality FB that features late sink. Hitters bury into ground which leads to very high GB rate. CB serves as legitimate K offering. Can be inefficient when going for K and needs to mix pitches better.

Guillon, Ismael — SP — Cincinnati
EXP MLB DEBUT: 2015 | POTENTIAL: #3 starter | 7D

Thrws L Age 21
2008 NDFA, Venezuela
88-92 FB +++
CU +++
CB ++

Year	Lev	Team	W	L	Sv	IP	K	ERA	WHIP	BF/G	OBA	H%	S%	xERA	Ctl	Dom	Cmd	hr/9	BPV
2010	Rk	Reds	3	3	0	57	73	3.32	1.09	18.6	195	30	67	1.82	3.6	11.5	3.2	0.2	127
2011	Rk	Billings	3	6	0	63	61	6.57	1.97	20.1	305	36	69	6.87	6.6	8.7	1.3	1.6	-3
2012	Rk	Billings	4	1	0	51	63	2.29	1.24	18.8	213	32	81	2.43	4.2	11.1	2.6	0.2	104
2012	A	Dayton	2	0	0	25	27	2.55	1.18	24.6	240	32	81	3.15	2.6	9.9	3.9	0.7	126

Long and lean Venezuelan hurler had an impressive breakout. Has a dominant arm and struck out almost a batter an inning, but also walked 46 in 63 IP. Works off good low-90s FB and a plus CU. Needs to develop a quality breaking ball and improve his control, but already has a good 1-2 punch.

Gutierrez, Carlos — RP — Chicago (N)
EXP MLB DEBUT: 2013 | POTENTIAL: Setup reliever | 6B

Thrws R Age 26
2008 (1-C) Miami-FL
90-96 FB ++++
79-83 SL ++
80-82 CU +

Year	Lev	Team	W	L	Sv	IP	K	ERA	WHIP	BF/G	OBA	H%	S%	xERA	Ctl	Dom	Cmd	hr/9	BPV
2009	AA	New Britain	1	3	0	52	32	6.19	1.64	10.6	296	33	63	5.43	4.1	5.5	1.3	1.0	6
2010	AA	New Britain	5	8	2	122	81	4.57	1.52	16.6	283	33	69	4.46	3.7	6.0	1.6	0.5	26
2010	AAA	Rochester	0	0	0	4	6	2.25	1.75	9.1	307	49	86	4.82	4.5	13.5	3.0	0.0	140
2011	AAA	Rochester	2	3	0	62	57	4.62	1.46	6.2	254	33	66	3.65	4.5	8.2	1.8	0.3	45
2012	AAA	Rochester	2	2	0	16	20	5.06	1.00	6.1	224	30	50	2.85	1.7	11.3	6.7	1.1	175

Big, strong RP who underwent shoulder surgery and will be back early in '13. Deceptive cross-fire delivery produces heavy sink and movement on sinker. Hitters rarely elevate, and his extreme GB tendencies could lead to prominent role. Does not have good secondaries and relies too much on sinker.

Hahn, Jesse — SP — Tampa Bay
EXP MLB DEBUT: 2015 | POTENTIAL: #3 starter / Setup reliever | 8D

Thrws R Age 23
2010 (6) Virginia Tech
91-98 FB ++++
80-85 CB +++
80-85 CU ++

Year	Lev	Team	W	L	Sv	IP	K	ERA	WHIP	BF/G	OBA	H%	S%	xERA	Ctl	Dom	Cmd	hr/9	BPV
2008	NCAA	Virginia Tech	3	7	0	64	36	4.64	1.48	19.7	279	31	68	4.35	3.5	5.1	1.4	0.6	14
2009	NCAA	Virginia Tech	1	2	1	24	23	6.00	1.96	6.7	334	42	69	6.55	4.9	8.6	1.8	0.8	42
2010	NCAA	Virginia Tech	5	4	0	73	76	3.70	1.25	22.8	256	33	72	3.56	2.5	9.4	3.8	0.7	120
2012	A-	Hudson Valley	2	2	0	52	55	2.77	1.02	14.3	206	29	70	1.64	2.6	9.5	3.7	0.0	119

Power SP who has intriguing velocity, pitch movement, and stuff, but missed most of last three years with TJ surgery and broken foot. Was old for level and teased hitters with FB that he located low in zone. Uses two-seamer to induce gb and can blow four-seamer by batters up in zone. Hard CB shows potential.

Hale, David — SP — Atlanta
EXP MLB DEBUT: 2014 | POTENTIAL: #4 starter | 7D

Thrws R Age 25
2009 (3) Princeton
92-94 FB +++
SL ++++
CU +

Year	Lev	Team	W	L	Sv	IP	K	ERA	WHIP	BF/G	OBA	H%	S%	xERA	Ctl	Dom	Cmd	hr/9	BPV
2009	NCAA	Princeton	2	3	0	41	47	4.43	1.60	22.5	263	37	71	4.25	5.3	10.4	2.0	0.4	62
2009	Rk	Danville	2	1	1	16	12	1.13	0.75	8.2	134	17	83	0.21	2.8	6.8	2.4	0.0	64
2010	A	Rome	5	8	5	94	69	4.13	1.51	14.5	269	33	70	3.80	4.2	6.6	1.6	0.1	23
2011	A+	Lynchburg	4	6	0	101	86	4.10	1.35	15.0	271	33	71	4.09	2.7	7.7	2.9	0.8	84
2012	AA	Mississippi	8	4	0	146	124	3.77	1.29	22.2	228	28	72	3.25	4.1	7.7	1.9	0.7	44

SP with plus arm strength and easy velocity on his low-90s FB. Complements the heater with a plus SL and an improved CU. Took a huge step forward in the 2nd half, going 3-1 with a 3.28 ERA and made the SL All-Star squad. Needs to show better command of his FB and CU, but has some upside.

Haley, Trey — RP — Cleveland
EXP MLB DEBUT: 2013 | POTENTIAL: Setup reliever/Closer | 7D

Thrws R Age 23
2008 (2) HS (TX)
92-99 FB ++++
80-83 CB +++
82-84 CU ++

Year	Lev	Team	W	L	Sv	IP	K	ERA	WHIP	BF/G	OBA	H%	S%	xERA	Ctl	Dom	Cmd	hr/9	BPV
2011	A	Lake County	0	0	1	13	17	2.84	1.03	6.1	123	21	69	0.74	5.7	12.1	2.1	0.0	82
2011	A+	Kinston	1	1	1	29	27	3.77	1.46	6.5	236	31	73	3.45	5.3	8.5	1.6	0.3	26
2012	Rk	Indians	1	0	0	6	10	7.50	1.67	6.7	321	54	50	4.82	3.0	15.0	5.0	0.0	207
2012	A+	Carolina	0	0	2	17	16	1.04	0.81	5.2	141	20	86	0.41	3.1	8.3	2.7	0.0	83
2012	AA	Akron	3	1	0	15	23	1.76	1.37	7.1	188	33	86	2.28	6.5	13.5	2.1	0.0	87

Power-armed RP who was converted from SP in '11 and now letting FB fly. Has lots of movement in wild delivery, but has vicious, heavy FB. Since move to pen, has induced more gb and K rate increasing. Throws from ¾ slot which helps avg power CB. Control and command still need work and has athleticism.

Heaney, Andrew — SP — Miami
EXP MLB DEBUT: 2015 | POTENTIAL: #2 starter | 8C

Thrws L Age 22
2012 (1) Oklahoma State
90-92 FB ++++
CB ++
CU ++

Year	Lev	Team	W	L	Sv	IP	K	ERA	WHIP	BF/G	OBA	H%	S%	xERA	Ctl	Dom	Cmd	hr/9	BPV
2010	NCAA	Oklahoma St	5	4	1	66	55	5.16	1.58	18.3	302	36	68	5.28	3.3	7.5	2.3	0.9	64
2011	NCAA	Oklahoma St	7	4	0	67	51	4.03	1.49	14.4	290	35	71	4.23	3.1	6.9	2.2	0.3	58
2012	NCAA	Oklahoma St	8	2	0	118	140	1.60	0.81	28.6	182	27	82	1.11	1.7	10.6	6.4	0.3	164
2012	Rk	GCL Marlins	0	0	0	7	9	2.57	1.29	14.4	262	39	78	3.01	2.6	11.6	4.5	0.0	157
2012	A	Greensboro	1	2	0	20	21	4.95	1.45	21.4	307	41	62	4.11	1.8	9.5	5.3	0.0	140

Smart collegiate SP knows how to get hitters out. FB sits in the low-90s and tops out at 95 mph. Holds his velocity well and mixes in a deceptive CB and a CU with good late sink. Can throw all three for strikes and keeps hitters on their heels with pitch selection. Throws strikes and sets up hitters effectively.

Heath, Deunte — RP — Chicago (A)

EXP MLB DEBUT: 2012 | POTENTIAL: Setup reliever | 7C

Thrws R Age 27
2006 (19) Tennessee
90-97 FB ++++
79-83 SL +++
77-80 CB +
CU

Year	Lev	Team	W	L	Sv	IP	K	ERA	WHIP	BF/G	OBA	H%	S%	xERA	Ctl	Dom	Cmd	hr/9	BPV
2009	AAA	Gwinnett	0	1	0	19	18	9.64	2.09	13.1	339	42	51	7.15	5.8	8.7	1.5	1.0	18
2010	AA	Birmingham	2	4	2	58	84	3.12	1.40	6.2	232	36	79	3.48	5.0	13.1	2.6	0.6	119
2011	AAA	Charlotte	4	7	1	103	117	4.73	1.56	15.0	253	33	72	4.58	5.4	10.3	1.9	1.1	56
2012	AAA	Charlotte	4	3	3	67	74	1.48	1.00	7.1	199	27	89	2.02	2.7	9.9	3.7	0.5	124
2012	MLB	Chicago (A)	0	0	0	2	1	4.50	1.00	2.5	151	0	100	5.26	4.5	4.5	1.0	4.5	-23

Big, strong RP who had career year. Move to bullpen re-ignited him and hard stuff plays up in short stints. Can register Ks with FB and solid-avg SL while he also uses subpar CB and CU. Can be subject to flyballs as he leaves pitches up, though lively FB tough to elevate when located down in zone.

Heckathorn, Kyle — RP — Milwaukee

EXP MLB DEBUT: 2013 | POTENTIAL: #5 starter/reliever | 6C

Thrws R Age 25
2009 (1-S) Kennesaw St
88-93 FB ++
83-85 SL ++
CU ++

Year	Lev	Team	W	L	Sv	IP	K	ERA	WHIP	BF/G	OBA	H%	S%	xERA	Ctl	Dom	Cmd	hr/9	BPV
2010	A	Wisconsin	6	6	0	85	67	2.96	1.24	20.3	255	32	75	3.03	2.4	7.1	2.9	0.2	80
2010	A+	Brevard County	4	0	0	39	23	3.00	1.28	20.0	267	31	76	3.35	2.3	5.3	2.3	0.2	51
2011	A+	Brevard County	5	6	0	80	65	3.95	1.29	21.8	267	32	72	4.00	2.4	7.3	3.1	0.9	86
2011	AA	Huntsville	0	4	0	36	24	7.18	1.71	23.5	305	33	60	6.39	4.2	5.9	1.4	1.7	11
2012	AA	Huntsville	5	11	0	119	88	4.75	1.38	14.3	274	33	65	3.97	2.9	6.6	2.3	0.5	60

Workhorse SP fared better, but doesn't miss many bats. Reached the high 90s in college, but is in the low-90s as a pro. Also uses a CT, hard SL, and CU. Struggled to put hitters away despite good stuff. Struggles with FB command and mechanics resulted in a move to relief and could play swing role.

Hellweg, Johnny — SP — Milwaukee

EXP MLB DEBUT: 2013 | POTENTIAL: #3 starter/power reliever | 9E

Thrws R Age 24
2008 (16) Florida CC
94-97 FB ++++
83-85 CB ++
CU ++

Year	Lev	Team	W	L	Sv	IP	K	ERA	WHIP	BF/G	OBA	H%	S%	xERA	Ctl	Dom	Cmd	hr/9	BPV
2009	A	Cedar Rapids	0	0	2	7	7	1.35	1.65	6.0	175	25	91	2.88	9.4	9.4	1.0	0.0	-67
2010	A	Cedar Rapids	2	4	16	44	66	4.33	1.49	4.6	140	24	70	2.45	9.3	13.6	1.5	0.4	12
2011	A+	Inland Empire	6	4	0	89	113	3.73	1.50	13.8	229	34	73	3.31	5.9	11.4	1.9	0.2	62
2012	AA	Arkansas	5	10	0	120	88	3.38	1.38	23.9	237	28	76	3.53	4.5	6.6	1.5	0.6	15
2012	AA	Huntsville	2	1	0	20	17	2.70	1.55	12.5	221	29	81	3.18	6.8	7.7	1.1	0.0	-27

Tall, skinny SP was part of the Greinke deal. Comes after hitters with a plus 94-97 FB that can hit 100 mph. Also has an average CB and CU. Struggles with control and walked 75 in 139.2 IP. Does use his size well to pitch down hill and keeps the ball on the ground. Need to improve CU and show better control.

Hembree, Heath — RP — San Francisco

EXP MLB DEBUT: 2013 | POTENTIAL: Power reliever | 8C

Thrws R Age 24
2010 (5) College of Charleston
93-96 FB ++++
84-86 SL ++++
CU ++

Year	Lev	Team	W	L	Sv	IP	K	ERA	WHIP	BF/G	OBA	H%	S%	xERA	Ctl	Dom	Cmd	hr/9	BPV
2010	Rk	Giants	0	0	3	11	22	0.82	0.82	3.3	225	50	89	1.28	0.0	18.0		0.0	342
2011	A+	San Jose	0	0	21	25	44	0.73	1.13	3.8	187	37	96	1.99	4.4	16.1	3.7	0.4	189
2011	AA	Richmond	1	1	17	29	34	2.83	1.15	4.1	198	29	75	2.17	4.1	10.7	2.6	0.3	100
2012	A+	San Jose	0	0	0	5	7	0.00	0.20	3.0	0	0	100	0.00	1.8	12.6	7.0	0.0	196
2012	AAA	Fresno	1	1	15	38	36	4.74	1.29	4.0	213	28	62	2.87	4.7	8.5	1.8	0.5	44

Strong-armed RP suffered flexor strain and was not right until August. FB tops out 99 mph, but can be overthrown. Has smoothed out his mechanics, but still struggles with control. If healthy, should compete for a roster spot and has good K potential.

Hensley, Ty — SP — New York (A)

EXP MLB DEBUT: 2016 | POTENTIAL: #2 starter | 9D

Thrws R Age 20
2012 (1) HS (OK)
90-97 FB +++
77-79 CB +++
82-85 CU ++

Year	Lev	Team	W	L	Sv	IP	K	ERA	WHIP	BF/G	OBA	H%	S%	xERA	Ctl	Dom	Cmd	hr/9	BPV
2012	Rk	GCL Yankees	1	2	0	12	14	3.00	1.25	9.8	191	26	79	2.75	5.3	10.5	2.0	0.8	65

Durable and aggressive youngster who throws hard and has impressive CB to match. Natural stuff needs time to develop along with FB location. FB can arrive flat and he often telegraphs CB. Has stuff to become #2 starter—velocity, breaking ball, arm speed. Also possesses advanced ability to hold velocity.

Heredia, Luis — SP — Pittsburgh

EXP MLB DEBUT: 2015 | POTENTIAL: #1 starter | 9D

Thrws R Age 18
2010 NDFA. Mexico
90-93 FB ++++
CB ++
83-85 CU ++

Year	Lev	Team	W	L	Sv	IP	K	ERA	WHIP	BF/G	OBA	H%	S%	xERA	Ctl	Dom	Cmd	hr/9	BPV
2011	Rk	GCL Pirates	1	2	0	30	23	4.75	1.55	11.0	247	29	70	4.35	5.6	6.8	1.2	0.9	-11
2012	A-	State College	4	2	0	66	40	2.71	1.10	18.6	221	26	75	2.33	2.7	5.4	2.0	0.3	42

Tall, lanky SP is just starting to harness his immense potential. Already features a mid-90s FB, with room for more. Also has a SL, CB, and a CU. The CU showed signs of improvement, but all offerings need refinement. At 17 there is still much work to do, but the upside remains substantial.

Hermsen, B.J. — SP — Minnesota

EXP MLB DEBUT: 2013 | POTENTIAL: #4 starter | 7D

Thrws R Age 23
2008 (6) HS (IA)
84-91 FB +++
77-79 CB ++
78-80 CU +++

Year	Lev	Team	W	L	Sv	IP	K	ERA	WHIP	BF/G	OBA	H%	S%	xERA	Ctl	Dom	Cmd	hr/9	BPV
2010	A	Beloit	4	6	0	72	46	5.00	1.39	25.3	295	33	64	4.51	1.9	5.8	3.1	0.8	71
2011	A	Beloit	11	7	0	125	81	3.10	1.30	24.5	271	31	78	3.91	2.2	5.8	2.6	0.7	63
2011	A+	Fort Myers	2	1	0	27	20	4.39	1.50	23.0	311	37	69	4.64	2.0	6.7	3.3	0.3	85
2012	A+	Fort Myers	1	0	0	23	12	0.78	0.91	21.5	198	22	95	1.70	2.0	4.7	2.4	0.4	50
2012	AA	New Britain	11	6	0	140	75	3.22	1.22	25.6	269	29	76	3.73	1.6	4.8	3.0	0.8	61

Tall, durable SP who doesn't throw hard, but knows how to mix and throw strikes. Has become more aggressive with FB early and spotting it to corners. Doesn't offer a plus pitch, though CU has shown significant improvement. Repeats delivery and arm slot and induces GB. Very low K rate limits upside.

Hernandez, Pedro — SP — Minnesota

EXP MLB DEBUT: 2012 | POTENTIAL: #5 starter/Setup reliever | 6B

Thrws L Age 24
2006 FA (Venezuela)
88-93 FB +++
78-82 SL ++
80-83 CU +++

Year	Lev	Team	W	L	Sv	IP	K	ERA	WHIP	BF/G	OBA	H%	S%	xERA	Ctl	Dom	Cmd	hr/9	BPV
2011	AAA	Tucson	2	1	0	18	7	6.00	1.89	21.2	356	36	71	7.50	3.0	3.5	1.2	1.5	0
2012	AA	Birmingham	7	2	0	69	37	2.75	1.25	23.3	260	28	81	3.71	2.4	4.8	2.1	0.8	42
2012	AAA	Charlotte	1	0	0	17	17	3.71	1.24	23.0	273	35	70	3.56	1.6	9.0	5.7	0.5	137
2012	MLB	Chicago (A)	0	1	0	4	2	18.00	3.25	24.3	515	49	50	19.69	2.3	4.5	2.0	6.8	38
2012	AAA	Rochester	0	2	0	17	11	5.19	1.50	18.7	338	39	64	5.27	0.5	5.7	11.0	0.5	107

Short, stocky SP who fits Twins mold of control-command pitcher with limited velo. Deceptive CU may be best pitch and can use in any count. Drops all three pitches into zone for strikes and proper pitch sequencing has been asset. Doesn't have wipeout breaking ball. Could eventually move to pen.

Heston, Chris — SP — San Francisco

EXP MLB DEBUT: 2014 | POTENTIAL: #4 starter | 7B

Thrws R Age 25
2009 (12) East Carolina
86-89 FB ++
CB ++
SL ++
CU

Year	Lev	Team	W	L	Sv	IP	K	ERA	WHIP	BF/G	OBA	H%	S%	xERA	Ctl	Dom	Cmd	hr/9	BPV
2009	NCAA	East Carolina	7	0	0	91	88	4.17	1.35	22.2	260	33	71	4.01	3.2	8.7	2.8	0.9	89
2009	Rk	Giants	1	5	0	35	34	4.11	1.14	12.6	253	32	60	2.30	2.6	8.7	3.4	0.0	106
2010	A	Augusta	5	13	0	149	124	3.75	1.30	23.6	277	34	70	3.66	2.0	7.5	3.8	0.4	99
2011	A+	San Jose	12	4	0	151	131	3.16	1.22	25.4	253	31	75	3.31	2.4	7.8	3.3	0.6	94
2012	AA	Richmond	9	8	0	149	135	2.24	1.10	23.3	228	30	78	2.26	2.4	8.2	3.4	0.1	100

Finesse RH knows how to pitch. FB rarely breaks 90 mph but has good sinking action. Mixes in a SL and a CU and keeps the ball down in the zone—3.1 GB/FB ratio. Had an impressive season at the proving grounds of Double-A and doesn't get nearly as much attention as he should.

Holmberg, David — SP — Arizona

EXP MLB DEBUT: 2014 | POTENTIAL: #3 starter | 8B

Thrws L Age 21
2009 (2) HS (FL)
88-92 FB +++
SL ++
80-83 CU ++++

Year	Lev	Team	W	L	Sv	IP	K	ERA	WHIP	BF/G	OBA	H%	S%	xERA	Ctl	Dom	Cmd	hr/9	BPV
2010	Rk	Great Falls	1	1	0	40	29	4.46	1.51	21.8	314	37	69	4.82	2.0	6.5	3.2	0.4	80
2011	A	South Bend	8	3	0	83	81	2.39	0.94	22.3	217	29	75	1.90	1.4	8.8	6.2	0.3	138
2011	A+	Visalia	4	6	0	71	76	4.67	1.51	23.8	266	35	64	4.26	4.4	9.6	2.2	0.6	71
2012	A+	Visalia	6	3	0	78	86	2.99	0.97	24.7	219	29	71	2.33	1.6	9.9	6.1	0.7	152
2012	AA	Mobile	5	5	0	95	67	3.60	1.34	26.3	280	32	75	4.15	2.2	6.3	2.9	0.8	73

Big, physical lefty continues to make rapid progress. Has as good low-90s sinking FB that he locates to both sides. Also has an average SL and a plus CU. Uses his height effectively along with an overhand delivery to pitch downhill. Repeats delivery consistently and is willing to pound the zone.

Holmes, Clay — SP — Pittsburgh

EXP MLB DEBUT: 2015 | POTENTIAL: #3 starter | 8D

Thrws R Age 20
2011 (9) HS, AL
90-95 FB ++++
CB ++
CU ++

Year	Lev	Team	W	L	Sv	IP	K	ERA	WHIP	BF/G	OBA	H%	S%	xERA	Ctl	Dom	Cmd	hr/9	BPV
2012	A-	State College	5	3	0	59	34	2.28	1.08	17.8	173	20	78	1.61	4.4	5.2	1.2	0.2	-8

Strong-bodied RHP has a low-90s FB that he throws with downhill tilt, getting plenty of GB outs and allowed just 1 HR in 59.1 innings. Also has a good SL that needs to become more consistent. Secondary stuff needs to be better and to miss more bats, but he did limit hitters to a .176 oppBAA.

Holt, Brad

RP | **New York (N)** | **EXP MLB DEBUT:** 2013 | **POTENTIAL:** Power reliever | **6D**

Thrws R Age 26
2008 (1-S) UNC-Wilmington

88-93	FB	+ + +
80-83	SL	+ +
79-82	CU	+ +

Year	Lev	Team	W	L	Sv	IP	K	ERA	WHIP	BF/G	OBA	H%	S%	xERA	Ctl	Dom	Cmd	hr/9	BPV
2010	A+	St. Lucie	2	9	0	65	62	7.48	1.91	22.0	271	35	58	5.25	7.8	8.6	1.1	0.6	-37
2010	AA	Binghamton	1	5	0	30	25	10.20	2.20	15.1	337	41	50	7.07	6.9	7.5	1.1	0.6	-33
2011	AA	Binghamton	8	8	0	94	74	4.71	1.41	11.7	221	26	66	3.47	5.5	7.1	1.3	0.7	-2
2012	AA	Binghamton	2	1	1	48	42	3.40	1.49	5.3	242	30	78	3.83	5.3	7.9	1.5	0.6	18
2012	AAA	Buffalo	0	0	1	5	3	10.13	2.81	5.0	423	48	60	9.75	6.8	5.1	0.8	0.0	-73

Former 1st rounder was moved to relief with modest results. Still has a good low-90s FB and a decent SL, but struggles with location and secondary offerings have not improved. Move to RP looks permanent and allows his FB to play up, but poor Ctl makes long-term success unlikely regardless of the role.

Hope, Mason

SP | **Miami** | **EXP MLB DEBUT:** 2015 | **POTENTIAL:** #3 starter | **8D**

Thrws R Age 21
2011 (5) HS, OK

90-93	FB	+ + +
71-73	SL	+ +
74-76	CB	+ +
70-72	CU	+ +

Year	Lev	Team	W	L	Sv	IP	K	ERA	WHIP	BF/G	OBA	H%	S%	xERA	Ctl	Dom	Cmd	hr/9	BPV
2012	A-	Jamestown	3	4	0	71	53	2.90	1.39	21.4	264	32	78	3.46	3.4	6.7	2.0	0.1	46

5th rounder had a decent debut and has a good low-90s FB. Also throws an above-average CB and an ineffective CU. Has a quick arm and nice athleticism, but throws across his body and needs better mechanics. Keeps the ball down, but lack of dominance make him a mid-rotation guy at best.

Houser, Adrian

SP | **Houston** | **EXP MLB DEBUT:** 2015 | **POTENTIAL:** #3 starter | **8C**

Thrws R Age 20
2011 (2) HS (OK)

90-95	FB	+ + + +
76-78	CB	+ + +
79-83	CU	+ +

Year	Lev	Team	W	L	Sv	IP	K	ERA	WHIP	BF/G	OBA	H%	S%	xERA	Ctl	Dom	Cmd	hr/9	BPV
2011	Rk	GCL Astros	1	2	0	22	25	4.03	1.52	16.2	276	39	71	3.82	4.0	10.1	2.5	0.0	91
2011	Rk	Greeneville	1	2	0	26	19	4.56	1.56	18.7	257	31	69	4.01	5.3	6.7	1.3	0.4	-4
2012	Rk	Greeneville	3	4	0	58	54	4.19	1.31	21.8	245	32	65	3.02	3.6	8.4	2.3	0.2	72

Very tall SP with raw pitching mechanics and plenty of arm strength. Throws downhill with excellent speed and has feel to cut and sink FB. Induces high number of GB and keeps ball in yard. FB command needs work and could benefit from getting to chase CB. Could rocket up prospect charts if CU improves.

Howard, Dillon

SP | **Cleveland** | **EXP MLB DEBUT:** 2016 | **POTENTIAL:** #3 starter | **8E**

Thrws R Age 21
2011 (2) HS (AR)

85-94	FB	+ + +
78-82	CB	+ +
75-79	CU	+ + +

Year	Lev	Team	W	L	Sv	IP	K	ERA	WHIP	BF/G	OBA	H%	S%	xERA	Ctl	Dom	Cmd	hr/9	BPV
2012	Rk	Arizona Indians	1	7	0	41	35	7.90	2.02	16.6	360	43	59	7.08	4.0	7.7	1.9	0.7	50

Tall SP who never got going early and suffered from inconsistent velocity. Sat in low-90s in '11, but velocity dropped in '12. Keeps ball low and throws with clean arm so drop in heat a bit of concern. Has trouble staying on top of CB and will need weapon against RHP. CU remains solid-avg pitch with potential for plus.

Hultzen, Danny

SP | **Seattle** | **EXP MLB DEBUT:** 2013 | **POTENTIAL:** #2 starter | **8A**

Thrws L Age 23
2011 (1) Virginia

90-94	FB	+ + + +
80-82	SL	+ + +
83-87	CU	+ + + +

Year	Lev	Team	W	L	Sv	IP	K	ERA	WHIP	BF/G	OBA	H%	S%	xERA	Ctl	Dom	Cmd	hr/9	BPV
2009	NCAA	Virginia	9	1	0	95	107	2.17	1.22	22.6	247	34	83	3.00	2.6	10.1	3.8	0.4	128
2010	NCAA	Virginia	11	1	0	107	123	2.78	0.93	25.0	200	27	73	2.05	2.0	10.4	5.1	0.8	150
2011	NCAA	Virginia	12	3	0	118	165	1.37	0.84	24.0	186	30	84	1.14	1.8	12.6	7.2	0.2	197
2012	AA	Jackson	8	3	0	75	79	1.19	0.93	21.7	152	21	88	1.04	3.8	9.4	2.5	0.2	85
2012	AAA	Tacoma	1	4	0	49	57	5.92	1.89	19.1	263	37	67	4.91	8.0	10.5	1.3	0.4	-7

Advanced SP who had tale of two halves. Dominated AA with command and sequencing. Promoted to AAA and struggled to throw strikes. Uses height and arm slot to give hitters difficult look. Locates FB in lower half of zone. SL can be good at times and CU is best secondary pitch. Repeats arm speed.

Jackson, Jay

RP | **Chicago (N)** | **EXP MLB DEBUT:** 2013 | **POTENTIAL:** Reliever | **6D**

Thrws R Age 25
2008 (9) Furman

89-93	FB	+ + +
81-84	SL	+ +
75-77	CB	+ +
	CU	+

Year	Lev	Team	W	L	Sv	IP	K	ERA	WHIP	BF/G	OBA	H%	S%	xERA	Ctl	Dom	Cmd	hr/9	BPV
2009	AA	Tennessee	5	5	0	83	77	3.70	1.35	21.6	238	30	74	3.62	4.2	8.4	2.0	0.8	54
2009	AAA	Iowa	1	0	0	6	4	1.50	1.33	24.9	228	24	100	4.15	4.5	6.0	1.3	1.5	5
2010	AAA	Iowa	11	8	0	157	119	4.63	1.28	20.1	256	29	66	4.04	2.7	6.8	2.5	1.1	66
2011	AAA	Iowa	8	14	0	147	97	5.34	1.54	24.6	303	35	64	4.89	2.8	6.0	2.1	0.6	49
2012	AAA	Iowa	3	7	0	86	76	6.57	1.71	10.6	301	35	63	6.07	4.5	7.9	1.8	1.5	40

Stocky RP struggled despite good raw stuff. Nice low-90s FB and an inconsistent CB. Can still blow the FB by hitters at times, but can't find the strike zone. Command problems were made worse by gopheritis (14 home runs given up in 86.1 IP). Was moved to relief but the results weren't any better.

Jackson, Luke

SP | **Texas** | **EXP MLB DEBUT:** 2015 | **POTENTIAL:** #3 starter | **8D**

Thrws R Age 21
2010 (1-S) HS (FL)

88-95	FB	+ + +
79-83	CB	+ + +
	CU	+ +

Year	Lev	Team	W	L	Sv	IP	K	ERA	WHIP	BF/G	OBA	H%	S%	xERA	Ctl	Dom	Cmd	hr/9	BPV
2011	A	Hickory	5	6	0	75	78	5.64	1.75	18.0	282	36	69	5.49	5.8	9.4	1.6	1.1	31
2012	A	Hickory	5	5	0	64	72	4.92	1.50	21.3	259	35	66	4.05	4.6	10.1	2.2	0.6	75
2012	A+	Myrtle Beach	5	2	0	66	74	4.39	1.51	21.9	266	37	69	3.89	4.4	10.1	2.3	0.3	82

Strong, athletic SP who has tough downhill plane to plate and hard CB could become plus offering. Relies on CB too much at times and needs to establish FB early in count. Has trouble repeating delivery, thus hindering command. Can be inefficient by pursuing Ks. Has solid upside, but needs development.

Jaime, Juan

RP | **Atlanta** | **EXP MLB DEBUT:** 2014 | **POTENTIAL:** Reliever | **8E**

Thrws R Age 25
2007 NDFA, D.R.

95-98	FB	+ + + +
	CB	+
	CU	+

Year	Lev	Team	W	L	Sv	IP	K	ERA	WHIP	BF/G	OBA	H%	S%	xERA	Ctl	Dom	Cmd	hr/9	BPV
2008	Rk	GCL Nationals	2	1	0	19	23	4.74	1.79	10.9	230	33	73	4.31	8.5	10.9	1.3	0.5	-16
2009	A	Hagerstown	3	1	0	32	40	2.27	1.20	15.9	198	29	83	2.52	4.5	11.4	2.5	0.6	100
2009	A-	Vermont	2	1	0	24	36	1.88	1.25	16.3	181	32	83	1.90	5.6	13.5	2.4	0.0	109
2012	A+	Lynchburg	1	3	18	51	73	3.16	1.25	5.0	176	27	77	2.51	5.8	12.8	2.2	0.7	92

Missed the past two seasons with TJS, but was back in action in '12. Now working in relief with a plus mid-90s FB that touches 100 mph. Because of the amount time he missed, he is still somewhat unpolished and did walk 5.8 per nine, but also struck out 12.8 and has the power arm to be an impact reliever.

James, Chad

SP | **Miami** | **EXP MLB DEBUT:** 2014 | **POTENTIAL:** #2 starter | **9E**

Thrws L Age 22
2009 (1) HS, OK

90-93	FB	+ + +
80-82	SL	+
78-80	CU	+ +

Year	Lev	Team	W	L	Sv	IP	K	ERA	WHIP	BF/G	OBA	H%	S%	xERA	Ctl	Dom	Cmd	hr/9	BPV
2010	A	Greensboro	5	10	0	114	105	5.12	1.58	21.0	265	34	65	4.05	5.1	8.3	1.6	0.2	29
2011	A+	Jupiter	5	15	0	149	124	3.80	1.50	23.9	291	35	76	4.69	3.1	7.5	2.4	0.7	70
2012	A+	Jupiter	6	10	0	115	80	4.87	1.64	21.3	299	35	70	5.16	3.9	6.3	1.6	0.7	25

Lanky former 1st rounder continues to underwhelm. Has a decent low-90s FB, but velocity is down from HS. Scrapped his CB for a SL and mixes in a CU, both of which have potential, but remain inconsistent. Continues to struggle with Cmd and throws across his body. The clock is ticking.

Jenkins, Chad

SP | **Toronto** | **EXP MLB DEBUT:** 2012 | **POTENTIAL:** #4 starter | **7D**

Thrws R Age 25
2009 (1) Kennesaw State

88-93	FB	+ + +
81-86	SL	+ + +
78-80	CB	+ +
	CU	+ + +

Year	Lev	Team	W	L	Sv	IP	K	ERA	WHIP	BF/G	OBA	H%	S%	xERA	Ctl	Dom	Cmd	hr/9	BPV
2010	A+	Dunedin	2	6	0	62	42	4.33	1.46	20.5	293	33	72	4.77	2.6	6.1	2.3	0.9	57
2011	A+	Dunedin	4	5	0	67	44	3.07	1.26	25.0	272	32	76	3.53	1.9	5.9	3.1	0.4	73
2011	AA	New Hampshire	5	7	0	100	74	4.13	1.20	25.2	247	29	66	3.31	2.4	6.6	2.7	0.7	72
2012	AA	New Hampshire	5	9	0	114	57	4.96	1.54	24.9	310	33	71	5.69	2.4	4.5	1.8	1.3	33
2012	MLB	Blue Jays	1	3	0	32	16	4.50	1.34	10.2	262	27	71	4.55	3.1	4.5	1.5	1.4	15

Durable, dependable SP who reached TOR after middling campaign in Double-A. Sinker/SL pitcher who keeps ball low in zone and works efficiently. Keeps BB to a minimum by working corners of plate with FB. Hard SL can be out pitch, but he focuses on contact early in count. Very hittable stuff.

Jenkins, Tyrell

SP | **St. Louis** | **EXP MLB DEBUT:** 2015 | **POTENTIAL:** #2 starter | **8D**

Thrws R Age 20
2010 (1-S) HS, TX

93-96	FB	+ + + +
	CB	+ +
74-76	CU	+ +

Year	Lev	Team	W	L	Sv	IP	K	ERA	WHIP	BF/G	OBA	H%	S%	xERA	Ctl	Dom	Cmd	hr/9	BPV
2010	Rk	Johnson City	0	0	0	3	2	0.00	1.33	6.2	191	24	100	2.30	6.0	6.0	1.0	0.0	-36
2011	Rk	Johnson City	4	2	0	56	55	3.86	1.36	21.3	285	37	71	4.00	2.1	8.8	4.2	0.5	121
2012	A	Quad Cities	4	4	0	82	80	5.14	1.46	18.5	266	34	63	4.04	3.9	8.7	2.2	0.5	69

Athletic SP competes well with a 92-94 mph FB. Also throws a good 1-7 CB and a nice CU. Battled a shoulder injury that limited him to 19 starts. Has loose, easy arm action, which leads to easy velocity with nice deception. Some work to do yet, but the upside is substantial.

Johnson, Brian — SP — Boston

EXP MLB DEBUT: 2014 | POTENTIAL: #4 starter | 7B

Thrws L Age 22
2012 (1) Florida

88-93	FB	+++
80-83	SL	+++
73-78	CB	++
83-86	CU	++

Year	Lev	Team	W	L	Sv	IP	K	ERA	WHIP	BF/G	OBA	H%	S%	xERA	Ctl	Dom	Cmd	hr/9	BPV
2010	NCAA	Florida	6	4	0	74	51	4.03	1.38	19.4	298	34	74	4.86	1.7	6.2	3.6	1.1	84
2011	NCAA	Florida	8	3	0	80	72	3.61	1.17	19.9	258	33	69	3.11	1.7	8.1	4.8	0.5	119
2012	NCAA	Florida	8	5	0	90	73	3.90	1.17	21.1	255	30	68	3.42	1.8	7.3	4.1	0.8	101
2012	A-	Lowell	0	0	0	6	4	0.00	0.53	4.7	111	14	100	0.00	1.6	6.3	4.0	0.0	89

First round pick who suffered broken bones in face after being struck by line drive. Lacks athleticism, but has idea on how to set up hitters with advanced pitch sequencing and deception. Uses any pitch in any count and rarely beats himself with BB. Velocity is good and changes speeds fairly well.

Johnson, Erik — SP — Chicago (A)

EXP MLB DEBUT: 2014 | POTENTIAL: #3 starter | 8C

Thrws R Age 23
2011 (2) California

89-96	FB	+++
85-87	SL	++++
77-80	CB	++
80-83	CU	++

Year	Lev	Team	W	L	Sv	IP	K	ERA	WHIP	BF/G	OBA	H%	S%	xERA	Ctl	Dom	Cmd	hr/9	BPV
2010	NCAA	California	6	3	1	77	73	4.09	1.55	21.0	281	36	73	4.41	4.0	8.5	2.1	0.5	64
2011	NCAA	California	7	4	0	105	102	2.83	1.21	23.5	187	25	76	2.15	5.1	8.7	1.7	0.3	39
2011	Rk	Great Falls	0	0	0	2	2	4.50	2.50	5.3	415	52	80	8.75	4.5	9.0	2.0	0.0	59
2012	A	Kannapolis	2	2	0	43	39	2.30	1.35	19.9	243	30	85	3.55	4.0	8.2	2.1	0.6	58
2012	A+	Winston-Salem	4	3	0	49	48	2.74	1.07	24.0	236	32	72	2.16	1.8	8.8	4.8	0.0	126

Physical pitcher with power build. Needs to tweak delivery to make smoother and has some effort, but produces good FB with projection. Showed improved control while upgrading SL that is now legitimate swing and miss pitch. Still needs to enhance CB and CU and needs to sequence pitches better.

Johnson, Pierce — SP — Chicago (N)

EXP MLB DEBUT: 2016 | POTENTIAL: #3 starter | 8D

Thrws R Age 22
2012 (1-S) Missouri State

91-94	FB	++++
86-88	CT	+++
	CU	+

Year	Lev	Team	W	L	Sv	IP	K	ERA	WHIP	BF/G	OBA	H%	S%	xERA	Ctl	Dom	Cmd	hr/9	BPV
2010	NCAA	Missouri State	1	2	0	41	36	7.52	2.11	12.5	328	39	64	7.17	6.6	8.0	1.2	1.1	-18
2011	NCAA	Missouri State	6	5	2	76	72	4.76	1.51	18.2	273	35	67	4.08	4.0	8.6	2.1	0.4	63
2012	NCAA	Missouri State	4	6	0	100	119	2.53	1.13	28.1	232	34	76	2.33	2.5	10.7	4.3	0.1	143
2012	Rk	Cubs	0	0	0	3	2	0.00	1.33	6.2	321	38	100	4.07	0.0	6.0		0.0	126
2012	A-	Boise	0	0	0	8	12	4.50	1.63	8.9	307	49	69	4.51	3.4	13.5	4.0	0.0	170

6'3" righty zoomed up draft boards and ended up going to the Cubs at #43. Health concerns in the past, but was fine in '12. Has a good 92-94 FB that tops out at 96 mph. Also has a decent CB and a good downer CU. Saw limited action after being drafted, but has good potential and should move up quickly.

Johnson, Steve — SP — Baltimore

EXP MLB DEBUT: 2012 | POTENTIAL: #4 starter | 7C

Thrws R Age 25
2005 (13) HS (MD)

87-93	FB	+++
81-82	SL	+++
77-79	CB	++
82-84	CU	++

Year	Lev	Team	W	L	Sv	IP	K	ERA	WHIP	BF/G	OBA	H%	S%	xERA	Ctl	Dom	Cmd	hr/9	BPV
2010	AA	Bowie	7	8	0	145	128	5.09	1.53	22.5	260	30	71	5.05	4.8	7.9	1.6	1.5	30
2011	AA	Bowie	5	1	0	58	59	2.16	0.94	21.9	196	24	85	2.35	2.3	9.1	3.9	1.1	119
2011	AAA	Norfolk	2	7	0	87	63	5.57	1.69	23.2	291	34	67	5.18	4.8	6.5	1.3	0.7	4
2012	AAA	Norfolk	4	8	0	91	86	2.86	1.06	18.7	204	26	76	2.39	3.1	8.5	2.8	0.7	88
2012	MLB	Orioles	4	0	0	38	46	2.11	1.07	12.4	175	23	86	2.29	4.2	10.8	2.6	0.9	98

Big, durable pitcher who surprised in bigs. Leveraged increased K rate and vastly improved command. Showed ability to mix pitches with nice FB, 2 breaking balls, and fringy CU. Has confidence to use any pitch and quick arm generates movement. Throws with max effort and is extreme flyball pitcher.

Jones, Chris — RP — Atlanta

EXP MLB DEBUT: 2014 | POTENTIAL: Reliever | 6C

Thrws L Age 24
2007 (15) HS, FL

87-90	FB	+++
75-77	CB	++

Year	Lev	Team	W	L	Sv	IP	K	ERA	WHIP	BF/G	OBA	H%	S%	xERA	Ctl	Dom	Cmd	hr/9	BPV
2009	A+	Kinston	1	1	0	18	21	7.50	1.67	20.2	302	36	60	6.92	4.0	10.5	2.6	2.5	99
2010	A	Lake County	2	2	1	22	20	2.86	0.82	11.4	205	25	69	1.91	0.8	8.2	10.0	0.8	143
2010	A+	Kinston	4	3	2	68	65	2.39	1.29	9.0	239	32	81	2.99	3.6	8.6	2.4	0.3	77
2011	A+	Kinston	7	1	0	72	66	3.36	1.31	7.0	242	30	76	3.55	3.7	8.2	2.2	0.7	65
2012	AA	Mississippi	2	5	2	60	61	3.90	1.47	5.7	290	39	71	4.03	2.9	9.2	3.2	0.2	106

Came over from the Indians in '11 and immediately made a positive impression. Doesn't blow hitters away with his 87-90 mph FB, but he keeps them off balance and has some nice deception. Mixes in an average CB and a decent CU, all of which he commands well.

Jones, Zack — RP — Minnesota

EXP MLB DEBUT: 2015 | POTENTIAL: Setup reliever / Closer | 7D

Thrws R Age 22
2012 (4) San Jose State

91-96	FB	++++
82-85	SL	++
	CU	+

Year	Lev	Team	W	L	Sv	IP	K	ERA	WHIP	BF/G	OBA	H%	S%	xERA	Ctl	Dom	Cmd	hr/9	BPV
2010	NCAA	San Jose State	5	1	5	41	39	3.73	1.46	8.8	227	30	73	3.24	5.7	8.6	1.5	0.2	18
2011	NCAA	San Jose State	1	3	10	43	53	3.98	1.28	8.0	198	30	67	2.39	5.2	11.1	2.1	0.2	76
2012	NCAA	San Jose State	3	4	7	54	60	4.50	1.26	11.6	251	34	63	3.28	2.8	10.0	3.5	0.5	122
2012	Rk	Elizabethton	0	0	0	6	9	0.00	1.00	3.8	106	20	100	0.50	6.0	13.5	2.3	0.0	99
2012	A	Beloit	0	0	4	14	25	3.21	1.14	4.6	186	36	73	2.26	4.5	16.1	3.6	0.6	186

Athletic, strong-armed RP who throws everything hard and shows little feel. Explosive FB has electric late life, though has trouble commanding. When he's aggressive, he's tough to hit. When he nibbles, the FB flattens. Doesn't have great size and rough delivery gives him control problems.

Joseph, Donnie — RP — Kansas City

EXP MLB DEBUT: 2013 | POTENTIAL: Setup reliever | 7A

Thrws L Age 25
2009 (3) Houston

91-96	FB	++++
82-85	SL	+++
	CU	+

Year	Lev	Team	W	L	Sv	IP	K	ERA	WHIP	BF/G	OBA	H%	S%	xERA	Ctl	Dom	Cmd	hr/9	BPV
2010	AA	Carolina	1	0	1	7	7	5.14	1.29	4.1	262	35	56	3.04	2.6	9.0	3.5	0.0	111
2011	AA	Carolina	1	3	8	58	66	6.94	1.66	4.6	289	37	58	5.53	4.6	10.2	2.2	1.2	76
2012	AA	Pensacola	4	2	13	30	46	0.89	0.69	4.1	132	23	90	0.26	2.4	13.6	5.8	0.3	200
2012	AAA	Louisville	4	1	5	22	22	2.86	1.41	5.2	262	35	77	3.35	3.7	9.0	2.4	0.0	81
2012	AAA	Omaha	1	0	2	17	19	4.15	1.96	7.5	301	40	79	5.78	6.8	9.9	1.5	0.5	13

Power RP who rebounded from disastrous '11 and elevated prospect status. Projects to more than situational LHP due to electric stuff. Quick arm generates excellent velo and inconsistent SL shows glimpses of plus. Has tendency to overthrow and mechanics are less than ideal for consistent control.

Jungmann, Taylor — SP — Milwaukee

EXP MLB DEBUT: 2014 | POTENTIAL: #3 starter | 8D

Thrws R Age 23
2011 (1) Texas

90-94	FB	++++
80-83	SL	++
74-77	CB	++
81-85	CU	++

Year	Lev	Team	W	L	Sv	IP	K	ERA	WHIP	BF/G	OBA	H%	S%	xERA	Ctl	Dom	Cmd	hr/9	BPV
2009	NCAA	Texas	11	3	0	95	101	2.00	1.06	14.7	196	28	80	1.71	3.3	9.6	2.9	0.1	101
2010	NCAA	Texas	8	3	0	120	129	2.03	1.08	27.5	206	28	84	2.35	3.1	9.7	3.1	0.6	109
2011	NCAA	Texas	13	3	0	141	126	1.60	0.83	27.1	169	22	81	1.01	2.3	8.0	3.5	0.3	101
2012	A+	Brevard County	11	6	0	153	99	3.53	1.34	24.5	269	31	73	3.69	2.7	5.8	2.2	0.4	50

Tall, lean RH has a good low-90s sinking FB, but doesn't put hitters away. Throws strikes and has good SL, but a below-average CU. Showed good Ctl in his pro debut, but shaky Dom is a concern. Has the frame to develop into a workhorse starter though he does have some effort to delivery.

Karns, Nathan — SP — Washington

EXP MLB DEBUT: 2015 | POTENTIAL: #4 starter | 7C

Thrws R Age 25
2009 (12) Texas Tech

90-93	FB	+++
	CB	+++
	CU	++

Year	Lev	Team	W	L	Sv	IP	K	ERA	WHIP	BF/G	OBA	H%	S%	xERA	Ctl	Dom	Cmd	hr/9	BPV
2009	NCAA	Texas Tech	4	5	0	54	57	5.47	1.53	18.2	257	32	66	4.67	5.0	9.4	1.9	1.2	54
2011	Rk	GCL Nationals	0	0	0	19	26	0.00	0.43	12.1	37	7	100	0.00	2.9	12.5	4.3	0.0	166
2011	A-	Auburn	3	2	0	37	33	3.44	1.47	19.7	207	27	75	3.05	6.6	8.1	1.2	0.2	-15
2012	A	Hagerstown	3	0	2	44	61	2.03	0.99	15.4	155	26	79	1.18	4.3	12.4	2.9	0.2	126
2012	A+	Potomac	8	4	0	72	87	2.26	1.02	21.2	189	29	76	1.55	3.3	10.9	3.3	0.1	126

Fully recovered from TJS and FB now sits in the low-90s. Keeps hitters off-balance with a plus CB, a SL, and an average CU. Throws plenty of strikes and fared well at two A-ball stops. Even more impressively, he led the minors in oppBAA by limiting opposing hitters to a .174 average.

Kelly, Casey — SP — San Diego

EXP MLB DEBUT: 2012 | POTENTIAL: #3 starter | 8C

Thrws R Age 23
2008 (1) HS, FL

90-94	FB	++++
76-79	CB	++++
80-84	CU	+++

Year	Lev	Team	W	L	Sv	IP	K	ERA	WHIP	BF/G	OBA	H%	S%	xERA	Ctl	Dom	Cmd	hr/9	BPV
2011	AA	San Antonio	11	6	0	142	105	3.98	1.40	22.2	276	33	71	4.02	2.9	6.6	2.3	0.5	59
2012	Rk	Padres	0	1	0	9	7	4.00	1.11	11.8	283	35	60	2.91	0.0	7.0		0.0	144
2012	AA	San Antonio	0	1	0	17	18	3.78	0.84	20.3	190	26	54	1.51	1.6	9.7	6.0	0.5	149
2012	AAA	Tucson	0	0	0	12	14	2.25	1.00	22.9	262	38	75	2.30	0.0	10.5		0.0	207
2012	MLB	Padres	2	3	0	29	26	6.21	1.69	21.8	323	38	66	6.44	3.1	8.1	2.6	1.6	79

Former 1st rounder had his best season yet, but struggled when the Padres called him up. Features a 90-94 mph FB, a sinker, and a CB and scouts continue to rave about his potential. Still seems more like a mid-rotation guy, but made excellent progress in '12 and should have a rotation spot in 2013.

Kelly, Mike — SP — San Diego

EXP MLB DEBUT: 2016 | POTENTIAL: #3 starter | 7D

Thrws R Age 20
2011 (1-S) HS, FL

88-93	FB	+++
	CB	++
	CU	++

Year	Lev	Team	W	L	Sv	IP	K	ERA	WHIP	BF/G	OBA	H%	S%	xERA	Ctl	Dom	Cmd	hr/9	BPV
2012	Rk	Padres	0	5	0	44	37	7.11	1.78	15.7	302	37	57	5.26	5.1	7.5	1.5	0.4	16
2012	A	Fort Wayne	0	2	0	14	14	7.54	2.51	10.9	308	41	67	6.81	11.3	8.8	0.8	0.0	-129

Lean and projectable RH with a power arm. Has a nice low-90s FB with room for more as he matures. Gets good movement from a low 3/4 arm slot, but needs to refine his breaking ball and CU and learn how to pitch. Has some work to do, but has nice potential though was not effective in his pro debut.

Kickham, Mike — SP — San Francisco

EXP MLB DEBUT: 2014 | POTENTIAL: #5 Starter/reliever | 7C

Thrws L Age 24
2010 (6) Missouri State

- 90-92 FB +++
- 80-83 SL +++
- 80-82 CU +++

Year	Lev	Team	W	L	Sv	IP	K	ERA	WHIP	BF/G	OBA	H%	S%	xERA	Ctl	Dom	Cmd	hr/9	BPV
2010	NCAA	Missouri State	4	9	0	96	103	5.25	1.36	26.8	272	34	64	4.60	2.8	9.7	3.4	1.3	116
2010	Rk	Giants	0	0	0	2	3	11.59	2.58	4.2	378	53	50	8.16	7.7	11.6	1.5	0.0	18
2011	A	Augusta	5	10	0	112	103	4.11	1.33	22.1	262	33	70	3.85	3.0	8.3	2.8	0.7	87
2012	AA	Richmond	11	10	0	151	137	3.05	1.29	22.1	219	28	77	2.94	4.5	8.2	1.8	0.5	44

Physical lefty has a good low-90s FB and was impressive at AA. but struggled with control. Induces plenty of groundball outs (2.5 GB/FB ratio) and mixes in a nice SL and a much improved CU. Limited the opposition to a .219 oppBAA. Has some work to do, but interesting upside.

Kingham, Nick — SP — Pittsburgh

EXP MLB DEBUT: 2015 | POTENTIAL: #3 starter | 8D

Thrws R Age 21
2010 (4) HS, NV

- 90-93 FB +++
- CB ++
- CU ++

Year	Lev	Team	W	L	Sv	IP	K	ERA	WHIP	BF/G	OBA	H%	S%	xERA	Ctl	Dom	Cmd	hr/9	BPV
2010	Rk	GCL Pirates	0	0	0	3	2	0.00	1.00	5.7	262	32	100	2.35	0.0	6.0		0.0	126
2011	A-	State College	6	2	0	71	47	2.15	1.10	18.5	239	27	84	2.89	1.9	6.0	3.1	0.6	74
2012	A	West Virginia	6	8	0	127	117	4.39	1.19	18.9	243	29	65	3.55	2.6	8.3	3.3	1.1	98

Tall, skinny RH was lucky in '11 and unlucky in '12. FB sits at 90-93 but tops out at 95 mph. Also throws an above-average CU and a CB that is good but inconsistent. Gets good downhill tilt on his FB and was much better in the 2nd half, with a 3.69 ERA. Just needs to avoid big innings and to be more consistent.

Kirk, Austin — SP — Chicago (N)

EXP MLB DEBUT: 2013 | POTENTIAL: Reliever | 6C

Thrws L Age 23
2009 (3) HS, OK

- 88-91 FB ++
- 75-78 CB ++
- CU +

Year	Lev	Team	W	L	Sv	IP	K	ERA	WHIP	BF/G	OBA	H%	S%	xERA	Ctl	Dom	Cmd	hr/9	BPV
2010	A	Peoria	1	1	0	13	17	3.55	1.34	17.6	183	27	75	2.83	6.4	12.1	1.9	0.7	63
2010	A-	Boise	4	5	0	52	48	3.31	1.22	17.4	259	32	77	3.82	2.1	8.4	4.0	1.0	112
2011	A	Peoria	5	12	0	151	122	4.29	1.20	20.9	251	29	66	3.64	2.3	7.3	3.2	1.0	88
2012	A+	Daytona	7	3	0	129	78	3.13	1.30	24.2	248	29	75	3.11	3.3	5.4	1.6	0.2	26
2012	AA	Tennessee	2	0	0	23	13	3.09	1.29	19.2	215	22	81	3.56	4.6	5.0	1.1	1.2	-17

Control took a step backwards as his walk rate nearly doubled. Doesn't have overpowering stuff and his FB rarely breaks 90 mph though he does have some nice deception. Lack of a quality breaking ball limits his long-term develop and a move to relief seems likely.

Klein, Dan — RP — Baltimore

EXP MLB DEBUT: 2014 | POTENTIAL: Setup reliever | 7B

Thrws R Age 24
2010 (3) UCLA

- 88-94 FB +++
- 80-82 CB +++
- 81-84 SL +++
- 78-80 CU +++

Year	Lev	Team	W	L	Sv	IP	K	ERA	WHIP	BF/G	OBA	H%	S%	xERA	Ctl	Dom	Cmd	hr/9	BPV
2010	A-	Aberdeen	1	0	1	6	10	0.00	0.32	4.0	53	11	100	0.00	1.4	14.2	10.0	0.0	236
2011	A+	Frederick	0	1	0	16	21	1.15	0.77	8.0	169	23	100	1.64	1.7	12.1	7.0	1.1	189
2011	AA	Bowie	3	0	0	17	16	1.08	1.02	7.1	229	31	88	1.94	1.6	8.6	5.3	0.0	130

Athletic RP who missed entire season after multiple shoulder surgeries. Has only pitched 38 IP in last 3 years due to ailments. When healthy, uses clean, loose delivery to throw strikes. Owns deep arsenal for RP, though none are plus pitches. Lively FB is best pitch and has CU with nice depth and fade.

Kline, Branden — SP — Baltimore

EXP MLB DEBUT: 2014 | POTENTIAL: #3 starter / Setup reliever | 8D

Thrws R Age 21
2012 (2) Virginia

- 89-95 FB +++
- 80-82 SL +++
- 80-83 CB +++
- 80-82 CU +

Year	Lev	Team	W	L	Sv	IP	K	ERA	WHIP	BF/G	OBA	H%	S%	xERA	Ctl	Dom	Cmd	hr/9	BPV
2010	NCAA	Virginia	5	1	3	65	56	3.62	1.14	11.7	228	27	73	3.30	2.8	7.8	2.8	1.1	83
2011	NCAA	Virginia	4	1	18	43	56	1.88	1.21	5.4	198	31	83	2.01	4.6	11.7	2.5	0.0	105
2012	NCAA	Virginia	7	3	0	94	94	3.56	1.37	24.5	243	32	73	3.35	4.1	9.0	2.2	0.4	69
2012	A-	Aberdeen	0	0	0	12	12	4.50	1.33	12.5	262	33	67	3.86	3.0	9.0	3.0	0.8	99

Athletic, tall SP who has makings of mid-rotation starter or knockout RP. FB is go-to pitch early in count and rounds out arsenal with SL, CB, and CU. Erratic CB shows flashes of dominance, but CU far from polished. Command and control come and go and smoother delivery could solve problems.

Koehler, Tom — SP — Miami

EXP MLB DEBUT: 2012 | POTENTIAL: #4 starter | 7C

Thrws R Age 27
2008 (18) Stony Brook

- 88-92 FB +++
- CB ++
- CU ++
- 82-84 CT ++

Year	Lev	Team	W	L	Sv	IP	K	ERA	WHIP	BF/G	OBA	H%	S%	xERA	Ctl	Dom	Cmd	hr/9	BPV
2009	A+	Jupiter	4	1	0	35	25	3.37	1.27	23.6	264	32	70	3.04	2.3	6.5	2.8	0.0	72
2010	AA	Jacksonville	16	2	0	159	145	2.61	1.17	22.6	238	30	80	3.03	2.6	8.2	3.2	0.6	96
2011	AAA	New Orleans	12	7	0	150	116	4.97	1.48	23.1	254	29	68	4.45	4.7	6.9	1.5	1.1	15
2012	AAA	New Orleans	12	11	0	151	138	4.17	1.42	22.9	266	33	73	4.28	3.6	8.2	2.3	0.9	68
2012	MLB	Miami	0	1	0	13	13	5.40	1.28	6.8	285	31	69	5.88	1.4	8.8	6.5	2.7	140

Polished RHP throws strikes, but is not overpowering. Pitches off an upper-80 FB and mixes in a SL, a CB, and a good CU. The SL is his best pitch and keeps hitters off-balance. Throws enough strikes that he could compete for a rotation spot for the retooling Marlins, but he doesn't miss enough bats.

Krol, Ian — SP — Oakland

EXP MLB DEBUT: 2014 | POTENTIAL: #4 starter | 7C

Thrws L Age 22
2009 (7) HS (IL)

- 86-91 FB +++
- 78-82 CB +++
- 78-81 CU +++

Year	Lev	Team	W	L	Sv	IP	K	ERA	WHIP	BF/G	OBA	H%	S%	xERA	Ctl	Dom	Cmd	hr/9	BPV
2010	A	Kane County	9	4	0	119	91	2.65	0.99	18.8	227	28	73	2.19	1.4	6.9	4.8	0.4	103
2010	A+	Stockton	1	0	0	20	20	3.66	1.37	20.6	245	30	79	4.32	4.1	9.2	2.2	1.4	72
2011	Rk	Athletics	0	0	0	5	6	0.00	0.00	4.7	0	0	100	0.00	0.0	10.8		0.0	212
2012	A+	Stockton	1	7	0	86	79	5.21	1.38	17.3	281	33	65	4.82	2.5	8.2	3.3	1.4	99
2012	AA	Midland	1	2	0	11	10	5.06	1.22	5.4	268	35	54	2.95	1.7	8.4	5.0	0.0	124

Athletic lefty who only pitched 5 innings in '11 due to elbow ailment and off-field incidents. Moved to bullpen and could be future role. Induces plenty of GB with lively FB. Spots FB to both sides of plate and can mix in solid-avg CB for Ks. Not overpowering and lacks projection, but has above average control.

Kukuk, Cody — SP — Boston

EXP MLB DEBUT: 2016 | POTENTIAL: #3 starter | 8E

Thrws L Age 20
2011 (7) HS (KS)

- 88-93 FB +++
- 81-84 SL +++
- 80-83 CU ++

Year	Lev	Team	W	L	Sv	IP	K	ERA	WHIP	BF/G	OBA	H%	S%	xERA	Ctl	Dom	Cmd	hr/9	BPV
2012	Rk	GCL Red Sox	2	0	0	10	16	0.90	0.60	6.8	96	20	83	0.00	2.7	14.4	5.3	0.0	204

Tall, projectable SP who made brief pro debut after being held back due to off-field issues. Loose arm generates quality FB with opp to add a few more ticks. Ball explodes out of hand, but lacks movement. Needs to work on release which would enhance hard SL. Shows improved CU, but still needs work.

Kurcz, Aaron — RP — Boston

EXP MLB DEBUT: 2014 | POTENTIAL: Setup reliever | 7B

Thrws R Age 22
2010 (10) JC of Southern NV

- 89-94 FB +++
- 70-75 CB ++
- 83-85 SL +++
- 80-82 CU ++

Year	Lev	Team	W	L	Sv	IP	K	ERA	WHIP	BF/G	OBA	H%	S%	xERA	Ctl	Dom	Cmd	hr/9	BPV
2010	NCAA	So Nevada	3	4	10	37	55	4.17	1.31	5.8	231	36	70	3.56	4.2	13.5	3.2	1.0	148
2010	Rk	Cubs	0	0	0	1	2	0.00	0.00	2.8	0	0	100	0.00	0.0	18.0		0.0	342
2010	A-	Boise	2	1	9	26	46	2.05	0.99	4.0	168	32	83	1.72	3.8	15.7	4.2	0.7	200
2011	A+	Daytona	5	4	0	82	91	3.28	1.23	10.4	224	30	75	3.00	3.7	9.9	2.7	0.7	97
2012	AA	Portland	3	4	4	50	72	3.04	1.37	7.3	228	35	80	3.44	4.8	12.9	2.7	0.7	119

Unheralded RP who throws from ¾ slot and across body, but hitters don't see pitches well. Quick arm makes up for smallish frame and generates quality mph FB. Lacks reliable secondary, but SL shows improvement. Needs to prove health after ending season in July due to pulled rotator cuff.

Lamb, John — SP — Kansas City

EXP MLB DEBUT: 2014 | POTENTIAL: #3 starter | 8D

Thrws L Age 23
2008 (5) HS (CA)

- 88-95 FB +++
- 77-79 CB +++
- 78-81 CU ++++

Year	Lev	Team	W	L	Sv	IP	K	ERA	WHIP	BF/G	OBA	H%	S%	xERA	Ctl	Dom	Cmd	hr/9	BPV
2010	A+	Wilmington	6	3	0	75	90	1.45	0.99	21.9	219	32	85	1.83	1.8	10.8	6.0	0.1	164
2010	AA	NW Arkansas	2	1	0	33	26	5.45	1.52	20.4	284	34	63	4.47	3.5	7.1	2.0	0.5	50
2011	AA	NW Arkansas	1	2	0	35	22	3.09	1.31	18.1	251	28	79	3.71	3.3	5.7	1.7	0.8	30
2012	Rk	Idaho Falls	0	1	0	7	8	7.37	1.50	15.8	303	36	56	6.48	2.5	9.8	4.0	2.5	129
2012	Rk	Royals	0	0	0	6	6	6.35	1.41	6.0	273	38	50	3.50	3.2	9.5	3.0	0.0	104

Tall SP who returned in Aug after TJ surgery. Velo and feel slowly returning and could regain prospect status. At peak, commands FB to both sides of plate and drops in solid CB for strikes. Deceptive CU is plus pitch and has confidence to use in any count. FB tends to lose sink at higher velocities.

Langfield, Dan — RP — Cincinnati

EXP MLB DEBUT: 2014 | POTENTIAL: Setup reliever | 7C

Thrws R Age 22
2012 (3) Memphis

- 92-95 FB +++
- SL +++
- CB ++
- CU ++

Year	Lev	Team	W	L	Sv	IP	K	ERA	WHIP	BF/G	OBA	H%	S%	xERA	Ctl	Dom	Cmd	hr/9	BPV
2012	Rk	Billings	3	0	0	37	54	2.68	1.19	9.9	206	34	77	2.26	4.1	13.1	3.2	0.2	143

Short RP from Memphis was one of the better power arms in the '12 draft. Has a heavy mid-90s FB, but it can be straight and hittable. Also has a good hard SL and an inconsistent CB. Throws with some effort and his control can be erratic, but in his debut he was able to get plenty of swings and misses.

Lara, Braulio — SP — Miami

EXP MLB DEBUT: 2014 | POTENTIAL: #4 starter | 7D

Thrws L Age 24
2008 FA (DR)

Velo	Pitch	Grade
90-95	FB	+++
81-84	CB	++
82-85	CU	++

Year	Lev	Team	W	L	Sv	IP	K	ERA	WHIP	BF/G	OBA	H%	S%	xERA	Ctl	Dom	Cmd	hr/9	BPV
2010	Rk	Princeton	6	4	0	66	58	2.18	1.12	20.0	208	27	81	2.20	3.4	7.9	2.3	0.3	68
2011	A	Bowling Green	5	11	0	120	111	4.94	1.43	20.5	256	32	65	4.03	4.1	8.3	2.0	0.7	56
2012	A+	Charlotte	6	10	0	112	82	5.71	1.62	19.9	280	32	65	4.98	4.7	6.6	1.4	0.9	11

Smooth starter who offers solid pitch mix. Posted reverse splits and had trouble locating FB within strike zone. K rate dropped as he pitched from behind in count. Solid FB has good movement, but tough to command. Uses clean arm to throw below avg CB and CU, though both have avg potential.

Lebron, Ramon — RP — Detroit

EXP MLB DEBUT: 2015 | POTENTIAL: Setup reliever | 8E

Thrws R Age 24
2006 FA (DR)

Velo	Pitch	Grade
90-96	FB	++++
82-85	SL	++
81-83	CU	+++

Year	Lev	Team	W	L	Sv	IP	K	ERA	WHIP	BF/G	OBA	H%	S%	xERA	Ctl	Dom	Cmd	hr/9	BPV
2010	A	West Michigan	4	5	0	47	55	6.85	1.88	17.1	273	36	63	5.56	7.4	10.5	1.4	1.0	6
2010	A-	Connecticut	1	1	1	11	20	8.43	2.06	7.4	285	52	57	6.04	8.4	16.9	2.0	0.8	94
2011	A	West Michigan	3	1	1	34	44	1.84	1.08	6.1	157	24	83	1.47	5.0	11.5	2.3	0.3	91
2012	A	West Michigan	0	0	1	33	33	5.18	1.91	6.0	205	28	71	4.14	10.6	9.0	0.8	0.3	-107
2012	A-	Connecticut	1	1	0	16	16	5.74	1.28	7.1	199	22	59	3.84	5.2	9.2	1.8	1.7	44

Max effort RP who has arm strength and quick action, but fails to throw strikes. Regressed across board, but hopeful he'll improve now healthy. FB has both velo and movement, though difficult to command low in zone. Hitters find him tough to hit with deceptive CU that could become above avg.

Lee, Chen — RP — Cleveland

EXP MLB DEBUT: 2013 | POTENTIAL: Setup reliever | 7A

Thrws R Age 26
2009 FA (Taiwan)

Velo	Pitch	Grade
89-95	FB	++++
80-82	SL	+++
	CU	+

Year	Lev	Team	W	L	Sv	IP	K	ERA	WHIP	BF/G	OBA	H%	S%	xERA	Ctl	Dom	Cmd	hr/9	BPV
2009	A+	Kinston	4	6	2	83	97	3.35	1.14	7.3	222	31	71	2.64	3.0	10.5	3.5	0.5	125
2010	AA	Akron	5	4	0	73	82	3.22	1.11	6.5	224	30	73	2.79	2.7	10.2	3.7	0.7	127
2011	AA	Akron	2	1	0	40	56	2.50	0.96	6.5	194	32	73	1.54	2.5	12.7	5.1	0.2	179
2011	AAA	Columbus	4	0	1	32	43	2.27	1.20	6.1	225	34	83	2.85	3.4	12.2	3.6	0.6	146
2012	AAA	Columbus	2	0	0	7	8	2.57	0.86	5.1	202	25	80	2.39	1.3	10.3	8.0	1.3	168

Short RP whose season ended in April after TJ surgery. Produces plenty of velo with fast arm and uncorks FB from low ¾ slot to add deception. Keeps ball down and all pitches exhibit movement. Has trouble staying on top of SL and Ks generated more from deception. Throws strikes and rarely beats himself.

Lee, Zach — SP — Los Angeles (N)

EXP MLB DEBUT: 2014 | POTENTIAL: #2 starter | 9D

Thrws R Age 21
2010 (1) HS, TX

Velo	Pitch	Grade
89-92	FB	+++
75-78	CB	+++
81-84	SL	+++
	CU	+++

Year	Lev	Team	W	L	Sv	IP	K	ERA	WHIP	BF/G	OBA	H%	S%	xERA	Ctl	Dom	Cmd	hr/9	BPV
2011	A	Great Lakes	9	6	0	109	91	3.47	1.22	18.3	247	30	73	3.39	2.6	7.5	2.8	0.7	82
2012	A+	Rancho Cuc	2	3	0	55	52	4.55	1.27	18.8	278	33	69	4.59	1.6	8.5	5.2	1.5	126
2012	AA	Chattanooga	4	3	0	66	51	4.25	1.39	21.2	271	32	71	4.21	3.0	7.0	2.3	0.8	62

Physical RH has a plus low-90s FB. Also has a nice CT and an improved CU that could be plus down the road. Simple, repeatable mechanics produce good control. Works both sides of the plate and has good feel for his FB. Also mixes in a CB and a SL both of which have potential.

Leesman, Charles — SP — Chicago (A)

EXP MLB DEBUT: 2013 | POTENTIAL: #4 starter | 7D

Thrws L Age 26
2008 (11) Xavier

Velo	Pitch	Grade
86-91	FB	+++
79-83	SL	++
75-78	CB	++
75-79	CU	++++

Year	Lev	Team	W	L	Sv	IP	K	ERA	WHIP	BF/G	OBA	H%	S%	xERA	Ctl	Dom	Cmd	hr/9	BPV
2009	A	Kannapolis	13	5	0	158	117	3.08	1.41	24.7	271	33	77	3.72	3.3	6.7	2.0	0.2	49
2010	A+	Winston-Salem	9	4	0	85	39	5.10	1.68	22.4	291	32	69	5.09	4.7	4.1	0.9	0.6	-34
2010	AA	Birmingham	5	2	0	64	51	2.69	1.05	22.4	207	26	73	1.90	2.8	7.2	2.6	0.1	71
2011	AA	Birmingham	10	7	0	152	113	4.03	1.53	24.5	259	32	72	3.87	4.9	6.7	1.4	0.2	6
2012	AAA	Charlotte	12	10	0	135	103	2.47	1.34	21.6	253	30	83	3.58	3.5	6.9	2.0	0.5	48

Tall, savvy SP who finished 2nd in IL in ERA. Effectively moves ball around strike zone and deceives hitters by changing speeds and eye levels. Plus CU is best offering and he drops it in for strikes. FB velocity is below avg but he commands it. Maintains stuff deep and will need better breaking ball for RHH.

Lehman, Patrick — RP — Washington

EXP MLB DEBUT: 2013 | POTENTIAL: Reliever | 6B

Thrws R Age 26
2009 (13) George Washington

Velo	Pitch	Grade
88-92	FB	+++
	SL	++
	CU	++

Year	Lev	Team	W	L	Sv	IP	K	ERA	WHIP	BF/G	OBA	H%	S%	xERA	Ctl	Dom	Cmd	hr/9	BPV
2010	A+	Potomac	5	4	0	87	88	4.84	1.32	17.2	261	32	67	4.46	2.9	9.1	3.1	1.4	103
2011	A+	Potomac	2	0	7	16	11	1.72	0.57	4.1	169	21	67	0.14	0.0	6.3		0.0	132
2011	AA	Harrisburg	1	2	6	34	34	3.71	0.76	4.2	187	24	50	1.28	1.1	9.0	8.5	0.5	151
2012	AA	Harrisburg	0	0	4	8	9	1.17	0.78	3.5	156	19	100	1.58	2.3	10.6	4.5	1.2	145
2012	AAA	Syracuse	1	0	1	43	29	3.32	1.36	4.9	256	30	77	3.76	3.5	6.0	1.7	0.6	31

Crafty and effective RP proved reliable at AA and AAA and should see action in the majors. Throws a low-90s FB, an average SL, and decent CU. He has nice polish and is a strike throwing machine (53 BB/223 K in minor league career). Keeps the ball down in the zone and gets lots of ground ball outs.

Light, Pat — SP — Boston

EXP MLB DEBUT: 2015 | POTENTIAL: #3 starter | 8D

Thrws R Age 22
2012 (1-S) Monmouth

Velo	Pitch	Grade
88-96	FB	++++
84-86	SL	+++
79-82	CU	+

Year	Lev	Team	W	L	Sv	IP	K	ERA	WHIP	BF/G	OBA	H%	S%	xERA	Ctl	Dom	Cmd	hr/9	BPV
2010	NCAA	Monmouth	2	6	1	57	33	6.12	1.62	23.2	314	35	61	5.43	3.0	5.2	1.7	0.8	31
2011	NCAA	Monmouth	4	5	0	76	61	4.04	1.32	22.4	280	34	69	3.85	2.0	7.3	3.6	0.5	94
2012	NCAA	Monmouth	8	3	0	101	102	2.40	0.99	27.6	227	31	75	2.08	1.4	9.1	6.4	0.3	143
2012	A-	Lowell	0	2	0	30	30	2.37	1.06	9.8	240	32	77	2.44	1.5	8.9	6.0	0.3	138

Slender power pitcher who may eventually end up in pen due to electric stuff, but will be tried as SP for time being. Throws consistent strikes with plus FB despite difficulty in repeating arm slot. SL has moments of swing-and-miss. Generally throws from mid ¾ slot and needs to change speeds more effectively.

Lopez, Jorge — SP — Milwaukee

EXP MLB DEBUT: 2016 | POTENTIAL: #3 starter | 7D

Thrws R Age 20
2011 (2) HS, P.R.

Velo	Pitch	Grade
88-92	FB	+++
	CB	+++
	CU	+

Year	Lev	Team	W	L	Sv	IP	K	ERA	WHIP	BF/G	OBA	H%	S%	xERA	Ctl	Dom	Cmd	hr/9	BPV
2012	Rk	Brewers	1	3	2	25	20	5.33	1.54	15.8	274	33	65	4.54	4.3	7.1	1.7	0.7	31

Tall, skinny RH has a good a low-90s FB and a potentially plus CB. He has a loose, easy arm action and should add velocity once he fills out. Will need to work on developing consistent mechanics and refining his CU, but does have some interesting upside, though he struggled in his pro debut.

Lorin, Brett — RP — Arizona

EXP MLB DEBUT: 2014 | POTENTIAL: Reliever | 6D

Thrws R Age 26
2008 (5) Long Beach State

Velo	Pitch	Grade
88-92	FB	++
	SL	+++
	CU	++

Year	Lev	Team	W	L	Sv	IP	K	ERA	WHIP	BF/G	OBA	H%	S%	xERA	Ctl	Dom	Cmd	hr/9	BPV
2009	A	Clinton	5	4	0	89	87	2.44	0.97	21.0	196	24	81	2.27	2.5	8.8	3.5	0.9	108
2010	Rk	GCL Pirates	0	0	0	7	10	1.29	0.57	7.9	48	0	100	0.13	3.9	12.9	3.3	1.3	145
2010	A	West Virginia	2	3	0	42	32	5.18	1.42	14.7	298	34	65	4.93	1.9	6.9	3.6	1.1	90
2011	A+	Bradenton	7	6	1	117	99	2.84	1.04	18.1	237	29	74	2.61	1.5	7.6	5.2	0.5	115
2012	AA	Mobile	3	10	0	103	70	6.40	1.58	15.6	305	34	59	5.42	3.1	6.1	2.0	1.1	46

Lorin regressed after a nice breakout in '11. Does have a decent 90-92 mph sinking FB, but did not miss many bats at AA. Struggles can be traced to lack of dominance and sub-par command. Was moved to relief late in the season, where he fared a bit better. Will likely remain in that role.

Lotzkar, Kyle — SP — Cincinnati

EXP MLB DEBUT: 2013 | POTENTIAL: #4 starter | 8D

Thrws R Age 23
2007 (1-S) HS, Canada

Velo	Pitch	Grade
88-93	FB	++++
79-82	SU	+++
79-83	CU	+

Year	Lev	Team	W	L	Sv	IP	K	ERA	WHIP	BF/G	OBA	H%	S%	xERA	Ctl	Dom	Cmd	hr/9	BPV
2010	Rk	Billings	2	0	0	20	33	0.45	0.50	16.6	124	23	100	0.00	0.9	14.9	16.5	0.5	261
2010	Rk	Reds	1	1	0	24	27	3.33	1.32	12.6	226	31	74	2.97	4.4	10.0	2.3	0.4	78
2011	A	Dayton	3	2	0	67	72	4.32	1.14	18.9	213	27	65	3.05	3.4	9.7	2.9	1.1	102
2012	A+	Bakersfield	3	0	0	26	27	2.39	1.22	21.3	229	30	83	3.06	3.4	9.2	2.7	0.7	92
2012	AA	Pensacola	4	6	0	86	96	5.21	1.51	20.7	240	31	68	4.47	5.5	10.0	1.8	1.3	49

Has been plagued by health problems since being drafted, but managed to log a career high 112.2 IP. Quick arm action provides plus movement to FB and SL. Worked hard to improve and smooth out mechanics, but still throws across his body. Does provide some deception, but needs to stay healthy.

Loux, Barret — SP — Chicago (N)

EXP MLB DEBUT: 2014 | POTENTIAL: #4 starter | 7C

Thrws R Age 24
2011 FA (Texas A&M)

Velo	Pitch	Grade
89-94	FB	+++
78-81	CB	++
82-84	SL	+++
	CU	+++

Year	Lev	Team	W	L	Sv	IP	K	ERA	WHIP	BF/G	OBA	H%	S%	xERA	Ctl	Dom	Cmd	hr/9	BPV
2008	NCAA	Texas A&M	6	2	0	90	81	4.18	1.23	22.9	230	28	68	3.42	3.5	8.1	2.3	1.0	69
2009	NCAA	Texas A&M	3	3	0	48	62	4.13	1.33	16.6	241	36	68	3.20	3.9	11.6	3.0	0.4	121
2010	NCAA	Texas A&M	11	2	0	105	136	2.83	1.07	24.0	209	31	75	2.34	2.9	11.7	4.0	0.6	149
2011	A+	Myrtle Beach	8	5	0	109	127	3.80	1.28	21.3	256	36	70	3.41	2.8	10.5	3.7	0.5	131
2012	AA	Frisco	14	1	0	127	100	3.47	1.27	20.8	251	30	74	3.53	2.9	7.1	2.4	0.7	67

Durable SP who throws with good angle and repeats simple delivery to keep command and control intact. Easy arm generates avg velocity and has ability to properly mix in CB, SL, and CU with good fade. K rate has declined and FB can be straight. Needs polish to secondary offerings.

Lovegrove, Kieran — SP — Cleveland
EXP MLB DEBUT: 2017 | POTENTIAL: #3 starter | 8E

Thrws R Age 18
2012 (3) HS (CA)

Velo	Pitch	Grade
86-94	FB	++
83-86	SL	+++
82-85	CU	+++

Year	Lev	Team	W	L	Sv	IP	K	ERA	WHIP	BF/G	OBA	H%	S%	xERA	Ctl	Dom	Cmd	hr/9	BPV
2012	Rk	Indians	0	2	0	21	18	6.00	1.76	12.0	321	40	64	5.54	3.9	7.7	2.0	0.4	53

Projectable SP who has fine natural stuff, but will need time to develop. Pitches with inconsistent velo and needs to iron out mechanics. Lacks strength to hold velo, but has frame to grow. Can register Ks with hard SL and CU has makings of becoming avg. Tends to telegraph pitches.

Lowell, Charlie — SP — Miami
EXP MLB DEBUT: 2015 | POTENTIAL: #4 starter | 6C

Thrws L Age 22
2011 (6) Wichita State

Velo	Pitch	Grade
89-93	FB	+++
	SL	++
	CU	++

Year	Lev	Team	W	L	Sv	IP	K	ERA	WHIP	BF/G	OBA	H%	S%	xERA	Ctl	Dom	Cmd	hr/9	BPV
2011	NCAA	Wichita State	10	5	0	103	124	2.79	1.20	24.4	224	33	75	2.39	3.5	10.8	3.1	0.1	118
2011	Rk	GCL Marlins	0	1	0	1	2	40.60	4.51	4.9	516	70	0	16.45	13.5	13.5	1.0	0.0	-104
2011	A-	Jamestown	0	0	0	2	4	0.00	1.50	4.3	151	38	100	2.16	9.0	18.0	2.0	0.0	99
2012	A	Greensboro	5	5	0	110	117	4.35	1.36	19.9	225	30	69	3.43	4.8	9.6	2.0	0.7	60
2012	A+	Jupiter	0	0	0	5	5	1.80	1.00	19.1	221	25	100	3.48	1.8	9.0	5.0	1.8	131

Big, stocky lefty has a strong frame and a good low-90s FB. Will mix in an above-average SL and a show-me CU. Gets good downhill tilt, keeping the ball down in the zone, but struggled with control. If control improves, could develop into a solid, durable back-end starter.

Maddox, Austin — RP — Boston
EXP MLB DEBUT: 2015 | POTENTIAL: Setup reliever | 7C

Thrws R Age 22
2012 (3) Florida

Velo	Pitch	Grade
90-96	FB	++++
83-86	SL	++
82-84	CU	++

Year	Lev	Team	W	L	Sv	IP	K	ERA	WHIP	BF/G	OBA	H%	S%	xERA	Ctl	Dom	Cmd	hr/9	BPV
2011	NCAA	Florida	3	0	5	27	21	0.67	0.85	4.7	208	27	91	1.27	1.0	7.0	7.0	0.0	117
2012	NCAA	Florida	3	3	12	55	57	2.44	0.94	6.5	208	28	76	1.93	1.8	9.3	5.2	0.5	137
2012	Rk	GCL Red Sox	0	1	0	5	4	1.80	1.00	6.4	221	28	80	1.80	1.8	7.2	4.0	0.0	99
2012	A-	Lowell	0	0	0	3	4	0.00	1.00	11.5	191	31	100	1.40	3.0	12.0	4.0	0.0	153

Durable RP who served as closer in college and has attack philosophy to have similar role as pro. Can be more thrower than pitcher, but raw arm strength is desirable in short stints. Throws quality strikes with FB while mixing in promising CU and slurvy SL. Can leave pitches up in zone.

Madrid, Roman — RP — San Diego
EXP MLB DEBUT: 2014 | POTENTIAL: Setup reliever | 7B

Thrws R Age 22
2012 (7) Central Florida

Velo	Pitch	Grade
91-94	FB	+++
85-87	SL	+++

Year	Lev	Team	W	L	Sv	IP	K	ERA	WHIP	BF/G	OBA	H%	S%	xERA	Ctl	Dom	Cmd	hr/9	BPV
2010	NCAA	Texas A&M-CC	0	3	1	13	13	18.23	3.08	5.2	435	51	37	12.57	8.1	8.8	1.1	2.0	-43
2011	NCAA	McLennan CC	3	2	9	28	39	2.89	1.50	5.8	233	--	--	--	5.8	12.5	2.2	--	87
2012	NCAA	Central Florida	5	2	3	45	46	1.00	1.18	5.6	221	30	92	2.42	3.4	9.2	2.7	0.2	92
2012	A-	Eugene	7	0	13	37	44	2.89	0.99	4.6	198	30	68	1.47	2.7	10.6	4.0	0.0	137

Short, but strong-bodied RH reliever pounds the strike zone with a good 91-94 mph fastball, but his best offering is a nasty hard SL that gets plenty of swings-and-misses. Was lights-out in his pro debut, posting a 4.0 Cmd while striking out 10.6 per nine and notching 13 saves.

Magill, Matt — SP — Los Angeles (N)
EXP MLB DEBUT: 2014 | POTENTIAL: #5 starter | 7C

Thrws R Age 23
2008 (31) HS, CA

Velo	Pitch	Grade
88-91	FB	++
	SL	++++
	CU	+

Year	Lev	Team	W	L	Sv	IP	K	ERA	WHIP	BF/G	OBA	H%	S%	xERA	Ctl	Dom	Cmd	hr/9	BPV
2008	Rk	GCL Dodgers	1	2	1	30	25	3.34	1.31	11.2	264	32	76	3.72	2.7	7.6	2.8	0.6	81
2009	Rk	Ogden	6	3	0	72	55	4.00	1.24	19.5	225	26	70	3.27	3.8	6.9	1.8	0.9	41
2010	A	Great Lakes	7	4	2	126	135	3.28	1.10	20.6	196	25	74	2.61	3.7	9.6	2.6	0.9	91
2011	A+	Rancho Cuc	11	5	0	139	126	4.33	1.49	23.1	284	35	73	4.79	3.4	8.1	2.4	1.0	74
2012	AA	Chattanooga	11	8	0	146	168	3.75	1.28	23.1	235	33	71	3.13	3.8	10.3	2.8	0.5	103

Tall RH continues to make steady progress and struck out 168 in '12. Gets swings and misses despite below-average FB velocity. Best pitch is a plus SL and also has a decent CU. Keeps the ball down and gets lots of GB outs. SL/CU guys have a hard time remaining starters, but Magill hasn't faltered yet.

Magnifico, Damien — RP — Milwaukee
EXP MLB DEBUT: 2014 | POTENTIAL: Setup reliever | 7C

Thrws R Age 22
2012 (5) Oklahoma

Velo	Pitch	Grade
95-97	FB	+++
	SL	++
	CU	+

Year	Lev	Team	W	L	Sv	IP	K	ERA	WHIP	BF/G	OBA	H%	S%	xERA	Ctl	Dom	Cmd	hr/9	BPV
2012	Rk	Helena	0	3	0	22	25	5.81	1.66	10.8	256	34	65	4.67	6.2	10.4	1.7	0.8	37

Strong fireballer comes after hitters with a plus upper-90s FB that reaches 100 mph. FB tends to be flat and doesn't control it as well as needed, but does mix in a decent power SL. Max-effort delivery and previous elbow make him a health risk, but did strike out 10.4 per nine. Could have an impact.

Manzanillo, Santo — RP — Milwaukee
EXP MLB DEBUT: 2013 | POTENTIAL: Setup reliever | 6D

Thrws R Age 24
2005 NDFA, D.R.

Velo	Pitch	Grade
94-96	FB	++++
83-85	SL	+++

Year	Lev	Team	W	L	Sv	IP	K	ERA	WHIP	BF/G	OBA	H%	S%	xERA	Ctl	Dom	Cmd	hr/9	BPV
2011	A+	Brevard County	1	0	10	41	43	1.52	1.09	5.8	210	28	88	2.28	3.0	9.4	3.1	0.4	104
2011	AA	Huntsville	0	1	7	20	19	2.21	1.23	4.1	185	22	87	2.77	5.3	8.4	1.6	0.9	26
2012	Rk	Brewers	0	1	0	3	2	10.11	1.50	5.8	347	42	25	4.92	0.0	6.7		0.0	139
2012	A	Wisconsin	2	1	0	6	2	7.50	1.67	6.7	228	21	56	5.02	7.5	3.0	0.4	1.5	-131
2012	AA	Huntsville	0	4	1	13	10	6.08	1.73	5.0	257	29	67	5.37	6.8	6.8	1.0	1.4	-43

Short, strong-armed reliever took a huge step back. Control problem resurfaced and made '11 look like an anomaly. Attacks hitters with a 95-98 mph FB that tops out at 100 mph. His breaking ball will need to improve if he is to make an impact in the majors and that future looks much less likely than a year ago.

Maples, Dillon — SP — Chicago (N)
EXP MLB DEBUT: 2015 | POTENTIAL: #3 starter | 8D

Thrws R Age 21
2011 (14) HS, SC

Velo	Pitch	Grade
93-95	FB	++++
75-78	CB	+++
80-83	CU	+++

Year	Lev	Team	W	L	Sv	IP	K	ERA	WHIP	BF/G	OBA	H%	S%	xERA	Ctl	Dom	Cmd	hr/9	BPV
2012	Rk	Cubs	0	1	0	10	12	4.36	1.55	7.5	171	26	69	2.57	8.7	10.5	1.2	0.0	-29

Maples spent much of the year in extended spring training refining his mechanics. Has a plus FB that tops out at 97 mph. Also has a nice CB and a potentially plus CU. Mechanics remain a work in progress, but has nice athleticism. Should make his full-season debut in 2013.

Marinez, Jhan — RP — Chicago (A)
EXP MLB DEBUT: 2010 | POTENTIAL: Closer | 8D

Thrws R Age 24
2006 FA (DR)

Velo	Pitch	Grade
92-98	FB	++++
86-89	SL	+++
	CU	+

Year	Lev	Team	W	L	Sv	IP	K	ERA	WHIP	BF/G	OBA	H%	S%	xERA	Ctl	Dom	Cmd	hr/9	BPV
2010	AA	Jacksonville	1	0	6	17	20	2.16	0.96	4.2	161	23	80	1.48	3.8	10.8	2.9	0.5	110
2010	MLB	Florida	1	1	0	3	3	6.74	2.25	3.4	285	31	80	8.94	10.1	10.1	1.0	3.4	-73
2011	AA	Jacksonville	3	8	3	58	74	3.57	1.53	4.5	223	31	80	4.15	6.5	11.5	1.8	1.1	49
2012	AAA	Charlotte	4	2	4	63	65	2.86	1.10	6.2	180	23	77	2.21	4.3	9.3	2.2	0.7	69
2012	MLB	Chicago (A)	0	0	0	3	1	0.00	1.50	5.8	210	23	100	2.96	6.7	3.4	0.5	0.0	-103

Loose-armed RP with velo to succeed in late innings and improved BB rate. Proved tough to hit with FB/SL combo and offers some deception with whip-like delivery. Can overthrow SL and needs to stay on top of pitch. Rarely changes speeds and is flyball pitcher, though HR haven't been problem.

Markel, Parker — SP — Tampa Bay
EXP MLB DEBUT: 2014 | POTENTIAL: #4 starter / Setup reliever | 7B

Thrws R Age 22
2010 (39) Yavapai JC

Velo	Pitch	Grade
90-96	FB	+++
82-86	SL	+++
81-84	CU	+++

Year	Lev	Team	W	L	Sv	IP	K	ERA	WHIP	BF/G	OBA	H%	S%	xERA	Ctl	Dom	Cmd	hr/9	BPV
2010	Rk	GCL Rays	2	0	0	10	13	1.74	1.06	5.7	215	33	82	1.86	2.6	11.3	4.3	0.0	151
2011	A-	Hudson Valley	3	4	0	57	44	3.14	1.13	17.4	206	25	73	2.41	3.6	6.9	1.9	0.5	45
2012	A	Bowling Green	11	5	0	120	96	3.53	1.26	20.4	257	31	72	3.34	2.6	7.2	2.8	0.5	79

Tall, strong SP who seems destined for bullpen where power stuff could play up. Heavy sinker can be used to register Ks, especially from low ¾ slot, but has proven difficult to locate. Gets fair share of gb with deceptive CU. Lacks stamina and inability to maintain velocity late in games.

Marlowe, Chris — RP — San Francisco
EXP MLB DEBUT: 2013 | POTENTIAL: Setup reliever | 7B

Thrws R Age 23
2011 (5) Oklahoma State

Velo	Pitch	Grade
92-95	FB	++++
81-84	CB	+++

Year	Lev	Team	W	L	Sv	IP	K	ERA	WHIP	BF/G	OBA	H%	S%	xERA	Ctl	Dom	Cmd	hr/9	BPV
2011	NCAA	Oklahoma St	3	3	4	41	71	5.05	1.44	7.3	178	33	64	2.94	7.5	15.6	2.1	0.7	97
2011	Rk	Giants	1	0	0	3	5	0.00	1.33	4.2	262	46	100	3.10	3.0	15.0	5.0	0.0	207
2012	A	Augusta	1	9	2	84	86	4.20	1.49	12.0	219	29	72	3.50	6.3	9.3	1.5	0.5	13

Short, strong-armed RP has good dominance, but struggles with control. Does have a good mid-90s heater he locates well along with a power CB, but CU is a work in progress. Worked both as a starter and a reliever. Long-term his role is likely as a reliever where concerns about durabilty will not be an issue.

Maronde, Nick — SP — Los Angeles (A)

EXP MLB DEBUT: 2012 | **POTENTIAL:** #3 starter | **8C**

Thrws L Age 23
2011 (3) Florida

- 87-95 FB ++++
- 80-85 SL +++
- 80-82 CU +++

Year	Lev	Team	W	L	Sv	IP	K	ERA	WHIP	BF/G	OBA	H%	S%	xERA	Ctl	Dom	Cmd	hr/9	BPV
2011	Rk	Orem	5	0	0	46	50	2.14	1.10	16.5	216	28	87	2.88	2.9	9.7	3.3	1.0	114
2012	Rk	Angels	0	1	0	8	9	1.13	0.63	9.2	117	18	80	0.00	2.3	10.1	4.5	0.0	140
2012	A+	Inland Empire	3	1	0	59	60	1.82	0.91	22.1	193	25	84	1.79	2.1	9.1	4.3	0.6	124
2012	AA	Arkansas	3	2	0	32	21	3.34	1.30	19.0	300	35	73	3.91	0.8	5.8	7.0	0.3	101
2012	MLB	Los Angeles (A)	0	0	0	6	7	1.50	1.50	2.2	262	38	89	3.56	4.5	10.5	2.3	0.0	86

Athletic SP who pitched on four levels and ended season in LAA bullpen. Could be RP with plus FB and knockout SL, but will stay in rotation to develop CU. Throws with loose arm which adds movement. Hard SL gets Ks, but can get flat and left up. Has plus-plus control, but can fall in love with FB and be inefficient.

Marshall, Brett — SP — New York (A)

EXP MLB DEBUT: 2014 | **POTENTIAL:** #4 starter | **7B**

Thrws R Age 23
2008 (6) HS (TX)

- 89-94 FB +++
- 82-85 SL +++
- 78-81 CU +++

Year	Lev	Team	W	L	Sv	IP	K	ERA	WHIP	BF/G	OBA	H%	S%	xERA	Ctl	Dom	Cmd	hr/9	BPV
2010	Rk	GCL Yankees	0	0	0	8	8	2.25	1.25	16.3	210	29	80	2.28	4.5	9.0	2.0	0.0	59
2010	A	Charleston (Sc)	4	2	0	72	56	2.50	1.03	21.3	204	25	75	1.90	2.8	7.0	2.5	0.3	70
2010	A+	Tampa	0	0	0	4	6	4.50	1.25	16.3	307	49	60	3.56	0.0	13.5		0.0	261
2011	A+	Tampa	9	7	0	140	114	3.78	1.35	21.7	264	33	71	3.62	3.1	7.3	2.4	0.4	66
2012	AA	Trenton	13	7	0	158	120	3.52	1.29	24.1	253	29	75	3.74	3.0	6.8	2.3	0.9	59

Short SP who throws from repeatable, high ¾ slot and succeeds with pitchability. Sinker/SL combo is solid, but CU may be best pitch. Throws CU with same arm speed as FB and is weapon against LHH. K rate doesn't project due to lack of out pitch and has elevated HR rate despite GB tendencies.

Marshall, Evan — RP — Arizona

EXP MLB DEBUT: 2013 | **POTENTIAL:** Possible closer | **7B**

Thrws R Age 23
2011 (4) Kansas State

- 91-95 FB +++
- 82-85 CB +++
- 82-84 CU ++

Year	Lev	Team	W	L	Sv	IP	K	ERA	WHIP	BF/G	OBA	H%	S%	xERA	Ctl	Dom	Cmd	hr/9	BPV
2011	NCAA	Kansas State	5	5	1	61	55	1.62	1.03	7.8	215	29	83	1.80	2.4	8.1	3.4	0.0	100
2011	A-	Yakima	0	0	2	12	13	0.75	1.00	4.2	228	32	92	1.87	1.5	9.8	6.5	0.0	153
2011	A+	Visalia	0	1	4	17	18	1.59	1.12	4.5	226	29	94	3.13	2.6	9.5	3.6	1.1	118
2011	AA	Mobile	0	0	0	2	0	0.00	1.00	7.6	262	26	100	2.41	0.0	0.0		0.0	18
2012	AA	Mobile	6	3	16	49	27	3.51	1.46	5.0	286	32	75	4.20	3.0	5.0	1.7	0.4	28

Strong, hard-throwing RP held his own at AA, notching 16 saves. Has a good 92-95 mph FB, a hard CB, and a usable CU. While he fared well at AA, his K rate declined and will need to miss more bats as he moves up. The raw stuff is above-average and he is being groomed as a future closer.

Martin, Cody — SP — Atlanta

EXP MLB DEBUT: 2015 | **POTENTIAL:** #3 starter | **8D**

Thrws R Age 23
2011 (7) Gonzaga

- 90-94 FB +++
- 83-85 SL +++
- CB ++
- CU ++

Year	Lev	Team	W	L	Sv	IP	K	ERA	WHIP	BF/G	OBA	H%	S%	xERA	Ctl	Dom	Cmd	hr/9	BPV
2010	NCAA	Gonzaga	5	7	0	88	89	6.55	1.69	28.4	311	39	62	5.94	3.8	9.1	2.4	1.2	80
2011	NCAA	Gonzaga	2	1	12	52	63	0.86	0.94	7.9	169	26	92	1.17	3.3	10.8	3.3	0.2	125
2011	Rk	Danville	0	0	3	9	14	0.00	0.33	3.5	73	15	100	0.00	1.0	14.0	14.0	0.0	243
2011	A	Rome	1	0	6	24	35	1.48	0.90	6.5	208	32	90	2.04	1.5	12.9	8.8	0.7	211
2012	A+	Lynchburg	12	7	0	107	123	2.93	1.18	19.5	235	32	77	2.96	2.9	10.3	3.6	0.6	127

Strong-armed college reliever was moved into a starting role and seemed to thrive. Worked hard to get in better shape and added depth and bite to his hard SL. FB sits at 90-94 mph and also mixes in a CB and a CU. The CB and CU need work, but he throws strikes and kept hitters off balance.

Martin, Ethan — SP — Philadelphia

EXP MLB DEBUT: 2013 | **POTENTIAL:** #2 starter | **8C**

Thrws R Age 24
2008 (1) HS, GA

- 90-95 FB ++++
- 82-84 SL ++++
- 80-84 SP +++

Year	Lev	Team	W	L	Sv	IP	K	ERA	WHIP	BF/G	OBA	H%	S%	xERA	Ctl	Dom	Cmd	hr/9	BPV
2010	A+	Inland Empire	9	14	0	113	105	6.35	1.77	20.8	273	34	63	5.17	6.4	8.3	1.3	0.8	-6
2011	A+	Rancho Cuc	4	4	0	55	61	7.36	1.85	16.1	295	38	61	6.17	6.1	10.0	1.6	1.3	34
2011	AA	Chattanooga	5	3	2	40	43	4.02	1.49	8.3	214	28	74	3.55	6.5	9.6	1.5	0.7	16
2012	AA	Chattanooga	8	6	0	118	112	3.58	1.27	24.1	211	28	71	2.71	4.7	8.5	1.8	0.4	46
2012	AA	Reading	5	0	0	40	35	3.18	1.18	22.7	206	25	75	2.72	4.1	7.9	1.9	0.7	51

Was part of the Victorino deal and showed signs of progress. Has a plus mid-90s FB, a SL, CB, and CU, all of which are erratic. Inconsistent mechanics and poor control hold him back, but can be very tough to hit and struck out 147 in 157.2 IP. Still has 1st round stuff and is a breakout candidate in 2013.

Martinez, Carlos — SP — St. Louis

EXP MLB DEBUT: 2014 | **POTENTIAL:** #1 starter | **9C**

Thrws R Age 21
2010 NDFA, D.R.

- 94-98 FB +++++
- 78-81 CB ++++
- CU +++

Year	Lev	Team	W	L	Sv	IP	K	ERA	WHIP	BF/G	OBA	H%	S%	xERA	Ctl	Dom	Cmd	hr/9	BPV
2011	A	Quad Cities	3	2	0	39	50	2.33	1.06	18.8	198	31	78	1.86	3.3	11.6	3.6	0.2	139
2011	A+	Palm Beach	3	3	0	46	48	5.28	1.72	20.9	274	37	68	4.66	5.9	9.4	1.6	0.4	29
2012	A+	Palm Beach	2	2	0	33	34	3.00	1.18	18.9	238	33	72	2.45	2.7	9.3	3.4	0.0	111
2012	AA	Springfield	4	3	0	71	58	2.90	1.18	19.0	236	28	78	3.14	2.8	7.3	2.6	0.8	75

Talented RH has an electric arm and put together a solid season. Blows hitters away with a upper-90s fastball, a plus CB, and an improved CU. Did miss time with shoulder tendinitis. Uses a high leg kick to generate torque and deception. Not pretty to watch, but the results are very good.

Martinez, Fabio — SP — Cleveland

EXP MLB DEBUT: 2014 | **POTENTIAL:** #2 starter/Closer | **9E**

Thrws R Age 23
2007 FA (DR)

- 90-97 FB ++++
- 80-83 SL ++++
- 79-83 CU ++

Year	Lev	Team	W	L	Sv	IP	K	ERA	WHIP	BF/G	OBA	H%	S%	xERA	Ctl	Dom	Cmd	hr/9	BPV
2009	Rk	Angels	3	2	0	61	92	3.26	1.34	18.0	208	36	74	2.57	5.3	13.6	2.6	0.1	119
2010	A	Cedar Rapids	7	3	0	103	141	3.92	1.51	22.4	215	33	74	3.46	6.6	12.3	1.9	0.5	60
2011	Rk	Angels	0	0	0	2	2	0.00	1.29	4.8	233	30	100	2.68	3.9	7.7	2.0	0.0	53
2012	A+	Inland Empire	0	5	0	23	23	10.72	2.56	15.2	289	37	55	7.38	12.7	9.1	0.7	0.8	-161
2012	A+	Carolina	0	2	0	6	7	8.53	2.05	3.9	219	32	54	4.40	11.4	10.0	0.9	0.0	-110

Tall SP who returned in June after myriad injuries limited him to 2 IP in '11. Acquired off waivers in Aug but still has upside with hard stuff. Lacks feel for CU and has experienced problems with BB and LHH. Thrives with high arm slot and downward angle, especially with heavy FB and hard SL.

Mata, Angel — SP — Minnesota

EXP MLB DEBUT: 2017 | **POTENTIAL:** #3 starter | **8E**

Thrws R Age 20
2010 FA (Venezuela)

- 88-94 FB +++
- 79-82 CB ++
- 80-81 CU ++

Year	Lev	Team	W	L	Sv	IP	K	ERA	WHIP	BF/G	OBA	H%	S%	xERA	Ctl	Dom	Cmd	hr/9	BPV
2011	Rk	GCL Twins	0	1	0	37	30	1.46	1.14	12.2	181	24	86	1.67	4.6	7.3	1.6	0.0	25
2012	Rk	Elizabethton	4	3	0	53	55	3.38	1.22	16.6	171	20	78	2.86	5.7	9.3	1.6	1.2	30

Tall, powerful SP who will likely simmer in minors for several years. Has potential for three avg to slightly above avg pitches, led by very heavy FB. Throws with quick arm that produces ideal pitch movement. Trouble repeating delivery causes issues with CU. Profiles as avg pitch along with CB.

Mateo, Luis — SP — New York (N)

EXP MLB DEBUT: 2015 | **POTENTIAL:** #2 starter | **9D**

Thrws R Age 23
2008 NDFA, D.R.

- 92-95 FB +++
- SL +++
- CU +

Year	Lev	Team	W	L	Sv	IP	K	ERA	WHIP	BF/G	OBA	H%	S%	xERA	Ctl	Dom	Cmd	hr/9	BPV
2012	A-	Brooklyn	4	5	0	73	85	2.45	0.90	22.7	216	31	72	1.69	1.1	10.4	9.4	0.2	176

Failed international signing caused him to fly under the radar, but has top-shelf stuff. Works off his 92-95 FB and complements it with a plus hard SL. Needs to refine his CU, but it shows potential. Was lights-out in debut, showing plus command and over-matched hitters in the NYPL. Great find by the Mets.

Matthews, Kevin — SP — Texas

EXP MLB DEBUT: 2015 | **POTENTIAL:** #4 starter | **7C**

Thrws L Age 20
2011 (1) HS (GA)

- 87-93 FB +++
- 79-83 CB +++
- CU +++

Year	Lev	Team	W	L	Sv	IP	K	ERA	WHIP	BF/G	OBA	H%	S%	xERA	Ctl	Dom	Cmd	hr/9	BPV
2011	Rk	Rangers	1	0	0	12	12	1.50	1.25	7.0	228	29	93	3.21	3.8	9.0	2.4	0.8	79
2011	A-	Spokane	0	3	0	17	18	2.70	1.62	14.8	229	33	81	3.44	7.0	9.7	1.4	0.0	3
2012	A	Hickory	3	4	1	74	66	4.38	1.74	17.8	238	31	73	4.10	7.8	8.0	1.0	0.2	-48

Small, athletic SP who had issues with throwing strikes. Needs to find consistent release point and may need to refine delivery. Despite flyballs, only allowed 2 HR. Has solid pitch mix that projects to better results. Quick arm produces FB movement and can get hitters to chase CB. Best pitch may be CU.

Matz, Stephen — SP — New York (N)

EXP MLB DEBUT: 2015 | **POTENTIAL:** #2 starter | **8E**

Thrws L Age 22
2009 (2) HS, NY

- 90-94 FB ++++
- SL +++
- CB ++
- 73-75 CU ++

Year	Lev	Team	W	L	Sv	IP	K	ERA	WHIP	BF/G	OBA	H%	S%	xERA	Ctl	Dom	Cmd	hr/9	BPV
2012	Rk	Kingsport	2	1	0	29	34	1.55	1.14	19.1	164	24	88	1.75	5.3	10.6	2.0	0.3	65

2nd round pick finally made pro debut with respectable results. FB is dynamic and sits in the mid-90s and topping out at 98 mph. Also showed a decent SL, CB, and CU. Was shut-down in July with more shoulder soreness, but pitched in instructional ball without any discomfort. Still has all kinds of potential.

Matzek, Tyler — SP — Colorado

EXP MLB DEBUT: 2014 | POTENTIAL: #2 starter | 8E

Thrws L Age 22
2009 (1) HS, CA

Velo	Pitch	Grade
91-95	FB	++++
80-83	SL	++++
74-76	CB	+++
	CU	++

Year	Lev	Team	W	L	Sv	IP	K	ERA	WHIP	BF/G	OBA	H%	S%	xERA	Ctl	Dom	Cmd	hr/9	BPV
2010	A	Asheville	5	1	0	89	88	2.92	1.39	20.9	198	25	81	3.05	6.2	8.9	1.4	0.6	9
2011	A	Asheville	5	4	0	64	74	4.36	1.48	23.0	200	28	70	3.13	7.0	10.4	1.5	0.4	15
2011	A+	Modesto	0	3	0	33	37	9.82	2.42	17.3	268	34	59	7.26	12.5	10.1	0.8	1.4	-139
2012	A+	Modesto	6	8	0	142	153	4.62	1.61	22.5	250	34	70	4.10	6.0	9.7	1.6	0.4	30

Talented lefty continues to be all over the map. Has good velocity, topping out at 96, to go along with a decent mix of SL, CB, and CU. Misses bats effectively and consistently, but inconsistent mechanics and release point means he can't find the strike zone. Was better than in '11, but still walked too many.

Maurer, Brandon — SP — Seattle

EXP MLB DEBUT: 2014 | POTENTIAL: #3 starter | 8C

Thrws R Age 23
2008 (23) HS (CA)

Velo	Pitch	Grade
91-95	FB	+++
83-86	SL	+++
77-79	CB	++
	CU	++

Year	Lev	Team	W	L	Sv	IP	K	ERA	WHIP	BF/G	OBA	H%	S%	xERA	Ctl	Dom	Cmd	hr/9	BPV
2010	Rk	Arizona	0	1	0	11	14	1.64	0.91	10.3	205	32	80	1.34	1.6	11.5	7.0	0.0	180
2010	A	Clinton	0	1	0	4	6	2.08	1.15	8.6	291	39	100	5.03	0.0	12.5		2.1	242
2011	A	Clinton	1	3	0	37	44	3.41	1.14	20.9	212	30	70	2.45	3.4	10.7	3.1	0.5	119
2011	A+	High Desert	2	4	0	42	37	6.38	1.37	19.7	283	32	56	5.15	2.3	7.9	3.4	1.7	96
2012	AA	Jackson	9	2	0	138	117	3.20	1.31	23.7	255	32	75	3.28	3.1	7.6	2.4	0.3	71

Athletic SP who has seen status rise with combo of pitch mix and control. Throws four pitches for strikes and has confidence in solid-avg FB. Injury prone in past, but no major surgeries. Has effort in delivery, but repeats it and shows good command. Uses two breaking balls, but needs to hone CU.

May, Trevor — SP — Minnesota

EXP MLB DEBUT: 2013 | POTENTIAL: #1 starter | 9D

Thrws R Age 23
2008 (4) HS, WA

Velo	Pitch	Grade
92-95	FB	++++
74-78	CB	+++
80-82	CU	+++

Year	Lev	Team	W	L	Sv	IP	K	ERA	WHIP	BF/G	OBA	H%	S%	xERA	Ctl	Dom	Cmd	hr/9	BPV
2009	A	Lakewood	4	1	0	77	95	2.56	1.31	21.3	210	31	81	2.73	5.0	11.1	2.2	0.3	82
2010	A	Lakewood	7	3	0	65	92	2.91	1.09	23.1	218	34	74	2.33	2.8	12.7	4.6	0.4	173
2010	A+	Clearwater	5	5	0	70	90	5.01	1.63	19.5	212	30	70	4.07	7.8	11.6	1.5	0.9	15
2011	A+	Clearwater	10	8	0	151	208	3.63	1.24	22.8	221	34	71	2.81	4.0	12.4	3.1	0.5	133
2012	AA	Reading	10	13	0	150	151	4.87	1.45	22.8	248	30	70	4.50	4.7	9.1	1.9	1.3	55

Tall, strong SP who wasn't able to duplicate breakout of '11, but has great arm. Owns plus FB with heavy, late life. Power CB can be swing-and-miss pitch, though CU remains below avg. Struggles to repeat mechanics, which leads to command issues. Also can leave ball up in zone and get hammered.

Mazzoni, Cory — SP — New York (N)

EXP MLB DEBUT: 2014 | POTENTIAL: #4 starter | 7D

Thrws R Age 23
2011 (2) NC State

Velo	Pitch	Grade
90-94	FB	+++
72-75	CB	+++
	CU	++

Year	Lev	Team	W	L	Sv	IP	K	ERA	WHIP	BF/G	OBA	H%	S%	xERA	Ctl	Dom	Cmd	hr/9	BPV
2011	NCAA	NC State	6	6	0	115	137	3.30	1.05	27.7	220	31	70	2.46	2.3	10.8	4.7	0.6	150
2011	A-	Brooklyn	1	0	0	6	10	0.00	1.17	4.0	228	42	100	2.23	3.0	15.0	5.0	0.0	207
2011	A+	St. Lucie	1	1	0	7	8	2.57	1.14	4.6	262	34	86	3.87	1.3	10.3	8.0	1.3	168
2012	A+	St. Lucie	5	1	0	64	48	3.25	1.26	21.6	263	32	74	3.40	2.3	6.8	3.0	0.4	79
2012	AA	Binghamton	5	5	0	81	56	4.46	1.36	24.1	283	32	69	4.51	2.2	6.2	2.8	1.0	70

Short RH has a plus FB that tops out at 97 mph. He complements it with a decent CB and a split-CU. Started the season well in the FSL, but scuffled when moved up to AA and FB tends to be flat when elevated. Throws plenty of strikes, but needs to refine and trust his secondary offerings to have success.

McCullers, Lance — SP — Houston

EXP MLB DEBUT: 2016 | POTENTIAL: #2 starter / Closer | 9D

Thrws R Age 19
2012 (1-S) HS (FL)

Velo	Pitch	Grade
92-99	FB	++++
84-88	SL	++++
81-84	CU	+

Year	Lev	Team	W	L	Sv	IP	K	ERA	WHIP	BF/G	OBA	H%	S%	xERA	Ctl	Dom	Cmd	hr/9	BPV
2012	Rk	GCL Astros	0	1	0	11	12	1.64	1.09	10.8	244	34	83	2.29	1.6	9.8	6.0	0.0	151
2012	Rk	Greeneville	0	3	0	15	17	4.80	1.33	15.6	191	24	67	3.39	6.0	10.2	1.7	1.2	40

Athletic pitcher who thrives with outstanding FB/SL combo that can dominate. Showed touch and feel for power stuff while throwing quality strikes. Delivery gets out of whack when overthrowing and can rely on FB too much. Power arsenal could be lethal in late innings, though will be given chance to start.

McGough, Scott — RP — Miami

EXP MLB DEBUT: 2014 | POTENTIAL: reliever | 6C

Thrws R Age 23
2011 (5) Oregon

Velo	Pitch	Grade
90-94	FB	+++
77-80	CB	+++
	CU	++

Year	Lev	Team	W	L	Sv	IP	K	ERA	WHIP	BF/G	OBA	H%	S%	xERA	Ctl	Dom	Cmd	hr/9	BPV
2011	NCAA	Oregon	3	6	5	58	62	3.59	1.34	7.7	242	34	70	2.89	3.9	9.7	2.5	0.0	87
2011	Rk	Ogden	1	1	2	6	8	4.76	1.41	4.0	333	50	63	4.40	0.0	12.7		0.0	247
2011	A	Great Lakes	0	4	8	20	25	2.21	1.18	4.1	239	34	83	2.86	2.7	11.1	4.2	0.4	145
2012	A+	Rancho Cuc	3	5	5	47	48	3.99	1.50	5.8	252	33	74	3.98	4.9	9.1	1.8	0.6	49
2012	A+	Jupiter	2	1	1	17	8	3.24	1.38	4.7	288	33	74	3.69	2.2	4.3	2.0	0.0	37

Short reliever has a low-90s FB, a power CB, and decent CU. He competes well and throws all three for strikes. Held up well in the CAL and looked even better after being traded to the Marlins. Uses plus arm speed to get good velocity from small frame and should continue to move up.

McGuire, Deck — SP — Toronto

EXP MLB DEBUT: 2013 | POTENTIAL: #3 starter | 8D

Thrws R Age 24
2010 (1) Georgia Tech

Velo	Pitch	Grade
88-94	FB	+++
80-83	SL	+++
77-80	CB	++
	CU	++

Year	Lev	Team	W	L	Sv	IP	K	ERA	WHIP	BF/G	OBA	H%	S%	xERA	Ctl	Dom	Cmd	hr/9	BPV
2009	NCAA	Georgia Tech	11	2	0	100	118	3.50	1.27	25.6	233	32	74	3.26	3.7	10.6	2.9	0.7	109
2010	NCAA	Georgia Tech	9	4	0	113	118	2.96	1.13	27.8	228	29	79	3.17	2.6	9.4	3.6	1.0	116
2011	A+	Dunedin	7	4	0	105	102	2.75	1.21	22.2	232	29	81	3.18	3.3	8.8	2.7	0.8	88
2011	AA	New Hampshire	2	1	0	21	22	4.35	1.31	21.3	255	31	74	4.63	3.0	9.6	3.1	1.7	108
2012	AA	New Hampshire	5	15	0	144	97	5.88	1.56	22.5	285	31	64	5.37	3.9	6.1	1.6	1.4	23

Tall, durable SP who has talent to earn role in bigs. Was victim of flyballs and HR while hitting fat part of plate. Mixes pitches well and maintains velo deep into games. Lacks high ceiling, but has four effective pitches at disposal including SL that can generate Ks. Needs to throw more strikes early in count.

McNeil, Ryan — SP — Chicago (N)

EXP MLB DEBUT: 2016 | POTENTIAL: #4 starter | 7D

Thrws R Age 19
2012 (3) HS, CA

Velo	Pitch	Grade
90-92	FB	+++
	SL	++
	CU	++

Year	Lev	Team	W	L	Sv	IP	K	ERA	WHIP	BF/G	OBA	H%	S%	xERA	Ctl	Dom	Cmd	hr/9	BPV
2012	Rk	Cubs	1	0	0	20	18	1.35	1.45	10.7	252	32	93	3.75	4.5	8.1	1.8	0.5	42

Strong, atheltic HS righty was a 3rd round pick. Isn't overpowering, but does have a good 90-92 mph FB that was up to the task in rookie ball. Has good FB command with nice late movement. SL has some potential and has shown some feel for a CU. Had a 0.53 ERA in August.

McNutt, Trey — SP — Chicago (N)

EXP MLB DEBUT: 2013 | POTENTIAL: #4 starter/setup reliever | 8D

Thrws R Age 23
2009 (32) Shelton State CC

Velo	Pitch	Grade
90-98	FB	+++
	CB	+++
	CU	++

Year	Lev	Team	W	L	Sv	IP	K	ERA	WHIP	BF/G	OBA	H%	S%	xERA	Ctl	Dom	Cmd	hr/9	BPV
2010	A	Peoria	6	0	0	60	70	1.51	1.12	18.1	204	30	85	1.87	3.6	10.6	2.9	0.0	110
2010	A+	Daytona	4	0	0	41	49	2.63	0.93	17.1	201	28	74	1.96	2.0	10.8	5.4	0.7	158
2010	AA	Tennessee	0	1	0	16	13	5.74	1.60	23.1	322	38	65	5.81	2.3	7.5	3.3	1.1	90
2011	AA	Tennessee	5	6	0	95	65	4.55	1.67	18.6	309	36	72	5.19	3.7	6.2	1.7	0.5	29
2012	AA	Tennessee	9	8	0	95	66	4.26	1.45	11.9	258	29	74	4.50	4.3	6.3	1.5	1.1	15

Big, physical RH has good raw stuff, but doesn't dominate. Inconsistent mechanics and release point result in poor command. Mid-90s FB has potential, but tends to be overthrown. Power CB can also be plus, but CU remains below average. Frustratingly ineffective despite potential.

McPherson, Kyle — SP — Pittsburgh

EXP MLB DEBUT: 2012 | POTENTIAL: #4 starter | 7B

Thrws R Age 25
2007 (14) HS, AL

Velo	Pitch	Grade
88-92	FB	+++
73-75	CB	+++
80-83	CU	+++

Year	Lev	Team	W	L	Sv	IP	K	ERA	WHIP	BF/G	OBA	H%	S%	xERA	Ctl	Dom	Cmd	hr/9	BPV
2011	A+	Bradenton	4	1	0	72	60	2.89	0.95	22.5	235	29	70	2.31	0.8	7.5	10.0	0.5	133
2011	AA	Altoona	8	5	0	89	82	3.02	1.07	21.7	229	29	74	2.75	2.1	8.3	3.9	0.7	110
2012	AA	Altoona	3	5	0	49	46	4.07	1.21	21.8	282	35	69	4.01	0.9	8.5	9.2	0.9	146
2012	AAA	Indianapolis	0	1	0	18	17	0.98	0.82	22.2	175	22	93	1.26	2.0	8.3	4.3	0.5	115
2012	MLB	Pittsburgh	0	2	0	26	21	2.73	1.18	10.5	244	28	82	3.51	2.4	7.2	3.0	1.0	83

Tall RH made his MLB debut and looked good doing so. Fringy FB velocity is mitigated by good command and mix of CB and an effective CU. Pinpoint accuracy and is able to hit all parts of the strike zone. Continued to maintain a Cmd ratio north of 3.0 and could develop into a reliable, workhorse starter.

Melotakis, Mason — RP — Minnesota

EXP MLB DEBUT: 2014 | POTENTIAL: Setup reliever | 7D

Thrws L Age 22
2012 (2) Northwestern State

Velo	Pitch	Grade
90-96	FB	+++
79-81	SL	+++
80-83	CU	+

Year	Lev	Team	W	L	Sv	IP	K	ERA	WHIP	BF/G	OBA	H%	S%	xERA	Ctl	Dom	Cmd	hr/9	BPV
2010	NCAA	Northwestern St	0	0	0	25	14	3.28	1.46	7.5	294	31	84	5.35	2.6	5.1	2.0	1.5	41
2011	NCAA	Northwestern St	1	3	5	41	45	3.98	1.57	7.4	286	39	74	4.51	4.0	10.0	2.5	0.4	90
2012	NCAA	Northwestern St	4	4	7	62	70	3.63	1.05	10.4	212	29	67	2.47	2.6	10.2	3.9	0.7	130
2012	Rk	Elizabethton	1	1	0	7	10	1.35	0.60	3.3	96	19	75	0.00	2.7	13.5	5.0	0.0	188
2012	A	Beloit	3	1	1	17	24	2.08	1.10	5.2	235	33	94	3.63	2.1	12.5	6.0	1.6	186

Aggressive pitcher who will be tried as starter in '13 despite closer mentality and stuff. Pitches with solid FB and intimidates by pitching inside. Counters FB with hard but inconsistent SL. Move to rotation could be good in order for him to work on subpar CU. Short arm action limits projection.

Mendez, Roman — SP — Texas

EXP MLB DEBUT: 2014 — POTENTIAL: #3 starter — 8C

Thrws R Age 22
2007 FA (DR)

- 91-96 FB ++++
- 82-87 SL +++
- 82-84 CU ++

Year	Lev	Team	W	L	Sv	IP	K	ERA	WHIP	BF/G	OBA	H%	S%	xERA	Ctl	Dom	Cmd	hr/9	BPV
2010	A	Greenville	0	2	0	15	18	11.40	2.60	13.6	407	50	59	11.63	6.0	10.8	1.8	3.0	50
2011	A	Hickory	9	1	1	117	130	3.31	1.38	18.9	262	35	77	3.78	3.5	10.0	2.9	0.5	105
2012	Rk	Rangers	0	1	0	9	7	3.00	0.89	11.1	216	25	71	2.41	1.0	7.0	7.0	1.0	117
2012	A+	Myrtle Beach	4	6	1	70	71	5.14	1.34	16.2	259	33	62	3.99	3.2	9.1	2.8	0.9	96
2012	AA	Frisco	2	0	1	12	9	1.46	0.97	9.4	187	19	100	2.71	2.9	6.6	2.3	1.5	57

Quick-armed SP with athleticism in wiry frame. Throws across body and suffers control problems at times. Slot can be inconsistent. When on, can be difficult to hit. Quick FB has natural cutting action while hard SL can be dominant. Has good separation between FB and CU, but lacks deception.

Meo, Anthony — SP — Arizona

EXP MLB DEBUT: 2014 — POTENTIAL: #3 starter/setup reliever — 8D

Thrws R Age 23
2011 (2) Coastal Carolina

- 92-95 FB +++
- 87-98 SL +++
- 81-83 CB ++
- 83-85 CU ++

Year	Lev	Team	W	L	Sv	IP	K	ERA	WHIP	BF/G	OBA	H%	S%	xERA	Ctl	Dom	Cmd	hr/9	BPV
2010	NCAA	Coastal Carolina	13	2	0	97	94	2.61	1.20	21.6	231	30	80	2.94	3.2	8.8	2.8	0.6	90
2011	NCAA	Coastal Carolina	10	3	0	108	115	2.16	1.13	26.7	230	31	82	2.59	2.6	9.6	3.7	0.4	120
2011	Rk	Missoula	0	0	0	2	1	0.00	0.00	5.6	0	0	100	0.00	0.0	4.5		0.0	99
2011	Rk	Diamondbacks	0	0	0	1	2	0.00	0.00	2.8	0	0	100	0.00	0.0	18.0		0.0	342
2012	A+	Visalia	9	8	0	140	153	4.11	1.46	23.1	253	33	74	4.27	4.6	9.8	2.2	1.0	72

Lean RH survied a stint in the CAL and showed good Dom. Works off a plus 92-94 FB that tops at 96 and mixes in a plus hard SL that can be swing-and-miss. CU and CB are average, but give him a 4-pitch mix. Improved mechanics give him a chance, but control is problematic.

Mercedes, Melvin — RP — Detroit

EXP MLB DEBUT: 2015 — POTENTIAL: Setup reliever — 8E

Thrws R Age 22
2008 FA (DR)

- 89-96 FB ++++
- 81-83 SL +++
- CU +

Year	Lev	Team	W	L	Sv	IP	K	ERA	WHIP	BF/G	OBA	H%	S%	xERA	Ctl	Dom	Cmd	hr/9	BPV
2010	A	West Michigan	1	2	3	20	12	5.03	1.78	6.0	224	27	69	3.82	8.7	5.5	0.6	0.0	-118
2011	A	West Michigan	0	0	0	2	1	10.78	2.40	4.4	389	45	50	7.98	5.4	5.4	1.0	0.0	-31
2011	A-	Connecticut	3	1	3	34	21	2.67	1.43	6.8	252	30	79	3.29	4.3	5.6	1.3	0.0	4
2012	A	West Michigan	0	3	9	64	43	2.80	1.20	7.0	229	27	77	2.81	3.2	6.0	1.9	0.4	39
2012	A+	Lakeland	0	0	0	1	0	0.00	2.00	4.8	262	26	100	4.93	9.0	0.0	0.0	0.0	-225

Big, strong RP whose results starting to show. Has excellent upside with potential for two plus offerings, highlighted by heavy FB and hard SL. Should lead to higher K rate, but focus on FB command has led to contact. Needs offspeed pitch to counter LHH. Control has improved dramatically.

Merejo, Luis — RP — Atlanta

EXP MLB DEBUT: 2016 — POTENTIAL: Setup reliever — 7C

Thrws L Age 18
2011 NDFA, D.R.

- 88-93 FB +++
- CB ++
- CU +++

Year	Lev	Team	W	L	Sv	IP	K	ERA	WHIP	BF/G	OBA	H%	S%	xERA	Ctl	Dom	Cmd	hr/9	BPV
2012	Rk	GCL Braves	0	5	0	41	53	4.61	1.15	16.3	247	37	57	2.67	2.0	11.6	5.9	0.2	174

Short, lefty RP had an impressive debut. FB sits at 88-93 mph and he could add more velocity as he fills out. Mixes in a good, but inconsistent CB and a decent CU. Comes right after hitters by pounding the zone and his FB is described as sneaky-fast.

Meyer, Ajay — RP — Toronto

EXP MLB DEBUT: 2015 — POTENTIAL: Setup reliever — 7C

Thrws R Age 25
2011 FA (Ashland, OH)

- 85-91 FB +++
- 79-82 SL +++
- 74-77 CB +++
- 80-81 CU +

Year	Lev	Team	W	L	Sv	IP	K	ERA	WHIP	BF/G	OBA	H%	S%	xERA	Ctl	Dom	Cmd	hr/9	BPV
2011	Rk	Bluefield	4	2	0	66	55	3.02	1.14	20.0	251	31	74	2.93	1.8	7.5	4.2	0.4	106
2012	A	Lansing	3	3	33	56	57	3.67	1.07	4.1	228	28	70	3.09	2.1	9.1	4.4	1.1	126

Very tall, thin RP who led MWL in saves. Owns below average velo for late innings RP but has impeccable control. Throws from ¾ slot to add movement and can drop down to make SL more effective. Can have trouble taming moving parts in delivery. Throws two breaking balls of varying velocity.

Meyer, Alex — SP — Minnesota

EXP MLB DEBUT: 2015 — POTENTIAL: #1 starter — 9C

Thrws R Age 23
2011 (1) Kentucky

- 94-97 FB ++++
- 82-85 SL +++
- CB ++
- 83-85 CU ++

Year	Lev	Team	W	L	Sv	IP	K	ERA	WHIP	BF/G	OBA	H%	S%	xERA	Ctl	Dom	Cmd	hr/9	BPV
2009	NCAA	Kentucky	1	4	1	60	80	5.73	1.64	20.5	240	33	68	5.02	6.8	12.1	1.8	1.5	52
2010	NCAA	Kentucky	5	3	0	51	63	7.06	1.86	19.9	291	40	61	5.71	6.4	11.1	1.8	0.9	47
2011	NCAA	Kentucky	7	5	0	101	110	2.94	1.23	29.2	215	30	75	2.44	4.1	9.8	2.4	0.2	84
2012	A	Hagerstown	7	4	0	90	107	3.10	1.13	19.8	211	30	72	2.36	3.4	10.7	3.1	0.4	119
2012	A+	Potomac	3	2	0	39	32	2.31	1.03	21.4	209	26	79	2.15	2.5	7.4	2.9	0.5	82

Tall, angular SP who was acquired from WAS in Nov. Has nasty, electric FB that can dominate early in count. Improvement of SL gives him two plus pitches to register Ks. Throws from ¾ slot and keeps ball on ground. Long limbs make repeating delivery difficult. Owns very high upside with big K ability.

Miller, Aaron — SP — Los Angeles (N)

EXP MLB DEBUT: 2013 — POTENTIAL: #4 starter/setup reliever — 8D

Thrws L Age 25
2009 (1-S) Baylor

- 90-95 FB +++
- 83-85 SL +++
- CU ++

Year	Lev	Team	W	L	Sv	IP	K	ERA	WHIP	BF/G	OBA	H%	S%	xERA	Ctl	Dom	Cmd	hr/9	BPV
2010	A+	Inland Empire	6	4	0	102	99	2.92	1.22	21.6	210	27	77	2.70	4.2	8.8	2.1	0.5	61
2010	AA	Chattanooga	1	4	0	23	22	7.04	2.00	18.5	302	37	65	6.52	7.0	8.6	1.2	1.2	-17
2011	Rk	Dodgers	1	0	0	2	3	0.00	1.00	7.6	151	27	100	0.94	4.5	13.5	3.0	0.0	140
2011	A+	Rancho Cuc	3	2	0	34	30	3.97	1.62	15.1	278	35	75	4.61	4.8	7.9	1.7	0.5	32
2012	AA	Chattanooga	6	6	0	121	110	4.45	1.55	21.2	255	32	72	4.31	5.3	8.2	1.5	0.7	23

Frustratingly inconsistent as he has all the tools to thrive. Starts with a plus mid-90s FB and a nasty hard SL. Was healthy after missing extended action with a sports hernia but command was erratic. Located his FB well in the past, but will need to clean up his mechanics and become more consistent.

Miller, Matt — SP — Milwaukee

EXP MLB DEBUT: 2014 — POTENTIAL: #5 starter — 6C

Thrws R Age 24
2010 (5) Michigan

- 90-92 FB ++
- 80-82 SL +++
- CU ++

Year	Lev	Team	W	L	Sv	IP	K	ERA	WHIP	BF/G	OBA	H%	S%	xERA	Ctl	Dom	Cmd	hr/9	BPV
2010	NCAA	Michigan	3	3	0	64	51	5.06	1.73	17.1	315	38	70	5.50	3.9	7.2	1.8	0.6	41
2010	Rk	Helena	7	2	0	71	53	4.06	1.28	20.8	239	28	70	3.58	3.5	6.7	1.9	0.9	43
2011	A	Wisconsin	6	8	0	111	89	4.38	1.41	21.4	246	30	67	3.47	4.5	7.2	1.6	0.3	27
2012	A	Wisconsin	10	7	0	132	95	3.68	1.29	24.6	262	31	72	3.58	2.6	6.5	2.5	0.5	65
2012	A+	Brevard County	1	2	0	20	20	7.20	1.90	23.6	369	46	61	7.15	2.3	9.0	4.0	0.9	119

Strong RH held his own in the MWL, but given his age and collegiate experience it was not particularly impressive. Has good control of a low-90s FB, but it tends to be straight and doesn't miss bats. Complements the FB with a slurve and an average CU. A move to relief could be his only hope of reaching the majors.

Miller, Shelby — SP — St. Louis

EXP MLB DEBUT: 2012 — POTENTIAL: #1 starter — 9B

Thrws R Age 22
2009 (1) HS, TX

- 93-97 FB ++++
- 75-77 CB ++++
- 83-85 CU +++

Year	Lev	Team	W	L	Sv	IP	K	ERA	WHIP	BF/G	OBA	H%	S%	xERA	Ctl	Dom	Cmd	hr/9	BPV
2010	A	Quad Cities	7	5	0	104	140	3.62	1.25	17.7	248	37	72	3.29	2.8	12.1	4.2	0.6	159
2011	A+	Palm Beach	2	3	0	53	81	2.89	1.13	23.3	211	36	74	2.27	3.4	13.8	4.1	0.3	174
2011	AA	Springfield	9	3	0	87	89	2.70	1.21	21.8	228	31	77	2.59	3.4	9.2	2.7	0.2	92
2012	AAA	Memphis	11	10	0	137	160	4.74	1.38	21.2	264	34	71	4.76	3.3	10.5	3.2	1.6	119
2012	MLB	St. Louis	1	0	0	14	16	1.32	0.95	8.6	189	29	85	1.27	2.6	10.5	4.0	0.0	137

One of the best SP in the minors, despite mixed results in '12. Had a slow start, but a mechanical adjustment allowed him to thrive. Was 7-2 with a 2.88 ERA after the break with only 7 BB. Has a plus FB, good CB, and a CU which shows potential. Worked in relief in playoffs, but future is as starter.

Mitchell, Bryan — SP — New York (A)

EXP MLB DEBUT: 2015 — POTENTIAL: #3 starter — 8D

Thrws R Age 22
2009 (16) HS (NC)

- 88-94 FB +++
- 80-82 CB +++
- 84-85 CU ++

Year	Lev	Team	W	L	Sv	IP	K	ERA	WHIP	BF/G	OBA	H%	S%	xERA	Ctl	Dom	Cmd	hr/9	BPV
2010	Rk	GCL Yankees	2	1	0	42	36	3.67	1.20	16.8	192	24	69	2.37	4.8	7.8	1.6	0.4	30
2010	A-	Staten Island	0	1	0	4	3	6.75	2.00	19.3	383	46	63	6.85	2.3	6.8	3.0	0.0	79
2011	A-	Staten Island	1	3	0	62	59	4.09	1.56	19.3	272	34	75	4.55	4.5	8.6	1.9	0.7	51
2012	A	Charleston (Sc)	9	11	0	120	121	4.58	1.49	19.2	240	32	69	3.76	5.4	9.1	1.7	0.5	36

Live-armed athlete who thrives on ability to keep ball on ground with good sinker. FB velocity is only avg but exhibits natural late movement that is tough to elevate. Power CB can register Ks while CU in development stage. BB rate increased and needs to polish command in order to fool upper level hitters.

Mitchell, D.J. — SP — Seattle

EXP MLB DEBUT: 2012 — POTENTIAL: #4 starter — 7D

Thrws R Age 26
2008 (10) Clemson

- 87-91 FB +++
- 76-79 CB ++
- 80-82 SL +++
- 81-83 CU ++

Year	Lev	Team	W	L	Sv	IP	K	ERA	WHIP	BF/G	OBA	H%	S%	xERA	Ctl	Dom	Cmd	hr/9	BPV
2010	AAA	Scranton/W-B	2	0	0	18	16	3.57	1.47	25.3	276	36	73	3.71	3.6	8.1	2.3	0.0	68
2011	AAA	Scranton/W-B	13	9	0	161	112	3.18	1.35	24.0	254	30	77	3.65	3.5	6.2	1.8	0.6	36
2012	AAA	Scranton/W-B	6	4	0	86	72	5.04	1.33	23.7	260	31	62	3.93	3.0	7.6	2.5	0.8	72
2012	MLB	Yankees	0	0	0	5	2	3.85	2.14	5.8	347	35	89	8.38	5.8	3.9	0.7	1.9	-69
2012	AAA	Tacoma	3	2	0	49	33	2.96	1.23	24.7	230	26	79	3.21	3.5	6.1	1.7	0.7	33

Short, slender SP who is durable despite lack of size. Lacks frontline velocity and dominance, but knows how to sequence pitches. Lives off sinker/SL combo and pounds bottom half of strike zone with quality strikes. CU has potential to be another average offering.

Molina, Nestor — SP — Chicago (A)

EXP MLB DEBUT: 2013 | **POTENTIAL:** #4 starter | **7C**

Thrws R	Age 24		Year	Lev	Team	W	L	Sv	IP	K	ERA	WHIP	BF/G	OBA	H%	S%	xERA	Ctl	Dom	Cmd	hr/9	BPV
2006 FA (Venezuela)			2010	A+	Dunedin	0	0	0	4	3	2.08	1.62	9.6	364	43	86	5.53	0.0	6.2		0.0	130
88-93	FB	+++	2011	A+	Dunedin	10	3	0	108	115	2.58	1.07	20.1	250	33	79	2.96	1.2	9.6	8.2	0.7	159
75-78	CB	+++	2011	AA	New Hampshire	2	0	0	22	33	0.41	0.64	15.2	162	29	93	0.15	0.8	13.5	16.5	0.0	239
82-84	SP	+++	2012	AA	Birmingham	6	10	0	123	84	4.26	1.48	24.0	311	36	71	4.77	1.9	6.2	3.2	0.5	77
80-83	CU	+++	2012	AAA	Charlotte	0	1	0	4	4	13.50	2.50	21.3	444	49	50	13.64	2.3	9.0	4.0	4.5	119

Quick-armed SP with plus control and command. Keeps hitters off balance by mixing pitches and changing speeds with precision. Location is paramount as he lacks out pitch and LHH have dominated him. Falling K rate will likely be trend. Arsenal highlighted by average FB and hard SPL.

Montas, Francellis — SP — Boston

EXP MLB DEBUT: 2016 | **POTENTIAL:** #2 starter | **9E**

Thrws R	Age 20		Year	Lev	Team	W	L	Sv	IP	K	ERA	WHIP	BF/G	OBA	H%	S%	xERA	Ctl	Dom	Cmd	hr/9	BPV
2009 FA (DR)																						
92-99	FB	++++																				
82-84	SL	++																				
78-80	CB	+	2012	Rk	GCL Red Sox	1	5	0	41	41	3.98	1.13	13.4	229	32	61	2.21	2.7	9.1	3.4	0.0	110
85-87	CU	+	2012	A-	Lowell	0	0	0	4	4	0.00	1.63	16.3	326	44	100	4.87	2.5	9.8	4.0	0.0	128

Lean, strong SP who improved control. Still quite a bit away from big leagues, but has ability to dominate hitters with lively FB. Velo can waver and crude delivery needs to be smoother. FB shows explosive life and hard SL has promise. CB and CU are well below avg and may scrap CB.

Montero, Rafael — SP — New York (N)

EXP MLB DEBUT: 2015 | **POTENTIAL:** #3 starter | **8D**

Thrws R	Age 22		Year	Lev	Team	W	L	Sv	IP	K	ERA	WHIP	BF/G	OBA	H%	S%	xERA	Ctl	Dom	Cmd	hr/9	BPV
2011 NDFA, D.R.			2011	Rk	Kingsport	2	1	0	17	9	4.24	1.35	17.7	262	28	71	4.24	3.2	4.8	1.5	1.1	18
91-93	FB	+++	2011	Rk	GCL Mets	1	2	1	31	32	1.45	1.10	17.3	243	34	85	2.30	1.7	9.3	5.3	0.9	138
	SL	++	2011	A-	Brooklyn	1	0	0	5	5	3.60	0.80	9.1	175	18	67	2.44	1.8	9.0	5.0	1.8	131
	CU	++	2012	A	Savannah	6	3	0	71	54	2.52	0.97	22.5	233	28	75	2.34	1.0	6.8	6.8	0.5	113
			2012	A+	St. Lucie	5	2	0	51	56	2.13	0.91	23.6	197	28	77	1.59	2.0	9.9	5.1	0.4	144

Short RH from the D.R. has easy arm action that results good low-90s FB with nice arm-side run. Pairs the FB with a SL, CB, and a seldom used CU. Slight hesitation in delivery gives him deception, but also slows his tempo. Has plus command of all pitches and walked just 19 while striking out 110.

Montgomery, Mark — RP — New York (A)

EXP MLB DEBUT: 2013 | **POTENTIAL:** Closer | **8C**

Thrws R	Age 22		Year	Lev	Team	W	L	Sv	IP	K	ERA	WHIP	BF/G	OBA	H%	S%	xERA	Ctl	Dom	Cmd	hr/9	BPV
2011 (11) Longwood			2011	NCAA	Longwood	1	0	10	30	48	0.89	0.73	4.9	123	24	86		3.0	14.2	4.8	0.0	194
90-94	FB	+++	2011	A	Charleston (Sc)	0	0	14	24	41	1.85	1.15	4.4	199	32	82	1.83	4.1	15.2	3.7	0.0	181
82-85	SL	++++	2011	A-	Staten Island	0	0	1	4	10	2.25	1.25	4.1	210	70	80	2.15	4.5	22.5	5.0	0.0	302
	CU	+	2012	A+	Tampa	4	1	14	40	61	1.34	0.97	4.9	168	30	85	1.04	3.6	13.6	3.8	0.0	167
			2012	AA	Trenton	3	1	24	38	1.88	0.75	5.7	151	27	76	0.66	2.3	14.3	6.3	0.4	214	

Short RP who is on fast track. Spent entire career in bullpen where FB/SL combo dominates hitters. RHH and LHH both hit under .200 and they also have trouble elevating sinking FB. Velocity is only average and CU is non-existent, though vicious SL is among minors best breaking balls.

Montgomery, Mike — SP — Tampa Bay

EXP MLB DEBUT: 2013 | **POTENTIAL:** #3 starter | **8D**

Thrws L	Age 24		Year	Lev	Team	W	L	Sv	IP	K	ERA	WHIP	BF/G	OBA	H%	S%	xERA	Ctl	Dom	Cmd	hr/9	BPV
2008 (1-S) HS (CA)			2010	A+	Wilmington	2	0	0	25	33	1.09	0.73	21.9	168	28	83	0.45	1.5	12.0	8.3	0.0	195
88-95	FB	+++	2010	AA	NW Arkansas	5	4	0	60	48	3.47	1.37	19.3	250	30	76	3.68	3.9	7.2	1.8	0.6	42
74-78	CB	+++	2011	AAA	Omaha	5	11	0	151	129	5.32	1.50	23.2	270	32	65	4.54	4.1	7.7	1.9	0.9	45
81-83	CU	++++	2012	AA	NW Arkansas	2	6	0	58	44	6.67	1.55	25.4	297	32	60	5.98	3.3	6.8	2.1	1.9	53
			2012	AAA	Omaha	3	6	0	92	67	5.69	1.67	24.2	298	34	67	5.66	4.2	6.6	1.6	1.2	22

Tall, durable SP whose performance is head-scratching as his pitch mix is still quite good. Uses easy arm action and mixes in pitch effectively low in zone. CU remains strong and thrown with same arm speed as FB. Problems stem from erratic mechanics and release point. Has arsenal to register Ks.

Mooneyham, Brett — SP — Washington

EXP MLB DEBUT: 2015 | **POTENTIAL:** #3 starter | **7D**

Thrws L	Age 23		Year	Lev	Team	W	L	Sv	IP	K	ERA	WHIP	BF/G	OBA	H%	S%	xERA	Ctl	Dom	Cmd	hr/9	BPV
2012 (3) Stanford			2009	NCAA	Stanford	6	3	0	67	72	4.14	1.49	22.3	195	26	73	3.32	7.2	9.6	1.3	0.7	-4
90-93	FB	+++	2010	NCAA	Stanford	3	7	0	87	99	5.07	1.59	22.5	237	32	68	4.22	6.4	10.2	1.6	0.8	29
	CB	++	2012	NCAA	Stanford	7	6	0	83	90	4.75	1.42	23.5	252	33	66	3.83	4.2	9.7	2.3	0.6	79
	CU	++	2012	A-	Auburn	2	2	0	42	29	2.55	1.23	17.1	232	27	80	2.92	3.4	6.2	1.8	0.4	37

Strong lefty doesn't have overpowering stuff. Comes after hitters with an 88-92 mph FB. Throws both a SL and a CB, but neither are consistently reliable and mixes in an average CU. Had a decent pro debut, but was not dominant. He has some nice potential, but will need to refine his CU to have success.

Moore, Navery — RP — Atlanta

EXP MLB DEBUT: 2015 | **POTENTIAL:** Reliever | **7C**

Thrws R	Age 22		Year	Lev	Team	W	L	Sv	IP	K	ERA	WHIP	BF/G	OBA	H%	S%	xERA	Ctl	Dom	Cmd	hr/9	BPV
2011 (14) Vanderbilt			2009	NCAA	Vanderbilt	0	0	0	5	2	7.20	2.00	8.0	262	25	67	6.58	9.0	3.6	0.4	1.8	-160
92-96	FB	+++	2010	NCAA	Vanderbilt	2	0	0	13	16	9.23	2.13	6.3	296	43	52	5.63	8.5	11.4	1.3	0.0	-8
	CB	+	2011	NCAA	Vanderbilt	4	2	11	30	25	1.21	1.01	4.1	177	21	93	1.88	3.6	7.6	2.1	0.6	56
	CU	+	2012	A	Rome	8	3	0	103	84	3.86	1.25	16.1	223	28	67	2.69	3.9	7.4	1.9	0.3	44

Injury plagued RH has a good mid-90s FB when healthy and had a nice pro debut. Worked as both as a starter and a reliever. Complements the FB with a below-average breaking ball and a CU. Given his injury history and plus FB, Moore profiles better as a reliever, but does have a nice power arm.

Morey, Robert — SP — Miami

EXP MLB DEBUT: 2015 | **POTENTIAL:** #5 starter | **7D**

Thrws R	Age 24		Year	Lev	Team	W	L	Sv	IP	K	ERA	WHIP	BF/G	OBA	H%	S%	xERA	Ctl	Dom	Cmd	hr/9	BPV
2010 (5) Virginia			2009	NCAA	Virginia	3	0	2	68	84	3.32	1.18	15.0	214	31	73	2.76	3.7	11.2	3.0	0.7	119
86-91	FB	+++	2010	NCAA	Virginia	9	4	0	99	77	4.20	1.27	25.2	232	27	69	3.56	3.7	7.0	1.9	1.0	43
71-73	SL	+++	2010	A	Greensboro	1	3	0	44	41	3.65	1.29	15.2	265	32	76	4.23	2.4	8.3	3.4	1.2	102
80-82	CU	++	2011	A	Greensboro	7	7	0	140	107	5.14	1.54	23.5	290	34	67	4.97	3.3	6.9	2.1	0.9	52
			2012	A+	Jupiter	8	3	0	89	57	3.84	1.42	20.9	279	32	72	4.01	2.9	5.8	2.0	0.4	43

Polished RH isn't overpowering, but gets by despite average stuff. FB sits at 86-91 mph, though he can occasionally get a bit more. Complements the heat with an average SL and an average CU. Doesn't have the size or stuff to dominate at higher levels, but could carve out a role at the back end of a rotation.

Morgan, Adam — SP — Philadelphia

EXP MLB DEBUT: 2015 | **POTENTIAL:** #3 starter | **8C**

Thrws L	Age 23		Year	Lev	Team	W	L	Sv	IP	K	ERA	WHIP	BF/G	OBA	H%	S%	xERA	Ctl	Dom	Cmd	hr/9	BPV
2011 (3) Alabama			2010	NCAA	Alabama	7	5	0	90	72	6.18	1.61	22.2	307	35	64	6.02	3.2	7.2	2.3	1.6	61
91-93	FB	++++	2011	NCAA	Alabama	5	7	0	97	77	4.64	1.34	25.2	275	34	63	3.73	2.4	7.1	3.0	0.4	81
80-83	SL	+++	2011	A-	Williamsport	3	3	0	54	43	2.01	1.04	18.8	217	27	81	2.18	2.3	7.2	3.1	0.3	84
	CU	+++	2012	A+	Clearwater	4	10	0	123	140	3.29	1.07	22.8	229	32	69	2.52	2.0	10.2	5.0	0.5	147
			2012	AA	Reading	4	1	0	36	29	3.53	1.26	24.3	253	31	72	3.34	2.8	7.3	2.6	0.5	75

Lefty showed improved velocity and FB now tops out at 94. Doesn't really have a plus secondary pitch, but succeeds due to ability to command and keep hitters off balance. CU and CB have potential to be above-average and he has exceeded expectations.

Morris, Bryan — RP — Pittsburgh

EXP MLB DEBUT: 2012 | **POTENTIAL:** Reliever | **7C**

Thrws R	Age 26		Year	Lev	Team	W	L	Sv	IP	K	ERA	WHIP	BF/G	OBA	H%	S%	xERA	Ctl	Dom	Cmd	hr/9	BPV
2006 (1-C) Motlow St CC			2010	A+	Bradenton	3	0	0	45	40	0.60	0.99	21.2	227	30	93	1.83	1.4	8.1	5.7	0.0	125
88-94	FB	+++	2010	AA	Altoona	6	4	0	89	84	4.25	1.33	19.4	257	32	70	3.94	3.1	8.5	2.7	0.9	86
80-83	SL	+++	2011	AA	Altoona	3	4	3	78	64	3.35	1.35	9.3	247	31	74	3.22	3.8	7.4	1.9	0.2	48
			2012	AAA	Indianapolis	2	2	5	81	79	2.67	1.15	7.0	250	31	81	3.36	1.9	8.8	4.6	0.9	125
			2012	MLB	Pittsburgh	0	0	0	5	6	1.80	0.80	3.6	124	20	75	0.20	3.6	10.8	3.0	0.0	115

Strong, durable RH is turning into a effective reliever. Attacks hitters with a 90-95 mph FB and a good CB. Solid command of FB and CB resulted in a good Cmd ratio and enabled him to make his MLB debut. At 25 he will need to make the Bucs pen in 2013, but should provide someone with a good bullpen arm if not.

Munson, Kevin — RP — Arizona

EXP MLB DEBUT: 2013 | **POTENTIAL:** Reliever | **7D**

Thrws R	Age 24		Year	Lev	Team	W	L	Sv	IP	K	ERA	WHIP	BF/G	OBA	H%	S%	xERA	Ctl	Dom	Cmd	hr/9	BPV
2010 (4) James Madison			2010	A	South Bend	2	0	3	16	17	1.10	0.80	4.9	148	19	92	0.96	2.8	9.4	3.4	0.6	112
90-94	FB	+++	2010	A+	Visalia	0	0	0	1	0			4.9							0.0		
	SL	+++	2011	A+	Visalia	4	3	0	54	76	4.02	1.58	5.6	225	35	75	3.90	6.9	12.7	1.9	0.7	62
			2011	AA	Mobile	0	0	0	3	2	0.00	1.33	6.2	262	32	100	3.19	3.0	6.0	2.0	0.0	45
			2012	AA	Mobile	3	5	3	53	64	6.28	1.55	5.3	269	38	57	4.25	4.6	10.9	2.4	0.5	90

Short righty RP imploded, posting a 6.28 ERA at AA. FB tops out at 95 mph. SL has nice swing and miss potential and good late depth. Short arm action and inconsistent mechanics undermine his power potential and time is running out.

Murphy, Griffin — SP — Toronto

EXP MLB DEBUT: 2016 | POTENTIAL: #3 starter | **8E**

Thrws L | Age 22
2010 (2) HS (CA)

87-92	FB	+++
73-76	CB	+++
	CU	++

Year	Lev	Team	W	L	Sv	IP	K	ERA	WHIP	BF/G	OBA	H%	S%	xERA	Ctl	Dom	Cmd	hr/9	BPV
2011	Rk	GCL Blue Jays	2	2	0	41	39	4.39	1.56	16.3	293	35	76	5.42	3.5	8.6	2.4	1.3	77
2012	Rk	Bluefield	1	2	1	37	42	1.70	1.00	9.4	187	27	83	1.60	3.2	10.2	3.2	0.2	117
2012	A-	Vancouver	0	0	0	2	2	3.86	0.86	4.3	233	30	50	1.59	0.0	7.7		0.0	157

Tall, projectable LHP who was knocked around, but offers upside. Adept at changing speeds and moving ball around plate, but can be hit hard without precise location. FB should gain velocity with added strength and could benefit by quickening delivery. Slow CB is true out pitch, but is inconsistent.

Musgrove, Joe — SP — Houston

EXP MLB DEBUT: 2016 | POTENTIAL: #3 starter | **8E**

Thrws R | Age 20
2011 (1-S) HS (CA)

90-96	FB	+++
77-81	CB	+++
80-82	SL	++
	CU	+++

Year	Lev	Team	W	L	Sv	IP	K	ERA	WHIP	BF/G	OBA	H%	S%	xERA	Ctl	Dom	Cmd	hr/9	BPV
2011	Rk	GCL Blue Jays	0	1	0	22	16	4.57	0.97	10.3	218	26	50	2.08	1.7	6.6	4.0	0.4	93
2011	Rk	Bluefield	1	0	0	3	2	0.00	1.00	11.5	191	24	100	1.46	3.0	6.0	2.0	0.0	45
2012	Rk	Bluefield	0	0	0	8	9	1.13	0.63	13.8	181	27	80	0.36	0.0	10.1		0.0	200
2012	Rk	Greeneville	0	1	0	9	10	7.00	2.00	10.8	356	48	61	6.30	4.0	10.0	2.5	0.0	90

Big, durable SP who has deep repertoire, though no pitch grades as plus at present. Heavy FB shows potential and could evolve into above avg offering, but needs to sharpen command. Has two breaking pitches at disposal and CB is better now. Changes speeds fairly well and repeats arm speed.

Mutz, Nick — RP — Los Angeles (A)

EXP MLB DEBUT: 2015 | POTENTIAL: Setup reliever | **7D**

Thrws R | Age 23
2011 (9) Dakota State

90-95	FB	+++
82-85	SL	+++
86-87	CT	+++
	CU	+

Year	Lev	Team	W	L	Sv	IP	K	ERA	WHIP	BF/G	OBA	H%	S%	xERA	Ctl	Dom	Cmd	hr/9	BPV
2011	Rk	Orem	2	3	2	23	25	2.31	1.07	7.6	233	28	90	3.56	1.9	9.6	5.0	1.5	140
2012	Rk	Angels	0	3	0	10	8	10.45	1.65	5.1	325	40	29	4.91	2.6	7.0	2.7	0.0	73
2012	A	Cedar Rapids	0	1	1	11	5	11.81	3.00	6.9	464	50	58	12.01	5.1	4.2	0.8	0.8	-43

Quick-armed RP who suffered through miserable season before shutting it down in June. Was hit hard and often as FB velo declined and SL wasn't sharp. Worked on smoother delivery and finding consistent release point and had success, but still doesn't change speeds effectively. Has impressive arm strength.

Neal, Zach — SP — Miami

EXP MLB DEBUT: 2014 | POTENTIAL: #4 starter | **7D**

Thrws R | Age 24
2010 (17) Oklahoma

88-93	FB	+++
	SL	+++
	CB	++
	CU	++

Year	Lev	Team	W	L	Sv	IP	K	ERA	WHIP	BF/G	OBA	H%	S%	xERA	Ctl	Dom	Cmd	hr/9	BPV
2010	Rk	GCL Marlins	1	0	0	11	16	0.84	0.84	13.0	210	36	89	1.21	0.8	13.5	16.0	0.0	238
2010	A-	Jamestown	1	1	0	21	21	1.74	1.02	19.8	246	33	85	2.55	0.9	9.1	10.5	0.4	159
2011	A	Greensboro	7	6	0	119	84	4.16	1.39	22.8	270	31	72	4.28	3.1	6.4	2.0	0.9	49
2012	A+	Jupiter	4	1	0	45	33	1.21	1.14	19.7	246	30	92	2.86	2.0	6.6	3.3	0.4	83
2012	AA	Jacksonville	4	6	0	69	45	3.80	1.30	13.5	285	33	71	3.91	1.6	5.9	3.8	0.5	82

Athletic hurler doesn't overpower hitters, but has enough stuff to keep them honest and has good deception with a high leg kick. Holds his own by throwing strikes and keeping hitters off-balance. FB tops at 92, but has some tailing action. Not the highest upside in the system, but does project as a solid innings-eater.

Nelson, Jimmy — SP — Milwaukee

EXP MLB DEBUT: 2014 | POTENTIAL: #3 starter | **7C**

Thrws R | Age 24
2010 (2) Alabama

90-94	FB	++++
82-84	SL	+++
	CU	++
		++

Year	Lev	Team	W	L	Sv	IP	K	ERA	WHIP	BF/G	OBA	H%	S%	xERA	Ctl	Dom	Cmd	hr/9	BPV
2010	NCAA	Alabama	9	3	0	110	98	4.01	1.30	25.2	262	31	73	4.23	2.7	8.0	3.0	1.2	89
2010	Rk	Helena	2	0	3	27	33	3.71	1.61	9.9	285	40	78	4.80	4.4	11.1	2.5	0.7	100
2011	A	Wisconsin	8	9	0	146	120	4.38	1.45	24.0	262	32	69	3.97	4.0	7.4	1.8	0.6	43
2012	A+	Brevard County	4	4	0	81	77	2.21	1.08	24.4	215	28	80	2.24	2.8	8.5	3.1	0.3	97
2012	AA	Huntsville	2	4	0	46	42	3.91	1.54	20.1	208	27	74	3.37	7.2	8.2	1.1	0.4	-30

Big-bodied RH uses his height to generate good velocity on his sinking FB. Also has a good SL, but CU remains a work in progress. Continues to struggle with command, but was much more efficient in the FSL. Will need to show that improvements are legit and can be repeated in 2013.

Nicolino, Justin — SP — Miami

EXP MLB DEBUT: 2015 | POTENTIAL: #2 starter | **8B**

Thrws L | Age 21
2010 (2) HS, FL

89-92	FB	+++
	CB	++
75-78	CU	++++

Year	Lev	Team	W	L	Sv	IP	K	ERA	WHIP	BF/G	OBA	H%	S%	xERA	Ctl	Dom	Cmd	hr/9	BPV
2011	A	Lansing	1	1	0	9	9	3.11	1.50	12.5	310	42	77	4.28	2.1	9.3	4.5	0.0	130
2011	A-	Vancouver	5	1	0	52	64	1.03	0.75	15.5	159	25	85	0.42	1.9	11.0	5.8	0.0	165
2012	A	Lansing	10	4	0	124	119	2.46	1.07	17.3	242	31	78	2.64	1.5	8.6	5.7	0.4	132

Tall, slender SP who led MWL in ERA. Spots FB to both sides and teases hitters with mature sequencing. Commands solid-avg CB and plus CU. Keeps ball on ground with sinker. Had reverse splits in '12 and may continue due to superb CU. K rate likely to decline unless he adds velo or polishes CB.

Nolin, Sean — SP — Toronto

EXP MLB DEBUT: 2014 | POTENTIAL: #4 starter | **7C**

Thrws L | Age 23
2010 (6) San Jacinto JC

88-95	FB	+++
79-82	CB	++
81-84	SL	+++
80-82	CU	+++

Year	Lev	Team	W	L	Sv	IP	K	ERA	WHIP	BF/G	OBA	H%	S%	xERA	Ctl	Dom	Cmd	hr/9	BPV
2010	Rk	GCL Blue Jays	0	0	0	2	4	0.00	1.00	7.6	151	38	100	0.90	4.5	18.0	4.0	0.0	221
2010	A-	Auburn	0	2	0	19	22	6.05	1.76	14.8	314	43	62	4.99	4.2	10.2	2.4	0.0	89
2011	A	Lansing	4	4	1	108	113	3.49	1.23	17.5	250	33	73	3.43	2.6	9.4	3.6	0.7	117
2012	A+	Dunedin	9	0	0	86	90	2.19	1.08	19.8	228	30	84	2.75	2.2	9.4	4.3	0.7	128
2012	AA	New Hampshire	1	0	0	15	18	1.20	1.00	19.1	175	27	87	1.24	3.6	10.8	3.0	0.0	115

Strong, deceptive LHP who may lack plus offering, but retires hitters with deep arsenal thrown from tough arm angle. Spots FB to all quadrants of strike zone. Can drop in SL and CB for strikes, though SL is more of chase pitch. Repeating arm speed on CU gives it avg status and keeps hitters off-guard.

Norris, Daniel — SP — Toronto

EXP MLB DEBUT: 2016 | POTENTIAL: #2 starter | **9E**

Thrws L | Age 20
2011 (2) HS (TN)

90-96	FB	++++
75-78	CB	+++
81-83	CU	+++

Year	Lev	Team	W	L	Sv	IP	K	ERA	WHIP	BF/G	OBA	H%	S%	xERA	Ctl	Dom	Cmd	hr/9	BPV
2012	Rk	Bluefield	2	3	0	35	38	7.97	1.63	14.2	308	40	49	5.54	3.3	9.8	2.9	1.0	104
2012	A-	Vancouver	0	1	0	8	5	10.56	2.48	20.3	393	46	53	8.26	5.9	5.9	1.0	0.0	-35

Very projectable LHP who lives in lower half of strike zone with commandable FB and complements sinker with potential plus CB and solid-avg CU. Throws with quick arm and pitches exhibit good movement. Lacks extension in delivery and crude mechanics need to be upgraded to realize potential.

Nuding, Zach — SP — New York (A)

EXP MLB DEBUT: 2014 | POTENTIAL: #4 starter | **7C**

Thrws R | Age 23
2010 (30) Weatherford JC

88-96	FB	++++
81-84	SL	++
78-84	CU	++

Year	Lev	Team	W	L	Sv	IP	K	ERA	WHIP	BF/G	OBA	H%	S%	xERA	Ctl	Dom	Cmd	hr/9	BPV
2011	Rk	GCL Yankees	0	0	0	7	8	2.57	0.86	8.6	233	34	67	1.56	0.0	10.3		0.0	203
2011	A	Charleston (Sc)	7	6	0	98	82	4.48	1.33	20.4	239	28	68	3.81	4.0	7.5	1.9	1.0	44
2011	A+	Tampa	0	0	0	3	1	0.00	1.33	12.5	262	29	100	3.22	3.0	3.0	1.0	0.0	-9
2012	Rk	GCL Yankees	1	0	0	14	11	1.26	1.19	14.4	182	23	88	1.82	5.0	6.9	1.4	0.0	7
2012	A+	Tampa	8	3	0	86	66	3.89	1.34	22.3	269	33	70	3.60	2.7	6.9	2.5	0.3	69

Big, hefty SP who showed improved control and command of three pitch arsenal. Could eventually move to bullpen where power stuff could play up. Uses height to throw heavy FB with good angle and downhill plane, but can hang inconsistent SL. Could stand to improve CU to battle LHH better.

Oberholtzer, Brett — SP — Houston

EXP MLB DEBUT: 2013 | POTENTIAL: #4 starter | **7C**

Thrws L | Age 24
2008 (8) HS (DE)

88-92	FB	+++
79-82	SL	++
77-79	CB	+++
83-84	CU	+++

Year	Lev	Team	W	L	Sv	IP	K	ERA	WHIP	BF/G	OBA	H%	S%	xERA	Ctl	Dom	Cmd	hr/9	BPV
2010	A+	Myrtle Beach	6	6	2	113	107	4.15	1.25	20.9	279	36	66	3.72	1.4	8.5	5.9	0.6	133
2011	AA	Mississippi	9	9	0	128	93	3.74	1.26	24.8	248	30	70	3.21	3.0	6.6	2.2	0.4	56
2011	AA	Corpus Christi	2	3	0	27	28	5.27	1.39	19.2	266	34	63	4.29	3.3	9.2	2.8	1.0	95
2012	AA	Corpus Christi	5	3	0	77	68	4.21	1.32	24.5	272	32	73	4.49	2.5	7.9	3.2	1.3	95
2012	AAA	Oklahoma City	5	7	0	90	69	4.52	1.38	25.1	293	33	71	4.98	1.9	6.9	3.6	1.3	91

Durable-framed SP who is more about moxie and pitchability than natural stuff. Needs to find weapon to combat RHH, though generally commands four pitches. Offers deception in delivery and isn't afraid to come inside. Velo isn't awe-inspring, but he has good location and control. Can get Ks with CB and SL.

Odorizzi, Jake — SP — Tampa Bay

EXP MLB DEBUT: 2012 | POTENTIAL: #3 starter | **8B**

Thrws R | Age 23
2008 (1-S) HS (IL)

90-94	FB	++++
78-81	SL	+++
73-76	CB	+++
80-84	CU	+++

Year	Lev	Team	W	L	Sv	IP	K	ERA	WHIP	BF/G	OBA	H%	S%	xERA	Ctl	Dom	Cmd	hr/9	BPV
2011	A+	Wilmington	5	4	0	78	103	2.87	1.15	20.7	235	35	76	2.74	2.5	11.8	4.7	0.5	163
2011	AA	NW Arkansas	5	3	0	69	54	4.72	1.28	23.5	254	28	69	4.54	2.9	7.1	2.5	1.7	68
2012	AA	NW Arkansas	4	2	0	38	47	3.32	0.97	20.6	201	29	66	1.90	2.4	11.1	4.7	0.5	154
2012	AAA	Omaha	11	3	0	107	88	2.93	1.35	23.6	258	30	83	4.10	3.4	7.4	2.2	1.0	60
2012	MLB	Kansas City	0	1	0	7	4	4.91	1.64	16.3	279	30	73	5.36	4.9	4.9	1.0	1.2	-26

Tall, athletic SP who locates FB effectively and can cut and sink it early in count. Can overthrow and elevate FB when gunning for Ks and may need to rely on pitching to contact. Repeating delivery enhances look and feel for hard SL and CB while providing deception to nifty CU. Rarely beats himself.

Ogando, Jochi — SP — Seattle

EXP MLB DEBUT: 2017 | POTENTIAL: #2 starter | 9E

Thrws R Age 20
2009 FA (DR)

Velo	Pitch	Grade
92-97	FB	++++
79-82	CB	++
84-87	SL	++
82-84	CU	+

Year	Lev	Team	W	L	Sv	IP	K	ERA	WHIP	BF/G	OBA	H%	S%	xERA	Ctl	Dom	Cmd	hr/9	BPV
2011	Rk	Mariners	1	4	0	25	15	5.84	1.95	14.7	248	29	68	4.90	9.1	5.5	0.6	0.4	-130
2012	Rk	Pulaski	2	3	0	50	39	4.17	1.45	17.7	259	32	70	3.77	4.2	7.1	1.7	0.4	33

Long, lean SP who will simmer in minors for several years, but has exciting upside. Still more of a thrower than pitcher and lacks second pitch to complement plus FB. Quick arm produces velo and late movement, but rarely throws CB/SL for strikes. Lacks feel for CU and struggles with LHH (.338).

Olacio, Jefferson — SP — Chicago (A)

EXP MLB DEBUT: 2016 | POTENTIAL: #2 starter | 9E

Thrws L Age 19
2010 FA (DR)

Velo	Pitch	Grade
89-95	FB	++++
80-82	CB	++
84-85	CU	++

Year	Lev	Team	W	L	Sv	IP	K	ERA	WHIP	BF/G	OBA	H%	S%	xERA	Ctl	Dom	Cmd	hr/9	BPV
2012	Rk	Bristol	2	6	0	59	55	5.03	1.61	21.8	255	32	68	4.34	5.8	8.4	1.4	0.6	13
2012	A	Kannapolis	1	5	0	37	34	5.35	1.86	11.6	292	36	71	5.62	6.3	8.3	1.3	0.7	-4

Tall, raw SP who was among youngest players in Low-A before demotion to short-season. Has intimidating size and power arm. Could add a few more ticks with smoother delivery. Throws with max effort which aids in deception, but hampers control. Needs second pitch to complement plus FB.

Oliver, Andrew — SP — Pittsburgh

EXP MLB DEBUT: 2010 | POTENTIAL: #3 starter | 8D

Thrws L Age 25
2009 (2) Oklahoma State

Velo	Pitch	Grade
90-96	FB	++++
82-84	SL	++
81-84	CU	+++

Year	Lev	Team	W	L	Sv	IP	K	ERA	WHIP	BF/G	OBA	H%	S%	xERA	Ctl	Dom	Cmd	hr/9	BPV
2010	AAA	Toledo	3	4	0	53	49	3.23	1.28	24.2	223	27	79	3.49	4.2	8.3	2.0	1.0	53
2010	MLB	Detroit	0	4	0	22	18	7.36	1.77	20.2	295	34	58	5.92	5.3	7.4	1.4	1.2	7
2011	AAA	Toledo	8	12	0	147	143	4.71	1.56	24.8	264	33	71	4.62	4.9	8.8	1.8	0.9	43
2011	MLB	Detroit	0	1	0	10	5	6.51	1.96	23.1	287	26	75	7.78	7.4	4.7	0.6	2.8	-99
2012	AAA	Toledo	5	9	0	118	112	4.88	1.62	18.7	236	30	69	4.04	6.7	8.5	1.3	0.5	-9

Aggressive, durable LHP who was moved to bullpen in Aug. Tough to make hard contact against (.235 oppBA), but below avg command and control haunt. Has excellent velocity and CU can be solid-avg pitch with consistent arm speed and slot. Scrapped CB in favor of SL and had mixed results.

Oliveros, Lester — RP — Minnesota

EXP MLB DEBUT: 2011 | POTENTIAL: Setup reliever | 7E

Thrws R Age 25
2005 FA (Venezuela)

Velo	Pitch	Grade
90-96	FB	+++
80-84	SL	+++
77-80	CU	+++

Year	Lev	Team	W	L	Sv	IP	K	ERA	WHIP	BF/G	OBA	H%	S%	xERA	Ctl	Dom	Cmd	hr/9	BPV
2011	MLB	Detroit Tigers	0	0	0	8	4	5.63	1.50	3.8	262	30	58	3.62	4.5	4.5	1.0	0.0	-23
2011	MLB	Minnesota	0	0	0	13	9	4.05	1.50	5.8	257	31	70	3.54	4.7	6.1	1.3	0.0	0
2012	AA	New Britain	1	1	2	19	16	1.42	0.89	5.4	157	21	82	0.81	3.3	7.6	2.3	0.0	65
2012	AAA	Rochester	1	2	6	29	35	3.07	1.09	6.0	225	32	73	2.62	2.5	10.7	4.4	0.6	145
2012	MLB	Minnesota	0	0	0	2	1	5.39	1.20	6.7	175	21	50	1.78	5.4	5.4	1.0	0.0	-31

Strong, strocky RP who underwent TJ surgery in August and likely out for entire '13. With improved break and consistency on SL, now has three avg pitches. Despite athleticism, has max effort delivery and will need to be tamed upon return. Pitches up too often and is extreme flyballer. Throws good strikes.

Olmsted, Michael — RP — Milwaukee

EXP MLB DEBUT: 2013 | POTENTIAL: Setup reliever | 7C

Thrws R Age 26
2007 (9) Cypress JC

Velo	Pitch	Grade
88-93	FB	+++
80-82	SL	++
72-74	CB	+++

Year	Lev	Team	W	L	Sv	IP	K	ERA	WHIP	BF/G	OBA	H%	S%	xERA	Ctl	Dom	Cmd	hr/9	BPV
2008	A	Savannah	1	0	0	9	11	3.86	1.61	20.7	313	42	79	5.50	2.9	10.6	3.7	1.0	131
2011	Rk	GCL Red Sox	1	0	2	4	4	0.00	0.50	4.4	81	12	100	0.00	2.3	9.0	4.0	0.0	119
2011	A	Greenville	1	0	4	28	44	1.59	0.92	5.9	175	32	81	1.00	2.9	14.0	4.9	0.0	192
2012	A+	Salem	0	2	16	39	61	2.29	0.84	4.4	184	32	72	1.11	1.8	14.0	7.6	0.2	220
2012	AA	Portland	1	2	3	20	31	0.00	0.90	5.3	163	30	100	0.82	3.2	14.0	4.4	0.0	184

Tall, large-framed RP who finished 3rd in CAR in saves. Signed to big league contract by MIL in offseason. Doesn't have velo usually seen in closer. However, has proven difficult to hit by using two varieties of breaking balls—hard SL and slow CB. Tends to keep hitters off balance and keeps BB to minimum.

Omogrosso, Brian — RP — Chicago (A)

EXP MLB DEBUT: 2012 | POTENTIAL: Setup reliever | 7D

Thrws R Age 29
2006 (6) Indiana State

Velo	Pitch	Grade
90-97	FB	++++
85-87	SL	++
	CU	+

Year	Lev	Team	W	L	Sv	IP	K	ERA	WHIP	BF/G	OBA	H%	S%	xERA	Ctl	Dom	Cmd	hr/9	BPV
2010	AA	Birmingham	0	1	0	3	3	3.00	1.00	3.8	191	27	67	1.43	3.0	9.0	3.0	0.0	99
2011	AA	Birmingham	0	2	2	43	53	2.51	1.21	5.6	229	33	80	2.78	3.3	11.1	3.3	0.4	127
2011	AAA	Charlotte	1	1	0	22	19	4.03	1.43	8.6	276	34	71	4.00	3.2	7.7	2.4	0.4	69
2012	AAA	Charlotte	0	2	9	47	59	4.56	1.16	5.7	244	35	60	2.99	2.3	11.2	4.9	0.6	158
2012	MLB	White Sox	0	0	0	21	18	2.57	1.38	5.2	252	29	88	4.37	3.9	7.7	2.0	1.3	53

Big, strong RP who enjoyed breakout season with improved control and increased K rate. Tweaked mechanics to provide more power and saw slight increase in velo. Throws from low ¾ slot which aids in pitch movement and can get hitters to swing and miss against FB and SL. No feel for changing speeds.

Oramas, Juan — SP — San Diego

EXP MLB DEBUT: 2013 | POTENTIAL: #4 starter | 7C

Thrws L Age 23
2006 NDFA, Mexico

Velo	Pitch	Grade
89-92	FB	+++
	CB	++
	CU	++

Year	Lev	Team	W	L	Sv	IP	K	ERA	WHIP	BF/G	OBA	H%	S%	xERA	Ctl	Dom	Cmd	hr/9	BPV
2010	A	Fort Wayne	0	1	0	15	25	1.20	0.80	10.9	175	34	83	0.69	1.8	15.0	8.3	0.0	239
2010	A+	Lake Elsinore	7	3	0	84	90	3.00	1.07	13.6	213	27	78	2.86	2.8	9.6	3.5	1.1	116
2011	AA	San Antonio	10	5	0	105	102	3.10	1.21	22.2	251	32	78	3.52	2.4	8.8	3.6	0.9	111
2011	AAA	Tucson	0	1	0	4	4	14.71	2.18	18.3	403	39	40	14.60	2.5	9.8	4.0	7.4	128
2012	AA	San Antonio	3	4	0	35	33	6.37	1.56	19.3	281	34	60	5.20	4.1	8.4	2.1	1.3	59

Short LH reliever hit a wall in repeat of AA. Calling card had been his plus command, but, that vanished and he walked 4.1 per nine. FB tops out in the low-90s, but can be hard to hit because of deception. Also throws a CB and an decent CU. Will need to regroup and prove that '12 was a fluke.

Ortega, Jose — RP — Detroit

EXP MLB DEBUT: 2012 | POTENTIAL: Setup reliever | 7D

Thrws R Age 24
2006 FA (Venezuela)

Velo	Pitch	Grade
92-97	FB	++++
82-86	SL	++
82-84	CU	++

Year	Lev	Team	W	L	Sv	IP	K	ERA	WHIP	BF/G	OBA	H%	S%	xERA	Ctl	Dom	Cmd	hr/9	BPV
2010	A+	Lakeland	2	1	0	19	20	0.95	1.11	7.5	207	29	90	1.88	3.3	9.5	2.9	0.0	99
2010	AA	Erie	1	0	0	24	19	3.04	1.23	6.4	248	30	78	3.43	2.7	7.2	2.7	0.8	76
2011	AAA	Toledo	1	3	0	50	44	6.30	1.76	6.9	302	36	65	6.01	4.9	7.9	1.6	1.3	29
2012	AAA	Toledo	5	8	1	63	68	5.74	2.03	6.7	301	40	71	6.00	7.3	9.8	1.3	0.6	-4
2012	MLB	Detroit	0	0	0	3	4	3.37	1.50	5.8	285	36	100	7.02	3.4	13.5	4.0	3.4	170

Short, strong RP who has plus-plus FB that he uses aggressively. Quick arm produces powerful late movement. Can rely on FB too much and will need to develop power SL and well below avg CU. Mature hitters can wait out FB and crush secondary pitches. Has upside in late inning role, but needs major polish.

Osich, Josh — RP — San Francisco

EXP MLB DEBUT: 2014 | POTENTIAL: reliever | 7C

Thrws L Age 24
2011 (6) Oregon State

Velo	Pitch	Grade
93-95	FB	++++
	SL	++
	CU	++

Year	Lev	Team	W	L	Sv	IP	K	ERA	WHIP	BF/G	OBA	H%	S%	xERA	Ctl	Dom	Cmd	hr/9	BPV
2008	NCAA	Oregon State	0	2	0	25	19	7.56	2.36	10.8	319	36	69	7.97	9.4	6.8	0.7	1.4	-112
2009	NCAA	Oregon State	0	0	1	26	34	2.05	1.22	6.3	168	24	87	2.33	5.8	11.6	2.0	0.7	70
2011	NCAA	Oregon State	6	4	0	77	79	3.64	1.25	19.5	223	30	71	2.88	4.0	9.3	2.3	0.5	77
2012	A+	San Jose	0	2	1	32	34	3.62	1.39	5.0	272	37	73	3.70	3.1	9.5	3.1	0.3	106

Strong lefty RP has a good 92-95 mph FB and a nice, if inconsistent, SL. CU never really progressed and is not needed in relief role. Can sometimes struggle with location and did walk 3.0 per nine, but also struck out 9.5 per nine.

Osuna, Roberto — SP — Toronto

EXP MLB DEBUT: 2017 | POTENTIAL: #2 starter | 9D

Thrws R Age 18
2011 FA (Mexico)

Velo	Pitch	Grade
88-95	FB	+++
80-82	SL	++
84-85	CU	++++

Year	Lev	Team	W	L	Sv	IP	K	ERA	WHIP	BF/G	OBA	H%	S%	xERA	Ctl	Dom	Cmd	hr/9	BPV
2012	Rk	Bluefield	1	0	0	24	24	1.50	1.00	13.1	210	28	87	2.00	2.3	9.0	4.0	0.4	119
2012	A-	Vancouver	1	0	0	20	25	3.20	1.17	15.7	202	30	73	2.38	4.1	11.4	2.8	0.5	113

Advanced SP who found success in first year in US despite youth. Possesses rare feel and pitchability for hurler his age and has mature frame. Thrives with solid FB and plus CU. Locates CU with good arm speed down in strike zone and is potent weapon against LHH. SL and conditioning need to get better.

Owens, Henry — SP — Boston

EXP MLB DEBUT: 2015 | POTENTIAL: #3 starter | 8C

Thrws L Age 20
2011 (1-S) HS (CA)

Velo	Pitch	Grade
88-94	FB	+++
68-76	CB	+++
80-82	CU	+++

Year	Lev	Team	W	L	Sv	IP	K	ERA	WHIP	BF/G	OBA	H%	S%	xERA	Ctl	Dom	Cmd	hr/9	BPV
2012	A	Greenville	12	5	0	102	130	4.87	1.45	18.9	259	36	67	4.20	4.2	11.5	2.8	0.9	113

Tall, lean SP who posted impressive numbers in first pro experience. Has advanced feel for pitching and is evidenced by solid-avg three pitch mix. Doesn't command or locate FB yet, but has deception in delivery which allows offerings to play up. Not a fireballer, but has good velo for lefty. Flyball tendencies.

Owens, Rudy — SP — Houston

EXP MLB DEBUT: 2013 | POTENTIAL: #5 starter | 6B

Thrws L Age 25
2006 (28) Chandler-Gilbert CC

Velo	Pitch	Grade
85-91	FB	+++
75-77	CB	++
78-80	CU	+++

Year	Lev	Team	W	L	Sv	IP	K	ERA	WHIP	BF/G	OBA	H%	S%	xERA	Ctl	Dom	Cmd	hr/9	BPV
2009	A+	Lynchburg	1	1	0	23	22	3.86	1.33	16.1	306	37	75	4.88	0.8	8.5	11.0	1.2	150
2010	AA	Altoona	12	6	0	150	132	2.46	0.98	21.9	227	28	78	2.44	1.4	7.9	5.7	0.7	123
2011	AAA	Indianapolis	9	7	0	112	71	5.05	1.43	22.8	289	33	65	4.59	2.6	5.7	2.2	0.8	51
2012	AAA	Indianapolis	8	5	0	117	85	3.14	1.17	24.6	253	29	77	3.51	1.9	6.5	3.4	0.9	84
2012	AAA	Oklahoma City	2	3	0	46	23	4.34	1.25	23.2	250	25	70	4.13	2.8	4.5	1.6	1.4	25

Tall, strong SP who spent second year AAA. Velo isn't as prevalent as in previous years and doesn't have strikeout pitch. Flyball tendencies also could cause HR problems. Regardless, exhibits pinpoint control of three pitches and works efficiently. Pitches to contact with FB while mixing in below avg CB and nice CU.

Paulino, Brenny — SP — Detroit

EXP MLB DEBUT: 2016 | POTENTIAL: #3 starter | 8D

Thrws R Age 20
2009 FA (DR)

Velo	Pitch	Grade
89-97	FB	++++
75-80	CB	++
	CU	++

Year	Lev	Team	W	L	Sv	IP	K	ERA	WHIP	BF/G	OBA	H%	S%	xERA	Ctl	Dom	Cmd	hr/9	BPV
2011	Rk	GCL Tigers	4	3	0	46	45	2.36	1.14	16.4	209	28	78	2.17	3.5	8.9	2.5	0.2	82
2011	A+	Lakeland	0	2	0	5	7	21.95	3.38	16.5	375	53	28	10.11	15.2	11.8	0.8	0.0	-180

Tall, projectable, and lean SP did not pitch due to minor shoulder surgery. When healthy, throws with loose, quick arm from high ¾ slot. Uses height to advantage and keeps ball low. Quick FB shows electric life, but needs to find consistent secondary offering. Elevates CB and crude CU needs upgrade to retire LHH.

Paxton, James — SP — Seattle

EXP MLB DEBUT: 2013 | POTENTIAL: #2 starter | 9C

Thrws L Age 24
2010 (4) Kentucky

Velo	Pitch	Grade
91-98	FB	++++
76-79	CB	++++
82-84	CU	+++

Year	Lev	Team	W	L	Sv	IP	K	ERA	WHIP	BF/G	OBA	H%	S%	xERA	Ctl	Dom	Cmd	hr/9	BPV
2008	NCAA	Kentucky	4	2	1	52	43	2.92	1.36	12.9	238	29	81	3.56	4.3	7.4	1.7	0.7	35
2009	NCAA	Kentucky	5	3	0	78	115	5.86	1.31	24.9	273	40	57	4.41	2.3	13.2	5.8	1.3	194
2011	A	Clinton	3	3	0	56	80	2.73	1.34	23.3	222	36	78	2.76	4.8	12.9	2.7	0.2	119
2011	AA	Jackson	3	0	0	39	51	1.85	1.05	21.6	203	31	85	2.10	3.0	11.8	3.9	0.5	149
2012	AA	Jackson	9	4	0	106	110	3.05	1.41	21.4	243	32	79	3.49	4.6	9.3	2.0	0.4	62

Tall LHP with potential for three plus pitches. Continues to post high K rate due to natural stuff and improving command. Establishes FB early in count to set up plus CB. Can register Ks with both FB and CB while CU can also get occasional swing and miss. Key to future success hinges on ability to locate pitches.

Payano, Victor — SP — Texas

EXP MLB DEBUT: 2017 | POTENTIAL: #2 starter | 9E

Thrws L Age 20
2010 FA (DR)

Velo	Pitch	Grade
86-92	FB	+++
76-78	CB	++
80-82	CU	++

Year	Lev	Team	W	L	Sv	IP	K	ERA	WHIP	BF/G	OBA	H%	S%	xERA	Ctl	Dom	Cmd	hr/9	BPV
2011	A-	Spokane	2	5	0	48	43	5.44	1.67	14.4	281	33	70	5.51	5.1	8.1	1.6	1.3	26
2012	A	Hickory	6	8	1	105	97	4.63	1.51	18.2	247	31	70	4.06	5.3	8.3	1.6	0.7	24

Very projectable, fluid SP who doesn't throw hard, but should add ticks as he refines delivery. Has long levers that make delivery difficult to repeat, but hides ball well. Locates FB fairly well, but seems to aim ball at times. Secondary pitches need upgrade. CB could use more bite and needs to use CU more.

Peacock, Brad — SP — Oakland

EXP MLB DEBUT: 2011 | POTENTIAL: #3 starter | 8D

Thrws R Age 25
2006 (41) Palm Beach CC

Velo	Pitch	Grade
91-95	FB	++++
77-80	CB	+++
81-84	CU	+++

Year	Lev	Team	W	L	Sv	IP	K	ERA	WHIP	BF/G	OBA	H%	S%	xERA	Ctl	Dom	Cmd	hr/9	BPV
2010	AA	Harrisburg	2	2	0	39	30	4.65	1.42	23.4	232	26	70	4.10	5.1	7.0	1.4	1.2	5
2011	AA	Harrisburg	10	2	0	99	129	2.01	0.86	22.7	182	28	78	1.29	2.1	11.8	5.6	0.4	173
2011	AAA	Syracuse	5	1	0	48	48	3.19	1.25	21.7	210	26	78	3.16	4.5	9.0	2.0	0.9	59
2011	MLB	Nationals	2	0	0	12	4	0.75	1.08	15.6	171	19	92	1.48	4.5	3.0	0.7	0.0	-50
2012	AAA	Sacramento	12	9	0	135	139	6.01	1.58	21.2	279	35	62	5.03	4.4	9.3	2.1	1.1	66

Very athletic SP who had horrendous season after breakout '11. Exhibits plus arm strength that pumps FB w/ movement. Had trouble controlling FB and increased BB rate. Solid CU features depth and fade while sharp CB can get Ks. Can rely on FB too much and will need to learn better pitch sequencing.

Peavey, Greg — SP — New York (N)

EXP MLB DEBUT: 2014 | POTENTIAL: #4 starter | 6D

Thrws R Age 24
2010 (6) Oregon State

Velo	Pitch	Grade
88-93	FB	++++
84-85	SL	+++
	CU	++

Year	Lev	Team	W	L	Sv	IP	K	ERA	WHIP	BF/G	OBA	H%	S%	xERA	Ctl	Dom	Cmd	hr/9	BPV
2009	NCAA	Oregon State	4	3	0	63	42	5.74	1.55	21.1	284	33	62	4.71	3.9	6.0	1.6	0.7	22
2010	NCAA	Oregon State	6	3	0	99	72	3.64	1.27	27.0	258	31	70	3.23	2.6	6.5	2.5	0.3	65
2011	A	Savannah	6	2	0	78	69	3.12	1.10	21.9	254	32	71	2.81	1.3	8.0	6.3	0.3	127
2011	A+	St. Lucie	5	4	0	59	39	3.97	1.37	19.0	284	34	69	3.74	2.3	5.9	2.6	0.2	63
2012	AA	Binghamton	8	8	0	144	84	5.06	1.43	24.5	294	32	66	4.96	2.3	5.3	2.3	1.1	50

Compact RH stalled at AA as lack of dominance caught up with him. Locates his upper-80 FB well and complements it with a sharp SL and decent CU. His SL while good, can flatten out when he overthrows it and he struck out just 5.3 per nine. He will likely repeat Double-A and could be moved to relief.

Pena, Ariel — SP — Milwaukee

EXP MLB DEBUT: 2014 | POTENTIAL: #4 starter/Power reliever | 8D

Thrws R Age 24
2007 NDFA, D.R.

Velo	Pitch	Grade
92-95	FB	++++
84-86	SL	+++
	CU	+

Year	Lev	Team	W	L	Sv	IP	K	ERA	WHIP	BF/G	OBA	H%	S%	xERA	Ctl	Dom	Cmd	hr/9	BPV
2010	A+	Rancho Cuc	0	1	0	10	8	8.71	2.23	17.4	256	32	57	5.34	11.3	7.0	0.6	0.0	-162
2011	A+	Inland Empire	10	6	0	152	180	4.45	1.55	24.5	265	37	71	4.28	4.8	10.7	2.2	0.6	80
2011	AAA	Salt Lake	0	0	0	4	3	2.25	2.75	22.3	383	46	91	8.74	9.0	6.8	0.8	0.0	-104
2012	AA	Arkansas	6	6	0	114	111	2.99	1.20	24.2	228	28	80	3.40	3.3	8.7	2.6	1.1	86
2012	AA	Huntsville	0	2	0	32	29	7.24	1.95	22.0	305	36	64	6.65	6.4	8.1	1.3	1.4	-10

Tall, durable SP struggled after coming over to the Brewers in the Grienke trade. Comes after hitters with a good 92-94 sinking FB. Also has a plus hard SL and a CU that lacks deception. Inconsistent mechanics and release point can lead to struggles with control, but raw stuff is good enough to start.

Peralta, Wily — SP — Milwaukee

EXP MLB DEBUT: 2012 | POTENTIAL: #3 starter | 8D

Thrws R Age 24
2005 NDFA, D.R.

Velo	Pitch	Grade
92-95	FB	++++
80-83	SL	+++
	CU	+++

Year	Lev	Team	W	L	Sv	IP	K	ERA	WHIP	BF/G	OBA	H%	S%	xERA	Ctl	Dom	Cmd	hr/9	BPV
2010	AA	Huntsville	2	3	0	42	29	3.61	1.58	23.3	265	30	81	4.85	5.1	6.2	1.2	1.1	-9
2011	AA	Huntsville	9	7	0	120	117	3.46	1.29	23.4	239	31	74	3.37	3.6	8.8	2.4	0.7	79
2011	AAA	Nashville	2	0	0	31	40	2.03	1.03	23.9	194	31	78	1.51	3.2	11.6	3.6	0.0	141
2012	AAA	Nashville	7	11	0	147	143	4.66	1.58	23.1	271	35	70	4.44	4.8	8.8	1.8	0.6	47
2012	MLB	Milwaukee	2	1	0	29	23	2.48	1.21	19.5	227	29	77	2.40	3.4	7.1	2.1	0.0	54

Struggled with control at AAA, but was effective when recalled and seems a lock to make the '13 rotation. When going well, he has a plus 92-95 mph that has nice, late sink and a quality SL. If he can refine his CU and SL he has the raw stuff to dominante in the majors, but there is a lot of work to be done.

Perez, Carlos — RP — Atlanta

EXP MLB DEBUT: 2013 | POTENTIAL: Reliever | 7D

Thrws L Age 21
2010 NDFA, D.R.

Velo	Pitch	Grade
86-90	FB	++
	CB	++
	CU	+++

Year	Lev	Team	W	L	Sv	IP	K	ERA	WHIP	BF/G	OBA	H%	S%	xERA	Ctl	Dom	Cmd	hr/9	BPV
2010	Rk	Danville	2	0	0	32	27	1.13	1.06	20.7	181	24	88	1.49	3.9	7.6	1.9	0.0	48
2010	A	Rome	0	1	0	7	4	3.86	1.57	15.4	288	31	80	5.38	3.9	5.1	1.3	1.3	6
2011	A	Rome	4	10	1	125	109	4.82	1.63	19.9	281	35	70	4.67	4.8	7.8	1.7	0.5	31
2012	Rk	Danville	3	2	0	31	50	2.05	1.14	7.6	188	35	80	1.69	4.4	14.7	3.3	0.0	163
2012	A	Rome	0	3	0	19	12	12.79	2.74	15.1	381	42	51	10.02	9.0	5.7	0.6	1.4	-123

Perez has a FB that sits in the 88-92 mph with nice sinking action. He mixes in an average CB and flashed a plus CU. CB and CU don't need to be as good in relief, but at 21 Perez needs to figure things out soon. He will likely head back to Low-A Rome for his 4th stint, but he could move up quickly.

Perez, Martin — SP — Texas

EXP MLB DEBUT: 2012 | POTENTIAL: #2 starter | 9D

Thrws L Age 22
2007 FA (Venezuela)

Velo	Pitch	Grade
90-96	FB	+++
77-80	CB	+++
80-82	CU	++++

Year	Lev	Team	W	L	Sv	IP	K	ERA	WHIP	BF/G	OBA	H%	S%	xERA	Ctl	Dom	Cmd	hr/9	BPV
2010	AA	Frisco	5	8	0	100	101	5.96	1.68	18.7	294	37	65	5.50	4.5	9.1	2.0	1.1	60
2011	AA	Frisco	4	2	0	88	83	3.16	1.31	21.5	243	31	77	3.43	3.7	8.5	2.3	0.6	71
2011	AAA	Round Rock	4	4	0	49	37	6.43	1.88	23.0	343	40	65	6.49	3.7	6.8	1.9	0.7	41
2012	AAA	Round Rock	7	6	0	127	69	4.25	1.40	24.4	254	28	70	3.93	4.0	4.9	1.2	0.7	-1
2012	MLB	Texas	1	4	0	38	25	5.45	1.63	14.1	305	35	66	5.23	3.6	5.9	1.7	0.7	29

Durable, strong LHP who is till very young and reached majors at age 21. Has clean, quick delivery that produces excellent velo and pitch movement. Has experienced problems with command of secondary pitches and K rate has suffered. Lively FB is excellent offering while plus CU is best secondary pitch in org.

Peterson, Dave — RP — Atlanta

EXP MLB DEBUT: 2015 | POTENTIAL: Reliever | 6D

Thrws R Age 23
2012 (8) College of Charleston

Velo	Pitch	Grade
92-95	FB	+++
76-78	CB	++

Year	Lev	Team	W	L	Sv	IP	K	ERA	WHIP	BF/G	OBA	H%	S%	xERA	Ctl	Dom	Cmd	hr/9	BPV
2009	NCAA	Col/Charleston	7	3	0	77	47	5.73	1.52	25.7	320	36	62	5.40	1.8	5.5	3.1	0.9	70
2010	NCAA	Col/Charleston	8	3	0	87	68	5.30	1.40	24.4	290	36	58	3.84	2.2	7.1	3.2	0.1	86
2011	NCAA	Col/Charleston	5	6	0	88	56	4.52	1.51	25.3	294	34	69	4.47	3.0	5.7	1.9	0.4	41
2012	NCAA	Col/Charleston	1	3	10	40	40	3.40	1.18	5.0	222	30	70	2.48	3.4	9.1	2.7	0.2	89
2012	A	Rome	4	1	8	28	23	1.93	1.14	5.5	210	27	81	2.03	3.5	7.4	2.1	0.0	56

8th round pick has a nice 92-95 mph FB. He works mostly off his FB and commands it well to both sides of the plate. CB and CU are below-average and will need to improve for him to transition back into a starting role. The Braves used him in relief in his pro debut, where he was very effective.

Petricka, Jacob — SP — Chicago (A)

EXP MLB DEBUT: 2014 | POTENTIAL: #3 starter | 8D

Thrws R Age 25
2010 (2) Indiana State
90-96 FB ++++
80-83 CB +++
82-84 CU ++

Year	Lev	Team	W	L	Sv	IP	K	ERA	WHIP	BF/G	OBA	H%	S%	xERA	Ctl	Dom	Cmd	hr/9	BPV
2011	Rk	Bristol	0	0	0	4	5	0.00	1.00	7.6	262	39	100	2.29	0.0	11.3		0.0	221
2011	A	Kannapolis	3	1	0	42	48	2.81	1.25	21.2	249	36	75	2.76	2.8	10.4	3.7	0.0	129
2011	A+	Winston-Salem	4	7	0	68	46	4.39	1.43	22.1	271	32	68	3.94	3.5	6.1	1.8	0.4	35
2012	A+	Winston-Salem	5	5	0	83	84	5.33	1.68	19.6	285	38	66	4.57	5.0	9.1	1.8	0.2	47
2012	AA	Birmingham	3	3	0	58	27	5.46	1.70	26.1	279	29	69	5.40	5.5	4.2	0.8	1.1	-54

Tall, lean SP who has better pitch mix than numbers indicate. Uses height to throw downhill and induce GB. Can be overpowering with FB and occasional plus CB. K rate is erratic and consistent CB could solve that. Lacks confidence in CU, but can be average pitch with good arm speed.

Pettibone, Jon — SP — Philadelphia

EXP MLB DEBUT: 2015 | POTENTIAL: #3 starter | 7C

Thrws R Age 22
2008 (3) HS, CA
89-93 FB +++
80-83 SL +
CU ++

Year	Lev	Team	W	L	Sv	IP	K	ERA	WHIP	BF/G	OBA	H%	S%	xERA	Ctl	Dom	Cmd	hr/9	BPV
2009	A-	Williamsport	2	4	0	35	36	5.35	1.50	17.0	271	37	60	3.70	4.1	9.2	2.3	0.0	73
2010	A	Lakewood	8	6	0	131	84	3.50	1.18	21.9	235	27	72	3.10	2.8	5.8	2.0	0.7	46
2011	A+	Clearwater	10	11	0	161	115	2.96	1.14	23.6	247	30	73	2.75	1.9	6.4	3.4	0.3	82
2012	AA	Reading	9	7	0	117	81	3.30	1.21	24.9	258	30	74	3.47	2.1	6.2	3.0	0.7	74
2012	AAA	Lehigh Valley	4	1	0	42	32	2.55	1.25	24.6	206	26	77	2.26	4.7	6.8	1.5	0.0	14

Lanky RH continues to impress despite the lack of an overpowering FB or high K rate. FB sits at 88-92, but he locates well. Mixes in a SL, CT, and a decent CU. Has good pitchability and keeps hitters off balance, but the lack of a swing-and-miss offering gives him a small margin for error.

Pike, Tyler — SP — Seattle

EXP MLB DEBUT: 2017 | POTENTIAL: #4 starter | 7C

Thrws L Age 19
2012 (3) HS (FL)
88-93 FB +++
73-76 CB +++
CU ++

Year	Lev	Team	W	L	Sv	IP	K	ERA	WHIP	BF/G	OBA	H%	S%	xERA	Ctl	Dom	Cmd	hr/9	BPV
2012	Rk	Mariners	2	1	0	51	57	1.78	1.09	18.0	192	28	83	1.81	3.7	10.1	2.7	0.2	100

Athletic, advanced LHP who led AZL in ERA. Repeats arm speed and mechanics effectively and relies more on pitchability than natural stuff. Has confidence in all pitches, including CU, but best pitch may be slow CB. Posted high K rate and low oppBA due to advanced pitch mixing and ability to locate FB.

Pill, Tyler — SP — New York (N)

EXP MLB DEBUT: 2014 | POTENTIAL: #4 starter | 7D

Thrws R Age 23
2011 (4) Cal State Fullerton
88-92 FB +++
85-87 CT ++
CB ++
CU ++

Year	Lev	Team	W	L	Sv	IP	K	ERA	WHIP	BF/G	OBA	H%	S%	xERA	Ctl	Dom	Cmd	hr/9	BPV
2011	NCAA	Cal St/Fullerton	6	1	0	91	99	2.08	1.00	21.7	220	30	80	2.14	1.9	9.8	5.2	0.4	144
2011	Rk	GCL Mets	0	0	0	2	1	4.50	1.50	4.3	347	39	67	4.95	0.0	4.5		0.0	99
2011	A-	Brooklyn	1	0	0	7	9	3.86	1.00	3.8	168	27	57	1.15	3.9	11.6	3.0	0.0	122
2012	A	Savannah	3	4	0	52	54	2.61	1.24	23.3	278	37	80	3.63	1.4	9.4	6.8	0.5	150
2012	A+	St. Lucie	6	1	0	61	51	2.05	1.09	21.8	235	29	82	2.48	2.1	7.5	3.6	0.3	97

Short RHP continues to put up solid numbers. FB sits at 88-92, but has some nice deception and good command. Complements the FB with a CU, CB, and CT—none of which project to be plus. Does throw strikes and could end up as a solid back-end starter. AA will give him a good test in '13.

Pimentel, Carlos — RP — Texas

EXP MLB DEBUT: 2013 | POTENTIAL: Setup reliever | 7D

Thrws R Age 23
2006 FA (DR)
89-95 FB +++
81-84 SL ++
82-83 CU +++

Year	Lev	Team	W	L	Sv	IP	K	ERA	WHIP	BF/G	OBA	H%	S%	xERA	Ctl	Dom	Cmd	hr/9	BPV
2009	A	Hickory	5	4	1	123	101	2.93	1.26	17.9	257	30	82	3.95	2.6	7.4	2.9	1.1	82
2010	A+	Bakersfield	7	7	0	123	97	4.96	1.59	23.6	287	33	71	5.21	4.1	7.1	1.7	1.1	35
2010	AA	Frisco	0	1	0	4	2	11.25	1.50	17.3	307	18	33	10.63	2.3	4.5	2.0	6.8	38
2011	AA	Frisco	7	9	0	142	110	4.74	1.46	21.8	242	28	69	4.12	5.1	7.0	1.4	0.9	7
2012	AA	Frisco	8	3	1	88	92	2.55	1.25	10.3	189	26	80	2.40	5.3	9.4	1.8	0.4	44

Effectively wild pitcher who seems to have found niche in bullpen. K rate increased in new role. Held hitters to .188 oppBA due to sneaky quick FB and decent SL with late break. Also has hint of deception that allows offerings to play up. Needs to hone command and throw SL for strikes.

Pimentel, Stolmy — SP — Pittsburgh

EXP MLB DEBUT: 2014 | POTENTIAL: #3 starter | 8D

Thrws R Age 23
2006 FA (DR)
88-96 FB +++
81-84 SL +++
78-82 CU +++

Year	Lev	Team	W	L	Sv	IP	K	ERA	WHIP	BF/G	OBA	H%	S%	xERA	Ctl	Dom	Cmd	hr/9	BPV
2009	A	Greenville	10	7	0	118	103	3.82	1.39	20.7	289	35	75	4.57	2.2	7.9	3.6	0.9	100
2010	A+	Salem	9	11	0	129	102	4.06	1.26	20.2	249	29	69	3.53	2.9	7.1	2.4	0.8	67
2011	A+	Salem	6	4	0	52	35	4.53	1.28	19.2	255	28	69	4.27	2.8	6.1	2.2	1.4	52
2011	AA	Portland	0	9	0	50	30	9.12	1.95	16.0	346	37	52	7.38	4.1	5.4	1.3	1.4	4
2012	AA	Portland	6	7	0	116	86	4.59	1.36	22.0	261	31	66	3.88	3.3	6.7	2.0	0.7	50

Aggressive, slender SP who improved in return trip to AA. Rediscovered success with CU that shows outstanding depth. Repeats arm speed and adds hint of deception to keep hitters off guard. Has a tendency to rear back and overthrow FB and command can be issue. LHH have given him problems.

Portillo, Adys — SP — San Diego

EXP MLB DEBUT: 2013 | POTENTIAL: #3 starter | 7D

Thrws R Age 21
2008 NDFA, Venezuela
87-92 FB ++++
CB ++
CU ++

Year	Lev	Team	W	L	Sv	IP	K	ERA	WHIP	BF/G	OBA	H%	S%	xERA	Ctl	Dom	Cmd	hr/9	BPV
2010	A	Fort Wayne	0	0	0	2	1	4.50	1.50	8.6	262	18	100	7.85	4.5	4.5	1.0	4.5	-23
2010	A-	Eugene	2	6	0	62	62	4.79	1.53	19.3	239	32	67	3.63	5.8	9.0	1.6	0.3	23
2011	A	Fort Wayne	3	11	0	82	97	7.11	1.75	16.4	277	37	59	5.43	6.0	10.6	1.8	1.1	47
2012	A	Fort Wayne	6	6	0	92	81	1.87	1.08	19.9	173	22	83	1.71	4.4	8.0	1.8	0.3	42
2012	AA	San Antonio	2	5	0	35	26	7.20	1.69	19.7	256	29	56	4.96	6.4	6.7	1.0	1.0	-35

Projectable hurler had mixed results. Was impressive at Low-A, but crashed and burned at AA. FB velo jumped from 88-92 last year to 94-98 mph. Secondary offerings still very much in progress, though CU and CB have potential. Struggles with mechanics and control. Lots of upside, but work to be done.

Pryor, Stephen — RP — Seattle

EXP MLB DEBUT: 2012 | POTENTIAL: Setup reliever | 8D

Thrws R Age 23
2010 (5) Tennessee Tech
93-98 FB ++++
87-91 CT +++
80-82 CB +++
82-86 CU +

Year	Lev	Team	W	L	Sv	IP	K	ERA	WHIP	BF/G	OBA	H%	S%	xERA	Ctl	Dom	Cmd	hr/9	BPV
2011	AA	Jackson	2	1	6	23	27	1.19	0.71	4.7	123	20	81	0.00	2.8	10.7	3.9	0.0	136
2012	A+	High Desert	0	0	0	3	3	6.74	1.12	5.3	0	0	33	0.00	10.1	10.1	1.0	0.0	-73
2012	AA	Jackson	1	0	7	16	24	1.13	0.75	5.2	134	25	83	0.15	2.8	13.5	4.8	0.0	185
2012	AAA	Tacoma	0	0	3	20	20	0.00	1.10	4.9	163	23	100	1.37	5.0	9.0	1.8	0.0	46
2012	MLB	Seattle	3	1	0	23	27	3.91	1.52	3.8	253	31	83	5.34	5.1	10.6	2.1	2.0	71

Big, durable RP who reached SEA on basis of heavy FB. Only allowed two HR in minor league career, but allowed five with SEA. Despite low HR rate, is flyball pitcher, but has velo to pitch up. Aggressively locates FB and has nasty CT with electric action. Hard CB is go-to pitch late in count, but doesn't change speeds well.

Purke, Matt — SP — Washington

EXP MLB DEBUT: 2015 | POTENTIAL: #2 starter | 8D

Thrws L Age 22
2011 (3) TCU
91-94 FB ++++
78-81 SL ++
76-78 CU +++

Year	Lev	Team	W	L	Sv	IP	K	ERA	WHIP	BF/G	OBA	H%	S%	xERA	Ctl	Dom	Cmd	hr/9	BPV
2010	NCAA	TCU	16	0	0	116	142	3.02	1.07	22.7	217	31	72	2.34	2.6	11.0	4.2	0.5	145
2011	NCAA	TCU	5	1	0	53	61	1.71	1.06	18.6	195	28	85	1.94	3.4	10.4	3.1	0.3	113
2012	A	Hagerstown	0	2	0	15	14	5.87	1.76	23.4	258	32	65	4.74	7.0	8.2	1.2	0.6	-24

Struggled in his junior year at TCU and in his pro debut before being diagnosed with a shoulder injury that required surgery. Since being drafted, velocity has been in the low-90s and command abysmal. Surgery could correct the problem though we will have to wait and see if the velocity comes back.

Quackenbush, Kevin — RP — San Diego

EXP MLB DEBUT: 2014 | POTENTIAL: Reliever | 7B

Thrws R Age 24
2011 (8) South Florida
90-93 FB ++++
SL ++
CU ++

Year	Lev	Team	W	L	Sv	IP	K	ERA	WHIP	BF/G	OBA	H%	S%	xERA	Ctl	Dom	Cmd	hr/9	BPV
2010	NCAA	South Florida	2	5	4	34	49	4.54	1.46	5.8	240	37	70	3.89	5.1	13.1	2.6	0.8	117
2011	NCAA	South Florida	1	2	12	33	45	0.81	0.63	4.1	130	22	86	0.00	1.9	12.2	6.4	0.0	186
2011	A	Fort Wayne	1	1	9	21	38	0.84	0.84	4.3	166	35	89	0.69	2.5	16.0	6.3	0.0	238
2011	A-	Eugene	1	0	9	21	33	0.44	0.92	4.5	182	34	95	1.07	2.6	14.4	5.5	0.0	206
2012	A+	Lake Elsinore	3	2	27	58	70	0.94	1.11	4.4	205	31	92	2.00	3.4	10.9	3.2	0.2	122

Tall, strong-armed RP continued his dominance, striking out 10.9 per nine and limiting opposing hitters to a .205 oppBA. Uses 90-93 mph FB with great effect. Hides the ball well and has nice deception. Also throws a SL, and a CU. Has developed into one of the best relievers in the minors.

Quintana, Zachary — SP — Milwaukee

EXP MLB DEBUT: 2016 | POTENTIAL: #5 starter | 6C

Thrws R Age 19
2012 (3) HS, NV
90-94 FB +++
SL +
CU +

Year	Lev	Team	W	L	Sv	IP	K	ERA	WHIP	BF/G	OBA	H%	S%	xERA	Ctl	Dom	Cmd	hr/9	BPV
2012	Rk	Brewers	3	4	1	43	39	5.82	1.52	14.5	265	33	60	4.27	4.6	8.1	1.8	0.6	40

Short RH was a 3rd round pick in '12, but struggled with control in pro debut, walking 4.6 per nine. Does have a good, heavy FB that sits at 90-93 mph. Also mixes in sharp CB, and a decent CU. Has easy, repeatable mechanics, but needs to throw strikes and improve his CU.

Ramirez, J.C. — RP — Philadelphia

Thrws R Age 24 | 2005 NDFA, Venezuela | EXP MLB DEBUT: 2013 | POTENTIAL: reliever | 6C

- 92-94 FB +++
- 77-80 SL ++
- CU +

Year	Lev	Team	W	L	Sv	IP	K	ERA	WHIP	BF/G	OBA	H%	S%	xERA	Ctl	Dom	Cmd	hr/9	BPV
2010	A+	Clearwater	4	3	0	64	55	4.06	1.24	23.8	258	33	65	3.15	2.4	7.7	3.2	0.3	92
2010	AA	Reading	3	4	0	78	60	5.45	1.45	25.5	289	33	65	5.07	2.8	7.0	2.5	1.3	68
2011	AA	Reading	11	13	0	144	89	4.50	1.38	23.3	262	29	69	4.19	3.4	5.6	1.6	0.9	25
2012	AA	Reading	0	2	3	27	18	3.62	1.22	6.9	200				4.6	5.9	1.3	1.0	
2012	AAA	Lehigh Valley	3	2	1	40	34	4.28	1.33	5.7	250				3.8	7.6	2	0.7	

Tall, strong RH was part of the Cliff Lee trade and features a 92-94 mph sinking FB, a SL, and a CU. The SL and CU still need work and he struggled at times throwing strikes. Was moved to relief, but the results were pedestrian. Has power stuff, but needs to become more consistent and miss more bats.

Ramirez, Jose — SP — New York (A)

Thrws R Age 23 | 2007 FA (DR) | EXP MLB DEBUT: 2015 | POTENTIAL: #3 starter | 8D

- 90-95 FB +++
- 81-83 SL ++
- CU +++

Year	Lev	Team	W	L	Sv	IP	K	ERA	WHIP	BF/G	OBA	H%	S%	xERA	Ctl	Dom	Cmd	hr/9	BPV
2009	A+	Tampa	0	0	0	3	2	0.00	0.33	9.5	106	13	100	0.00	0.0	6.0		0.0	126
2010	A	Charleston (Sc)	6	5	0	115	105	3.60	1.29	21.5	246	32	70	3.06	3.3	8.2	2.5	0.2	77
2011	A	Charleston (Sc)	5	7	0	79	74	4.90	1.47	22.6	274	34	68	4.63	3.6	8.4	2.3	1.0	71
2011	A+	Tampa	0	5	0	24	25	8.14	1.89	19.1	338	42	56	6.76	4.1	9.2	2.3	1.1	75
2012	A+	Tampa	7	6	0	99	94	3.19	1.24	19.1	248	32	76	3.34	2.7	8.6	3.1	0.6	98

Slender, projectable SP who finished with 2.18 ERA after April. Can be lights out with solid avg FB thrown with loose arm. Improved FB location, though has tendency to aim. SL lacks depth and needs upgrading to get Ks in upper levels. Throws CU with good arm speed and features late movement.

Ramirez, Neil — SP — Texas

Thrws R Age 24 | 2007 (1-S) HS (VA) | EXP MLB DEBUT: 2013 | POTENTIAL: #4 starter | 7C

- 90-96 FB +++
- 74-78 CB +++
- 83-85 CU ++

Year	Lev	Team	W	L	Sv	IP	K	ERA	WHIP	BF/G	OBA	H%	S%	xERA	Ctl	Dom	Cmd	hr/9	BPV
2011	A+	Myrtle Beach	0	0	0	5	9	0.00	0.43	15.2	71	19	100	0.00	1.9	17.3	9.0	0.0	278
2011	AA	Frisco	1	0	0	19	24	1.89	1.11	12.4	195	29	85	2.16	3.8	11.4	3.0	0.5	120
2011	AAA	Round Rock	4	3	0	74	86	3.63	1.32	17.1	231	32	74	3.38	4.2	10.4	2.5	0.7	91
2012	AA	Frisco	2	5	0	49	45	4.20	1.28	15.5	253	30	70	3.92	2.9	8.2	2.8	1.1	87
2012	AAA	Round Rock	6	8	0	74	63	7.66	1.47	21.2	272	31	47	5.04	3.8	7.7	2.0	1.5	54

Tall, lean RHP who was hammered in AAA before demotion to AA where he righted ship. Extreme flyballer who saw K rate drop and needs to firm up release point to regain command. Throws with good angle to plate and has nice FB. CB is out pitch and CU shows incremental improvement.

Ramirez, Noe — SP — Boston

Thrws R Age 23 | 2011 (4) Cal St Fullerton | EXP MLB DEBUT: 2015 | POTENTIAL: #4 starter | 8E

- 86-93 FB +++
- 80-85 SL ++
- 81-84 CU ++++

Year	Lev	Team	W	L	Sv	IP	K	ERA	WHIP	BF/G	OBA	H%	S%	xERA	Ctl	Dom	Cmd	hr/9	BPV
2009	NCAA	Cal St/Fullerton	9	2	0	111	100	3.33	1.03	21.3	224	27	71	2.74	2.0	8.1	4.2	0.9	112
2010	NCAA	Cal St/Fullerton	12	1	0	106	119	2.54	1.04	25.7	235	31	79	2.77	1.6	10.1	6.3	0.8	156
2011	NCAA	Cal St/Fullerton	8	3	0	83	91	1.74	0.85	23.3	182	27	77	0.93	2.0	9.9	5.1	0.0	143
2012	A	Greenville	2	7	0	85	82	4.15	1.28	21.7	272	33	72	4.35	2.0	8.7	4.3	1.3	120

Extreme flyball pitcher possesses long and lean frame that could add more oomph to FB. Plus, deceptive CU is go-to pitch with arm speed and can throw for strikes. Keeps LHH at bay, but RHH hit him hard, particularly with HR. Prospect outlook could improve with better breaking ball and stamina.

Ranaudo, Anthony — SP — Boston

Thrws R Age 23 | 2010 (1-S) LSU | EXP MLB DEBUT: 2014 | POTENTIAL: #3 starter | 8C

- 88-96 FB +++
- 78-82 CB ++++
- 81-83 CU ++

Year	Lev	Team	W	L	Sv	IP	K	ERA	WHIP	BF/G	OBA	H%	S%	xERA	Ctl	Dom	Cmd	hr/9	BPV
2009	NCAA	Louisiana State	12	3	0	124	159	3.04	1.15	26.0	210	29	79	3.02	3.6	11.5	3.2	1.1	127
2010	NCAA	Louisiana State	5	3	0	52	54	7.32	1.68	15.5	292	36	58	5.94	4.7	9.4	2.0	1.6	60
2011	A	Greenville	4	1	0	46	50	3.33	1.11	18.1	212	28	72	2.68	3.1	9.8	3.1	0.8	110
2011	A+	Salem	5	5	0	81	67	4.33	1.36	21.2	259	31	68	3.83	3.3	7.4	2.2	0.7	62
2012	AA	Portland	1	3	0	38	27	6.69	1.81	19.4	278	32	63	5.50	6.5	6.5	1.0	1.0	-40

Very tall SP whose season ended in July due to tired arm. Suffers from inconsistent secondary pitches and erratic release point. Natural stuff is quite good. When on, he uses height to pitch downhill and keeps FB low. Has ability to dominate with FB and CB while CU could develop into third legitimate offering.

Rasmussen, Rob — SP — Los Angeles (N)

Thrws L Age 24 | 2010 (2) UCLA | EXP MLB DEBUT: 2013 | POTENTIAL: #4 starter / Setup reliever | 7D

- 90-93 FB +++
- 77-79 CB ++
- 84-87 SL +++
- CU +++

Year	Lev	Team	W	L	Sv	IP	K	ERA	WHIP	BF/G	OBA	H%	S%	xERA	Ctl	Dom	Cmd	hr/9	BPV
2010	NCAA	UCLA	11	3	0	109	128	2.72	1.13	22.7	222	30	80	2.87	2.9	10.5	3.7	0.8	130
2010	A	Greensboro	0	0	0	7	4	1.35	1.20	5.4	242	29	88	2.59	2.7	5.4	2.0	0.0	42
2011	A+	Jupiter	12	10	0	148	118	3.64	1.42	22.5	251	30	75	3.82	4.3	7.2	1.7	0.6	31
2012	A+	Jupiter	4	7	0	88	75	3.90	1.36	22.9	251	31	72	3.67	3.7	7.7	2.1	0.6	57
2012	AA	Corpus Christi	4	4	0	54	44	4.80	1.40	20.8	275	32	67	4.45	3.0	7.3	2.4	1.0	69

Diminutive, consistent LHP who makes up for lack of size with solid repertoire and ability to work in lower half of K zone. Sets up hitters by pitching off FB and complementing with hard SL and fringy CB. Pitches inside and has enough arm to hold velocity late. Could be interesting situational reliever.

Ray, Robbie — SP — Washington

Thrws L Age 21 | 2010 (12) HS, TN | EXP MLB DEBUT: 2014 | POTENTIAL: #5 starter | 7D

- 91-94 FB +++
- 72-74 CB +++
- CU +++

Year	Lev	Team	W	L	Sv	IP	K	ERA	WHIP	BF/G	OBA	H%	S%	xERA	Ctl	Dom	Cmd	hr/9	BPV
2011	A	Hagerstown	2	3	0	89	95	3.13	1.22	18.0	221	30	74	2.62	3.8	9.6	2.5	0.3	87
2012	A+	Potomac	4	12	0	106	86	6.56	1.62	21.3	290	34	60	5.42	4.2	7.3	1.8	1.2	37

Thin, athletic lefty hit a wall in '12 and almost nothing went well. Fringy control in the past turned into a problem. FB lacks plus velocity and his CB is inconsistent and slurvy. CU has potential, but was not effective because he was behind too often. Does get some nice deception from his whip-like arm action.

Reed, Chris — SP — Los Angeles (N)

Thrws L Age 23 | 2011 (1) Stanford | EXP MLB DEBUT: 2014 | POTENTIAL: #3 starter/power reliever | 8C

- 90-94 FB ++++
- 85-86 SL +++
- 75-78 CU ++

Year	Lev	Team	W	L	Sv	IP	K	ERA	WHIP	BF/G	OBA	H%	S%	xERA	Ctl	Dom	Cmd	hr/9	BPV
2010	NCAA	Stanford	2	0	0	21	14	6.10	1.84	5.1	283	33	65	5.17	6.5	6.1	0.9	0.4	-49
2011	NCAA	Stanford	6	2	9	50	48	2.54	1.01	6.8	200	27	73	1.72	2.7	8.7	3.2	0.2	101
2011	A+	Rancho Cuc	0	1	0	7	9	7.71	1.86	10.9	313	43	58	6.42	5.1	11.6	2.3	1.3	87
2012	A+	Rancho Cuc	1	4	0	35	38	3.09	1.11	19.7	202	28	71	2.08	3.6	9.8	2.7	0.3	97
2012	AA	Chattanooga	0	4	0	35	29	4.84	1.44	12.6	237	29	65	3.60	5.1	7.4	1.5	0.5	13

Competitive lefty continues to transition from college closer to SP. Started well in the CAL and made the Futures Games before struggling with control at AA. Has a good FB, a plus SL, and decent CU. Funky delivery with poor front-side mechanics add some deception, but also explain the control issues.

Rhee, Dae-Eun — SP — Chicago (N)

Thrws R Age 24 | 2007 NDFA, Korea | EXP MLB DEBUT: 2014 | POTENTIAL: #5 starter/reliever | 7D

- 88-92 FB ++
- CB +++
- CU +++

Year	Lev	Team	W	L	Sv	IP	K	ERA	WHIP	BF/G	OBA	H%	S%	xERA	Ctl	Dom	Cmd	hr/9	BPV
2009	Rk	Cubs	0	0	0	5	3	7.71	1.93	7.4	233	28	56	4.30	9.6	5.8	0.6	0.0	-138
2009	A-	Boise	0	1	0	4	4	11.25	2.25	10.1	415	45	57	12.35	2.3	9.0	4.0	4.5	119
2010	A+	Daytona	5	13	0	114	70	5.27	1.44	18.7	279	31	64	4.53	3.1	5.5	1.8	0.9	32
2011	A+	Daytona	8	7	0	128	117	4.02	1.36	21.4	267	33	71	3.97	3.0	8.2	2.7	0.7	85
2012	AA	Tennessee	9	8	0	142	78	4.81	1.54	23.0	295	32	71	5.26	3.2	4.9	1.5	1.1	20

Rhee had Tommy John surgery in '09 and was slow to recover. He is back to 100% now, but no longer has the same velocity on his FB. Heater is now in the 88-92 range though he does have a good breaking ball and a decent CU. Dom rate slipped to 4.9 in '12 and his time as a starter could be limited.

Rienzo, Andre — SP — Chicago (A)

Thrws R Age 25 | 2006 FA (Brazil) | EXP MLB DEBUT: 2013 | POTENTIAL: #4 starter | 7C

- 90-94 FB +++
- 80-82 CT +++
- 77-79 CB +++
- 78-82 CU ++

Year	Lev	Team	W	L	Sv	IP	K	ERA	WHIP	BF/G	OBA	H%	S%	xERA	Ctl	Dom	Cmd	hr/9	BPV
2010	A	Kannapolis	8	4	0	101	125	3.65	1.26	20.6	250	36	70	3.20	2.9	11.1	3.9	0.4	142
2011	A+	Winston-Salem	6	5	0	116	118	3.41	1.50	20.0	248	33	76	3.68	5.1	9.2	1.8	0.3	45
2012	A+	Winston-Salem	3	0	0	25	31	1.08	0.96	23.6	194	30	88	1.34	2.5	11.2	4.4	0.0	151
2012	AA	Birmingham	4	3	0	72	72	3.26	1.24	22.4	217	29	72	2.58	4.1	9.0	2.2	0.3	69
2012	AAA	Charlotte	0	0	0	7	10	0.00	1.05	25.8	210	36	100	1.73	2.7	13.5	5.0	0.0	188

Tall, very thin SP who served 50 game suspension due to PED. Possesses lively FB and complements with average CT and CB. CU has flashes of being OK, but often slows arm. Best pitch is CB that he uses to get Ks. Lean frame brings questions of durability and move to bullpen could be in offing.

Rivero, Felipe — SP — Tampa Bay

Thrws L Age 22 | 2008 FA (Venezuela) | EXP MLB DEBUT: 2015 | POTENTIAL: #3 starter | 8D

- 87-94 FB +++
- 75-78 CB ++++
- 81-83 CU ++

Year	Lev	Team	W	L	Sv	IP	K	ERA	WHIP	BF/G	OBA	H%	S%	xERA	Ctl	Dom	Cmd	hr/9	BPV
2011	Rk	Princeton	3	3	0	60	57	4.62	1.28	17.7	273	34	66	4.16	1.9	8.5	4.4	1.0	119
2012	A	Bowling Green	8	8	0	113	98	3.41	1.27	17.2	265	33	73	3.42	2.3	7.8	3.4	0.4	96

Short, thin LHP who lives in lower half of K zone and induces GB while limiting the long ball. Quick arm produces sufficient velo and movement while plus CB ranks among best in org. Throws all pitches for strikes and has mature feel for pitch sequencing. CU is still in development phase.

Roach, Donn — SP — San Diego

EXP MLB DEBUT: 2014 | POTENTIAL: #4 starter | 7B

Thrws R Age 23
2010 (3) Arizona

Velo	Pitch	Grade
90-92	FB	+++
	SP	++
73-75	CB	+

Year	Lev	Team	W	L	Sv	IP	K	ERA	WHIP	BF/G	OBA	H%	S%	xERA	Ctl	Dom	Cmd	hr/9	BPV
2010	Rk	Orem	4	1	0	54	59	6.04	1.49	14.5	297	39	59	5.00	2.7	9.9	3.7	1.0	124
2011	A	Cedar Rapids	5	5	2	70	68	3.46	1.32	6.5	269	36	72	3.35	2.6	8.7	3.4	0.1	106
2012	A+	Inland Empire	5	0	0	42	29	2.16	0.94	26.1	235	28	76	2.02	0.6	6.3	9.7	0.2	113
2012	A+	Lake Elsinore	5	1	0	47	44	1.74	1.11	23.0	238	31	84	2.47	2.1	8.5	4.0	0.2	113
2012	AA	San Antonio	1	1	0	17	5	1.59	1.00	16.2	158	17	82	1.13	4.2	2.6	0.6	0.0	-49

Former 3rd round pick continues to be surprisingly effective. Uses a heavy 90-93 mph sinking FB and a splitter. Secondary offerings are not advanced and both CB and CU need work. Has a good approach with clean, repeatable mechanics and nice long-term potential.

Robles, Hansel — SP — New York (N)

EXP MLB DEBUT: 2015 | POTENTIAL: #3 starter | 8D

Thrws R Age 22
2008 NDFA, D.R.

Velo	Pitch	Grade
92-95	FB	+++
83-86	SL	++
84-86	CU	+++

Year	Lev	Team	W	L	Sv	IP	K	ERA	WHIP	BF/G	OBA	H%	S%	xERA	Ctl	Dom	Cmd	hr/9	BPV
2011	Rk	Kingsport	3	1	1	37	42	2.68	1.19	9.9	212	29	79	2.59	3.9	10.2	2.6	0.5	97
2012	A-	Brooklyn	6	1	0	73	66	1.11	0.78	21.8	187	25	84	0.84	1.2	8.2	6.6	0.0	132

Short, stocky Dominican righty was one of the more impressive hulers in the NYPL, posting a 1.11 ERA in 12 starts. Has a plus 92-95 mph sinking FB that he locates very effectively. Also has a good hard SL with good late break and is showing feel for a CU. Posted a 6.6 Cmd and is gaining attention.

Rodgers, Brady — SP — Houston

EXP MLB DEBUT: 2015 | POTENTIAL: #4 starter | 7E

Thrws R Age 22
2012 (3) Arizona State

Velo	Pitch	Grade
88-92	FB	+++
75-78	CB	++
82-84	SL	+++
	CU	++

Year	Lev	Team	W	L	Sv	IP	K	ERA	WHIP	BF/G	OBA	H%	S%	xERA	Ctl	Dom	Cmd	hr/9	BPV
2010	NCAA	Arizona State	4	3	3	73	67	2.11	0.88	12.2	205	27	77	1.65	1.4	8.3	6.1	0.4	131
2011	NCAA	Arizona State	8	4	0	92	83	2.85	0.97	24.8	236	31	68	2.00	0.9	8.1	9.2	0.1	141
2012	NCAA	Arizona State	0	1	0	8	4	1.08	0.72	29.5	175	20	83	0.60	1.1	4.3	4.0	0.0	67
2012	NCAA	Arizona State	10	2	0	107	75	2.36	0.97	28.9	228	28	75	2.08	1.3	6.3	5.0	0.3	98
2012	A-	Tri City	7	2	0	62	49	2.89	1.14	20.6	254	30	77	3.26	1.6	7.1	4.5	0.7	102

Tall, slender RHP who has polish and advanced command. Effectively spots FB for strikes in lower half of strike zone and induces large amount of GB. Won't blow ball by hitters, but won't beat himself with BB. Secondary pitches show promise, though none are dominant, swing-and-miss offerings.

Rodgers, Colin — SP — Kansas City

EXP MLB DEBUT: 2016 | POTENTIAL: #4 starter | 7C

Thrws L Age 19
2012 (3) HS (LA)

Velo	Pitch	Grade
88-93	FB	+++
75-77	CB	+++
79-83	CU	++

Year	Lev	Team	W	L	Sv	IP	K	ERA	WHIP	BF/G	OBA	H%	S%	xERA	Ctl	Dom	Cmd	hr/9	BPV
2012	Rk	Burlington	3	1	0	48	25	2.05	1.16	17.5	227	25	83	2.65	3.0	4.7	1.6	0.4	21

Short, advanced LHP who throws with quick, loose arm and peppers strike zone with quality pitches. Not much hope for additional velo, but FB works well with late sink. Limits flyballs by keeping ball down and sharp, power CB can get Ks. Though CU is below average at present, shows feel for pitch.

Rodriguez, Armando — RP — New York (N)

EXP MLB DEBUT: 2013 | POTENTIAL: reliever | 7C

Thrws R Age 25
2007 NDFA, D.R.

Velo	Pitch	Grade
88-92	FB	+++
85-87	CT	++
78-81	SL	+
75-77	CU	++

Year	Lev	Team	W	L	Sv	IP	K	ERA	WHIP	BF/G	OBA	H%	S%	xERA	Ctl	Dom	Cmd	hr/9	BPV
2009	A	Savannah	2	1	0	17	24	2.16	0.84	20.3	96	18	71	0.01	4.9	13.0	2.7	0.0	120
2010	A	Savannah	8	9	0	146	152	3.08	1.11	21.2	220	30	71	2.33	2.8	9.4	3.3	0.3	110
2011	A+	St. Lucie	4	4	0	75	74	3.96	1.19	18.8	221	26	72	3.50	3.5	8.9	2.6	1.3	84
2012	AA	Binghamton	2	3	1	73	77	3.22	1.09	8.4	221	26	80	3.51	2.6	9.5	3.7	1.6	119
2012	AAA	Buffalo	0	0	0	4	2	2.08	1.15	17.2	197	23	80	1.94	4.2	4.2	1.0	0.0	-19

Tall, strong, RH was moved into a relief with good results. Came into camp in better shape and added some zip to his low-90s FB. Locates the FB well and complements it with a CT, a SL, and a CU. Attacks hitters to both sides of the plate and is tough to hit. He has strong frame and competes well.

Rodriguez, Eduardo — SP — Baltimore

EXP MLB DEBUT: 2014 | POTENTIAL: #4 starter | 7B

Thrws L Age 20
2010 FA (Venezuela)

Velo	Pitch	Grade
88-94	FB	+++
79-83	SL	+++
80-84	CU	+++

Year	Lev	Team	W	L	Sv	IP	K	ERA	WHIP	BF/G	OBA	H%	S%	xERA	Ctl	Dom	Cmd	hr/9	BPV
2011	Rk	GCL Orioles	1	1	1	45	46	1.81	1.01	15.5	182	26	80	1.34	3.4	9.3	2.7	0.0	92
2011	A-	Aberdeen	0	0	0	4	4	6.75	1.75	18.3	347	41	67	7.65	2.3	9.0	4.0	2.3	119
2012	A	Delmarva	5	7	0	107	73	3.70	1.24	19.8	254	30	69	3.17	2.5	6.1	2.4	0.3	60

Durable, strong LHP who was one of youngest players in SAL, yet stood out for improved velo and control. Possesses mature arsenal for age and hint of deception allows pitches to play up. Moves ball around K zone with lively FB. K rate muted due to erratic SL, though CU could evolve into above avg pitch.

Rodriguez, Julio — SP — Philadelphia

EXP MLB DEBUT: 2014 | POTENTIAL: #4 starter | 7D

Thrws R Age 22
2008 (8) HS, P.R.

Velo	Pitch	Grade
87-90	FB	++
70-72	CB	++++
73-75	SL	++
77-79	CU	++

Year	Lev	Team	W	L	Sv	IP	K	ERA	WHIP	BF/G	OBA	H%	S%	xERA	Ctl	Dom	Cmd	hr/9	BPV
2009	Rk	GCL Phillies	1	2	0	50	56	3.08	1.01	17.3	204	26	75	2.61	2.5	10.1	4.0	1.1	132
2010	A	Lakewood	5	1	0	56	90	1.44	0.96	16.4	168	30	87	1.31	3.5	14.4	4.1	0.3	182
2010	A-	Williamsport	2	2	0	34	36	2.65	1.18	19.4	207	28	79	2.55	4.0	9.5	2.4	0.5	82
2011	A+	Clearwater	16	7	0	157	168	2.76	1.01	22.2	188	25	76	2.11	3.2	9.7	3.0	0.7	105
2012	AA	Reading	7	7	0	134	136	4.23	1.47	19.8	243	31	73	4.12	5.1	9.1	1.8	0.9	45

Tall RH took a step back in '12. Does not blow people away, but does have a plus CB and locates a low-90s FB. Doesn't use lower half effectively and the lack of control cost him. Gets plenty of swings-and-misses on his CB, but often it dives out of the zone and hitters laid-off as the season progressed.

Rodriguez, Paco — RP — Los Angeles (N)

EXP MLB DEBUT: 2012 | POTENTIAL: reliever | 7B

Thrws L Age 22
2012 (2) Florida

Velo	Pitch	Grade
90-92	FB	+++
85-88	CT	++
	SL	++

Year	Lev	Team	W	L	Sv	IP	K	ERA	WHIP	BF/G	OBA	H%	S%	xERA	Ctl	Dom	Cmd	hr/9	BPV
2011	NCAA	Florida	4	2	2	38	44	1.91	1.14	4.7	226	32	85	2.64	2.9	10.5	3.7	0.5	130
2012	NCAA	Florida	3	2	4	62	81	2.18	1.00	7.0	219	34	77	1.87	1.9	11.8	6.2	0.1	179
2012	A	Great Lakes	0	0	2	6	10	0.00	0.67	3.5	191	37	100	0.53	0.0	15.0		0.0	288
2012	AA	Chattanooga	1	0	3	14	22	1.32	0.95	3.4	154	30	85	0.84	4.0	14.5	3.7	0.0	172
2012	MLB	Los Angeles (N)	0	1	0	7	6	1.35	1.05	2.4	136	19	86	3.78	5.4	8.1	1.5	0	25

Lefty RP has a good 90-92 mph FB, a decent SL and good control. Primary calling card is an unusual delivery that involves lots of deception and a low 3/4 arm slot. Struck out 32 in 19.2 IP and was one of the first players in the draft to reach the majors where he got into 11 games for the Dodgers.

Rodriguez, Santos — RP — Chicago (A)

EXP MLB DEBUT: 2013 | POTENTIAL: Setup reliever | 7C

Thrws L Age 25
2006 FA (DR)

Velo	Pitch	Grade
91-98	FB	++++
79-82	SL	+++
84-85	CU	++

Year	Lev	Team	W	L	Sv	IP	K	ERA	WHIP	BF/G	OBA	H%	S%	xERA	Ctl	Dom	Cmd	hr/9	BPV
2011	A+	Winston-Salem	2	3	2	62	49	3.77	1.66	6.9	286	34	78	4.89	4.8	7.1	1.5	0.6	17
2012	AA	Birmingham	2	4	8	64	60	2.81	1.03	6.7	155	18	77	1.91	4.6	8.4	1.8	0.8	45
2012	AAA	Charlotte	0	0	0	7	9	3.68	1.23	5.9	253	37	67	2.75	2.5	11.1	4.5	0.0	151

Live-armed RP who saw K rate improve after surprising drop-off in '11. Can be tough to make hard contact against due to deception and wild arm action. Throws plus FB for strikes and uses SL as K pitch. Repeats arm speed on CU and has shown improvement. Flyball tendencies could become problematic.

Rodriguez, Wilking — SP — Tampa Bay

EXP MLB DEBUT: 2015 | POTENTIAL: #4 starter | 7D

Thrws R Age 23
2007 FA (Venezuela)

Velo	Pitch	Grade
89-95	FB	++++
76-79	CB	++
	CU	++

Year	Lev	Team	W	L	Sv	IP	K	ERA	WHIP	BF/G	OBA	H%	S%	xERA	Ctl	Dom	Cmd	hr/9	BPV
2009	Rk	Princeton	1	6	0	56	52	3.21	1.00	16.5	218	27	71	2.51	1.9	8.4	4.3	0.8	116
2010	A	Bowling Green	4	10	0	106	93	4.23	1.29	19.9	267	32	69	4.00	2.4	7.9	3.3	0.9	96
2011	A	Bowling Green	0	3	0	37	34	4.66	1.42	17.3	269	34	67	4.16	3.4	8.3	2.4	0.7	75
2011	A-	Hudson Valley	1	1	0	8	9	6.48	1.44	17.7	299	41	50	3.95	2.2	9.7	4.5	0.0	135
2012	A+	Charlotte	0	4	0	34	29	5.56	1.21	19.6	0.213				4.0	7.7	1.9	0.8	

Injury-prone SP who saw season end in May after shoulder ailment. Hasn't pitched much in last 2 yrs and was outrighted off 40-man roster. When healthy, shows FB with tailing action that is tough to elevate. Changes speeds, but prefers to go with hard FB/CB. Leaves secondary pitches up in zone.

Rogers, Mark — SP — Milwaukee

EXP MLB DEBUT: 2010 | POTENTIAL: #1 starter | 8D

Thrws R Age 27
2004 (1) HS, ME

Velo	Pitch	Grade
92-95	FB	++++
83-86	SL	+++
73-76	CB	+++
80-83	CU	++

Year	Lev	Team	W	L	Sv	IP	K	ERA	WHIP	BF/G	OBA	H%	S%	xERA	Ctl	Dom	Cmd	hr/9	BPV
2011	Rk	Brewers	0	0	0	13	11	4.85	1.38	10.9	262	32	65	3.95	3.5	7.6	2.2	0.7	62
2011	A+	Brevard County	0	3	0	16	17	9.37	2.27	16.6	323	38	61	8.50	8.3	9.4	1.1	2.2	-37
2011	AAA	Nashville	0	2	0	15	12	13.20	2.87	17.1	332	40	50	8.66	13.2	7.2	0.5	0.6	-209
2012	AAA	Nashville	6	6	0	95	74	4.72	1.48	22.8	255	29	71	4.60	4.6	7.0	1.5	1.2	19
2012	MLB	Milwaukee	3	1	0	39	41	3.92	1.28	22.9	247	31	73	3.90	3.2	9.5	2.9	1.2	101

Athletic, power pitcher continues to be frustratingly inconsistent. For much of the year, he looked indifferent at AAA, but was good when the Brewers called him up. Still has a good 92-95 mph FB, a power SL, CB, and CU. At 26 the clock is ticking, but has the stuff and experience for a breakout.

Rollins, David — SP — Houston

EXP MLB DEBUT: 2015 | POTENTIAL: #4 starter | 7D

Thrws L Age 23
2011 (24) San Jacinto JC
- 88-91 FB +++
- 81-83 SL ++
- 82-84 CU +++

Year	Lev	Team	W	L	Sv	IP	K	ERA	WHIP	BF/G	OBA	H%	S%	xERA	Ctl	Dom	Cmd	hr/9	BPV
2011	Rk	Bluefield	3	0	0	22	18	1.25	0.65	18.8	164	19	92	1.03	0.8	7.5	9.0	0.8	130
2011	A-	Vancouver	1	0	0	14	11	2.57	1.21	18.8	288	36	76	3.25	0.6	7.1	11.0	0.0	128
2012	A	Lansing	6	1	0	78	75	2.78	1.29	17.7	226	30	78	2.79	4.2	8.7	2.1	0.2	62
2012	A	Lexington	1	3	0	31	25	3.48	1.16	20.6	236	26	77	3.76	2.6	7.3	2.8	1.5	78

Steady LHP who sizzled in stellar, sleeper season. Doesn't possess frontline velo or stuff, but throws solid sinker and keeps ball out of air. Ability to coordinate offerings make him tough to hit, though command still work in progress. Could have breakout if he irons out mechanics and improves SL.

Romero, Enny — SP — Tampa Bay

EXP MLB DEBUT: 2015 | POTENTIAL: #3 starter | 8C

Thrws L Age 22
2008 FA (DR)
- 90-97 FB +++
- 78-84 CB +++
- 80-83 CU +++

Year	Lev	Team	W	L	Sv	IP	K	ERA	WHIP	BF/G	OBA	H%	S%	xERA	Ctl	Dom	Cmd	hr/9	BPV
2009	Rk	GCL Rays	2	4	0	39	33	4.81	1.50	15.4	255	32	67	3.93	4.8	7.6	1.6	0.5	24
2010	Rk	Princeton	4	1	0	69	72	1.95	0.94	20.0	207	28	79	1.70	1.8	9.3	5.1	0.3	137
2010	A-	Hudson Valley	1	0	0	5	4	1.80	1.20	20.1	66	9	83	0.71	9.0	7.2	0.8	0.0	-95
2011	A	Bowling Green	5	5	0	114	140	4.26	1.51	19.0	244	34	72	4.01	5.4	11.1	2.1	0.7	72
2012	A+	Charlotte	5	7	0	126	107	3.93	1.31	20.8	200	25	69	2.66	5.4	7.6	1.4	0.4	9

Long, lean, and projectable SP who uses smooth arm action to register Ks and weak contact. Possesses erratic delivery which hinders command, but natural stuff is as good as any in org. K rate fell while walks increased but held hitters to .210 oppBA. FB is sneaky quick while hard CB is knockout secondary.

Rondon, Bruce — RP — Detroit

EXP MLB DEBUT: 2013 | POTENTIAL: Closer | 8B

Thrws R Age 22
2007 FA (Venezuela)
- 94-100 FB +++++
- 84-87 SL +++
- 87-89 CU ++

Year	Lev	Team	W	L	Sv	IP	K	ERA	WHIP	BF/G	OBA	H%	S%	xERA	Ctl	Dom	Cmd	hr/9	BPV
2010	A+	Lakeland	0	0	2	7	7	1.35	0.60	5.7	96	8	100	0.71	2.7	9.4	3.5	1.3	115
2011	A	West Michigan	2	2	19	40	61	2.03	1.40	4.1	163	30	84	2.08	7.7	13.7	1.8	0.0	59
2012	A+	Lakeland	1	0	15	23	34	1.93	0.94	4.0	154	26	81	1.20	3.9	13.1	3.4	0.4	150
2012	AA	Erie	0	1	12	22	23	0.83	1.11	4.1	197	27	96	2.15	3.7	9.6	2.6	0.4	89
2012	AAA	Toledo	1	0	2	8	9	2.25	1.50	3.8	181	23	91	3.63	7.9	10.1	1.3	1.1	-12

Big-bodied RP who peppers K zone with exceptional FB that features late life. Hitters rarely make quality contact against it and improvement of secondary pitches, especially SL, make him particularly potent. Still experiences bouts of erratic control, but dominant velocity and high K totals are OK trade-off.

Rondon, Hector — SP — Chicago (N)

EXP MLB DEBUT: 2013 | POTENTIAL: #4 starter | 7D

Thrws R Age 25
2006 FA (Venezuela)
- 88-94 FB +++
- 79-82 SL +++
- 77-80 CB ++
- 79-82 CU +++

Year	Lev	Team	W	L	Sv	IP	K	ERA	WHIP	BF/G	OBA	H%	S%	xERA	Ctl	Dom	Cmd	hr/9	BPV
2009	AAA	Columbus	4	5	0	74	64	4.00	1.29	25.5	284	34	72	4.28	1.6	7.7	4.9	1.0	115
2010	AAA	Columbus	1	3	0	32	33	8.53	1.83	21.0	350	39	61	8.98	2.8	9.4	3.3	3.4	110
2011	A-	Mahoning Val	0	0	0	3	2	3.00	1.00	5.7	262	32	67	2.35	0.0	6.0		0.0	126
2012	Rk	Indians	0	0	0	3	6	0.00	0.33	4.7	0	0	100	0.00	3.0	18.0	6.0	0.0	261
2012	AA	Akron	0	0	0	4	3	2.25	1.25	8.1	262	33	80	2.97	2.3	6.8	3.0	0.0	79

Tall, lean SP who has only 41 IP last 3 years due to multiple arm surgeries and was picked in Rule 5 draft. Starting to regain velo and feel which were best attributes prior to injuries. Throws good strikes with avg pitch mix and repeats delivery very. Changes speeds and can get get Ks with FB and CB.

Rosario, Jose — SP — Chicago (N)

EXP MLB DEBUT: 2015 | POTENTIAL: #4 starter/setup reliever | 8D

Thrws R Age 22
2008 NDFA, D.R.
- 91-95 FB ++++
- SL +++
- CU +

Year	Lev	Team	W	L	Sv	IP	K	ERA	WHIP	BF/G	OBA	H%	S%	xERA	Ctl	Dom	Cmd	hr/9	BPV
2009	Rk	Cubs	2	1	1	17	21	4.76	1.24	6.3	238	34	60	3.07	3.2	11.1	3.5	0.5	132
2009	A+	Daytona	0	0	0	3	3	0.00	1.00	5.7	106	15	100	0.55	6.0	9.0	1.5	0.0	18
2010	Rk	Cubs	1	2	0	27	33	7.57	1.65	11.1	287	40	51	4.90	4.6	10.9	2.4	0.7	89
2011	A-	Boise	6	3	2	64	50	3.53	1.34	17.6	272	34	71	3.45	2.5	7.1	2.8	0.1	77
2012	A	Peoria	6	8	0	111	95	4.22	1.43	23.6	285	35	70	4.29	2.8	7.7	2.8	0.6	82

Short, athletic SP held his own in the MWL and has some of the best velocity in the system. FB sits in the 90-94 range and tops out at 97 mph. Mixes in a SL that can gets plenty of swings-and-misses and a below average CU. FB has nice sinking action and he gets plenty of ground ball outs.

Rosenbaum, Danny — SP — Colorado

EXP MLB DEBUT: 2014 | POTENTIAL: #4 starter | 6C

Thrws L Age 25
2009 (22) Xavier
- 88-91 FB +++
- CB ++
- CU ++

Year	Lev	Team	W	L	Sv	IP	K	ERA	WHIP	BF/G	OBA	H%	S%	xERA	Ctl	Dom	Cmd	hr/9	BPV
2010	A	Hagerstown	2	5	0	101	84	2.32	1.22	22.7	250	31	82	3.14	2.5	7.5	3.0	0.4	85
2010	A+	Potomac	3	2	0	43	31	2.09	1.12	21.2	224	27	83	2.53	2.7	6.5	2.4	0.4	61
2011	A+	Potomac	6	5	0	132	108	2.59	1.17	26.3	233	29	77	2.63	2.8	7.4	2.6	0.3	75
2011	AA	Harrisburg	3	1	0	39	27	2.29	0.97	24.8	196	24	74	1.43	2.5	6.2	2.5	0.0	61
2012	AA	Harrisburg	8	10	0	155	99	3.94	1.31	24.7	272	32	69	3.70	2.3	5.7	2.5	0.5	60

Short RH was picked-up in the Rule 5 draft and has a chance to stick. Throws a decent sinking 88-92 mph FB, a SL, and a CU. Breaking ball needs more consistency, but the CU is good. Nice pitchability RH who throws strikes and has career 1.19 WHIP and does not give up many free passes.

Rosenthal, Trevor — SP — St. Louis

EXP MLB DEBUT: 2012 | POTENTIAL: #2 starter/closer | 9C

Thrws R Age 23
2009 (21) Cowley County CC
- 93-99 FB +++++
- 80-83 CB +++
- 75-78 CU ++

Year	Lev	Team	W	L	Sv	IP	K	ERA	WHIP	BF/G	OBA	H%	S%	xERA	Ctl	Dom	Cmd	hr/9	BPV
2010	Rk	Johnson City	3	0	1	32	30	2.25	0.94	12.0	203	27	76	1.68	2.0	8.4	4.3	0.3	117
2011	A	Quad Cities	7	7	0	120	133	4.11	1.25	22.2	246	34	66	3.21	2.9	9.9	3.4	0.5	118
2012	AA	Springfield	8	6	0	94	83	2.78	1.11	21.7	202	25	77	2.37	3.5	7.9	2.2	0.6	65
2012	AAA	Memphis	0	0	0	15	21	4.20	1.07	19.4	206	32	60	2.30	3.0	12.6	4.2	0.6	164
2012	MLB	St. Louis	0	2	0	23	25	2.78	0.93	4.5	180	24	74	1.85	2.8	9.9	3.6	0.8	122

Doesn't get as much attention as he should. Has a plus FB that tops out at 100 mph and a nice power CB. Attacks the strike zone and has good movement on all of his offerings. Gets good torque from his lower half to generate plus arm speed and easy velocity. Combines plus stuff with good Cmd.

Rosin, Seth — RP — Philadelphia

EXP MLB DEBUT: 2014 | POTENTIAL: reliever | 7B

Thrws R Age 24
2010 (4) Minnesota
- 91-93 FB +++
- CB ++
- CU ++

Year	Lev	Team	W	L	Sv	IP	K	ERA	WHIP	BF/G	OBA	H%	S%	xERA	Ctl	Dom	Cmd	hr/9	BPV
2010	NCAA	Minnesota	9	4	0	103	95	4.72	1.09	25.2	256	31	59	3.53	1.0	8.3	7.9	1.1	139
2010	A-	Salem-Keizer	1	1	0	11	9	4.91	0.91	6.8	225	29	40	1.62	0.8	7.4	9.0	0.0	128
2011	A	Augusta	2	3	2	89	93	3.34	1.25	9.3	244	33	72	2.98	3.0	9.4	3.1	0.3	105
2012	A+	San Jose	2	1	10	56	68	4.31	1.19	6.6	236	32	66	3.33	2.9	10.9	3.8	1.0	136
2012	A+	Clearwater	0	1	0	12	7	3.00	0.92	14.9	171	21	64	1.04	3.0	5.3	1.8	0.0	32

Spent the year working in relief and survived the CAL. Features a 91-93 mph FB, decent SL, and average CU. Throws strikes with regularity, but FB lacks movement. Move to relief allows his FB/SL combination to play up. Moved from the Giants to the Phillies as part of the Hunter Pence deal.

Ross, Joe — SP — San Diego

EXP MLB DEBUT: 2015 | POTENTIAL: #3 starter | 9D

Thrws R Age 20
2011 (1) HS, CA
- 91-94 FB ++++
- 78-82 SL +++
- CU +++

Year	Lev	Team	W	L	Sv	IP	K	ERA	WHIP	BF/G	OBA	H%	S%	xERA	Ctl	Dom	Cmd	hr/9	BPV
2011	Rk	Padres	0	0	0	1	0	0.00	2.00	4.8	415	41	100	7.58	0.0	0.0		0.0	18
2012	Rk	Padres	0	0	0	1	1												
2012	A	Fort Wayne	0	2	0	27	27	6.26	1.61	20.2	300	38	60	5.02	3.6	8.9	2.5	0.7	80
2012	A-	Eugene	0	2	0	27	28	2.02	0.94	12.5	175	24	79	1.41	3.0	9.4	3.1	0.3	106

25th pick in '11 was slowed with shoulder inflammation. When he got on the mound, was one of the better pitchers in the NWL. Features a nice 91-94 FB, a plus power SL, and an inconsistent CU. Showed improved command, but mechanics need to be more consistent and needs to prove he is durable.

Ruffin, Chance — RP — Seattle

EXP MLB DEBUT: 2011 | POTENTIAL: Setup reliever | 7B

Thrws R Age 24
2010 (1-S) Texas
- 88-94 FB +++
- 81-83 SL ++++
- 76-78 CB ++
- CU ++

Year	Lev	Team	W	L	Sv	IP	K	ERA	WHIP	BF/G	OBA	H%	S%	xERA	Ctl	Dom	Cmd	hr/9	BPV
2011	AA	Erie	3	3	10	34	43	2.12	1.15	4.4	193	28	84	2.30	4.2	11.4	2.7	0.5	109
2011	AAA	Toledo	0	0	9	15	17	1.84	1.36	4.7	253	35	89	3.67	3.7	10.4	2.8	0.6	106
2011	MLB	Detroit	0	0	0	4	3	4.90	1.36	7.7	326	29	100	8.82	0.0	7.4		4.9	150
2011	MLB	Seattle	1	0	0	14	15	3.86	1.57	4.7	248	31	80	4.77	5.8	9.6	1.7	1.3	35
2012	AAA	Tacoma	0	5	1	71	54	5.99	1.56	6.2	273	32	62	4.86	4.5	6.9	1.5	1.0	21

Short, aggressive RP who got off to slow start, but was very good last two months. Has impact stuff at back-end of bullpen with FB and dynamite SL. Can sometimes use SL to set up FB. Command has regressed and has noted struggles against LHH (.294). Can be hit hard when he leaves pitches up.

Salazar, Danny — SP — Cleveland

EXP MLB DEBUT: 2014 | POTENTIAL: #3 starter | 8D

Thrws R Age 23
2006 FA (DR)
- 91-96 FB ++++
- 84-86 SL ++
- 82-85 CU +++

Year	Lev	Team	W	L	Sv	IP	K	ERA	WHIP	BF/G	OBA	H%	S%	xERA	Ctl	Dom	Cmd	hr/9	BPV
2010	A	Lake County	1	1	0	32	23	4.45	1.45	19.7	272	28	78	5.45	3.6	6.4	1.8	1.9	36
2011	Rk	Indians	0	0	0	7	11	2.70	1.20	5.4	242	39	86	3.76	2.7	14.8	5.5	1.3	212
2011	A	Lake County	0	2	0	8	7	3.38	1.25	10.9	262	34	70	2.96	2.3	7.9	3.5	0.0	99
2012	A+	Carolina	1	2	0	54	53	2.68	1.21	13.5	233	30	79	2.94	3.2	8.9	2.8	0.5	92
2012	AA	Akron	4	0	0	34	23	1.85	0.97	21.5	207	25	81	1.82	2.1	6.1	2.9	0.3	70

Sleeper prospect who missed most of '10 and '11 after TJS. Broke out by inducing GB and increasing K rate. Buries quick FB low in strike zone despite short frame and throws power SL with conviction. Has been tough on LHH due to solid-avg CU, but needs to find consistency with SL and setting up hitters.

Salcedo, Adrian — SP — Minnesota

EXP MLB DEBUT: 2015 | POTENTIAL: #4 starter | **7D**

Thrws R | Age 22 | 2007 FA (DR)
89-93 FB +++
80-83 SL +++
CU ++

Year	Lev	Team	W	L	Sv	IP	K	ERA	WHIP	BF/G	OBA	H%	S%	xERA	Ctl	Dom	Cmd	hr/9	BPV
2010	Rk	Elizabethton	4	3	1	66	65	3.27	0.98	15.7	228	30	66	2.22	1.4	8.9	6.5	0.4	141
2010	A+	Fort Myers	1	3	0	27	16	6.26	1.83	21.2	353	39	66	6.80	2.6	5.3	2.0	1.0	42
2011	A	Beloit	6	6	0	135	92	2.93	1.17	18.6	256	31	74	2.95	1.8	6.1	3.4	0.3	80
2012	Rk	GCL Twins	0	1	0	5	4	3.38	1.50	7.7	318	39	75	4.43	1.7	6.8	4.0	0.0	94
2012	A+	Fort Myers	0	1	0	25	14	6.40	1.89	14.9	316	36	64	5.75	5.3	5.0	0.9	0.4	-36

Tall, thin SP whose season ended with elbow and shoulder ailments. When healthy, shows pitchability and ability to locate FB down. Extreme GB tendencies combined with plus control give him value in rotation. Throws with clean delivery and sufficient velocity, though lacks knockout offering. Needs strength.

Sample, Tyler — RP — Kansas City

EXP MLB DEBUT: 2014 | POTENTIAL: Setup reliever | **7D**

Thrws R | Age 24 | 2008 (3) HS (CO)
90-94 FB ++++
79-82 CB +++
81-83 CU +

Year	Lev	Team	W	L	Sv	IP	K	ERA	WHIP	BF/G	OBA	H%	S%	xERA	Ctl	Dom	Cmd	hr/9	BPV
2009	Rk	Burlington	4	2	1	51	44	2.84	1.07	16.4	192	34	73	1.95	3.6	7.8	2.2	0.4	63
2009	Rk	Royals	0	1	0	4	5	6.75	2.25	10.1	383	53	67	7.43	4.5	11.3	2.5	0.0	99
2010	A	Burlington	6	10	0	121	115	4.69	1.65	20.8	235	30	71	4.17	7.1	8.6	1.2	0.6	-19
2011	A+	Wilmington	7	12	0	130	86	5.25	1.57	21.2	284	32	66	4.80	4.0	5.9	1.5	0.8	17
2012	A+	Wilmington	1	9	0	99	91	5.84	1.59	15.5	272	32	65	5.16	4.8	8.3	1.7	1.3	37

Big-bodied RHP who repeated High-A and moved to bullpen in June. More comfortable in short stints where plus FB plays up. Effectively uses height to throw on downhill plane and makes FB explode out of hand with electric life. CB can have big break, but hangs it often. Lots of moving parts in delivery.

Sampson, Keyvius — SP — San Diego

EXP MLB DEBUT: 2014 | POTENTIAL: #3 starter | **8D**

Thrws R | Age 22 | 2009 (4) HS, FL
90-93 FB ++++
73-75 CB ++
CU +++

Year	Lev	Team	W	L	Sv	IP	K	ERA	WHIP	BF/G	OBA	H%	S%	xERA	Ctl	Dom	Cmd	hr/9	BPV
2009	Rk	Padres	0	0	0	3	3	3.00	0.33	4.7	106	15	0	0.00	0.0	9.0		0.0	180
2009	A-	Eugene	0	0	0	5	5	3.60	1.20	10.1	175	25	67	1.76	5.4	9.0	1.7	0.0	34
2010	A-	Eugene	3	3	0	43	58	3.56	1.21	17.3	224	33	73	3.10	3.6	12.1	3.4	0.8	140
2011	A	Fort Wayne	12	3	0	118	143	2.90	1.10	19.3	196	28	75	2.29	3.7	10.9	2.9	0.6	113
2012	AA	San Antonio	8	11	0	122	122	5.00	1.35	19.6	238	30	63	3.64	4.2	9.0	2.1	0.8	66

Talented RH was skipped over High-A and was inconsistent in AA debut. Led the league in K, but got roughed up and walked too many. Has a good 90-94 mph FB with late movement. Mixes in an average CB and a plus CU. Will vary arm slot and breaking ball needs to be more effective, but has potential.

Sanburn, Nolan — SP — Oakland

EXP MLB DEBUT: 2014 | POTENTIAL: #3 starter | **8C**

Thrws R | Age 21 | 2012 (2) Arkansas
90-97 FB +++
83-85 SL +++
80-82 CB +++
CU +

Year	Lev	Team	W	L	Sv	IP	K	ERA	WHIP	BF/G	OBA	H%	S%	xERA	Ctl	Dom	Cmd	hr/9	BPV
2011	NCAA	Arkansas	2	4	8	32	35	3.62	1.33	5.6	235	32	73	3.31	4.2	9.7	2.3	0.6	81
2012	NCAA	Arkansas	4	1	0	41	49	2.43	1.25	7.5	202	31	78	2.17	4.9	10.8	2.2	0.0	82
2012	A-	Vermont	0	1	0	19	19	3.86	1.55	11.7	304	38	78	5.23	2.9	9.2	3.2	1.0	105

Short, aggressive RHP who was college RP, but will develop in rotation. Will need to prove durability and stamina, but has arm strength to accomplish. Plus FB is key pitch and spots it well low. Complements heater with power CB and SL that register Ks. Needs to develop below avg CU.

Sanchez, Aaron — SP — Toronto

EXP MLB DEBUT: 2015 | POTENTIAL: #2 starter | **9C**

Thrws R | Age 21 | 2010 (1-S) HS (CA)
91-96 FB ++++
78-83 CB ++++
81-84 CU ++

Year	Lev	Team	W	L	Sv	IP	K	ERA	WHIP	BF/G	OBA	H%	S%	xERA	Ctl	Dom	Cmd	hr/9	BPV
2010	Rk	GCL Blue Jays	0	2	0	19	28	1.42	1.63	10.6	262	41	93	4.31	5.7	13.3	2.3	0.5	103
2010	A-	Auburn	0	0	0	6	9	4.50	1.50	13.0	191	34	67	2.65	7.5	13.5	1.8	0.0	59
2011	Rk	Bluefield	3	2	1	43	43	5.48	1.48	16.7	272	35	63	4.45	3.8	9.1	2.4	0.8	79
2011	A-	Vancouver	0	1	0	12	13	4.63	1.37	16.3	196	29	63	2.40	6.2	10.0	1.6	0.0	32
2012	A	Lansing	8	5	0	90	97	2.49	1.27	14.8	201	28	80	2.50	5.1	9.7	1.9	0.3	55

Athletic, projectable RHP whose stuff improved across board with velo increasing. Plus FB is located low with easy, smooth delivery. Plus CB is legit wipeout offering while CU thrown with good arm speed. Command is below average at present and he can overthrow.

Sanchez, Angel — SP — Los Angeles (N)

EXP MLB DEBUT: 2014 | POTENTIAL: #2 starter | **8D**

Thrws R | Age 23 | 2010 NDFA, D.R.
90-93 FB +++
CB +++
80-83 CU +++

Year	Lev	Team	W	L	Sv	IP	K	ERA	WHIP	BF/G	OBA	H%	S%	xERA	Ctl	Dom	Cmd	hr/9	BPV
2011	A	Great Lakes	8	4	0	99	84	2.82	1.12	19.5	205	26	75	2.34	3.5	7.6	2.2	0.5	60
2012	A+	Rancho Cuc	6	12	0	130	103	6.58	1.60	21.3	300	33	62	6.09	3.5	7.1	2.0	1.8	51

Was unable to repeat his breakout of '11 and got pounded in the CAL. FB sits at 90-93 and has a plus CU and a decent CB. Surrendered 26 HR, but otherwise peripherals looked similar. Still slender and doesn't finish his pitches so there is a bit of effort in his delivery, but the raw tools remain very good.

Sanchez, Jesus — RP — Milwaukee

EXP MLB DEBUT: 2013 | POTENTIAL: Reliever | **7C**

Thrws R | Age 25 | 2004 NDFA, Venezuela
90-93 FB +++
SL ++
CU +++

Year	Lev	Team	W	L	Sv	IP	K	ERA	WHIP	BF/G	OBA	H%	S%	xERA	Ctl	Dom	Cmd	hr/9	BPV
2010	A+	Clearwater	9	7	0	129	84	2.99	1.10	22.0	230	26	74	2.76	2.3	5.8	2.5	0.6	61
2011	AA	Huntsville	4	7	1	99	66	4.91	1.53	14.3	271	30	70	4.91	4.3	6.0	1.4	1.2	11
2012	AA	Huntsville	3	2	11	45	41	1.59	1.04	5.5	210	27	87	2.13	2.6	8.1	3.2	0.4	95
2012	AAA	Nashville	4	1	0	26	23	1.71	1.22	5.3	237	31	84	2.53	3.1	7.9	2.6	0.0	76

Converted catcher has emerged as one of the better relief prospects. FB sits in the 90-93 mph range and he mixed in an above-average CU and a decent SL. Commands all three offerings well and keeps the ball down. He gave up just two HR while earning 11 saves and looks like a set-up reliever.

Sanchez, Victor — SP — Seattle

EXP MLB DEBUT: 2016 | POTENTIAL: #3 starter | **8C**

Thrws R | Age 18 | 2011 FA (Venezuela)
90-94 FB ++++
82-84 SL ++
83-87 CU +++

Year	Lev	Team	W	L	Sv	IP	K	ERA	WHIP	BF/G	OBA	H%	S%	xERA	Ctl	Dom	Cmd	hr/9	BPV
2012	A-	Everett	6	2	0	85	69	3.18	1.13	22.4	224	27	73	2.66	2.9	7.3	2.6	0.5	72

Short SP with thick-build who was youngest player in league. Frame leaves much room for projection, but has good arsenal. Changes speeds with advanced CU and can drop hard SL in for strikes. FB is bread and butter with excellent location. Still work to do to improve overall repertoire.

Sappington, Mark — SP — Los Angeles (A)

EXP MLB DEBUT: 2015 | POTENTIAL: #4 starter | **7B**

Thrws R | Age 22 | 2012 (5) Rockhurst
91-97 FB ++++
77-79 CB +++
81-84 CU ++
CU

Year	Lev	Team	W	L	Sv	IP	K	ERA	WHIP	BF/G	OBA	H%	S%	xERA	Ctl	Dom	Cmd	hr/9	BPV
2012	Rk	Orem	1	1	0	37	34	5.15	1.28	10.0	231	29	59	3.31	3.9	8.3	2.1	0.7	62

Durable, big-framed SP who uses height well and is extreme GBer. FB is among best in org with quick arm and downward angle. Hitters rarely elevate it, especially with excellent velo. Avg CB has moments where it misses bats and CU showed promise. Has moving parts in delivery and can slow arm speed on CU.

Sawyer, Nick — RP — Tampa Bay

EXP MLB DEBUT: 2015 | POTENTIAL: Setup reliever | **7C**

Thrws R | Age 21 | 2012 (40) Howard JC
90-96 FB +++
82-87 SL +++
CU +

Year	Lev	Team	W	L	Sv	IP	K	ERA	WHIP	BF/G	OBA	H%	S%	xERA	Ctl	Dom	Cmd	hr/9	BPV
2012	Rk	Princeton	2	1	5	24	50	0.37	0.66	5.6	80	24	94	0.00	3.7	18.5	5.0	0.0	251
2012	Rk	GCL Rays	1	0	0	5	6	0.00	1.07	6.1	186	30	100	1.52	3.9	11.6	3.0	0.0	122
2012	A	Bowling Green	1	0	0	3	3	0.00	1.00	5.7	106	15	100	0.55	6.0	9.0	1.5	0.0	18

Short, athletic RP who had incredible debut despite low draft slot. Posted high Dom with solid-avg FB/SL combo. Rarely changes speeds and peppers strike zone with hard stuff. Hard SL is legitimate out pitch. Arm speed is quite good, but crude, max effort delivery keeps him in bullpen.

Scahill, Rob — RP — Colorado

EXP MLB DEBUT: 2012 | POTENTIAL: Reliever | **6C**

Thrws R | Age 25 | 2009 (8) Bradley
92-95 FB ++++
83-86 SL ++
CU ++

Year	Lev	Team	W	L	Sv	IP	K	ERA	WHIP	BF/G	OBA	H%	S%	xERA	Ctl	Dom	Cmd	hr/9	BPV
2009	A-	Tri-City	1	4	0	63	58	3.14	1.24	17.0	246	32	74	2.98	2.9	8.3	2.9	0.3	90
2010	A+	Modesto	10	7	0	156	140	4.73	1.49	24.9	282	35	67	4.33	3.4	8.1	2.4	0.5	71
2011	AA	Tulsa	12	11	0	161	104	3.92	1.39	25.1	266	30	73	4.03	3.4	5.8	1.7	0.7	32
2012	AAA	Col Springs	9	11	0	152	159	5.68	1.59	23.1	282	37	63	4.69	4.4	9.4	2.1	0.7	69
2012	MLB	Colorado	0	0	0	9	4	1.04	1.15	5.7	223	26	90	2.24	3.1	4.2	1.3	0.0	9

Strong-armed RH has a nice 90-94 mph FB with sinking action. Struggled in the hitter-friendly PCL, but did make his MLB. Complements FB with a nice SL and keeps the ball down to generate GB outs. Also has a power SL and a CB. 2.5 GB/FB ratio gives him a chance in Coors.

Scarpetta, Cody — SP — Milwaukee

EXP MLB DEBUT: 2014 | POTENTIAL: #3 starter | 8D

Thrws R Age 24
2007 (11) HS, IL
90-94 FB +++
75-78 CB ++++
CU ++

Year	Lev	Team	W	L	Sv	IP	K	ERA	WHIP	BF/G	OBA	H%	S%	xERA	Ctl	Dom	Cmd	hr/9	BPV
2008	Rk	Brewers	1	0	0	16	27	0.57	1.02	10.0	153	32	94	1.00	4.6	15.5	3.4	0.0	173
2009	A	Wisconsin	4	11	0	105	116	3.43	1.31	16.7	219	30	74	2.94	4.7	9.9	2.1	0.4	70
2009	AA	Huntsville	0	0	0	5	1	5.40	1.20	20.1	262	23	60	4.58	1.8	1.8	1.0	1.8	2
2010	A+	Brevard County	7	12	0	128	142	3.87	1.46	20.3	250	35	72	3.57	4.7	10.0	2.1	0.3	71
2011	AA	Huntsville	8	5	0	117	98	3.85	1.38	21.3	233	28	73	3.47	4.7	7.5	1.6	0.6	27

Stocky RH has plus raw stuff, but struggled with command. Has a nice 90-94 mph sinking FB and also throws a good 12-6 and a CU that needs work. Command issues will catch up with him eventually if they don't improve, but so far he has been effectively wild and has yet to post an ERA over 4.00 as a pro.

Schrader, Clayton — RP — Baltimore

EXP MLB DEBUT: 2013 | POTENTIAL: Setup reliever | 7C

Thrws R Age 23
2010 (10) San Jacinto JC
90-95 FB +++
80-81 CB +++
83-85 SL +++
CU +

Year	Lev	Team	W	L	Sv	IP	K	ERA	WHIP	BF/G	OBA	H%	S%	xERA	Ctl	Dom	Cmd	hr/9	BPV
2010	A-	Aberdeen	1	0	1	8	10	0.00	1.00	4.4	151	24	100	0.97	4.5	11.3	2.5	0.0	99
2011	A	Delmarva	1	1	2	22	38	2.05	1.09	7.2	151	29	83	1.54	5.3	15.5	2.9	0.4	154
2011	A+	Frederick	1	1	3	24	35	1.13	1.13	6.3	106	18	92	1.17	7.1	13.1	1.8	0.4	62
2012	A+	Frederick	1	1	4	35	51	1.29	1.34	6.3	168	30	89	2.00	6.9	13.1	1.9	0.0	67
2012	AA	Bowie	1	0	1	23	17	2.74	1.70	5.5	188	23	84	3.54	9.4	6.7	0.7	0.4	-116

Short, stocky RP who pitches aggressively with nifty sinker/slider combo. Has four pitches in pen, though rarely uses CU. Posts high K rates and keeps ball in ballpark despite flyball tendencies. Can elevate both breaking balls and throws across body which severely hinders control. Hard stuff and has tenacity.

Schugel, A.J. — SP — Los Angeles (A)

EXP MLB DEBUT: 2013 | POTENTIAL: #5 starter | 6B

Thrws R Age 24
2010 (25) Central Arizona JC
89-93 FB +++
77-81 SL +++
CU ++

Year	Lev	Team	W	L	Sv	IP	K	ERA	WHIP	BF/G	OBA	H%	S%	xERA	Ctl	Dom	Cmd	hr/9	BPV
2010	Rk	Orem	2	2	1	7	9	8.59	1.91	5.8	279	41	50	4.83	7.4	11.1	1.5	0.0	18
2010	Rk	Angels	0	0	2	16	12	1.72	1.28	5.8	253	32	85	2.92	2.9	6.9	2.4	0.0	65
2011	A	Cedar Rapids	4	3	1	90	80	2.59	1.24	14.7	223	29	78	2.61	3.9	8.0	2.1	0.2	57
2011	A+	Inland Empire	1	2	0	20	15	5.03	1.42	20.9	284	34	63	4.15	2.7	6.9	2.5	0.5	67
2012	AA	Arkansas	6	8	0	140	109	2.89	1.23	21.0	228	27	78	3.00	3.5	7.0	2.0	0.6	49

Savvy RHP who led TL in ERA despite lack of plus offering in three pitch repertoire. Is adept at throwing strikes, getting ahead in the count, and letting hitters make weak contact against his avg breaking ball. Avg FB exhibits nice tail, but has tendency to elevate SL and CU. Offers a hint of deception and hides ball.

Scoggins, Reid — RP — Los Angeles (A)

EXP MLB DEBUT: 2015 | POTENTIAL: Closer | 7E

Thrws R Age 22
2012 (15) Howard JC
91-96 FB ++++
83-86 SL ++
CU +

Year	Lev	Team	W	L	Sv	IP	K	ERA	WHIP	BF/G	OBA	H%	S%	xERA	Ctl	Dom	Cmd	hr/9	BPV
2012	Rk	Angels	1	0	0	17	34	4.24	1.59	5.0	213	48	70	3.08	7.4	18.0	2.4	0.0	142
2012	A	Cedar Rapids	0	0	0	3	7	5.41	2.10	5.5	242	56	71	4.73	10.8	18.9	1.8	0.0	67

Power armed RP who returned after missing '11 due to TJS. Posted extremely high K rate while rarely getting hitters to put ball in air. Plus FB is good not just for velo, but filthy late movement. Secondary pitches are far from polished and command is atrocious. Fits mold of late innings RP.

Scott, Tayler — SP — Chicago (N)

EXP MLB DEBUT: 2015 | POTENTIAL: #4 starter | 7D

Thrws R Age 21
2011 (5) HS, AZ
90-92 FB +++
76-78 CB ++
CU +++

Year	Lev	Team	W	L	Sv	IP	K	ERA	WHIP	BF/G	OBA	H%	S%	xERA	Ctl	Dom	Cmd	hr/9	BPV
2011	Rk	Cubs	0	0	0	4	2	7.36	1.36	7.7	279	32	40	3.51	2.5	4.9	2.0	0.0	40
2012	A-	Boise	5	1	0	71	43	2.52	1.33	19.7	247	29	79	2.99	3.7	5.4	1.5	0.0	17

Tall, lanky right-hander was a 5th round pick in the deep '11 draft. He isn't overpowering, but understands how to pitch and has a solid three-pitch mix that includes a 90-92 mph FB, CB, and CU. He has good athleticism and a clean, repeatable delivery. Will need better command to duplicate these results.

Seaton, Ross — SP — Houston

EXP MLB DEBUT: 2013 | POTENTIAL: #4 starter | 7E

Thrws R Age 23
2008 (3) HS (TX)
90-94 FB +++
82-85 SL ++
81-86 CU ++

Year	Lev	Team	W	L	Sv	IP	K	ERA	WHIP	BF/G	OBA	H%	S%	xERA	Ctl	Dom	Cmd	hr/9	BPV
2009	A	Lexington	8	10	0	137	88	3.29	1.29	23.4	262	30	76	3.76	2.6	5.8	2.3	0.7	53
2010	A+	Lancaster	6	13	0	146	85	6.64	1.66	23.4	324	35	61	6.23	2.8	5.2	1.9	1.4	37
2011	AA	Corpus Christi	4	9	0	155	97	5.23	1.39	23.3	278	30	64	4.58	2.7	5.6	2.1	1.1	46
2012	AA	Corpus Christi	8	8	0	146	106	4.07	1.27	23.9	274	31	71	4.18	1.9	6.5	3.4	1.0	84
2012	AAA	Oklahoma City	0	1	0	23	11	3.09	1.33	24.2	267	29	79	3.99	2.7	4.2	1.6	0.8	21

Tall, projectable SP who remains a prospect due to control and pitchability. Hasn't developed as much velocity as expected, but has fine location. SL can be very good at times and very bad at others. Flyballs and HR have been problems and subpar K rate is concern. Needs to refine CU to combat LHH.

Selman, Sam — SP — Kansas City

EXP MLB DEBUT: 2015 | POTENTIAL: #3 starter | 8C

Thrws L Age 22
2012 (2) Vanderbilt
91-96 FB ++++
82-86 SL ++++
81-83 CU ++

Year	Lev	Team	W	L	Sv	IP	K	ERA	WHIP	BF/G	OBA	H%	S%	xERA	Ctl	Dom	Cmd	hr/9	BPV
2012	Rk	Idaho Falls	5	4	0	60	89	2.09	1.11	18.2	209	35	80	2.02	3.3	13.3	4.0	0.1	168

Tall, deceptive LHP who led league in Ks. Pitches effectively down in K zone with high arm slot and has above avg velocity that allows SL to be even more effective. Both FB and SL register Ks while keeping ball out of air when contact made. Hides ball well in delivery, but needs to polish CU.

Shreve, Colby — RP — Philadelphia

EXP MLB DEBUT: 2013 | POTENTIAL: Reliever | 6D

Thrws R Age 25
2008 (6) S Nevada CC
89-95 FB +++
80-83 SL ++
79-82 CU ++

Year	Lev	Team	W	L	Sv	IP	K	ERA	WHIP	BF/G	OBA	H%	S%	xERA	Ctl	Dom	Cmd	hr/9	BPV
2011	A	Lakewood	5	5	2	72	65	2.75	1.36	9.1	259	33	81	3.67	3.4	8.1	2.4	0.5	73
2011	A+	Clearwater	1	1	0	13	14	3.55	1.50	7.8	309	37	88	6.27	2.1	9.9	4.7	2.1	139
2012	A	Lakewood	2	1	0	15	16	3.60	1.27	10.2	221	28	76	3.58	4.2	9.6	2.3	1.2	77
2012	A+	Clearwater	1	1	2	20	19	2.25	1.15	6.1	232	27	90	3.57	2.7	8.6	3.2	1.4	99
2012	AA	Reading	3	1	2	43	29	4.40	1.58	6.8	262	31	71	4.20	5.2	6.1	1.2	0.4	-14

Tall, skinny right-handed reliever scuffeld when he hit Double-A. Has a lively 90-95 mph FB and a nice SL. Shows ability to mix speeds well, but needs to spin ball better and repeat his ¾ arm slot. Walks went up and strikeouts down when he moved up and middle relief role seems his likely future.

Simpson, Hayden — SP — Chicago (N)

EXP MLB DEBUT: 2015 | POTENTIAL: #5 starter | 6D

Thrws R Age 24
2010 (1) S. Arkansas
90-93 FB +++
82-84 SL ++
CB ++
CU ++

Year	Lev	Team	W	L	Sv	IP	K	ERA	WHIP	BF/G	OBA	H%	S%	xERA	Ctl	Dom	Cmd	hr/9	BPV
2011	Rk	Cubs	0	4	0	18	11	8.15	2.09	7.9	343	39	58	6.84	5.6	5.6	1.0	0.5	-32
2011	A	Peoria	1	6	0	61	46	5.72	1.68	17.2	305	35	68	5.93	4.0	6.8	1.7	1.3	33
2012	A-	Boise	2	4	2	44	47	6.18	1.67	13.1	293	37	64	5.61	4.5	9.7	2.1	1.2	70
2012	A+	Daytona	2	3	1	39	16	6.98	2.07	13.5	319	33	67	7.00	6.7	3.7	0.6	1.2	-97

Nothing has gone right since being the 16th overall pick in '10. FB velocity is now more often in the 90-93 mph range. Once had a pair of above-average breaking balls, but neither are effective anymore. Was moved to relief in '12, but the results were about the same. Chalk this one up as a bust.

Sims, Luke — SP — Atlanta

EXP MLB DEBUT: 2016 | POTENTIAL: #2 starter | 9D

Thrws R Age 19
2012 (1) HS, GA
90-93 FB ++++
76-78 CB +++
CU ++

Year	Lev	Team	W	L	Sv	IP	K	ERA	WHIP	BF/G	OBA	H%	S%	xERA	Ctl	Dom	Cmd	hr/9	BPV
2012	Rk	GCL Braves	0	0	0	7	10	1.29	0.43	7.6	92	9	100	0.15	1.3	12.9	10.0	1.3	215
2012	Rk	Danville	2	4	0	27	29	4.33	1.41	14.3	255	34	69	3.86	4.0	9.7	2.4	0.7	84

Athletic RH with poise and mound presence. FB tops out at 94 mph with good, late movement. He also has a plus three-quarter CB with good rotation and a decent CU. Is aggressive on the mound and fared well in his pro debut. If the CU continues to improve, he has the power arm to be an impact starter.

Sisco, Jake — SP — Cleveland

EXP MLB DEBUT: 2015 | POTENTIAL: #4 starter | 7C

Thrws R Age 21
2011 (3) Merced JC
88-94 FB +++
77-81 CB +++
80-84 SL +++
CU ++

Year	Lev	Team	W	L	Sv	IP	K	ERA	WHIP	BF/G	OBA	H%	S%	xERA	Ctl	Dom	Cmd	hr/9	BPV
2011	Rk	Indians	2	4	0	34	31	5.24	1.66	12.8	292	38	65	4.43	4.5	8.1	1.8	0.0	44
2012	A-	Mahoning Val	1	6	0	77	45	5.03	1.44	21.9	272	30	65	4.26	3.5	5.3	1.5	0.7	18

Lean SP who is very inconsistent and worked on delivery and FB command. Got knocked around and K rate saw major decline. FB works with heavy sink and hitters bury into ground. Has promising SL and CB and could develop into plus pitches. Slows arm speed on poor CU.

Skaggs, Tyler — SP — Arizona

EXP MLB DEBUT: 2012 | POTENTIAL: #3 starter | 8B

Thrws L Age 21
2009 (1) HS, CA

Velo	Pitch	Grade
88-93	FB	+++
70-73	CB	++++
78-80	CU	+++

Year	Lev	Team	W	L	Sv	IP	K	ERA	WHIP	BF/G	OBA	H%	S%	xERA	Ctl	Dom	Cmd	hr/9	BPV
2011	A+	Visalia	5	5	0	101	125	3.22	1.14	23.5	222	32	72	2.64	3.0	11.2	3.7	0.5	137
2011	AA	Mobile	4	1	0	58	73	2.50	1.04	22.3	217	31	79	2.40	2.3	11.4	4.9	0.6	160
2012	AA	Mobile	5	4	0	70	71	2.84	1.21	21.6	243	30	82	3.55	2.7	9.2	3.4	1.0	110
2012	AAA	Reno	4	2	0	53	45	2.90	1.23	23.7	248	30	79	3.38	2.7	7.7	2.8	0.7	83
2012	MLB	Arizona	1	3	0	29	21	5.83	1.47	21.0	266	28	65	5.31	4.0	6.4	1.6	1.8	26

Tall lefty with easy velocity and smooth mechanics. Held his own in MLB debut. FB isn't overpowering, but has some nice deception. Locates well and isn't afraid to pitch inside. SL and CU are only average, but CB is plus and gives him a chance to be a solid big-league starter.

Slaats, Josh — SP — Colorado

EXP MLB DEBUT: 2013 | POTENTIAL: #4 starter | 6D

Thrws R Age 24
2010 (5) Hawaii

Velo	Pitch	Grade
88-93	FB	++
	SL	+++
	CU	+++

Year	Lev	Team	W	L	Sv	IP	K	ERA	WHIP	BF/G	OBA	H%	S%	xERA	Ctl	Dom	Cmd	hr/9	BPV
2010	NCAA	Hawaii	5	4	0	74	75	3.77	1.42	18.5	257	35	71	3.41	4.0	9.1	2.3	0.1	74
2010	A-	Tri-City	1	3	0	32	42	1.95	0.93	15.1	180	27	82	1.62	2.8	11.7	4.2	0.6	153
2011	A	Asheville	7	3	0	125	103	4.18	1.49	24.5	277	33	74	4.59	3.7	7.4	2.0	0.9	52
2012	A-	Tri-City	0	3	0	38	31	4.30	1.51	13.6	242	30	70	3.59	5.5	7.4	1.3	0.2	3
2012	A+	Modesto	1	2	0	33	32	7.91	2.12	20.4	326	40	62	7.13	6.8	8.7	1.3	1.1	-9

Big and strong RH hurler has a nice low-90s FB, SL, and CU. The SL and CU need refinement, but has good size and raw stuff. Struggled in the CAL and wasn't much better when sent down. CB can be plus at times, but is inconsistent. Complete lack of control explains the step backwards.

Smith, Josh — SP — Cincinnati

EXP MLB DEBUT: 2014 | POTENTIAL: #5 starter | 6C

Thrws R Age 25
2010 (21) Lipscomb

Velo	Pitch	Grade
88-92	FB	+++
	CB	++++
	CU	+

Year	Lev	Team	W	L	Sv	IP	K	ERA	WHIP	BF/G	OBA	H%	S%	xERA	Ctl	Dom	Cmd	hr/9	BPV
2010	NCAA	Lipscomb	8	4	0	104	124	4.66	1.37	31.2	259	36	66	3.85	3.5	10.7	3.1	0.7	117
2010	Rk	Billings	1	2	0	21	28	2.14	1.24	7.1	213	32	84	2.66	4.3	12.0	2.8	0.4	118
2010	A	Dayton	1	1	1	13	15	2.13	1.10	7.1	183	25	85	2.25	4.3	10.7	2.5	0.7	95
2011	A	Dayton	14	7	0	142	166	2.97	1.09	21.4	233	32	74	2.74	2.1	10.5	5.0	0.6	151
2012	A+	Bakersfield	9	8	0	147	140	3.80	1.29	22.4	256	32	73	3.83	2.8	8.6	3.0	0.9	96

21st round pick goes after hitters with a low-90s FB, a plus CB, and an average CU. Survived and even thrived in the CAL with a good CB and an average FB shows that he is a savvy hurler who knows how to limit damage. At 24 was old for this level so the real test will come when he hits AA in 2013.

Smith, Kyle — SP — Kansas City

EXP MLB DEBUT: 2016 | POTENTIAL: #4 starter | 7D

Thrws R Age 20
2011 (4) HS (FL)

Velo	Pitch	Grade
87-93	FB	+++
77-80	CB	+++
79-82	CU	++

Year	Lev	Team	W	L	Sv	IP	K	ERA	WHIP	BF/G	OBA	H%	S%	xERA	Ctl	Dom	Cmd	hr/9	BPV
2012	Rk	Idaho Falls	1	0	0	5	11	1.80	0.80	18.1	175	49	75	0.64	1.8	19.8	11.0	0.0	326
2012	A	Kane County	4	3	0	67	87	2.94	1.22	20.9	246	36	76	3.00	2.7	11.6	4.4	0.4	155

Athletic, polished SP who thrived in Low-A by repeating delivery and throwing all pitches for strikes. Quick arm produces movement and has confidence to pitch backwards by using CB to set up FB and CU. Avg velo, but he has proven command and control of FB. Profiles as back-end starter as K rate likely to fall.

Smoker, Josh — RP — Washington

EXP MLB DEBUT: 2013 | POTENTIAL: Reliever | 6C

Thrws L Age 24
2007 (1-S) HS, GA

Velo	Pitch	Grade
85-89	FB	+++
78-81	SL	++
72-76	CB	+++
81-83	SP	+++

Year	Lev	Team	W	L	Sv	IP	K	ERA	WHIP	BF/G	OBA	H%	S%	xERA	Ctl	Dom	Cmd	hr/9	BPV
2010	A	Hagerstown	3	10	3	91	92	6.50	1.77	14.0	292	35	65	6.08	5.5	9.1	1.6	1.5	32
2011	A+	Potomac	5	2	2	51	56	2.31	1.36	4.6	183	24	86	2.91	6.6	9.9	1.5	0.7	20
2012	Rk	GCL Nationals	1	0	0	5	3	1.80	0.80	9.1	175	21	75	0.79	1.8	5.4	3.0	0.0	67
2012	A	Hagerstown	0	1	1	3	1	15.00	2.33	7.7	262	21	33	8.56	12.0	3.0	0.3	3.0	-252
2012	A+	Potomac	0	0	0	2	2	10.78	1.80	3.9	298	42	33	4.83	5.4	10.8	2.0	0.0	67

Lefty has not lived up to expectations. At one point had a good low-90s FB with a CB, splitter, and a CU, but shoulder injuries took their toll. FB now sits in the upper-80s and he struggles to throw strikes. If healthy, he could be a good LOOGY but was not picked in the Rule 5 draft.

Smoral, Matthew — SP — Toronto

EXP MLB DEBUT: 2017 | POTENTIAL: #3 starter | 8E

Thrws L Age 19
2012 (1-S) HS (OH)

Velo	Pitch	Grade
90-95	FB	+++
80-83	SL	+++
80-85	CU	++

Year	Lev	Team	W	L	Sv	IP	K	ERA	WHIP	BF/G	OBA	H%	S%	xERA	Ctl	Dom	Cmd	hr/9	BPV
2012		Did not play																	

Tall, lanky SP who hasn't pitched in game action since early in spring '12 due to foot surgery. Could be lethal on hitters due to height and low ¾ angle to plate. Throws with easy arm that results in quality FB and excellent SL. Repeating delivery has been difficult due to long levers and needs CU.

Snell, Blake — SP — Tampa Bay

EXP MLB DEBUT: 2016 | POTENTIAL: #3 starter | 8C

Thrws L Age 20
2011 (1-S) HS (WA)

Velo	Pitch	Grade
88-95	FB	++++
80-83	SL	+++
77-80	CB	++
82-85	CU	++

Year	Lev	Team	W	L	Sv	IP	K	ERA	WHIP	BF/G	OBA	H%	S%	xERA	Ctl	Dom	Cmd	hr/9	BPV
2011	Rk	GCL Rays	1	2	0	26	26	3.08	1.56	10.5	288	38	78	4.09	3.8	8.9	2.4	0.0	76
2012	Rk	Princeton	5	1	0	47	53	2.09	1.08	16.8	203	27	85	2.47	3.2	10.1	3.1	0.8	112

Lean, wiry LHP who pitches aggressively with impressive arsenal, highlighted by plus FB and top-notch SL. Produces velo with quick arm and FB exhibits movement. Needs to improve CU to retire RHH, but LHH only hit .100 against him. Could add strength to frame and needs to trust secondary offerings.

Snodgress, Scott — SP — Chicago (A)

EXP MLB DEBUT: 2014 | POTENTIAL: #4 starter | 7B

Thrws L Age 23
2011 (5) Stanford

Velo	Pitch	Grade
89-95	FB	+++
80-82	CB	+++
	CU	++

Year	Lev	Team	W	L	Sv	IP	K	ERA	WHIP	BF/G	OBA	H%	S%	xERA	Ctl	Dom	Cmd	hr/9	BPV
2010	NCAA	Stanford	1	2	1	37	38	5.59	1.68	7.6	240	32	65	4.19	7.1	9.2	1.3	0.5	-6
2011	NCAA	Stanford	2	2	2	31	38	4.65	1.77	5.7	236	34	72	4.18	8.1	11.0	1.4	0.3	-3
2011	Rk	Great Falls	3	3	0	59	68	3.34	1.31	15.3	267	36	77	3.88	2.6	10.3	4.0	0.8	134
2012	A	Kannapolis	3	3	0	99	84	3.64	1.36	21.8	236	30	73	3.24	4.5	7.6	1.7	0.4	35
2012	A+	Winston-Salem	4	0	0	42	44	1.50	0.98	19.9	180	24	87	1.64	3.2	9.4	2.9	0.4	101

Tall, fresh-armed LHP who exudes athleticism in repeatable delivery and has consistent arm slot and release point. Offers hint of deception in delivery that allows pitch mix to play up. Can pitch inside with FB and has enough break on CB to make solid K offering. CU has potential to become third avg pitch.

Snow, Forrest — SP — Seattle

EXP MLB DEBUT: 2013 | POTENTIAL: #4 starter / Setup reliever | 7C

Thrws R Age 24
2010 (36) Washington

Velo	Pitch	Grade
87-93	FB	+++
74-77	CB	++
80-83	SL	++
82-86	CU	+++

Year	Lev	Team	W	L	Sv	IP	K	ERA	WHIP	BF/G	OBA	H%	S%	xERA	Ctl	Dom	Cmd	hr/9	BPV
2011	A	Clinton	2	7	0	75	71	3.62	1.08	22.4	227	29	66	2.54	2.3	8.6	3.7	0.5	110
2011	A+	High Desert	2	3	0	33	20	8.10	1.86	26.0	343	36	58	7.54	3.5	5.4	1.5	1.9	20
2011	AAA	Tacoma	1	2	0	35	36	5.35	1.25	16.0	254	32	58	3.79	2.5	9.2	3.6	1.0	114
2012	AA	Jackson	4	5	0	61	43	4.43	1.48	13.8	262	31	68	3.82	4.3	6.3	1.5	0.3	17
2012	AAA	Tacoma	1	4	0	57	56	8.42	1.89	20.5	302	37	55	6.33	6.0	8.9	1.5	1.3	15

Tall, lean RHP who was demoted to AA and regained footing. May eventually end up in pen where velo could increase. Spots FB well and uses height and slot to give deceptive angle. Breaking balls need to be refined and has trouble throwing for strikes. CU is best secondary offering, but doesn't fool LHH.

Solano, Javier — RP — Los Angeles (N)

EXP MLB DEBUT: 2013 | POTENTIAL: Reliever | 7C

Thrws R Age 23
2008 NDFA, Mexico

Velo	Pitch	Grade
89-93	FB	+++
75-78	CB	+++
	CU	++
	SL	+

Year	Lev	Team	W	L	Sv	IP	K	ERA	WHIP	BF/G	OBA	H%	S%	xERA	Ctl	Dom	Cmd	hr/9	BPV
2010	A+	Inland Empire	1	1	0	45	49	3.22	1.14	8.0	250	34	71	2.88	1.8	9.9	5.4	0.4	147
2010	AA	Chattanooga	2	0	0	20	23	2.29	1.02	5.8	224	30	83	2.71	1.8	10.5	5.8	0.9	158
2011	A+	Rancho Cuc	2	3	0	44	45	4.09	1.43	7.2	303	39	72	4.58	1.8	9.2	5.0	0.6	134
2011	AA	Chattanooga	1	0	1	33	27	3.03	1.41	7.3	246	31	78	3.40	4.4	7.4	1.7	0.3	33
2012	AA	Chattanooga	3	0	0	63	60	2.73	1.20	6.6	247	32	79	3.16	2.4	8.6	3.5	0.6	107

Short, right-handed reliever continues to put up impressive numbers. Comes after hitters with a good two-pitch mix that includes a 90-93 mph FB and a 75-78 mph power CB. Does mix in a CU, but it is more of a show-me offering. Could reach the majors in 2013 as a middle reliever.

Soliman, Manuel — SP — Minnesota

EXP MLB DEBUT: 2015 | POTENTIAL: #3 starter | 8E

Thrws R Age 23
2007 FA (DR)

Velo	Pitch	Grade
88-94	FB	+++
77-79	CB	+++
79-82	CU	++

Year	Lev	Team	W	L	Sv	IP	K	ERA	WHIP	BF/G	OBA	H%	S%	xERA	Ctl	Dom	Cmd	hr/9	BPV
2010	Rk	Elizabethton	5	2	0	65	74	3.48	1.05	20.9	205	28	68	2.36	2.9	10.3	3.5	0.7	124
2011	A	Beloit	7	11	0	136	120	3.97	1.31	20.1	250	30	73	4.01	3.3	7.9	2.4	1.1	72
2012	A+	Fort Myers	0	1	0	5	5	5.40	2.40	13.1	332	40	82	8.60	9.0	9.0	1.0	1.8	-63

Live-armed RHP who was shut down after surgery on labrum in pitching shoulder. Converted from 3B to mound in '09 and has shown feel for pitching. Offers projection with frame and arm action and could add ticks to both FB and slow CB. Can be efficient to a fault and might find value in missing bats.

Solis, Sammy — SP — Washington
EXP MLB DEBUT: 2013 | POTENTIAL: #3 starter | 8C

Thrws L Age 24
2010 (1-S) San Diego

Velo	Pitch	Grade
92-94	FB	++++
80-82	CU	+++
78-80	CB	++

Year	Lev	Team	W	L	Sv	IP	K	ERA	WHIP	BF/G	OBA	H%	S%	xERA	Ctl	Dom	Cmd	hr/9	BPV
2010	A	Hagerstown	0	0	0	4	3	0.00	0.50	6.6	151	19	100	0.00	0.0	6.8		0.0	140
2011	A	Hagerstown	2	1	0	40	40	4.02	1.26	23.5	255	33	69	3.52	2.7	8.9	3.3	0.7	106
2011	A+	Potomac	6	2	0	56	53	2.72	1.28	23.1	277	35	82	3.99	1.8	8.5	4.8	0.8	123

Athletic lefty had TJS in '12. Prior to the injury, had a nice 92-94 FB. Complements the heater with a plus CB and decent CU. At 6'5", 230 he has good size and solid mechanics. He should be ready to resume action in the spring and has the potential to develop into a mid-rotation lefty.

Soto, Giovanni — SP — Cleveland
EXP MLB DEBUT: 2013 | POTENTIAL: #5 starter | 7D

Thrws L Age 22
2009 (21) HS (PR)

Velo	Pitch	Grade
86-91	FB	+++
85-88	CT	+++
87-91	SL	++
	CU	++

Year	Lev	Team	W	L	Sv	IP	K	ERA	WHIP	BF/G	OBA	H%	S%	xERA	Ctl	Dom	Cmd	hr/9	BPV
2010	A	West Michigan	6	6	0	83	76	2.61	1.21	20.8	243	32	78	2.81	2.7	8.3	3.0	0.2	93
2010	A	Lake County	3	2	0	31	31	3.77	1.06	20.1	201	23	71	3.07	3.2	9.0	2.8	1.5	94
2011	Rk	Indians	0	0	0	5	7	1.80	1.00	6.4	221	36	80	1.75	1.8	12.6	7.0	0.0	196
2011	A+	Kinston	4	4	0	64	64	3.23	1.20	17.2	237	30	75	3.16	3.0	9.0	3.0	0.7	100
2012	AA	Akron	6	9	0	121	100	3.93	1.32	22.8	245	29	71	3.61	3.6	7.4	2.0	0.7	53

Tall, slender SP who threw no hitter. Won't blow ball by anybody, but moves around strike zone and gets hitters to chase CT and OK SL. Long levers give deception and improved FB command a bright spot. Slurvy SL could be firmed up, though he lacks dominant pitch for K. Quality sinker allows him for GB.

Spruill, Zeke — SP — Atlanta
EXP MLB DEBUT: 2013 | POTENTIAL: #3 starter | 7C

Thrws R Age 23
2008 (2) HS, GA

Velo	Pitch	Grade
90-94	FB	+++
76-83	SL	+++
79-82	CU	++

Year	Lev	Team	W	L	Sv	IP	K	ERA	WHIP	BF/G	OBA	H%	S%	xERA	Ctl	Dom	Cmd	hr/9	BPV
2010	Rk	GCL Braves	0	0	0	3	1	3.00	1.67	6.7	321	35	80	4.94	3.0	3.0	1.0	0.0	-9
2010	A+	Myrtle Beach	3	5	0	65	41	5.54	1.48	20.0	312	36	61	4.81	1.8	5.7	3.2	0.6	72
2011	A+	Lynchburg	7	9	0	130	92	3.19	1.01	24.8	228	27	69	2.38	1.6	6.4	4.0	0.5	90
2011	AA	Mississippi	3	2	0	45	16	3.20	1.38	27.0	262	27	78	3.89	3.4	3.2	0.9	0.6	-16
2012	AA	Mississippi	9	11	0	162	106	3.67	1.26	24.4	257	30	70	3.36	2.6	5.9	2.3	0.4	55

Lanky RH works efficiently and understands how to attack hitters. Pounds the strike zone with a plus sinking FB and complements it with a CU and an improved but inconsistent SL. Pitches to contact instead of attempting to overpower. At times becomes a two-pitch pitcher and needs to use CU more effectively.

Stephenson, Robert — SP — Cincinnati
EXP MLB DEBUT: 2015 | POTENTIAL: #2 starter | 9D

Thrws R Age 20
2011 (1) HS, CA

Velo	Pitch	Grade
94-96	FB	++++
73-75	CB	++
78-80	CU	++++

Year	Lev	Team	W	L	Sv	IP	K	ERA	WHIP	BF/G	OBA	H%	S%	xERA	Ctl	Dom	Cmd	hr/9	BPV
2012	Rk	Billings	1	0	0	31	37	2.05	0.98	16.6	203	29	82	2.04	2.3	10.9	4.6	0.6	150
2012	A-	Dayton	2	4	0	34	35	4.19	1.37	18.0	248	31	72	4.05	3.9	9.2	2.3	1.0	77

RH has an electric stuff had a nice pro debut. Delivery can be max-effort at times, but allows him to pump his FB into the mid-90s. Also has a nice CB that has potential to be above-average and a plus CU. Made huge strides with CU and improved command. If the CB comes along, could be a top-end starter.

Sterling, Felix — SP — Cleveland
EXP MLB DEBUT: 2015 | POTENTIAL: #3 starter | 8E

Thrws R Age 20
2009 FA (DR)

Velo	Pitch	Grade
89-95	FB	++++
83-86	SL	++
82-84	CU	+++

Year	Lev	Team	W	L	Sv	IP	K	ERA	WHIP	BF/G	OBA	H%	S%	xERA	Ctl	Dom	Cmd	hr/9	BPV
2010	Rk	Indians	2	3	0	51	57	3.16	1.17	17.1	217	30	72	2.47	3.5	10.0	2.9	0.4	103
2011	Rk	Indians	2	3	0	26	31	4.10	1.29	18.0	259	35	71	3.96	2.7	10.6	3.9	1.0	135
2011	A	Lake County	2	3	0	41	35	4.14	1.35	19.2	210	25	71	3.38	5.4	7.6	1.4	0.9	8
2012	Rk	Indians	3	0	2	22	31	1.66	0.97	13.7	186	32	81	1.26	2.9	12.9	4.4	0.0	171
2012	A	Lake County	4	8	1	93	71	6.58	1.55	16.9	284	32	59	5.40	3.9	6.9	1.8	1.5	37

Big, strong SP who can dominate, but needs time. Began in Low-A before demotion to rookie ball to iron out mechanics. Possesses pure arm strength that generates plus FB, though command is below avg. Allows lots of HR with FB and developing SL while CU has solid promise with depth and fade.

Stewart, Ethan — SP — Philadelphia
EXP MLB DEBUT: 2015 | POTENTIAL: #5 starter | 7D

Thrws L Age 22
2010 (47) New Mexico JC

Velo	Pitch	Grade
88-92	FB	+++
	CB	++
	CU	++

Year	Lev	Team	W	L	Sv	IP	K	ERA	WHIP	BF/G	OBA	H%	S%	xERA	Ctl	Dom	Cmd	hr/9	BPV
2011	Rk	GCL Phillies	4	4	0	55	54	3.62	1.43	21.1	270	34	77	4.28	3.5	8.9	2.6	0.8	85
2011	A-	Williamsport	1	0	0	9	6	2.00	1.67	20.2	262	29	93	4.97	6.0	6.0	1.0	1.0	-36
2012	A	Lakewood	5	9	0	116	81	3.89	1.42	20.4	235	27	73	3.62	5.0	6.3	1.3	0.6	-3

Projectable LH took a step back in '12. Has a nice low-90s FB and a CB and CU that show potential. Front-side mechanics are not good and led to lack of control. Is crafty and managed to post a sub-4.00 ERA despite a 1.42 WHIP. Has some potential, but needs refinement.

Stilson, John — RP — Toronto
EXP MLB DEBUT: 2014 | POTENTIAL: Setup reliever | 7D

Thrws R Age 22
2011 (3) Texas A&M

Velo	Pitch	Grade
91-96	FB	+++
84-87	SL	++
80-82	CU	+++

Year	Lev	Team	W	L	Sv	IP	K	ERA	WHIP	BF/G	OBA	H%	S%	xERA	Ctl	Dom	Cmd	hr/9	BPV
2010	NCAA	Texas A&M	9	1	10	79	114	0.80	0.94	9.0	186	31	93	1.39	2.6	13.0	5.0	0.2	181
2011	NCAA	Texas A&M	5	2	1	91	92	1.68	1.14	24.1	226	31	84	2.28	2.9	9.1	3.2	0.1	104
2012	A+	Dunedin	3	0	0	54	47	2.82	1.38	17.6	268	34	79	3.68	3.1	7.8	2.5	0.3	73
2012	AA	New Hampshire	2	4	1	50	44	5.04	1.54	12.8	277	33	69	4.91	4.1	7.9	1.9	1.1	49

Tall, aggressive RP who made it to AA in first pro season. Tried his hand as SP and performed well, but seems destined for bullpen. Lacks durability with max-effort delivery and has trouble repeating arm slot. Pitches aggressively inside with quality FB and hard SL. Sinking CU may be best pitch.

Stowell, Bryce — RP — Cleveland
EXP MLB DEBUT: 2013 | POTENTIAL: Setup reliever | 7B

Thrws R Age 26
2008 (22) UC Irvine

Velo	Pitch	Grade
90-96	FB	++++
82-84	SL	+++
	CU	+

Year	Lev	Team	W	L	Sv	IP	K	ERA	WHIP	BF/G	OBA	H%	S%	xERA	Ctl	Dom	Cmd	hr/9	BPV
2010	AAA	Columbus	1	1	0	20	28	5.49	1.42	4.9	165	25	62	3.03	7.8	12.8	1.6	0.9	39
2011	A	Lake County	0	1	0	17	26	2.60	1.04	6.7	141	26	72	0.94	5.2	13.5	2.6	0.0	121
2011	A-	Mahoning Val	0	0	1	2	3	0.00	1.00	7.6	151	27	100	0.94	4.5	13.5	3.0	0.0	140
2011	AA	Akron	1	0	0	19	28	1.86	1.14	5.9	180	29	86	2.05	4.7	13.0	2.8	0.5	127
2012	AA	Akron	2	1	2	29	44	3.72	1.10	4.6	220	32	74	3.44	2.8	13.7	4.9	1.6	188

Quick-armed, athletic RP who was strictly monitored due to history of ailments. Durability is big concern, but has plenty in arsenal to succeed. Very high K rate result of velocity and deception. Max-effort delivery difficult to repeat, but minimizes BB. Inconsistent SL could use polish.

Straily, Dan — SP — Oakland
EXP MLB DEBUT: 2012 | POTENTIAL: #3 starter | 8C

Thrws R Age 24
2009 (24) Marshall

Velo	Pitch	Grade
87-93	FB	+++
80-83	SL	+++
	CU	+++

Year	Lev	Team	W	L	Sv	IP	K	ERA	WHIP	BF/G	OBA	H%	S%	xERA	Ctl	Dom	Cmd	hr/9	BPV
2010	A	Kane County	10	7	0	148	149	4.32	1.34	22.0	248	32	69	3.75	3.7	9.1	2.4	0.8	81
2011	A+	Stockton	11	9	0	161	154	3.87	1.24	23.3	261	33	69	3.45	2.2	8.6	3.9	0.6	113
2012	AA	Midland	3	4	0	85	108	3.38	1.09	23.8	225	33	70	2.64	2.4	11.4	4.7	0.6	158
2012	AAA	Sacramento	6	3	0	67	82	2.02	0.88	22.5	175	26	79	1.32	2.6	11.1	4.3	0.4	148
2012	MLB	Oakland	2	1	0	39	32	3.89	1.32	23.3	245	24	85	5.28	3.7	7.3	2.0	2.5	51

Tall, poised SP who lacks true plus pitch, but mixes well and keeps hitters off-balance with varying speeds and locations. Locates FB down in K zone and uses height effectively. Has nice feel for big-breaking SL, but can be too inconsistent. Nice CU gives him quality third pitch. Throws lots of strikes.

Stratton, Chris — SP — San Francisco
EXP MLB DEBUT: 2015 | POTENTIAL: #3 starter | 8D

Thrws R Age 22
2012 (1) Mississippi State

Velo	Pitch	Grade
90-93	FB	+++
	CB	++
	SL	+++
		++

Year	Lev	Team	W	L	Sv	IP	K	ERA	WHIP	BF/G	OBA	H%	S%	xERA	Ctl	Dom	Cmd	hr/9	BPV
2010	NCAA	Mississippi St	5	3	0	78	76	5.29	1.61	24.8	276	34	68	5.02	4.8	8.7	1.8	1.0	45
2011	NCAA	Mississippi St	5	7	0	74	74	5.21	1.44	21.1	279	36	63	4.34	3.1	9.0	2.8	0.7	94
2012	NCAA	Mississippi St	11	2	1	110	127	2.38	0.99	24.6	214	30	78	2.20	2.1	10.4	5.1	0.6	150
2012	A-	Salem-Keizer	0	1	0	16	16	2.76	1.47	8.8	233	30	83	3.64	5.5	8.8	1.6	0.6	28

1st round pick is a polished collegiate RH with a good 91-93 FB. Mixes in a plus SL, a CB, and CU. The SL is already a swing-and-miss offering. Has good command and should develop into a solid mid-rotation starter. Has a good feel for pitching and could move up quickly.

Stripling, Ross — SP — Los Angeles (N)
EXP MLB DEBUT: 2015 | POTENTIAL: #4 starter | 7C

Thrws R Age 23
2012 (5) Texas A&M

Velo	Pitch	Grade
90-92	FB	+++
73-75	CB	+++
	CU	++

Year	Lev	Team	W	L	Sv	IP	K	ERA	WHIP	BF/G	OBA	H%	S%	xERA	Ctl	Dom	Cmd	hr/9	BPV
2012	Rk	Ogden	1	0	0	36	37	1.24	0.88	9.6	202	28	84	1.26	1.5	9.2	6.2	0.0	143

Polished finesse right-hander from Texas A&M. Has a decent 90-92 mph FB, a CU, and a really good CB that generates weak contact. He comes right after hitters and controls his FB well. CU improved in his pro debut where he had good success, posting a 1.24 ERA with 6 BB/37 K in 36.1 IP.

Stroman, Marcus — RP — Toronto

EXP MLB DEBUT: 2013 | POTENTIAL: Closer | 8C

Thrws R Age 22 | 2012 (1) Duke

- 90-96 FB +++
- 87-89 CT +++
- 84-86 SL ++++
- CU ++

Year	Lev	Team	W	L	Sv	IP	K	ERA	WHIP	BF/G	OBA	H%	S%	xERA	Ctl	Dom	Cmd	hr/9	BPV
2010	NCAA	Duke	6	4	3	58	64	5.31	1.42	14.4	260	34	64	4.36	3.9	10.0	2.6	1.1	92
2011	NCAA	Duke	3	4	4	64	90	2.80	1.24	15.4	245	39	76	2.80	2.9	12.6	4.3	0.1	165
2012	NCAA	Duke	6	5	0	98	136	2.39	1.11	27.5	231	36	80	2.59	2.4	12.5	5.2	0.5	178
2012	A-	Vancouver	1	0	0	11	15	3.18	0.97	6.1	200	32	64	1.43	2.4	11.9	5.0	0.0	168
2012	AA	New Hampshire	2	0	0	8	8	3.38	1.75	4.6	262	32	85	5.26	6.8	9.0	1.3	1.1	-2

Short, athletic RP who will miss time after suspension for PED. Possesses extremely quick arm that produces velo and pitch movement. Able to spot FB to all quadrants of strike zone, but SL is go-to pitch. Power SL features hard break and tough to hit. Rounds out arsenal with hard CT and subpar CU.

Struck, Nick — SP — Chicago (N)

EXP MLB DEBUT: 2014 | POTENTIAL: #4 starter | 6C

Thrws R Age 23 | 2009 (39) Mt. Hood CC

- 88-91 FB ++
- CB ++
- SL ++
- CU ++

Year	Lev	Team	W	L	Sv	IP	K	ERA	WHIP	BF/G	OBA	H%	S%	xERA	Ctl	Dom	Cmd	hr/9	BPV
2010	A+	Daytona	1	2	0	14	12	5.14	1.50	20.2	275	30	72	5.59	3.9	7.7	2.0	1.9	53
2011	A+	Daytona	6	2	0	50	47	3.42	1.42	21.2	281	36	75	3.98	2.9	8.5	2.9	0.4	93
2011	AA	Tennessee	1	1	0	35	26	2.31	1.37	24.5	299	37	81	3.81	1.5	6.7	4.3	0.0	97
2011	AAA	Iowa	2	4	0	62	38	5.20	1.57	22.8	302	35	65	4.65	3.2	5.5	1.7	0.3	31
2012	AA	Tennessee	14	10	0	156	123	3.18	1.18	22.2	242	29	76	3.29	2.5	7.1	2.8	0.8	77

Short RH had a nice season at AA, going 14-10 with a 3.18 ERA. Has a nice four-pitch mix that includes a low-90s FB, SL, CB, and CU all of which can be effective, but none of which are plus. His abilty to throw strikes with four offerings gives him some potential either as a back-end starter or set-up reliever.

Suarez, Larry — RP — Chicago (N)

EXP MLB DEBUT: 2014 | POTENTIAL: Reliever | 7D

Thrws R Age 23 | 2006 NDFA, Venezuela

- 89-95 FB +++
- 80-83 SL ++
- 80-82 CU +

Year	Lev	Team	W	L	Sv	IP	K	ERA	WHIP	BF/G	OBA	H%	S%	xERA	Ctl	Dom	Cmd	hr/9	BPV
2011	A	Peoria	0	0	1	16	23	0.00	1.13	6.3	224	35	106	2.62	2.8	12.9	4.6	0.6	175
2011	A+	Daytona	1	1	0	12	12	3.00	1.33	6.2	278	31	92	5.49	2.3	9.0	4.0	2.3	119
2011	AA	Tennessee	0	2	0	16	11	7.31	1.75	12.2	328	37	58	6.29	3.4	6.2	1.8	1.1	38
2012	A	Peoria	3	2	5	43	38	4.15	1.59	6.6	282	35	73	4.50	4.4	7.9	1.8	0.4	42
2012	A+	Daytona	0	3	0	11	3	13.50	2.91	6.1	433	45	50	11.04	6.7	2.5	0.4	0.8	-119

Tall, strong-bodied reliever continues to hold his own despite very pedestian stuff. Has a nice mid-90s FB and the quick arm action to snap-off a nasty SL. Control took a step back in '12 and he was sent from High-A back down to Low-A in the MWL. Did have 5 saves but profiles more as middle relief.

Sulbaran, JC — SP — Kansas City

EXP MLB DEBUT: 2014 | POTENTIAL: #3 starter | 8D

Thrws R Age 23 | 2008 (30) HS (FL)

- 88-93 FB +++
- 79-81 CB +++
- 84-86 CU ++

Year	Lev	Team	W	L	Sv	IP	K	ERA	WHIP	BF/G	OBA	H%	S%	xERA	Ctl	Dom	Cmd	hr/9	BPV
2009	A	Dayton	5	5	0	93	100	5.24	1.56	19.3	265	32	72	5.50	5.0	9.7	2.0	1.8	59
2010	A	Dayton	4	6	0	79	83	4.99	1.60	21.9	259	34	69	4.42	5.6	9.4	1.7	0.7	37
2011	A+	Bakersfield	9	6	0	137	155	4.60	1.39	22.2	266	36	67	3.95	3.3	10.2	3.1	0.7	113
2012	A+	Pensacola	7	7	0	105	111	4.04	1.48	23.7	255	31	78	4.80	4.6	9.5	2.1	1.5	64
2012	AA	NW Arkansas	0	4	0	26	24	7.62	2.12	21.4	310	35	69	8.13	7.6	8.3	1.1	2.4	-38

Big, strong RHP with ability to register Ks and gets hitters to bury ball into ground. Best pitch is FB that features nifty late sink. Complements FB with CB that can be plus pitch at times, but too erratic. Development of CU will dictate future role as SP or late-innings RP.

Summers, Matt — SP — Minnesota

EXP MLB DEBUT: 2015 | POTENTIAL: #5 starter | 6B

Thrws R Age 23 | 2011 (4) UC-Irvine

- 88-93 FB +++
- 87-89 CT +++
- 77-80 SL ++
- CU +++

Year	Lev	Team	W	L	Sv	IP	K	ERA	WHIP	BF/G	OBA	H%	S%	xERA	Ctl	Dom	Cmd	hr/9	BPV
2010	NCAA	California-Irvine	2	2	0	31	32	8.51	1.89	6.9	316	39	55	6.74	5.3	9.4	1.8	1.5	44
2011	NCAA	California-Irvine	10	2	0	104	90	1.74	0.91	25.8	180	24	80	1.16	2.6	7.8	3.0	0.1	88
2011	Rk	Elizabethton	1	1	6	21	36	0.87	0.77	3.7	159	33	88	0.44	2.2	15.7	7.2	0.0	241
2012	A	Beloit	9	4	0	109	71	3.55	1.26	23.4	251	28	73	3.55	2.8	5.9	2.1	0.7	48
2012	A+	Fort Myers	2	3	0	39	26	4.81	1.81	20.2	293	31	78	6.33	5.7	5.9	1.0	1.6	-29

Athletic, durable RHP who was moved to rotation and saw K rate drop. Posted 15.7 Dom as RP in '11 and may move back to pen where short arm action and pitch mix could be more suitable. Can cut and sink FB effectively. Deceptive CU gives him solid offspeed pitch, but needs better SL.

Surkamp, Eric — SP — San Francisco

EXP MLB DEBUT: 2011 | POTENTIAL: #5 starter | 7B

Thrws L Age 25 | 2008 (6) NC State

- 87-90 FB +++
- 75-78 CB +++
- CU ++

Year	Lev	Team	W	L	Sv	IP	K	ERA	WHIP	BF/G	OBA	H%	S%	xERA	Ctl	Dom	Cmd	hr/9	BPV
2008	A-	Salem-Keizer	0	2	0	14	16	6.43	1.79	12.9	336	45	63	6.02	3.2	10.3	3.2	0.6	116
2009	A	Augusta	11	5	0	131	169	3.30	1.28	23.4	259	38	74	3.35	2.7	11.6	4.3	0.4	155
2010	A+	San Jose	4	2	0	101	108	3.11	1.00	22.8	217	29	69	2.13	2.0	9.6	4.9	0.4	138
2011	A+	San Jose	1	0	0	6	5	0.00	0.83	21.9	191	25	100	1.03	1.5	7.5	5.0	0.0	113
2011	AA	Richmond	10	4	0	142	165	2.02	1.08	24.1	215	31	82	2.20	2.8	10.4	3.8	0.3	131

Had TJS and missed the whole season. Prior to the injury had carved out a role as a strike-thrower who knew how to attack hiters. FB is in the 87-90 mph range, but has good late sink to it. Complements it with a plus CB, and a CU. Has some nice deception with a low 3/4 delivery from the LH side.

Swagerty, Jordan — RP — St. Louis

EXP MLB DEBUT: 2013 | POTENTIAL: reliever | 8C

Thrws R Age 23 | 2010 (2) Arizona State

- 88-95 FB ++++
- 83-85 CU +++
- CB ++

Year	Lev	Team	W	L	Sv	IP	K	ERA	WHIP	BF/G	OBA	H%	S%	xERA	Ctl	Dom	Cmd	hr/9	BPV
2011	A	Quad Cities	3	1	0	30	30	1.50	0.67	20.9	175	23	83	0.98	0.6	9.0	15.0	0.6	164
2011	A+	Palm Beach	2	2	5	54	52	1.82	1.07	9.6	215	29	82	2.04	2.7	8.6	3.3	0.2	101
2011	AA	Springfield	0	0	3	9	7	2.89	1.39	4.4	233	27	83	3.86	4.8	6.8	1.4	1.0	9

Missed all of '12 with TJS. Should return to action by mid-'13. Prior to the injury featured a low-90s sinking FB that ran in on hitters quicky. Best pitch was a plus slurve that has big, late break. Also has a nice CU. Solid three-pitch mix gives him a chance to start once he reaches the majors.

Syndergaard, Noah — SP — New York (N)

EXP MLB DEBUT: 2014 | POTENTIAL: #2 starter | 8B

Thrws R Age 20 | 2010 (1-S) HS (TX)

- 92-98 FB ++++
- 80-82 CB +++
- 81-85 CU +++

Year	Lev	Team	W	L	Sv	IP	K	ERA	WHIP	BF/G	OBA	H%	S%	xERA	Ctl	Dom	Cmd	hr/9	BPV
2010	Rk	GCL Blue Jays	0	1	0	13	6	2.70	1.13	10.5	226	26	73	2.22	2.7	4.1	1.5	0.0	18
2011	Rk	Bluefield	4	0	0	32	37	1.41	1.06	17.7	203	29	88	1.98	3.1	10.4	3.4	0.3	122
2011	A	Lansing	0	0	0	9	9	3.00	1.11	17.7	240	33	70	2.30	2.0	9.0	4.5	0.0	126
2011	A-	Vancouver	1	2	0	18	22	2.00	1.11	17.7	228	34	80	2.13	2.5	11.0	4.4	0.0	149
2012	A	Lansing	8	5	1	104	122	2.60	1.08	15.0	217	31	75	2.17	2.7	10.6	3.9	0.3	136

Big, durable SP who finished 3rd in MWL in Ks. Has potential to be dominant with three avg to plus offerings. FB exhibits lots of sink and cut while he throws downhill due to height. Extreme GBer, he can also register Ks with big-breaking CB. Can be erratic, but hitters chase CB. Exhibits good body control.

Tago, Peter — SP — Colorado

EXP MLB DEBUT: 2015 | POTENTIAL: #3 starter | 7D

Thrws R Age 21 | 2010 (2) HS, CA

- 91-94 FB +++
- 73-75 CB ++
- CU ++

Year	Lev	Team	W	L	Sv	IP	K	ERA	WHIP	BF/G	OBA	H%	S%	xERA	Ctl	Dom	Cmd	hr/9	BPV
2011	A	Asheville	3	5	0	90	58	7.07	1.77	21.8	257	28	59	5.16	7.2	5.8	0.8	1.0	-72
2012	A-	Tri-City	2	7	0	72	37	5.47	1.48	22.2	250	28	61	3.88	4.9	4.6	0.9	0.5	-30

RH with good velocity and movement on FB. Continues to struggle with control, but does have some projecabilty. Has a loose delivery and clean arm action. Needs to tighten the rotation on his CB. Can sometimes get under his breaking ball. He has shown a nice CU but it too needs refinement.

Taillon, Jameson — SP — Pittsburgh

EXP MLB DEBUT: 2013 | POTENTIAL: #1 starter | 9C

Thrws R Age 21 | 2010 (1) HS, TX

- 94-97 FB ++++
- 80-83 CB ++++
- CU +++
- ++

Year	Lev	Team	W	L	Sv	IP	K	ERA	WHIP	BF/G	OBA	H%	S%	xERA	Ctl	Dom	Cmd	hr/9	BPV
2011	A	West Virginia	2	3	0	93	97	3.98	1.20	16.2	254	33	69	3.53	2.1	9.4	4.4	0.9	130
2012	A+	Bradenton	6	8	0	125	98	3.82	1.17	21.7	236	28	68	3.09	2.7	7.1	2.6	0.7	73
2012	AA	Altoona	3	0	0	17	18	1.59	0.71	20.0	187	27	75	0.63	0.5	9.5	18.0	0.0	175

Tall, athletic SP has a plus FB that hits 99 mph. Also has a good slurvy SL and a nice power CB. At 6'6", 230 he has the size and power frame to both dominate and be durable. Gets good downhill tilt that makes his FB and SL difficult to elevate. Control was much better in '12 and the future looks very bright.

Tapia, Domingo — SP — New York (N)

EXP MLB DEBUT: 2015 | POTENTIAL: #3 starter/setup reliever | 7C

Thrws R Age 21 | 2009 NDFA, D.R.

- 95-98 FB ++++
- CB +
- CU +

Year	Lev	Team	W	L	Sv	IP	K	ERA	WHIP	BF/G	OBA	H%	S%	xERA	Ctl	Dom	Cmd	hr/9	BPV
2010	Rk	GCL Mets	4	3	0	47	29	3.45	1.26	19.2	270	32	69	3.11	1.9	5.6	2.9	0.0	66
2011	Rk	Kingsport	5	5	0	50	30	3.78	1.32	18.8	262	30	71	3.67	2.9	5.4	1.9	0.5	37
2011	A-	Brooklyn	1	0	0	6	6	0.00	0.83	21.9	228	31	100	1.45	0.0	9.0		0.0	180
2012	A	Savannah	6	5	0	109	101	3.98	1.14	21.5	231	30	62	2.43	2.7	8.4	3.2	0.2	97

Skinny RH has a plus two-seam FB and an good CU. Throws from a low ¾ arm slot. Uses a whip like motion to get good movement on his FB, but stops his delivery on the back end. Put up solid numbers and might have the best FB in the system, but funky mechanics could lead to a move to the pen.

Taylor, Logan — RP — New York (N)

EXP MLB DEBUT: 2015 | POTENTIAL: Reliever | 7D

Thrws R Age 21
2012 (11) HS, OK

90-94	FB	++++
75-78	CB	++
80-83	CU	+

Year	Lev	Team	W	L	Sv	IP	K	ERA	WHIP	BF/G	OBA	H%	S%	xERA	Ctl	Dom	Cmd	hr/9	BPV
2012	A-	Brooklyn	2	0	0	19	19	0.93	0.67	5.2	168	24	85	0.35	0.9	8.8	9.5	0.0	152

Tall, heavy-set RP has a good FB/CB combination. Mixes in a CU and locate all three well. Consistency and conditioning will be an issue going forward. Had a nice debut, with a 0.93 ERA, walking 2 and striking out 19. Will go as far as his command takes him.

Teheran, Julio — SP — Atlanta

EXP MLB DEBUT: 2012 | POTENTIAL: #1 starter | 9D

Thrws R Age 22
2007 NDFA, D.R.

90-93	FB	++++
75-79	CB	+++
79-82	CU	+++
80-83	SL	++

Year	Lev	Team	W	L	Sv	IP	K	ERA	WHIP	BF/G	OBA	H%	S%	xERA	Ctl	Dom	Cmd	hr/9	BPV
2010	AA	Mississippi	3	2	0	40	38	3.38	1.15	22.7	205	27	70	2.39	3.8	8.6	2.2	0.5	69
2011	AAA	Gwinnett	15	3	0	145	122	2.55	1.18	23.2	232	29	78	2.68	3.0	7.6	2.5	0.3	74
2011	MLB	Atlanta	1	1	0	20	10	5.03	1.47	16.9	275	27	72	5.45	3.7	4.6	1.3	1.8	2
2012	AAA	Gwinnett	7	9	0	131	97	5.08	1.44	21.5	283	32	67	4.92	3.0	6.7	2.3	1.2	58
2012	MLB	Atlanta	0	0	0	6	5	5.69	0.95	11.9	219	28	33	1.64	1.4	7.1	5.0	0.0	108

FB velocity was down from previous years and was in the low-90s. Does get good movement and can drop his CB in for strikes. CU is one of the best in the minors, but poor front-side mechanics resulted in struggles with control. Questions about his make-up came up and scouts were at a loss to explain the results.

Tepesch, Nick — SP — Texas

EXP MLB DEBUT: 2014 | POTENTIAL: #4 starter | 7B

Thrws R Age 24
2010 (14) Missouri

89-94	FB	+++
78-80	CB	+++
84-88	CT	+++
	CU	++

Year	Lev	Team	W	L	Sv	IP	K	ERA	WHIP	BF/G	OBA	H%	S%	xERA	Ctl	Dom	Cmd	hr/9	BPV
2010	NCAA	Missouri	6	6	0	99	75	4.20	1.37	27.5	280	33	71	4.29	2.5	6.8	2.8	0.8	75
2011	A	Hickory	7	5	0	138	118	4.03	1.30	19.7	274	33	71	4.11	2.1	7.7	3.6	0.9	98
2012	A+	Myrtle Beach	5	3	0	72	59	2.89	1.20	24.0	252	31	76	3.05	2.3	7.4	3.3	0.4	90
2012	AA	Frisco	6	3	0	90	68	4.28	1.36	23.6	276	32	71	4.38	2.6	6.8	2.6	1.0	70

Tall, strong SP who is solid sleeper with deep pitch mix and ability to mix. Extreme GBer with heavy FB thrown on downward plane. Has proper slot for solid CB and has hard CT to give hitters different look. Can slow arm speed on CU and generally lacks deception. Has been hittable, but pitches efficiently.

Thompson, Jake — SP — Detroit

EXP MLB DEBUT: 2017 | POTENTIAL: #3 starter | 8C

Thrws R Age 19
2012 (2) HS (TX)

88-94	FB	+++
82-84	SL	+++
80-83	CU	+++

Year	Lev	Team	W	L	Sv	IP	K	ERA	WHIP	BF/G	OBA	H%	S%	xERA	Ctl	Dom	Cmd	hr/9	BPV
2012	Rk	GCL Tigers	1	2	0	28	31	1.91	0.85	14.8	149	21	78	0.88	3.2	9.8	3.1	0.3	109

Tall, physical SP with solid combo of athleticism and pitchability. Peppers strike zone with three solid offerings and could develop plus SL with more experience. Has tendency to telegraph SL by changing arm angle, but FB has heavy life down in zone. Advanced feel for CU gives him ideal pitch to attack LHH.

Thornburg, Tyler — SP — Milwaukee

EXP MLB DEBUT: 2012 | POTENTIAL: #3 starter | 8C

Thrws R Age 24
2010 (3) Charleston Southern

91-94	FB	++++
75-78	CB	+++
	CU	++

Year	Lev	Team	W	L	Sv	IP	K	ERA	WHIP	BF/G	OBA	H%	S%	xERA	Ctl	Dom	Cmd	hr/9	BPV
2011	A	Wisconsin	7	0	0	69	76	1.57	1.08	22.3	202	28	87	2.11	3.3	10.0	3.0	0.4	109
2011	A+	Brevard County	3	6	0	68	84	3.57	1.15	22.5	190	27	70	2.39	4.4	11.1	2.5	0.7	100
2012	AA	Huntsville	8	1	0	75	71	3.00	1.08	22.5	212	27	75	2.56	2.9	8.5	3.0	0.7	94
2012	AAA	Nashville	2	3	0	38	42	3.58	1.35	19.7	263	37	72	3.44	3.1	10.0	3.2	0.2	115
2012	MLB	Brewers	0	0	0	22	20	4.50	1.41	11.6	279	28	87	6.67	2.9	8.2	2.9	3.3	88

Short but athletic RH put together another impressive season. Has a plus FB that hits 97 mph. Complements the heater with a power CB and an inconsistent CU. Comes after hitters from a high 3/4 arm slot that adds deception. Can be downright nasty and has good command of all three offerings.

Tillman, Daniel — RP — Los Angeles (A)

EXP MLB DEBUT: 2014 | POTENTIAL: Closer | 8D

Thrws R Age 24
2010 (2) Florida Southern

90-95	FB	++++
78-84	SL	+++
80-82	CU	++

Year	Lev	Team	W	L	Sv	IP	K	ERA	WHIP	BF/G	OBA	H%	S%	xERA	Ctl	Dom	Cmd	hr/9	BPV
2010	Rk	Orem	2	2	10	32	50	1.95	1.02	5.6	201	36	79	1.55	2.8	13.9	5.0	0.0	193
2011	A	Cedar Rapids	5	3	12	66	70	2.04	1.28	7.6	221	31	83	2.61	4.3	9.5	2.2	0.1	72
2011	A+	Inland Empire	1	0	2	8	8	4.50	1.13	4.5	237	29	63	3.36	2.3	9.0	4.0	1.1	119
2012	A+	Inland Empire	1	1	8	24	31	1.88	1.00	4.2	129	21	79	0.74	5.3	11.6	2.2	0.0	86
2012	AA	Arkansas	1	5	0	19	21	12.11	2.17	4.8	297	37	41	7.08	8.8	9.8	1.1	1.4	-45

Loose-armed RP who fared much better in High-A upon demotion. Profiles as K pitcher with dominant stuff. Plus FB features vicious sink and thrown with incredible arm speed from ¾ slot. Provides deception and can locate SL low in K zone. Has trouble throwing strikes and needs overall refinement.

Tirado, Alberto — SP — Toronto

EXP MLB DEBUT: 2017 | POTENTIAL: #4 starter | 7D

Thrws R Age 18
2011 FA (DR)

90-96	FB	+++
80-82	SL	++
	CU	+++

Year	Lev	Team	W	L	Sv	IP	K	ERA	WHIP	BF/G	OBA	H%	S%	xERA	Ctl	Dom	Cmd	hr/9	BPV
2012	Rk	GCL Blue Jays	1	2	0	37	34	2.68	1.08	13.1	212	28	73	1.88	2.9	8.3	2.8	0.0	88
2012	Rk	Bluefield	2	0	0	11	5	2.45	0.82	13.3	114	13	67	0.22	4.1	4.1	1.0	0.0	-19

Lean, athletic SP who showed advanced command for age and could add more velocity as his body and mechanics develop. Already throws hard and has arm speed to use solid-avg CU early in count. Needs to develop SL to wipe out RHH. Has tendency to get on side of SL and mature hitters lay off it.

Tonkin, Mike — RP — Minnesota

EXP MLB DEBUT: 2014 | POTENTIAL: Setup reliever | 7C

Thrws R Age 23
2008 (30) HS (CA)

90-96	FB	++++
80-83	SL	++
	CU	+++

Year	Lev	Team	W	L	Sv	IP	K	ERA	WHIP	BF/G	OBA	H%	S%	xERA	Ctl	Dom	Cmd	hr/9	BPV
2010	Rk	Elizabethton	1	0	1	25	26	1.08	0.88	9.3	203	28	90	1.60	1.4	9.4	6.5	0.4	148
2010	A	Beloit	3	6	0	65	40	4.29	1.45	21.3	293	33	72	4.83	2.5	5.5	2.2	1.0	50
2011	A	Beloit	4	3	2	77	69	3.87	1.38	6.7	275	35	71	3.80	2.8	8.1	2.9	0.4	88
2012	A	Beloit	3	0	6	39	53	1.38	0.97	6.7	209	33	86	1.75	2.1	12.2	5.9	0.2	182
2012	A+	Fort Myers	1	1	6	30	44	2.97	1.15	5.5	219	35	76	2.67	3.3	13.1	4.0	0.6	165

Tall, athletic RP who dominated on two levels and continues to fly under radar despite high K rate. Pitches aggressively with plus FB and mixes in above avg CU with depth. Throws from deceptive low ¾ slot that makes FB play up. Keeps ball down and minimizes BB, but will need to improve SL.

Torres, Alex — SP — Tampa Bay

EXP MLB DEBUT: 2011 | POTENTIAL: #3 starter | 8D

Thrws L Age 25
2005 FA (Venezuela)

87-93	FB	+++
78-82	CB	++
79-83	CU	++++

Year	Lev	Team	W	L	Sv	IP	K	ERA	WHIP	BF/G	OBA	H%	S%	xERA	Ctl	Dom	Cmd	hr/9	BPV
2009	AA	Montgomery	0	2	0	9	7	3.11	1.38	18.2	223	26	82	3.76	5.2	7.3	1.4	1.0	9
2010	AA	Montgomery	11	6	0	143	150	3.47	1.44	22.5	253	33	77	3.84	4.4	9.5	2.1	0.6	69
2011	AAA	Durham	9	7	0	146	156	3.08	1.48	23.3	245	33	80	3.71	5.1	9.6	1.9	0.4	53
2012	Rk	GCL Rays	0	1	0	11	17	3.18	0.92	13.2	175				3.2	13.5	4.3	0.0	
2012	AAA	Durham	3	7	0	69	91	7.30	1.93	12.6	261				8.2	11.9	1.4	0.8	

Short, strong SP whose overall numbers weren't very good, but has the offerings to be dynamic dominator. Performed better out of pen, but still has hope of starting. Generates plenty of Ks with lively FB and plus CU. Delivery produces movement and deception along with arm speed. Lacks feel for CB.

Travieso, Nick — SP — Cincinnati

EXP MLB DEBUT: 2016 | POTENTIAL: #3 starter | 8D

Thrws R Age 18
2012 (1) HS, FL

91-94	FB	+++
82-85	SL	+++
	CU	++

Year	Lev	Team	W	L	Sv	IP	K	ERA	WHIP	BF/G	OBA	H%	S%	xERA	Ctl	Dom	Cmd	hr/9	BPV
2012	Rk	Reds	0	2	0	21	14	4.71	1.19	10.5	252	27	64	3.91	2.1	6.0	2.8	1.3	68

14th overall pick in the draft has a good feel for pitching. Pitches off his solid 91-94 mph FB that has good downward tilt. He also has the makings of good hard SL. His CU has potential but needs refinement. Mechanics are simple and repeatable, but struggles with control and needs to increase his tempo.

Treinen, Blake — SP — Oakland

EXP MLB DEBUT: 2014 | POTENTIAL: #3 starter | 8E

Thrws R Age 25
2011 (7) South Dakota State

90-97	FB	+++
82-86	SL	+++
82-85	CU	++

Year	Lev	Team	W	L	Sv	IP	K	ERA	WHIP	BF/G	OBA	H%	S%	xERA	Ctl	Dom	Cmd	hr/9	BPV
2010	NCAA	SoDakota State	7	1	0	75	82	6.09	1.57	27.5	286	37	61	4.97	3.9	9.8	2.5	1.0	88
2011	NCAA	SoDakota State	7	3	0	84	84	3.00	1.26	26.4	255	34	75	3.08	2.7	9.0	3.4	0.2	108
2011	Rk	Athletics	0	0	0	3	7	0.00	1.33	4.2	262	67	100	3.04	3.0	21.0	7.0	0.0	315
2011	A	Burlington	1	1	2	27	29	3.67	1.00	5.7	208	29	62	1.93	2.3	9.7	4.1	0.3	129
2012	A+	Stockton	7	7	0	103	92	4.37	1.35	17.9	285	35	70	4.44	2.0	8.0	4.0	1.0	108

Tall righty who was moved to RP in Aug, but likely to return to rotation. Needs to find pitch to counter LHH (.303 oppBA). Owns pure arm strength and excellent hard stuff, led by FB that features heavy sink. Can take a few ticks off for additional movement. SL has nice break, but CU is far from polished.

Tropeano, Nick — SP — Houston — EXP MLB DEBUT: 2014 — POTENTIAL: #3 starter — 8C

Thrws R Age 22
2011 (5) Stony Brook

Velo	Pitch	Grade
88-94	FB	+++
81-83	SL	++
81-85	CU	++++

Year	Lev	Team	W	L	Sv	IP	K	ERA	WHIP	BF/G	OBA	H%	S%	xERA	Ctl	Dom	Cmd	hr/9	BPV
2010	NCAA	Stony Brook	8	4	0	100	106	2.44	1.05	27.6	213	28	80	2.41	2.6	9.6	3.7	0.6	120
2011	NCAA	Stony Brook	12	1	0	93	119	1.84	0.94	24.9	194	30	81	1.54	2.3	11.5	5.0	0.3	163
2011	A-	Tri City	3	2	0	53	63	2.36	1.18	17.8	218	32	79	2.35	3.5	10.6	3.0	0.2	114
2012	A	Lexington	6	4	0	87	97	2.78	1.18	23.3	238	33	76	2.73	2.7	10.0	3.7	0.3	126
2012	A+	Lancaster	6	3	0	71	69	3.31	1.32	24.4	265	33	79	4.12	2.7	8.8	3.3	1.0	104

Tall, lean SP who throws strikes and fools hitters with well above avg CU. Gets separation from FB and CU by maintaining arm speed. Throws on downhill plane and tough for hitters to elevate. FB command is superb, but needs to stay on top of modest SL to maintain K rate at upper levels.

Turley, Nik — SP — New York (A) — EXP MLB DEBUT: 2014 — POTENTIAL: #4 starter — 7B

Thrws L Age 23
2008 (50) HS (CA)

Velo	Pitch	Grade
87-92	FB	+++
77-79	CB	+++
79-83	CU	++

Year	Lev	Team	W	L	Sv	IP	K	ERA	WHIP	BF/G	OBA	H%	S%	xERA	Ctl	Dom	Cmd	hr/9	BPV
2010	A-	Staten Island	4	4	0	62	47	4.38	1.39	21.7	247	31	65	3.13	4.2	6.9	1.6	0.0	27
2011	A	Charleston (Sc)	4	6	0	82	82	2.51	1.11	21.5	232	29	82	3.01	2.3	9.0	3.9	0.9	117
2011	A+	Tampa	0	0	0	7	5	6.14	1.64	16.3	347	39	64	6.43	1.2	6.1	5.0	1.2	95
2012	A+	Tampa	9	5	0	112	116	2.89	1.26	19.9	235	31	78	3.14	3.5	9.3	2.6	0.6	90
2012	AA	Trenton	1	0	0	5	1	5.40	1.80	23.1	362	38	67	6.00	1.8	1.8	1.0	0.0	2

Large-framed LHP who led FSL in ERA. Struggled with BB, but hitters fail to make hard contact against pitch mix. Moves ball around with FB and CB serves as K offering. Stands 6'6" and uses overhand delivery for deception. Throws downhill and can induce GB. Could move to bullpen.

Tuttle, Dan — SP — Cincinnati — EXP MLB DEBUT: 2014 — POTENTIAL: reliever — 6D

Thrws R Age 22
2009 (5) HS, NC

Velo	Pitch	Grade
89-94	FB	+++
79-82	SL	++
	CU	++

Year	Lev	Team	W	L	Sv	IP	K	ERA	WHIP	BF/G	OBA	H%	S%	xERA	Ctl	Dom	Cmd	hr/9	BPV
2009	Rk	GCL Reds	1	2	0	32	30	1.67	1.30	14.8	260	34	88	3.31	2.8	8.4	3.0	0.3	93
2010	Rk	Billings	5	3	0	58	52	4.32	1.49	19.3	261	32	73	4.42	4.5	8.0	1.8	0.9	42
2011	Rk	Reds	3	1	0	23	35	3.91	1.22	18.6	227	39	64	2.35	3.5	13.7	3.9	0.0	169
2011	A	Dayton	4	3	0	57	50	4.87	1.38	21.9	264	33	62	3.61	3.3	7.8	2.4	0.3	70
2012	A	Dayton	1	3	0	34	20	5.03	1.38	17.9	267	30	64	4.14	3.2	5.3	1.7	0.8	28

RH hit a wall in '12 in repeat of MWL. Features a low-90s FB, hard-breaking SL, and a potential CU. Whip-like delivery generates good movement, but leads to struggles with control. Was suspended for 50 games for a second violatoin of baseball's drug policy and at 21 future is unclear.

Underwood, Duane — SP — Chicago (N) — EXP MLB DEBUT: 2016 — POTENTIAL: #3 starter — 7D

Thrws R Age 18
2012 (2) HS, GA

Velo	Pitch	Grade
91-94	FB	++++
73-75	CB	++
	CU	++

Year	Lev	Team	W	L	Sv	IP	K	ERA	WHIP	BF/G	OBA	H%	S%	xERA	Ctl	Dom	Cmd	hr/9	BPV
2012	Rk	Cubs	0	1	0	9	7	5.19	1.50	7.5	223	26	67	4.06	6.2	7.3	1.2	1.0	-19

Strong-armed HS right-hander has a potential. FB sits at 91-94 and can go as high as 97 mph. Shows the potential for a plus CB and an average CU, but both are inconsistent. Does have good athleticism but needs to repeat his mechanics and smooth out the rough edges.

Urbina, Juan — RP — New York (N) — EXP MLB DEBUT: 2014 — POTENTIAL: Reliever — 7D

Thrws L Age 20
2009 NDFA, Venezuela

Velo	Pitch	Grade
88-91	FB	+++
75-77	CB	++
80-83	CU	++
	SL	

Year	Lev	Team	W	L	Sv	IP	K	ERA	WHIP	BF/G	OBA	H%	S%	xERA	Ctl	Dom	Cmd	hr/9	BPV
2010	Rk	GCL Mets	5	3	0	48	38	5.03	1.41	18.6	284	33	65	4.55	2.6	7.1	2.7	0.9	75
2011	Rk	Kingsport	4	6	0	56	49	5.95	1.57	20.5	301	35	65	5.69	3.2	7.9	2.5	1.4	73
2012	Rk	Kingsport	1	0	0	12	18	5.11	2.03	6.6	206	35	72	4.15	11.7	13.1	1.1	0.0	-61
2012	A-	Brooklyn	0	0	0	5	5	3.60	1.40	7.0	221	31	71	2.79	5.4	9.0	1.7	0.0	34

Projectable LH has been slow to develop. Does have a decent FB that tops out at 93, but control is spotty. Best pitch is a CU that he uses effectively. Also has a CB and a SL, but both need work. Inconsistent mechanics resulted in move to relief, but subpar control continues to undermine effectiveness.

Urena, Jose — SP — Miami — EXP MLB DEBUT: 2015 — POTENTIAL: #4 starter — 8D

Thrws R Age 21
2008 NDFA, D.R.

Velo	Pitch	Grade
90-94	FB	++++
	SL	++
	CU	++

Year	Lev	Team	W	L	Sv	IP	K	ERA	WHIP	BF/G	OBA	H%	S%	xERA	Ctl	Dom	Cmd	hr/9	BPV
2011	A-	Jamestown	4	7	0	73	48	4.33	1.42	20.5	265	31	69	3.91	3.6	5.9	1.7	0.5	28
2012	A	Greensboro	9	6	2	138	101	3.38	1.24	20.8	268	31	75	3.84	1.9	6.6	3.5	0.8	85

Lean RH hurler held his own in full-season debut. Generates easy velocity on FB that tops out at 97. FB tends to straighten out when overthrown, but showed nice progress. Also has a nice SL and an inconsistent CU. If his off-speed stuff improves he could have an impact once he reaches S. Florida.

Valdespina, Jose — SP — Texas — EXP MLB DEBUT: 2016 — POTENTIAL: #4 starter / Setup reliever — 7D

Thrws R Age 21
2011 FA(DR)

Velo	Pitch	Grade
90-97	FB	++++
80-82	SL	++
81-83	CU	+

Year	Lev	Team	W	L	Sv	IP	K	ERA	WHIP	BF/G	OBA	H%	S%	xERA	Ctl	Dom	Cmd	hr/9	BPV
2012	A-	Spokane	3	6	0	60	54	5.58	1.69	18.0	285	36	65	4.82	5.1	8.1	1.6	0.5	26

Very tall SP who is quite raw, but has arm action and velo. More thrower than pitcher. Plus FB is best pitch and he can be guilty of overthrowing. When thrown for strikes, can be dominant. SL shows flashes of being true out pitch while he lacks feel and touch of CU. Could be intriguing late reliever.

Velasquez, Vincent — SP — Houston — EXP MLB DEBUT: 2016 — POTENTIAL: #3 starter — 8D

Thrws R Age 21
2010 (2) HS (CA)

Velo	Pitch	Grade
89-95	FB	++++
75-78	CB	+++
81-84	CU	+++

Year	Lev	Team	W	L	Sv	IP	K	ERA	WHIP	BF/G	OBA	H%	S%	xERA	Ctl	Dom	Cmd	hr/9	BPV
2010	Rk	Greeneville	2	2	0	29	25	3.07	0.99	14.0	225	26	76	2.97	1.5	7.7	5.0	1.2	115
2012	A-	Tri City	4	1	0	46	51	3.35	1.18	20.3	223	31	71	2.63	3.4	10.1	3.0	0.4	108

Big, athletic, and projectable SP who returned after missing entire '11 season due to TJS. Ailment didn't hinder quick arm action and velo is back with vicious late life. Could throw harder with additional mechanical refinement. CB can register Ks, but needs to stay on top of it. Repeats arm speed on effective CU.

Ventura, Yordano — SP — Kansas City — EXP MLB DEBUT: 2014 — POTENTIAL: #2 starter — 9D

Thrws R Age 22
2008 FA (DR)

Velo	Pitch	Grade
93-98	FB	++++
79-83	CB	+++
82-85	CU	+++

Year	Lev	Team	W	L	Sv	IP	K	ERA	WHIP	BF/G	OBA	H%	S%	xERA	Ctl	Dom	Cmd	hr/9	BPV
2010	Rk	Royals	4	2	0	53	58	3.25	1.25	15.3	248	34	75	3.24	2.9	9.9	3.4	0.5	118
2011	A	Kane County	4	6	0	84	88	4.27	1.26	18.1	256	33	67	3.69	2.6	9.4	3.7	0.9	118
2012	Rk	Royals	0	0	0	4	7	2.45	1.09	14.3	225	47	75	1.98	2.5	17.2	7.0	0.0	261
2012	A+	Wilmington	3	5	0	76	98	3.30	1.23	19.3	235	33	76	3.29	3.3	11.6	3.5	0.8	137
2012	AA	NW Arkansas	1	2	0	29	25	4.60	1.23	19.8	218	28	60	2.62	4.0	7.7	1.9	0.3	48

Short, aggressive SP with outstanding natural stuff and velocity. Can be fun to watch with plus FB and CB that make hitters swing and miss. Can dominate deep into games with quick arm action, though can be inefficient with pitch mix. Needs to use CU more and effort in delivery may eventually lead to pen.

VerHagen, Drew — SP — Detroit — EXP MLB DEBUT: 2015 — POTENTIAL: #4 starter — 7C

Thrws R Age 22
2012 (4) Vanderbilt

Velo	Pitch	Grade
90-97	FB	++++
79-83	CB	++
80-83	CU	++

Year	Lev	Team	W	L	Sv	IP	K	ERA	WHIP	BF/G	OBA	H%	S%	xERA	Ctl	Dom	Cmd	hr/9	BPV
2010	NCAA	Oklahoma	0	0	0	13	13	3.38	1.50	9.6	271	35	79	4.35	4.1	8.8	2.2	0.7	67
2012	NCAA	Vanderbilt	6	3	2	69	37	3.50	1.33	10.6	247	28	72	3.22	3.6	4.8	1.3	0.3	6
2012	Rk	GCL Tigers	0	0	0	4	2	2.25	1.25	8.1	307	35	80	3.65	0.0	4.5		0.0	99
2012	A+	Lakeland	0	3	0	27	17	3.67	1.26	13.8	208	25	68	2.31	4.7	5.7	1.2	0.0	-6

Tall, durable SP who may not project to high K rate, but effectively keeps ball on ground and rarely allows HR. Keeps hitters guessing by mixing pitches well, though FB is only plus offering. Crude mechanics limit effectiveness of CB that shows OK break, but rarely thrown for strikes. CU has potential to become avg.

Verrett, Logan — SP — New York (N) — EXP MLB DEBUT: 2015 — POTENTIAL: #5 starter — 7C

Thrws R Age 23
2011 (3) Baylor

Velo	Pitch	Grade
88-92	FB	+++
	SL	++
	CU	+++

Year	Lev	Team	W	L	Sv	IP	K	ERA	WHIP	BF/G	OBA	H%	S%	xERA	Ctl	Dom	Cmd	hr/9	BPV
2009	NCAA	Baylor	7	1	3	54	64	5.14	1.69	12.3	323	43	71	5.89	3.1	10.6	3.4	1.0	124
2010	NCAA	Baylor	5	3	1	91	97	3.28	1.22	22.9	256	34	74	3.26	2.3	9.6	4.2	0.5	130
2011	NCAA	Baylor	7	6	0	101	96	2.93	1.24	24.2	250	32	77	3.18	2.8	8.5	3.1	0.4	97
2012	A	Savannah	3	2	0	65	67	3.06	1.02	22.6	238	30	75	2.96	1.3	9.3	7.4	1.0	152
2012	A+	St. Lucie	2	0	0	39	26	2.09	0.88	23.8	216	24	83	2.32	0.9	6.1	6.5	0.9	102

6'3" RH from Baylor was good in pro debut. FB is only average and sits in the 88-92 mph range, but he locates it well and compliments it with a SL and a CU—both of which are at least average. Has clean, repeatable delivery and throws without effort. Will stick as a starter for now and could move up quickly.

Vizcaino, Arodys

SP | **Chicago (N)** | EXP MLB DEBUT: 2011 | POTENTIAL: #3 starter/Setup Reliever | **9D**

Thrws R Age 22
2007 NDFA, D.R.

89-96	FB	++++
80-83	CB	++++
83-85	CU	++

Year	Lev	Team	W	L	Sv	IP	K	ERA	WHIP	BF/G	OBA	H%	S%	xERA	Ctl	Dom	Cmd	hr/9	BPV
2010	A+	Myrtle Beach	0	0	0	14	11	4.61	1.39	19.2	293	35	67	4.39	2.0	7.2	3.7	0.7	95
2011	A+	Lynchburg	2	2	0	40	37	2.45	1.02	17.2	214	27	79	2.38	2.2	8.3	3.7	0.7	106
2011	AA	Mississippi	2	3	0	50	55	3.81	1.25	18.4	239	33	69	3.14	3.3	10.0	3.1	0.5	109
2011	AAA	Gwinnett	1	0	0	7	8	1.29	1.00	4.5	262	34	100	3.51	0.0	10.3		1.3	203
2012	MLB	Atlanta	1	1	0	17	17	4.67	1.44	4.5	239	32	67	4.37	4.7	8.8	1.9	0.5	46

Short, strong-armed hurler missed all of '12 following TJS. Was then traded from the Braves to the Cubs. Prior to the injury featured a plus 92-95 mph FB, an above-average CB, and an inconsistent CU. Whether in relief or as a starter, he is still just 21 and has the potential to be an impact arm.

Von Rosenberg, Zack

SP | **Pittsburgh** | EXP MLB DEBUT: 2014 | POTENTIAL: #4 starter | **7D**

Thrws R Age 22
2009 (6) HS, LA

87-91	FB	++
74-76	CB	+++
	CU	+++

Year	Lev	Team	W	L	Sv	IP	K	ERA	WHIP	BF/G	OBA	H%	S%	xERA	Ctl	Dom	Cmd	hr/9	BPV
2009	Rk	GCL Pirates	0	0	0	1	1	0.00	0.00	2.8	0	0	100	0.00	0.0	9.0		0.0	180
2010	A-	State College	1	6	0	59	39	3.20	1.24	18.4	265	31	75	3.56	2.0	5.9	3.0	0.6	72
2011	A	West Virginia	5	9	0	126	114	5.73	1.32	19.3	288	34	59	4.78	1.6	8.2	5.0	1.4	120
2012	A	West Virginia	5	7	0	87	60	4.36	1.36	21.3	278	31	71	4.55	2.5	6.2	2.5	1.1	63

Tall RH was better in his repeat of Low-A, but did see his K rate drop. FB has good velocity and now sits in the 90-92 mph but tends to be flat and elevated. Does have a plus CU and the makings of a nice slurvy CB. Cut his home run total from 19 to 11, but at 21 he will need to take a step up in 2013.

Wacha, Michael

SP | **St. Louis** | EXP MLB DEBUT: 2014 | POTENTIAL: #2 starter | **9D**

Thrws R Age 22
2012 (1) Texas A&M

90-94	FB	++++
	SL	++
	CB	++
	CU	++++

Year	Lev	Team	W	L	Sv	IP	K	ERA	WHIP	BF/G	OBA	H%	S%	xERA	Ctl	Dom	Cmd	hr/9	BPV
2011	NCAA	Texas A&M	9	4	0	130	123	2.29	1.13	27.0	242	32	79	2.59	2.1	8.5	4.1	0.2	115
2012	NCAA	Texas A&M	9	1	0	113	116	2.06	1.01	27.2	229	31	80	2.22	1.6	9.2	5.8	0.3	141
2012	Rk	GCL Cardinals	0	0	0	5	7	1.80	0.80	6.0	221	30	100	2.94	0.0	12.6		1.8	245
2012	A+	Palm Beach	0	0	0	8	16	0.00	0.25	6.1	42	13	100	0.00	1.1	18.0	16.0	0.0	312
2012	AA	Springfield	0	0	0	8	17	1.13	0.75	7.1	117	35	83	0.00	3.4	19.1	5.7	0.0	271

1st rounder from Texas A&M was fantastic in his debut. Uses a big leg kick and fires from a ¾ arm slot. Gets nice downward tilt on a 90-94 mph FB. Also has a good CB, a SL, and CU. Showed plus command in his debut, but has struggled in that area in the past. Will be fun to watch in '13.

Wagner, Tyler

SP | **Milwaukee** | EXP MLB DEBUT: 2016 | POTENTIAL: #4 starter/setup reliever | **7D**

Thrws R Age 22
2012 (4) Utah

91-94	FB	++++
	SL	++
	CU	++

Year	Lev	Team	W	L	Sv	IP	K	ERA	WHIP	BF/G	OBA	H%	S%	xERA	Ctl	Dom	Cmd	hr/9	BPV
2012	Rk	Helena	1	4	0	49	47	7.77	1.75	15.9	315	39	54	6.02	4.1	8.7	2.1	1.1	65

The 6-3, 200 pound Wagner has an explosive 91-94 mph FB and a power SL. He worked mostly in relief at Utah, but the Brewers drafted him as a starter. Mixes in an average SL and a decent CU, but got lit up in his pro debut and needs to refine his approach. PIO hitters raked to the tune of .304 oppBAA.

Walker, Taijuan

SP | **Seattle** | EXP MLB DEBUT: 2014 | POTENTIAL: #1 starter | **9C**

Thrws R Age 20
2010 (1-S) HS (CA)

91-98	FB	+++++
80-82	CB	+++
84-87	CU	++

Year	Lev	Team	W	L	Sv	IP	K	ERA	WHIP	BF/G	OBA	H%	S%	xERA	Ctl	Dom	Cmd	hr/9	BPV
2010	Rk	Arizona Mariners	1	1	0	7	9	1.29	0.71	6.2	92	16	80	0.00	3.9	11.6	3.0	0.0	122
2011	A	Clinton	6	5	0	97	113	2.89	1.12	21.1	202	29	74	2.19	3.6	10.5	2.9	0.4	109
2012	AA	Jackson	7	10	0	127	118	4.69	1.37	21.2	258	32	67	4.01	3.6	8.4	2.4	0.9	73

Athletic, electric SP who bypassed High-A. Few can match athleticism and upside with potential for three above avg offerings. Exceptional FB may be best in minors with explosive velocity and life. Can dominate with hard CB, but needs to find consistency. Has clean delivery and should post very high K rates.

Warren, Adam

SP | **New York (A)** | EXP MLB DEBUT: 2012 | POTENTIAL: #4 starter | **7B**

Thrws R Age 25
2009 (4) North Carolina

87-95	FB	+++
80-82	SL	+++
76-80	CB	++
77-80	CU	++

Year	Lev	Team	W	L	Sv	IP	K	ERA	WHIP	BF/G	OBA	H%	S%	xERA	Ctl	Dom	Cmd	hr/9	BPV
2010	A+	Tampa	7	5	0	81	67	2.22	1.10	21.2	240	30	79	2.49	1.9	7.4	3.9	0.2	101
2010	AA	Trenton	4	2	0	54	59	3.15	1.20	21.8	242	33	73	2.85	2.7	9.8	3.7	0.3	122
2011	AAA	Scranton/W-B	6	8	0	152	111	3.60	1.30	23.2	252	29	74	3.69	3.1	6.6	2.1	0.8	51
2012	AAA	Scranton/W-B	7	8	0	153	107	3.71	1.40	24.8	279	33	74	4.20	2.7	6.3	2.3	0.6	58
2012	MLB	Yankees	0	0	0	2	1	23.18	4.29	16.6	549	52	50	24.38	7.7	3.9	0.5	7.7	-121

Durable, athletic sinkerballer who lacks plus stuff and doesn't project to K pitcher, but throws heavy ball and SL with late break. Peppers strike zone and deceptive arm speed can keep hitters off balance. Holds velo deep into games and could carve out career as situational reliever without an improved CU.

Watson, Shane

SP | **Philadelphia** | EXP MLB DEBUT: 2016 | POTENTIAL: #4 starter | **7D**

Thrws R Age 19
2012 (1-S) HS, CA

89-93	FB	+++
75-78	CB	++
82-84	CU	++

Year	Lev	Team	W	L	Sv	IP	K	ERA	WHIP	BF/G	OBA	H%	S%	xERA	Ctl	Dom	Cmd	hr/9	BPV
2012	Rk	GCL Phillies	0	1	0	7	8	1.29	0.86	5.1	202	30	83	1.18	1.3	10.3	8.0	0.0	168

RH was a supplemental 1st round pick and saw limited action in his debut. Has a nice low-90s FB that tops out a 96. Also has a power CB that is plus at times. Looks to have a strong, durable 6'4", 200 frame and if his CU progresses he projects as a possible mid-rotation starter down the road.

Webster, Allen

SP | **Boston** | EXP MLB DEBUT: 2014 | POTENTIAL: #2 starter | **9D**

Thrws R Age 23
2008 (18) HS (NC)

90-96	FB	++++
83-86	SL	+++
77-80	CB	++
82-84	CU	+++

Year	Lev	Team	W	L	Sv	IP	K	ERA	WHIP	BF/G	OBA	H%	S%	xERA	Ctl	Dom	Cmd	hr/9	BPV
2010	A	Great Lakes	12	9	0	131	114	2.88	1.31	20.9	243	31	78	3.24	3.6	7.8	2.2	0.4	61
2011	A+	Rancho Cucamonga	5	2	0	54	62	2.33	1.24	24.4	232	33	82	2.83	3.5	10.3	3.0	0.3	110
2011	AA	Chattanooga	6	3	0	91	73	5.04	1.51	21.9	282	34	66	4.55	3.6	7.2	2.0	0.7	52
2012	AA	Chattanooga	6	8	0	122	117	3.55	1.45	19.3	259	34	73	3.50	4.2	8.7	2.1	0.1	60
2012	AA	Portland	0	1	0	9	12	8.00	1.89	21.2	339	47	56	6.65	4.0	12.0	3.0	1.0	126

Smooth, quick-armed SP repeated AA and started slowly in first two months. Was terrific rest of season. Pitch sequencing needs to be firmed up, but has excellent repertoire with plus sinker. Very high GB tendencies by living low and gets hitters to chase hard, biting SL. Control should improve as he repeats delivery.

Weickel, Walker

SP | **San Diego** | EXP MLB DEBUT: 2016 | POTENTIAL: #3 starter | **8D**

Thrws R Age 19
2012 (1-S) HS, FL

91-94	FB	+++
	CB	++++
	CU	++

Year	Lev	Team	W	L	Sv	IP	K	ERA	WHIP	BF/G	OBA	H%	S%	xERA	Ctl	Dom	Cmd	hr/9	BPV
2012	Rk	Arizona Padres	1	3	0	14	12	4.50	1.57	6.8	288	37	68	4.15	3.9	7.7	2.0	0.0	53

Long, lanky supplemental 1st rounder isn't overpowering despite his 6'6" frame. Tempo is slow and front-side mechanics could be better. Has a decent upper-80 FB, an average CB, and a rudimentary CU. Does have some projectabilty due to size and track record, but more likely profiles as a back-end guy.

Wells, Ben

SP | **Chicago (N)** | EXP MLB DEBUT: 2014 | POTENTIAL: #3 starter | **7D**

Thrws R Age 20
2010 (7) HS, AK

88-92	FB	+++
	CB	++
	CU	++

Year	Lev	Team	W	L	Sv	IP	K	ERA	WHIP	BF/G	OBA	H%	S%	xERA	Ctl	Dom	Cmd	hr/9	BPV
2011	A-	Boise	4	4	0	77	53	4.66	1.32	20.0	276	32	63	3.78	2.2	6.2	2.8	0.5	69
2012	Rk	Arizona Cubs	0	0	0	1	3	0.00	1.00	3.8	0	0	100	0.00	9.0	27.0	3.0	0.0	261
2012	A	Peoria	3	2	1	44	36	3.27	1.36	15.3	279	35	73	3.49	2.5	7.4	3.0	0.0	84

Bulky righty relies on a heavy 90-93 sinking FB. The Cubs continue to use him cautiously as he builds up arm strength. Secondary offerings are not advanced. CB and CU both need work, but has a good approach and clean, repeatable mechanics. Could be moved to relief down the road.

West, Matt

RP | **Texas** | EXP MLB DEBUT: 2015 | POTENTIAL: Setup reliever | **7D**

Thrws R Age 24
2007 (2) HS (TX)

90-98	FB	+++
82-84	SL	+++
	CU	++

Year	Lev	Team	W	L	Sv	IP	K	ERA	WHIP	BF/G	OBA	H%	S%	xERA	Ctl	Dom	Cmd	hr/9	BPV
2011	A-	Spokane	1	2	9	26	35	3.12	0.92	4.2	239	34	71	2.76	0.3	12.1	35.0	1.0	227
2011	A+	Myrtle Beach	0	0	0	1	0	0.00	1.00	3.8	262	26	100	2.41	0.0	0.0		0.0	18
2012	A+	Myrtle Beach	0	3	0	20	14	6.64	1.67	5.4	239	28	58	4.15	7.1	6.2	0.9	0.4	-62

Strong, compact RP who saw limited action and eventually underwent TJ surgery, thus likely to miss all '13. Converted to RP in '11 and has shown feel for K zone and aggressive nature of late relief. Uses FB early in count to set up solid-avg SL with good depth. FB tends to be straight and CU still in early phase.

Wheeler, Zack — SP — New York (N)

EXP MLB DEBUT: 2013 | POTENTIAL: #1 starter | 9C

Thrws R Age 23
2009 (1) HS, GA

Velo	Pitch	Grade
93-95	FB	++++
78-82	SL	+++
83-85	CU	++

Year	Lev	Team	W	L	Sv	IP	K	ERA	WHIP	BF/G	OBA	H%	S%	xERA	Ctl	Dom	Cmd	hr/9	BPV
2010	A	Augusta	3	3	0	59	70	3.99	1.45	11.9	221	33	69	2.90	5.8	10.7	1.8	0.0	54
2011	A+	San Jose	7	5	0	88	98	3.99	1.38	23.1	230	31	72	3.50	4.8	10.0	2.1	0.7	69
2011	A+	St. Lucie	2	2	0	27	31	2.00	1.15	17.9	255	37	81	2.58	1.7	10.3	6.2	0.0	159
2012	AA	Binghamton	10	6	0	116	117	3.26	1.16	24.3	220	30	70	2.32	3.3	9.1	2.7	0.2	91
2012	AAA	Buffalo	2	2	0	33	31	3.27	1.18	22.0	198	25	73	2.49	4.4	8.5	1.9	0.5	52

Tall, lanky RH has emerged as the organization's top prospect. FB sits at 93-95 and can hit 98 with good late life. Scrapped his power CB for a tight SL and mixes in an average CU. Simple, repeatable mechanics allow him to generate easy velocity. Has been lights-out since being traded.

Whitenack, Robert — SP — Chicago (N)

EXP MLB DEBUT: 2014 | POTENTIAL: #3 starter | 8D

Thrws R Age 24
2009 (8) SUNY Westbury

Velo	Pitch	Grade
88-92	FB	++
	CB	+++
80-83	SL	++
	CU	++

Year	Lev	Team	W	L	Sv	IP	K	ERA	WHIP	BF/G	OBA	H%	S%	xERA	Ctl	Dom	Cmd	hr/9	BPV
2010	A	Peoria	8	7	1	103	63	4.96	1.28	20.2	259	30	59	3.42	2.6	5.5	2.1	0.4	46
2010	A+	Daytona	3	1	0	40	28	2.04	1.06	22.0	222	26	83	2.40	2.3	6.4	2.8	0.5	71
2011	A+	Daytona	3	0	0	23	25	1.17	0.52	19.2	145	22	75	0.00	0.4	9.8	25.0	0.0	184
2011	AA	Tennessee	4	0	0	38	22	2.39	1.19	21.6	231	27	80	2.67	3.1	5.3	1.7	0.2	29
2012	A+	Daytona	1	6	0	51	31	5.96	1.89	16.1	326	37	68	6.22	4.7	5.4	1.1	0.7	-12

6'5" right-hander struggled in his first taste of the FSL, going 1-6 with a 5.96 ERA. Has a decent 88-92 mph FB, a good CB, SL, and CU. He does have some room for projection as he fills out, but for now he struggles to command all of his offerings and will likely repeat High-A.

Whiting, Boone — SP — St. Louis

EXP MLB DEBUT: 2014 | POTENTIAL: #4 starter/reliever | 7D

Thrws R Age 23
2010 (18) Centenary

Velo	Pitch	Grade
86-91	FB	++
	SL	++
	CU	++

Year	Lev	Team	W	L	Sv	IP	K	ERA	WHIP	BF/G	OBA	H%	S%	xERA	Ctl	Dom	Cmd	hr/9	BPV
2010	Rk	Johnson City	5	3	0	54	68	3.50	1.09	16.3	262	36	72	3.47	0.8	11.3	13.6	1.0	200
2011	A	Quad Cities	5	2	4	120	122	2.41	0.89	14.8	195	26	76	1.76	1.8	9.2	5.1	0.6	134
2012	Rk	GCL Cardinals	0	0	0	7	11	7.71	1.57	7.7	336	51	50	6.05	1.3	14.1	11.0	1.3	238
2012	A	Quad Cities	1	0	0	16	14	0.56	0.50	17.7	134	18	88	0.00	0.6	7.9	14.0	0.0	145
2012	AA	Springfield	0	0	0	12	9	1.50	1.17	23.9	245	31	86	2.54	2.3	6.8	3.0	0.0	79

RH does not have an overpowering FB but throws a ton of strikes. He was sidelined with forearm and shoulder soreness that limited him to 35 IP. Has high 3/4 delivery and features an upper-80 heater. Also has a decent SL and a good CU that gives him a chance. Now has a career K/BB ratio of 34 BB/224 K.

Wieland, Joe — SP — San Diego

EXP MLB DEBUT: 2012 | POTENTIAL: #3 starter | 8B

Thrws R Age 23
2008 (4) HS, NV

Velo	Pitch	Grade
88-93	FB	+++
80-83	CB	+++
79-82	CU	+++

Year	Lev	Team	W	L	Sv	IP	K	ERA	WHIP	BF/G	OBA	H%	S%	xERA	Ctl	Dom	Cmd	hr/9	BPV
2011	A+	Myrtle Beach	6	3	0	86	96	2.10	0.96	23.1	244	33	83	2.65	0.4	10.1	24.0	0.7	188
2011	AA	Frisco	4	0	0	44	36	1.23	1.05	24.3	220	27	91	2.29	2.3	7.4	3.3	0.4	90
2011	AA	San Antonio	3	1	0	26	18	2.77	1.12	20.5	239	29	72	2.33	2.1	6.2	3.0	0.0	74
2012	AAA	Tucson	0	1	0	8	11	3.52	1.56	16.8	316	48	75	4.51	2.3	12.9	5.5	0.0	187
2012	MLB	Padres	0	4	0	28	24	4.55	1.26	22.6	250	28	70	4.36	2.9	7.8	2.7	1.6	79

A strike-throwing machine who dominates without an overpowering fastball. Heater sits in the 88-92 range, but has good late tailing action. Complements the FB with a good CB and a nice CU. Got off to a solid start with the Padres, but blew out his elbow in May and had TJS in July and will miss all of 2013.

Wiles, Collin — SP — Texas

EXP MLB DEBUT: 2017 | POTENTIAL: #3 starter | 8E

Thrws R Age 19
2012 (1-S) HS (KS)

Velo	Pitch	Grade
86-90	FB	++
80-82	SL	+++
	CU	+++

Year	Lev	Team	W	L	Sv	IP	K	ERA	WHIP	BF/G	OBA	H%	S%	xERA	Ctl	Dom	Cmd	hr/9	BPV
2012	Rk	Rangers	1	1	0	37	25	6.87	1.64	11.7	317	36	56	5.46	2.9	6.1	2.1	0.7	49

Tall, athletic SP who is all about projection in lean frame. FB is below avg at present due to lack of frontline velocity, though has clean arm and could add ticks later. Pitch movement is good and throws consistent strikes. SL has potential to become more than avg. Has advanced CU for age and is tough on LHH.

Wilk, Adam — SP — Detroit

EXP MLB DEBUT: 2011 | POTENTIAL: #5 starter | 6A

Thrws L Age 25
2009 (11) Long Beach State

Velo	Pitch	Grade
85-91	FB	+++
82-86	CT	+++
79-80	CB	++
80-82	CU	+++

Year	Lev	Team	W	L	Sv	IP	K	ERA	WHIP	BF/G	OBA	H%	S%	xERA	Ctl	Dom	Cmd	hr/9	BPV
2010	AA	Erie	2	0	0	24	14	1.14	0.63	27.2	130	15	86	0.25	1.9	5.3	2.8	0.4	62
2011	AAA	Toledo	8	6	0	103	76	3.24	1.16	22.7	266	30	79	4.04	1.2	6.7	5.4	1.3	105
2011	MLB	Detroit	0	0	0	13	10	5.40	1.28	10.9	271	29	64	5.07	2.0	6.8	3.3	2.0	85
2012	AAA	Toledo	7	11	0	150	128	2.77	1.01	23.9	226	27	76	2.61	1.7	7.7	4.6	0.8	111
2012	MLB	Detroit	0	3	0	11	7	8.18	2.18	18.3	404	41	70	10.82	2.5	5.7	2.3	3.3	55

Tall, savvy LHP who defies expectations with pitchability. Has limited stuff, but keeps hitters off balance by exquisite mixing and well above avg control and command. Has feel for quality CU and messes with hitters timing by moving ball around. FB velo is subpar and lacks put away pitch, but gets hitters out.

Williams, Corey — RP — Minnesota

EXP MLB DEBUT: 2014 | POTENTIAL: Setup reliever | 7D

Thrws L Age 23
2011 (3) Vanderbilt

Velo	Pitch	Grade
89-94	FB	+++
82-84	SL	+++
	CU	++

Year	Lev	Team	W	L	Sv	IP	K	ERA	WHIP	BF/G	OBA	H%	S%	xERA	Ctl	Dom	Cmd	hr/9	BPV
2010	NCAA	Vanderbilt	1	0	1	17	17	2.65	1.18	5.7	226	31	75	2.29	3.2	9.0	2.8	0.0	94
2011	NCAA	Vanderbilt	2	0	2	38	37	4.46	1.15	5.2	217	28	60	2.56	3.3	8.7	2.6	0.5	86
2011	Rk	Elizabethton	1	1	1	12	11	3.86	1.46	7.1	267	35	71	3.55	3.9	8.5	2.2	0.0	67
2012	A	Beloit	4	4	17	62	68	3.47	1.41	5.6	238	32	77	3.71	4.8	9.8	2.1	0.7	66

Groundball-inducing RP with clean arm and ability to retire LHH (.179 oppBA). Throws with max effort and will live in pen where hard stuff is effective. Tailing and sinking FB could become quicker with refined mechanics and hard SL could register Ks even at high levels of minors. Lacks feel for changing speeds.

Wilson, Alex — RP — Boston

EXP MLB DEBUT: 2013 | POTENTIAL: Setup reliever/Closer | 7B

Thrws R Age 26
2009 (2) Texas A&M

Velo	Pitch	Grade
91-98	FB	++++
81-85	SL	+++
82-86	CU	+

Year	Lev	Team	W	L	Sv	IP	K	ERA	WHIP	BF/G	OBA	H%	S%	xERA	Ctl	Dom	Cmd	hr/9	BPV
2010	AA	Portland	4	5	0	78	56	6.66	1.65	21.9	301	33	62	6.16	3.9	6.4	1.6	1.7	28
2011	AA	Portland	9	4	0	112	99	3.05	1.25	21.7	246	30	77	3.35	3.0	8.0	2.7	0.6	81
2011	AAA	Pawtucket	1	0	0	21	24	3.43	1.24	21.3	243	33	75	3.46	3.0	10.3	3.4	0.9	122
2012	AAA	Pawtucket	5	3	1	73	78	3.72	1.50	7.8	271	37	75	4.04	4.1	9.7	2.4	0.4	82

Short, strong RHP was converted to RP in '12 and saw velo increase. FB exhibits excellent sink and complements heater with solid-avg SL. Both FB and tight SL can register Ks. Needs pitch to combat LHH (.316 oppBA) and violent delivery has been difficult to repeat. Has right mentality for late innings role.

Wimmers, Alex — SP — Minnesota

EXP MLB DEBUT: 2015 | POTENTIAL: #4 starter | 7E

Thrws R Age 24
2010 (1) Ohio State

Velo	Pitch	Grade
88-92	FB	+++
77-80	CB	+++
79-82	CU	+++

Year	Lev	Team	W	L	Sv	IP	K	ERA	WHIP	BF/G	OBA	H%	S%	xERA	Ctl	Dom	Cmd	hr/9	BPV
2010	A+	Fort Myers	2	0	0	16	23	0.57	0.70	13.8	120	22	91	0.00	2.9	13.2	4.6	0.0	178
2011	Rk	GCL Twins	0	0	0	1	1	0.00	1.00	3.8	0	0	100	0.00	9.0	9.0	1.0	0.0	-63
2011	A+	Fort Myers	2	3	1	41	39	4.20	1.23	13.7	196	23	69	3.11	4.9	8.6	1.8	1.1	42
2012	Rk	GCL Twins	0	1	0	1	0			6.9							0.0		
2012	AA	New Britain	0	0	0	4	3	4.16	1.85	20.2	329	35	86	7.46	4.2	6.2	1.5	2.1	18

Tall SP who will likely miss entire '13 season after TJ surgery in Aug. Had pronounced bout of wildness in '11, but seems to have gotten control back. Still has best CU in system with advanced feel. Possesses good bite and break on average CB while FB has enough jump and sink to be effective when healthy.

Winkler, Danny — SP — Colorado

EXP MLB DEBUT: 2015 | POTENTIAL: #4 starter/reliever | 7C

Thrws R Age 23
2011 (20) Central Florida

Velo	Pitch	Grade
91-94	FB	+++
81-83	SL	++++
	CU	++

Year	Lev	Team	W	L	Sv	IP	K	ERA	WHIP	BF/G	OBA	H%	S%	xERA	Ctl	Dom	Cmd	hr/9	BPV
2011	NCAA	Central Florida	3	4	0	82	92	4.70	1.32	19.0	268	37	62	3.52	2.6	10.1	3.8	0.3	128
2011	Rk	Casper	4	3	0	57	65	3.92	1.45	20.4	284	37	75	4.63	3.0	10.2	3.4	0.9	121
2012	A	Asheville	11	10	0	145	136	4.46	1.37	24.4	271	33	69	4.30	2.9	8.4	2.9	1.0	91

Short righty attacks hitters with a 91-93 mph FB and a plus SL. Keeps the ball down in the zone and gets swings-and-misses with his SL. Profiles as a back-end starter, but knows how to pitch and keep hitters off-balance.

Wisler, Matt — SP — San Diego

EXP MLB DEBUT: 2016 | POTENTIAL: #3 starter | 8C

Thrws R Age 20
2011 (7) HS, OH

Velo	Pitch	Grade
91-94	FB	+++
	CB	+++
	CU	++

Year	Lev	Team	W	L	Sv	IP	K	ERA	WHIP	BF/G	OBA	H%	S%	xERA	Ctl	Dom	Cmd	hr/9	BPV
2011	Rk	Padres	0	0	0	0	0												
2012	A	Fort Wayne	5	4	0	114	113	2.53	1.08	18.5	228	31	75	2.15	2.2	8.9	4.0	0.1	119

7th round pick looks to be a late-blooming gem. FB velocity jumped from upper-80s in HS to 96 mph in the MWL. Also has a plus CB and does a good job of throwing strikes and setting hitters up. FB sits in the low-90s and CU has potential. Posted a 4.0 Cmd in full-season debut and has surprising potential.

Withrow, Chris — RP — Los Angeles (N)

EXP MLB DEBUT: 2013 | POTENTIAL: Setup reliever | 8D

Thrws R Age 24
2007 (1) HS, TX

Velo	Pitch	Grade
89-94	FB	++++
74-78	CB	+++
79-81	CU	+++

Year	Lev	Team	W	L	Sv	IP	K	ERA	WHIP	BF/G	OBA	H%	S%	xERA	Ctl	Dom	Cmd	hr/9	BPV
2009	A+	Inland Empire	6	6	0	86	105	4.69	1.45	19.4	247	36	66	3.52	4.7	10.9	2.3	0.3	88
2009	AA	Chattanooga	2	2	0	27	26	3.95	1.32	18.8	237	30	71	3.41	4.0	8.6	2.2	0.7	65
2010	AA	Chattanooga	4	9	0	130	120	5.97	1.66	21.5	285	35	64	5.16	4.8	8.3	1.7	0.9	39
2011	AA	Chattanooga	6	6	0	129	130	4.20	1.45	22.0	234	31	71	3.60	5.2	9.1	1.7	0.6	40
2012	AA	Chattanooga	3	3	2	60	64	4.65	1.47	11.7	235	32	67	3.55	5.4	9.6	1.8	0.5	45

Athletic SP with plus velocity and ability to dominate, but struggles with control. FB sits at 90-95 and hits 98 with late movement. CB can be plus, but tends to be inconsistent and CU needs work. Was moved to relief with better results. Pectoral injury ended his season, but should be ready by spring.

Wittgren, Nick — RP — Miami

EXP MLB DEBUT: 2014 | POTENTIAL: Reliever | 7D

Thrws R Age 22
2012 (9) Purdue

Velo	Pitch	Grade
89-93	FB	++++
	SL	++

Year	Lev	Team	W	L	Sv	IP	K	ERA	WHIP	BF/G	OBA	H%	S%	xERA	Ctl	Dom	Cmd	hr/9	BPV
2011	NCAA	Purdue	2	3	12	51	55	3.18	1.12	6.9	246	34	71	2.73	1.8	9.7	5.5	0.4	145
2012	NCAA	Purdue	3	0	10	41	39	1.76	1.15	6.3	232	31	83	2.30	2.6	8.6	3.3	0.0	101
2012	A	Greensboro	0	0	2	6	13	0.00	0.33	3.2	56	20	100	0.00	1.5	19.5	13.0	0.0	329
2012	A-	Jamestown	0	2	11	25	34	1.46	1.13	5.7	256	40	86	2.55	1.5	12.4	8.5	0.0	202

Long, lean 6'3" 200# right-hander from Purdue had an excellent professional debut, posting a 1.17 ERA with 5 BB/47 K in 30.2 IP. FB isn't plus and sits in the low-90s but he has some nice deception and a decent CB. Notched 13 saves in 23 games and could move up quickly.

Wojciechowski, Asher — SP — Houston

EXP MLB DEBUT: 2013 | POTENTIAL: #4 starter | 7B

Thrws R Age 24
2010 (1-S) The Citadel

Velo	Pitch	Grade
89-94	FB	+++
80-85	SL	+++
81-84	CU	++

Year	Lev	Team	W	L	Sv	IP	K	ERA	WHIP	BF/G	OBA	H%	S%	xERA	Ctl	Dom	Cmd	hr/9	BPV
2010	NCAA	The Citadel	12	3	0	126	155	3.58	1.14	29.3	239	34	70	3.00	2.3	11.1	4.8	0.7	156
2010	A-	Auburn	0	0	0	12	11	0.75	0.83	14.6	151	21	90	0.58	3.0	8.3	2.8	0.0	86
2011	A+	Dunedin	11	9	0	130	96	4.70	1.43	22.2	298	34	69	4.93	2.1	6.6	3.1	1.0	80
2012	A+	Dunedin	7	3	0	93	76	3.57	1.21	20.9	257	32	69	3.07	2.1	7.3	3.5	0.3	93
2012	AA	Corpus Christi	2	2	0	44	34	2.06	1.01	20.9	196	25	77	1.52	2.9	7.0	2.4	0.0	66

Big, strong SP who was promoted to AA upon acquisition from TOR. Could eventually end up in bullpen where FB and hard SL could play up. Hasn't shown much of touch or feel for CU and often rushes delivery. Throws strikes with all pitches, but can pitch tentatively instead of aggressively attacking hitters with his FB/SL.

Wood, Alex — SP — Atlanta

EXP MLB DEBUT: 2014 | POTENTIAL: #4 starter | 8D

Thrws L Age 22
2012 (2) Georgia

Velo	Pitch	Grade
90-94	FB	++++
	SL	++
	CU	+++

Year	Lev	Team	W	L	Sv	IP	K	ERA	WHIP	BF/G	OBA	H%	S%	xERA	Ctl	Dom	Cmd	hr/9	BPV
2010	NCAA	Georgia	0	0	0	1	1			3.9							1.0		
2011	NCAA	Georgia	6	7	0	101	79	4.44	1.39	28.5	289	34	69	4.46	2.2	7.0	3.2	0.8	84
2012	NCAA	Georgia	7	3	0	102	100	2.73	1.13	25.3	248	33	76	2.79	1.8	8.8	4.8	0.4	126
2012	A	Rome	4	3	0	53	52	2.22	1.01	15.5	208	28	77	1.80	2.4	8.9	3.7	0.2	113

Tall, athletic lefty with unorthodox delivery. Has a plus FB that sits at 90-94 mph and tops out at 96 mph along with a decent CU and below-average SL. Had a good pro debut going 4-3 with a 2.22 ERA, 14 BB/52 K in 52.2 IP. If he can smooth out his mechanics he has nice long-term potential.

Wood, Austin — SP — Los Angeles (A)

EXP MLB DEBUT: 2015 | POTENTIAL: #4 starter | 7D

Thrws R Age 22
2011 (6) USC

Velo	Pitch	Grade
91-96	FB	++++
81-83	SL	++
80-82	CU	++

Year	Lev	Team	W	L	Sv	IP	K	ERA	WHIP	BF/G	OBA	H%	S%	xERA	Ctl	Dom	Cmd	hr/9	BPV
2011	NCAA	USC	5	7	0	77	50	5.61	1.61	21.3	293	34	62	4.55	4.0	5.8	1.5	0.2	16
2011	Rk	Orem	0	0	0	1	1	20.30	3.01	3.9	516	52	33	19.09	0.0	6.8		6.8	140
2012	A	Cedar Rapids	5	12	0	128	109	4.30	1.54	21.4	258	33	70	3.91	5.1	7.7	1.5	0.3	19

Tall SP who had inconsistent season and finished 2nd in MWL in BB. Has impressive, pure stuff, but has trouble keeping mechanics in check. FB is best pitch, but loses sink and movement at higher velo. SL and CU have potential to be solid offerings, though needs to mix better and learn how to set up hitters.

Workman, Brandon — SP — Boston

EXP MLB DEBUT: 2014 | POTENTIAL: #4 starter | 7B

Thrws R Age 24
2010 (2) Texas

Velo	Pitch	Grade
89-95	FB	+++
86-89	CT	+++
75-77	CB	+++
83-84	CU	++

Year	Lev	Team	W	L	Sv	IP	K	ERA	WHIP	BF/G	OBA	H%	S%	xERA	Ctl	Dom	Cmd	hr/9	BPV
2009	NCAA	Texas	3	5	0	75	82	3.48	1.15	14.9	215	28	72	2.86	3.4	9.8	2.9	0.8	104
2010	NCAA	Texas	12	2	0	105	101	3.35	1.16	24.5	249	32	72	3.11	2.0	8.7	4.4	0.6	121
2011	A	Greenville	6	7	0	131	115	3.71	1.23	20.4	257	32	71	3.49	2.3	7.9	3.5	0.7	99
2012	A+	Salem	7	7	0	114	107	3.40	1.09	22.2	245	31	71	3.07	1.6	8.5	5.4	0.8	128
2012	AA	Portland	3	1	0	25	23	3.96	1.12	19.7	246	31	65	3.09	1.8	8.3	4.6	0.7	118

Tall, thin SP who was BOS minor league pitcher of year. Pure arm strength is asset for FB and holding velo deep. Rarely walks hitters and can throw four pitches in any count. Development of CT has been key, but can leave FB up. Slow CB has its moments and will need to repeat arm speed on CU.

Wright, Mike — SP — Baltimore

EXP MLB DEBUT: 2014 | POTENTIAL: #3 starter | 8D

Thrws R Age 23
2011 (3) East Carolina

Velo	Pitch	Grade
89-95	FB	+++
82-85	SL	+++
	CU	+++

Year	Lev	Team	W	L	Sv	IP	K	ERA	WHIP	BF/G	OBA	H%	S%	xERA	Ctl	Dom	Cmd	hr/9	BPV
2011	Rk	GCL Orioles	0	0	0	1	1	0.00	0.00	2.8	0	0	100	0.00	0.0	9.0		0.0	180
2011	A	Delmarva	1	1	0	14	12	10.53	1.83	15.9	353	40	41	7.69	2.6	7.9	3.0	2.0	89
2011	A-	Aberdeen	2	1	0	31	29	3.77	1.13	17.5	249	31	69	3.29	1.7	8.4	4.8	0.9	123
2012	A+	Frederick	5	2	0	46	35	2.91	1.12	22.8	265	32	76	3.23	1.0	6.8	7.0	0.6	114
2012	AA	Bowie	5	3	0	62	45	4.91	1.41	22.0	288	33	67	4.70	2.5	6.5	2.6	1.0	69

Long, strong RHP with intriguing upside as SP or RP. Uses height well to throw downhill and keep ball low. Relies on sinker/SL combo to induce GB. May lack a K pitch, but better sequencing could keep hitters off-guard. Throws too many strikes and needs to upgrade CU to have success against LHH.

Yambati, Robinson — SP — Kansas City

EXP MLB DEBUT: 2015 | POTENTIAL: #3 starter | 8E

Thrws R Age 22
2008 FA (DR)

Velo	Pitch	Grade
90-96	FB	+++
80-82	SL	+++
	CU	++

Year	Lev	Team	W	L	Sv	IP	K	ERA	WHIP	BF/G	OBA	H%	S%	xERA	Ctl	Dom	Cmd	hr/9	BPV
2009	Rk	Royals	2	3	1	27	18	8.89	2.01	11.0	347	39	54	7.15	4.6	5.9	1.3	1.0	0
2010	Rk	Royals	8	2	0	66	64	2.71	1.16	18.9	258	35	74	2.67	1.6	8.7	5.3	0.0	130
2011	Rk	Burlington	0	5	0	18	9	18.85	3.11	13.1	469	48	37	14.51	5.6	4.6	0.8	3.1	-51
2012	A	Kane County	2	1	2	45	33	3.22	1.28	11.4	241	30	73	2.95	3.4	6.6	1.9	0.2	45
2012	A+	Wilmington	2	1	5	25	31	2.16	1.28	6.0	238	36	81	2.68	3.6	11.2	3.1	0.0	122

Tall, lean RHP who primarily worked out of bullpen. K rate increased and stymied LHH despite less than stellar CU. Generates lots of leverage and power in ¾ delivery and keeps ball low to induce GB. Hard SL can be potent and gets Ks against hitters from both sides. Inconsistent velo has been problem.

Ybarra, Tyler — RP — Toronto

EXP MLB DEBUT: 2015 | POTENTIAL: Setup reliever | 7D

Thrws L Age 23
2008 (43) HS (KS)

Velo	Pitch	Grade
87-92	FB	+++
81-83	SL	+++
80-82	CU	++

Year	Lev	Team	W	L	Sv	IP	K	ERA	WHIP	BF/G	OBA	H%	S%	xERA	Ctl	Dom	Cmd	hr/9	BPV
2009	Rk	GCL Blue Jays	2	4	0	20	11	6.64	1.92	6.0	336	38	63	6.22	4.4	4.9	1.1	0.4	-14
2011	Rk	Bluefield	2	0	0	46	54	2.15	1.09	12.8	208	30	81	2.19	3.1	10.6	3.4	0.4	124
2012	A	Lansing	3	2	2	44	57	2.27	1.47	7.2	236	35	85	3.50	5.4	11.7	2.2	0.4	85

Tall, lean RP who is sleeper. Needs to be challenged due to age and could advance quickly. Works fast with lively FB and has nasty SL that dominates LHH. BB have haunted him and he's had trouble repeating delivery that features effort. Could be solid situational guy, but has pitch mix to project to more.

Zimmer, Kyle — SP — Kansas City

EXP MLB DEBUT: 2014 | POTENTIAL: #2 starter | 9C

Thrws R Age 21
2012 (1) San Francisco

Velo	Pitch	Grade
92-99	FB	++++
80-81	CB	+++
82-84	SL	+++
83-85	CU	+++

Year	Lev	Team	W	L	Sv	IP	K	ERA	WHIP	BF/G	OBA	H%	S%	xERA	Ctl	Dom	Cmd	hr/9	BPV
2010	NCAA	San Francisco	0	0	0	5	7	8.44	1.50	4.6	347	47	43	6.47	0.0	11.8		1.7	231
2011	NCAA	San Francisco	6	4	1	92	89	3.73	1.28	18.8	265	35	69	3.33	2.4	8.7	3.7	0.3	112
2012	NCAA	San Francisco	5	3	0	88	104	2.85	1.04	26.2	231	33	72	2.29	1.7	10.6	6.1	0.3	162
2012	Rk	Royals	1	0	0	10	13	0.90	0.50	11.1	151	25	80	0.00	0.0	11.7		0.0	229
2012	A	Kane County	2	3	0	30	29	2.43	1.42	20.9	289	38	83	4.04	2.4	8.8	3.6	0.3	111

Tall, athletic SP with plenty of projection and upside. Electric and quick arm produces plus-plus velo and late FB movement. Uses hard SL and late-breaking CB. CU has potential to become best secondary offering. Controls all pitches and needs to be more efficient. Repeats delivery and keeps BB to minimum.

Zych, Tony — RP — Chicago (N)

EXP MLB DEBUT: 2013 | POTENTIAL: Possible closer | 7C

Thrws R Age 22
2011 (4) Louisville

Velo	Pitch	Grade
94-97	FB	++++
83-85	SL	+++

Year	Lev	Team	W	L	Sv	IP	K	ERA	WHIP	BF/G	OBA	H%	S%	xERA	Ctl	Dom	Cmd	hr/9	BPV
2011	NCAA	Louisville	0	2	13	30	30	3.00	1.43	4.6	255	34	79	3.60	4.2	9.0	2.1	0.3	67
2011	Rk	Cubs	0	0	0	2	3	4.50	1.50	4.3	262	43	67	3.53	4.5	13.5	3.0	0.0	140
2011	A-	Boise	0	0	0	2	2	0.00	0.50	3.3	0	0	100	0.00	4.5	9.0	2.0	0.0	59
2012	A+	Daytona	3	3	6	37	36	3.19	1.06	5.3	236	32	67	2.14	1.7	8.8	5.1	0.0	131
2012	AA	Tennessee	2	1	0	25	28	4.38	1.54	5.4	272	38	70	4.15	4.4	10.2	2.3	0.4	84

Reliever with a plus 94-97 mph FB and a good SL. Throws from a low 3/4 slot adding some nice deception and good movement. Jumped from rookie ball to High-A where he pitched effectively, earning him a mid-season promotion to AA. Clearly on the fast-track to the majors and has been good so far.

MAJOR LEAGUE EQUIVALENTS

In his 1985 *Baseball Abstract,* Bill James introduced the concept of major league equivalencies. His assertion was that, with the proper adjustments, a minor leaguer's statistics could be converted to an equivalent major league level performance with a great deal of accuracy.

Because of wide variations in the level of play among different minor leagues, it is difficult to get a true reading on a player's potential. For instance, a .300 batting average achieved in the high-offense Pacific Coast League is not nearly as much of an accomplishment as a similar level in the Eastern League. MLEs normalize these types of variances, for all statistical categories.

The actual MLEs are not projections. They represent how a player's previous performance might look at the major league level. However, the MLE stat line can be used in forecasting future performance in just the same way as a major league stat line would.

The model we use contains a few variations to James' version and updates all of the minor league and ballpark factors. In addition, we designed a module to convert pitching statistics, which is something James did not originally do.

Do MLEs really work?

Used correctly, MLEs are excellent indicators of potential. But just like we cannot take traditional major league statistics at face value, the same goes for MLEs. The underlying measures of base skill — batting eye ratios, pitching command ratios, etc. — are far more accurate in evaluating future talent than raw home runs, batting averages or ERAs.

The charts we present here also provide the unique perspective of looking at up to five years' worth of data. Ironically, the longer the history, the less likely the player is a legitimate prospect — he should have made it to the majors before compiling a long history in AA and/or AAA ball. Of course, the shorter trends are more difficult to read despite them often belonging to players with higher ceilings. But even here we can find small indications of players improving their skills, or struggling, as they rise through more difficult levels of competition. Since players — especially those with any talent — are promoted rapidly through major league systems, a two or three-year scan is often all we get to spot any trends.

Here are some things to look for as you scan these charts:

Target players who...

- spent a full year in AA and then a full year in AAA
- had consistent playing time from one year to the next
- improved their base skills as they were promoted

Raise the warning flag for players who...

- were stuck at a level for multiple seasons, or regressed
- displayed marked changes in playing time from one year to the next
- showed large drops in BPIs from one year to the next

Players are listed on the charts if they spent at least part of 2007-2011 in Triple-A or Double-A and had at least 100 AB or 30 IP within those two levels. Each is listed with the organization with which they finished the season.

Only statistics accumulated in Triple-A and Double-A ball are included (players who split a season are indicated as a/a); Single-A stats are excluded.

Each player's actual AB and IP totals are used as the base for the conversion. However, it is more useful to compare performances using common levels, so rely on the ratios and sabermetric gauges. Complete explanations of these formulas appear in the Glossary.

BATTER	B	Yr	Age	Pos	Lev	Tm	AB	R	H	D	T	HR	RBI	BB	K	SB	CS	BA	OB	Slg	OPS	bb%	Ct%	Eye	PX	SX	RC/G	BPV
Adams,David	R	10	23	2B	aa	NYY	152	25	40	13	2	3	26	16	27	4	2	264	333	432	765	9%	83%	0.59	116	132	5.17	83
		12	25	2B	aa	NYY	327	34	86	19	0	7	37	30	61	2	1	263	325	387	712	8%	81%	0.49	86	42	3.67	26
Adams,Matt	L	12	24	1B	aaa	STL	258	30	70	18	0	12	37	12	66	2	1	272	303	483	786	4%	74%	0.18	149	48	4.32	42
Adrianza,Ehire	B	12	23	SS	aa	SF	451	46	91	21	4	2	28	35	99	14	4	203	261	285	546	7%	78%	0.35	61	116	1.88	12
Aguilar,Jesus	R	12	22	1B	aa	CLE	72	11	20	6	0	3	12	12	26	0	0	277	381	471	852	14%	64%	0.47	166	26	5.22	28
Almonte,Zoilo	B	11	22	OF	aa	NYY	175	18	40	10	1	3	18	11	49	3	1	226	273	336	610	6%	72%	0.24	77	83	3.17	-10
		12	23	OF	aa	NYY	419	51	105	20	1	19	56	20	113	12	4	250	285	439	724	5%	73%	0.18	129	88	3.72	33
Anderson,Lars	L	08	21	1B	aa	BOS	133	22	40	14	0	4	24	23	34	1	0	304	407	501	908	15%	75%	0.69	141	46	8.21	57
		09	22	1B	aa	BOS	447	42	102	26	0	7	43	54	92	2	0	228	311	334	645	11%	79%	0.58	76	42	3.78	15
		10	23	1B	a/a	BOS	471	47	120	40	2	11	53	38	96	2	3	254	310	416	726	8%	80%	0.40	115	52	4.53	43
		11	24	1B	aaa	BOS	491	53	120	33	2	11	63	65	131	4	0	245	333	385	717	12%	73%	0.50	97	67	4.76	16
		12	25	1B	aaa	CLE	396	39	82	23	1	6	44	48	125	1	0	207	292	320	613	11%	69%	0.38	95	49	2.41	-12
Anderson,Leslie	L	10	28	OF	a/a	TAM	303	28	76	13	1	6	28	17	47	3	1	250	289	360	649	5%	85%	0.36	73	60	3.67	27
		11	29	1B	aaa	TAM	462	32	98	18	0	9	45	15	78	1	4	211	236	308	544	3%	83%	0.19	64	29	2.31	1
		12	30	OF	aaa	TAM	444	44	104	16	0	10	39	18	74	0	4	234	264	335	599	4%	83%	0.24	64	27	2.52	2
Arenado,Nolan	R	12	21	3B	aa	COL	516	49	148	38	1	12	49	34	57	0	2	287	332	434	766	6%	89%	0.60	94	26	4.16	53
Asche,Cody	L	12	22	3B	aa	PHI	263	33	71	18	2	8	37	17	62	1	1	269	315	449	764	6%	76%	0.28	125	70	3.93	41
Avery,Xavier	L	10	20	OF	aa	BAL	107	8	24	5	0	3	14	5	25	8	0	221	257	356	613	5%	76%	0.20	87	91	3.44	14
		11	21	OF	aa	BAL	557	63	137	29	2	4	23	42	163	32	15	245	298	324	622	7%	71%	0.26	60	107	3.32	-21
		12	22	OF	aaa	BAL	390	51	88	12	4	8	31	45	111	20	7	226	306	338	644	10%	72%	0.41	78	124	2.91	9
Barfield,Jeremy	R	11	23	OF	aa	OAK	495	39	104	20	2	7	51	29	103	1	1	210	254	302	557	6%	79%	0.28	62	48	2.58	-6
		12	24	OF	aa	OAK	482	50	109	24	1	9	48	27	96	1	0	225	266	333	599	5%	80%	0.28	75	46	2.46	6
Beckham,Tim	R	12	22	SS	aaa	TAM	285	33	65	9	1	5	23	24	79	5	0	227	286	315	602	8%	72%	0.30	64	87	2.72	-17
Bell,Josh	B	10	24	3B	aaa	BAL	316	34	79	22	0	12	40	18	63	2	5	251	291	431	722	5%	80%	0.28	118	40	4.13	39
		11	25	3B	aaa	BAL	395	47	87	10	1	16	43	29	133	3	0	220	274	374	648	7%	66%	0.22	89	76	3.56	-25
		12	26	3B	aaa	ARI	360	36	81	22	2	8	45	22	94	2	6	226	271	360	631	6%	74%	0.24	100	58	2.41	7
Belnome,Vince	L	11	23	2B	aa	SD	267	42	72	15	1	11	46	37	72	0	6	269	359	458	817	12%	73%	0.51	118	41	5.68	25
		12	24	DH	aaa	SD	258	19	55	8	1	3	22	31	89	3	1	211	296	285	581	11%	65%	0.35	62	58	2.39	-48
Beltre,Engel	L	10	21	OF	aa	TEX	181	12	45	4	4	1	12	8	19	7	2	250	283	336	619	4%	89%	0.42	49	150	3.36	52
		11	22	OF	aa	TEX	437	49	92	14	6	1	21	21	109	12	6	210	247	272	519	5%	75%	0.20	42	145	2.20	-12
		12	23	OF	aa	TEX	564	63	137	16	16	12	43	21	124	28	11	244	270	390	660	4%	78%	0.17	85	146	2.76	33
Benson,Joe	R	10	23	OF	aa	MIN	373	50	81	17	5	17	38	29	90	11	11	217	274	426	700	7%	76%	0.32	123	139	3.57	60
		11	23	OF	aa	MIN	400	50	98	26	3	10	49	42	118	9	10	244	316	397	713	10%	70%	0.36	101	102	4.18	15
		12	24	OF	a/a	MIN	236	18	37	8	2	4	22	19	78	6	3	159	223	259	481	8%	67%	0.25	76	107	1.36	-21
Bethancourt,Christian	R	12	21	C	aa	ATL	268	26	60	5	1	2	23	10	50	7	6	224	251	266	518	3%	81%	0.19	28	82	1.87	-18
Bogaerts,Xander	R	12	20	SS	aa	BOS	92	10	30	11	0	4	15	1	22	1	1	324	330	579	909	1%	77%	0.04	187	44	5.51	73
Bradley,Jackie	L	12	22	OF	aa	BOS	229	31	60	17	2	5	24	29	52	7	3	260	343	412	755	11%	77%	0.56	110	94	3.80	50
Brantly,Rob	L	12	23	C	a/a	MIA	362	27	94	21	1	4	33	17	57	0	3	260	293	351	644	4%	84%	0.29	66	27	2.80	8
Brentz,Bryce	R	12	24	OF	a/a	BOS	473	51	126	31	1	13	62	33	150	6	6	267	314	419	734	6%	68%	0.22	123	58	3.71	4
Brown,Gary	R	12	24	OF	aa	SF	538	64	135	31	2	6	37	34	99	29	20	250	295	345	640	6%	82%	0.34	70	104	2.61	28
Calhoun,Kole	L	12	25	OF	aaa	LAA	410	51	94	23	4	9	47	28	106	8	4	229	279	367	645	6%	74%	0.27	99	105	2.69	22
Castellanos,Alex	R	11	25	OF	aa	LA	475	72	122	29	4	16	60	26	144	10	2	257	296	435	731	5%	70%	0.18	113	134	4.57	21
		12	26	2B	aaa	LA	344	44	84	19	3	10	31	27	106	10	10	245	299	406	705	7%	69%	0.25	121	104	3.07	21
Castellanos,Nick	R	12	20	OF	aa	DET	322	29	78	13	1	6	21	11	77	4	4	244	269	344	614	3%	76%	0.15	71	67	2.59	-10
Castro,Leandro	R	12	23	OF	aa	PHI	478	51	120	32	1	8	55	13	79	10	10	251	271	370	641	3%	83%	0.17	84	75	2.59	31
Cavazos-Galvez,B	R	11	24	1B	aa	LA	411	43	93	22	3	10	44	8	75	9	13	226	241	364	605	2%	82%	0.11	91	102	2.54	36
		12	25	OF	a/a	LA	256	30	60	11	2	7	29	7	49	4	1	236	257	379	636	3%	81%	0.15	90	93	2.78	31
Chambers,Adron	L	10	24	OF	a/a	STL	321	46	76	8	4	4	25	29	51	11	6	238	302	324	626	8%	84%	0.58	51	134	3.40	37
		11	25	OF	aaa	STL	426	51	95	15	3	6	30	37	105	15	15	222	285	318	603	8%	75%	0.35	62	111	2.83	2
		12	26	OF	aaa	STL	357	42	91	14	1	2	31	38	96	9	5	255	326	316	642	10%	73%	0.39	50	83	3.00	-22
Chiang,Chih-Hsien	L	10	22	OF	aa	BOS	438	40	106	37	1	8	48	23	46	1	0	242	280	386	666	5%	89%	0.50	105	47	3.77	68
		11	23	OF	aa	SEA	451	63	118	38	3	13	69	25	107	6	5	261	300	447	747	5%	76%	0.24	127	98	4.63	49
		12	24	OF	a/a	SEA	449	32	93	20	2	5	37	18	94	2	5	207	237	295	532	4%	79%	0.19	63	51	1.77	-8
Choice,Michael	R	12	23	OF	aa	OAK	359	45	87	13	2	7	43	26	101	4	1	242	292	345	637	7%	72%	0.25	75	84	2.96	-13
Colon,Christian	R	11	22	SS	aa	KC	491	51	111	13	2	5	45	33	54	12	8	226	275	291	566	6%	89%	0.62	43	87	2.70	31
		12	23	SS	a/a	KC	290	27	75	9	2	4	24	25	30	9	7	260	318	345	663	8%	90%	0.81	50	79	3.15	40
Cox,Zack	L	11	22	3B	aa	STL	352	35	83	15	0	6	31	19	78	0	1	236	275	331	606	5%	78%	0.25	65	31	3.12	-14
		12	23	3B	a/a	MIA	394	32	86	25	1	7	34	18	101	1	0	219	253	340	593	4%	74%	0.18	94	45	2.26	-3
Crumbliss,Conner	L	12	25	OF	aa	OAK	470	68	99	17	5	7	33	89	117	17	9	210	336	310	645	16%	75%	0.76	69	111	2.74	23
Culberson,Charlie	R	11	22	2B	aa	SF	553	59	133	33	2	8	48	19	138	12	4	241	266	352	618	3%	75%	0.14	79	98	3.19	1
		12	23	2B	aaa	COL	476	44	108	22	5	8	40	13	99	9	4	226	246	348	594	3%	79%	0.13	81	105	2.23	20
Cunningham,Todd	B	12	23	OF	aa	ATL	466	65	130	21	5	2	43	33	58	20	9	279	326	360	686	7%	87%	0.56	53	121	3.39	44
Danks,Jordan	L	09	23	OF	aa	CHW	284	43	63	11	1	6	17	32	65	6	3	221	300	328	628	10%	77%	0.50	69	94	3.46	14
		10	24	OF	aaa	CHW	445	47	92	23	2	7	32	32	127	12	7	207	260	313	573	7%	71%	0.25	73	99	2.67	-11
		11	25	OF	aaa	CHW	463	51	102	21	4	13	51	48	184	14	5	221	294	366	660	9%	60%	0.26	90	125	3.76	-29
		12	26	OF	aaa	CHW	218	31	61	15	1	8	25	40	80	5	4	278	390	458	849	16%	63%	0.50	152	67	5.15	28
Darnell,James	R	10	23	3B	aa	SD	373	39	83	18	1	8	43	39	60	2	0	223	297	339	636	10%	84%	0.65	77	57	3.60	35
		11	24	3B	a/a	SD	422	54	99	21	1	13	52	47	99	1	1	234	311	383	693	10%	77%	0.48	95	48	4.22	19
		12	25	3B	aaa	SD	116	15	23	4	0	4	14	11	32	1	1	199	270	347	617	9%	73%	0.36	101	50	1.77	6
Davis,Kentrail	L	12	24	OF	aa	MIL	438	43	105	21	5	6	32	44	141	15	12	241	309	354	663	9%	68%	0.31	89	104	2.75	-6
Decker,Jaff	L	11	21	OF	aa	SD	496	67	95	23	1	13	69	82	168	11	6	192	306	321	627	14%	66%	0.49	83	88	3.46	-12
		12	22	OF	aa	SD	147	23	23	2	2	2	7	33	42	5	2	154	309	236	546	18%	71%	0.78	54	116	1.89	1
Dickerson,Corey	L	12	23	OF	aa	COL	266	34	72	16	3	13	32	15	51	6	3	271	311	497	807	5%	81%	0.30	139	100	4.37	77
Dietrich,Derek	L	12	23	2B	aa	TAM	133	18	31	6	1	3	14	6	41	0	1	235	266	364	630	4%	69%	0.13	97	75	2.59	-14
Eaton,Adam	L	11	23	OF	aa	ARI	212	22	57	7	4	3	20	21	38	7	7	268	334	376	711	9%	82%	0.55	65	131	4.29	39
		12	24	OF	a/a	ARI	528	89	170	42	5	5	33	39	88	30	13	323	370	448	818	7%	83%	0.45	91	124	4.82	59
Erickson,Gorman	B	11	23	C	aa	LA	142	13	32	7	0	5	19	8	25	1	0	229	268	381	649	5%	82%	0.30	96	36	3.53	28
		12	24	C	aa	LA	274	20	55	13	1	2	20	34	63	1	2	200	287	277	565	11%	77%	0.53	61	34	2.00	-10

BATTER	B	Yr	Age	Pos	Lev	Tm	AB	R	H	D	T	HR	RBI	BB	K	SB	CS	BA	OB	Slg	OPS	bb%	Ct%	Eye	PX	SX	RC/G	BPV
Fairley,Wendell	L	11	23	OF	aa	SF	98	9	24	3	2	0	6	7	29	2	2	245	293	312	605	6%	70%	0.23	42	140	3.02	-29
		12	24	OF	aa	SF	109	5	22	5	0	0	8	11	37	1	1	198	272	241	513	9%	66%	0.29	47	29	1.67	-70
Federowicz,Tim	R	11	24	C	a/a	LA	422	40	94	21	0	9	44	28	100	1	0	223	272	335	607	6%	76%	0.28	77	36	3.16	-8
		12	25	C	aaa	LA	412	43	92	26	0	7	46	30	110	0	1	222	276	336	611	7%	73%	0.28	91	36	2.40	-8
Fields,Daniel	L	12	21	OF	aa	DET	106	11	26	4	0	2	6	10	22	7	1	241	309	322	631	9%	80%	0.48	56	83	3.24	8
Flores,Wilmer	R	12	21	3B	aa	NYM	251	31	66	15	2	7	28	16	33	0	0	261	306	412	718	6%	87%	0.50	92	49	3.61	50
Franklin,Nick	B	12	21	SS	a/a	SEA	472	52	115	28	6	9	45	40	122	10	4	244	304	384	688	8%	74%	0.33	102	107	3.04	28
Fuentes,Reymond	L	12	21	OF	aa	SD	473	42	87	17	3	3	27	44	152	28	10	184	253	252	505	8%	68%	0.29	56	123	1.68	-28
Galvez,Jonathan	R	12	21	2B	aa	SD	312	38	78	17	2	4	28	27	81	10	3	249	308	357	665	8%	74%	0.33	83	98	3.08	9
Garcia,Avisail	R	12	21	OF	aa	DET	215	26	62	8	3	5	18	6	39	7	4	289	307	423	730	3%	82%	0.14	81	115	3.77	33
Garcia,Leury	B	12	21	2B	aa	TEX	377	45	105	12	11	2	24	18	81	25	7	280	313	381	694	5%	79%	0.22	62	149	3.35	20
Gennett,Scooter	L	12	22	2B	aa	MIL	533	55	142	29	2	4	36	24	80	9	5	267	298	351	649	4%	85%	0.30	60	74	2.98	21
Gillaspie,Conor	L	10	23	3B	aa	SF	491	50	132	24	7	7	58	31	59	0	4	269	313	387	701	6%	88%	0.53	76	72	4.26	49
		11	24	3B	aaa	SF	428	40	103	18	4	7	39	42	92	6	11	240	307	350	657	9%	79%	0.45	71	82	3.53	16
		12	25	3B	aaa	SF	413	40	92	15	2	8	33	26	65	0	0	222	269	329	599	6%	84%	0.41	66	45	2.50	18
Gillies,Tyson	L	10	22	OF	aa	PHI	105	11	21	2	1	2	5	4	18	2	2	202	232	298	530	4%	83%	0.23	55	111	2.12	19
		12	24	OF	aa	PHI	276	45	72	11	6	3	18	14	60	6	7	262	297	379	677	5%	78%	0.23	76	134	2.82	25
Gindl,Caleb	L	10	22	OF	aa	MIL	463	49	111	30	1	7	48	46	65	8	6	240	308	354	663	9%	86%	0.71	83	67	3.81	50
		11	23	OF	aaa	MIL	472	59	122	19	3	11	42	46	111	4	6	258	323	384	707	9%	77%	0.41	80	79	4.37	13
		12	24	OF	aaa	MIL	452	43	104	25	4	10	40	30	114	3	1	231	279	370	649	6%	75%	0.26	99	78	2.76	16
Gomes,Yan	R	11	24	C	a/a	TOR	290	24	59	16	1	9	36	18	94	0	0	202	249	358	606	6%	68%	0.19	100	31	2.97	-26
		12	25	C	aaa	TOR	305	29	81	24	1	9	38	16	88	3	0	267	304	443	747	5%	71%	0.19	137	57	3.84	24
Gomez,Hector	R	11	23	SS	aa	COL	425	32	89	21	5	11	35	13	98	11	4	210	233	361	593	3%	77%	0.13	94	126	2.71	29
Gonzalez,Elevys	B	12	23	2B	aa	PIT	148	8	26	5	1	2	12	11	43	1	3	175	233	254	486	7%	71%	0.26	62	51	1.33	-36
Goodwin,Brian	L	12	22	OF	aa	WAS	166	14	34	7	1	4	12	14	52	2	3	203	265	332	597	8%	68%	0.27	98	65	2.21	-11
Green,Grant	R	11	24	SS	aa	OAK	530	53	124	27	1	6	43	27	140	4	9	234	271	321	592	5%	74%	0.19	63	53	2.80	-28
		12	25	OF	aaa	OAK	524	50	124	23	4	9	52	23	91	9	11	236	268	351	619	4%	83%	0.25	73	87	2.42	25
Green,Taylor	L	09	23	3B	aa	MIL	306	28	71	14	0	4	35	29	32	0	1	232	299	317	616	9%	90%	0.91	61	24	3.34	33
		10	24	3B	aa	MIL	393	40	88	25	1	11	64	37	57	0	2	224	292	377	668	9%	85%	0.65	102	33	3.76	53
		11	25	3B	a/a	MIL	431	54	120	31	1	17	65	41	93	1	0	279	341	469	810	9%	79%	0.44	125	41	5.96	45
		12	26	3B	aaa	MIL	282	18	65	15	0	6	22	22	69	1	4	230	286	344	630	7%	75%	0.32	85	18	2.62	-8
Gregorius,Didi	L	12	22	SS	a/a	CIN	501	59	123	19	9	6	45	34	88	3	6	245	293	357	650	6%	82%	0.39	69	87	2.67	26
Guyer,Brandon	R	09	23	OF	aa	CHC	189	18	32	12	1	1	12	8	30	6	6	171	204	259	463	4%	84%	0.26	68	115	1.48	36
		10	24	OF	aa	CHC	369	56	109	35	4	10	42	20	41	22	4	297	333	489	822	5%	89%	0.50	132	150	6.17	119
		11	25	OF	aaa	TAM	388	60	102	24	4	10	47	27	94	12	7	263	311	429	740	7%	76%	0.29	107	140	4.61	45
		12	26	OF	aaa	TAM	85	7	21	2	1	2	10	5	18	2	0	243	287	369	656	6%	79%	0.29	77	72	3.19	11
Gyorko,Jedd	R	11	23	3B	aa	SD	236	30	55	9	0	5	29	20	61	1	0	231	292	329	621	8%	74%	0.33	65	49	3.42	-18
		12	24	3B	a/a	SD	499	58	122	22	0	20	73	39	118	4	5	245	301	408	709	7%	76%	0.33	107	42	3.58	20
Hamilton,Billy	B	12	22	SS	aa	CIN	175	29	47	4	4	1	13	32	47	45	17	271	384	359	743	15%	73%	0.68	55	174	4.00	22
Havens,Reese	L	10	24	2B	aa	NYM	68	9	20	2	1	4	9	4	11	0	3	288	327	519	846	5%	83%	0.35	128	97	5.16	78
		11	25	2B	aa	NYM	211	26	49	12	1	4	18	19	71	1	0	232	296	354	650	8%	66%	0.27	83	72	3.75	-27
		12	26	2B	aa	NYM	325	31	53	10	0	7	29	42	132	1	1	162	257	261	519	11%	59%	0.32	86	33	1.78	-59
Hazelbaker,Jeremy	L	11	24	OF	aa	BOS	354	42	81	18	2	8	29	30	117	25	9	229	289	360	649	8%	67%	0.25	85	130	3.55	-7
		12	25	OF	a/a	BOS	466	63	114	24	5	15	54	27	137	29	13	245	287	410	697	6%	71%	0.20	119	138	3.18	32
Head,Miles	R	12	21	3B	aa	OAK	213	20	51	8	2	4	22	13	84	0	1	239	282	343	625	6%	61%	0.15	89	61	2.67	-54
Hechavarria,Adeiny	R	10	21	SS	aa	TOR	253	27	61	10	1	2	26	9	32	5	4	240	266	311	577	3%	87%	0.29	51	87	2.72	26
		11	22	SS	a/a	TOR	572	53	129	24	7	6	41	24	113	14	17	225	256	322	578	4%	80%	0.21	64	116	2.51	17
		12	23	SS	aaa	TOR	443	54	117	17	5	4	43	26	100	6	2	263	304	354	658	6%	77%	0.26	63	100	3.08	3
Hernandez,Cesar	B	12	22	2B	a/a	PHI	532	52	142	28	9	2	47	26	86	18	16	266	300	363	664	5%	84%	0.30	65	115	2.66	33
Herrmann,Chris	L	12	25	C	aa	MIN	490	70	114	22	1	7	47	45	102	2	1	234	298	323	621	8%	79%	0.44	64	60	2.72	5
Hicks,Aaron	B	12	23	OF	aa	MIN	472	80	120	19	9	9	49	64	128	26	12	255	344	392	736	12%	73%	0.50	93	144	3.64	35
Holt,Brock	L	11	23	2B	aa	PIT	511	50	132	27	7	1	32	39	90	15	11	258	311	343	654	7%	82%	0.44	62	120	3.67	32
		12	24	SS	a/a	PIT	477	54	147	28	5	2	41	39	64	13	15	308	360	401	761	8%	87%	0.61	65	87	3.94	42
Hood,Destin	R	12	22	OF	aa	WAS	355	37	79	19	2	3	37	19	93	5	1	223	263	310	573	5%	74%	0.20	70	96	2.14	-8
Iglesias,Jose	R	10	20	SS	aa	BOS	221	23	60	11	2	0	10	6	34	4	2	270	290	340	630	3%	85%	0.18	54	103	3.46	20
		11	21	SS	aaa	BOS	357	30	80	10	0	1	27	18	60	10	4	225	263	261	523	5%	83%	0.30	29	76	2.35	-10
		12	22	SS	aaa	BOS	353	39	90	10	1	1	20	23	49	10	3	255	300	294	594	6%	86%	0.47	28	89	2.74	8
Jackson,Brett	L	10	22	OF	aa	CHC	228	35	56	12	3	5	21	23	47	14	5	246	315	390	705	9%	79%	0.49	92	157	4.34	59
		11	23	OF	a/a	CHC	431	57	100	20	3	14	39	49	154	14	8	232	311	392	703	10%	64%	0.32	99	116	4.19	-7
		12	24	OF	aaa	CHC	407	47	89	18	9	11	34	34	180	19	6	219	279	391	670	8%	56%	0.19	149	142	2.79	3
Jackson,Ryan	R	11	23	SS	aa	STL	533	41	117	27	2	6	46	28	104	1	0	219	258	312	571	5%	80%	0.27	67	52	2.76	3
		12	24	SS	aaa	STL	445	44	99	19	1	7	34	33	86	1	0	223	277	313	590	7%	81%	0.38	63	49	2.45	4
James,Jiwan	B	12	23	OF	aa	PHI	381	43	83	13	4	5	24	16	128	6	9	217	249	306	556	4%	66%	0.13	70	102	1.89	-38
Jensen,Kyle	R	11	23	OF	aa	FLA	80	10	17	1	1	3	7	5	28	1	0	211	261	370	631	6%	65%	0.20	85	100	3.31	-26
		12	24	OF	aa	MIA	445	55	87	18	2	17	66	57	184	1	1	197	287	357	645	11%	59%	0.31	135	55	2.81	-17
Jimenez,Luis	R	11	23	3B	aa	LAA	490	52	126	35	1	15	79	22	79	13	7	258	289	424	714	4%	84%	0.27	112	79	4.19	59
		12	24	3B	aaa	LAA	485	52	118	30	1	10	57	12	83	11	8	244	263	373	637	3%	83%	0.15	88	85	2.61	35
Jones,Mycal	R	11	24	OF	aa	ATL	373	46	78	21	1	5	26	41	105	12	7	209	288	309	597	10%	72%	0.39	72	92	3.03	-6
		12	25	OF	aa	ATL	85	9	10	0	0	0	0	7	29	6	6	120	190	120	310	8%	66%	0.25	0	111	0.54	-87
Joseph,Corban	L	10	22	2B	aa	NYY	111	9	20	5	2	0	11	13	27	1	0	182	269	264	532	11%	76%	0.49	56	121	2.51	8
		11	23	2B	aa	NYY	499	59	121	33	5	5	46	48	116	3	3	243	309	356	665	9%	77%	0.41	81	93	3.89	19
		12	24	2B	a/a	NYY	413	47	100	25	1	14	49	55	78	0	1	243	332	409	741	12%	81%	0.70	108	34	3.79	46
Joseph,Tommy	R	12	21	C	aa	PHI	404	35	93	22	0	9	38	27	105	0	4	231	280	353	632	6%	74%	0.26	91	18	2.62	-11
Kieschnick,Roger	L	10	23	OF	aa	SF	223	19	52	8	3	3	20	15	49	2	3	233	280	334	614	6%	78%	0.30	63	95	3.12	6
		11	24	OF	aa	SF	459	58	105	20	5	13	53	28	134	11	8	228	272	376	648	6%	71%	0.21	91	126	3.34	7
		12	25	OF	aaa	SF	222	33	54	11	3	9	27	16	82	0	2	243	293	440	733	7%	63%	0.19	152	87	3.45	15
Kobernus,Jeff	R	12	24	2B	aa	WAS	330	33	82	9	1	1	15	14	63	33	12	247	279	291	570	4%	81%	0.23	32	121	2.42	-4

BATTER	B	Yr	Age	Pos	Lev	Tm	AB	R	H	D	T	HR	RBI	BB	K	SB	CS	BA	OB	Slg	OPS	bb%	Ct%	Eye	PX	SX	RC/G	BPV
Kozma,Peter	R	09	21	SS	aa	STL	407	40	77	13	2	4	29	33	65	3	2	189	250	261	511	8%	84%	0.51	48	76	2.19	14
		10	22	SS	aa	STL	503	53	105	24	1	9	56	43	84	10	2	209	271	314	585	8%	83%	0.51	72	86	2.97	34
		11	23	SS	aaa	STL	398	34	70	14	1	2	33	26	101	1	2	176	227	233	460	6%	75%	0.26	42	61	1.72	-35
Krauss,Marc	L	11	24	OF	aa	ARI	433	48	91	23	6	11	45	44	136	1	3	210	283	367	649	9%	69%	0.32	98	99	3.48	3
		12	25	OF	a/a	HOU	432	59	93	25	1	14	52	56	140	5	6	215	305	376	682	11%	68%	0.40	125	70	2.99	17
Lagares,Juan	R	11	22	OF	aa	NYM	162	16	53	10	3	1	17	4	33	8	2	324	340	442	782	2%	80%	0.12	80	140	5.69	31
		12	23	OF	aa	NYM	499	56	114	23	4	3	39	29	104	17	11	228	271	311	582	5%	79%	0.28	60	113	2.13	12
Laird,Brandon	R	10	23	3B	a/a	NYY	531	72	133	24	1	24	85	36	96	2	2	251	299	432	731	6%	82%	0.38	109	54	4.52	46
		11	24	3B	aaa	NYY	462	43	109	24	0	16	58	15	93	0	0	236	259	389	648	3%	80%	0.16	98	22	3.43	13
		12	25	3B	aaa	NYY	503	42	110	26	1	13	60	27	117	1	0	219	259	357	616	5%	77%	0.23	95	40	2.54	7
Lake,Junior	R	11	21	SS	aa	CHC	242	31	54	9	1	5	13	10	64	14	2	222	252	330	582	4%	73%	0.15	69	144	2.93	2
		12	22	SS	aa	CHC	405	45	103	24	3	8	41	29	114	17	13	255	305	388	693	7%	72%	0.25	101	100	3.06	13
LaMarre,Ryan	R	12	24	OF	aa	CIN	482	58	115	20	2	5	27	51	136	26	11	238	311	318	630	10%	72%	0.38	63	108	2.80	-9
Lambo,Andrew	L	09	21	OF	aa	LA	492	61	115	35	1	10	53	34	84	3	3	234	284	372	656	7%	83%	0.41	97	64	3.61	44
		10	22	OF	aa	PIT	272	31	67	11	1	5	29	19	55	1	1	246	296	349	645	7%	80%	0.35	68	59	3.63	6
		11	23	OF	a/a	PIT	437	43	90	25	0	8	46	33	113	4	3	207	263	321	584	7%	74%	0.30	80	54	2.81	-7
		12	24	OF	aa	PIT	92	11	20	3	1	3	13	11	20	0	1	219	302	364	666	11%	78%	0.55	88	61	2.98	24
Lee,Hak-Ju	L	11	21	SS	aa	TAM	100	12	17	1	3	1	5	8	24	4	2	172	235	272	507	8%	76%	0.35	50	240	2.02	33
		12	22	SS	aa	TAM	475	55	111	13	9	3	30	41	114	30	10	233	294	318	612	8%	76%	0.36	55	147	2.57	10
Leon,Sandy	B	12	23	C	a/a	WAS	187	19	54	16	0	2	19	16	30	1	0	288	344	410	755	8%	84%	0.53	92	34	4.06	37
Linares,Juan Carlos	R	10	26	OF	aa	BOS	46	2	9	4	0	1	3	0	10	1	1	200	200	340	540	0%	79%	0.00	102	4	1.96	-0
		11	27	OF	aaa	BOS	60	6	12	5	1	2	9	3	14	0	1	204	243	419	662	5%	77%	0.22	140	100	3.03	61
Lin,Che-Hsuan	R	10	22	OF	aa	BOS	458	65	115	18	3	1	25	53	45	19	15	251	329	310	639	10%	90%	1.18	44	106	3.53	50
		11	23	OF	a/a	BOS	466	55	103	17	2	1	28	45	70	22	8	221	289	276	566	9%	85%	0.64	41	113	2.86	26
		12	24	OF	aaa	BOS	396	35	90	11	4	2	25	34	72	12	4	228	289	288	577	8%	82%	0.47	40	101	2.33	8
Liriano,Rymer	R	12	21	OF	aa	SD	183	19	39	8	2	2	16	17	58	8	1	214	281	314	595	8%	69%	0.29	80	119	2.42	-7
Lough,David	L	09	23	OF	aa	KC	236	32	70	13	1	7	25	10	23	10	5	295	323	444	767	4%	90%	0.42	96	101	5.07	78
		10	24	OF	aaa	KC	460	48	111	14	8	8	43	30	55	11	6	242	288	357	645	6%	88%	0.54	68	131	3.53	60
		11	25	OF	aaa	KC	456	60	122	22	9	6	45	24	55	10	9	268	305	393	698	5%	88%	0.44	80	145	4.05	71
		12	26	OF	aaa	KC	491	46	110	16	10	6	46	17	74	17	5	225	250	331	581	3%	85%	0.22	61	138	2.19	38
Lutz,Zach	R	12	26	3B	aaa	NYM	244	25	55	12	1	7	26	30	89	0	0	227	312	372	684	11%	63%	0.34	118	33	3.28	-18
Mahoney,Joseph	L	10	23	1B	aa	BAL	191	24	56	11	1	8	24	13	31	7	1	292	337	482	819	6%	84%	0.42	118	95	6.16	73
		11	24	1B	aa	BAL	315	36	83	21	4	10	56	20	92	6	2	262	307	451	758	6%	71%	0.22	121	118	4.91	29
		12	25	1B	aaa	BAL	491	46	117	26	1	9	47	28	106	3	2	238	279	350	630	5%	78%	0.27	80	51	2.73	6
Mahtook,Mikie	R	12	23	OF	aa	TAM	153	14	33	9	1	3	20	9	35	3	3	215	257	343	600	5%	77%	0.25	92	79	2.14	18
Marisnick,Jake	R	12	21	OF	aa	TOR	223	21	49	11	3	2	13	9	49	12	4	218	248	315	563	4%	78%	0.19	69	134	1.98	17
Marrero,Chris	R	09	21	1B	aa	WAS	75	8	19	6	0	1	10	7	16	0	1	256	320	377	697	9%	79%	0.45	92	36	4.16	20
		10	22	1B	aa	WAS	524	65	142	27	0	15	73	38	88	1	3	271	320	408	729	7%	83%	0.43	90	34	4.68	30
		11	23	1B	aaa	WAS	483	48	129	27	0	11	56	46	106	2	2	267	330	392	723	9%	78%	0.43	86	35	4.73	11
		12	24	1B	a/a	WAS	149	12	32	7	1	1	12	12	34	0	0	216	274	290	565	7%	77%	0.35	58	41	2.07	-16
Marte,Alfredo	R	11	22	OF	aa	ARI	43	3	9	1	0	1	4	3	11	1	0	205	255	279	533	6%	75%	0.27	46	40	2.49	-36
		12	23	OF	aa	ARI	398	53	107	24	3	16	59	26	79	5	7	269	313	466	779	6%	80%	0.33	125	77	4.03	58
Marte,Jefry	R	12	21	3B	aa	NYM	462	50	96	16	2	7	48	34	81	7	6	208	263	301	564	7%	82%	0.42	59	86	2.12	18
Martinez,Francisco	R	11	21	3B	aa	SEA	477	68	124	19	5	8	57	19	118	8	11	259	288	369	656	4%	75%	0.16	69	124	3.44	4
		12	22	3B	aa	SEA	352	50	73	15	1	2	21	40	96	25	8	207	288	267	555	10%	73%	0.42	52	121	2.20	-9
Martin,Leonys	L	11	23	OF	a/a	TEX	287	36	74	14	3	3	29	18	35	13	11	257	302	356	658	6%	88%	0.52	68	119	3.43	55
		12	24	OF	aaa	TEX	231	34	72	16	2	10	30	17	43	7	10	314	361	522	882	7%	81%	0.39	132	86	5.06	72
Matthes,Kent	R	12	25	OF	aa	COL	336	36	68	18	2	16	33	18	84	5	2	203	243	408	651	5%	75%	0.21	135	89	2.65	47
McCann,James	R	12	22	C	aa	DET	220	12	39	11	0	2	15	6	46	2	2	179	202	250	452	3%	79%	0.14	56	43	1.21	-18
Mercer,Jordy	R	10	24	3B	aa	PIT	485	53	119	28	1	2	52	24	57	6	1	245	281	319	600	5%	88%	0.42	59	81	3.18	35
		11	25	SS	a/a	PIT	491	60	105	26	1	14	52	27	86	7	7	215	255	357	613	5%	83%	0.31	93	83	2.92	42
		12	26	SS	aaa	PIT	209	22	51	12	1	3	21	15	50	2	6	245	297	354	651	7%	76%	0.31	83	63	2.59	6
Mesa,Melky	R	11	24	OF	aa	NYY	386	45	84	20	2	8	35	28	145	14	15	217	271	345	615	7%	63%	0.20	84	114	2.79	-33
		12	25	OF	a/a	NYY	458	61	105	22	1	20	52	28	134	17	5	229	274	416	690	6%	71%	0.21	131	109	3.31	34
Milligan,Adam	L	12	24	OF	aa	ATL	102	3	16	4	0	1	7	7	44	0	0	153	205	219	423	6%	57%	0.15	71	5	1.09	-99
Mitchell,Jared	L	12	24	OF	a/a	CHW	455	56	96	21	9	10	54	70	209	17	7	210	315	365	681	13%	54%	0.33	142	127	2.86	-4
Moore,Jeremy	L	11	24	OF	aaa	LAA	426	49	100	19	10	10	43	13	133	14	12	235	258	393	651	3%	69%	0.10	94	193	3.11	16
Morris,Hunter	L	12	24	1B	aa	MIL	522	61	140	37	5	24	89	32	137	2	1	268	311	491	802	6%	74%	0.24	154	65	4.35	52
Myers,Wil	R	12	22	OF	a/a	KC	522	75	146	24	6	25	83	47	149	5	3	279	338	492	830	8%	72%	0.31	143	90	4.98	46
Neal,Thomas	R	10	23	OF	aa	SF	525	60	144	38	1	10	60	39	84	10	5	274	325	407	732	7%	84%	0.47	95	73	4.78	50
		11	24	OF	aaa	CLE	256	31	63	12	2	1	20	11	65	6	7	247	277	327	605	4%	74%	0.17	58	110	2.88	-12
		12	25	OF	aa	CLE	405	68	114	23	1	10	45	40	81	11	9	281	346	414	760	9%	80%	0.49	91	85	4.12	38
Nick,David	R	12	22	2B	aa	ARI	458	39	106	22	2	4	34	22	91	10	5	231	265	316	581	5%	80%	0.24	62	85	2.23	7
Olt,Mike	R	12	24	3B	aa	TEX	354	50	93	16	1	25	64	48	109	3	0	262	350	521	872	12%	69%	0.44	176	61	5.78	62
Parker,Stephen	L	11	24	3B	a/a	OAK	529	52	122	24	1	6	52	48	133	1	1	231	295	319	614	8%	75%	0.36	62	43	3.33	-20
		12	25	3B	aaa	OAK	328	29	67	10	4	4	32	22	112	3	1	204	254	298	552	6%	66%	0.20	73	95	1.99	-35
Peguero,Francisco	R	11	23	OF	aa	SF	285	29	81	11	6	4	31	4	49	7	1	285	296	407	703	1%	83%	0.08	75	151	4.39	41
		12	24	OF	aaa	SF	449	31	99	17	7	3	46	10	96	1	0	222	238	310	548	2%	79%	0.10	59	77	1.90	-9
Perez,Eury	R	12	22	OF	a/a	WAS	510	45	144	17	2	0	33	12	84	38	16	283	299	325	624	2%	84%	0.14	32	107	2.95	-2
Phelps,Cord	B	10	23	2B	a/a	CLE	442	51	118	25	4	6	42	31	56	3	7	266	315	379	694	7%	87%	0.56	77	75	4.10	49
		11	24	2B	aaa	CLE	378	39	94	22	3	10	48	40	102	2	7	250	321	400	721	10%	73%	0.39	98	63	4.35	10
		12	25	2B	aaa	CLE	503	61	116	30	2	11	46	52	110	7	5	230	302	363	666	9%	78%	0.48	94	74	2.92	31
Pirela,Jose	R	11	22	SS	aa	NYY	468	40	101	18	3	7	36	20	95	7	8	215	248	313	561	4%	80%	0.22	64	81	2.46	5
		12	23	2B	aa	NYY	317	44	83	17	2	7	26	21	53	7	3	263	309	398	707	6%	83%	0.40	86	96	3.52	45
Profar,Jurickson	B	12	19	SS	aa	TEX	480	65	134	26	7	14	53	57	78	14	4	279	355	447	803	11%	84%	0.73	102	112	4.61	74
Rendon,Anthony	R	12	22	3B	aa	WAS	68	11	10	3	1	2	2	9	17	0	0	147	242	319	561	11%	76%	0.51	111	92	1.85	43
Rincon,Edinson	R	12	22	3B	aa	SD	494	36	121	25	0	7	38	19	92	1	7	246	273	341	614	4%	81%	0.20	68	19	2.51	-5

BATTER	B	Yr	Age	Pos	Lev	Tm	AB	R	H	D	T	HR	RBI	BB	K	SB	CS	BA	OB	Slg	OPS	bb%	Ct%	Eye	PX	SX	RC/G	BPV
Robertson,Daniel	R	11	26	OF	aa	SD	438	67	94	17	3	3	30	40	66	14	7	214	280	289	570	8%	85%	0.61	52	128	2.77	39
		12	27	OF	aaa	SD	490	45	108	20	3	1	24	33	77	12	10	220	268	279	548	6%	84%	0.42	44	86	1.90	13
Robinson,Clint	L	11	26	1B	aaa	KC	503	59	133	30	0	14	68	39	102	1	1	264	317	407	724	7%	80%	0.38	95	38	4.66	23
		12	27	1B	aaa	KC	487	46	111	30	1	8	44	52	77	1	0	229	303	340	643	10%	84%	0.67	77	35	2.76	30
Rodriguez,Henry	B	11	21	2B	aa	CIN	278	27	72	16	1	4	26	18	49	13	3	259	303	364	667	6%	82%	0.37	76	94	4.00	33
		12	22	3B	a/a	CIN	345	35	90	14	0	5	29	13	59	7	4	261	287	343	630	4%	83%	0.21	57	65	2.90	6
Romero,Stefen	R	12	24	2B	aa	SEA	216	34	66	13	3	10	44	13	44	5	3	307	346	536	882	6%	79%	0.29	142	108	5.48	77
Romine,Andrew	B	10	25	SS	aa	LAA	383	42	94	13	2	2	26	37	54	16	11	246	313	306	619	9%	86%	0.69	43	96	3.32	27
		11	26	SS	aaa	LAA	381	41	81	7	1	2	22	27	105	14	7	213	264	255	519	7%	72%	0.25	28	99	2.28	-43
		12	27	SS	aaa	LAA	351	35	74	8	3	2	24	15	58	14	13	210	242	273	515	4%	84%	0.25	38	115	1.62	9
Romine,Austin	R	10	22	C	aa	NYY	455	54	110	26	0	9	58	32	76	2	0	242	292	360	652	7%	83%	0.42	82	52	3.74	29
		11	23	C	a/a	NYY	351	36	89	11	0	6	40	27	69	2	2	253	306	334	640	7%	80%	0.39	54	39	3.62	-7
		12	24	C	aaa	NYY	61	5	12	2	0	3	7	6	11	0	0	190	267	352	618	10%	82%	0.58	94	6	2.72	25
Ruf,Darin	R	12	26	1B	aa	PHI	489	68	128	27	1	28	76	48	123	1	0	262	328	495	823	9%	75%	0.39	153	45	4.96	55
Russell,Kyle	L	10	24	OF	aa	LA	273	26	55	19	1	7	20	20	93	2	2	200	255	352	607	7%	66%	0.22	103	66	2.95	-18
		11	25	OF	a/a	LA	432	42	83	24	2	12	45	31	188	1	1	191	246	341	587	7%	57%	0.17	97	89	2.78	-55
		12	26	OF	a/a	LA	247	28	48	14	0	7	29	27	88	3	2	194	275	342	617	10%	64%	0.31	124	62	2.38	-3
Saladino,Tyler	R	12	23	SS	a/a	CHW	467	66	99	15	3	4	37	72	123	32	9	211	317	281	598	13%	74%	0.59	52	127	2.59	3
Sanchez,Carlos	B	12	20	SS	a/a	CHW	158	19	51	11	1	0	12	10	31	6	5	324	364	401	765	6%	80%	0.31	65	87	4.13	13
Schafer,Logan	L	11	25	OF	a/a	MIL	359	45	93	18	4	4	30	25	53	11	9	260	308	366	673	7%	85%	0.47	72	120	3.76	50
		12	26	OF	aaa	MIL	464	55	109	20	7	9	31	23	87	12	8	236	271	367	638	5%	81%	0.26	82	119	2.56	37
Schoop,Jonathan	R	12	21	2B	aa	BAL	485	54	109	22	1	12	45	39	108	4	3	224	282	348	630	7%	78%	0.36	84	57	2.74	12
Shaw,Travis	L	12	22	1B	aa	BOS	110	11	24	14	0	2	10	17	36	1	1	222	328	412	740	14%	68%	0.48	174	36	3.02	49
Short,Brandon	R	11	23	OF	aa	CHW	526	62	124	26	4	12	49	32	142	17	10	235	279	369	648	6%	73%	0.22	86	114	3.41	9
		12	24	OF	a/a	CHW	48	4	10	2	0	0	2	2	9	1	0	200	229	237	466	4%	80%	0.19	33	60	1.53	-24
Silverio,Alfredo	R	11	24	OF	aa	LA	533	65	133	35	9	11	61	21	109	8	14	249	277	414	691	4%	80%	0.19	107	138	3.56	55
Singleton,Jonathan	L	12	21	1B	aa	HOU	461	69	115	24	3	16	58	65	146	5	2	250	343	422	765	12%	68%	0.44	128	84	4.16	27
Skipworth,Kyle	L	11	21	C	aa	FLA	396	26	71	11	1	8	36	27	165	0	4	179	231	273	504	6%	58%	0.16	58	36	1.97	-95
	L	12	22	C	aa	MIA	420	48	79	14	2	15	51	31	156	1	1	187	243	338	581	7%	63%	0.20	116	63	2.24	-21
Soto,Neftali	R	11	22	1B	a/a	CIN	396	51	97	16	2	25	58	19	110	0	1	244	279	483	761	5%	72%	0.17	138	57	4.59	27
	R	12	23	1B	aaa	CIN	465	43	100	26	0	12	46	32	132	2	1	214	265	347	612	6%	72%	0.24	101	38	2.49	-6
Springer,George	R	12	23	OF	aa	HOU	73	6	13	3	0	1	4	4	28	3	2	184	229	281	510	6%	61%	0.15	84	69	1.61	-55
Taveras,Oscar	L	12	20	OF	aa	STL	477	67	137	33	5	17	76	35	60	8	1	287	336	484	820	7%	87%	0.59	117	104	4.79	90
Taylor,Michael	R	09	24	OF	a/a	PHI	428	61	124	25	3	19	70	39	61	18	6	291	350	495	845	8%	86%	0.64	126	110	6.43	95
		10	25	OF	aaa	OAK	464	54	99	20	4	4	53	35	67	11	7	213	268	298	566	7%	86%	0.52	59	111	2.66	39
		11	26	OF	aaa	OAK	349	33	72	12	0	10	42	30	98	9	6	207	269	327	596	8%	72%	0.30	75	65	2.89	-16
		12	27	OF	aaa	OAK	449	53	98	24	1	7	44	58	133	12	4	218	307	323	630	11%	70%	0.43	86	85	2.72	0
Thompson,Trayce	R	12	21	OF	aa	CHW	68	9	16	3	1	3	5	9	24	3	0	235	328	428	756	12%	64%	0.38	144	105	4.21	29
Tovar,Wilfredo	R	12	21	SS	aa	NYM	193	17	40	9	1	0	22	9	24	2	1	209	244	270	514	4%	88%	0.37	44	79	1.64	21
Townsend,Tyler	L	12	24	1B	aa	BAL	73	8	16	2	0	5	10	7	27	0	0	217	289	443	732	9%	64%	0.28	161	13	3.95	8
Triunfel,Carlos	R	10	20	SS	aa	SEA	470	41	108	10	1	5	34	10	43	2	10	230	247	289	536	2%	91%	0.24	38	46	2.16	14
		11	21	SS	a/a	SEA	506	37	120	24	2	4	32	20	102	4	8	237	265	315	580	4%	80%	0.19	57	56	2.70	-8
		12	22	SS	aaa	SEA	496	54	107	26	1	7	46	17	104	2	2	215	242	313	555	3%	79%	0.17	72	67	1.99	2
Valle,Sebastian	R	12	22	C	a/a	PHI	388	31	89	14	1	14	48	11	125	0	0	229	250	380	630	3%	68%	0.09	110	26	2.69	-26
Van Slyke,Scott	R	10	24	OF	a/a	LA	255	21	48	9	1	3	22	12	32	3	3	188	223	264	487	4%	87%	0.36	51	72	1.85	22
		11	25	OF	aa	LA	457	58	128	37	2	14	65	44	123	4	6	280	343	461	803	9%	73%	0.36	123	65	5.64	30
		12	26	OF	aaa	LA	358	40	87	26	0	11	40	27	80	3	4	244	296	408	704	7%	78%	0.33	117	52	3.22	36
Vazquez,Christian	R	12	22	C	aa	BOS	73	9	14	4	0	0	4	7	9	0	0	198	264	256	520	8%	87%	0.70	48	44	1.66	18
Villar,Jonathan	B	11	20	SS	aa	HOU	324	38	66	14	2	8	19	21	109	10	6	204	253	328	581	6%	66%	0.19	79	111	2.65	-23
		12	21	SS	aa	HOU	326	40	74	6	2	9	37	26	97	29	9	228	285	335	620	7%	70%	0.27	71	125	2.95	-8
Vitters,Josh	R	12	23	3B	aaa	CHC	415	40	109	28	2	13	50	23	87	4	3	263	301	431	732	5%	79%	0.26	114	60	3.65	38
Wates,Austin	R	12	24	OF	aa	HOU	359	41	91	14	3	5	34	22	84	12	13	255	297	352	650	6%	77%	0.26	67	100	2.73	4
Wheeler,Ryan	L	10	22	3B	aa	ARI	67	7	16	3	0	3	9	4	13	0	0	239	282	418	700	6%	81%	0.31	109	20	4.09	29
		11	23	3B	aa	ARI	480	50	124	28	2	12	64	32	112	2	3	258	304	398	703	6%	78%	0.28	93	54	4.24	12
		12	24	3B	aaa	ARI	362	34	104	23	3	9	55	15	78	2	1	288	317	448	764	4%	78%	0.20	109	65	4.12	30
Witherspoon,Travis	R	12	23	OF	aa	LAA	208	25	38	8	1	5	19	21	59	8	4	181	256	307	563	9%	72%	0.35	89	109	1.99	10
Wong,Kolten	L	12	22	2B	aa	STL	523	62	130	20	4	6	41	36	81	16	12	249	297	339	637	6%	84%	0.44	58	100	2.75	29
Zunino,Mike	R	12	21	C	aa	SEA	51	6	16	4	0	3	7	5	8	0	0	309	368	537	905	9%	84%	0.60	140	11	6.31	72

PITCHER	Th	Yr	Age	Lev	Org	W	L	G	Sv	IP	H	ER	HR	BB	K	ERA	WHIP	BF/G	OBA	bb/9	K/9	Cmd	HR/9	H%	S%	BPV
Adams,Austin	R	11	25	aa	CLE	11	10	26	0	136	176	71	6	67	106	4.72	1.79	24.6	307	4.5	7.0	1.6	0.4	38%	73%	57
Alderson,Tim	R	09	21	aa	PIT	9	2	20	0	111	123	53	9	24	56	4.32	1.32	23.6	275	1.9	4.5	2.3	0.7	31%	68%	55
		10	22	aa	PIT	7	6	18	0	89	125	64	10	25	49	6.46	1.68	22.8	324	2.5	4.9	2.0	1.0	36%	61%	31
		11	23	aa	PIT	0	4	42	0	74	80	40	6	26	46	4.88	1.43	7.7	269	3.2	5.5	1.7	0.7	31%	66%	49
		12	24	a/a	PIT	5	4	28	3	89	113	54	9	28	51	5.44	1.59	14.0	310	2.9	5.2	1.8	0.9	34%	66%	36
Allen,Cody	R	12	24	a/a	CLE	3	2	29	3	39	28	11	4	9	37	2.52	0.95	5.1	202	2.1	8.5	4.1	1.0	25%	79%	122
Ames,Steven	R	11	23	aa	LA	2	2	28	5	33	34	9	3	10	35	2.47	1.32	4.9	260	2.6	9.8	3.7	0.7	35%	84%	117
		12	24	aa	LA	3	3	54	18	63	60	13	2	13	60	1.84	1.14	4.6	251	1.8	8.5	4.7	0.3	33%	85%	146
Anderson,Chase	R	12	25	aa	ARI	5	4	21	0	104	111	43	11	26	78	3.73	1.32	20.5	275	2.2	6.7	3.0	0.9	32%	75%	75
Archer,Chris	R	10	22	aa	CHC	8	2	13	0	70	53	16	2	38	58	2.06	1.30	22.7	206	4.9	7.5	1.5	0.3	27%	84%	83
		11	23	a/a	TAM	9	7	27	0	147	160	73	11	83	112	4.43	1.65	25.0	272	5.1	6.9	1.4	0.6	33%	73%	51
		12	24	aaa	TAM	7	9	25	0	128	112	59	6	61	118	4.18	1.35	21.4	237	4.3	8.3	1.9	0.4	30%	68%	85
Aumont,Phillippe	R	10	21	aa	PHI	1	6	11	0	49	60	45	4	37	32	8.23	1.97	21.9	295	6.8	5.9	0.9	0.7	34%	56%	27
		11	22	a/a	PHI	2	5	43	7	54	49	19	2	24	67	3.11	1.37	5.4	239	4.1	11.2	2.8	0.4	36%	77%	121
		12	23	aaa	PHI	3	1	41	15	44	41	27	4	35	50	5.51	1.71	4.9	245	7.2	10.2	1.4	0.7	33%	68%	75
Barnes,Scott	L	09	22	aa	CLE	2	2	6	0	31	42	27	8	15	26	7.79	1.83	24.7	316	4.3	7.5	1.7	2.3	35%	61%	4
		10	23	aa	CLE	6	11	26	0	138	142	92	14	59	110	5.98	1.46	23.2	261	3.8	7.1	1.9	0.9	31%	59%	57
		11	24	a/a	CLE	8	4	18	0	99	97	44	12	37	89	4.04	1.36	23.5	252	3.4	8.1	2.4	1.1	31%	73%	72
		12	25	aaa	CLE	2	3	31	2	52	42	26	1	23	54	4.54	1.25	6.8	224	3.9	9.4	2.4	0.2	31%	61%	112
Bauer,Trevor	R	11	20	aa	ARI	1	1	4	0	17	21	15	2	7	23	8.07	1.70	19.3	303	3.9	12.2	3.1	1.1	44%	51%	101
		12	21	a/a	ARI	12	2	22	0	130	113	37	9	55	136	2.54	1.29	24.3	236	3.8	9.4	2.5	0.6	31%	82%	98
Belfiore,Michael	L	12	24	aa	BAL	5	1	28	2	47	50	18	2	21	41	3.43	1.50	7.3	273	4.0	7.7	1.9	0.5	34%	77%	74
Betances,Dellin	R	11	23	a/a	NYY	4	9	25	0	126	120	66	12	74	119	4.69	1.54	22.5	246	5.3	8.5	1.6	0.9	31%	70%	65
		12	24	a/a	NYY	6	9	27	0	131	172	120	17	106	102	8.20	2.12	24.0	317	7.2	7.0	1.0	1.2	37%	61%	18
Black,Victor	R	12	24	aa	PIT	2	3	51	13	60	48	14	2	29	66	2.08	1.28	4.8	220	4.4	9.9	2.3	0.3	31%	84%	109
Boxberger,Brad	R	12	24	aaa	SD	2	2	37	5	43	38	12	0	18	54	2.48	1.28	4.8	235	3.7	11.2	3.0	0.0	36%	78%	138
Brasier,Ryan	R	10	23	aa	LAA	7	12	28	0	142	147	96	31	67	78	6.08	1.51	22.5	262	4.2	4.9	1.2	2.0	27%	65%	-2
		11	24	a/a	LAA	2	2	50	19	52	49	18	3	21	43	3.16	1.33	4.5	241	3.7	7.3	2.0	0.5	30%	77%	78
		12	25	aaa	LAA	7	3	55	13	60	69	28	1	22	44	4.21	1.53	4.7	292	3.3	6.6	2.0	0.1	36%	70%	75
Brewer,Charles	R	11	23	aa	ARI	5	1	11	0	52	53	17	2	18	40	2.90	1.37	20.4	259	3.1	6.8	2.2	0.4	32%	79%	80
		12	24	a/a	ARI	11	7	27	0	151	218	107	29	34	96	6.38	1.67	25.1	339	2.0	5.7	2.8	1.7	36%	65%	29
Britton,Drake	L	12	23	aa	BOS	4	7	16	0	85	104	46	3	39	64	4.94	1.69	23.9	303	4.2	6.8	1.6	0.4	36%	69%	58
Buckel,Cody	R	12	20	aa	TEX	5	5	13	0	69	64	36	9	23	58	4.72	1.26	21.7	247	3.0	7.6	2.5	1.2	29%	65%	68
Bundy,Dylan	R	12	20	aa	BAL	2	0	3	0	17	15	7	1	7	11	3.64	1.36	23.2	244	4.0	6.1	1.5	0.6	28%	74%	57
Burgos,Hiram	R	12	25	a/a	MIL	8	3	21	0	130	128	41	8	46	94	2.86	1.34	25.7	259	3.2	6.5	2.0	0.6	31%	80%	67
Cabrera,Edwar	L	12	25	a/a	COL	11	5	21	0	130	111	57	28	37	92	3.99	1.15	24.5	234	2.6	6.4	2.5	2.0	23%	76%	40
Capps,Carter	R	12	22	a/a	SEA	2	3	39	19	51	43	7	2	12	68	1.31	1.06	5.1	229	2.0	11.9	5.9	0.3	35%	89%	194
Carpenter,Chris	R	11	26	a/a	CHC	3	4	32	2	43	48	31	5	27	27	6.64	1.77	6.2	279	5.7	5.6	1.0	1.1	31%	63%	19
		12	27	a/a	BOS	1	0	17	4	18	12	4	1	9	15	2.23	1.19	4.2	193	4.6	7.8	1.7	0.6	24%	84%	80
Carson,Robert	L	10	21	aa	NYM	1	6	10	0	48	69	44	6	22	25	8.22	1.89	23.2	329	4.1	4.7	1.1	1.1	36%	55%	7
		11	22	aa	NYM	4	11	25	0	128	159	71	12	51	79	5.01	1.64	23.4	298	3.6	5.6	1.6	0.8	34%	70%	36
		12	23	a/a	NYM	1	2	41	10	51	64	22	3	19	43	3.80	1.62	5.6	306	3.3	7.5	2.2	0.5	37%	76%	71
Castillo,Richard	R	11	22	aa	STL	1	1	24	0	44	59	18	3	18	36	3.70	1.75	8.6	314	3.7	7.3	2.0	0.6	39%	79%	60
		12	23	aa	STL	7	5	19	0	110	137	49	7	32	54	4.03	1.53	25.2	306	2.6	4.5	1.7	0.6	34%	74%	39
Castro,Simon	R	10	22	a/a	SD	7	7	26	0	140	128	52	7	41	101	3.34	1.21	22.2	238	2.6	6.5	2.5	0.5	29%	72%	84
		11	23	a/a	SD	7	8	22	0	115	127	61	10	30	84	4.74	1.37	22.4	274	2.4	6.5	2.8	0.7	33%	65%	75
		12	24	a/a	CHW	7	5	20	0	115	147	64	8	31	76	5.01	1.55	25.1	311	2.5	5.9	2.4	0.6	36%	67%	60
Chaffee,Ryan	R	12	24	aa	LAA	5	1	37	0	43	29	17	3	28	46	3.54	1.33	4.8	193	5.9	9.7	1.6	0.7	25%	75%	87
Chapman,Kevin	L	11	23	aa	KC	1	2	25	3	40	40	24	4	20	41	5.34	1.50	7.0	257	4.4	9.2	2.1	1.0	33%	65%	73
		12	24	aa	HOU	6	3	49	2	58	53	18	2	30	50	2.76	1.44	5.0	245	4.7	7.7	1.6	0.3	31%	81%	78
Cingrani,Tony	L	12	23	aa	CIN	5	3	16	0	89	71	28	9	41	87	2.81	1.26	22.8	221	4.2	8.8	2.1	0.9	27%	82%	80
Cisnero,Jose	R	12	23	a/a	HOU	13	7	28	0	148	151	60	8	58	128	3.63	1.41	22.4	265	3.5	7.8	2.2	0.5	33%	74%	81
Clemens,Paul	R	11	23	a/a	HOU	8	7	26	0	144	138	63	12	57	108	3.92	1.36	23.7	248	3.6	6.7	1.9	0.7	30%	72%	64
		12	24	a/a	HOU	11	10	27	0	143	197	92	22	40	89	5.79	1.66	23.8	328	2.5	5.6	2.2	1.4	36%	67%	28
Cleto,Maikel	R	11	22	a/a	STL	7	5	20	0	106	97	45	6	49	87	3.86	1.38	22.7	239	4.2	7.4	1.8	0.5	30%	72%	73
		12	23	aaa	STL	3	2	45	2	54	55	33	3	21	55	5.61	1.42	5.1	266	3.6	9.3	2.6	0.6	35%	59%	94
Cloyd,Tyler	R	11	24	aa	PHI	6	3	18	0	107	114	38	7	15	81	3.18	1.21	24.5	269	1.2	6.9	5.5	0.6	33%	75%	139
		12	25	a/a	PHI	15	1	26	0	167	153	53	18	43	93	2.88	1.18	25.7	246	2.3	5.0	2.1	1.0	26%	80%	52
Cohoon,Mark	L	10	23	aa	NYM	5	4	13	0	71	78	33	5	14	46	4.18	1.31	23.1	274	1.8	5.8	3.2	0.7	32%	68%	82
		11	24	a/a	NYM	5	14	27	0	146	197	93	17	54	80	5.72	1.72	25.1	316	3.3	4.9	1.5	1.0	35%	68%	21
		12	25	a/a	NYM	8	12	25	0	155	181	77	14	31	69	4.50	1.37	25.9	293	1.8	4.0	2.2	0.8	31%	68%	43
Cole,Gerrit	R	12	22	a/a	PIT	4	6	13	0	65	69	27	2	23	54	3.73	1.42	21.2	273	3.2	7.5	2.3	0.3	34%	72%	86
Colome,Alexander	R	11	22	aa	TAM	3	4	9	0	52	43	25	5	26	27	4.25	1.33	24.5	221	4.5	4.7	1.1	0.8	24%	69%	38
		12	23	a/a	TAM	8	4	17	0	92	90	39	3	41	78	3.82	1.43	22.9	258	4.0	7.6	1.9	0.3	32%	72%	80
Colvin,Brody	R	12	22	aa	PHI	1	4	7	0	33	48	45	6	22	14	12.50	2.14	23.1	341	6.1	3.8	0.6	1.7	35%	38%	-29
Corcino,Daniel	R	12	22	aa	CIN	8	8	26	0	143	132	62	12	67	111	3.92	1.39	23.2	245	4.2	7.0	1.6	0.7	29%	73%	60
Cosart,Jarred	R	11	21	aa	HOU	1	2	7	0	36	34	19	4	12	20	4.60	1.24	21.6	241	2.9	4.8	1.7	0.9	27%	64%	44
		12	22	a/a	HOU	6	7	21	0	115	111	40	3	45	81	3.17	1.36	22.8	256	3.6	6.4	1.8	0.2	31%	76%	73
Crosby,Casey	L	11	23	aa	DET	9	7	25	0	132	138	70	12	74	99	4.78	1.61	23.9	264	5.1	6.8	1.3	0.8	32%	71%	47
		12	24	aaa	DET	7	9	22	0	126	132	69	13	65	89	4.96	1.57	25.1	271	4.7	6.4	1.4	0.9	31%	70%	39
De Fratus,Justin	R	10	23	aa	PHI	1	0	20	6	24	19	7	2	5	24	2.60	0.99	4.7	212	1.9	8.9	4.8	0.7	28%	77%	145
		11	24	a/a	PHI	6	3	51	15	75	73	30	4	25	81	3.61	1.31	6.2	250	3.0	9.7	3.2	0.5	34%	73%	115
		12	25	aaa	PHI	0	1	17	3	22	19	8	2	3	18	3.36	1.01	4.9	234	1.4	7.5	5.5	1.0	27%	71%	138
De La Rosa,Dane	R	10	27	aa	TAM	9	3	47	4	73	90	23	4	31	53	2.82	1.67	7.1	298	3.9	6.5	1.7	0.4	36%	84%	57
		11	28	aaa	TAM	6	5	52	6	70	78	31	9	28	65	4.01	1.51	6.0	275	3.6	8.3	2.3	1.1	34%	77%	64
		12	29	aaa	TAM	0	4	54	20	68	46	27	2	46	66	3.56	1.35	5.2	193	6.1	8.8	1.4	0.3	26%	73%	90
Drake,Oliver	R	11	24	a/a	BAL	3	5	13	0	66	94	48	11	26	40	6.51	1.81	24.0	328	3.5	5.4	1.6	1.4	36%	66%	12
		12	25	aa	BAL	1	1	3	0	18	10	4	1	4	12	1.84	0.75	21.4	158	2.0	6.0	2.9	0.6	18%	80%	103

PITCHER	Th	Yr	Age	Lev	Org	W	L	G	Sv	IP	H	ER	HR	BB	K	ERA	WHIP	BF/G	OBA	bb/9	K/9	Cmd	HR/9	H%	S%	BPV
Familia,Jeurys	R	11	22	aa	NYM	4	4	17	0	88	88	35	9	32	84	3.57	1.37	22.1	256	3.3	8.6	2.6	0.9	33%	77%	83
		12	23	aaa	NYM	9	9	28	0	137	153	73	7	66	105	4.82	1.60	21.6	284	4.3	6.9	1.6	0.5	34%	69%	59
Faulk,Kenny	L	12	25	aa	DET	1	0	40	4	58	70	36	6	33	53	5.66	1.77	6.6	299	5.1	8.3	1.6	0.9	37%	68%	53
Font,Wilmer	R	12	22	aa	TEX	2	0	10	1	15	11	6	1	7	24	3.85	1.19	6.0	200	4.4	14.4	3.3	0.8	34%	69%	147
Frazier,Parker	R	12	24	aa	COL	5	14	27	0	167	239	111	30	46	72	5.96	1.71	28.0	337	2.5	3.9	1.6	1.6	34%	69%	-5
Gardner,Joe	R	11	23	aa	COL	10	11	25	0	134	157	74	8	53	65	4.98	1.57	24.0	287	3.5	4.4	1.2	0.6	32%	67%	33
		12	24	aa	COL	8	8	28	1	138	171	95	21	45	77	6.18	1.56	21.6	304	2.9	5.0	1.7	1.4	32%	62%	20
Gast,John	L	11	22	aa	STL	4	4	13	0	79	77	31	7	28	46	3.52	1.33	25.9	250	3.2	5.2	1.6	0.7	28%	75%	48
		12	23	a/a	STL	13	7	28	0	161	175	77	13	54	106	4.33	1.42	24.4	278	3.0	6.0	2.0	0.7	32%	70%	55
Geltz,Steven	R	10	23	aa	LAA	1	0	16	0	18	10	6	0	15	30	2.97	1.37	4.9	158	7.4	14.8	2.0	0.0	32%	76%	154
		11	24	a/a	LAA	3	3	34	0	48	39	22	5	15	56	4.03	1.11	5.7	215	2.8	10.4	3.8	0.9	30%	65%	126
Gibson,Kyle	R	10	23	a/a	MIN	7	5	19	0	108	111	44	5	26	72	3.66	1.27	23.8	260	2.2	6.0	2.8	0.4	31%	70%	85
		11	24	aaa	MIN	3	8	18	0	95	125	59	10	28	72	5.61	1.60	24.0	309	2.7	6.8	2.6	0.9	37%	65%	61
Gilmartin,Sean	L	12	22	a/a	ATL	6	10	27	0	157	169	77	15	38	99	4.39	1.32	24.1	276	2.2	5.7	2.6	0.9	31%	68%	62
Graham,J.R.	R	12	22	aa	ATL	3	1	9	0	45	40	19	2	17	37	3.85	1.26	20.6	238	3.4	7.4	2.2	0.4	30%	69%	85
Gray,Sonny	R	11	22	aa	OAK	1	0	5	0	20	15	1	0	5	16	0.44	1.04	15.8	209	2.4	7.1	2.9	0.0	28%	95%	117
		12	23	a/a	OAK	6	9	27	0	152	170	76	7	56	85	4.48	1.48	24.2	284	3.3	5.1	1.5	0.4	32%	69%	48
Grimm,Justin	R	12	24	a/a	TEX	11	6	25	0	135	146	53	6	31	82	3.51	1.32	22.3	278	2.1	5.5	2.6	0.4	32%	73%	74
Guerra,Deolis	R	09	20	aa	MIN	6	3	12	0	62	68	42	4	17	42	6.06	1.36	22.2	271	2.5	6.1	2.5	0.6	32%	53%	72
		10	21	a/a	MIN	2	13	24	0	127	167	92	17	41	75	6.54	1.63	24.1	310	2.9	5.3	1.8	1.2	35%	61%	27
		11	22	aa	MIN	8	7	37	1	95	107	60	8	27	79	5.72	1.41	11.1	279	2.5	7.5	2.9	0.8	34%	59%	82
		12	23	a/a	MIN	4	3	36	1	70	74	39	7	22	59	4.95	1.37	8.2	272	2.9	7.6	2.7	0.9	33%	64%	76
Gutierrez,Carlos	R	09	23	aa	MIN	1	3	22	0	52	73	45	6	26	25	7.84	1.90	11.4	325	4.5	4.4	1.0	1.1	36%	58%	5
		10	24	a/a	MIN	5	8	34	2	126	157	70	7	52	71	5.01	1.65	16.9	299	3.7	5.1	1.4	0.5	34%	69%	39
		11	25	aaa	MIN	2	3	43	0	62	70	38	2	33	44	5.50	1.65	6.6	278	4.8	6.4	1.3	0.3	34%	64%	58
		12	26	aaa	MIN	2	2	10	0	16	16	12	2	3	16	6.72	1.22	6.5	264	1.9	8.8	4.8	1.2	32%	44%	119
Haley,Trey	R	12	22	aa	CLE	3	1	9	0	15	12	4	0	11	20	2.29	1.51	7.4	215	6.6	11.7	1.8	0.0	34%	83%	119
Hale,David	R	12	25	aa	ATL	8	4	27	0	146	147	79	13	72	104	4.86	1.50	23.3	264	4.5	6.4	1.4	0.8	30%	68%	48
Heath,Deunte	R	08	23	aa	ATL	4	5	13	0	66	88	48	5	33	39	6.60	1.82	24.1	312	4.5	5.3	1.2	0.7	36%	63%	28
		09	24	a/a	ATL	2	6	32	1	98	128	73	7	54	76	6.71	1.85	14.6	308	4.9	6.9	1.4	0.7	37%	62%	45
		10	25	aa	CHW	2	4	39	2	57	63	28	6	37	68	4.37	1.75	6.8	275	5.8	10.6	1.8	0.9	38%	76%	76
		11	26	aaa	CHW	4	7	30	1	103	124	70	17	74	96	6.15	1.93	16.6	293	6.5	8.4	1.3	1.5	36%	71%	28
		12	27	aaa	CHW	4	3	36	3	67	63	16	6	26	60	2.21	1.32	7.7	250	3.5	8.0	2.3	0.8	31%	88%	77
Heckathorn,Kyle	R	11	23	aa	MIL	0	4	7	0	36	50	33	8	17	21	8.08	1.85	24.7	321	4.2	5.2	1.2	1.9	34%	58%	-8
		12	24	aa	MIL	5	11	35	0	119	148	76	8	40	76	5.76	1.57	15.0	306	3.0	5.7	1.9	0.6	35%	62%	50
Hembree,Heath	R	11	22	aa	SF	1	1	28	17	29	23	11	1	13	29	3.52	1.26	4.3	217	4.1	9.1	2.2	0.3	30%	71%	103
		12	23	aaa	SF	1	1	39	15	38	30	19	2	17	31	4.55	1.24	4.0	218	4.1	7.3	1.8	0.4	27%	61%	81
Hernandez,Pedro	L	11	22	a/a	SD	5	3	13	0	59	63	23	5	14	45	3.50	1.30	19.3	267	2.1	6.9	3.2	0.7	32%	75%	90
		12	23	a/a	MIN	8	4	19	0	103	128	46	8	22	54	4.00	1.46	23.2	306	2.0	4.8	2.4	0.7	34%	73%	53
Heston,Chris	R	12	24	aa	SF	9	8	25	0	149	151	49	2	41	113	2.94	1.29	24.4	264	2.5	6.8	2.7	0.1	33%	76%	97
Holmberg,David	L	12	21	aa	ARI	5	5	15	0	95	118	46	9	22	58	4.38	1.48	27.2	307	2.1	5.5	2.6	0.9	34%	72%	55
Hultzen,Danny	L	12	23	a/a	SEA	9	7	25	0	124	95	46	4	74	121	3.33	1.37	20.8	214	5.4	8.8	1.6	0.3	29%	75%	91
Jackson,Jay	R	12	25	aaa	CHC	3	7	37	0	86	122	74	15	44	62	7.68	1.92	11.1	333	4.6	6.4	1.4	1.6	37%	61%	8
Jenkins,Chad	R	11	24	aa	TOR	5	7	16	0	100	110	57	9	28	63	5.11	1.37	26.9	272	2.5	5.7	2.2	0.8	31%	63%	56
		12	25	aa	TOR	5	9	20	0	114	177	82	22	33	47	6.42	1.83	26.6	354	2.6	3.7	1.4	1.7	36%	68%	-14
Johnson,Steve	R	11	24	a/a	BAL	7	8	27	0	146	170	88	18	63	99	5.42	1.60	24.4	285	3.9	6.1	1.6	1.1	33%	68%	33
		12	25	aaa	BAL	4	8	19	0	91	84	41	10	34	68	4.05	1.29	19.8	246	3.3	6.7	2.0	1.0	28%	71%	60
Jones,Chris	L	12	24	aa	ATL	2	5	45	2	60	82	33	1	20	52	4.92	1.70	6.0	327	3.0	7.8	2.6	0.2	41%	69%	86
Kelly,Casey	R	10	21	aa	BOS	3	5	21	0	95	124	60	10	31	72	5.68	1.63	20.6	309	3.0	6.9	2.3	0.9	37%	65%	56
		11	22	aa	SD	11	6	27	0	142	153	58	6	43	95	3.70	1.38	22.6	269	2.7	6.0	2.2	0.4	32%	72%	73
		12	23	a/a	SD	0	1	5	0	29	24	10	1	3	28	3.02	0.92	21.5	226	0.9	8.9	9.9	0.2	30%	66%	264
Kickham,Mike	L	12	24	aa	SF	11	10	28	0	151	144	67	9	77	115	4.00	1.47	23.1	254	4.6	6.9	1.5	0.5	30%	73%	61
Kirk,Austin	L	12	22	aa	CHC	2	0	5	0	23	21	10	3	12	11	3.71	1.40	19.7	238	4.7	4.3	0.9	1.3	24%	79%	14
Kurcz,Aaron	R	12	22	aa	BOS	3	4	29	4	50	50	22	5	27	62	3.95	1.53	7.6	260	4.9	11.0	2.2	0.8	36%	76%	92
Lamb,John	L	10	20	aa	KC	2	1	7	0	33	38	21	2	11	24	5.71	1.50	20.8	283	3.1	6.6	2.1	0.5	34%	60%	67
		11	21	aa	KC	1	2	8	0	35	35	12	3	12	18	3.20	1.33	18.6	254	3.0	4.7	1.6	0.7	29%	77%	46
Leesman,Charles	L	10	23	aa	CHW	5	2	11	0	63	57	25	1	22	44	3.52	1.24	23.9	235	3.1	6.2	2.0	0.1	29%	69%	83
		11	24	aa	CHW	10	7	27	0	152	183	90	6	95	96	5.34	1.83	26.7	292	5.6	5.7	1.0	0.3	35%	69%	42
		12	25	aaa	CHW	12	10	26	0	135	165	53	12	64	87	3.53	1.70	23.5	303	4.3	5.8	1.4	0.8	34%	81%	34
Lee,Chen	R	10	24	aa	CLE	5	4	44	0	72	67	30	6	22	71	3.73	1.23	6.8	241	2.7	8.8	3.3	0.8	31%	71%	105
		11	25	a/a	CLE	6	1	44	1	71	62	23	3	24	80	2.87	1.21	6.7	230	3.0	10.1	3.3	0.4	33%	76%	129
Lee,Zach	R	12	21	aa	LA	4	3	13	0	66	75	35	6	20	44	4.74	1.46	21.6	289	2.8	6.1	2.2	0.8	33%	68%	55
Lehman,Patrick	R	11	25	aa	WAS	1	2	29	6	34	27	18	2	4	27	4.70	0.90	4.5	211	1.1	7.2	6.5	0.6	26%	45%	175
		12	26	a/a	WAS	1	0	45	5	51	56	21	5	19	29	3.78	1.47	4.9	280	3.4	5.2	1.5	0.8	31%	76%	38
Lorin,Brett	R	12	25	aa	ARI	3	10	29	0	103	155	95	15	36	56	8.36	1.87	16.6	349	3.2	4.9	1.5	1.3	38%	54%	9
Lotzkar,Kyle	R	12	23	aa	CIN	4	6	18	0	86	93	66	16	56	83	6.92	1.73	21.8	277	5.8	8.6	1.5	1.7	32%	62%	32
Loux,Barret	R	12	23	aa	TEX	14	1	25	0	127	144	64	14	44	81	4.55	1.48	21.8	287	3.1	5.8	1.9	1.0	32%	71%	42
Manzanillo,Santo	R	11	23	aa	MIL	0	1	20	7	20	14	6	2	12	17	2.49	1.30	4.3	196	5.3	7.4	1.4	1.0	23%	86%	61
Marinez,Jhan	R	10	22	aa	FLA	1	0	15	6	16	10	5	1	7	18	2.78	1.05	4.3	175	3.9	10.0	2.6	0.6	25%	75%	117
		11	23	aa	FLA	3	8	56	3	58	51	25	7	43	67	3.89	1.62	4.7	233	6.6	10.4	1.6	1.0	32%	79%	73
		12	24	aaa	CHW	4	2	40	4	63	49	28	7	36	56	4.01	1.35	6.6	216	5.2	8.0	1.5	1.0	26%	73%	61
Maronde,Nick	L	12	23	aa	LAA	3	2	7	0	32	46	15	1	3	18	4.26	1.52	20.1	336	0.9	4.9	5.8	0.3	38%	71%	129
Marshall,Brett	R	12	22	aa	NYY	13	7	27	0	158	173	75	19	54	103	4.27	1.43	24.9	279	3.1	5.8	1.9	1.1	31%	73%	41
Marshall,Evan	R	12	22	aa	ARI	6	3	42	16	49	63	23	2	16	23	4.31	1.62	5.1	316	2.9	4.3	1.5	0.4	35%	73%	36
Martinez,Carlos	R	12	21	aa	STL	4	3	15	0	71	65	24	5	21	50	3.02	1.21	19.2	245	2.7	6.3	2.4	0.6	28%	77%	74
Martin,Ethan	R	11	22	aa	LA	5	3	21	2	40	32	18	3	25	38	3.92	1.40	8.3	213	5.5	8.5	1.5	0.6	28%	72%	78
		12	23	aa	PHI	13	6	27	0	158	133	71	9	78	126	4.03	1.34	24.3	231	4.5	7.2	1.6	0.5	28%	69%	71
Maurer,Brandon	R	12	22	aa	SEA	9	2	24	0	138	153	60	4	50	106	3.92	1.47	24.6	282	3.3	6.9	2.1	0.3	34%	72%	77

PITCHER	Th	Yr	Age	Lev	Org	W	L	G	Sv	IP	H	ER	HR	BB	K	ERA	WHIP	BF/G	OBA	bb/9	K/9	Cmd	HR/9	H%	S%	BPV
May,Trevor	R	12	23	aa	PHI	10	13	28	0	150	157	94	24	77	129	5.64	1.56	23.4	271	4.6	7.8	1.7	1.4	31%	67%	40
Mazzoni,Cory	R	12	23	aa	NYM	5	5	14	0	81	96	42	9	18	46	4.66	1.42	24.4	298	2.0	5.1	2.5	1.0	33%	69%	51
McGuire,Deck	R	11	22	aa	TOR	2	1	4	0	21	23	12	4	7	20	5.17	1.43	22.5	273	3.1	8.5	2.8	2.0	32%	71%	52
		12	23	aa	TOR	5	15	28	0	144	189	117	27	63	84	7.30	1.75	23.5	318	3.9	5.2	1.3	1.7	34%	60%	1
McPherson,Kyle	R	11	24	aa	PIT	8	5	16	0	89	87	36	7	21	65	3.65	1.21	23.1	251	2.1	6.5	3.1	0.7	30%	71%	86
		12	25	a/a	PIT	3	6	12	0	67	81	33	7	9	48	4.37	1.34	23.2	299	1.3	6.5	5.1	0.9	34%	69%	115
Miller,Aaron	L	10	23	aa	LA	1	4	6	0	23	30	19	3	18	17	7.26	2.06	19.1	308	6.9	6.8	1.0	1.2	36%	65%	19
		12	25	aa	LA	6	6	25	0	121	137	72	11	71	89	5.34	1.71	22.0	286	5.2	6.6	1.3	0.8	33%	69%	40
Miller,Shelby	R	11	21	aa	STL	9	3	16	0	87	69	22	1	28	77	2.30	1.12	21.9	214	2.9	8.0	2.7	0.1	29%	78%	113
		12	22	aaa	STL	11	10	27	0	137	145	74	20	48	137	4.86	1.41	21.4	273	3.2	9.0	2.9	1.3	33%	69%	75
Mitchell,D.J.	R	12	25	aaa	SEA	9	6	23	0	134	136	65	10	47	90	4.34	1.36	24.4	264	3.1	6.0	1.9	0.7	30%	68%	58
Molina,Nestor	R	11	22	aa	TOR	2	0	5	0	22	14	1	0	2	29	0.49	0.71	16.0	175	0.8	12.0	14.7	0.0	29%	92%	400
		12	23	a/a	CHW	6	11	23	0	127	196	82	12	31	77	5.82	1.79	25.4	354	2.2	5.5	2.5	0.9	40%	67%	44
Montgomery,Mark	R	12	22	aa	NYY	3	1	15	1	24	14	6	1	6	32	2.27	0.83	5.8	169	2.3	12.2	5.3	0.5	26%	74%	191
Montgomery,Michael	L	10	21	aa	KC	5	4	13	0	59	60	25	4	23	42	3.80	1.40	19.7	258	3.5	6.4	1.8	0.6	31%	73%	62
		11	22	aaa	KC	5	11	28	0	151	166	93	13	63	107	5.54	1.52	23.9	275	3.7	6.4	1.7	0.8	33%	63%	51
		12	23	a/a	KC	5	12	27	0	150	198	113	22	62	90	6.77	1.74	25.3	320	3.7	5.4	1.5	1.3	35%	62%	15
Morgan,Adam	L	12	22	aa	PHI	4	1	6	0	36	38	16	2	11	25	4.01	1.35	24.8	272	2.7	6.4	2.4	0.5	32%	70%	73
Morris,Bryan	R	10	23	aa	PIT	6	4	19	0	89	100	49	9	30	68	5.00	1.46	20.5	278	3.0	6.9	2.3	0.9	33%	67%	60
		11	24	aa	PIT	3	4	35	3	78	84	35	2	33	50	4.05	1.50	9.8	269	3.8	5.8	1.5	0.2	33%	71%	61
		12	25	aaa	PIT	2	2	46	5	81	93	32	9	18	60	3.52	1.37	7.4	290	2.0	6.7	3.4	1.0	33%	78%	78
Munson,Kevin	R	12	23	aa	ARI	3	5	44	3	53	65	46	4	27	54	7.87	1.73	5.5	302	4.6	9.1	2.0	0.6	39%	51%	73
Nelson,Jimmy	R	12	23	aa	MIL	2	4	10	0	46	39	24	2	38	37	4.65	1.67	20.6	231	7.4	7.2	1.0	0.5	28%	71%	59
Nolin,Sean	L	12	23	aa	TOR	1	0	3	0	15	11	2	0	6	16	1.49	1.11	19.6	199	3.6	9.3	2.6	0.0	28%	85%	125
Oberholtzer,Brett	L	11	22	aa	HOU	11	12	27	0	155	152	68	8	46	107	3.95	1.28	24.1	251	2.7	6.2	2.3	0.5	30%	69%	75
		12	23	a/a	HOU	10	10	28	0	167	194	79	23	36	118	4.29	1.38	25.0	293	2.0	6.4	3.3	1.2	33%	73%	67
Odorizzi,Jake	R	11	21	aa	KC	5	3	12	0	69	69	37	11	20	45	4.90	1.30	24.2	257	2.6	5.9	2.3	1.4	28%	66%	43
		12	22	a/a	KC	15	5	26	0	145	143	54	12	48	112	3.31	1.31	23.1	259	2.9	6.9	2.4	0.8	31%	77%	71
Oliveros,Lester	R	10	22	aa	DET	1	2	24	14	25	22	16	3	20	31	5.74	1.67	4.8	231	7.2	11.1	1.6	1.1	32%	67%	76
		11	23	a/a	MIN	3	3	34	5	48	55	24	7	21	47	4.50	1.58	6.3	281	3.9	8.8	2.2	1.2	35%	75%	62
		12	24	a/a	MIN	2	3	32	8	48	40	16	2	16	42	2.98	1.15	6.0	227	2.9	7.8	2.7	0.4	29%	74%	102
Oliver,Andrew	L	11	24	aaa	DET	8	12	26	0	147	179	99	18	82	115	6.06	1.77	26.5	294	5.0	7.0	1.4	1.1	35%	67%	35
		12	25	aaa	DET	5	9	28	0	118	124	81	8	90	87	6.17	1.81	19.5	271	6.9	6.7	1.0	0.6	32%	65%	43
Olmsted,Michael	R	12	25	aa	BOS	1	2	14	3	20	14	0	0	8	25	0.00	1.07	5.6	197	3.4	11.2	3.3	0.0	31%	100%	152
Omogrosso,Brian	R	08	24	aa	CHW	2	3	17	1	39	41	23	3	27	22	5.34	1.75	10.7	265	6.3	5.0	0.8	0.7	30%	69%	27
		09	25	a/a	CHW	7	2	17	0	78	100	62	8	47	59	7.15	1.88	22.1	305	5.5	6.8	1.2	1.0	36%	61%	32
		10	26	aa	CHW	0	1	3	0	3	2	1	0	1	3	3.45	1.15	4.1	208	3.4	7.8	2.3	0.0	28%	67%	108
		11	27	a/a	CHW	1	3	42	2	65	78	31	4	29	58	4.27	1.64	7.1	290	4.0	7.9	2.0	0.6	37%	74%	68
		12	28	aaa	CHW	0	2	33	9	47	59	37	5	16	47	6.98	1.58	6.3	306	3.0	8.9	2.9	0.9	38%	54%	81
Oramas,Juan	L	11	21	a/a	SD	10	6	20	0	108	99	34	9	25	97	2.85	1.15	22.0	238	2.1	8.1	3.9	0.7	30%	78%	116
		12	22	aa	SD	3	4	8	0	35	41	25	4	15	30	6.43	1.59	19.5	290	3.9	7.6	1.9	1.1	34%	59%	52
Ortega,Jose	R	10	22	aa	DET	1	0	15	0	23	25	9	2	7	16	3.49	1.38	6.6	270	2.7	6.2	2.3	0.8	32%	77%	63
		11	23	aaa	DET	1	3	33	0	50	72	44	8	27	36	7.93	1.98	7.4	330	4.9	6.5	1.3	1.5	38%	60%	13
		12	24	aaa	DET	5	8	45	1	63	90	49	4	51	54	7.10	2.24	7.1	336	7.3	7.8	1.1	0.6	41%	67%	38
Owens,Rudy	L	10	23	aa	PIT	12	6	26	0	150	138	47	11	22	111	2.82	1.07	23.0	240	1.3	6.7	5.0	0.7	29%	76%	133
		11	24	aaa	PIT	9	7	21	0	112	148	73	10	31	56	5.88	1.59	24.1	310	2.5	4.5	1.8	0.8	35%	62%	33
		12	25	aaa	HOU	10	8	27	0	163	164	62	18	36	89	3.41	1.23	24.5	263	2.0	4.9	2.5	1.0	28%	76%	54
Paxton,James	L	11	23	aa	SEA	3	0	7	0	39	31	9	2	13	45	2.05	1.12	22.5	214	3.0	10.4	3.5	0.4	31%	83%	135
		12	24	aa	SEA	9	4	21	0	106	115	46	5	58	96	3.88	1.63	22.5	277	4.9	8.1	1.6	0.5	35%	76%	69
Peacock,Brad	R	11	23	a/a	WAS	15	3	25	0	147	113	47	10	46	147	2.88	1.09	23.5	208	2.8	9.0	3.2	0.6	28%	75%	116
		12	24	aaa	OAK	12	9	28	0	135	159	93	14	64	118	6.23	1.65	21.5	295	4.2	7.9	1.8	0.9	36%	62%	54
Peavey,Greg	R	12	24	aa	NYM	8	8	25	0	144	185	86	17	34	68	5.40	1.52	25.0	313	2.1	4.2	2.0	1.1	33%	66%	26
Pena,Ariel	R	12	23	aa	MIL	6	8	26	0	147	153	76	22	66	122	4.67	1.50	24.4	270	4.1	7.5	1.8	1.3	31%	73%	44
Peralta,Wily	R	10	21	aa	MIL	2	3	8	0	42	47	19	5	24	26	4.06	1.69	24.2	277	5.1	5.6	1.1	1.1	31%	79%	24
		11	22	a/a	MIL	11	7	26	0	151	134	55	9	56	141	3.26	1.26	24.2	233	3.3	8.4	2.5	0.5	31%	75%	96
		12	23	aaa	MIL	7	11	28	0	147	177	92	11	80	123	5.62	1.76	24.0	300	4.9	7.5	1.5	0.6	36%	67%	53
Perez,Martin	L	10	19	aa	TEX	5	8	24	0	99	125	76	14	46	96	6.93	1.72	19.2	301	4.2	8.7	2.1	1.2	38%	60%	53
		11	20	a/a	TEX	8	6	27	0	137	158	68	10	52	105	4.49	1.53	22.6	283	3.4	6.9	2.0	0.7	34%	71%	62
		12	21	aaa	TEX	7	6	22	0	127	133	67	12	54	58	4.76	1.48	24.8	271	3.8	4.1	1.1	0.8	29%	68%	23
Petricka,Jacob	R	12	24	aa	CHW	3	3	10	0	58	74	43	9	39	23	6.68	1.97	27.6	312	6.2	3.6	0.6	1.4	32%	68%	-15
Pimentel,Carlos	R	11	22	aa	TEX	7	9	28	0	142	143	87	17	79	93	5.47	1.56	22.8	256	5.0	5.9	1.2	1.1	29%	66%	31
		12	23	aa	TEX	8	3	35	1	88	70	33	5	55	75	3.34	1.41	10.7	219	5.6	7.6	1.4	0.6	27%	77%	69
Pimentel,Stolmy	R	11	21	aa	BOS	0	9	15	0	50	80	55	7	22	26	9.81	2.03	16.6	354	3.9	4.6	1.2	1.3	39%	50%	-3
		12	22	aa	BOS	6	7	22	0	116	136	77	10	43	74	5.97	1.55	23.0	295	3.3	5.7	1.7	0.8	33%	61%	43
Portillo,Adys	R	12	21	aa	SD	2	5	8	0	35	35	28	3	24	24	7.20	1.69	19.7	262	6.2	6.1	1.0	0.8	30%	56%	35
Pryor,Stephen	R	11	22	aa	SEA	2	1	17	6	23	10	3	0	7	24	1.30	0.73	4.9	128	2.7	9.6	3.6	0.0	20%	80%	162
		12	23	a/a	SEA	1	0	27	10	36	20	2	0	16	39	0.55	0.99	5.1	163	4.0	9.8	2.5	0.0	24%	94%	133
Ramirez,J.C.	R	10	22	aa	PHI	3	4	13	0	77	96	51	12	23	51	5.95	1.54	26.5	299	2.7	5.9	2.2	1.4	34%	64%	36
		11	23	aa	PHI	11	13	26	0	144	160	81	16	53	75	5.04	1.48	24.4	276	3.3	4.7	1.4	1.0	30%	67%	28
		12	24	a/a	PHI	3	4	45	4	67	66	37	7	32	44	5.00	1.46	6.4	259	4.3	5.8	1.4	0.9	29%	67%	39
Ramirez,Neil	R	11	22	a/a	TEX	5	3	24	0	93	82	36	7	41	93	3.50	1.31	16.5	230	3.9	9.0	2.3	0.7	30%	75%	89
		12	23	a/a	TEX	8	13	28	0	123	145	105	23	48	88	7.70	1.57	19.3	295	3.5	6.4	1.8	1.7	32%	52%	23
Ranaudo,Anthony	R	12	23	aa	BOS	1	3	9	0	38	50	37	5	28	23	8.88	2.06	20.4	318	6.7	5.4	0.8	1.1	35%	55%	8
Reed,Chris	L	12	22	aa	LA	0	4	12	0	35	34	21	2	19	25	5.46	1.50	12.7	255	4.8	6.4	1.3	0.5	30%	62%	55
Rhee,Dae-Eun	R	12	23	aa	CHC	9	8	27	0	142	195	93	21	53	66	5.90	1.74	24.1	327	3.3	4.2	1.2	1.3	34%	68%	2
Rienzo,Andre	R	12	24	a/a	CHW	4	3	14	0	78	74	34	3	41	71	3.90	1.46	24.0	251	4.7	8.1	1.7	0.3	32%	72%	81
Roach,Donn	R	12	23	aa	SD	1	1	4	0	17	10	3	0	8	4	1.64	1.03	16.4	167	4.2	2.4	0.6	0.0	18%	82%	48
Rodriguez,Armando	R	12	24	a/a	NYM	2	3	35	1	77	66	28	12	21	64	3.32	1.14	8.7	234	2.5	7.4	3.0	1.5	26%	79%	72

PITCHER	Th	Yr	Age	Lev	Org	W	L	G	Sv	IP	H	ER	HR	BB	K	ERA	WHIP	BF/G	OBA	bb/9	K/9	Cmd	HR/9	H%	S%	BPV
Rodriguez,Julio	R	12	22	aa	PHI	7	7	29	0	134	134	71	15	74	119	4.80	1.55	20.2	262	4.9	8.0	1.6	1.0	31%	71%	55
Rodriguez,Santos	L	12	24	a/a	CHW	2	4	42	8	71	48	30	8	41	59	3.79	1.25	6.9	194	5.2	7.5	1.5	1.0	22%	73%	61
Rogers,Mark	R	10	24	a/a	MIL	6	8	25	0	116	100	53	3	74	100	4.08	1.50	20.5	228	5.8	7.8	1.3	0.2	30%	71%	77
		12	26	aaa	MIL	6	6	18	0	95	113	64	16	54	61	6.06	1.75	24.2	296	5.1	5.7	1.1	1.5	32%	68%	8
Rondon,Bruce	R	12	22	aa	DET	1	1	30	14	30	23	5	2	15	27	1.43	1.28	4.1	213	4.7	8.0	1.7	0.6	26%	93%	78
Rondon,Hector	R	9	22	a/a	CLE	11	10	27	0	146	158	66	11	29	130	4.05	1.28	22.7	270	1.8	8.0	4.6	0.7	34%	69%	124
		10	22.6	aaa	CLE	1	3	7	0	31	50	30	10	10	30	8.79	1.89	21.5	352	2.7	8.8	3.2	3.0	40%	59%	14
Rosario,Jose	R	10	24.6	a/a	FLA	5	5	18	0	85	102	43	8	42	61	4.57	1.69	21.8	291	4.5	6.5	1.4	0.9	34%	74%	40
Rosenthal,Trevor	R	12	22	a/a	STL	8	6	20	0	109	82	37	6	40	89	3.08	1.13	21.5	212	3.3	7.3	2.2	0.5	26%	73%	88
Ruffin,Chance	R	11	23	aa	DET	3	3	44	19	49	43	13	2	22	49	2.46	1.32	4.7	231	4.0	9.1	2.3	0.6	31%	84%	93
		12	24	aaa	SEA	0	5	50	1	71	79	47	7	33	47	5.93	1.59	6.2	284	4.2	6.0	1.4	0.9	32%	62%	38
Salazar,Danny	R	12	22	aa	CLE	4	0	6	0	34	30	9	1	8	20	2.41	1.11	22.3	236	2.2	5.3	2.4	0.3	27%	78%	81
Sampson,Keyvius	R	12	21	aa	SD	8	11	26	0	122	112	68	9	55	112	5.00	1.36	19.7	244	4.0	8.2	2.0	0.7	31%	63%	78
Sanchez,Jesus	R	11	24	aa	MIL	4	7	30	1	99	118	62	14	48	57	5.64	1.68	15.2	290	4.4	5.2	1.2	1.3	32%	69%	14
		12	25	a/a	MIL	7	3	52	11	72	68	16	2	24	54	2.04	1.28	5.6	252	3.0	6.7	2.3	0.3	31%	85%	84
Scahill,Rob	R	11	24	aa	COL	12	11	27	0	161	189	83	14	59	81	4.63	1.54	26.5	287	3.3	4.5	1.4	0.8	32%	71%	30
		12	25	aaa	COL	9	11	29	0	152	189	106	13	72	121	6.30	1.72	23.8	307	4.3	7.2	1.7	0.7	37%	62%	50
Scarpetta,Cody	R	11	23	aa	MIL	8	5	23	0	117	111	56	9	61	86	4.33	1.47	22.4	246	4.7	6.6	1.4	0.7	30%	71%	55
Schrader,Clayton	R	12	22	aa	BAL	1	0	19	1	23	17	8	1	23	14	3.17	1.73	5.5	205	9.0	5.6	0.6	0.4	24%	82%	47
Seaton,Ross	R	11	22	aa	HOU	4	9	28	0	155	173	89	18	42	85	5.16	1.39	23.9	277	2.4	5.0	2.0	1.0	31%	64%	41
		12	23	aaa	HOU	8	9	29	0	169	186	73	18	35	101	3.86	1.30	24.1	280	1.8	5.4	2.9	1.0	31%	73%	64
Shreve,Colby	R	12	24	aa	PHI	3	1	28	2	43	50	25	2	25	24	5.19	1.74	7.0	290	5.3	5.1	1.0	0.5	33%	69%	34
Skaggs,Tyler	L	11	20	aa	ARI	4	1	10	0	58	48	17	4	14	64	2.67	1.06	23.0	220	2.1	9.9	4.7	0.6	31%	77%	150
		12	21	a/a	ARI	9	6	22	0	122	119	41	12	33	100	3.01	1.24	22.6	256	2.4	7.4	3.0	0.9	30%	79%	85
Snow,Forrest	R	11	23	aaa	SEA	1	2	9	0	35	32	17	3	8	32	4.38	1.14	15.9	236	2.1	8.2	3.9	0.7	30%	62%	117
		12	24	a/a	SEA	5	9	32	0	118	145	93	10	68	86	7.08	1.81	17.0	305	5.2	6.6	1.3	0.7	36%	59%	38
Solano,Javier	R	10	20	aa	LA	2	0	13	0	19	16	5	2	4	20	2.23	1.04	5.9	224	1.8	9.4	5.2	0.9	29%	84%	149
		11	21	aa	LA	1	0	19	1	33	30	11	1	14	24	2.93	1.35	7.3	242	3.7	6.6	1.8	0.2	30%	77%	76
		12	22	aa	LA	3	0	38	0	63	64	21	4	16	52	3.08	1.27	6.8	266	2.3	7.4	3.3	0.6	32%	77%	97
Soto,Giovanni	L	12	21	aa	CLE	6	9	22	0	121	130	68	11	50	87	5.07	1.48	23.7	276	3.7	6.5	1.8	0.8	32%	66%	51
Stilson,John	R	12	22	aa	TOR	2	4	17	1	50	62	34	7	23	39	6.14	1.69	13.3	305	4.1	7.0	1.7	1.3	35%	65%	33
Stowell,Bryce	R	10	24	aa	CLE	2	1	31	7	42	29	13	2	28	52	2.87	1.35	5.8	191	6.0	11.2	1.9	0.4	29%	79%	111
		11	25	aa	CLE	1	0	13	0	19	14	5	1	11	23	2.33	1.30	6.3	203	5.0	10.6	2.1	0.5	30%	83%	108
		12	26	aa	CLE	2	1	25	2	29	30	17	6	10	35	5.27	1.37	4.9	266	3.1	10.8	3.5	1.9	33%	68%	83
Straily,Dan	R	12	24	a/a	OAK	9	7	25	0	152	120	50	8	41	161	2.98	1.06	23.6	218	2.4	9.5	3.9	0.5	29%	72%	136
Suarez,Larry	R	11	22	aa	CHC	0	2	6	0	16	24	15	2	6	9	8.21	1.87	12.8	341	3.3	5.3	1.6	1.2	38%	55%	16
Surkamp,Eric	L	11	24	aa	SF	10	4	23	0	142	133	42	6	46	135	2.63	1.26	25.8	242	2.9	8.6	2.9	0.4	32%	79%	109
Taillon,Jameson	R	12	21	aa	PIT	3	0	3	0	17	12	4	0	1	15	1.90	0.79	20.4	206	0.5	7.8	15.4	0.0	27%	73%	383
Teheran,Julio	R	10	20	aa	ATL	3	2	7	0	40	29	15	2	15	37	3.48	1.11	23.0	199	3.5	8.4	2.4	0.4	27%	68%	104
		11	20	aaa	ATL	15	3	25	0	145	136	48	5	47	111	2.98	1.27	24.2	244	2.9	6.9	2.4	0.3	31%	76%	87
		12	21	aaa	ATL	7	9	26	0	131	156	79	17	41	87	5.43	1.50	21.8	297	2.8	6.0	2.1	1.2	33%	65%	41
Thornburg,Tyler	R	12	24	a/a	MIL	10	4	21	0	113	111	49	8	39	96	3.90	1.33	22.3	259	3.1	7.7	2.5	0.7	32%	71%	82
Tillman,Daniel	R	12	23	aa	LAA	1	5	20	0	19	27	33	3	20	18	15.43	2.42	5.1	333	9.1	8.3	0.9	1.6	39%	31%	10
Ventura,Yordano	R	12	21	aa	KC	1	2	6	0	29	25	17	1	13	21	5.25	1.29	20.1	235	3.9	6.4	1.7	0.3	28%	56%	73
Vizcaino,Arodys	R	11	21	a/a	ATL	3	3	17	0	57	56	25	4	17	56	3.90	1.29	14.0	252	2.8	8.9	3.2	0.6	33%	70%	107
Walker,Taijuan	R	12	20	aa	SEA	7	10	25	0	127	138	78	12	50	110	5.57	1.49	21.8	279	3.6	7.8	2.2	0.9	34%	62%	66
Warren,Adam	R	10	23	aa	NYY	4	2	10	0	54	56	23	2	16	52	3.77	1.33	23.0	261	2.7	8.7	3.2	0.3	35%	71%	112
		11	24	aaa	NYY	6	8	27	0	152	180	83	19	59	91	4.92	1.56	25.3	288	3.5	5.4	1.6	1.1	32%	71%	29
		12	25	aaa	NYY	7	8	26	0	153	205	83	15	50	86	4.87	1.67	26.4	322	3.0	5.1	1.7	0.9	36%	72%	30
Webster,Allen	R	11	21	aa	LA	6	3	18	0	91	103	49	6	30	65	4.88	1.46	22.2	279	3.0	6.4	2.1	0.6	34%	66%	65
		12	22	aa	BOS	6	9	29	0	131	158	73	2	62	110	5.02	1.68	20.3	299	4.3	7.6	1.8	0.2	38%	68%	73
Wheeler,Zack	R	12	22	a/a	NYM	12	8	25	0	149	120	55	4	52	124	3.30	1.16	23.7	222	3.2	7.5	2.4	0.2	28%	70%	99
Whitenack,Robert	R	11	23	aa	CHC	4	0	7	0	38	36	11	1	13	18	2.74	1.29	22.7	246	3.1	4.4	1.4	0.3	28%	78%	55
Wilk,Adam	L	11	24	aaa	DET	8	6	18	0	103	126	48	18	14	61	4.17	1.37	24.5	296	1.3	5.4	4.3	1.6	32%	76%	71
		12	25	aaa	DET	7	11	24	0	150	148	58	15	29	100	3.49	1.18	24.9	260	1.7	6.0	3.5	0.9	29%	73%	86
Wilson,Alex	R	10	24	aa	BOS	4	5	16	0	78	108	67	15	33	47	7.72	1.81	23.1	322	3.8	5.4	1.4	1.8	35%	59%	-1
		11	25	a/a	BOS	10	4	25	0	133	146	58	11	46	98	3.89	1.45	23.2	273	3.1	6.6	2.1	0.7	33%	74%	63
		12	26	aaa	BOS	5	3	40	1	73	99	43	4	37	61	5.33	1.86	8.5	325	4.5	7.6	1.7	0.5	40%	70%	57
Withrow,Chris	R	10	21	aa	LA	4	9	27	0	129	153	88	12	66	98	6.13	1.70	22.1	289	4.6	6.8	1.5	0.8	35%	63%	44
		11	22	aa	LA	6	6	25	0	129	114	59	7	64	115	4.10	1.38	22.1	233	4.5	8.0	1.8	0.5	30%	70%	80
		12	23	aa	LA	3	3	22	2	60	59	36	3	34	54	5.35	1.55	11.9	257	5.2	8.1	1.6	0.5	33%	64%	72
Wojciechowski,Asher	R	12	24	aa	HOU	2	2	8	0	44	33	12	0	13	29	2.38	1.05	21.1	209	2.7	5.9	2.2	0.0	26%	75%	94
Wood,Austin	L	11	25	aa	DET	5	5	50	6	63	67	27	6	28	48	3.84	1.52	5.6	269	4.0	6.9	1.7	0.8	32%	76%	55
		12	26	a/a	DET	1	0	20	0	23	36	14	1	17	21	5.53	2.27	5.9	354	6.5	8.1	1.2	0.4	44%	75%	45
Workman,Brandon	R	12	24	aa	BOS	3	1	5	0	25	28	15	2	5	19	5.36	1.35	20.8	287	1.9	6.8	3.6	0.8	34%	60%	88
Wright,Mike	R	12	22	aa	BAL	5	3	12	0	62	79	39	8	16	38	5.68	1.53	22.6	311	2.4	5.5	2.3	1.2	34%	64%	40
Zych,Tony	R	12	22	aa	CHC	2	1	20	0	25	30	14	1	12	24	5.27	1.70	5.6	299	4.5	8.8	2.0	0.4	39%	67%	77

This section of the book may be the smallest as far as word count is concerned, but may be the most important, as this is where players' skills and potential are tied together and ranked against their peers. The rankings that follow are divided into long-term potential in the major leagues and shorter-term fantasy value.

HQ100: Lists the top 100 minor league prospects in terms of long-range potential in the major leagues. The overall list is the work of five minor-league analysts at BaseballHQ.com (Rob Gordon, Jeremy Deloney, Brent Hershey, Colby Garrapy and Chris Mallonee). The two authors then also provide their own personal lists.

ORGANIZATIONAL: Lists the top 15 minor league prospects within each organization in terms of long-range potential in the major leagues.

POSITIONAL: Lists the top 15 prospects, by position, in terms of long-range potential in the major leagues.

TOP POWER: Lists the top 25 prospects that have the potential to hit for power in the major leagues, combining raw power, plate discipline, and at the ability to make their power game-usable.

TOP BA: Lists the top 25 prospects that have the potential to hit for high batting average in the major leagues, combining contact ability, plate discipline, hitting mechanics and strength.

TOP SPEED: Lists the top 25 prospects that have the potential to steal bases in the major leagues, combining raw speed and base-running instincts.

TOP FASTBALL: Lists the top 25 pitchers that have the best fastball, combining velocity and pitch movement.

TOP BREAKING BALL: Lists the top 25 pitchers that have the best breaking ball, combining pitch movement, strikeout potential, and consistency.

2013 TOP FANTASY PROSPECTS: Lists the top 100 minor league prospects that will have the most value to their respective fantasy teams in 2013.

TOP 100 ARCHIVE: Takes a look back at the top 100 lists from the past eight years.

The rankings in this book are the creation of the minor league department at BaseballHQ.com. While several baseball personnel contributed player information to the book, no opinions were solicited or received in comparing players.

THE HQ100: TOP PROSPECTS OF 2013

1	Jurickson Profar	SS	TEX		51	Jake Marisnick	OF	MIA
2	Dylan Bundy	SP	BAL		52	Trevor Story	SS	COL
3	Wil Myers	OF	TAM		53	Kevin Gausman	SP	BAL
4	Gerrit Cole	SP	PIT		54	Trevor Rosenthal	SP	STL
5	Oscar Taveras	OF	STL		55	Alex Meyer	SP	MIN
6	Taijuan Walker	SP	SEA		56	Jorge Soler	OF	CHC
7	Trevor Bauer	SP	CLE		57	Matt Davidson	3B	ARI
8	Jose Fernandez	SP	MIA		58	Brett Jackson	OF	CHC
9	Travis d'Arnaud	C	NYM		59	Michael Choice	OF	OAK
10	Miguel Sano	3B	MIN		60	David Dahl	OF	COL
11	Zack Wheeler	SP	NYM		61	Mason Williams	OF	NYY
12	Christian Yelich	OF	MIA		62	Robert Stephenson	SP	CIN
13	Tyler Skaggs	SP	ARI		63	Chris Archer	SP	TAM
14	Francisco Lindor	SS	CLE		64	Oswaldo Arcia	OF	MIN
15	Javier Baez	SS	CHC		65	Zach Lee	SP	LA
16	Shelby Miller	SP	STL		66	Tony Cingrani	SP	CIN
17	Nick Castellanos	OF	DET		67	Jesse Biddle	SP	PHI
18	Xander Bogaerts	SS	BOS		68	Gregory Polanco	OF	PIT
19	Jameson Taillon	SP	PIT		69	Addison Russell	SS	OAK
20	Danny Hultzen	SP	SEA		70	Robbie Erlin	SP	SD
21	Jonathan Singleton	1B	HOU		71	Courtney Hawkins	OF	CHW
22	Mike Zunino	C	SEA		72	Brian Goodwin	OF	WAS
23	Billy Hamilton	OF	CIN		73	Martin Perez	SP	TEX
24	Anthony Rendon	3B	WAS		74	Luis Heredia	SP	PIT
25	Mike Olt	3B	TEX		75	Yasiel Puig	OF	LA
26	Byron Buxton	OF	MIN		76	Wilmer Flores	3B	NYM
27	Nolan Arenado	3B	COL		77	Justin Nicolino	SP	MIA
28	Carlos Correa	SS	HOU		78	Max Fried	SP	SD
29	Archie Bradley	SP	ARI		79	Adam Eaton	OF	ARI
30	Julio Teheran	SP	ATL		80	Gary Brown	OF	SF
31	Matt Barnes	SP	BOS		81	Casey Kelly	SP	SD
32	Gary Sanchez	C	NYY		82	Lucas Giolito	SP	WAS
33	Jackie Bradley	OF	BOS		83	Wily Peralta	SP	MIL
34	Carlos Martinez	SP	STL		84	Michael Wacha	SP	STL
35	Bubba Starling	OF	KC		85	Austin Hedges	C	SD
36	Jake Odorizzi	SP	TAM		86	Kyle Gibson	SP	MIN
37	Jedd Gyorko	3B	SD		87	Hak-Ju Lee	SS	TAM
38	Alen Hanson	SS	PIT		88	Dan Straily	SP	OAK
39	George Springer	OF	HOU		89	Kyle Crick	SP	SF
40	Nick Franklin	2B	SEA		90	Avisail Garcia	OF	DET
41	Aaron Sanchez	SP	TOR		91	Cody Buckel	SP	TEX
42	Albert Almora	OF	CHC		92	Tyler Thornburg	SP	MIL
43	Kaleb Cowart	3B	LAA		93	Allen Webster	SP	BOS
44	Taylor Guerrieri	SP	TAM		94	Jarred Cosart	SP	HOU
45	Kyle Zimmer	SP	KC		95	Bruce Rondon	RP	DET
46	Noah Syndergaard	SP	NYM		96	Delino DeShields	2B	HOU
47	Kolten Wong	2B	STL		97	A.J. Cole	SP	OAK
48	Tyler Austin	OF	NYY		98	Manny Banuelos	SP	NYY
49	James Paxton	SP	SEA		99	Yordano Ventura	SP	KC
50	Rymer Liriano	OF	SD		100	Trevor May	SP	MIN

ROB GORDON'S TOP 100

#	Name	Pos	Team	#	Name	Pos	Team
1	Jurickson Profar	SS	TEX	51	Tony Cingrani	LHP	CIN
2	Oscar Taveras	OF	STL	52	Robert Stephenson	RHP	CIN
3	Wil Myers	OF	TAM	53	Wilmer Flores	3B	NYM
4	Dylan Bundy	RHP	BAL	54	Carlos Correa	SS	HOU
5	Jose Fernandez	RHP	MIA	55	Taylor Guerrieri	RHP	TAM
6	Travis D'Arnaud	C	NYM	56	Aaron Sanchez	RHP	TOR
7	Mike Zunino	C	SEA	57	Joey Gallo	3B	TEX
8	Gerrit Cole	RHP	PIT	58	Miles Head	3B	OAK
9	Trevor Bauer	RHP	CLE	59	George Springer	OF	HOU
10	Taijuan Walker	RHP	SEA	60	Addison Russell	SS	OAK
11	Xander Bogaerts	3B	BOS	61	Alex Meyer	RHP	MIN
12	Javier Baez	SS	CHC	62	Brian Goodwin	OF	WAS
13	Anthony Rendon	3B	WAS	63	Julio Teheran	RHP	ATL
14	Shelby Miller	RHP	STL	64	Dan Vogelbach	1B	CHC
15	Miguel Sano	3B	MIN	65	Justin Nicolino	LHP	MIA
16	Billy Hamilton	OF	CIN	66	Brett Jackson	OF	CHC
17	Christian Yelich	CF	MIA	67	Kevin Gausman	RHP	BAL
18	Nick Castellanos	3B/OF	DET	68	Jessie Biddle	LHP	PHI
19	Zack Wheeler	RHP	NYM	69	Luis Heredia	RHP	PIT
20	Tyler Skaggs	LHP	ARI	70	Austin Hedges	C	SD
21	Mike Olt	3B	TEX	71	Joc Pederson	OF	LA
22	Nolan Arenado	3B	COL	72	Daniel Corcino	RHP	CIN
23	Jonathan Singleton	1B	HOU	73	Zach Lee	RHP	LA
24	Jameson Taillon	RHP	PIT	74	Cody Buckel	RHP	TEX
25	Carlos Martinez	RHP	STL	75	Michael Wacha	RHP	STL
26	Francisco Lindor	SS	CLE	76	Matt Davidson	3B	ARI
27	Trevor Story	SS	COL	77	James Paxton	LHP	SEA
28	Byron Buxton	OF	MIN	78	Kolten Wong	2B	STL
29	Archie Bradley	RHP	ARI	79	Michael Choice	OF	OAK
30	Danny Hultzen	LHP	SEA	80	Brad Miller	SS	SEA
31	Bubba Starling	OF	KC	81	Casey Kelly	RHP	SD
32	Gregory Polanco	OF	PIT	82	Trevor May	RHP	MIN
33	Jedd Gyorko	3B	SD	83	Kaleb Cowart	3B	LAA
34	Matt Barnes	RHP	BOS	84	Gary Brown	OF	SF
35	Albert Almora	OF	CHC	85	Jarred Cosart	RHP	HOU
36	Jake Odorizzi	RHP	TAM	86	Martin Perez	LHP	TEX
37	Gary Sanchez	C	NYY	87	A.J. Cole	RHP	OAK
38	Oswaldo Arcia	OF	MIN	88	Courtney Hawkins	OF	CHW
39	Alen Hanson	SS/2B	PIT	89	Leonys Martin	OF	TEX
40	Jackie Bradley Jr	OF	BOS	90	Kyle Parker	OF	COL
41	Tyler Austin	OF	NYY	91	Eddie Rosario	2B	MIN
42	Jorge Soler	OF	CHC	92	Chris Archer	RHP	TAM
43	Yasiel Puig	OF	LA	93	Yordano Ventura	RHP	KC
44	David Dahl	OF	COL	94	Dan Straily	RHP	OAK
45	Rymer Liriano	OF	SD	95	Tyler Thornburg	RHP	MIL
46	Mason Williams	OF	NYY	96	Daniel Norris	LHP	TOR
47	Robbie Erlin	LHP	SD	97	Kyle Crick	RHP	SF
48	Nick Franklin	SS	SEA	98	Bruce Rondon	RHP	DET
49	Noah Syndergaard	RHP	NYM	99	Corey Seager	3B	LA
50	Trevor Rosenthal	RHP	STL	100	Matt Wisler	RHP	SD

JEREMY DELONEY'S TOP 100

#	Name	Pos	Team	#	Name	Pos	Team
1	Dylan Bundy	RHP	BAL	51	Nick Franklin	INF	SEA
2	Jurickson Profar	SS	TEX	52	Tyler Austin	OF	NYY
3	Gerrit Cole	RHP	PIT	53	Robert Stephenson	RHP	CIN
4	Oscar Taveras	OF	STL	54	Adam Eaton	OF	ARI
5	Wil Myers	OF	TAM	55	Kyle Crick	RHP	SF
6	Trevor Bauer	RHP	CLE	56	Jake Marisnick	OF	MIA
7	Francisco Lindor	SS	CLE	57	Max Fried	LHP	SD
8	Christian Yelich	OF	MIA	58	Jorge Soler	OF	CHC
9	Miguel Sano	3B	MIN	59	Aaron Sanchez	RHP	TOR
10	Mike Zunino	C	SEA	60	Gregory Polanco	OF	PIT
11	Jose Fernandez	RHP	MIA	61	Tyler Thornburg	RHP	MIL
12	Anthony Rendon	3B	WAS	62	Brett Jackson	OF	CHC
13	Jonathan Singleton	1B	HOU	63	Yasiel Puig	OF	LA
14	Taijuan Walker	RHP	SEA	64	Michael Choice	OF	OAK
15	Javier Baez	SS	CHC	65	Bubba Starling	OF	KC
16	Tyler Skaggs	LHP	ARI	66	Carlos Martinez	RHP	STL
17	Danny Hultzen	LHP	SEA	67	Zach Lee	RHP	LA
18	Kyle Zimmer	RHP	KC	68	Oswaldo Arcia	OF	MIN
19	Zack Wheeler	RHP	NYM	69	Bruce Rondon	RHP	DET
20	Jameson Taillon	RHP	PIT	70	Trevor Rosenthal	RHP	STL
21	Travis d'Arnaud	C	NYM	71	J.R. Graham	RHP	ATL
22	Nick Castellanos	3B/OF	DET	72	Kyle Gibson	RHP	MIN
23	Shelby Miller	RHP	STL	73	Avisail Garcia	OF	DET
24	Byron Buxton	OF	MIN	74	Matt Davidson	3B	ARI
25	Carlos Correa	SS	HOU	75	Gary Brown	OF	SF
26	Xander Bogaerts	SS	BOS	76	Chris Archer	RHP	TAM
27	Nolan Arenado	3B	COL	77	Corey Seager	3B	LA
28	Michael Wacha	RHP	STL	78	Jarred Cosart	RHP	HOU
29	Jedd Gyorko	3B	SD	79	Kevin Gausman	RHP	BAL
30	Matt Barnes	RHP	BOS	80	Luke Sims	RHP	ATL
31	James Paxton	LHP	SEA	81	Jesse Biddle	LHP	PHI
32	Trevor Story	SS	COL	82	Cody Buckel	RHP	TEX
33	Mike Olt	3B	TEX	83	Arodys Vizcaino	RHP	CHC
34	Julio Teheran	RHP	ATL	84	Casey Kelly	RHP	SD
35	George Springer	OF	HOU	85	Addison Russell	SS	OAK
36	Lucas Giolito	RHP	WAS	86	Noah Syndergaard	RHP	NYM
37	Jake Odorizzi	RHP	TAM	87	Alex Meyer	RHP	MIN
38	Kolten Wong	2B	STL	88	Wilmer Flores	3B	NYM
39	Archie Bradley	RHP	ARI	89	Justin Nicolino	LHP	MIA
40	Gary Sanchez	C	NYY	90	Martin Perez	LHP	TEX
41	Kaleb Cowart	3B	LAA	91	Domingo Santana	OF	HOU
42	Jackie Bradley	OF	BOS	92	Andrew Heaney	LHP	MIA
43	Taylor Guerrieri	RHP	TAM	93	Jonathan Schoop	INF	BAL
44	David Dahl	OF	COL	94	Lance McCullers	RHP	HOU
45	Courtney Hawkins	OF	CHW	95	Luis Heredia	RHP	PIT
46	Albert Almora	OF	CHC	96	Brian Goodwin	OF	WAS
47	Alen Hanson	SS	PIT	97	Tony Cingrani	LHP	CIN
48	Billy Hamilton	OF	CIN	98	Allen Webster	RHP	BOS
49	Robbie Erlin	LHP	SD	99	Jeurys Familia	RHP	NYM
50	Wily Peralta	RHP	MIL	100	Yordano Ventura	RHP	KC

TOP PROSPECTS BY ORGANIZATION

AL EAST

BALTIMORE ORIOLES
1. Dylan Bundy, RHP
2. Kevin Gausman, RHP
3. Jonathan Schoop, SS
4. Xavier Avery, OF
5. Nick Delmonico, 1B
6. Branden Kline, RHP
7. Tim Berry, LHP
8. Adrian Marin, SS
9. Parker Bridwell, RHP
10. Christian Walker, 1B
11. Glynn Davis, OF
12. L.J. Hoes, OF
13. Mike Wright, RHP
14. Eduardo Rodriguez, LHP
15. Jason Esposito, 3B

BOSTON RED SOX
1. Xander Bogaerts, SS
2. Matt Barnes, RHP
3. Jackie Bradley, OF
4. Allen Webster, RHP
5. Garin Cecchini, 3B
6. Henry Owens, LHP
7. Blake Swihart, C
8. Bryce Brentz, OF
9. Anthony Ranaudo, RHP
10. Brandon Workman, RHP
11. Deven Marrero, SS
12. Aaron Kurcz, RHP
13. Jose Iglesias, SS
14. Brandon Jacobs, OF
15. Alex Wilson, RHP

NEW YORK YANKEES
1. Gary Sanchez, C
2. Tyler Austin, OF
3. Mason Williams, OF
4. Manny Banuelos, LHP
5. Mark Montgomery, RHP
6. Ty Hensley, RHP
7. Slade Heathcott, OF
8. Jose Campos, RHP
9. Ramon Flores, OF
10. Angelo Gumbs, 2B
11. Corey Black, RHP
12. Ravel Santana, OF
13. Bryan Mitchell, RHP
14. Zoilo Almonte, OF
15. Brett Marshall, RHP

TAMPA BAY RAYS
1. Wil Myers, OF
2. Taylor Guerrieri, RHP
3. Jake Odorizzi, RHP
4. Chris Archer, RHP
5. Richie Shaffer, 3B
6. Hak-Ju Lee, SS
7. Mikie Mahtook, OF
8. Alex Colome, RHP
9. Drew Vettleson, OF
10. Blake Snell, LHP
11. Enny Romero, LHP
12. Ryan Brett, 2B
13. Tyler Goeddel, 3B
14. Mike Montgomery, LHP
15. Felipe Rivero, LHP

TORONTO BLUE JAYS
1. Aaron Sanchez, RHP
2. Roberto Osuna, RHP
3. Daniel Norris, LHP
4. D.J. Davis, OF
5. Marcus Stroman, RHP
6. Deck McGuire, RHP
7. Chris Hawkins, OF
8. Adonys Cardona, RHP
9. Jake Anderson, OF
10. Matt Dean, 3B
11. Dwight Smith, OF
12. Matt Smoral, LHP
13. Anthony Alford, OF
14. Kevin Pillar, OF
15. Chase DeJong, RHP

AL CENTRAL

CHICAGO WHITE SOX
1. Courtney Hawkins, OF
2. Trayce Thompson, OF
3. Carlos Sanchez, 2B/SS
4. Keenyn Walker, OF
5. Erik Johnson, RHP
6. Jared Mitchell, OF
7. Keon Barnum, 1B
8. Scott Snodgress, LHP
9. Chris Beck, RHP
10. Jake Petricka, RHP
11. Jhan Marinez, RHP
12. Andre Rienzo, RHP
13. Andy Wilkins, 1B
14. Brandon Brennan, RHP
15. Joey DeMichele, 2B

CLEVELAND INDIANS
1. Trevor Bauer, RHP
2. Francisco Lindor, SS
3. Dorssys Paulino, SS
4. Mitch Brown, RHP
5. Luigi Rodriguez, OF
6. Tyler Naquin, OF
7. Ronny Rodriguez, 2B/SS
8. Danny Salazar, RHP
9. Chen Lee, RHP
10. Giovanny Urshela, 3B
11. Cody Allen, RHP
12. Bryce Stowell, RHP
13. Scott Barnes, LHP
14. Alex Monsalve, C
15. Tony Wolters, SS

DETROIT TIGERS
1. Nick Castellanos, OF
2. Bruce Rondon, RHP
3. Avisail Garcia, OF
4. Austin Schotts, OF
5. Danry Vasquez, OF
6. Casey Crosby, LHP
7. Jake Thompson, RHP
8. Eugenio Suarez, SS
9. Steven Moya, OF
10. Tyler Collins, OF
11. Brenny Paulino, RHP
12. Harold Castro, 2B
13. Drew VerHagen, RHP
14. Melvin Mercedes, RHP
15. Kenny Faulk, LHP

KANSAS CITY ROYALS
1. Kyle Zimmer, RHP
2. Bubba Starling, OF
3. Yordano Ventura, RHP
4. Adalberto Mondesi, SS
5. Miguel Almonte, RHP
6. Sam Selman, LHP
7. Alexis Rivera, OF
8. Jorge Bonifacio, OF
9. Donnie Joseph, LHP
10. Christian Colon, 2B/SS
11. Jason Adam, RHP
12. Chris Dwyer, LHP
13. J.C. Sulbaran, RHP
14. Cheslor Cuthbert, 3B
15. John Lamb, LHP

MINNESOTA TWINS
1. Miguel Sano, 3B
2. Byron Buxton, OF
3. Oswaldo Arcia, OF
4. Kyle Gibson, RHP
5. Alex Meyer, RHP
6. Trevor May, RHP
7. J.O. Berrios, RHP
8. Eddie Rosario, 2B
9. Aaron Hicks, OF
10. Jorge Polanco, SS
11. Travis Harrison, 3B
12. Luke Bard, RHP
13. Max Kepler, OF
14. J.T. Chargois, RHP
15. Mike Tonkin, RHP

AL WEST

HOUSTON ASTROS
1. Jonathan Singleton, 1B
2. Carlos Correa, SS
3. George Springer, OF
4. Jarred Cosart, RHP
5. Domingo Santana, OF
6. Lance McCullers, RHP
7. Delino DeShields, 2B
8. Nick Tropeano, RHP
9. Mike Foltynewicz, RHP
10. Jonathan Villar, SS
11. Rio Ruiz, 3B
12. Adrian Houser, RHP
13. Asher Wojciechowski, RHP
14. Vincent Velasquez, RHP
15. Carlos Perez, C

LOS ANGELES ANGELS
1. Kaleb Cowart, 3B
2. C.J. Cron, 1B
3. Taylor Lindsey, 2B
4. Nick Maronde, RHP
5. Randal Grichuk, OF
6. R.J. Alvarez, RHP
7. Travis Witherspoon, OF
8. Daniel Tillman, RHP
9. Cam Bedrosian, RHP
10. Alex Yarbrough, 2B
11. Luis Jimenez, 3B
12. Mark Sappington, RHP
13. A.J. Schugel, RHP
14. Wendell Soto, SS
15. Michael Clevinger, RHP

OAKLAND ATHLETICS
1. Michael Choice, OF
2. Addison Russell, SS
3. Grant Green, 2B
4. A.J. Cole, RHP
5. Nolan Sanburn, RHP
6. Dan Straily, RHP
7. Sonny Gray, RHP
8. Matt Olson, 1B
9. Max Stassi, C
10. Brad Peacock, RHP
11. Renato Nunez, 3B
12. Michael Taylor, OF
13. Miles Head, 3B
14. Daniel Robertson, SS/3B
15. Chris Bostick, 2B/SS

SEATTLE MARINERS
1. Mike Zunino, C
2. Taijuan Walker, RHP
3. Danny Hultzen, LHP
4. James Paxton, LHP
5. Nick Franklin, 2B
6. Carter Capps, RHP
7. Brandon Maurer, RHP
8. Brad Miller, SS
9. Victor Sanchez, RHP
10. Stephen Pryor, RHP
11. Stefen Romero, 2B
12. Guillermo Pimentel, OF
13. Vince Catricala, 3B
14. Leon Landry, OF
15. Tyler Marlette, C

TEXAS RANGERS
1. Jurickson Profar, SS
2. Mike Olt, 3B
3. Cody Buckel, RHP
4. Martin Perez, LHP
5. Lewis Brinson, OF
6. Roman Mendez, RHP
7. C.J. Edwards, RHP
8. Joey Gallo, 3B
9. Nomar Mazara, OF
10. Leonys Martin, OF
11. Jorge Alfaro, C/1B
12. Hanser Alberto, SS
13. Luke Jackson, RHP
14. Wilmer Font, RHP
15. Luis Sardinas, 2B/SS

TOP PROSPECTS BY ORGANIZATION

NL EAST

ATLANTA BRAVES
1. Julio Teheran, RHP
2. Sean Gilmartin, LHP
3. Lucas Sims, RHP
4. J.R. Graham, RHP
5. Christian Bethancourt, C
6. Zeke Spruill, RHP
7. Alex Wood, LHP
8. Jose Peraza, SS
9. Joey Terdoslavich, 1B
10. Edward Salcedo, 3B
11. Nick Ahmed, SS
12. Todd Cunningham, OF
13. Matt Lipka, OF
14. Josh Elander, C
15. Bryan de la Rosa, C

MIAMI MARLINS
1. Christian Yelich, OF
2. Jose Fernandez, RHP
3. Jake Marisnick, OF
4. Justin Nicolino, LHP
5. Andrew Heaney, LHP
6. Adam Conley, LHP
7. Marcell Ozuna, OF
8. Adeiny Hechavarria, SS
9. Rob Brantly, C
10. Jacob Realmuto, C
11. Jose Urena, RHP
12. Chad James, LHP
13. Mason Hope, RHP
14. Jesus Solorzano, OF
15. Zack Cox, 3B

NEW YORK METS
1. Zack Wheeler, RHP
2. Travis d'Arnaud, C
3. Noah Syndergaard, RHP
4. Wilmer Flores, 3B
5. Brandon Nimmo, OF
6. Jeurys Familia, RHP
7. Michael Fulmer, RHP
8. Gavin Cecchini, SS
9. Rafael Montero, RHP
10. Matt den Dekker, OF
11. Cesar Puello, OF
12. Reese Havens, 2B
13. Domingo Tapia, RHP
14. Cory Vaughn, OF
15. Juan Lagares, OF

PHILADELPHIA PHILLIES
1. Jesse Biddle, LHP
2. Maikel Franco, 3B
3. Tommy Joseph, C
4. Adam Morgan, LHP
5. Phillippe Aumont, RHP
6. Sebastian Valle, C
7. Ethan Martin, RHP
8. Jon Pettibone, RHP
9. Justin De Fratus, RHP
10. Cody Asche, 3B
11. Brody Colvin, RHP
12. Shane Watson, RHP
13. Darin Ruf, 1B
14. Roman Quinn, SS
15. Larry Greene, OF

WASHINGTON NATIONALS
1. Anthony Rendon, 3B
2. Brian Goodwin, OF
3. Lucas Giolito, RHP
4. Matt Skole, 3B
5. Michael Taylor, OF
6. Eury Perez, OF
7. Nathan Karns, RHP
8. Chris Marrero, 1B
9. Destin Hood, OF
10. Sammy Solis, LHP
11. Matt Purke, LHP
12. Robbie Ray, LHP
13. Tony Renda, 2B
14. Brett Mooneyham, LHP
15. Brandon Miller, OF

NL CENTRAL

CHICAGO CUBS
1. Javier Baez, SS
2. Albert Almora, OF
3. Jorge Soler, OF
4. Dan Vogelbach, 1B
5. Arodys Vizcaino, RHP
6. Brett Jackson, OF
7. Christian Villanueva, 3B
8. Pierce Johnson, RHP
9. Matt Szczur, OF
10. Dillon Maples, RHP
11. Gioskar Amaya, 2B
12. Trey McNutt, RHP
13. Jose Rosario, RHP
14. Duane Underwood, RHP
15. Josh Vitters, 3B

CINCINNATI REDS
1. Billy Hamilton, OF
2. Robert Stephenson, RHP
3. Tony Cingrani, LHP
4. Daniel Corcino, RHP
5. Nick Travieso, RHP
6. Jesse Winker, OF
7. Ryan Wright, 2B
8. Kyle Lotzkar, RHP
9. Tanner Rahier, 3B
10. Yorman Rodriguez, OF
11. Jeff Gelalich, OF
12. Drew Cisco, RHP
13. Ryan LaMarre, OF
14. Dan Langfield, RHP
15. Neftali Soto, 1B

MILWAUKEE BREWERS
1. Tyler Thornburg, RHP
2. Wily Peralta, RHP
3. Taylor Jungmann, RHP
4. Clint Coulter, C
5. Jed Bradley, LHP
6. Victor Roache, OF
7. Johnny Hellweg, RHP
8. Mark Rogers, RHP
9. Ariel Pena, RHP
10. Logan Schafer, OF
11. Hunter Morris, 1B
12. Jimmy Nelson, RHP
13. Scooter Gennett, 2B
14. Drew Gagnon, RHP
15. Kentrail Davis, OF

PITTSBURGH PIRATES
1. Gerrit Cole, RHP
2. Jameson Taillon, RHP
3. Gregory Polanco, OF
4. Alen Hanson, SS
5. Luis Heredia, RHP
6. Josh Bell, OF
7. Wyatt Mathisen, C
8. Barrett Barnes, OF
9. Tyler Glasnow, RHP
10. Nick Kingham, RHP
11. Dilson Herrera, 2B
12. Kyle McPherson, RHP
13. Alex Dickerson, 1B
14. Clay Holmes, RHP
15. Bryan Morris, RHP

ST. LOUIS CARDINALS
1. Oscar Taveras, OF
2. Shelby Miller, RHP
3. Carlos Martinez, RHP
4. Trevor Rosenthal, RHP
5. Kolten Wong, 2B
6. Matt Adams, 1B
7. Michael Wacha, RHP
8. Tyrell Jenkins, RHP
9. Patrick Wisdom, 3B
10. Ryan Jackson, SS
11. James Ramsey, OF
12. Steve Bean, C
13. Colin Walsh, 2B
14. Carson Kelly, 3B
15. Jordan Swagerty, RHP

NL WEST

ARIZONA DIAMONDBACKS
1. Tyler Skaggs, LHP
2. Archie Bradley, RHP
3. Adam Eaton, OF
4. Didi Gregorius, SS
5. Matt Davidson, 3B
6. David Holmberg, LHP
7. Stryker Trahan, C
8. Chris Owings, SS
9. Andrew Chafin, LHP
10. Michael Perez, C
11. A.J. Pollock, OF
12. Chase Anderson, RHP
13. Socrates Brito, OF
14. Anthony Meo, RHP
15. Alfredo Marte, OF

COLORADO ROCKIES
1. Nolan Arenado, 3B
2. Trevor Story, SS
3. David Dahl, OF
4. Kyle Parker, OF
5. Chad Bettis, RHP
6. Will Swanner, C
7. Eddie Butler, RHP
8. Tom Murphy, C
9. Rafael Ortega, OF
10. Tim Wheeler, OF
11. Ryan Wheeler, 1B/3B
12. Tyler Anderson, LHP
13. Rosell Herrera, SS
14. Tyler Matzek, LHP
15. Jayson Aquino, LHP

LOS ANGELES DODGERS
1. Yasiel Puig, OF
2. Zach Lee, RHP
3. Joc Pederson, OF
4. Chris Reed, LHP
5. Corey Seager, 3B
6. Onelki Garcia, LHP
7. Chris Withrow, RHP
8. Zach Bird, RHP
9. Aaron Miller, LHP
10. Angel Sanchez, RHP
11. Alex Santana, 3B
12. Matt Magill, RHP
13. Alex Castellanos, 2B
14. Paco Rodriguez, LHP
15. Ross Stripling, RHP

SAN DIEGO PADRES
1. Jedd Gyorko, 3B
2. Rymer Liriano, OF
3. Robbie Erlin, LHP
4. Austin Hedges, C
5. Casey Kelly, RHP
6. Max Fried, LHP
7. Cory Spangenberg, 2B
8. Joe Ross, RHP
9. Adys Portillo, RHP
10. Joe Wieland, RHP
11. Keyvius Sampson, RHP
12. Matt Wisler, RHP
13. Jace Peterson, SS
14. Zach Eflin, RHP
15. Matt Andriese, RHP

SAN FRANCISCO GIANTS
1. Gary Brown, OF
2. Clayton Blackburn, RHP
3. Kyle Crick, RHP
4. Chris Stratton, RHP
5. Francisco Peguero, OF
6. Joe Panik, SS
7. Heath Hembree, RHP
8. Chris Heston, RHP
9. Chris Marlowe, RHP
10. Eric Surkamp, LHP
11. Andrew Susac, C
12. Mike Kickham, LHP
13. Martin Agosta, RHP
14. Mac Williamson, OF
15. Josh Osich, LHP

TOP PROSPECTS BY POSITION

CATCHER
1. Travis d'Arnaud, NYM
2. Mike Zunino, SEA
3. Gary Sanchez, NYY
4. Austin Hedges, SD
5. Jorge Alfaro, TEX
6. Christian Bethancourt, ATL
7. Rob Brantly, MIA
8. Blake Swihart, BOS
9. Tommy Joseph, PHI
10. Stryker Trahan, ARI
11. Steve Bean, STL
12. Wyatt Mathisen, PIT
13. Max Stassi, OAK
14. Sebastian Valle, PHI
15. Carlos Perez, HOU

FIRST BASE
1. Jonathan Singleton, HOU
2. Dan Vogelbach, CHC
3. C.J. Cron, LAA
4. Matt Adams, STL
5. Nick Delmonico, BAL
6. Matt Olson, OAK
7. Hunter Morris, MIL
8. Alex Dickerson, PIT
9. Darin Ruf, PHI
10. Keon Barnum, CHW
11. Ryan Wheeler, COL
12. Chris Marrero, WAS
13. Joey Terdoslavich, ATL
14. O'Koyea Dickson, LA
15. Ronald Guzman, TEX

SECOND BASE
1. Nick Franklin, SEA
2. Kolten Wong, STL
3. Delino DeShields, HOU
4. Eddie Rosario, MIN
5. Cory Spangenberg, SD
6. Grant Green, OAK
7. Carlos Sanchez, CHW
8. Derek Dietrich, MIA
9. Dilson Herrera, PIT
10. Christian Colon, KC
11. Ryan Brett, TAM
12. Scooter Gennett, MIL
13. Alex Castellanos, LA
14. Stefen Romero, SEA
15. Rougned Odor, TEX

THIRD BASE
1. Miguel Sano, MIN
2. Anthony Rendon, WAS
3. Mike Olt, TEX
4. Nolan Arenado, COL
5. Jedd Gyorko, SD
6. Kaleb Cowart, LAA
7. Matt Davidson, ARI
8. Wilmer Flores, NYM
9. Joey Gallo, TEX
10. Miles Head, OAK
11. Corey Seager, LA
12. Maikel Franco, PHI
13. Richie Shaffer, TAM
14. Stephen Piscotty, STL
15. Garin Cecchini, BOS

SHORTSTOP
1. Jurickson Profar, TEX
2. Francisco Lindor, CLE
3. Javier Baez, CHC
4. Xander Bogaerts, BOS
5. Carlos Correa, HOU
6. Alen Hanson, PIT
7. Trevor Story, COL
8. Addison Russell, OAK
9. Hak-Ju Lee, TAM
10. Brad Miller, SEA
11. Adalberto Mondesi, KC
12. Dorssys Paulino, CLE
13. Jonathan Schoop, BAL
14. Didi Gregorius, ARI
15. Roman Quinn, PHI

OUTFIELD
1. Wil Myers, TAM
2. Oscar Taveras, STL
3. Christian Yelich, MIA
4. Nick Castellanos, DET
5. Billy Hamilton, CIN
6. Byron Buxton, MIN
7. Jackie Bradley, BOS
8. Bubba Starling, KC
9. George Springer, HOU
10. Albert Almora, CHC
11. Tyler Austin, NYY
12. Rymer Liriano, SD
13. Jake Marisnick, MIA
14. Jorge Soler, CHC
15. Brett Jackson, CHC
16. Michael Choice, OAK
17. David Dahl, COL
18. Mason Williams, NYY
19. Oswaldo Arcia, MIN
20. Gregory Polanco, PIT
21. Courtney Hawkins, CHW
22. Brian Goodwin, WAS
23. Yasiel Puig, LA
24. Adam Eaton, ARI
25. Gary Brown, SF
26. Avisail Garcia, DET
27. Leonys Martin, TEX
28. Aaron Hicks, MIN
29. Bryce Brentz, BOS
30. Joc Pederson, LA
31. Brandon Nimmo, NYM
32. Marcell Ozuna, MIA
33. Josh Bell, PIT
34. Kyle Parker, COL
35. Domingo Santana, HOU
36. Trayce Thompson, CHW
37. Lewis Brinson, TEX
38. Drew Vettleson, TAM
39. Barrett Barnes, PIT
40. Slade Heathcott, NYY
41. Jorge Bonifacio, KC
42. Trayce Thompson, CHW
43. Mikie Mahtook, TAM
44. Ariel Ovando, HOU
45. Randal Grichuk, LAA

STARTING PITCHER
1. Dylan Bundy, BAL
2. Gerrit Cole, PIT
3. Taijuan Walker, SEA
4. Trevor Bauer, CLE
5. Jose Fernandez, MIA
6. Zack Wheeler, NYM
7. Tyler Skaggs, ARI
8. Shelby Miller, STL
9. Jameson Taillon, PIT
10. Danny Hultzen, SEA
11. Archie Bradley, ARI
12. Julio Teheran, ATL
13. Matt Barnes, BOS
14. Carlos Martinez, STL
15. Jake Odorizzi, TAM
16. Aaron Sanchez, TOR
17. Taylor Guerrieri, TAM
18. Kyle Zimmer, KC
19. Noah Syndergaard, NYM
20. James Paxton, SEA
21. Kevin Gausman, BAL
22. Trevor Rosenthal, STL
23. Alex Meyer, MIN
24. Robert Stephenson, CIN
25. Chris Archer, TAM
26. Zach Lee, LA
27. Tony Cingrani, CIN
28. Jesse Biddle, PHI
29. Robbie Erlin, SD
30. Martin Perez, TEX

31. Luis Heredia, PIT
32. Justin Nicolino, MIA
33. Max Fried, SD
34. Casey Kelly, SD
35. Lucas Giolito, WAS
36. Wily Peralta, MIL
37. Michael Wacha, STL
38. Kyle Gibson, MIN
39. Dan Straily, OAK
40. Kyle Crick, SF
41. Cody Buckel, TEX
42. Tyler Thornburg, MIL
43. Allen Webster, BOS
44. Jarred Cosart, HOU
45. A.J. Cole, OAK

46. Manny Banuelos, NYY
47. Yordano Ventura, KC
48. Trevor May, MIN
49. Daniel Corcino, CIN
50. Arodys Vizcaino, CHC
51. J.R. Graham, ATL
52. Roberto Osuna, TOR
53. Luke Sims, ATL
54. Daniel Norris, TOR
55. Luke Jackson, TEX
56. J.O. Berrios, MIN
57. Tyrell Jenkins, STL
58. Sean Gilmartin, ATL
59. Andrew Heaney, MIA
60. Johnny Hellweg, MIL

61. Lance McCullers, HOU
62. Jeurys Familia, NYM
63. Matt Wisler, SD
64. Nick Tropeano, HOU
65. Joe Ross, SD
66. Ty Hensley, NYY
67. Clayton Blackburn, SF
68. Adam Morgan, PHI
69. Sonny Gray, OAK
70. Mike Foltynewicz, HOU
71. Casey Crosby, DET
72. Joe Wieland, SD
73. Ariel Pena, MIL
74. Mike Montgomery, TAM
75. Chris Stratton, SF

RELIEF PITCHER
1. Bruce Rondon, DET
2. Carter Capps, SEA
3. Marcus Stroman, TOR
4. Phillippe Aumont, PHI
5. Brad Boxberger, SD
6. Heath Hembree, SF
7. Mark Montgomery, NYY
8. Kevin Quackenbush, SD
9. Paco Rodriguez, LA
10. Chen Lee, CLE
11. Cody Allen, CLE
12. Donnie Joseph, KC
13. Justin De Fratus, PHI
14. Aaron Kurcz, BOS
15. Stephen Pryor, SEA

TOP PROSPECTS BY SKILLS

TOP POWER

Joey Gallo, 3B, TEX
Miguel Sano, 3B, MIN
Wil Myers, OF, TAM
Mike Olt, 3B, TEX
Darin Ruf, 1B, PHI
Jonathan Singleton, 1B, HOU
Oscar Taveras, OF, STL
Dan Vogelbach, 1B, CHC
Matt Adams, 1B, STL
C.J. Cron, 1B, LAA
Gary Sanchez, C, NYY
Kaleb Cowart, 3B, LAA
Matt Davidson, 3B, ARI
Xander Bogaerts, SS, BOS
Travis d'Arnaud, C, NYM
Mike Zunino, C, SEA
Jedd Gyorko, 3B, SD
Kyle Parker, OF, COL
Michael Choice, OF, OAK
George Springer, OF, HOU
David Dahl, OF, COL
Marcell Ozuna, OF, MIA
Domingo Santana, OF, HOU
Trayce Thompson, OF, CHW
Oswaldo Arcia, OF, MIN

TOP BA

Christian Yelich, OF, MIA
Nick Castellanos, OF, DET
Oscar Taveras, OF, STL
Jurickson Profar, SS, TEX
Albert Almora, OF, CHC
Richie Shaffer, 3B, TAM
Mike Zunino, C, SEA
Wil Myers, OF, TAM
Anthony Rendon, 3B, WAS
Francisco Lindor, SS, CLE
Jedd Gyorko, 3B, SD
Adam Eaton, OF, ARI
Javier Baez, SS, CHC
Trevor Story, SS, COL
Oswaldo Arcia, OF, MIN
Courtney Hawkins, OF, CHW
Gregory Polanco, OF, PIT
Jonathan Singleton, 1B, HOU
Tyler Austin, OF, NYY
Carlos Correa, SS, HOU
Dan Vogelbach, 1B, CHC
Eddie Rosario, 2B, MIN
Kaleb Cowart, 3B, LAA
Mason Williams, OF, NYY
Carlos Sanchez, 2B/SS, CHW

TOP SPEED

Billy Hamilton, OF, CIN
Delino DeShields, 2B, HOU
Eury Perez, OF, WAS
Byron Buxton, OF, MIN
Gary Brown, OF, SF
D.J. Davis, OF, TOR
Gregory Polanco, OF, PIT
Jurickson Profar, SS, TEX
Leonys Martin, OF, TEX
Mason Williams, OF, NYY
Francisco Lindor, SS, CLE
Carlos Correa, SS, HOU
Theo Bowe, OF, CIN
Austin Schotts, OF, DET
George Springer, OF, HOU
Aaron Hicks, OF, MIN
Alen Hanson, SS, PIT
James Baldwin, OF, LA
Slade Heathcott, OF, NYY
Jonathan Villar, SS, HOU
Xavier Avery, OF, BAL
Matt Szczur, OF, CHC
Keenyn Walker, OF, CHW
Brett Jackson, OF, CHC
Hak-Ju Lee, SS, TAM

TOP FASTBALL

Dylan Bundy, RHP, BAL
Gerrit Cole, RHP, PIT
Taijuan Walker, RHP, SEA
Bruce Rondon, RHP, DET
Alex Meyer, RHP, MIN
Carlos Martinez, RHP, STL
Jameson Taillon, RHP, PIT
Jose Fernandez, RHP, MIA
Yordano Ventura, RHP, KC
Kyle Zimmer, RHP, KC
Lance McCullers, RHP, HOU
Carter Capps, RHP, SEA
Kyle Crick, RHP, SF
Zack Wheeler, RHP, NYM
Aaron Sanchez, RHP, TOR
Trevor Rosenthal, RHP, STL
Archie Bradley, RHP, ARI
Jarred Cosart, RHP, HOU
Noah Syndergaard, RHP, NYM
Robert Stephenson, RHP, CIN
Kevin Gausman, RHP, BAL
Matt Barnes, RHP, BOS
Chris Archer, RHP, TAM
James Paxton, LHP, SEA
Cody Allen, RHP, CLE

TOP BREAKING BALL

Dylan Bundy, RHP, BAL
Gerrit Cole, RHP, PIT
Chris Archer, RHP, TAM
Jameson Taillon, RHP, PIT
Lance McCullers, RHP, HOU
Casey Crosby, LHP, DET
James Paxton, LHP, SEA
Tyler Skaggs, LHP, ARI
Jose Fernandez, RHP, MIA
Aaron Sanchez, RHP, TOR
Zack Wheeler, RHP, NYM
Archie Bradley, RHP, ARI
Mark Montgomery, RHP, NYY

Erik Johnson, RHP, CHW
Ariel Pena, RHP, MIL
Sam Selman, LHP, KC
Taylor Guerrieri, RHP, TAM
Sonny Gray, RHP, OAK
Andrew Chafin, LHP, ARI
Kyle Crick, RHP, SF
Chris Dwyer, LHP, KC
Danny Hultzen, LHP, SEA
Martin Perez, LHP, TEX
Garrett Gould, RHP, LAD
Marcus Stroman, RHP, TOR
Carlos Martinez, RHP, STL

2013 TOP FANTASY PROSPECTS

1	Wil Myers (OF, TAM)	51	Grant Green (INF/OF, OAK)
2	Tyler Skaggs (LHP, ARI)	52	Christian Colon (INF, KC)
3	Dan Straily (RHP, OAK)	53	James Darnell (OF, SD)
4	Jake Odorizzi (RHP, TAM)	54	Phillippe Aumont (RHP, PHI)
5	Shelby Miller (RHP, STL)	55	Josh Vitters (3B, CHC)
6	Trevor Bauer (RHP, CLE)	56	Ryan Wheeler (3B, COL)
7	Jurickson Profar (SS, TEX)	57	Nick Maronde (LHP, LAA)
8	Zack Wheeler (RHP, NYM)	58	Tim Wheeler (OF, COL)
9	Travis d'Arnaud (C, NYM)	59	Zack Cox (3B, MIA)
10	Dylan Bundy (RHP, BAL)	60	Bruce Rondon (RHP, DET)
11	Gerrit Cole (RHP, PIT)	61	Edwar Cabrera (RHP, COL)
12	Julio Teheran (RHP, ATL)	62	Chris Owings (SS, ARI)
13	Casey Kelly (RHP, SD)	63	Tony Sanchez (C, PIT)
14	Brett Jackson (OF, CHC)	64	A.J. Pollock (OF, ARI)
15	Wily Peralta (RHP, MIL)	65	Charlie Culberson (2B, COL)
16	Tyler Thornburg (RHP, MIL)	66	Hak-Ju Lee (SS, TAM)
17	Avisail Garcia (OF, DET)	67	Matt Davidson (3B, ARI)
18	Danny Hultzen (LHP, SEA)	68	Darin Ruf (1B, PHI)
19	Kyle Gibson (RHP, MIN)	69	Daniel Corcino (RHP, CIN)
20	Jeurys Familia (RHP, NYM)	70	George Springer (OF, HOU)
21	Jonathan Singleton (1B, HOU)	71	Mike Zunino (C, SEA)
22	Billy Hamilton (SS/OF, CIN)	72	Gary Brown (OF, SF)
23	Rob Brantly (C, MIA)	73	Sonny Gray (RHP, OAK)
24	Nolan Arenado (3B, COL)	74	Lars Anderson (1B, ARI)
25	Martin Perez (LHP, TEX)	75	Trevor May (RHP, MIN)
26	Jedd Gyorko (3B, SD)	76	Oswaldo Arcia (OF, MIN)
27	Mike Olt (3B, TEX)	77	Brad Peacock (RHP, OAK)
28	Carlos Martinez (RHP, STL)	78	Andy Oliver (LHP, PIT)
29	Tony Cingrani (LHP, CIN)	79	Matt den Dekker (OF, NYM)
30	Robbie Erlin (LHP, SD)	80	Casey Crosby (LHP, DET)
31	Matt Adams (1B, STL)	81	Eury Perez (OF, WAS)
32	Trevor Rosenthal (RHP, STL)	82	Hunter Morris (1B, MIL)
33	Chris Archer (RHP, TAM)	83	Chris Marrero (1B, WAS)
34	Leonys Martin (OF, TEX)	84	Logan Schafer (OF, MIL)
35	Nick Franklin (SS, SEA)	85	Alex Castellanos (OF, LA)
36	Oscar Taveras (OF, STL)	86	Justin De Fratus (RHP, PHI)
37	Anthony Rendon (3B, WAS)	87	Mike Montgomery (LHP, TAM)
38	Kyle McPherson (RHP, PIT)	88	Scott Van Slyke (1B, LA)
39	Mark Rogers (RHP, MIL)	89	Heath Hembree (RHP, SF)
40	Adam Eaton (OF, ARI)	90	L.J. Hoes (OF, BAL)
41	James Paxton (LHP, SEA)	91	Adam Warren (RHP, NYY)
42	Joe Wieland (RHP, SD)	92	Mark Montgomery (RHP, NYY)
43	Taijuan Walker (RHP, SEA)	93	Alex Colome (RHP, TAM)
44	Rudy Owens (LHP, HOU)	94	Brandon Guyer (OF, TAM)
45	Nick Castellanos (3B/OF, DET)	95	Charlie Leesman (LHP, CHW)
46	Jackie Bradley (OF, BOS)	96	Carlos Sanchez (INF, CHW)
47	Kolten Wong (2B, STL)	97	Jhan Marinez (RHP, CHW)
48	Bryce Brentz (OF, BOS)	98	Donnie Joseph (LHP, KC)
49	Jarred Cosart (RHP, HOU)	99	Carter Capps (RHP, SEA)
50	Aaron Hicks (OF, MIN)	100	Cody Asche (3B, PHI)

TOP 100 PROSPECTS ARCHIVE

2012

1. Bryce Harper (OF, WAS)
2. Matt Moore (LHP, TAM)
3. Mike Trout (OF, LAA)
4. Julio Teheran (RHP, ATL)
5. Jesus Montero (C, NYY)
6. Jurickson Profar (SS, TEX)
7. Manny Machado (SS, BAL)
8. Gerrit Cole (RHP, PIT)
9. Devin Mesoraco (C, CIN)
10. Wil Myers (OF, KC)

11. Miguel Sano (3B, MIN)
12. Jacob Turner (RHP, DET)
13. Anthony Rendon (3B, WAS)
14. Trevor Bauer (RHP, ARI)
15. Nolan Arenado (3B, COL)
16. Jameson Taillon (RHP, PIT)
17. Shelby Miller (RHP, STL)
18. Dylan Bundy (RHP, BAL)
19. Brett Jackson (OF, CHC)
20. Drew Pomeranz (LHP, COL)

21. Martin Perez (LHP, TEX)
22. Yonder Alonso (1B, SD)
23. Taijuan Walker (RHP, SEA)
24. Danny Hultzen (LHP, SEA)
25. Gary Brown (OF, SF)
26. Anthony Rizzo (1B, CHC)
27. Bubba Starling (OF, KC)
28. Travis d'Arnaud (C, TOR)
29. Mike Montgomery (LHP, KC)
30. Jake Odorizzi (RHP, KC)

31. Hak-Ju Lee (SS, TAM)
32. Jonathan Singleton (1B, HOU)
33. Garrett Richards (RHP, LAA)
34. Manny Banuelos (LHP, NYY)
35. James Paxton (LHP, SEA)
36. Jarrod Parker (RHP, OAK)
37. Carlos Martinez (RHP, STL)
38. Jake Marisnick (OF, TOR)
39. Yasmani Grandal (C, SD)
40. Trevor May (RHP, PHI)

41. Gary Sanchez (C, NYY)
42. Mike Olt (3B, TEX)
43. Wilin Rosario (C, COL)
44. John Lamb (LHP, KC)
45. Francisco Lindor (SS, CLE)
46. Dellin Betances (RHP, NYY)
47. Michael Choice (OF, OAK)
48. Arodys Vizcaino (RHP, ATL)
49. Trayvon Robinson (OF, SEA)
50. Matt Harvey (RHP, NYM)

51. Will Middlebrooks (3B, BOS)
52. Jedd Gyorko (3B, SD)
53. Randall Delgado (RHP, ATL)
54. Zack Wheeler (RHP, NYM)
55. Zach Lee (RHP, LA)
56. Tyler Skaggs (LHP, ARI)
57. Nick Castellanos (3B, DET)
58. Robbie Erlin (LHP, SD)
59. Christian Yelich (OF, MIA)
60. Anthony Gose (OF, TOR)

61. Addison Reed (RHP, CHW)
62. Javier Baez (SS, CHC)
63. Starling Marte (OF, PIT)
64. Kaleb Cowart (3B, LAA)
65. George Springer (OF, HOU)
66. Jarred Cosart (RHP, HOU)
67. Jean Segura (2B, LAA)
68. Kolten Wong (2B, STL)
69. Nick Franklin (SS, SEA)
70. Alex Torres (RHP, TAM)

71. Rymer Liriano (OF, SD)
72. Josh Bell (OF, PIT)
73. Leonys Martin (OF, TEX)
74. Joe Wieland (RHP, SD)
75. Joe Benson (OF, MIN)
76. Wily Peralta (RHP, MIL)
77. Tim Wheeler (OF, COL)
78. Oscar Taveras (OF, STL)
79. Xander Bogaerts (SS, BOS)
80. Archie Bradley (RHP, ARI)

81. Kyle Gibson (RHP, MIN)
82. Allen Webster (RHP, LA)
83. C.J. Cron (1B, LAA)
84. Grant Green (OF, OAK)
85. Brad Peacock (RHP, OAK)
86. Chris Dwyer (LHP, KC)
87. Billy Hamilton (SS, CIN)
88. A.J. Cole (RHP, OAK)
89. Aaron Hicks (OF, MIN)
90. Noah Syndergaard (RHP, TOR)

91. Tyrell Jenkins (RHP, STL)
92. Anthony Ranaudo (RHP, BOS)
93. Jed Bradley (LHP, MIL)
94. Nathan Eovaldi (RHP, LA)
95. Andrelton Simmons (SS, ATL)
96. Taylor Guerrieri (RHP, TAM)
97. Cheslor Cuthbert (3B, KC)
98. Edward Salcedo (3B, ATL)
99. Domingo Santana, OF, HOU)
100. Jesse Biddle (LHP, PHI)

2011

1. Bryce Harper (OF, WAS)
2. Domonic Brown (OF, PHI)
3. Jesus Montero (C, NYY)
4. Mike Trout (OF, LAA)
5. Jeremy Hellickson (RHP, TAM)
6. Aroldis Chapman (LHP, CIN)
7. Eric Hosmer (1B, KC)
8. Dustin Ackley (2B, SEA)
9. Desmond Jennings (OF, TAM)
10. Julio Teheran (RHP, ATL)

11. Mike Moustakas (3B, KC)
12. Brandon Belt (1B, SF)
13. Freddie Freeman (1B, ATL)
14. Michael Pineda (RHP, SEA)
15. Matt Moore (LHP, TAM)
16. Mike Montgomery (LHP, KC)
17. Brett Jackson (OF, CHC)
18. Nick Franklin (SS, SEA)
19. Jameson Taillon (RHP, PIT)
20. Jacob Turner (RHP, DET)

21. Shelby Miller (RHP, STL)
22. Martin Perez (LHP, TEX)
23. Wil Myers (C, KC)
24. Kyle Gibson (RHP, MIN)
25. Lonnie Chisenhall (3B, CLE)
26. Tyler Matzek (LHP, COL)
27. Brett Lawrie (2B, TOR)
28. Yonder Alonso (1B, CIN)
29. Jarrod Parker (RHP, ARI)
30. Jonathan Singleton (1B, PHI)

31. Tanner Scheppers (RHP,TEX)
32. Kyle Drabek (RHP, TOR)
33. Jason Knapp (RHP, CLE)
34. Manny Banuelos (LHP, NYY)
35. Alex White (RHP, CLE)
36. Jason Kipnis (2B, CLE)
37. Wilin Rosario (C, COL)
38. Manny Machado (SS, BAL)
39. Chris Sale (LHP, CHW)
40. Devin Mesoraco (C, CIN)

41. Tyler Chatwood (RHP, LAA)
42. John Lamb (LHP, KC)
43. Danny Duffy (LHP, KC)
44. Trevor May (RHP, PHI)
45. Mike Minor (LHP, ATL)
46. Jarred Cosart (RHP, PHI)
47. Tony Sanchez (C, PIT)
48. Brody Colvin (RHP, PHI)
49. Zach Britton (LHP, BAL)
50. Dee Gordon (SS, LA)

51. Miguel Sano (3B, MIN)
52. Grant Green (SS, OAK)
53. Danny Espinosa (SS, WAS)
54. Simon Castro (RHP, SD)
55. Derek Norris (C, WAS)
56. Chris Archer (RHP, CHC)
57. Jurickson Profar (SS, TEX)
58. Zack Cox (3B, STL)
59. Billy Hamilton (2B, CIN)
60. Gary Sanchez (C, NYY)

61. Zach Lee (RHP, LA)
62. Drew Pomeranz (LHP, CLE)
63. Randall Delgado (RHP, ATL)
64. Michael Choice (OF, OAK)
65. Nick Weglarz (OF, CLE)
66. Nolan Arenado (3B, COL)
67. Chris Carter (1B/OF, OAK)
68. Arodys Vizcaino (RHP, ATL)
69. Trey McNutt (RHP, CHC)
70. Dellin Betances (RHP, NYY)

71. Aaron Hicks (OF, MIN)
72. Aaron Crow (RHP, KC)
73. Jake McGee (LHP, TAM)
74. Lars Anderson (1B, BOS)
75. Fabio Martinez (RHP, LAA)
76. Ben Revere (OF, MIN)
77. Jordan Lyles (RHP, HOU)
78. Casey Kelly (RHP, SD)
79. Trayvon Robinson (OF, LA)
80. Craig Kimbrel (RHP, ATL)

81. Jose Iglesias (SS, BOS)
82. Garrett Richards (RHP, LAA)
83. Allen Webster (RHP, LA)
84. Chris Dwyer (LHP, KC)
85. Alex Colome (RHP, TAM)
86. Zack Wheeler (RHP, SF)
87. Andy Oliver (LHP, DET)
88. Andrew Brackman (RHP,NYY)
89. Wilmer Flores (SS, NYM)
90. Christian Friedrich (LHP, COL)

91. Anthony Ranaudo (RHP, BOS)
92. Aaron Miller (LHP, LA)
93. Matt Harvey (RHP, NYM)
94. Mark Rogers (RHP, MIL)
95. Jean Segura (2B, LAA)
96. Hank Conger (C, LAA)
97. J.P. Arencibia (C, TOR)
98. Matt Dominguez (3B, FLA)
99. Jerry Sands (1B, LA)
100. Nick Castellanos (3B, DET)

TOP 100 PROSPECTS ARCHIVE

2010

1. Stephen Strasburg (RHP, WAS)
2. Jason Heyward (OF, ATL)
3. Jesus Montero (C, NYY)
4. Buster Posey (C, SF)
5. Justin Smoak (1B, TEX)
6. Pedro Alvarez (3B, PIT)
7. Carlos Santana (C, CLE)
8. Desmond Jennings (OF, TAM)
9. Brian Matusz (LHP, BAL)
10. Neftali Feliz (RHP, TEX)

11. Brett Wallace (3B, TOR)
12. Mike Stanton (OF. FLA)
13. M. Bumgarner (LHP, SF)
14. J. Hellickson (RHP, TAM)
15. Dustin Ackley (1B/OF, SEA)
16. Aroldis Chapman (LHP, CIN)
17. Yonder Alonso (1B, CIN)
18. Alcides Escobar (SS, MIL)
19. Brett Lawrie (2B, MIL)
20. Starlin Castro (SS, CHC)

21. Logan Morrison (1B, FLA)
22. Mike Montgomery (LHP, KC)
23. Domonic Brown (OF, PHI)
24. Josh Vitters (3B, CHC)
25. R. Westmoreland (OF, BOS)
26. Todd Frazier (3B/OF, CIN)
27. Eric Hosmer (1B, KC)
28. Freddie Freeman (1B, ATL)
29. Derek Norris (C, WAS)
30. Martin Perez (LHP, TEX)

31. Wade Davis (RHP, TAM)
32. Trevor Reckling (LHP, LAA)
33. Jordan Walden (RHP, LAA)
34. Mat Gamel (3B, MIL)
35. Tyler Flowers (C, CHW)
36. T. Scheppers (RHP, TEX)
37. Casey Crosby (LHP, DET)
38. Austin Jackson (OF, DET)
39. Devaris Gordon (SS, LA)
40. Kyle Drabek (RHP, TOR)

41. Ben Revere (OF, MIN)
42. Michael Taylor (OF, OAK)
43. Jacob Turner (RHP, DET)
44. Tim Beckham (SS, TAM)
45. Carlos Triunfel (SS, SEA)
46. Aaron Crow (RHP, KC)
47. Matt Moore (LHP, TAM)
48. Jarrod Parker (RHP, ARI)
49. F. Martinez (OF, NYM)
50. C. Friedrich (LHP, COL)

51. Jenrry Mejia (RHP, NYM)
52. Tyler Matzek (LHP, COL)
53. Brett Jackson (OF, CHC)
54. Aaron Hicks (OF, MIN)
55. Jhoulys Chacin (RHP, COL)
56. Josh Bell (3B, BAL)
57. Brandon Allen (1B, ARI)
58. Chris Carter (1B, OAK)
59. Jason Knapp (RHP, CLE)
60. Danny Duffy (LHP, KC)

61. Tim Alderson (RHP, PIT)
62. Matt Dominguez (3B, FLA)
63. Mike Moustakas (3B, KC)
64. Jake Arrieta (RHP, BAL)
65. Carlos Carrasco (RHP, CLE)
66. Wilmer Flores (SS, NYM)
67. Drew Storen (RHP, WAS)
68. Lonnie Chisenhall (3B, CLE)
69. Aaron Poreda (LHP, SD)
70. A. Cashner (RHP, CHC)

71. Tony Sanchez (C, PIT)
72. Julio Teheran (RHP, ATL)
73. Jose Tabata (OF, PIT)
74. Jason Castro (C, HOU)
75. Casey Kelly (RHP, BOS)
76. Alex White (RHP, CLE)
77. Jay Jackson (RHP, CHC)
78. Dan Hudson (RHP, CHW)
79. Brandon Erbe (RHP, BAL)
80. Zack Wheeler (RHP, SF)

81. Shelby Miller (RHP, STL)
82. Jordan Lyles (RHP, HOU)
83. Simon Castro (RHP, SD)
84. Aaron Miller (LHP, LA)
85. Michael Ynoa (RHP, OAK)
86. Ethan Martin (RHP, LA)
87. Scott Elbert (LHP, LA)
88. Nick Weglarz (OF, CLE)
89. Donavan Tate (OF, SD)
90. Jordan Danks (OF, CHW)

91. Hector Rondon (RHP, CLE)
92. Chris Heisey (OF, CIN)
93. Kyle Gibson (RHP, MIN)
94. Mike Leake (RHP, CIN)
95. Mike Trout (OF, LAA)
96. Jake McGee (LHP, TAM)
97. Chad James (LHP, FLA)
98. C. Bethancourt (C, NYY)
99. Miguel Sano (SS, MIN)
100. Noel Arguelles (LHP, KC)

2009

1. Matt Wieters (C, BAL)
2. David Price (LHP, TAM)
3. Rick Porcello (RHP, DET)
4. Colby Rasmus (OF, STL)
5. Madison Bumgarner (LHP, SF)
6. Neftali Feliz (RHP, TEX)
7. Jason Heyward (OF, ATL)
8. Andrew McCutchen (OF, PIT)
9. Pedro Alvarez (3B, PIT)
10. Cameron Maybin (OF, FLA)

11. Trevor Cahill (RHP, OAK)
12. Mike Moustakas (3B/SS, KC)
13. Jordan Zimmermann (RHP, WAS)
14. Travis Snider (OF, TOR)
15. Tim Beckham (SS, TAM)
16. Eric Hosmer (1B, KC)
17. Tommy Hanson (RHP, ATL)
18. Dexter Fowler (OF, COL)
19. Brett Anderson (LHP, OAK)
20. Carlos Triunfel (SS/2B, SEA)

21. Buster Posey (C, SF)
22. Chris Tillman (RHP, BAL)
23. Brian Matusz (LHP, BAL)
24. Justin Smoak (1B, TEX)
25. Jarrod Parker (RHP, ARI)
26. Derek Holland (LHP, TEX)
27. Lars Anderson (1B, BOS)
28. Michael Inoa (RHP, OAK)
29. Mike Stanton (OF, FLA)
30. Taylor Teagarden (C, TEX)

31. Gordon Beckham (SS, CHW)
32. Brett Wallace (3B, STL)
33. Matt LaPorta (OF, CLE)
34. Jordan Schafer (OF, ATL)
35. Carlos Santana (C, CLE)
36. Aaron Hicks (OF, MIN)
37. Adam Miller (RHP, CLE)
38. Elvis Andrus (SS, TEX)
39. Alcides Escobar (SS, MIL)
40. Wade Davis (RHP, TAM)

41. Austin Jackson (OF, NYY)
42. Jesus Montero (C, NYY)
43. Tim Alderson (RHP, SF)
44. Jhoulys Chacin (RHP, COL)
45. Phillippe Aumont (RHP, SEA)
46. James McDonald (RHP, LA)
47. Reid Brignac (SS, TAM)
48. Desmond Jennings (OF, TAM)
49. Fernando Martinez (OF, NYM)
50. JP Arencibia (C, TOR)

51. Wilmer Flores (SS, NYM)
52. Brett Cecil (LHP, TOR)
53. Aaron Poreda (LHP, CHW)
54. Jeremy Jeffress (RHP, MIL)
55. Michael Main (RHP, TEX)
56. Josh Vitters (3B, CHC)
57. Mat Gamel (3B, MIL)
58. Yonder Alonso (1B, CIN)
59. Gio Gonzalez (LHP, OAK)
60. Michael Bowden (RHP, BOS)

61. Angel Villalona (1B, SF)
62. Carlos Carrasco (RHP, PHI)
63. Jake Arrieta (RHP, BAL)
64. Jordan Walden (RHP, LAA)
65. Freddie Freeman (1B, ATL)
66. Logan Morrison (1B, FLA)
67. Shooter Hunt (RHP, MIN)
68. Junichi Tazawa (RHP, BOS)
69. Nick Adenhart (RHP, LAA)
70. Jose Tabata (OF, PIT)

71. Adrian Cardenas (SS/2B, OAK)
72. Chris Carter (3B/OF, OAK)
73. Ben Revere (OF, MIN)
74. Josh Reddick (OF, BOS)
75. Jeremy Hellickson (RHP, TAM)
76. Justin Jackson (SS, TOR)
77. Wilson Ramos (C, MIN)
78. Jason Castro (C, HOU)
79. Julio Borbon (OF, TEX)
80. Tyler Flowers (C, CHW)

81. Gorkys Hernandez (OF, ATL)
82. Neftali Soto (3B, CIN)
83. Henry Rodriguez (RHP, OAK)
84. Dan Duffy (LHP, KC)
85. Daniel Cortes (RHP, KC)
86. Dayan Viciedo (3B, CHW)
87. Matt Dominguez (3B, FLA)
88. Jordan Danks (OF, CHW)
89. Chris Coghlan (2B, FLA)
90. Brian Bogusevic (OF, HOU)

91. Ryan Tucker (RHP, FLA)
92. Jonathon Niese (LHP, NYM)
93. Martin Perez (LHP, TEX)
94. James Simmons (RHP, OAK)
95. Nick Weglarz (OF/1B, CLE)
96. Daniel Bard (RHP, BOS)
97. Yamaico Navarro (SS, BOS)
98. Jose Ceda (RHP, FLA)
99. Jeff Samardzija (RHP, CHC)
100. Jason Donald (SS, PHI)

TOP 100 PROSPECTS ARCHIVE

2008

1. Jay Bruce (OF, CIN)
2. Evan Longoria (3B, TAM)
3. Clay Buchholz (RHP, BOS)
4. Clayton Kershaw (LHP, LAD)
5. Joba Chamberlain (RHP, NYY)
6. Colby Rasmus (OF, STL)
7. Cameron Maybin (OF, FLA)
8. Homer Bailey (RHP, CIN)
9. David Price (LHP, TAM)
10. Andrew McCutchen (OF, PIT)

11. Brandon Wood (3B/SS, LAA)
12. Matt Wieters (C, BAL)
13. Jacoby Ellsbury (OF, BOS)
14. Travis Snider (OF, TOR)
15. Reid Brignac (SS, TAM)
16. Jacob McGee (LHP, TAM)
17. Wade Davis (RHP, TAM)
18. Adam Miller (RHP, CLE)
19. Rick Porcello (RHP, DET)
20. Franklin Morales (LHP, COL)

21. Carlos Triunfel (SS, SEA)
22. Andy LaRoche (3B/OF, LAD)
23. Jordan Schafer (OF, ATL)
24. Kosuke Fukodome (OF, CHC)
25. Jose Tabata (OF, NYY)
26. Carlos Gonzalez (OF, OAK)
27. Joey Votto (1B/OF, CIN)
28. Daric Barton (1B, OAK)
29. Angel Villalona (3B, SF)
30. Eric Hurley (RHP, TEX)

31. Nick Adenhart (RHP, LAA)
32. Fernando Martinez (OF, NYM)
33. Ross Detwiler (LHP, WAS)
34. Johnny Cueto (RHP, CIN)
35. Chris Marrero (OF, WAS)
36. Jason Heyward (OF, ATL)
37. Mike Moustakas (SS, KC)
38. Elvis Andrus (SS, TEX)
39. Taylor Teagarden (C, TEX)
40. Ian Kennedy (RHP, NYY)

41. Kasey Kiker (LHP, TEX)
42. Scott Elbert (LHP, LAD)
43. Justin Masterson (RHP, BOS)
44. Max Scherzer (RHP, ARI)
45. Brandon Jones (OF, ATL)
46. Josh Vitters (3B, CHC)
47. Jarrod Parker (RHP, ARI)
48. Matt Antonelli (2B, SD)
49. Gio Gonzalez (LHP, CHW)
50. Ian Stewart (3B, COL)

51. Chase Headley (3B, SD)
52. Anthony Swarzak (RHP, MIN)
53. Jair Jurrjens (RHP, DET)
54. Billy Rowell (3B, BAL)
55. Jeff Clement (C, SEA)
56. Tyler Colvin (OF, CHC)
57. Neil Walker (3B, PIT)
58. Geovany Soto (C/1B, CHC)
59. Steven Pearce (1B/OF, PIT)
60. Fautino de los Santos (RHP, CHW)

61. Manny Parra (LHP, MIL)
62. Matt LaPorta (OF, MIL)
63. Austin Jackson (OF, NYY)
64. Carlos Carrasco (RHP, PHI)
65. Jed Lowrie (SS/2B, BOS)
66. Deolis Guerra (RHP, NYM)
67. Jonathon Meloan (RHP, LAD)
68. Chin-Lung Hu (SS, LAD)
69. Blake Beaven (RHP, TEX)
70. Michael Main (RHP, TEX)

71. Gorkys Hernandez (OF, ATL)
72. Jeff Niemann (RHP, TAM)
73. Desmond Jennings (OF, TAM)
74. Radhames Liz (RHP, BAL)
75. Chuck Lofgren (LHP, CLE)
76. Luke Hochevar (RHP, KC)
77. Brent Lillibridge (SS, ATL)
78. Jaime Garcia (LHP, STL)
79. Bryan Anderson (C, STL)
80. Troy Patton (LHP, BAL)

81. Nolan Reimold (OF, BAL)
82. Matt Latos (RHP, SD)
83. Tommy Hanson (RHP, ATL)
84. Aaron Poreda (LHP, CHW)
85. Cole Rohrbough (LHP, ATL)
86. Lars Anderson (1B, BOS)
87. Chris Volstad (RHP, FLA)
88. Henry Sosa (RHP, SF)
89. Madison Bumgarner (LHP, SF)
90. Michael Bowden (RHP, BOS)

91. Hank Conger (C, LAA)
92. JR Towles (C, HOU)
93. Greg Reynolds (RHP, COL)
94. Adrian Cardenas (2B/SS, PHI)
95. Chris Nelson (SS, COL)
96. Ryan Kalish (OF, BOS)
97. Dexter Fowler (OF, COL)
98. James McDonald (RHP, LAD)
99. Beau Mills (3B/1B, CLE)
100. Michael Burgess (OF, WAS)

2007

1. Delmon Young (OF, TAM)
2. Alex Gordon (3B, KC)
3. Daisuke Matsuzaka (RHP, BOS)
4. Justin Upton (OF, ARI)
5. Homer Bailey (RHP, CIN)
6. Philip Hughes (RHP, NYY)
7. Brandon Wood (SS, LAA)
8. Jay Bruce (OF, CIN)
9. Billy Butler (OF, KC)
10. Cameron Maybin (OF, DET)

11. Andrew McCutchen (OF, PIT)
12. Troy Tulowitzki (SS, COL)
13. Evan Longoria (3B, TAM)
14. Jose Tabata (OF, NYY)
15. Reid Brignac (SS, TAM)
16. Chris Young (OF, ARI)
17. Adam Miller (RHP, CLE)
18. Mike Pelfrey (RHP, NYM)
19. Carlos Gonzalez (OF, ARI)
20. Tim Lincecum (RHP, SF)

21. Andy LaRoche (3B, LAD)
22. Fernando Martinez (OF, NYM)
23. Yovani Gallardo (RHP, MIL)
24. Colby Rasmus (OF, STL)
25. Ryan Braun (3B, MIL)
26. Scott Elbert (LHP, LAD)
27. Nick Adenhart (RHP, LAA)
28. Andrew Miller (LHP, DET)
29. Billy Rowell (3B, BAL)
30. John Danks (LHP, CHW)

31. Luke Hochevar (RHP, KC)
32. Erick Aybar (SS, LAA)
33. Jacoby Ellsbury (OF, BOS)
34. Eric Hurley (RHP, TEX)
35. Ian Stewart (3B, COL)
36. Clay Buchholz (RHP, BOS)
37. Elvis Andrus (SS, ATL)
38. Jason Hirsh (RHP, COL)
39. Hunter Pence (OF, HOU)
40. Franklin Morales (LHP, COL)

41. Adam Lind (OF, TOR)
42. Travis Snider (OF, TOR)
43. Jeff Niemann (RHP, TAM)
44. Clayton Kershaw (LHP, LAD)
45. James Loney (1B, LAD)
46. Chris Iannetta (C, COL)
47. Elijah Dukes (OF, TAM)
48. Chuck Lofgren (LHP, CLE)
49. Joey Votto (1B, CIN)
50. Jacob McGee (LHP, TAM)

51. Adam Jones (OF, SEA)
52. Brad Lincoln (RHP, PIT)
53. Brian Barton (OF, CLE)
54. Will Inman (RHP, MIL)
55. Wade Davis (RHP, TAM)
56. Donald Veal (LHP, CHC)
57. Michael Bowden (RHP, BOS)
58. Ryan Sweeney (OF, CHW)
59. Josh Fields (3B, CHW)
60. Jarrod Saltalamacchia (C, ATL)

61. Felix Pie (OF, CHC)
62. Brandon Erbe (RHP, BAL)
63. Giovanny Gonzalez (LHP, CHW)
64. Trevor Crowe (OF, CLE)
65. Travis Buck (OF, OAK)
66. Daric Barton (1B, OAK)
67. Kevin Kouzmanoff (3B, SD)
68. Jeff Clement (C, SEA)
69. Neil Walker (C, PIT)
70. Troy Patton (LHP, HOU)

71. Brandon Morrow (RHP, SEA)
72. Dustin Pedroia (2B, BOS)
73. Blake DeWitt (2B, LAD)
74. Carlos Carrasco (RHP, PHI)
75. Jonathon Meloan (RHP, LAD)
76. Hank Conger (C, LAA)
77. Sean Rodriguez (SS, LAA)
78. Humberto Sanchez (RHP, NYY)
79. Phil Humber (RHP, NYM)
80. Edinson Volquez (RHP, TEX)

81. Dustin Nippert (RHP, ARI)
82. Anthony Swarzak (RHP, MIN)
83. Chris Parmalee (OF/1B, MIN)
84. Ubaldo Jimenez (RHP, COL)
85. Dexter Fowler (OF, COL)
86. Drew Stubbs (OF, CIN)
87. Miguel Montero (C, ARI)
88. Carlos Gomez (OF, NYM)
89. Kevin Slowey (RHP, MIN)
90. Nolan Reimold (OF, BAL)

91. Daniel Bard (RHP, BOS)
92. Chris Nelson (SS, COL)
93. Cedric Hunter (OF, SD)
94. Angel Villanoa (3B, SF)
95. Jamie Garcia (LHP, STL)
96. Travis Wood (LHP, CIN)
97. Cesar Carillo (RHP, SD)
98. Pedro Beato (RHP, BAL)
99. Joba Chamberlain (RHP, NYY)
100. Kei Igawa (LHP, NYY)

TOP 100 PROSPECTS ARCHIVE

2006

1. Delmon Young (OF, TAM)
2. Justin Upton (OF/SS, ARI)
3. Brandon Wood (SS, LAA)
4. Ian Stewart (3B, COL)
5. Prince Fielder (1B, MIL)
6. Jeremy Hermida (OF, FLA)
7. Chad Billingsley (RHP, LAD)
8. Stephen Drew (SS, ARI)
9. Andy Marte (3B, BOS)
10. Francisco Liriano (LHP, MIN)

11. Alex Gordon (3B, KC)
12. Jarrod Saltalamacchia (C, ATL)
13. Carlos Quentin (OF, ARI)
14. Lastings Milledge (OF, NYM)
15. Conor Jackson (1B, ARI)
16. Joel Guzman (SS, LAD)
17. Nick Markakis (OF, BAL)
18. Adam Miller (RHP, CLE)
19. Matt Cain (RHP, SF)
20. Erick Aybar (SS, LAA)

21. Billy Butler (OF, KC)
22. Justin Verlander (RHP, DET)
23. Howie Kendrick (2B, LAA)
24. Andy LaRoche (3B, LAD)
25. Troy Tulowitski (SS, COL)
26. Jered Weaver (RHP, LAA)
27. Ryan Zimmerman (3B, WAS)
28. Chris Young (OF, ARI)
29. Elvis Andrus (SS, ATL)
30. Daric Barton (1B, OAK)

31. Scott Olson (LHP, FLA)
32. Jon Lester (LHP, BOS)
33. Cole Hamels (LHP, PHI)
34. Anthony Reyes (RHP, STL)
35. Mike Pelfrey (RHP, NYM)
36. Andrew McCutchen (OF, PIT)
37. Ryan Braun (3B, MIL)
38. Chris Nelson (SS, COL)
39. Kendry Morales (1B/OF, LAA)
40. Anibal Sanchez (RHP, FLA)

41. Hanley Ramirez (SS, FLA)
42. John Danks (LHP, TEX)
43. Edison Volquez (RHP, TEX)
44. Russell Martin (C, LAD)
45. Dustin Nippert (RHP, ARI)
46. Jon Papelbon (RHP, BOS)
47. Carlos Gonzales (OF, ARI)
48. Felix Pie (OF, CHC)
49. Yusmeiro Petit (RHP, FLA)
50. Dustin Pedroia (2B, BOS)

51. Joel Zumaya (RHP, DET)
52. Gio Gonzalez (LHP, PHI)
53. Hayden Penn (RHP, BAL)
54. Nolan Reimold (OF, BAL)
55. Homer Bailey (RHP, CIN)
56. Mark Pawelek (LHP, CHC)
57. Neil Walker (C, PIT)
58. Philip Hughes (RHP, NYY)
59. Jonathon Broxton (RHP, LAD)
60. Dustin McGowan (RHP, TOR)

61. Cameron Maybin (OF, DET)
62. Scott Elbert (LHP, LAD)
63. Andrew Lerew (RHP, ATL)
64. Yuniel Escobar (SS, ATL)
65. Jose Tabata (OF, NYY)
66. Craig Hansen (RHP, BOS)
67. Javier Herrera (OF, OAK)
68. James Loney (1B, LAD)
69. Matt Kemp (OF, LAD)
70. Jairo Garcia (RHP, OAK)

71. Ryan Sweeney (OF, CHW)
72. Thomas Diamond (RHP, TEX)
73. Cesar Carillo (RHP, SD)
74. Adam Loewen (LHP, BAL)
75. Chuck Tiffany (LHP, LAD)
76. Brian Anderson (OF, CHW)
77. Jeremy Sowers (LHP, CLE)
78. Matt Moses (3B, MIN)
79. Angel Guzman (RHP, CHC)
80. Jeff Clement (C, SEA)

81. Kenji Jojima (C, SEA)
82. Fernando Nieve (RHP, HOU)
83. Corey Hart (OF/3B, MIL)
84. Eric Duncan (3B, NYY)
85. Justin Huber (1B, KC)
86. Jeff Niemann (RHP, TAM)
87. Cliff Pennington (SS, OAK)
88. Jeff Mathis (C, LAA)
89. Troy Patton (LHP, HOU)
90. Jay Bruce (OF, CIN)

91. Colby Rasmus (OF, STL)
92. Jeff Bianchi (SS, KC)
93. Joaquin Arias (SS, TEX)
94. Eddy Martinez-Esteve (OF, SF)
95. Jason Kubel (OF, MIN)
96. Adam Jones (OF, SEA)
97. Ian Kinsler (2B, TEX)
98. Eric Hurley (RHP, TEX)
99. Anthony Swarzak (RHP, MIN)
100. Josh Barfield (2B, SD)

2005

1. Delmon Young (OF, TAM)
2. Casey Kotchman (1B, LAA)
3. Felix Hernandez (RHP, SEA)
4. Ian Stewart (3B, COL)
5. Andy Marte (3B, ATL)
6. Rickie Weeks (2B, MIL)
7. Adam Miller (RHP, CLE)
8. Prince Fielder (1B, MIL)
9. Scott Kazmir (LHP, TAM)
10. Dallas McPherson (3B, LAA)

11. Jeff Francis (LHP, COL)
12. Jeff Francouer (OF, ATL)
13. Chris Nelson (SS, COL)
14. Hanley Ramirez (SS, BOS)
15. Matt Cain (RHP, SF)
16. Edwin Jackson (RHP, LA)
17. Joel Guzman (SS, LA)
18. JJ Hardy (SS, MIL)
19. Carlos Quentin (OF, ARI)
20. Lastings Milledge (OF, NYM)

21. Jeremy Hermida (OF, FLA)
22. Daric Barton (C/1B, OAK)
23. James Loney (1B, LA)
24. Chad Billingsley (RHP, LA)
25. John Danks (LHP, TEX)
26. Josh Barfield (2B, SD)
27. Ervin Santana (RHP, LAA)
28. Ryan Sweeney (OF, CHW)
29. Kendry Morales (1B/OF, LAA)
30. Erick Aybar (SS, LAA)

31. Conor Jackson (OF, ARI)
32. Yuresimo Petit (RHP, NYM)
33. Anthony Reyes (RHP, STL)
34. Joe Blanton (RHP, OAK)
35. Michael Aubrey (1B, CLE)
36. Nick Swisher (OF, OAK)
37. Jason Kubel (OF, MIN)
38. Michael Hinckley (LHP, WAS)
39. Gavin Floyd (RHP, PHI)
40. Jose Capellan (RHP, MIL)

41. Dan Meyer (LHP, OAK)
42. Eric Duncan (3B, NYY)
43. Cole Hamels (LHP, PHI)
44. Jeremy Reed (OF, SEA)
45. Jesse Crain (RHP, MIN)
46. Franklin Gutierrez (OF, CLE)
47. Shin Soo Choo (OF, SEA)
48. Guillermo Quiroz (C, TOR)
49. Jeff Mathis (C, LAA)
50. Jeff Niemann (RHP, TAM)

51. JD Durbin (RHP, MIN)
52. Dustin McGowan (RHP, TOR)
53. Scott Olsen (LHP, FLA)
54. Francisco Rosario (RHP, TOR)
55. Aaron Hill (SS, TOR)
56. Jason Bartlett (SS, MIN)
57. Brian Anderson (OF, CHW)
58. Sergio Santos (SS, ARI)
59. Jered Weaver (RHP, LAA)
60. Justin Verlander (RHP, DET)

61. Russ Adams (SS, TOR)
62. Brandon League (RHP, TOR)
63. Brandon McCarthy (RHP, CHW)
64. Juan Dominguez (RHP, TEX)
65. Huston Street (RHP, OAK)
66. Jairo Garcia (RHP, OAK)
67. John Maine (RHP, BAL)
68. Javier Herrera (OF, OAK)
69. Chuck Tiffany (LHP, LA)
70. Angel Guzman (RHP, CHC)

71. Felix Pie (OF, CHC)
72. Josh Fields (3B, CHW)
73. Fernando Nieve (RHP, HOU)
74. Chris Burke (2B, HOU)
75. Ian Kinsler (SS, TEX)
76. Brian Dopirak (1B, CHC)
77. John VanBenscoten (RHP, PIT)
78. Zach Duke (LHP, PIT)
79. Greg Miller (LHP, LA)
80. Ryan Howard (1B, PHI)

81. Dan Johnson (1B, OAK)
82. Andy LaRoche (3B, LA)
83. Merkin Valdez (RHP, SF)
84. Homer Bailey (RHP, CIN)
85. Nick Marakis (OF, BAL)
86. Ubaldo Jimenez (RHP, COL)
87. Phil Humber (RHP, NYM)
88. Edwin Encarnacion (3B, CIN)
89. Kyle Davies (RHP, ATL)
90. Vince Sinisi (OF, TEX)

91. Thomas Diamond (RHP, TEX)
92. Stephen Drew (SS, ARI)
93. Denny Bautista (RHP, KC)
94. Matt Moses (3B, MIN)
95. Chris Snyder (C, ARI)
96. Billy Butler (3B, KC)
97. Brian McCann (C, ATL)
98. Mark Teahen (3B, KC)
99. Corey Hart (OF, MIL)
100. Matt Bush (SS, SD)

AVG: Batting Average (see also BA)

BA: Batting Average (see also AVG)

Base Performance Indicator (BPI): A statistical formula that measures an isolated aspect of a player's situation-independent raw skill or a gauge that helps capture the effects of random chance has on a skill. Although there are many such formulas, there are only a few that we are referring to when the term is used in this book. For pitchers, our BPI's are control (bb%), dominance (k/9), command (k/bb), opposition on base average (OOB), ground/line/fly ratios (G/L/F), and expected ERA (xERA). Random chance is measured witih the hit rate (H%) and strand rate (S%).

*Base Performance Value (BPV): A single value that describes a pitcher's overall raw skill level. This is more useful than any traditional statistical gauge to track performance trends and project future statistical output. The BPV formula combines and weights several BPIs:

(Dominance Rate x 6) + (Command ratio x 21) − Opposition HR Rate x 30) − ((Opp. Batting Average - .275) x 200)

The formula combines the individual raw skills of power, command, the ability to keep batters from reaching base, and the ability to prevent long hits, all characteristics that are unaffected by most external team factors. In tandem with a pitcher's strand rate, it provides a complete picture of the elements that contribute to a pitcher's ERA, and therefore serves as an accurate tool to project likely changes in ERA. **BENCHMARKS:** We generally consider a BPV of 50 to be the minimum level required for long-term success. The elite of bullpen aces will have BPV's in the excess of 100 and it is rare for these stoppers to enjoy long-term success with consistent levels under 75.

Batters Faced per Game *(Craig Wright)*

((IP x 2.82) + H + BB) / G

A measure of pitcher usage and one of the leading indicators for potential pitcher burnout.

Batting Average (BA, or AVG)

(H/AB)

Ratio of hits to at-bats, though it is a poor evaluative measure of hitting performance. It neglects the offensive value of the base on balls and assumes that all hits are created equal.

Batting Eye (Eye)

(Walks / Strikeouts)

A measure of a player's strike zone judgment, the raw ability to distinguish between balls and strikes. **BENCHMARKS:** The best hitters have eye ratios over 1.00 (indicating more walks than strikeouts) and are the most likely to be among a league's .300 hitters. At the other end of the scale are ratios

less than 0.50, which represent batters who likely also have lower BAs.

bb%: Walk rate (hitters)

bb/9: Opposition Walks per 9 IP

BF/Gm: Batters Faced Per Game

BPI: Base Performance Indicator

*BPV: Base Performance Value

Cmd: Command ratio

Command Ratio (Cmd)

(Strikeouts / Walks)

This is a measure of a pitcher's raw ability to get the ball over the plate. There is no more fundamental a skill than this, and so it is accurately used as a leading indicator to project future rises and falls in other gauges, such as ERA. Command is one of the best gauges to use to evaluate minor league performance. It is a prime component of a pitcher's base performance value. **BENCHMARKS:** Baseball's upper echelon of command pitchers will have ratios in excess of 3.0. Pitchers with ratios under 1.0 — indicating that they walk more batters than they strike out — have virtually no potential for long term success. If you make no other changes in your approach to drafting a pitching staff, limiting your focus to only pitchers with a command ratio of 2.0 or better will substantially improve your odds of success.

Contact Rate (ct%)

((AB - K) / AB)

Measures a batter's ability to get wood on the ball and hit it into the field of play. **BENCHMARK:** Those batters with the best contact skill will have levels of 90% or better. The hackers of society will have levels of 75% or less.

Control Rate (bb/9), or Opposition Walks per Game

BB Allowed x 9 / IP

Measures how many walks a pitcher allows per game equivalent. **BENCHMARK:** The best pitchers will have bb/9 levels of 3.0 or less.

ct%: Contact rate

Ctl: Control Rate

Dom: Dominance Rate

Dominance Rate (k/9), or Opposition Strikeouts per Game

(K Allowed x 9 / IP)

Measures how many strikeouts a pitcher allows per game equivalent. **BENCHMARK:** The best pitchers will have k/9 levels of 6.0 or higher.

Expected Earned Run Average (Gill and Reeve)

(.575 x H [per 9 IP]) + (.94 x HR [per 9 IP]) + (.28 x BB [per 9 IP]) - (.01 x K [per 9 IP]) - Normalizing Factor

"xERA represents the expected ERA of the pitcher based on a normal distribution of his statistics. It is not influenced by situation-dependent factors." xERA erases the inequity between starters' and relievers' ERA's, eliminating the effect that a pitcher's success or failure has on another pitcher's ERA.

Similar to other gauges, the accuracy of this formula changes with the level of competition from one season to the next. The normalizing factor allows us to better approximate a pitcher's actual ERA. This value is usually somewhere around 2.77 and varies by league and year. BENCHMARKS: In general, xERA's should approximate a pitcher's ERA fairly closely. However, those pitchers who have large variances between the two gauges are candidates for further analysis.

Extra-Base Hit Rate (X/H)

(2B + 3B + HR) / Hits

X/H is a measure of power and can be used along with a player's slugging percentage and isolated power to gauge a player's ability to drive the ball. BENCHMARKS: Players with above average power will post X/H of greater than 38% and players with moderate power will post X/H of 30% or greater. Weak hitters with below average power will have a X/H level of less than 20%.

Eye: Batting Eye

h%: Hit rate (batters)

H%: Hits Allowed per Balls in Play (pitchers)

Hit Rate (h% or H%)

(H—HR) / (AB – HR - K)

The percent of balls hit into the field of play that fall for hits.

hr/9: Opposition Home Runs per 9 IP

ISO: Isolated Power

Isolated Power (ISO)

(Slugging Percentage - Batting Average)

Isolated Power is a measurement of power skill. Subtracting a player's BA from his SLG, we are essentially pulling out all the singles and single bases from the formula. What remains are the extra-base hits. ISO is not an absolute measurement as it assumes that two doubles is worth one home run, which certainly is not the case, but is another statistic that is a good measurement of raw power. BENCHMARKS: The game's top sluggers will tend to have ISO levels over .200. Weak hitters will be under .100.

k/9: Dominance rate (opposition strikeouts per 9 IP)

Major League Equivalency (Bill James)

A formula that converts a player's minor or foreign league statistics into a comparable performance in the major leagues. These are not projections, but conversions of current performance.

Contains adjustments for the level of play in individual leagues and teams. Works best with Triple-A stats, not quite as well with Double-A stats, and hardly at all with the lower levels. Foreign conversions are still a work in process. James' original formula only addressed batting. Our research has devised conversion formulas for pitchers, however, their best use comes when looking at BPI's, not traditional stats.

MLE: Major League Equivalency

OBP: On Base Percentage (batters)

OBA: Opposition Batting Average (pitchers)

On Base Percentage (OBP)

(H + BB) / (AB + BB)

Addressing one of the two deficiencies in BA, OBP gives value to those events that get batters on base, but are not hits. By adding walks (and often, hit batsmen) into the basic batting average formula, we have a better gauge of a batter's ability to reach base safely. An OBP of .350 can be read as "this batter gets on base 35% of the time."

Why this is a more important gauge than batting average? When a run is scored, there is no distinction made as to how that runner reached base. So, two thirds of the time—about how often a batter comes to the plate with the bases empty—a walk really is as good as a hit. BENCHMARKS: We all know what a .300 hitter is, but what represents "good" for OBP? That comparable level would likely be .400, with .275 representing the level of futility.

On Base Plus Slugging Percentage (OPS): A simple sum of the two gauges, it is considered as one of the better evaluators of overall performance. OPS combines the two basic elements of offensive production — the ability to get on base (OBP) and the ability to advance baserunners (SLG). BENCHMARKS: The game's top batters will have OPS levels over .900. The worst batters will have levels under .600.

Opposition Batting Average (OBA)

(Hits Allowed / ((IP x 2.82) + Hits Allowed))

A close approximation of the batting average achieved by opposing batters against a particular pitcher. BENCHMARKS: The converse of the benchmark for batters, the best pitchers will have levels under .250; the worst pitchers levels over .300.

Opposition Home Runs per Game (hr/9)

(HR Allowed x 9 / IP)

Measures how many home runs a pitcher allows per game equivalent. BENCHMARK: The best pitchers will have hr/9 levels of under 1.0.

Opposition On Base Average (OOB)

(Hits Allowed + BB) / ((IP x 2.82) + H + BB)

A close approximation of the on base average achieved by opposing batters against a particular pitcher. BENCHMARK: The best pitchers will have levels under .300; the worst pitchers levels over .375.

Opposition Strikeouts per Game: See Dominance Rate.

Opposition Walks per Game: See Control Rate.

OPS: On Base Plus Slugging Percentage

RC: Runs Created

RC/G: Runs Created Per Game

Runs Created *(Bill James)*

(H + BB - CS) x (Total bases + (.55 x SB)) / (AB + BB)

A formula that converts all offensive events into a total of runs scored. As calculated for individual teams, the result approximates a club's actual run total with great accuracy.

Runs Created Per Game *(Bill James)*

Runs Created / ((AB - H + CS) / 25.5)

RC expressed on a per-game basis might be considered the hypothetical ERA compiled against a particular batter. **BENCHMARKS:** Few players surpass the level of a 10.00 RC/G in any given season, but any level over 7.50 can still be considered very good. At the bottom are levels below 3.00.

S%: Strand Rate

Save: There are six events that need to occur in order for a pitcher to post a single save...

1. The starting pitcher and middle relievers must pitch well.
2. The offense must score enough runs.
3. It must be a reasonably close game.
4. The manager must choose to put the pitcher in for a save opportunity.
5. The pitcher must pitch well and hold the lead.
6. The manager must let him finish the game.

Of these six events, only one is within the control of the relief pitcher. As such, projecting saves for a reliever has little to do with skill and a lot to do with opportunity. However, pitchers with excellent skills sets may create opportunity for themselves.

Situation Independent: Describing a statistical gauge that measures performance apart from the context of team, ballpark, or other outside variables. Strikeouts and Walks, inasmuch as they are unaffected by the performance of a batter's surrounding team, are considered situation independent stats.

Conversely, RBIs are situation dependent because individual performance varies greatly by the performance of other batters on the team (you can't drive in runs if there is nobody on base). Similarly, pitching wins are as much a measure of the success of a pitcher as they are a measure of the success of the offense and defense performing behind that pitcher, and are therefore a poor measure of pitching performance alone.

Situation independent gauges are important for us to be able to separate a player's contribution to his team and isolate his performance so that we may judge it on its own merits.

Slg: Slugging Percentage

Slugging Percentage (Slg)

(Singles + (2 x Doubles) + (3 x Triples) + (4 x HR)) / AB

A measure of the total number of bases accumulated per at bat. It is a misnomer; it is not a true measure of a batter's slugging ability because it includes singles. SLG also assumes that each type of hit has proportionately increasing value (i.e. a double is twice as valuable as a single, etc.) which is not true. **BENCHMARKS:** The top batters will have levels over .500. The bottom batters will have levels under .300.

Strand Rate (S%)

(H + BB - ER) / (H + BB - HR)

Measures the percentage of allowed runners a pitcher strands, which incorporates both individual pitcher skill and bullpen effectiveness. **BENCHMARKS:** The most adept at stranding runners will have S% levels over 75%. Once a pitcher's S% starts dropping down below 65%, he's going to have problems with his ERA. Those pitchers with strand rates over 80% will have artificially low ERAs, which will be prone to relapse.

Strikeouts per Game: See Opposition Strikeouts per game.

Walks + Hits per Innings Pitched (WHIP): The number of baserunners a pitcher allows per inning. **BENCHMARKS:** Usually, a WHIP of under 1.20 is considered top level and over 1.50 is indicative of poor performance. Levels under 1.00 — allowing fewer runners than IP — represent extraordinary performance and are rarely maintained over time.

Walk rate (bb%)

(BB / (AB + BB))

A measure of a batter's eye and plate patience. BENCHMARKS: The best batters will have levels of over 10%. Those with the least plate patience will have levels of 5% or less.

Walks per Game: See Opposition Walks per Game.

WHIP: Walks + Hits per Innings Pitched

Wins: There are five events that need to occur in order for a pitcher to post a single win...

1. He must pitch well, allowing few runs.
2. The offense must score enough runs.
3. The defense must successfully field all batted balls.
4. The bullpen must hold the lead.
5. The manager must leave the pitcher in for 5 innings, and not remove him if the team is still behind.

X/H: Extra-base Hit Rate

*xERA: Expected ERA

* Asterisked formulas have updated versions in the Baseball Forecaster. *However, those updates include statistics like Ground Ball Rate, Fly Ball Rate or Line Drive Rate, for which we do not have reliable data for minor leaguers. So we use the previous version of those formulas, as listed here, for the players in this book.*

TEAM	ORG	LEAGUE	LEV	TEAM	ORG	LEAGUE	LEV
Aberdeen	BAL	New York-Penn League	SS	Connecticut	DET	New York-Penn League	SS
Akron	CLE	Eastern League	AA	Corpus Christi	HOU	Texas League	AA
Albuquerque	LA	Pacific Coast League	AAA	Danville	ATL	Appalachian League	Rk
Altoona	PIT	Eastern League	AA	Dayton	CIN	Midwest League	A-
Arkansas	LAA	Texas League	AA	Daytona	CHC	Florida State League	A+
Asheville	COL	South Atlantic League	A-	Delmarva	BAL	South Atlantic League	A-
Auburn	WAS	New York-Penn League	SS	Dunedin	TOR	Florida State League	A+
Augusta	SF	South Atlantic League	A-	Durham	TAM	International League	AAA
AZL Angels	LAA	Arizona League	Rk	Elizabethton	MIN	Appalachian League	Rk
AZL Athletics	OAK	Arizona League	Rk	Erie	DET	Eastern League	AA
AZL Brewers	MIL	Arizona League	Rk	Eugene	SD	Northwest League	SS
AZL Cubs	CHC	Arizona League	Rk	Everett	SEA	Northwest League	SS
AZL Diamondbacks	ARI	Arizona League	Rk	Fort Myers	MIN	Florida State League	A+
AZL Dodgers	LA	Arizona League	Rk	Fort Wayne	SD	Midwest League	A-
AZL Giants	SF	Arizona League	Rk	Frederick	BAL	Carolina League	A+
AZL Indians	CLE	Arizona League	Rk	Fresno	SF	Pacific Coast League	AAA
AZL Mariners	SEA	Arizona League	Rk	Frisco	TEX	Texas League	AA
AZL Padres	SD	Arizona League	Rk	GCL Astros	HOU	Gulf Coast League	Rk
AZL Rangers	TEX	Arizona League	Rk	GCL Blue Jays	TOR	Gulf Coast League	Rk
AZL Reds	CIN	Arizona League	Rk	GCL Braves	ATL	Gulf Coast League	Rk
AZL Royals	KC	Arizona League	Rk	GCL Cardinals	STL	Gulf Coast League	Rk
Bakersfield	CIN	California League	A+	GCL Marlins	MIA	Gulf Coast League	Rk
Batavia	MIA	New York-Penn League	SS	GCL Nationals	WAS	Gulf Coast League	Rk
Beloit	OAK	Midwest League	A-	GCL Orioles	BAL	Gulf Coast League	Rk
Billings	CIN	Pioneer League	Rk	GCL Phillies	PHI	Gulf Coast League	Rk
Binghamton	NYM	Eastern League	AA	GCL Pirates	PIT	Gulf Coast League	Rk
Birmingham	CHW	Southern League	AA	GCL Rays	TAM	Gulf Coast League	Rk
Bluefield	TOR	Appalachian League	Rk	GCL Red Sox	BOS	Gulf Coast League	Rk
Boise	CHC	Northwest League	SS	GCL Tigers	DET	Gulf Coast League	Rk
Bowie	BAL	Eastern League	AA	GCL Twins	MIN	Gulf Coast League	Rk
Bowling Green	TAM	Midwest League	A-	GCL Yankees	NYY	Gulf Coast League	Rk
Bradenton	PIT	Florida State League	A+	Grand Junction	COL	Pioneer League	Rk
Brevard County	MIL	Florida State League	A+	Great Falls	CHW	Pioneer League	Rk
Bristol	CHW	Appalachian League	Rk	Great Lakes	LA	Midwest League	A-
Brooklyn	NYM	New York-Penn League	SS	Greeneville	HOU	Appalachian League	Rk
Buffalo	TOR	International League	AAA	Greensboro	MIA	South Atlantic League	A-
Burlington	KC	Appalachian League	Rk	Greenville	BOS	South Atlantic League	A-
Burlington	LAA	Midwest League	A-	Gwinnett	ATL	International League	AAA
Carolina	CLE	Carolina League	A+	Hagerstown	WAS	South Atlantic League	A-
Cedar Rapids	MIN	Midwest League	A-	Harrisburg	WAS	Eastern League	AA
Charleston	NYY	South Atlantic League	A-	Helena	MIL	Pioneer League	Rk
Charlotte	CHW	International League	AAA	Hickory	TEX	South Atlantic League	A-
Charlotte	TAM	Florida State League	A+	High Desert	SEA	California League	A+
Chattanooga	LA	Southern League	AA	Hillsboro	ARI	Northwest League	SS
Clearwater	PHI	Florida State League	A+	Hudson Valley	TAM	New York-Penn League	SS
Clinton	SEA	Midwest League	A-	Huntsville	MIL	Southern League	AA
Colorado Springs	COL	Pacific Coast League	AAA	Idaho Falls	KC	Pioneer League	Rk
Columbus	CLE	International League	AAA	Indianapolis	PIT	International League	AAA

TEAM	ORG	LEAGUE	LEV	TEAM	ORG	LEAGUE	LEV
Inland Empire	LAA	California League	A+	Pulaski	SEA	Appalachian League	Rk
Iowa	CHC	Pacific Coast League	AAA	Quad Cities	HOU	Midwest League	A-
Jackson	SEA	Southern League	AA	Rancho Cucamonga	LA	California League	A+
Jacksonville	MIA	Southern League	AA	Reading	PHI	Eastern League	AA
Jamestown	PIT	New York-Penn League	SS	Reno	ARI	Pacific Coast League	AAA
Johnson City	STL	Appalachian League	Rk	Richmond	SF	Eastern League	AA
Jupiter	MIA	Florida State League	A+	Rochester	MIN	International League	AAA
Kane County	CHC	Midwest League	A-	Rome	ATL	South Atlantic League	A-
Kannapolis	CHW	South Atlantic League	A-	Round Rock	TEX	Pacific Coast League	AAA
Kingsport	NYM	Appalachian League	Rk	Sacramento	OAK	Pacific Coast League	AAA
Lake County	CLE	Midwest League	A-	Salem	BOS	Carolina League	A+
Lake Elsinore	SD	California League	A+	Salem-Keizer	SF	Northwest League	SS
Lakeland	DET	Florida State League	A+	Salt Lake	LAA	Pacific Coast League	AAA
Lakewood	PHI	South Atlantic League	A-	San Antonio	SD	Texas League	AA
Lancaster	HOU	California League	A+	San Jose	SF	California League	A+
Lansing	TOR	Midwest League	A-	Savannah	NYM	South Atlantic League	A-
Las Vegas	NYM	Pacific Coast League	AAA	Scranton/Wilkes-Barre	NYY	International League	AAA
Lehigh Valley	PHI	International League	AAA	South Bend	ARI	Midwest League	A-
Lexington	KC	South Atlantic League	A-	Spokane	TEX	Northwest League	SS
Louisville	CIN	International League	AAA	Springfield	STL	Texas League	AA
Lowell	BOS	New York-Penn League	SS	St. Lucie	NYM	Florida State League	A+
Lynchburg	ATL	Carolina League	A+	State College	STL	New York-Penn League	SS
Mahoning Valley	CLE	New York-Penn League	SS	Staten Island	NYY	New York-Penn League	SS
Memphis	STL	Pacific Coast League	AAA	Stockton	OAK	California League	A+
Midland	OAK	Texas League	AA	Syracuse	WAS	International League	AAA
Mississippi	ATL	Southern League	AA	Tacoma	SEA	Pacific Coast League	AAA
Missoula	ARI	Pioneer League	Rk	Tampa	NYY	Florida State League	A+
Mobile	ARI	Southern League	AA	Tennessee	CHC	Southern League	AA
Modesto	COL	California League	A+	Toledo	DET	International League	AAA
Montgomery	TAM	Southern League	AA	Trenton	NYY	Eastern League	AA
Myrtle Beach	TEX	Carolina League	A+	Tri-City	COL	Northwest League	SS
Nashville	MIL	Pacific Coast League	AAA	Tri-City	HOU	New York-Penn League	SS
New Britain	MIN	Eastern League	AA	Tucson	SD	Pacific Coast League	AAA
New Hampshire	TOR	Eastern League	AA	Tulsa	COL	Texas League	AA
New Orleans	MIA	Pacific Coast League	AAA	Vancouver	TOR	Northwest League	SS
Norfolk	BAL	International League	AAA	Vermont	OAK	New York-Penn League	SS
Northwest Arkansas	KC	Texas League	AA	Visalia	ARI	California League	A+
Ogden	LA	Pioneer League	Rk	West Michigan	DET	Midwest League	A-
Oklahoma City	HOU	Pacific Coast League	AAA	West Virginia	PIT	South Atlantic League	A-
Omaha	KC	Pacific Coast League	AAA	Williamsport	PHI	New York-Penn League	SS
Orem	LAA	Pioneer League	Rk	Wilmington	KC	Carolina League	A+
Palm Beach	STL	Florida State League	A+	Winston-Salem	CHW	Carolina League	A+
Pawtucket	BOS	International League	AAA	Wisconsin	MIL	Midwest League	A-
Pensacola	CIN	Southern League	AA				
Peoria	STL	Midwest League	A-				
Portland	BOS	Eastern League	AA				
Potomac	WAS	Carolina League	A+				
Princeton	TAM	Appalachian League	Rk				

2013 FANTASY BASEBALL
WINNERS RESOURCE GUIDE

orders.baseballhq.com

10 REASONS
why winners rely on BASEBALL HQ PRODUCTS
for fantasy baseball information

1 **NO OTHER RESOURCE** provides you with more vital intelligence to help you win. Compare the depth of our offerings in these pages with any other information product or service.

2 **NO OTHER RESOURCE** provides more exclusive information, like cutting-edge component skills analyses, revolutionary strategies like the LIMA Plan, and innovative gaming formats like Rotisserie 500. *You won't find these anywhere else on the internet, guaranteed.*

3 **NO OTHER RESOURCE** has as long and consistent a track record of success in top national competitions... Our writers and readers have achieved 33 first place finishes, plus another 28 second and third place finishes since 1997. *No other resource comes remotely close.*

4 **NO OTHER RESOURCE** has as consistent a track record in projecting impact performances. In 2012, our readers had surprises like Everth Cabrera, Chris Davis, Edwin Encarnacion, Dexter Fowler, Yadier Molina, Trevor Plouffe, Wilin Rosario, Carlos Ruiz, Homer Bailey, A.J. Burnett, R.A. Dickey, Casey Janssen, Kris Medlen, Brandon Morrow, Jake Peavy, Max Scherzer and Chris Tillman on their teams, *and dozens more.*

5 **NO OTHER RESOURCE** is supported by more than 50 top writers and analysts — all paid professionals and proven winners, not weekend hobbyists or corporate staffers.

6 **NO OTHER RESOURCE** has a wider scope, providing valuable information not only for Rotisserie, but for alternative formats like simulations, salary cap contests, online games, points, head-to-head, dynasty leagues and others.

7 **NO OTHER RESOURCE** is as highly regarded by its peers in the industry. Baseball HQ is the *only* three-time winner of the Fantasy Sports Trade Association's "Best Fantasy Baseball Online Content" award and Ron Shandler has won two lifetime achievement awards.

8 **NO OTHER RESOURCE** is as highly regarded *outside* of the fantasy industry. Many Major League general managers are regular customers. We were advisors to the St. Louis Cardinals in 2004 and our former Minor League Director is now a scout for the organization.

9 **NO OTHER RESOURCE** has been creating fantasy baseball winners for as long as we have. Our 27 years of stability *guarantees your investment*.

10 Year after year, more than 90% of our customers report that Baseball HQ products and services have helped them improve their performance in their fantasy leagues. That's the bottom line.

FIRST PITCH
Forums and Conferences

Get a head start on the 2013 season with a unique opportunity to go one-on-one with some of the top writers and analysts in the fantasy baseball industry. First Pitch Forums bring the experts to some of the top cities in the USA for lively and informative symposium sessions.

These 3+ hour events combine player analysis with fantasy drafting, interactive activities and fun! You've never experienced anything so informative and entertaining! We've selected the top issues, topics, players and strategies that could make or break your fantasy season.

Our 2012 program identified many of last year's surprise players, such as Everth Cabrera, Andy Dirks, Chris Davis, Marco Estrada, Allen Craig, Trevor Plouffe, Lance Lynn, Tom Milone, Jarrod Saltalamacchia, Chris Sale, Jonathan Niese, Jake Peavy and Kris Medlen. For 2013, we will once again be on the lookout for game-changing impact players, based on...

- Playing time opportunity
- Injury prognoses
- Bullpen volatility
- Minor league scouting
- Statistical analysis
- Breakout profile modeling
- and much more!

Ron Shandler and *Baseball Injury Report's* Rick Wilton chair the sessions, bringing a dynamic energy to every event. They are joined by guest experts from BaseballHQ.com and some of the leading sports media sources, like ESPN.com, MLB.com, USA Today Sports Weekly, Baseball America, Rotowire.com, Mastersball.com, KFFL.com and Sirius/XM Radio.

What you get for your registration

- 3+ hours of baseball talk with some of the baseball industry's top writers and analysts
- The chance to have *your* questions answered, 1-on-1 with the experts
- The opportunity to network with fellow fantasy leaguers from your area
- Freebies and discounts from leading industry vendors

2013 SITES

Saturday, Feb. 16	**LOS ANGELES**
Sunday, Feb. 17	**SAN FRANCISCO**
Saturday, Feb. 23	**CHICAGO**
Friday, March 1	**WASHINGTON, DC**
Saturday, March 2	**NEW YORK area**
Sunday, March 3	**BOSTON**

REGISTRATION:
$39 per person in advance
$49 per person at the door

Don't forget - November 1-3 in Phoenix!

Program description, forum sites and directions at
http://www.baseballhq.com/ seminars/index.shtml